# Solaris 8:
# The Complete Reference

## About the Authors

**Paul A. Watters**, MAPS, M. Phil. (Cambridge), B.A. (Honors) (Tasmania), B.A. (Newcastle), recently submitted his Ph.D. in computer science at Macquarie University, Australia, in the area of artificial neural networks. The software he developed as part of his doctoral studies runs on high-end Solaris servers, providing simulation results through a web interface. In addition, he has eight years' systems management and application development experience in commercial and research and development organizations. Paul specializes in building e-commerce and Internet information systems based on Solaris, Java, and open standards such as CORBA. He has published many articles on computer science in leading international journals, including *Applied Signal Processing*, *Internet Research*, and *International Journal of Systems Science*. He is also a columnist and author for the trade journal *Inside Solaris*.

**Sriranga Veeraraghavan** works with the Voice Over IP Systems Software group at Empowertel Networks. He has also worked with the Network Management group at Cisco Systems. He has several years' experience developing software in C, Java, Perl, and Shell, and authored *Teach Yourself Shell Programming in 24 Hours*. Sriranga graduated from the University of California at Berkeley in 1997 with a degree in engineering, and is currently pursuing further studies at Stanford University.

## About the Contributing Author and Technical Reviewer

**Nalneesh Gaur** is a technical manager with the eRisk Solutions practice of Ernst & Young in Dallas, Texas. He is experienced with UNIX and Windows NT system administration, e-commerce architectures, UNIX/NT integration, e-commerce security, and web application development. Nalneesh has extensive experience with the Solaris and Windows NT environment. He is Sun Enterprise certified and a Microsoft Certified Systems Engineer (MCSE).

# Solaris 8:
# The Complete Reference

Paul A. Watters
Sriranga Veeraraghavan

Osborne/**McGraw-Hill**

Berkeley   New York   St. Louis   San Francisco
Auckland   Bogotá   Hamburg   London   Madrid
Mexico City   Milan   Montreal   New Delhi   Panama City
Paris   São Paulo   Singapore   Sydney
Tokyo   Toronto

Osborne/**McGraw-Hill**
2600 Tenth Street
Berkeley, California 94710
U.S.A.

For information on translations or book distributors outside the U.S.A., or to arrange
bulk purchase discounts for sales promotions, premiums, or fundraisers, please contact
Osborne/**McGraw-Hill** at the above address.

**Solaris 8: The Complete Reference**

4567890 CUS/CUS 043210

ISBN 0-07-212143-2

**Publisher**
  Brandon A. Nordin

**Vice President
and Editor-in-Chief**
  Scott Rogers

**Acquisitions Editor**
  Jane Brownlow

**Project Editors**
  Nancy McLaughlin
  Jenn Tust

**Acquisitions Coordinator**
  Tara Davis

**Technical Editor**
  Nalneesh Gaur

**Copy Editors**
  Doug Robert
  Lunaea Weatherstone

**Proofreader**
  Maggie Trapp

**Indexer**
  Valerie Robbins

**Computer Designers**
  Jani Beckwith
  Roberta Steele

**Illustrator**
  Michael T. Mueller

**Series Design**
  Peter F. Hancik

This book was composed with Corel VENTURA™ Publisher.

To my wife, Maya, and my
Godchildren, Shanice Espinosa and Matthew Watters.

# Contents at a Glance

# Contents

### Part I

### Getting Started with Solaris

**Part II**

**System Maintenance**

## Part III

### Basic Network Administration

## 14 The Dynamic Host Configuration Protocol  . . . . . . . . . .   423

## 15 Network Information Service (NIS+)  . . . . . . . . . . . . . . .   447

# Foreword

It's been an incredible journey for Sun Microsystems and its flagship operating system, Solaris. Sun released the first version of Solaris, based on a port of System V, release 4, in the early '90s and has built it into a truly world-class application platform, scaling from PCs to clusters of 64-way E10000s. Solaris was the first true assault on the "glass-house" mainframe world of proprietary architectures and astronomical prices. Every version has offered incremental improvements that keep Sun one step ahead of the competition—things like 64-bit processing, the journaling file system, great Java support, and network integration that is built in from the ground up.

And this is where this book comes in. *Solaris 8: The Complete Reference* guides you through the rich functionality of Solaris with real-world examples and techniques for getting the most out of your Solaris machines. There's enough here to satisfy everyone, from the Solaris experts needing a reference to beginners looking for a guide to tackling this powerful, complex operating system. Spanning all the core areas of Solaris, *Solaris 8: The Complete Reference* is an indispensable tool for both administrators and users.

—Garrett Suhm
Editor, *Inside Solaris*

# Acknowledgments

This book is the result of many years spent working with Solaris, since the good old days of BSD and SunOS 4.x. I would like to acknowledge the many bosses I've had over the years who have provided opportunities to work on solving problems with Solaris and UNIX, especially Professor Richard A. Heath (University of Newcastle), Professor James J. Wright (MHRI), Dr. Malti Patel (Macquarie University), Teresa White and Jonathon Wolfe (Whitewolf), David Doust (Neuroflex), and Gene Bagdonas (UAC). I'm convinced that optimal learning arises through hands-on experience, and the diversity of experience in my career has helped me appreciate the importance of operating systems at the core of all computing enterprises.

Professionally, I would like to thank the following individuals for technical advice over the years: Bruce Donaldson, Tim Gibbs, Ee Li Hong, Julian Jang, Matthew Langford, Steven Lee, Firaz Osman, and Gordon Rowell. Garrett Suhm, editor of *Inside Solaris*, has been inspirational in his enthusiasm for Solaris.

I would also like to thank the team at Osborne/McGraw-Hill, especially Jane Brownlow, Tara Davis, Nancy McLaughlin, and Jenn Tust. Their professionalism, attention to detail, and persistence with a challenging title will ensure that this text is readable and relevant to the information-technology industry.

My agency team at Studio B—Neil Salkind, Sherry and David Rogelberg, and Kristen Pickens—provided much-needed support and encouragement during the conception and execution of this project. Their high expectations and welcome assurances make writing a pleasure.

Finally, I would like to thank my parents, Walter and Judith Watters, and Cliff and Florenica Herewane, for their continuing support and encouragement. Special thanks to my wife, Maya, for her love and patience. Thanks also to my friend Karen Butler for her warmth and understanding.

# Introduction

Clients often ask why we choose Solaris as an operating environment. Is it a decision based on price? Is it an attraction to the latest gizmo features, each with its own four-letter acronym? Do we have a cozy arrangement with Sun Microsystems to promote their operating system? The answer to each of these questions is no, no, NO!

The operating system is at the very core of any computer system. It is the conceptual basis upon which applications are built, and it implements the critical software interface to hardware that makes computation possible. Thus, if your operating system fails, irrespective of the quality of your hardware or application software, your system as a whole will not deliver. That's why we firmly believe that reliable performance is the key criterion for the evaluation of any operating system.

We're not just talking about reliability in terms of a specific variable, such as uptime—we mean the confidence that comes from knowing that the applications you design will only fail if they have an internal bug. Solaris isn't perfect—far from it—but unlike other currently popular operating environments, Solaris does have the ability to isolate all potentially hazardous user or application activity from other users or applications. It is this logical isolation, built in to the system from the earliest days of UNIX, that gives us confidence.

The Solaris operating environment consists of all the tools, applications, and services that make use of the Sun Operating System (SunOS). SunOS is now in version 5—10 years ago, SunOS was only in version 4! This indicates that while operating environment numbers often appear to be highly inflated, the core operating system has only changed to enhance core functionality. Thus, much of the software written for SunOS 10 years ago would still be operable today. In the fast-changing world of the Internet economy, there is still room for the tried and steady solutions that allow system administrators to sleep comfortably at night.

Of course, SunOS has seen changes in recent years to keep pace with advances in hardware technology. Solaris now ships with both a 32-bit and a 64-bit kernel. Particularly for information systems that use databases and scientific research that is computationally intensive, 64-bit architectures have dramatically improved the performance of their Solaris systems. In many cases, the improvement in performance has come without any need to significantly redevelop source code: Applications tend to "inherit" the characteristics of the operating system in such cases.

This book will be a useful companion to the excellent reference material already provided by Sun on the documentation CD-ROM that accompanies the Solaris distribution. You can also download and/or search these documents at the Solaris documentation site (**http://docs.sun.com/**). You may be wondering why you need to buy this book if you already have the Sun Reference Guides, and there are three very good reasons. First, the authors are not employees of Sun Microsystems. We have written this book from the perspective of seasoned professionals who often use other operating systems and who are not dazzled by marketing propaganda. This book gives credit where credit is due, but also highlights some gaps in the operating environment. Let's use secure remote access as an example: Solaris 8 includes the latest Kerberos 5 authentication system, but fails to provide a secure shell for remote logins. We realize that many system administrators and UNIX users have a soft spot for Telnet, but honestly, what organization does not want to protect itself from packet-sniffed usernames and passwords? Fortunately, the third-party software we review for secure remote access does provide a high level of security and peace of mind.

Second, this book is not just a command reference (like the Solaris man pages), but actually aims to introduce a specific area of system operations and detail the advantages and disadvantages of software supplied with the Solaris distribution and other third-party software. We also attempt to explain why certain processes (such as backups) need to be performed, rather than just blindly describing the steps to be undertaken. We've also taken the liberty of excluding some of the purely command reference material. If you need to look up an option to a specific command, use the man pages—that's what they're designed for. However, if you want worked examples of actual commands, using the most common options, this book is for you.

Third, we have endeavored to cross-reference Solaris material with approaches found in other operating systems where this is useful. One of the hardest things for new users is trying to remember all the new commands and procedures that accompany a different operating system. We hope these users will be able to effectively reuse their knowledge in a useful way. For example, we have included material on print and file sharing with Microsoft Windows and Apple Macintosh systems so that administrators who work in heterogeneous environments can make use of existing investments in system hardware and print technology. We hope that this pragmatism for dealing with operational systems and common organizational scenarios will be useful for all readers.

This book is a comprehensive guide for beginning, intermediate, and advanced users of Solaris. Beginning users will find it useful to read the first few chapters outlining the advantages of Solaris and how to install Solaris on a new system. For example, you may be a new user of Solaris x86 who wants to learn more about choosing hardware and what kinds of installation options are available. An intermediate user probably knows what the advantages of Solaris are, but may be interested in learning more about a specific area of Solaris. For example, we cover the configuration of advanced network and Internet services, such as the **sendmail** mail transport agent and the Apache web server (including Java servlets). It is most likely that advanced users will use this book when they need to walk through a specific scenario—for instance, setting up an NIS+ domain, and making use of the Federated Naming System. In each of these cases, this book provides the background information and worked examples to allow Solaris users and administrators to make the best use of the operating environment for their specific needs.

We hope that you find this book a useful reference for many years.

The
# Complete
# Reference

Solaris 8

# Part I

## Getting Started with Solaris

The
Complete
Reference

Solaris 8

# Chapter 1

## Introduction to Solaris 8

Operating systems are the building blocks of computer systems and provide the interface between user applications and computer hardware. Solaris 8 is a multiuser, multitasking operating system, developed and sold by Sun Microsystems (**http://www.sun.com/**), and it is one implementation of the UNIX operating system that draws on both the System V (AT&T) and Berkeley (BSD) systems. It has risen from little more than a research project to become the dominant UNIX operating system in the international marketplace today. Solaris 8 is the latest in a long line of operating environment releases that are based around the SunOS operating system, which is currently in version 5.8. Solaris is commonly found in large corporations and educational institutions that require concurrent, multiuser access on individual hosts, and between hosts connected over the Internet. However, it is also rapidly being adopted by small businesses and individual developers through Sun's promotion of the "Free Solaris" program. In this book, when we refer to Solaris 8, many of the commands and procedures will apply equally to earlier versions of Solaris 2.x. Commands for Solaris 1.x are specified only where relevant.

Many desktop computer users have never heard the word "Sun" in the context of computing, nor are they usually familiar with the term "Solaris" as an operating environment. However, almost every time an Internet user sends an email message, or opens a file from a networked server running Sun's Network File System (NFS) product, Solaris 8 is transparently supporting many of today's existing Internet applications. In the enterprise computing industry, Sun is synonymous with highly available, highly reliable performance hardware, and Solaris 8 is often the operating environment of choice to support database servers and application servers. Sun's hardware solutions are based around the SPARC and UltraSPARC integrated circuit technologies, which currently support up to 64 processors in a single server system (the E10000 StarFire configuration). Sun also supports common industry standards in software development, including the Common Desktop Environment (CDE), as shown in Figure 1-1.

In recent times, two of Sun's innovations have moved the spotlight from the server room to the desktop. First, Sun's development of the Java programming language—which promises "write once, read anywhere" application execution across any platform that supports the Java virtual machine—has revolutionized the development of networked applications. In addition, Java *applets* (small encapsulated applications that execute client-side) now appear on many web pages, and *servlets* power the back end of many three-tier applications, such as CRM and complex HR applications.

Second, Sun is promoting a "free" version of Solaris 8 for the SPARC and Intel hardware platforms. This means organizations that have been previously committed to using Microsoft Windows or SCO OpenServer on the Intel platform, for example, can reuse the servers currently deployed with these operations by installing Solaris 8 for Intel. It has also made Solaris 8 more accessible for desktop users, who may wish to take advantage of Sun's other free offering, the StarOffice productivity suite. StarOffice is competitive to Microsoft Office, since it contains word processing, spreadsheet, presentation, and database components that are fully integrated. The StarOffice

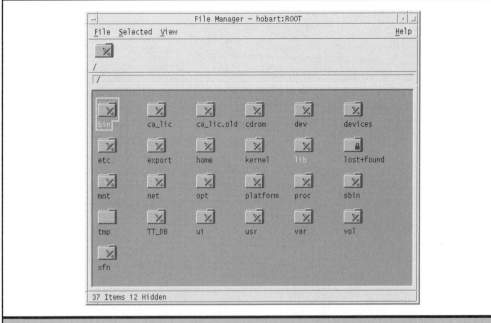

**Figure 1-1.**   *The Common Desktop Environment (CDE)*

interface is shown in Figure 1-2. In addition, StarOffice runs on many different platforms and in eight languages, meaning that a user on a Sun SPARCstation can share documents seamlessly with users on Linux and Microsoft Windows. The combination of a solid operating system with a best-of-breed productivity suite has given Solaris 8 new exposure in the desktop market.

This book is a complete reference for the Solaris 8 operating environment and for the SunOS 5.8 operating system, meaning that we will try to cover, in detail, the operational aspects of Solaris and SunOS. If you simply need to look up a command's options, you can usually make use of Sun's own online manual pages (also known as man pages), which can be accessed by typing **man** *command*, where *command* is the command for which you require help. Alternatively, you can retrieve the text of man pages and user manuals online by using the search facility at **http://docs.sun.com/**, as shown in Figure 1-3. This reference will be most useful when you need to implement a specific solution, and you need practical, tried and tested solutions. For example, in Chapter 20 we examine how to set up an anonymous FTP server, and in Chapter 16 we look at securing remote access. Although Solaris 8 comes with a set of remote access tools and servers by default, these are not always the best tools, in terms of security, that should be used in a production environment. For example, while FTP is fine for transferring files around a local area network, remote exchanges of data should be

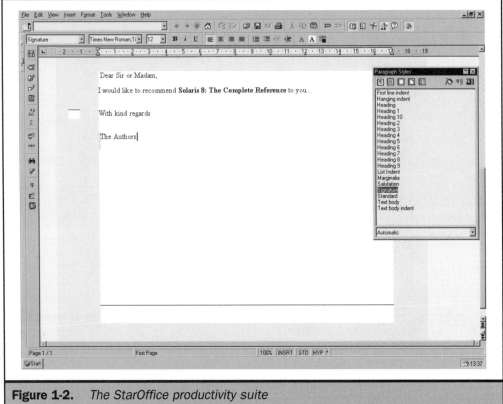

**Figure 1-2.** *The StarOffice productivity suite*

conducted using a secure file transfer system, such as **sftp**. In outlining a solution to a problem, we generally introduce Sun-supplied software first, and then discuss the installation and configuration of third-party alternatives.

If you've been keeping track of recent press releases, you may be wondering why Solaris has a version number of 8, while SunOS has a revision level of 5.8. Since the previous release of Solaris (Solaris 7), Sun has opted to number its releases sequentially with a single version number, based on the old minor revision number. This means that the release sequence for Solaris has been 2.5.1, 2.6, 7, and now 8. Thus, many sites will still be running Solaris 2.6 without feeling too far left behind, especially if they don't require the 64-bit functionality for the UltraSPARC processors provided with Solaris 7 and beyond. Sun does provide *jumbo patches* for previous operating system releases, which should always be installed when released to ensure that bugs (particularly security bugs) are resolved as soon as possible. Most of the commands and topics covered in this book for Solaris 8 are equally applicable to Solaris 7 and all previous releases of SunOS 5.x.

**Figure 1-3.**   *Locating Solaris reference material on docs.sun.com*

However, wherever possible, we have also included references to the SunOS 4.x
operating system, which was retrospectively labeled the Solaris 1.x platform. Many
installations have only started using SunOS 5.x in the past few years, and until Y2K
problems emerged with SunOS 4.x many sites still ran legacy applications on this
platform (especially if they preferred the BSD style SunOS 4.x to the System V style
SunOS 5.x operating system). Many Internet firewalls, mail servers, and news servers
still run on SPARC architecture CPUs, and some of these models are not supported by
the SunOS 5.x operating system. Making the decision to upgrade from SunOS 4.x to
SunOS 5.x was tough for many Sun installations.

Fortunately, with the release of Solaris 7 and 8, 64-bit computing has arrived,
and a stable platform has been arrived at. Many of the changes between Solaris 7
and 8 may appear cosmetic; for example, Larry Wall's Perl interpreter has been included
in the Solaris 8 distribution for the first time, meaning that a new generation of system
administrators will no longer have the pleasure of carrying out their first postinstallation
task. However, there are other quite important developments in the area of networking

and administration (such as the Solstice AdminSuite, as shown in Figure 1-4) that may not affect all users, but that are particularly important for the enterprise.

In this chapter, we will cover the background of the Solaris 8 operating environment, which really begins with the invention and widespread adoption of the UNIX operating system. In addition, we will address the means by which Solaris 8 can run cross-platform applications; for example, Solaris 8 for Intel is able to run Linux binary applications by using an application called Lxrun, which is freely available from Sun. Although earlier attempts to emulate other operating systems were largely unsuccessful (for example, WABI for emulating Microsoft Windows), Sun's development of Java can be seen as a strong commitment to cross-platform interoperability. Solaris 8 also provides many network management features that allow a Solaris 8 server to act as a primary or backup domain controller to manage Windows NT clients; for example, if you want the reliability of Solaris 8 coupled with the widespread adoption of Microsoft Windows as a desktop operating system.

Finally, we will review some of the many sites on the Internet that provide useful information, software packages, and further reading on many of the topics covered in this book.

## What Is UNIX?

It is hard to define what UNIX is because different vendors have historically introduced different features to arrive at the entities most users would think of as UNIX. However, it is easy enough to list the fundamental characteristics common to all UNIX and UNIX-like systems:

- They have a kernel, written in the C programming language, which mainly manages input/output processing, rather than being a complete operating system. The kernel has ultimate responsibility for allocating system resources to complete various tasks.

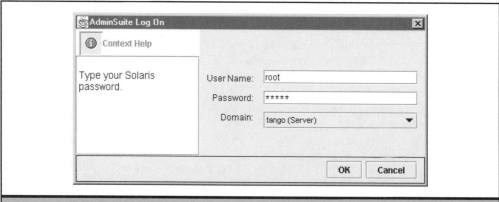

**Figure 1-4.**    *The Solstice AdminSuite launcher*

■ They have a hierarchical file system, which begins with a root directory and from which the branches of all other directories (and file systems) are mounted.

■ System hardware devices are represented logically on the file system as special files (such as /dev/pty, for pseudoterminals).

■ They are process based, with all services and user shells being represented by a single identifying number (the process ID, or PID).

■ They share a set of command-line utilities, which can be used for text and numeric processing of various kinds, such as **troff**, **col**, **cat**, **head**, and **tbl**.

■ User processes can be spawned from a shell, such as the Bourne shell, which interactively executes application programs.

■ Multiple processes can be executed concurrently by a single user and sent into the background by using the **&** operator.

■ Multiple users can execute commands concurrently by logging in from pseudoterminals.

Note that a graphical user interface is not necessarily a defining feature of UNIX, unlike other desktop operating systems, which place much stock in "look and feel," even though most UNIX systems support X11 graphics and the Common Desktop Environment (CDE). Figure 1-5 shows a typical CDE login screen.

The reasons for this distinction are largely historical and related to the UNIX design philosophy, as we will see later in this chapter. The layering of the various components of a UNIX system is shown in Figure 1-6.

Since UNIX was created by active developers, rather than operating system gurus, there was always a strong focus on creating an operating system to suit programmers' needs. A *Bell System Technical Journal* article in 1978 lists the key guiding principles of UNIX development:

■ Create small, self-contained programs that perform a single task. When a new task needs to be solved, either create a new program that performs it or combine tools from the toolset that already exists to arrive at a solution. This is a similar orientation to the current trend toward encapsulation and independent component building (such as Enterprise Java Beans), where complicated systems are built from smaller, interacting but logically independent modules.

■ Programs should accept data from standard input and write to standard output; thus, programs can be *chained* to process each other's output sequentially. Interactive input should be avoided in favor of command-line options that specify a program's actions to be performed. Presentation should be separated from what a program is trying to achieve. These ideas are consistent with the concept of piping, which is still fundamental to the operation of user shells. For example, the output of the **ls** command to list all files in a directory can be piped (using the pipe " | " symbol) to a program such as **grep**, to perform pattern matching. The number of pipes on a single command line instruction is not limited.

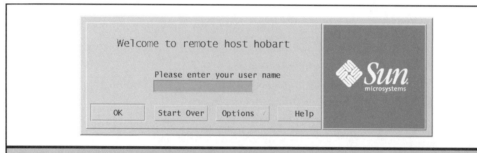

**Figure 1-6.**   *Common Desktop Environment (CDE) login screen*

■ Creating a new operating system or program should be undertaken on a scale of weeks, not years. The creative spirit that leads to cohesive design and implementation should be exploited. If software doesn't work, don't be afraid to build something better. This process of iterative revisions of programs has resurfaced in recent years with the rise of object-oriented development.

■ Make best use of all the tools available, rather than ask for more help. The motivation behind UNIX is to construct an operating system that supports the kinds of toolsets required for successful development.

This is not intended to be an exhaustive list of the characteristics that define UNIX. However, these features are central to understanding the importance UNIX developers often ascribe to the operating system. It is designed to be a programmer-friendly system.

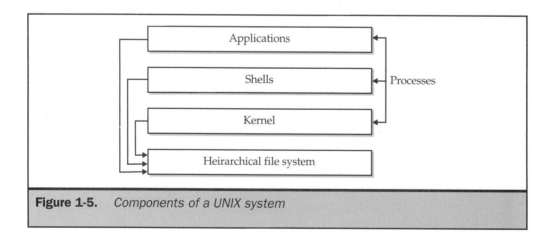

**Figure 1-5.**   *Components of a UNIX system*

# History of UNIX

UNIX was originally developed at Bell Laboratories as a private research project by a small group of people starting in the late 1960s. This group had experience with a number of different operating systems research efforts in the previous decade. Their goals with the UNIX project were to design an operating system to satisfy the objectives of transparency, simplicity, and modifiability with the use of a new third-generation programming language. At the time of conception, typical vendor-specific operating systems were extremely large, and all written in assembly language, making them difficult to maintain. Although the first attempts to write the UNIX kernel were based on assembly language, later versions were written in a high-level language called C, which was developed during the same era. Even today, most modern operating system kernels, such as the Linux kernel, are written in C. After the kernel was developed using the first C compiler, a complete operating environment was developed, including the many utilities associated with UNIX today (for example, the visual editor, **vi**). In this section, we examine the timeline leading to the development of UNIX and the origins of the two main flavors of UNIX: AT&T (System V) and BSD.

## Origins of UNIX

In 1969, Ken Thompson from AT&T's Bell Telephone Labs wrote the first version of the UNIX operating system, on a DEC PDP-7. Disillusioned with the inefficiency of the Multics (Multiplexed Information and Computing Service) project, Thompson decided to create a programmer-friendly operating system that limited the functions contained within the kernel and allowed greater flexibility in the design and implementation of applications. The PDP-7 was a modest system on which to build a new operating system: It only had an assembler and a loader, and would only allow a single-user login at any one time. It didn't even have a hard disk; the developers were forced to partition physical memory into an operating system segment and a RAM disk segment. Thus, the first UNIX file system was emulated entirely in RAM!

After successfully crafting a single-user version of UNIX on the PDP-7, Thompson and his colleague Dennis Ritchie ported the system to a much larger DEC PDP-11/20 system in 1970. This project was funded with the requirement of building a text-processing system for patents, the descendents of which still exist in text filters such as **troff**. The need to create application programs ultimately led to the development of the first C compiler by Ritchie, which was based on the B language. C was written with portability in mind; platform-specific libraries could be addressed using the same function call from source code that would also compile on another hardware platform. Although the PDP-11 was better than the PDP-7, it was still very modest compared to today's scientific calculators, as it has 24K of addressable memory, with 12K reserved for the operating system. By 1972, the number of worldwide UNIX installations had grown to 10.

The next major milestone in the development of UNIX was the rewriting of the kernel in C, by Ritchie and Thompson, in 1973. This explains why C and UNIX are strongly related: Even today, most UNIX applications are written in C, even though other programming languages have long been made available. Following the development of the C kernel, the owners of UNIX (AT&T) began licensing the source code to educational institutions within the United States and abroad. However, these licenses were often restrictive, and the releases were not widely advertised. There was no support offered, and no mechanism for officially fixing bugs. Since users had access to the source code, the ingenuity in hacking code—whose legacy exists today in community projects like Linux—gathered steam, particularly in the University of California at Berkeley. The issue of licensing and AT&T's control over UNIX would determine the future fragmentation of the operating system in years to come.

In 1975, the first distribution of UNIX software was made by the Berkeley group, and was known as the Berkeley Software Distribution (BSD). Berkeley was Ken Thompson's alma mater, and he teamed up with two graduate students (Bill Joy and Chuck Haley), who were later to become leading figures in the UNIX world. They worked on a UNIX Pascal compiler that was released as part of BSD, and Bill Joy also wrote the first version of **vi**, the visual editor, which continues to be popular.

In 1978, the seventh edition of the operating system was released, and it supported many different hardware architectures, including the IBM 360, Interdata 8/32, and Interdata 7/32. The version 7 kernel was a mere 40K in size, and included the following system calls: **_exit, access, acct, alarm, brk, chdir, chmod, chown, chroot, close, creat, dup, dup2, exec*, exit, fork, fstat, ftime, getegid, geteuid, getgid, getpid, getuid, gtty, indir, ioctl, kill, link, lock, lseek, mknod, mount, mpxcall, nice, open, pause, phys, pipe, pkoff, pkon, profil, ptrace, read, sbrk, setgid, setuid, signal, stat, stime, stty, sync, tell, time, times, umask, umount, unlink, utime, wait, write**. The full manual for version 7 is now available online at **http://plan9.bell-labs.com/7thEdMan/index.html**.

With the worldwide popularity of UNIX version 7, AT&T began to realize that UNIX might be a valuable commercial product, and attempted to restrict the teaching of UNIX from source code in university courses, thereby protecting valuable intellectual property. In addition, AT&T began to charge license fees for access to the UNIX source for the first time. This prompted the UCB group to create their own variant of UNIX: The BSD distribution now contained a full operating system in addition to the traditional applications that originally formed the distribution. As a result, version 7 forms the basis for all the UNIX versions currently available. This version of UNIX also contained a full Brian Kernighan and Ritchie C compiler and the Bourne shell. The branching of UNIX into AT&T and BSD flavors continues even today, although many commercial systems, such as SunOS, which are derived from BSD, have now adopted many System V features, as discussed below.

The most influential BSD versions of UNIX were 4.2, released in 1983, and 4.3, released in 1987. The DARPA-sponsored development of the Internet was largely undertaken on BSD UNIX, and most of the early commercial vendors of UNIX used BSD UNIX rather than paying license fees to AT&T. Indeed, many hardware platforms even today, right up to Cray supercomputers, can still run BSD out of the box. Other responses to the commercialization of UNIX included Andrew Tanenbaum's independent solution, which was to write a new UNIX-like operating system from scratch that would be compatible with UNIX, but without even one line of AT&T code.

Tanenbaum called it Minix, and Minix is still taught in operating systems courses today. Minix was also to play a crucial role in Linus Torvalds's experiments with his UNIX-like operating system, known today as Linux.

Bill Joy left Berkeley prior to the release of 4.2BSD, and modified the 4.1c system to form SunOS. In the meantime, AT&T continued with their commercial development of the UNIX platform. In 1983, they released the first System V Release 1, which had worked its way up to Release 3 by 1987. This is the release that several of the older generation of mainframe hardware vendors, such as HP and IBM, based their HP-UX and AIX systems upon, respectively. At this time, Sun and AT&T also began planning a future merging of the BSD and System V distributions. In 1990, AT&T released System V Release 4, which formed the basis for the SunOS 5.x release in 1992—this differed substantially from the previous SunOS 4.x systems, which were entirely based on BSD. Other vendors, such as IBM and DEC, eschewed this new cooperating and formed the Open Software Foundation (OSF).

In recent years, a new threat has emerged to the market dominance of UNIX systems: Microsoft's enterprise-level computing products, such as Windows NT and Windows 2000, are designed to deliver price-competitive alternatives to UNIX on inexpensive Intel hardware. In the same way that UNIX outgunned the dominant mainframe vendors with a faster, leaner operating system, Microsoft's strategy has also been based on arguments concerning Total Cost of Ownership (TCO), and a worldwide support scheme for an enormous installed base of desktop Microsoft Windows clients. However, the increasing popularity of Linux, and the release of Solaris 8 for Intel, has forced Microsoft to defend its platform publicly, and the future of enterprise operating systems is not clear. UNIX will have an important role to play in the future, however. As desktop computing systems rapidly become connected to the Internet, they will require the kinds of services typically available under operating systems such as Solaris 8. As part of their territorial defense of the UNIX environment, many former adversaries in the enterprise computing market, such as IBM, HP, and Sun, have agreed to work toward a Common Open Software Environment (COSE), which is designed to capitalize on the common features of UNIX provided by these vendors. By distributing common operating system elements such as the Common Desktop Environment, based on X11, these vendors will be looking to streamline their competing application APIs, and to support emerging enterprise data processing standards, such as the Object Management Group's CORBA object management service. Figure 1-7 shows the CORBA console from VisiBroker ORB (developed by Inprise), which allows distributed object management to be performed on the desktop using a GUI interface. More information on VisiBroker can be found at **http://www.inprise.com/**.

## Features of BSD

Solaris was originally derived from the BSD distribution from the University of California. Thus, commands in SunOS 4.x were very similar to those found in other BSD distribution, although these changed significantly in SunOS 5.x when System V Release 4 was adopted. For example, many veteran system administrators would still find themselves typing **ps aux** to display a process list, which is BSD style, rather than

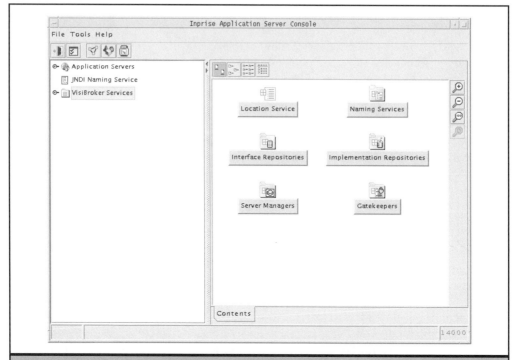

**Figure 1-7.**    *Managing distributed objects on the desktop with VisiBroker*

the newer **ps-eaf**, which is correct for SVR4. Before AT&T commercialized UNIX, the BSD distribution required elements of the AT&T system to form a fully operational system. By the early 1990s, the UCB groups had removed all dependencies on the AT&T system. This led to the development of many of the existing BSD systems available today, including FreeBSD and NetBSD.

The innovations pioneered at UCB included the development of a virtual memory system for UNIX, a fast file system (which supported long filenames and symbolic links), and the basic elements of a TCP/IP networking system (including authentication with Kerberos). The TCP/IP package included support for services like Telnet and FTP, and the **sendmail** mail transport agent, which used the Simple Mail Transfer Protocol (SMTP). In addition, alternative shells to the default Bourne shell—such as the C shell, which uses C-like constructs to process commands within an interpreted framework—were first seen in the BSD distribution, as were extensions to process management, such as job control. Standard terminal management libraries like termcap and curses also originated with BSD. Products from other vendors were introduced into BSD, including NFS clients and servers from Sun Microsystems. Later releases also included support for symmetric multiprocessing, thread management, and shared libraries.

It is often said that the BSD group gave rise to the community-oriented free software movement, which underlies many successful software projects being conducted around the world today. However, BSD is not the only attempt to develop a free version of UNIX. In 1984, Richard Stallman started developing the GNU (GNU is not UNIX) system, which was intended to be a replacement for UNIX and completely free. The GNU C and C++ compilers were some of the first to fully support industry (ANSI) standards, and the GNU Bourne Again shell has many more features than the original Bourne shell (the Bourne Again shell is shown in Figure 1-8). More information about the GNU project can be found at **http://www.gnu.org/**. In addition, there are several versions of BSD that are still freely distributed and available, such as FreeBSD.

## Features of System V Release 4

Solaris 8 integrates many features from the AT&T System V releases, including support of interprocess communication, which were missing in the BSD distributions. As we discussed earlier, many legal battles were fought over the UNIX name and source. System V was developed by the UNIX System Laboratories (USL), which was still majority-owned by AT&T in the early 1980s. However, Novell bought USL in early 1993. Eventually, USL sold UNIX to Novell, who ultimately sold it to X/Open. In 1991, the OSF-1 specification was released, and although DEC is the only major

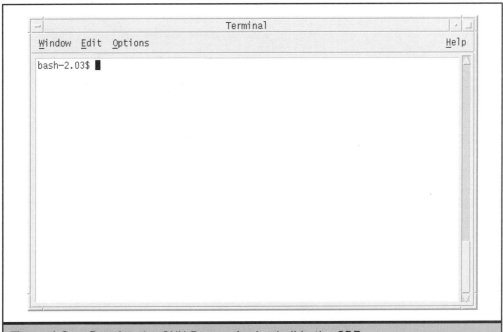

**Figure 1-8.**    *Running the GNU Bourne Again shell in the CDE*

manufacturer to fully implement the standard, there is much useful cross-fertilization between System V and other operating systems. Since Sun joined OSF in 1994, there has been new hope of standardizing UNIX services and APIs across platforms.

The major contributions of System V to the UNIX platform are:

- Enhancement of the Bourne shell, including shell functions
- The STREAMS and TLI libraries
- Remote file sharing (RFS)
- Improved memory paging
- The Application Binary Interface (ABI)

The major differences between SVR4 and BSD UNIX can be summarized as:

- **Boot scripts**   /etc/init.d in System V, /etc/rc.d in BSD
- **Default shell**   Bourne shell in System V, C shell in BSD
- **File system mount database**   /etc/mnttab in System V, /etc/mtab in BSD
- **Kernel name**   /unix in System V, /vmunix in BSD
- **Printing system**   lp in System V, **lpr** in BSD
- **String functions**   **memcopy** in System V, **bcopy** in BSD
- **Terminal initialization**   /etc/inittab in System V, /etc/ttys in BSD
- **Terminal control**   **termio** in System V, **termios** in BSD

## Solaris Innovations

Sun Microsystems was formed by former graduate students from Stanford and Berkeley, who used Stanford hardware and Berkeley software to develop the workstation market in the enterprise. It aimed to compete directly with the mainframe vendors by offering CPU speed and a mature operating system on the desktop, which was unprecedented. For a given price, greater performance could be obtained from the Sun workstations than was ever possible using mainframes. From one perspective, this success destroyed the traditional client-server market that used very dumb terminals to communicate with very clever but horrendously expensive mainframe systems. The vendors of proprietary systems, such as IBM and DEC, saw their market share rapidly decline in the enterprise market, as Sun delivered more bang per buck in performance. By 1986, UNIX was the dominant force at the expense of operating systems like VAX/VMS, although VMS would later come back to haunt UNIX installations in the form of Windows NT. When users could have a workstation with graphics instead of a dumb terminal, there were few arguments about adopting Sun.

However, Sun's innovation enabled departments and workgroups to take control of their own computing environments, and to develop productively with the

C programming language. Sun took BSD and transformed it into a commercial product, adding some useful innovations such as NFS along the way. This was similar in some ways to the approach of Linux companies who create distributions of useful software packages and bundle them with the Linux kernel. However, one significant difference between Sun and Red Hat Linux is that Sun has always been a company with a hardware focus: Its systems were designed with the SPARC chipset and (more recently) the UltraSPARC chipset in mind. This has enabled Sun to create very fast workstations and servers with typically lower CPU speeds than Intel, but faster and more efficient bus performance. Sun invests heavily in hardware design and implementation for an expected commercial reward—all the more so now that Sun gives away the Solaris 8 operating system.

The major innovations of SunOS 4.x can be summarized as:

- Implementation of the network file system (NFS version 2.0, running over UDP)
- The Open Windows 2.0 graphical user environment, based on X11
- The OpenBoot monitor
- The DeskSet utilities
- Multiprocessing support

The major innovations of SunOS 5.x can be summarized as:

- Support for symmetric multiprocessing of up to 128 processors
- The Open Windows 3.0 graphical user environment and OpenLook; integration with MIT X11R5, Motif, PostScript, and the Common Desktop Environment (CDE)
- The Network Information Service (NIS/NIS+)
- Kerberos integration for authentication
- Support for static and dynamic linking
- Full-moon clustering ensuring high availability
- The ability to serve NT clients as a primary domain controller
- Tooltalk
- Java, and support for GUI Java tools like Inprise's JBuilder (as shown in Figure 1-9)
- POSIX-compliant development environment, including single threads, multithreading, shared memory, and semaphores
- Real-time kernel processing
- X/OPEN-compliant command environment
- Compliance with UNIX 95 and UNIX 98 standards
- Support for very large (>2G) files
- Microsoft Windows emulation on the desktop with WABI

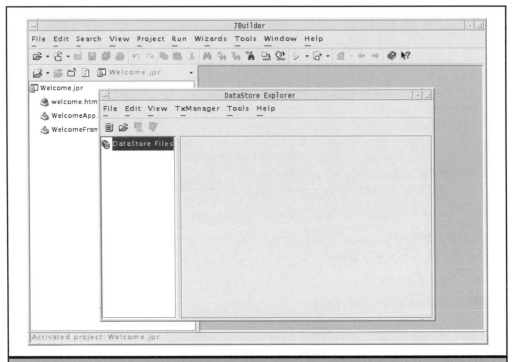

**Figure 1-9.**   *Inprise's JBuilder for Solaris makes building Java applications easy*

- Advanced volume management (**vold**)
- Standardized package administration and deployment tools
- Standardized patch management and integration
- Software-based power management
- Access control lists for resource authorization
- Support for centralized management of user home directories using the automounter
- Improvements to NFS (Version 3), running over TCP
- Support for advanced networking, such as ATM, frame relay, and gigabyte Ethernet
- JumpStart customization of local site installation and deployment
- 64-bit kernel architecture with Solaris 7 and later
- Simplifying backup and restore procedures
- Simplified site administration with the AdminSuite toolkit

## Hardware Support (SPARC and x86)

The classic CPU for Sun systems is the SPARC chip. Many systems in deployment today, including SPARC 5, 10, and 20, use different versions of the SPARC chip, with processor speeds of around 40–60 MHz. However, later systems, which use the UltraSPARC chipset, have processor speeds of up to 400 MHz. While this may not seem fast, the bus architectures of Sun systems are much faster than their PC counterparts, more than making up for apparently slower chip speeds. Many SPARC systems are still supported in Solaris 8, although it is advisable to check with Sun to determine whether older machines, such as IPCs and IPXs, will be supported in future releases. Sun 4 machines and older are no longer supported by Sun, but they may run one of the BSD releases or Linux. Some older machines, such as Classics, have a very loyal support base and are still actively supported.

With the introduction of Solaris 2.1 came support for the Intel platform, supporting ISA, EISA, MCA, and PCI bus types. This performed adequately on high-end 486 systems. Given the significant variation in types and manufacturers of PC hardware, not all devices are currently supported under Solaris 8. Newer innovations, such as the Universal Serial Bus (USB), may be supported in later releases. Solaris 8 for Intel runs very fast on modern Pentium-II and Pentium-III systems, meaning that Intel devotees now have a wider choice of operating systems if they don't want to buy Sun hardware. There was also a single port of Solaris to the PowerPC platform (with version 2.5.1), however, this failed to impress MacOS users and was deprecated in Solaris 2.6.

Solaris x86 users will require the Hardware Compatibility List (HCL) to determine whether or not their particular system or their peripheral devices are supported. This list can be found at

**http://access1.sun.com/drivers/hcl/hcl.html**

The HCL lists all tested systems, components, and peripherals known to work with Solaris x86. Chances are, if your hardware is not listed, it won't be supported. However, many Intel-based standards have been adopted by Sun, including the PCI bus, which is now integrated in the desktop Ultra workstations.

## Cross-Platform Interoperability

Solaris 8 supports several different kinds of cross-platform interoperability. For example, Sun recently released a product called Lxrun, which allows Linux binaries to be run under Solaris x86. This is very handy, as many database vendors, for example, have given away free versions of their database management products for Linux, but not for Solaris 8. Being able to exploit a free offer for one platform, and make use of it on Solaris 8, is a very handy cost saver indeed.

Sun also includes a binary compatibility package in Solaris 8 that allows Solaris 1.x applications to run without modification. However, success can depend on whether the application is statically or dynamically linked. It is not clear whether binary compatibility will continue to be supported in future releases of Solaris 8.

Of course, the greatest hope for the interoperability of different operating systems lies with the Java programming language developed by Sun. Starting life as the Oak Project, Java promises a "write once, run anywhere" platform, which means that an application compiled on Windows NT, for example, can be copied to Solaris 8 and executed without modification and recompilation. Even in the 1970s, when C was being implemented far and wide across different hardware platforms, it was often possible to transfer source and recompile it without modification, but binary compatibility was never achieved. The secret to Java's success is the two-stage compile and interpretation process, which differs from many other development environments. Java source is compiled on the source platform to an intermediary bytecode format, which can then be transferred to any other platform and interpreted by a Java Virtual Machine (JVM). Many software vendors, including SunSoft and Microsoft, have declared support for the Java platform, even though some vendors have failed to meet the specifications laid out by Sun. Until a standard is developed for Java, Sun will retain control over its direction, which is a risk for non-Solaris sites especially. However, Solaris 8 installations should have few qualms about integrating Java technology within their existing environments. With the release of free development tools, such as Inprise's JBuilder Foundation (**http://www.inprise.com/**), development in Java is daily becoming easier for experienced UNIX and C developers. Java is the best attempt yet at complete binary compatibility between operating systems and architectures.

# Sources for Additional Information

In this chapter, we have so far examined the history of UNIX and what distinguishes UNIX systems from other operating systems. We have traced the integration of both flavors of UNIX into the current Solaris 8 release. With the ever-rising popularity of Solaris 8, there are many web sites, mailing lists, and documentation sets that new and experienced users will find useful when trying to capitalize on an investment in Sun equipment or the latest Solaris 8 operating environment. In this section, we present some pointers to the main Internet sites where reliable information about Solaris 8 can be obtained.

## Sun Documentation/SunSites

Unlike some operating systems, Solaris 8 comes with a complete set of online reference manuals and user guides on the AnswerBook CD-ROM, which is distributed with all Solaris 8 releases (Intel and SPARC). The AnswerBooks are in PDF format and cover a wide range of system administration topics, including:

- Binary compatibility guide
- JumpStart guide

- Mail server guide
- Naming services guide
- NFS administration guide
- NIS+ guide
- SunShield security guide
- System administration guides
- TCP/IP guide
- Troubleshooting guides

There is also a set of user guides available on AnswerBook:

- Open Windows user guide
- CDE user guide
- CDE transition guide
- Power management user guide

Developers will also be pleased with the AnswerBook coverage for development issues:

- 64-bit developer's guide
- Device drivers guide
- Internationalization guide
- SPARC assembly language guide (yes, it is still included for the adventurous)
- STREAMS guide
- Source compatibility guide
- WebNFS developer's guide

Hardware maintenance and technical staff will find the hardware reference guides invaluable.

The best thing about the AnswerBook series is that they are available for download and interactive searching through **http://docs.sun.com/**. This means that if you are working in the field and you need to consult a guide, you don't need to carry around a CD-ROM or a printed manual. Just connect through the Internet and read the guide in HTML, or download and retrieve a PDF-format chapter or two.

The two main Sun sites for Solaris 8 are at **http://www.sun.com/solaris** (for SPARC users) and **http://www.sun.com/intel** (for Intel users). Both of these pages contain internal and external links that will be useful in finding more information about Solaris 8 and any current offerings. The Sun Developer Connection is a useful resource users can join to obtain special pricing and download many software components for free.

## Web Sites

There are also many third-party web sites available that deal exclusively with Sun and Solaris 8. For example, SunSunSun (**http://www.sunsunsun.net/**) sells secondhand and reconditioned Sun hardware for a song—as an example, they were recently clearing Classics for $85 per unit (these systems do run Solaris 8). Alternatively, if you are looking for a Solaris 8 FAQ, or a pointer to Sun information, try the Sun Help site (**http://www.sunhelp.org/**). If it's free, precompiled software you're after, check the Sun Freeware site (**http://www.sunfreeware.com/**) or one of the many mirrors. Here you can find the GNU C compiler in a precompiled package (Sun dropped the compiler from Solaris 1.x to Solaris 8, leading to the most frequently asked question on many Solaris 8 forums: "Why doesn't the Solaris 8 compiler work?"). For Solaris 8 for Intel users, there is also an archive of precompiled binaries available at

> **ftp://x86.cs.duke.edu/pub/solaris-x86/bins/**

In case you are interested in seeing what the pioneers of UNIX are doing these days, check out the home pages of these famous UNIX developers:

- Brian Kernighan: **http://cm.bell-labs.com/cm/cs/who/bwk/index.html**
- Dennis Ritchie: **http://cm.bell-labs.com/cm/cs/who/dmr/index.html**
- Ken Thompson: **http://cm.bell-labs.com/who/ken**

## USENET

USENET is a great resource for asking questions, finding answers, and contributing your skills and expertise to help others in need. This is not necessarily a selfless act; there will always be a Solaris 8 question you can't answer, and if you've helped others before, they will remember you. The comp.unix.solaris forum is the best USENET group for Solaris 8 information and discussion. The best source of practical Solaris 8 information is contained in the Solaris 8 FAQ, maintained by the legendary Casper Dik. The latest version can always be found at

> **http://www.wins.uva.nl/pub/solaris/solaris2/**

For Solaris 8 for Intel users, there is the less formal alt.solaris.x86 forum, where you won't be flamed for asking questions about dual-booting with Microsoft Windows or mentioning non-SPARC hardware. For Solaris x86, the best FAQ is at **http://sun.pmbc. com/faq/**. For both SPARC and Intel platforms, there is a comp.sys.sun.admin group dealing with system administration issues, which also has a FAQ available at **ftp://thor.ece.uc.edu/pub/sun-faq/FAQs**. You can easily read USENET news in CDE by using the Netscape Message Center, as shown in Figure 1-10.

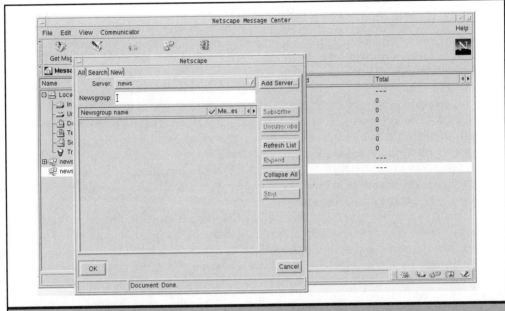

**Figure 1-10.**    *Reading USENET news with the Netscape Message Center*

## Mailing Lists

Mailing lists are a good way of meeting colleagues and engaging in discussions in
a threaded format. The Sun Manager's List is the most famous Sun list, containing
questions, answers, and most importantly, summaries of previous queries. All Solaris-
related topics are covered. Details are available at

> **ftp://ftp.cs.toronto.edu/pub/jdd/sun-managers/faq**

In addition, there is a Solaris 8 for x86 mailing list archived at

> **http://www.egroups.com/group/solarisonintel/**

This list has some great tips, tricks, and advice for those who are new to Solaris 8,
or who are having difficulties with specific hardware configurations.

## What's New in Solaris 8

Solaris 8 was first released through the Solaris Developer Connection as an "Early
Access" release, in the fourth quarter of 1999. The new operating system contains many

enhancements and new features compared to Solaris 7, on both the client and server side, and specifically for administrators. For example, StarOffice 5.1 is now included with the operating system distribution, as well as providing support for integration between personal organization applications and the new generation of "palm computing" devices. On the server side, Solaris now ships with the Apache web server installed, and runs Linux applications through lxrun. Security is overhauled with the inclusion of Kerberos version 5 (discussed more fully in Chapter 16), and IPSec for IPv4 and IPv6, which are also supported, making it easy to create virtual private networks through improved tunneling and encryption technologies. Developers will appreciate the inclusion of a Perl 5 interpreter, other popular tools released under the GNU license, and the Java 2 SDK. In this chapter, we will preview some of these new innovations, and highlight how administrators can ease the transition from Solaris 7 to Solaris 8.

Solaris has always been known as a server-based operating system. Its history and involvement with powering the Internet, and providing a reliable platform for database servers and client-server applications, are the characteristics that most Administrators would associate with Solaris. However, Solaris 8 has bought many improvements on the desktop as well, with further integration and support for standards-based CDE-based applications (in contrast to the old proprietary Open Windows system). Further support for multimedia is also provided, with facilities for MIDI audio, and streamed video supporting many popular formats. CDE support for interfacing with productivity applications hosted on mobile computing devices such as Palm is also provided in conjunction with CDE.

Of course, the biggest desktop announcement of 1999 was Sun's purchase of the Star Office suite from Star Division, and their decision to both ship it for free to the general public and to include it as an integral part of Solaris 8. In addition, Sun is promoting the Sun Ray client as a cost-effective alternative to desktop computing based around legacy PC architectures, with server provided with a departmental server (such as an E450). This approach promises to revolutionize the way many organizations currently (and often inconsistently) manage software updates, patches, and distribution. Figure 1-11 depicts the topology of the Sun Ray workgroup, and summarizes the main features. With the security and reliability of Solaris on the server side, the Solaris desktop will continue to see innovation in Solaris 8 and beyond.

# Star Office

Star Office is a complete office productivity suite, including integrated word processing, spreadsheet, database, presentation, formula rendering, image processing, and web page design applications. A big advantage is the ability to import existing documents from office packages distributed by alternative vendors (including Microsoft Office products). The interoperability between Star Office and competing products is also

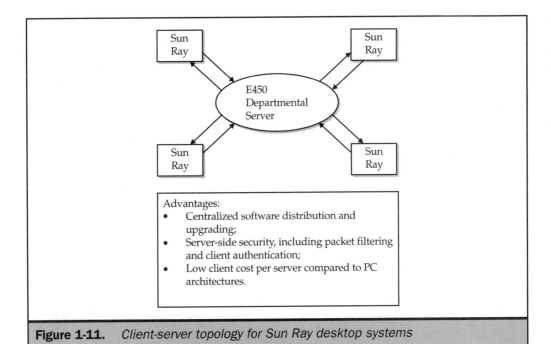

**Figure 1-11.**    *Client-server topology for Sun Ray desktop systems*

reflected in the cross-platform implementation of the product: In addition to running on Solaris, it is also available for OS/2, Linux, and Microsoft Windows computers. Reflecting its European roots, Star Office natively supports many different languages, including Dutch, English, French, German, Italian, Portuguese, Spanish, and Swedish. Figure 1-12 shows the opening screen of Star Office, from which users can create a new type of document, such as a spreadsheet or an image.

Creating a new StarBase database is easy: Just select the appropriate option from the menu, and a database design wizard appears (shown in Figure 1-13). Using a wizard makes creating a database very easy for novice users, and although the Star Office database is not an industrial strength server, it is perfectly adequate for routine administrative tasks such as creating customer contact and product description tables.

Star Office has some advantages over competing products: For example, it has the ability to render quite complex formulas through an innovative formula painter. The user simply selects the appropriate function and enters the appropriate arguments. In addition, more than one predicate can be combined to form complex expressions. In the example shown in Figure 1-14, a combined cubic-root and exponential function expression is constructed in just a few keystrokes.

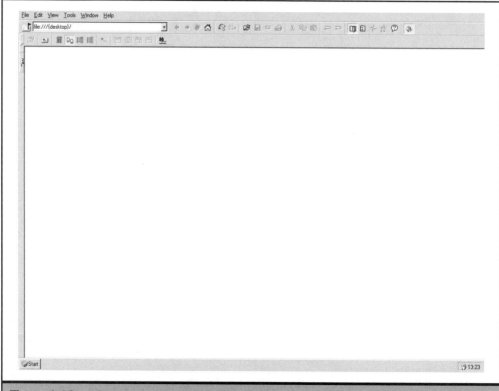

**Figure 1-12.** *Opening screen of the Star Office productivity suite*

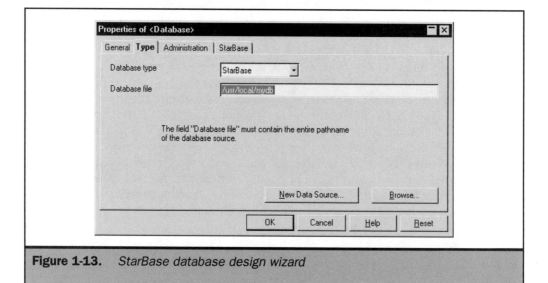

**Figure 1-13.** *StarBase database design wizard*

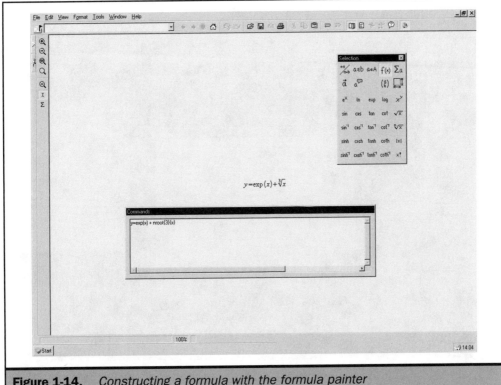

**Figure 1-14.**    *Constructing a formula with the formula painter*

Star Office also has the ability to design and publish web pages as new documents, or to export existing documents. In fact, an entire site can be created by using the wizards that are supplied as part of the HTML editing package. Figure 1-15 shows the first web site wizard screen, and demonstrates the wide variety of templates available through the program.

Although Star Office comes with complete online documentation and help, further information regarding Star Office can be found at the Star Office web center:

```
http://www.sun.com/staroffice
```

# Mobile Computing

The Solaris Operating Environment includes a number of enhancements to the Common Desktop Environment (CDE). Personal Digital Assistant (PDA) support synchronizes data (using PDASync) from most Palm Computing devices with the CDE textpad, calendar, mail, and address book. This enables Palm users to transfer

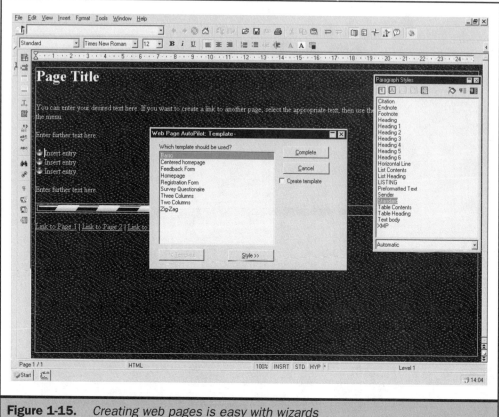

**Figure 1-15.**   *Creating web pages is easy with wizards*

data seamlessly between the desktop and the palmtop, previously a feature of traditionally desktop-oriented operating systems. PDASync is based around 3Com's HotSync technology, making synchronization possible with a single click.

Sun has also released the "K" Java virtual machine (KVM), which will allow Java developers on Solaris to easily port their Java 2 applications to mobile computing platforms, including Palm. The KVM forms part of the Java 2 Micro Edition suite, and has a small memory and disk footprint (i.e., less than 128K RAM). For further information regarding interoperability between Solaris and mobile computing devices using Java, see the KVM home page at:

```
http://java.sun.com/products/kvm/
```

# PC Support

Intel-based machines are not forgotten in Solaris 8, with the operating system being coreleased for the x86 and SPARC architectures. In addition, the workgroup integration software first released with Solaris 7 has now been improved and updated with Solaris 8. This means that PC networks that require a reliable server system for web, database, file, and application serving can make use of proven Solaris reliability and high availability. In addition, Solaris 8 x86 provides a cost-effective alternative to SPARC hardware, and can act as a "drop in" replacement for other server operating systems that also use Intel hardware. For example, the "PC NetLink" software, running on a Solaris server, provides many key networking services to PCs that are normally provided by NT server systems. These services include:

- Primary and backup domain control, enabling centralized sharing of user and resource database for department-sized workgroups
- Security and authentication using security identifiers for generating genuinely unique accounts
- Support for legacy networking protocols, like NetBIOS, and naming services like WINS
- NT file and print services

With the reliability and scalability of Solaris providing these basic network services for an existing PC network, many organizations are centralizing their server software around Solaris, as the same server can provide NetLink services to PCs whilst performing other tasks (such as database serving). For more information regarding NetLink, check the web site:

```
http://www.sun.com/interoperability/netlink/
```

There are several good reasons for using Solaris 8 as a server platform for PCs: First, viruses written for a PC platform are both physically and logically ineffective against Solaris, since the compiled codebase is different for both operating systems. In addition, even if the same codebase was shared (e.g., a rogue Java application executed from a remote shell), the Solaris authentication and identification system does not permit unprivileged users to write to system areas, preventing any malicious damage from occurring to the server. Second, Solaris provides packet-filtering technology that prevents network intruders from browsing internal networks, where PCs may freely broadcast and exchange information between each other.

One of the most exciting innovations in the new collaborative technology that accompanies Solaris 8 is WebNFS, literally "network file serving" through the web. WebNFS provides a standard file system for the World Wide Web, making it easy for users within the same building, or across the globe, to exchange data in a secure way, using industry standard clients. In fact, existing applications can be webified by gaining access to virtual remote file systems using an extension of Sun's original NFS system.

Solaris x86 platform for Intel systems is also gaining in popularity as a server and desktop solution. The dual compatibility policy that has ensured that most of the applications and techniques explained in this book apply to both SPARC and x86 architectures continues with Solaris 8. With the new operating system release, more device drivers are available for PC devices than ever before. For more details, see the Hardware Compatibility List (HCL):

```
http://soldc.sun.com/support/drivers/hcl/index.html
```

Solaris for Intel now supports more than 32GB of memory, and large disks over the current 8GB limit. Furthermore, Solaris 8 permits the use of an alternate boot disk and CD-ROM based reboots. More developments are taking place in terms of supporting the many different and varied PC hardware devices, such as USB and digital video.

# Server Tools

As always, Sun has released a new batch of server-side products to improve upon the existing functionality of Solaris. Of interest to those in the data center will be the new 2.2 release of Sun's "Cluster" product, which offers high system availability through management of hardware redundancy. This offering caters largely to the corporate world, however, developers who are more interested in championing open source technologies will also be pleased with the inclusion of lxrun, a platform for binary compatibility between Linux applications and the Solaris operating environment. Originally developed for UNIX systems distributed by the Santa Cruz Operation (SCO), lxrun allows applications developed for Linux, and released with a binary-only codebase, to be executed natively on the Solaris x86 platform without recompilation or modification. This will ultimately lead to a greater exchange of technology and ideas between Solaris and Linux users.

User and software management through CDE is continually being redeveloped: Solaris 8 contains an improved version of the admintool, which allows administrators to add and delete new users and groups, manage serial ports and printers, and add and delete software packages. Figure 1-16 demonstrates the software management capabilities of admintool.

## Clustering Technology

Increased reliability is often gained by the use of hardware redundancy, which can be achieved on a filesystem by filesystem basis by using a software solution, like DiskSuite, or a hardware-based solution, like an A1000 RAID drive. This allows partitions to be

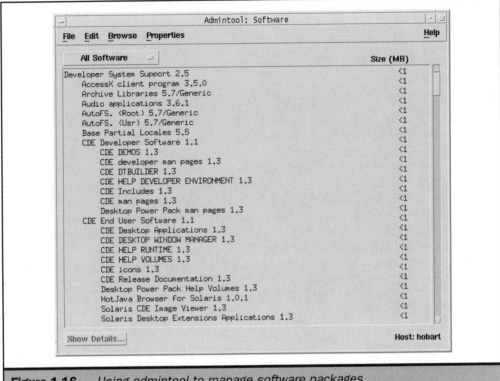

**Figure 1-16.**   *Using admintool to manage software packages*

actively mirrored so that in the event of a hardware failure, service can be rapidly resumed and missing data can be rapidly restored.

This approach is fine for single server systems that do not require close to 100 percent uptime. However, for mission critical applications, where the integrity of the whole server is at stake, it makes sense to invest in clustering technology. Quite simply, clusters are what the name suggests: groups of similar servers (or "nodes") that have similar function, and that share responsibility for providing system and application services. Clustering is commonly found in the financial world, where downtime is measured in hundreds of thousands of dollars, and not in minutes. Large organizations need to undertake a cost-benefit analysis to determine whether clustering is an effective technology for their needs. However, Sun has made the transition to clustering easier by integrating the Cluster product with Solaris 8.

Although Solaris 8 currently ships with Cluster 2.2, Cluster 3.0 will ship with a later Solaris 8 release. It offers even more functionality, with a clustered virtual file system, and cluster-wide load balancing. For more information on introducing clustering technology using Sun Cluster, see Paul Korzeniowski's technical article at:

```
http://www.sun.com/clusters/article/
```

# lxrun

One of the advantages of Solaris 8 for Intel x86 over its SPARC companion is the greater interoperability between computers based on Intel architectures. This means that there is greater potential for cooperation between Linux, operating on Intel, and Solaris, also operating on Intel. This potential has been realized recently with the efforts of Steve Ginzburg and Solaris engineers, who developed lxrun, which remaps system calls embedded in Linux software binaries to those appropriate for the Solaris environment. This means that Linux binaries can run without recompilation or modification on Solaris. In some ways, lxrun is like the Java virtual machine in that Linux applications execute through a layer that separates the application from the operating system. This means that your favorite Linux applications are now directly available through Solaris, including:

- KDE
- Gnome
- WordPerfect 7 and 8
- Applix
- Quake 2
- GIMP (as shown in Figure 1-17)

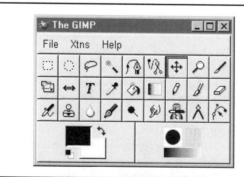

**Figure 1-17.**   *Running the GIMP under CDE*

For more information on lxrun, see its home page:

```
http://www.ugcs.caltech.edu/~steven/lxrun/
```

# Security Innovations

Security is a major concern for Solaris Administrators. The Internet is rapidly expanding with the new IPv6 protocol set to completely supercede IPv4 sometime in the next few years. This will allow very many more addresses to be available for Internet hosts than are currently available. It also means that the number of crackers, thieves, and rogue users will also increase exponentially. Solaris 8 prepares your network for this "virtual onslaught" by embracing IPv6, not only for its autoconfiguration and network numbering features, but because of the built-in security measures that form part of the protocol. In particular, authentication is a key issue after many highly publicized IP-spoofing breaches reported in the popular press over the past few years. A second layer of authentication for internal networks and intranets is provided in Solaris 8 by the provision of Kerberos version 5 clients and daemons. Previous releases, such as Solaris 7, only included support for Kerberos version 4, as reviewed in Chapter 16.

## Kerberos Version 5

Kerberos is the primary means of network authentication employed by many organizations to centralize authentication services. As a protocol, it is designed to provide strong authentication for client/server applications by using secret-key cryptography. Recall that Kerberos is designed to provide authentication to hosts inside and outside a firewall, as long as the appropriate realms have been created. The protocol requires a certificate-granting and validation system based around "tickets," which are distributed between clients and the server. A connection request from a client to a server takes a convoluted but secure route from a centralized authentication server before being forwarded to the target server. This ticket authorizes the client to request a specific service from a specific host, generally for a specific time period. A common analogy is a parking ticket machine that grants the drivers of motor vehicles permission to park in a specific street for one or two hours only.

Kerberos version 5 contains many enhancements over Kerberos version 4, including ticket renewal, removing some of the overhead involved in repetitive network requests. In addition, there is a pluggable authentication module, featuring support for RPC. The new version of Kerberos also provides both server and user level authentication, featuring a role-based access control feature that assigns access rights and permissions more stringently, ensuring system integrity. In addition to advances on the software front, Solaris 8 also provides integrated support for Kerberos and

Smart card technology using the Open Card Framework (OCF) 1.1. More information concerning Kerberos is available from MIT:

```
http://web.mit.edu/network/kerberos-form.html
```

# IPv6

IPv6, described in RFC 2471, is the replacement IP protocol for IPv4, which is currently deployed worldwide. The Internet relies on IP for negotiating many transport-related transactions on the Internet, including routing and the domain-name service. This means that host information is often stored locally (and inefficiently) at each network node. It is clearly important to establish a protocol that is more general in function, but more centralized for administration, and which can deal with the expanding requirements of the Internet. One of the growing areas of the Internet is obviously the number of hosts that need to be addressed: Many subnets are already exhausted, and the situation is likely to get worse. In addition, every IP address needs to be manually allocated to each individual machine on the Internet, which makes the usage of addresses within a subnet sparse and less than optimal. Clearly, there is a need for a degree of centralization when organizing IP addresses that can be handled through local administration, and through protocols like DHCP (Dynamic Host Configuration Protocol). However, one of the key improvements of IPv6 over IPv4 is its auto-configuration capabilities, which make it easier to configure entire subnets, and to renumber existing hosts. In addition, security is now included at the IP level, making host-to-host authentication more efficient and reliable, even allowing for data encryption. One way that this is achieved is by authentication header extensions: This allows a target host to determine whether or not a packet actually originates from a source host. This prevents common attacks, like IP spoofing and denial-of-service, and reduces reliance on a third-party firewall by locking in security at the packet level. Although IPv6 is included with the Solaris 8 distribution, it is also now available separately for Solaris:

```
http://playground.sun.com/pub/solaris2-ipv6/html/solaris2-ipv6.html
```

Tools are also included with Solaris 8 to assist with IPv4 to IPv6 migration.

# IPSec

Virtual Private Network (VPN) technology is also provided with Solaris 8 using IPSec. IPSec is compatible with both IPv4 and IPv6, making it easier to connect hosts using both new and existing networking protocols. IPSec consists of a combination of IP tunneling and encryption technologies to create sessions across the Internet that are as secure as possible. IP tunneling makes it difficult for unauthorized users (such as intruders) to access data that is being transmitted between two hosts on different sites: This is supported by encryption technologies and an improved method for exchanging keys using the Internet key exchange (IKE) method. IKE facilitates interprotocol negotiation and selection during host-to-host transactions, ensuring data integrity. By implementing encryption at the IP layer, it will be even more difficult for rogue users to pretend to be a target host, intercepting data with authorization.

## Overview of this Book

This book aims to be a complete reference for Solaris 8. That means that while we have attempted to broaden our coverage of all aspects of running, installing, and configuring Solaris 8, we have also had to be selective in the background information and worked examples that are presented. After learning the history of UNIX and Solaris 8 in this chapter, you no doubt want to know exactly what you can do with Solaris 8 (and more importantly, how you can achieve that).

Chapter 2 presents the basics of Solaris 8 installation. We cover the process of obtaining the Solaris 8 distribution from Sun Microsystems (including the free Solaris 8 promotion) and demonstrate step by step how to install Solaris 8 on both SPARC and Intel machines. Many readers will be installing Solaris 8 on x86 machines where Windows or Linux may already be installed, so this section will provide tips to ensure that the installation process will not harm existing information. This is particularly important when dual-booting between Solaris 8 and a second (or third) operating system.

After a successful installation, the first view many users have of Solaris 8 is the Common Desktop Environment (CDE). Chapter 3 discusses the process of logging in and using CDE. CDE is the now-default GUI environment on Solaris 8, but many readers will be unfamiliar with it if they have previously used Open Windows. We will cover the essentials of using CDE along with the GUI administration tool AdminTool.

Solaris 8 is partly based on System V UNIX from AT&T, and makes use of a flexible boot process, as covered in Chapter 4. Many books gloss over these processes; however, we walk through init states, startups, and shutdowns in detail, to ensure that your databases are correctly shut down, or alternatively, that you can shut down and secure your system in an emergency. Readers should definitely feel comfortable with tailoring the startup and shutdown of their systems before installing any further applications.

Solaris 8 provides many tools for process management, as presented in Chapter 5. In this chapter we will examine how these tools can be used as part of a standard system administration routine. We will also discuss the innovative /proc file system, and the associated tools that allow administrators to deal with misbehaving (and zombie) processes. This chapter will also discuss task automation and the real-time scheduling facility provided by Solaris 8.

Distributing software in packages has become extremely popular in recent years. In Chapter 6, we will introduce the concept of a software package and show the user how to add and remove third-party packages. We will also show how to create a package for distributing software in binary formats to other machines. Finally, we will discuss patches to installed software packages.

One of the most important and complicated tasks of a system administrator is managing devices. Chapter 7 will concentrate on providing up-to-date information on the wide range of media and devices available on Solaris 8 machines, including hard disk drives and CD-ROMs. Popular new media like Zip and Jaz disks and CD-Rs will also be covered in detail.

To start using a hard drive or removable disk, you need to create a file system. In Chapter 8, we will explain the different types of file systems available under Solaris 8 and show how to make new file systems. We will cover mounting and unmounting disks along with the volume manager, **vold**.

Once your file systems are installed and formatted, you need to monitor them for problems to identify potential problems before they mature. We will present strategies in Chapter 9 for monitoring problems and preventing them with quotas. We will also show you how to recover from disk crashes using **fsck**. Finally, this chapter will cover process and user accounting facilities that can be used as the basis for billing in a commercial environment.

Eventually, all machines crash, and when a crash happens you need to be able to recover quickly and restore functionality. Implementing a backup strategy is essential for recovering crashed systems quickly and efficiently. In Chapter 10, we will cover both the backup media and the different backup tools available on Solaris 8.

Sun's motto is "The Network Is The Computer," and Sun Solaris machines have networking built into them at the lowest levels. In Chapter 11, we will introduce the basics of configuring TCP/IP networking on a Solaris 8 machine. This will provide you with the foundation required to enable essential services on your machine. This chapter covers configuring a Solaris 8 machine for TCP/IP and will point you to tools used in debugging problems.

Being part of a TCP/IP network means that you have to move packets of information between your machine and others. This process is called routing. Chapter 12 will discuss the process of configuring network interfaces and enabling IP routing. We will show you how to manipulate the kernel's routing table statically and dynamically. Finally, we will cover the popular new topic of IP forwarding.

On TCP/IP networks, machines talk to one another using numerical addresses, but it is very difficult for people to remember the numerical address of a machine. Chapter 13 covers DNS, the system responsible for converting machine names into IP addresses. We will cover all aspects of DNS, including setting up primary, secondary, and caching name servers.

With the rise in the numbers of mobile computers like laptops and palmtops, the need for DHCP servers has increased exponentially. Chapter 14 provides an overview of DHCP. Then we will examine configuring a Solaris 8 system as a DHCP client and DHCP server.

The Network Information Service provides administrators with a easy way of controlling user and system information for a large number of machines. It allows for centralized maintenance of user information and host information. Chapter 15 will show you how to set up a NIS server and how to become part of a NIS system.

One of the greatest features of UNIX is that it supports many concurrent users. With TCP/IP enabled, users can log in to a system easily from the Internet. This brings about great flexibility and big security problems. Fortunately, it is possible to secure a Solaris 8 system so that only authorized users can connect to it. Chapter 16 will start by covering the standard tools and the security problems associated with them. It will then present a set of tools that will increase the level of security of your machine without reducing the flexibility of access.

NFS allows you to share your file systems seamlessly with other UNIX machines. Chapter 17 will show you how to configure machines to be NFS clients and NFS servers. It will also provide information on the automounter, which allows for mounting network resources on demand. In addition, we will also examine how to connect to a remote printer, setup a local printer, and make a local printer available for access by other Solaris servers by using the admintool.

Due to the exceptional performance and stability of Solaris 8 systems, they are often called upon to provide reliable file and print services for Macintosh and Windows machines. In Chapter 18, we will discuss the SMB and AppleTalk protocols along with the freely available SAMBA packages that allow Solaris 8 machines to provide Windows and Macintosh machines with file and print services.

Solaris 8 machines continue to be the preferred platform for mail servers. Chapter 19 will introduce the most popular mail servers and protocols used on Solaris 8, and explain their configuration and maintenance in detail. In particular, attention will be paid to the sendmail mail transport agent, whose configuration is often perplexing to experienced administrators.

FTP is the oldest and most common protocol for transferring files over the Internet. Chapter 20 will explain the protocol and show you how to set up an FTP site. We will also cover the popular topic of anonymous FTP and explain some of the alternative FTP servers designed to handle large amounts of anonymous FTP traffic.

The web is the hottest thing on the Internet, and Solaris 8 provides the most stable platform for hosting web content and providing web services. Chapter 21 will cover the HTTP protocol and the most popular and robust HTTP server available, Apache. We will cover basic installation and configuration, along with advanced topics such as user access, virtual hosts, proxies, and secure HTTP. In addition, we examine how to develop and deploy web-based applications using the CGI interface, and the servlt applications developed with Sun's Java programming language.

## Summary

Solaris 8 is an exciting, innovative operating environment for both SPARC and Intel-based processors. It can provide more functionality than existing desktop operating systems; however, there is an increased administrative overhead that must be considered. In this book, we hope to convey sound management practices and divulge practical techniques for solving many Solaris-related problems and implement the best-of-breed methods for all enterprise-level installations. By the end of this book, you should feel confident to manage all aspects of Solaris 8 system administration and feel confident in transferring those skills to the management of related operating systems, such as Linux.

# How to Find Out More

The main site for all Sun technologies is **http://www.sun.com/**. For further information on Java technologies, users should browse Sun's Java site at **http://java.sun.com/**. If you prefer an independent evaluation of Sun technologies, check out the Sun World site at **http://www.sunworld.com/** or Java technologies at **http://www.javaworld.com/**.

The
Complete
Reference

Solaris 8

# Chapter 2

## Installing Solaris

Many users of Solaris 8 will never have to install a server by themselves. However, with the release of "free" Solaris 8, many hobbyists will be installing their own systems. Although Solaris 8 comes preinstalled on new workstations from Sun, administrators will almost certainly need to upgrade the operating system during the life of the server. In this chapter, we will look at installing Solaris 8 on both x86-based and SPARC workstations. We will start with the preinstallation steps for x86 Solaris, which includes a discussion of the install procedure's hardware detection and configuration steps. The actual installation procedure is the same for both versions of Solaris, and we will cover it in the final section.

## Obtaining Solaris

Solaris is available in two versions: *commercial* and *noncommercial*.

The commercial version is required if you are going to be using Solaris in a corporate environment for business-related activities, such as for use on a departmental server or developer workstation. If you purchase a workstation or server from Sun, the latest version of Solaris is included along with your hardware. If you have older workstations or servers, you can purchase or upgrade to the latest version of Solaris. For more information about obtaining a copy of the commercial version of Solaris please consult the following web site:

**http://www.sun.com/solaris/how-to-buy.html**

The noncommercial version of Solaris is ideal for home or educational users. It allows you to obtain a complete copy of Solaris (not a restricted demo!), which is identical to the commercial version. The only difference is that the non-commercial version's license restricts you from using it for business-related activities. You can install and use Solaris on your workstation or PC at work for personal use.

The noncommercial version of Solaris is available from Sun for the cost of media and shipping only. Usually the cost (including shipping and handling) is about $20. In general, it will take from four to eight weeks for you to receive your copy of Solaris. If you order the x86 version the package will include the Solaris 8 installation CD set and a boot diskette. The boot diskette is required only for installing Solaris on x86-based systems; it is not required to run Solaris once it's been installed. If you have a bootable CD-ROM drive, you will not even require the boot disk: The installation CD-ROM can be used to boot the system. The package for SPARC workstations includes only the Solaris 8 installation CD set, since all SPARC workstations are able to boot from a CD-ROM. If you are interested in obtaining a copy of Solaris under the noncommercial license please refer to the following URL:

**http://www.sun.com/developers/solarispromo.html**

You may be wondering why any software company would want to practically give away its operating system. One of the main reasons that Sun started the "give-away" with its noncommercial license was to encourage users with ordinary PCs to try a robust alternative operating system. Sun believes that by giving the operating system away for noncommercial users, many developers will start using Solaris to develop applications. Since developers do not have to pay for Solaris, the cost of porting applications is reduced. As a result, a large number of applications have already been made available on Solaris. As the number of applications increases, many more users will be inclined to use Solaris instead of their current system. In addition, Sun is facing increasing pressure from other "free" operating systems, such as Linux, which is increasingly being deployed in commercial enterprises. For this reason, Solaris x86 is becoming more important in Sun's strategy to cater to the departmental and desktop markets.

# Preinstallation

There are at least two things you should do before installing Solaris in order to make the installation easier and faster to complete.

- Decide on a partitioning scheme for your hard drive.
- Collect network parameters about your system so that the installation can correctly configure your system during installation.

For SPARC-based workstations and servers, once you have completed these steps, you can start installing Solaris by inserting the Solaris 8 CD into each workstation's CD-ROM drive. For x86-based workstations, however, the installation of Solaris is not quite so easy, due to the wide range of hardware configurations available for x86-based workstations, and there are two additional preinstallation steps. The first is to verify that you have a complete distribution. The second is to verify that you have Solaris-compatible hardware.

## Deciding on Partitions for Your Hard Disk(s)

The first preinstallation step for Solaris involves determining the partitioning scheme you want to use for your hard drive(s). The Solaris installation allows you a great deal of flexibility in partitioning, so it is a good idea to determine the partitioning scheme before starting the installation.

### First, Deciding on a Distribution

The starting point for partitioning your hard drive or drives is to decide which version of the Solaris distribution you want to install. The four main versions, and their approximate sizes (including SWAP space), are listed in Table 2-1.

| Distribution | Approximate Size |
|---|---|
| Entire Distribution plus OEM | 800 MB |
| Entire Distribution | 790 MB |
| Developer System Support | 720 MB |
| End User System Support | 440 MB |

**Table 2-1.** *Solaris Distributions and Sizes*

The smallest distribution, End User System Support, should be adequate if you are not going to be developing C/C++ or Java applications. If you plan to develop applications yourself, or if you need to compile and install applications that are freely available, you should plan on installing the Developer System Support distribution. On systems with 1.5GB or greater disks, consider installing the Entire Distribution. This version includes extra documentation and demos that can be extremely useful. The Entire Distribution plus OEM is best if you plan to use special add-on cards or hardware upgrades designed specifically for Solaris. On systems without these cards or hardware upgrades, you do not need to install this distribution.

## Deciding on a Partition Scheme

Once you have decided which version of the Solaris distribution to install, you need to determine which partitions to create. Although it is possible to install and use Solaris on a single partition, this is normally a bad idea. Some of the common problems you can run into with a single partition are:

- Any user can fill up the partition.
- A rogue daemon can fill up the partition with its log file.

The first problem is not as severe as the second, since the system administrator can always delete the files of a user. Solaris reserves about 5 percent of the disk space available on your hard drive for use by root (the system administrator user). This allows root to continue using the system and fix the problem even if a user takes up all the available space for normal users. The second problem is much worse, since a rogue daemon can run as root, which means that it has access to the reserved portion of the hard disk. In this case your system may become unresponsive or unusable. In very rare cases, you would have to reboot your system from the Solaris installation CD in order to fix the problem.

With partitioning, you can segment a large hard drive into smaller and more manageable pieces. Basically, a hard drive partition marks different parts of the hard drive for use by different directories. This allows you to restrict users and daemons to specific partitions. If one of these partitions fills up, it will not affect the system, since other partitions will still have free space available. Normally you want to ensure that the main or root partition, /, has sufficient free space available at all times by creating one partition just for root and placing all other directories in separate partitions. The partitions most commonly created by Solaris administrators are given in Table 2-2.

Notice that you do not have to create the directories /bin and /sbin physically on the root filesystem. In Solaris these directories are mounted as /usr/bin and /usr/sbin respectively on the /usr filesystem. Keeping utilities separate from the kernel ensures that they do not fill up your root partition.

| Partition | Size | Purpose |
| --- | --- | --- |
| / | 64 MB to 128 MB | This is the root partition where essential files such as the kernel are stored. It should be large enough to hold the kernel and some additional files, with enough free space to handle a few large log files and core files from errant processes. |
| /home | 0 MB to 200+ MB | This partition is used to store user home directories. If you are not going to allow additional users on this machine, or if your users have home directories on other systems, you will not need to create this partition. If you are going to be allowing users to log in, then this partition should be large enough to hold your current number of users plus a few extra. Most sites allow about 15 MB to 20 MB per user. |
| /opt | 32 MB to 1+ GB | This partition is used to store optional applications to be installed on the local system. If you need to install several optional applications, this partition should be quite large. |
| /usr | 256 MB to 1+ GB | This partition stores the utilities that make up the heart of the Solaris system, including the "bin" and "sbin" subdirectories. If you intend to install some of your optional applications in /usr instead of in /opt, then this partition will need to be quite large. |

**Table 2-2.**   *Common Partitions on a Solaris System*

| Partition | Size | Purpose |
|-----------|------|---------|
| /var | 20 MB to 1+ GB | This partition is used to store volatile files, such as log files, mail files, and print jobs. If you are running a mail server or a print server, then you will need a large /var (1+ GB) to handle the temporary files. For other systems this partition should be large enough (128 MB to 256 MB) to store the log files of several different applications, but not so large that a rogue program can fill up your disk with hundreds of megabytes' worth of output. |

**Table 2-2.**   *Common Partitions on a Solaris System* (continued)

If you are using a new hard drive, then all you need to do is decide on the size of your partitions using Table 2-2 as a reference. If you are installing on an x86-based workstation with a hard drive that already has another operating system installed on it (for example, Windows), then you may need to repartition your hard drive *within* that operating system by using a utility like **fdisk** or **Partition Magic**. The most reliable method for installing Solaris on x86 systems is to install it on a separate hard drive dedicated to Solaris.

**Note**   *Once you have decided how to partition your hard drive or drives, write the information down so that you can provide it to the Solaris installation program during the actual install procedure described later in this chapter.*

## Determining Network Parameters

In order for your machine to function correctly on a network, whether it is a local area network (LAN) or the Internet, you will need to determine the network parameters given in Table 2-3. You will be using these parameters later, during the actual installation process, so write the information down as you gather it.

If you do not know the value of one of the parameters, please contact your network administrator or ISP for the correct values. Without the correct values, your system will not be usable.

| Parameter | Example | Description |
|---|---|---|
| Hostname | Natashia | Your system's hostname is the name that other people will use to access your machine. |
| IP Address | 10.8.11.2 | Your system's IP address is the numerical address that other computers will use to access your system. |
| Domain Name | Herewane.com | Your system's domain name is used to uniquely identify it by name for users accessing it from the Internet. |
| Subnet Mask | 255.255.255.0 | If your system is part of a subnet, you will need to obtain its subnet mask from your network administrator. |

**Table 2-3.** *Network Parameters for Solaris*

**Note** *If your machine will be configured to automatically obtain its network parameters using a Dynamic Host Configuration Protocol (DHCP) server, you do not need to know these values; the DHCP server will supply all of these parameters for you. Once the installation procedure is complete, however, you will need to follow the procedure given at the end of Chapter 14 in order to enable your system to use DHCP.*

# Additional Preinstallation for x86-Based Workstations

In addition to the two preinstallation steps that were just covered, for x86-based workstations you will need to perform two special steps. The first is to confirm that you have a complete distribution. The second is to verify that your hardware is compatible with Solaris.

## Verifying Your Distribution

If you ordered your copy of Solaris for x86 workstations using the URL given in the previous section, you should have received a Solaris 8 installation CD set and a boot diskette. You will need to have both the CD and a working boot diskette in order to install Solaris 8, if your CD-ROM is not bootable. In any case, you only ever need the boot diskette for installing Solaris 8; you do not need it in order to run Solaris 8 on your system.

**The Boot Diskette**    If you have problems with your boot diskette during the Solaris installation you can download a new copy of it from the following URL:

http://access1.sun.com/drivers/#26

The name of the file you need from that URL is boot.3. This file is a disk image and should be copied onto a 1.44 MB floppy using one of the following commands:
On a Solaris system, you will need to use a command similar to the following:

```
$ dd if=boot.3 of=/dev/fd0 bs=1440K
```

On a DOS/WINDOWS system, you will need to use a command like **rawrite.exe** in order to make a copy of the image (rawrite usually accompanies Linux distributions).
If you encounter problems making a disk image from the file boot.3, please check with Sun for more information, at the Sun support URL:

http://access1.sun.com/drivers/copytodisk.html

## Checking Hardware Compatibility

The second pre-installation step involves determining whether or not your system's hardware is compatible with Solaris 8. Solaris 8 includes drivers for a wide range of common x86 hardware and expansion cards. This section provides an overview of the general hardware compatibility requirements. For a complete list of hardware supported by Solaris, please check the URL:

http://access1.sun.com/drivers/hcl/hcl.html

If you are thinking about buying a new system to run Solaris but some aspect of your system isn't listed at this site, check it again later (as time allows) for the most recent support information. The site is frequently updated to add information about the latest cards and hardware platforms that are supported.
In general, most systems from Acer, Compaq, Dell, HP, and IBM are supported. Even if your particular machine is not from a supported vendor or is not featured on the "official" support list, if it meets the basic requirements you should be able to install and use Solaris without any problems.

**Supported Processors**    In order to install and run Solaris 8, your x86-based workstation should have one of the following processors:

- Intel Pentium, Pentium PRO, Pentium II, or Celeron
- AMD K5, K6, or K6-2
- Cyrix 5x86 or 6x86

**Memory Requirements**    Although the memory requirement for previous versions of Solaris was a minimum of 32M, 64M is required to install and run Solaris 8. This will be adequate to run many graphical applications and development tools, although for production systems, a minimum of 256 MB of RAM is recommended. For database applications, Solaris performs optimally on systems with 512 MB or greater.

**Supported Hard Drives and Removable Media**    Solaris supports almost all hard drives and removable media that are based on the Integrated Drive Electronics interface (IDE), the Enhanced Integrated Device Electronics interface (E-IDE, also called ATAPI by some vendors), and Small Computer System Interface (SCSI). If your hard drive is from a major vendor such as Seagate, Quantum, Fujitsu, Maxtor, or IBM, Solaris will be able to determine most of the parameters of your hard drive automatically. You may encounter problems with older hard drives or drives from smaller vendors.

Most CD-ROM drives with speeds greater than 2x will work fine with Solaris 8. You may encounter some problems with the older 1x CD-ROM drives or the newer 40x or greater CD-ROM drives. Also, since some older PC BIOS systems do not support booting from a CD-ROM directly, you may need a 1.44 MB floppy drive in your system in order to install Solaris.

**Supported Bus Types**    Solaris supports all major PC bus types, including the Industry Standard Architecture bus (ISA), the Extended Industry Standard Architecture bus (EISA), the Peripheral Component Interconnect bus (PCI), and Video Electronics Standards Association's Local Bus (VLB). The Micro-Channel bus and the Accelerated Graphics Port (AGP) are not supported by Solaris. It is advisable to install and run Solaris by using a video card in an ISA, EISA, or PCI slot.

**Add-on Card Support**    Although your bus type is most likely supported by Solaris, you may have video cards, network cards, sound cards, or modems that are not supported. Most popular cards by Adaptec, 3Com, SMC, Intel, and Creative Labs are supported, but please check the support URL given above for complete information regarding a particular card. Some of the more popular cards supported by Solaris are:

- Adaptec 1510, 1540, 2940, and 3940 SCSI adapters
- AMD's PCscsi and PCscsi II SCSI adapters
- AMD's PCnet-based Ethernet adapters
- Creative Labs Sound Blaster 16 and Sound Blaster PRO
- 3Com's Etherlink, Etherlink III, and Etherlink XL Ethernet adapters
- 3Com's TokenLinkIII token ring adapters
- D-Link's DE-530CT and DE-530CT+ Ethernet adapters
- Intel's EtherExpress 16 and EtherExpress PRO Ethernet adapters
- NetGear's FA310-based Ethernet adapters
- SMC's Elite32, EtherCard, and EtherPower Ethernet adapters
- Madge Networks Smart 16/4 token ring adapters

**Supported Video Cards** Since the number of manufactures and distributors for video cards is extremely high, Solaris supports video cards that are based on a particular video chipset rather than particular video cards. To determine the chipset of your video card, consult its manual or the web site of its manufacturer. Some of the more popular video chipsets supported by Solaris are:

- ATI 3D Rage, 3D Rage II, and 3D Rage PRO
- ATI Mach8, Mach32, and Mach64
- Chips and Technologies F65540, F65545, F65548, and F65550
- Cirrus Logic GD5420, GD5428, GD5429, GD5430, GD5434, GD5436, GD5446, GD5465, and GD5480
- Matrox MGA-2, MGA-3, MGA-Storm, and MGA-G100
- S3 Trio, Vision, Virge, Virge/DX, and Virge/VX

# Installing Solaris

After you have completed the preinstallation steps, decided on the partitioning scheme you'll want Solaris to create, and gathered your network parameters, you can start the actual Solaris installation process.

The actual installation process for Solaris 8 is nearly the same for both SPARC and x86-based systems, with the only difference being the hardware detection and configuration steps that Solaris performs on x86-based workstations before it begins the actual installation of the operating system. Those steps are discussed in the following section; after that I present the steps for installing to a SPARC-based system, and conclude with an example installation walkthrough, which is applicable to both x86-based systems and SPARC-based systems.

**Note** *If you are installing on an x86-based workstation, please read the next section, which provides you with an overview of the hardware detection and configuration process used by Solaris before the installation process starts. Once the hardware detection and configuration process has completed, you can proceed to the installation walkthrough section of this chapter. If you are installing Solaris on a SPARC-based workstation or server, please skip the following section and go directly to the section "Common Installation Procedures (SPARC/Intel)."*

## Installing to an x86 System

To start the installation process on an x86 system, insert your Solaris 8 installation CD into your CD-ROM drive. Depending on your CD-ROM drive, you may need to have your computer running in order to do this. In addition, on x86-based systems without a bootable CD-ROM drive, you will also need to insert the Solaris boot floppy into your computer's A: floppy drive. At this point you should reboot to start the required hardware detection and configuration process, and modify the BIOS settings if necessary to check for a bootable CD-ROM before booting from a floppy disk or hard drive.

When your machine boots from the floppy or CD-ROM drive, it will load the Solaris Device Configuration Assistant (DCA). You can use the DCA to perform the following tasks (the keyboard shortcut is given in parentheses):

- Scan and identify your hardware for installation (F2)
- Diagnose scan failures (F3)
- Add new drivers (F4)

At this point, you simply need to scan and identify your hardware for the installation, so you will need to press F2.

## Using the DCA

First the DCA will scan your bus type to determine if it is supported. Unless you have a Micro-Channel-based bus, this step will normally succeed. (Solaris does not support the Micro-Channel bus.) Once your bus type has been determined, the DCA scans your system to identify your hard drive, motherboard, mouse, keyboard, video card, and audio card. A progress bar will be displayed as the scan progresses.

If this step hangs, you will need to reboot your machine and then select the Diagnose scan failures option from the main DCA screen by pressing F3.

Once the scan completes successfully, the list of devices that were identified is displayed on the Identified Devices screen. This screen will contain a list similar to the following:

```
The following devices have been identified on this system. To
identify devices not on this list or to modify device
characteristics, chose Device Task. Platform types may be included
in this list.

    ISA: Floppy disk controller
    ISA: IDE controller
    ISA: IDE controller
    ISA: Motherboard
    ISA: PS/2 Mouse
    ISA: PnP bios: 16550-compatible serial controller
    ISA: PnP bios: 8514-compatible display controller
    ISA: PnP bios: Audio device
```

```
ISA: PnP bios: ECP 1.x compatible parallel port
ISA: System keyboard (US-English)
```

**The Device Task Screen**    From this screen you can change the properties of a particular device by pressing F4, which presents you with the Device Tasks screen that can be used for the following tasks:

- View/Edit Devices
- Set Keyboard Configuration
- Save Configuration
- Delete Saved Configuration
- Set Console Device

Unless you've already experienced problems from an earlier attempt to run Solaris from this same distribution, I suggest you accept the defaults detected by the DCA; they are the ones that are expected to work best for Solaris 8.

## Loading Drivers

Once you have finished configuring your devices, press F2 in the Identified Devices screen. The installation will pause as it loads the correct drivers for your system. Depending on the number of drivers that are required, the loading process may take anywhere from 30 seconds to a few minutes. Once the drivers have been loaded, you will be presented with the Boot Solaris screen, which contains a list of devices from which you can boot Solaris. The list will look similar to the following:

```
[ ] DISK: Target 0, TOSHIBA MK2103MAV
          on IDE controller on ISA bus at 1f0
[ ] CD  : Target 0, TOSHIBA CDROM XM-1202B 1635
          on IDE controller on ISA bus at 170
```

Of course, the make and model of your hard disk and CD-ROM will most likely be different than the ones shown in the above listing.

**Setting the Default Boot Device**    Unless a default boot device is set, you cannot automatically boot into Solaris. Before continuing with the installation, therefore, you should set your default boot device to one of the devices listed on the Boot Solaris screen. You can use the following procedure to set the boot device:

1. Press F4 in the Boot Solaris screen. You will be presented with the Boot Tasks screen.

2. In the Boot Tasks screen, select the first option, View/Edit Autoboot Settings, and press F2. You will be presented with the View/Edit Autoboot Settings screen.

3. In the View/Edit Autoboot Settings screen, select the Set Default Boot Device option and press F2. You will be presented with a list of bootable devices.

4. Select one of the devices in the list and press F2. You will be returned to the View/Edit Autoboot Settings screen.

5. In the View/Edit Autoboot Settings screen, select the Set Autoboot (ON/OFF) option and press F2. You will be presented with the Set Autoboot screen.

6. In the Set Autoboot screen, select ON and press F2. You will be returned to the View/Edit Autoboot Settings screen.

7. In the View/Edit Autoboot Settings screen, select the Accept Settings option and press F2.

8. You will be returned to the Boot Task Screen. Press F3 on this screen to load the new setting and resume the installation.

At this point you will be returned to the Boot Solaris screen. You should see the drive you selected highlighted. The drive is automatically assigned a drive number of zero to indicate its status as the default drive, as shown in this example:

```
[ ] DISK: (*) Target 0, TOSHIBA MK2103MAV
          on IDE controller on ISA bus at 1f0
```

## Common Installation Procedures (SPARC/Intel)

After completing the previous preconfiguration steps, your Intel system is ready to run the common Solaris installation program. In order to proceed with the installation, check that the Solaris 8 installation CD is in your CD-ROM drive and press F2. This will boot Solaris and prompt you for the installation mode. At this point, installation for Solaris x86 and SPARC is similar. The three available choices are:

■ Solaris Interactive

- Custom JumpStart
- Solaris WebStart

## Solaris Interactive Installation

The first option, Solaris Interactive, is available on both Intel x86 and SPARC systems that have the minimum memory and hard drive requirements. On SPARC systems this option will allow you to install Solaris even if you only have a text-only terminal connection to your machine. If you have a graphics monitor and a keyboard hooked up to your computer, the Solaris Interactive install will walk you through the installation using a graphical installation wizard. The installation wizard is based on a series of steps, and is quite similar to the installation wizards of other operating systems like Windows NT and the Mac OS.

In text mode, the Solaris Interactive installation uses text screens on the console in place of the graphical installation wizard on the monitor; the actual steps are exactly the same. In the "Installation Walkthrough" section later in this chapter, we examine the text-mode version of each of the graphical installation wizard's dialogs in code listings following the figures. In order to perform the installation in text mode, you will need either a text terminal such as a WYSE terminal or, alternatively, a PC or a terminal server connection. Performing the Solaris Interactive installation in text mode is available only for SPARC-based workstations.

A PC with a null modem cable (available at most computer stores) and terminal emulation software can be used as an alternative to an actual text terminal. The most common terminal emulation program used on a Windows PC is HyperTerminal. The most popular terminal emulation program on Macs is ZTerm. You can connect the null modem cable from the serial port on your PC (COM1 or COM2 port on a Windows/DOS machine, Printer/Modem ports on a MacOS machine) to the serial A port on your Sun workstation.

**Note**   *Older Sun workstations such as a SPARC 4, 5, 10, or 20 do not have multiple serial ports. Just connect the cable to the single serial port labeled A/B.*

If you have a terminal server such as a Cisco 500cs or 2500 and a null modem cable, you can use them to remotely access the console of your system. Terminal servers are computers or routers that have several serial ports and allow you to access these ports remotely via telnet. If your system is hooked up to a terminal server you will need to know the name or IP address of the terminal server and the port that your system is connected to. You should be able to get this information from your system administrator or your network administrator.

## JumpStart

The second option, Custom Jumpstart, is only useful at large Solaris installations where a centralized Solaris machine (a JumpStart server) has been preconfigured to automatically install Solaris on your machine. If there is a JumpStart server available on your network then you can use this option to install Solaris without any interaction. This option is not available when installing Solaris on a PC.

## WebStart

The third option, WebStart, provides a Java-based application interface that leads you through the installation process. This option is available on systems with greater than 64 MB of RAM. WebStart is similar to the Solaris Interactive installation, except that it makes better use of system graphical facilities than a standard installation wizard. Since many Solaris installations are performed with low-end graphics interfaces (such as a VT-100 terminal), we won't cover WebStart installation in depth in this book. However, details of WebStart are included in the Sun "Installation Guide."

# Installation Walkthrough

When your system starts the actual installation of the Solaris operating system, you will see the following message on your screen:

```
SunOS Release 5.8 Version Generic [UNIX(R) System V Release 4.0]
Copyright (c) 1983-2000, Sun Microsystems, Inc.
Configuring devices...
The system is coming up.  Please wait.
```

Depending on the speed of your CD-ROM drive, the initial system boot process can take up to five minutes. Most systems with 10x or greater CD-ROM drives will boot in about two minutes. After the system boots into the installation process, you will be presented with a set of questions, which I cover here in their order of appearance.

## Selecting a Language for the Installation

Once Solaris has booted from the CD you will be presented with the following message:

```
Select a Language
 0) English
 1) German
 2) Spanish
 3) French
 4) Italian
 5) Swedish
?
```

Type in the number corresponding to the language in which you want the installation to occur, and press ENTER.

*This prompt is for the language in which the installation will be conducted; it is not necessarily the language for your system. Unless you specifically purchased an international version, Solaris 8 will use English by default.*

Once you have selected a language for the installation, you will be asked to pick a locale. The locale determines how information such as time, date, spelling, and monetary values are displayed. In the United States the locale values that are most commonly used are 0 (ASCII) or 14 (ISO8859-1). The main difference between the ASCII and ISO locales is that the ISO locale allows you to use accented or umlaut characters. If you do not need to use these characters, the standard ASCII locale is sufficient.

## Configuring Networking

The second step in the installation is to configure the network parameters for your system. You should use the parameters that you determined earlier in the chapter to help you correctly answer the questions in this section.

**Setting the Hostname**   The first screen will ask you to enter the hostname of the machine:

```
Host Name

  On this screen you must enter your host name, which identifies
this system on the network.  The name must be unique within your
domain; creating a duplicate host name will cause problems on the
network after you install Solaris.

  A host name must be at least two characters; it can contain
etters, digits, and minus signs (-).

    Host name:
```

Enter the hostname of your machine at the prompt and press F2 to continue.

*During the first part of the Solaris installation the F2 key is used to proceed from one screen to another. If your keyboard does not support the F2 key you can use ESC-2 instead.*

**Enabling Networking**   The next screen will ask you whether or not your system is networked. If your machine is not networked, simply select NO and press F2; otherwise press F2 to continue with network configuration. The first networking parameter you will be asked for is the IP address of your system.

```
IP Address
  On this screen you must enter the Internet Protocol (IP) address
for this system. It must be unique and follow your site's address
conventions, or a system/network failure could result.

  IP addresses contain four sets of numbers separated by periods
(for example 129.200.9.1).

    IP address:
```

Enter the IP address for your machine, and press F2. After you have entered the IP address, you will be asked to confirm the values. Unless you made a mistake, press F2 after this to continue. Once you confirm the values, the Solaris installation configures your machine for networking. Depending on your system and network congestion, this process could take several minutes.

**Configuring Name Service**    After basic networking has been configured, you will be prompted for the Name Service used at your site:

```
Name Service

On this screen you must provide name service information.  Select
NIS+ or NIS if this system is known to the name server; select
Other if your site is using another name service (for example,
DCE or DNS); select None if your site is not using a name service,
or if it is not yet established.

> To make a selection, use the arrow keys to highlight the option
and press Return to mark it [X].

    Name service

    [ ] NIS+
    [ ] NIS (formerly yp)
    [X] Other
    [ ] None
```

If your system will be running either NIS or NIS+, you will need to know the NIS/NIS+ domain, and the IP address of your name server, in order to complete the configuration. You should obtain this information from your system administrator or your network administrator. For more information on NIS and NIS+, please see Chapter 15.

If your system will use an alternate method for name resolution, such as the Domain Name Service, you should choose the option Other. For more information about configuring DNS on your system once the installation completes, please see Chapter 13.

You should only select the None option if you do not want to use a centralized name service. Finally, since it is extremely easy to reconfigure name services after the installation, don't worry about choosing the wrong option for your site; you can always go back and fix it.

**Configuring the Subnet Mask**   After name service has been configured, you will be asked if your system is part of a subnet. This is the last step in the network configuration. If it is part of a subnet, press F2 to continue. Otherwise select NO and then press F2. If you are part of a subnet, the next screen will ask you to enter your subnet mask. Make sure that you enter the correct subnet mask for the network that your system will be a part of. If you enter an incorrect subnet mask your system will not be able to communicate with the rest of the network.

If your system requires a subnet mask, you should be able to get this information from your network administrator or your system administrator.

*You don't necessarily have to get the subnet mask from your network administrator. Another possibility is to look at the network configuration of a system that is already on the network and use the same subnet mask as that system.*

For more information on configuring networking on your system after the initial installation please see Chapters 11 and 12.

## Configuring the Time

The final step before the graphical installation wizard starts is to configure the local time for your machine. This is done using three separate screens. The first screen asks you for your general geographic area. The second asks you for your offset within that area. (For the United States this will be Eastern, Central, Mountain, or Pacific.) The third screen presents you with what your computer thinks is the correct time and allows you to adjust it, in case the computer's clock is out of sync. After you have entered the time information, you will be presented with a confirmation screen. If you made any mistakes you can go back and correct them; otherwise the Solaris install will finish configuring your machine and begin the actual installation using the web-based wizard. Once you have completed this configuration task the following message will be displayed:

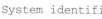

```
System identification is completed.
```

## Using the Graphical Installation Wizard

Once the installer has finished with the system identification process, the graphical installation wizard will start on your system. The steps in the graphical installation wizard are targeted toward making it easy for you to pick a distribution and partition your disks for that distribution. The text-mode equivalents for each of these dialogs are given in the code listings following the figures.

The first screen you will be presented with is the dialog shown in Figure 2-1. Click the Continue button in this dialog to begin partitioning your system's disks.

```
- Solaris Interactive Installation --------------------------------
  You'll be using the initial option for installing Solaris
  software on the system. The initial option overwrites the
  system disks when the new Solaris software is installed.

  On the following screens, you can accept the defaults or
  you can customize how Solaris software will be installed by:
        - Allocating space for diskless clients or AutoClient systems
        - Selecting the type of Solaris software to install
        - Selecting disks to hold software you've selected
        - Specifying how file systems are laid out on the disks

  After completing these tasks, a summary of your selections (called
  a profile) will be displayed.


  ------------------------------------------------------------------
      F2_Continue    F5_Exit    F6_Help
```

The next dialog that will appear is shown in Figure 2-2. This screen will ask you if you want to allocate client services. If your machine needs to support diskless clients such as network computers or X-terminals, click the Allocate button. Otherwise click the Continue button.

```
- Allocate Client Services? ---------------------------------------
  Do you want to allocate space for diskless clients and/or AutoClient
  systems?


  ------------------------------------------------------------------
    Esc-2_Continue Esc-3_Go Back Esc-4_Allocate Esc-5_Exit Esc-6_Help
```

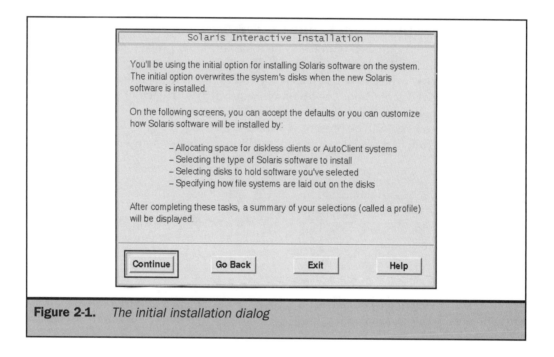

**Figure 2-1.** *The initial installation dialog*

The third dialog that is presented is shown in Figure 2-3. It asks you to select which distribution set of Solaris you want installed. Choose the distribution that you decided on earlier in the chapter as part of the first preinstallation step.

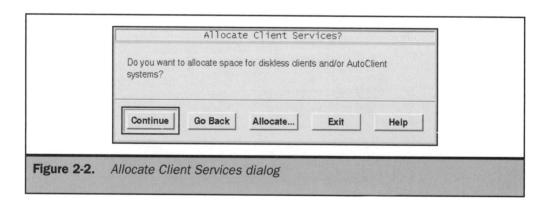

**Figure 2-2.** *Allocate Client Services dialog*

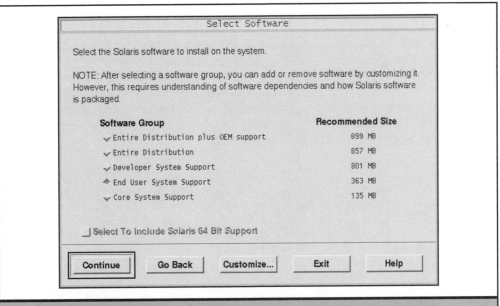

**Figure 2-3.**    *Select Software dialog*

```
- Select Software ------------------------------------------------------
  Select the Solaris software to install on the system.

  NOTE: After selecting a software group, you can add or remove
  software by customizing it. However, this requires understanding
  of software dependencies and how Solaris software is packaged.
  The software groups displaying 64-bit contain 64-bit support.


      [X]  Entire Distribution plus OEM support 64-bit  998.00 MB (F4 to Customize)
      [ ]  Entire Distribution 64-bit ................. 980.00 MB
      [ ]  Developer System Support 64-bit ............ 922.00 MB
      [ ]  End User System Support 64-bit ............. 562.00 MB
      [ ]  Core System Support ....................... 205.00 MB


 ------------------------------------------------------------------------
Esc-2_Continue Esc-3_Go Back Esc-4_Customize Esc-5_Exit Esc-6_Help
```

If you want to add to or remove certain portions of the packages that are installed, select the Customize button on this screen. In most cases, however, customization leads to problems after the installation has completed, so I recommend that you avoid it. Normally after selecting a distribution you should just click Continue.

After selecting a distribution you will be presented with the Select Disks dialog, show in Figure 2-4. Using this dialog you can select which hard drive you want to use to install Solaris. (If you have a hard drive that is dedicated to another operating system, make sure that it is not selected as an install drive.) Once you have selected your installation drives, click the Continue button.

```
- Select Disks --------------------------------------------------------
  On this screen you must select the disks for installing Solaris
  software.  Start by looking at the Suggested Minimum field; this
  value is the approximate space needed to install the software
  you've selected. Keep selecting disks until the Total Selected
  value exceeds the Suggested Minimum value.

         Disk Device (Size)          Available Space
         =============================================
         [X] c0t1d0    (638 MB)                638 MB   (F4 to edit)

                           Total Selected:     638 MB
                        Suggested Minimum:     740 MB


  ----------------------------------------------------------------------
Esc-2_Continue Esc-3_Go Back   Esc-5_Exit Esc-6_Help
```

At this point the Solaris install will present the dialog shown in Figure 2-5, which asks if you want to have it automatically lay out your file system. If you have a preference as to the layout of the file system, select the Manual Layout button; otherwise click the Auto Layout button.

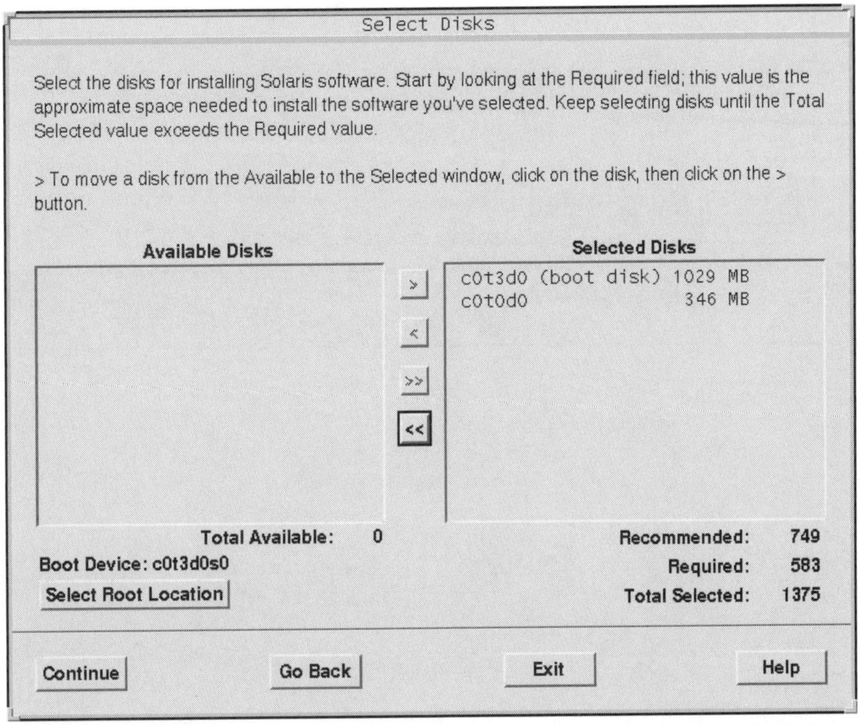

Select Disks

Select the disks for installing Solaris software. Start by looking at the Required field; this value is the approximate space needed to install the software you've selected. Keep selecting disks until the Total Selected value exceeds the Required value.

> To move a disk from the Available to the Selected window, click on the disk, then click on the > button.

**Available Disks**                          **Selected Disks**

>             c0t3d0 (boot disk) 1029 MB
<             c0t0d0             346 MB
>>
<<

|  |  |
|---|---|
| **Total Available:** 0 | **Recommended:** 749 |
| **Boot Device: c0t3d0s0** | **Required:** 583 |
| **Select Root Location** | **Total Selected:** 1375 |

Continue       Go Back       Exit       Help

**Figure 2-4.** *Select Disks dialog*

The Auto Layout option allows you to specify the partitions you want created and to modify their disk space layout by using the dialogs shown in Figures 2-6 and 2-7.

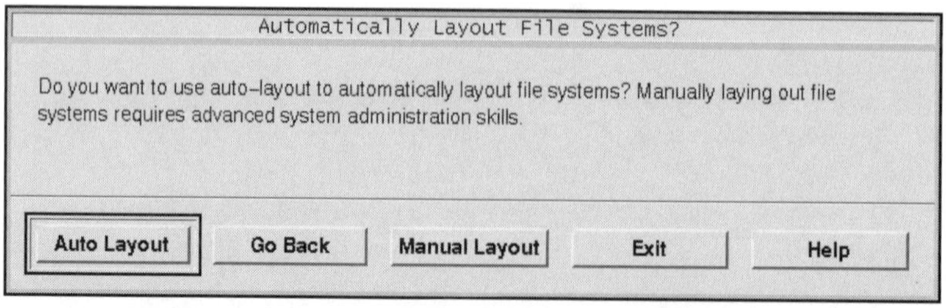

**Figure 2-5.** *The Auto Layout dialog*

```
- Automatically Layout File Systems -----------------------------
  On this screen you must select all the file systems you want
  auto-layout to create, or accept the default file systems shown.

  NOTE: For small disks, it may be necessary for auto-layout to
  break up some of the file systems you request into smaller file
  systems to fit the available disk space. So, after auto-layout
  completes, you may find file systems in the layout that you did
  not select from the list below.

          File Systems for Auto-layout
          ========================================
          [X]  /
          [ ]  /opt
          [X]  /usr
          [ ]  /usr/openwin
          [ ]  /var
          [X]  SWAP


  ----------------------------------------------------------------
      Esc-2_Continue    Esc-5_Cancel    Esc-6_Help
```

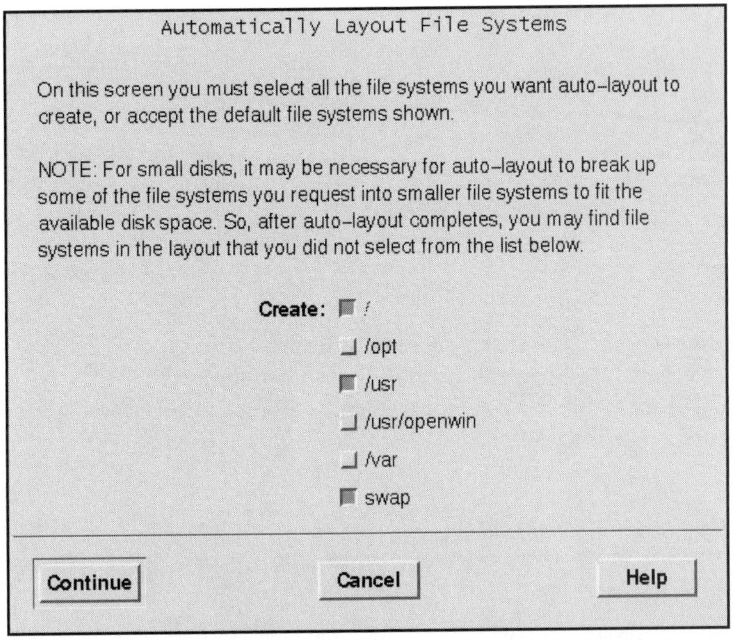

**Figure 2-6.**   *Create File Systems dialog*

```
- File System and Disk Layout ----------------------------------------
  The summary below is your current file system and disk layout,
  based on the information you've supplied.

  NOTE: If you choose to customize, you should understand file
  systems, their intended purpose on the disk, and how changing
  them may affect the operation of the system.
```

```
File system/Mount point            Disk/Slice            Size
===============================================================
/                                  c0t1d0s0             90 MB
/var                               c0t1d0s1             25 MB
overlap                            c0t1d0s2            638 MB
SWAP                               c0t1d0s3            147 MB
/usr                               c0t1d0s6            374 MB

---------------------------------------------------------------
Esc-2_Continue Esc-3_Go Back Esc-4_Customize Esc-5_Exit Esc-6_Help
```

If you want to modify the disk space allocations that were made by the Solaris installation, select the Customize button in the dialog shown in Figure 2-7. Otherwise click Continue. Once you have finished with any modifications, the Profile dialog shown in Figure 2-8 will be displayed.

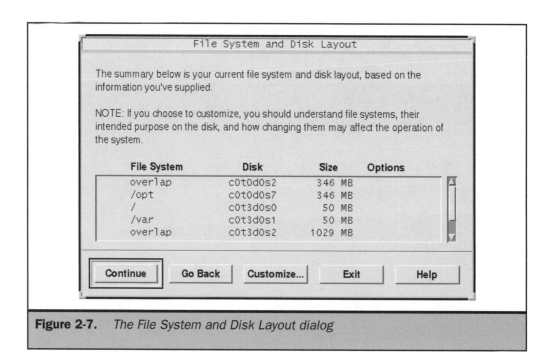

**Figure 2-7.** *The File System and Disk Layout dialog*

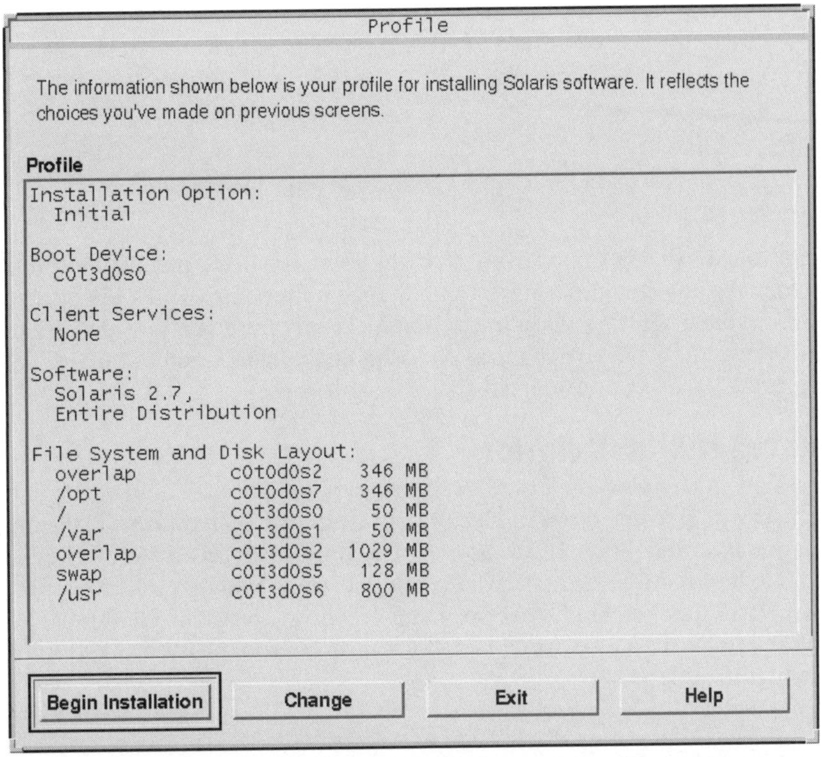

```
                              Profile

   The information shown below is your profile for installing Solaris software. It reflects the
   choices you've made on previous screens.

   Profile
   ┌─────────────────────────────────────────────────────────────┐
   │Installation Option:                                         │
   │  Initial                                                    │
   │                                                             │
   │Boot Device:                                                 │
   │  c0t3d0s0                                                   │
   │                                                             │
   │Client Services:                                             │
   │  None                                                       │
   │                                                             │
   │Software:                                                    │
   │  Solaris 2.7,                                               │
   │  Entire Distribution                                        │
   │                                                             │
   │File System and Disk Layout:                                 │
   │  overlap        c0t0d0s2     346 MB                         │
   │  /opt           c0t0d0s7     346 MB                         │
   │  /              c0t3d0s0      50 MB                         │
   │  /var           c0t3d0s1      50 MB                         │
   │  overlap        c0t3d0s2    1029 MB                         │
   │  swap           c0t3d0s5     128 MB                         │
   │  /usr           c0t3d0s6     800 MB                         │
   │                                                             │
   └─────────────────────────────────────────────────────────────┘

   ┌────────────────┐  ┌──────────┐  ┌──────────┐  ┌──────────┐
   │ Begin Installation │  │  Change  │  │   Exit   │  │   Help   │
   └────────────────┘  └──────────┘  └──────────┘  └──────────┘
```

**Figure 2-8.**   *The Profile dialog*

```
- Profile -------------------------------------------------------------
  The information shown below is your profile for installing Solaris
  software.  It reflects the choices you've made on previous screens.


========================================================================

                Installation Option: Initial
                        Boot Device: c0t1d0s0
                    Client Services: None
                           Software: Solaris 2.7, End User System Support 64-bit
```

```
File System and Disk Layout:  /           c0t1d0s0    54 MB
                              /var        c0t1d0s1    25 MB
                              SWAP        c0t1d0s3   183 MB
                              /usr        c0t1d0s6   374 MB

------------------------------------------------------------------

    Esc-2_Continue    Esc-4_Change    Esc-5_Exit    Esc-6_Help
```

You can use this dialog to make any changes you wish to the installation profile. If you want to make any changes, click on the Change button. This will walk you through the install from the beginning, allowing you to make any modifications that are required. If you do not want to make any changes, click the Begin Installation button (or, in text-mode, press ESC-2 to Continue, which is the same thing).

## Concluding the Installation

Once the installation begins, the progress bar, shown in Figure 2-9, will be displayed on your screen. It will give you a rough idea of how long the installation will take. Normally, the installation requires about half an hour to 45 minutes, but on an old machine it can take up to two hours. After the installation completes, you will be prompted to enter the root password for the first time. Make sure that you give a password that is easy for you to remember, but hard for others to guess. If you lose the root password, recovering it can be extremely difficult.

```
Solaris Initial Install



        MBytes Installed:      41.09
        MBytes Remaining:     576.91


            Installing:  Core Solaris, (Root)


    #######/
    |           |           |           |           |           |
    0          20          40          60          80         100
```

Once you have specified the root password, your system will reboot into Solaris 8. The environment that you will be presented with is called the Common Desktop Environment (CDE). With CDE you can use your computer to do a wide variety of tasks, such as managing your appointments, sending and receiving email, browsing the Internet, and managing your personal files and directories. The next chapter will give you an overview of CDE, starting with how to log in and use some of its features.

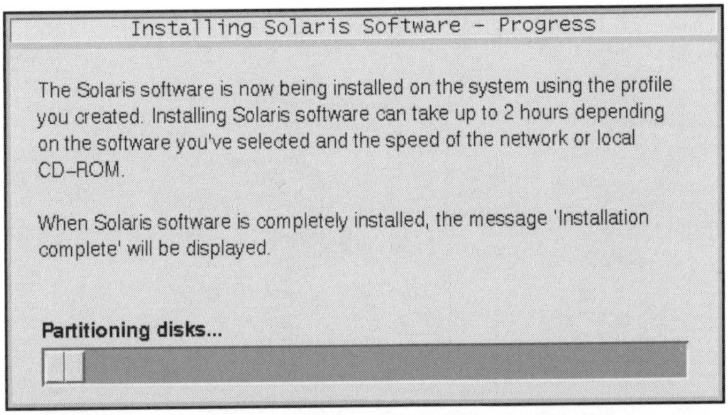

**Figure 2-9.** *Installation Progress Dialog*

## Summary

In this chapter we covered the installation procedure for Solaris on both SPARC and x86-based systems. We first examined the preinstallation steps common to both systems, and then we covered in detail the additional steps required for x86-based workstations. The second section of the chapter covered the installation of Solaris, with a screen-by-screen walkthrough of the process. This section started with the configuration of x86 hardware and concluded with the common installation procedures for both SPARC and x86-based systems. In the next chapter, you will learn how to get started using Solaris and its graphical user interface, CDE.

## How to Find Out More

There are several books that cover the installation of Solaris and its hardware compatibility. Some of the best references are:

Heslop, Brent D.; and Angell, David F. *Mastering Solaris 2.6.* (Sybex, 1993.)

Ledesma, Ron. *PC Hardware Configuration Guide: For DOS and Solaris.* (Prentice Hall, 1994.)

Winsor, Janice. *Solaris System Administrator's Guide.* (Macmillan Technical Publishing, 1998.)

Wong, Brian L. *Configuration and Capacity Planning for Solaris Servers.* (Prentice Hall, 1997.)

The
Complete
Reference

Solaris 8

# Chapter 3

## Getting Started

One of the myths about UNIX-based operating systems, including Solaris, is that the only method of interacting with the system is by means of an arcane and cryptic command-line interface. Although the command-line approach is actually one of the greatest strengths of such systems, it is no longer the only approach. Modern UNIX-based systems like Solaris come with a powerful graphical user interface called the Common Desktop Environment (CDE). This easy-to-use point-and-click interface allows you to access many UNIX features without having to use the command line at all.

In this chapter we will look at some of the CDE applications and features that are commonly used by administrators, and then we'll examine the default Solaris directory structure. These topics will help you get started using and administering a Solaris 8 system.

# The Common Desktop Environment

The basic user interface to the UNIX system is the command line, which you use to enter commands, options, and filenames for execution by the system. For experienced UNIX users the command-line interface (CLI) is extremely powerful, but it is simply daunting for new users; there are a lot of commands and options to learn to use UNIX systems effectively. I should point out that the command line was also the basic interface to DOS, so this approach is not restricted to UNIX-based systems. Although the DOS command line was much simpler than the UNIX command line, it still required users to memorize many commands to work effectively.

In the mid-1980s the introduction of the Apple Macintosh changed the way that users interacted with computers. The Macintosh used a graphical user interface (GUI) rather than a command line. Instead of memorizing complex commands and pathnames, users could click graphical representations of commands, called icons, to execute them. The Macintosh and, later, Microsoft Windows popularized the GUI concept to the extent that now it is considered the standard interface for typical users. Around the same time the Macintosh was first released, a research project was started at MIT to provide UNIX systems with a graphical user interface. This research project resulted in the development of the popular *X Window System*. The X Window System project adapted such GUI concepts as windows and icons to UNIX, while providing developers and corporations the ability to generate their own "windowing system," which determined the "look and feel" of a system.

The flexibility of the X Window System was also a big disadvantage. Since the X Window System provides only an interface for writing GUIs (or, in X Window System terminology, window managers), many different window managers with a wide range of "looks and feels" have been developed. Some of the more popular ones are TWM (Tom's Window Manager), OLWM (OpenLook Window Manager), and MWM (Motif Window Manager).

Tom's Window Manager (TWM) was one of the first window managers or GUIs to be written for the X Window System. It is a simple and fast windowing system that provides only the most basic functionality of a GUI. It offers no graphical icons, and it supports only a limited subset of window operations, including opening, closing, and resizing windows. Since its resource requirements are small, TWM was often used on slow systems that had to support many concurrent users.

The next major development was the OpenLook Window Manager. OLWM was developed using the OpenLook toolkit developed by Sun Microsystems and AT&T. The OpenLook toolkit was popular with developers, since it allowed graphical X Window System applications to be written quickly and easily. It also added many features, including graphical icons. Sun's implementation of OpenLook, called OpenWindows, was the standard GUI on Sun systems for much of the late 1980s and early 1990s.

An alternative to the OpenLook Toolkit, called the Motif Toolkit, was developed by the Open Software Foundation (OSF) in the late 1980s. It was designed to have a look and feel similar to that of Microsoft Windows and the OS/2 Presentation Manager. The similarities between the Motif Window Manager (MWM) and Microsoft Windows attracted many PC users to UNIX systems. Developers also found Motif to be easier to use than OpenLook, and by the early 1990s Motif had become the most popular windowing system available for UNIX and the X Window System. Unfortunately, not all vendors supported Motif as the default windowing system; this meant that applications programmers could not count on it being available on a user's system. The problem was even greater for users, for each UNIX vendor that supported Motif and MWM had its own slightly different implementation. Also, since each version of Motif shipped with different applications, users could not count on a standard editor, file manager, or terminal application.

In 1993, Hewlett-Packard, IBM, Novell, and SunSoft started the Common Open Software Environment (COSE) initiative in order to provide a common graphical user interface and applications programming environment. Eventually Digital, Fujitsu, and Hitachi also joined the COSE initiative. The main objective of COSE was to provide an entire computing environment, heavily based on icons and windows, that included a standard window manager based on MWM and a core set of applications familiar to users from Windows and the Mac OS. The first major result of this initiative was the Common Desktop Environment, version 1.0 (CDE 1.0).

CDE is a standard desktop, available on most UNIX platforms, that provides many basic applications with a common "look and feel" across all the versions of UNIX that support it. It also provides many common services for system administrators and application programmers. Currently Solaris 8 ships with CDE version 1.4. Earlier versions of CDE are available for HP-UX, Digital UNIX, and AIX. CDE 1.0 is also available for Linux and FreeBSD as add-on application packages from TriTeal, Work Group Solutions (WGS), and X Inside.

CDE has been the standard windowing system on Solaris since Solaris 2.5; with Solaris 8 it has been extensively improved in terms of speed and usability. In this section I will show you how to get started with CDE, and provide an overview of the key features of the environment.

# Logging into CDE

To start using CDE you must first log in, in much the same way as when you access a UNIX system via a text-only terminal or an application like **telnet**. The major difference is that instead of a text prompt CDE offers an easy-to-use graphical login screen. When you first access a UNIX system with the Common Desktop Environment, you will see a "login screen," similar to the one shown here, prompting you for a user name:

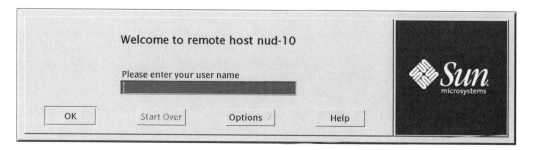

In order to access the system, you need to enter your user name in this text field. The prompt will then change and ask you for your password:

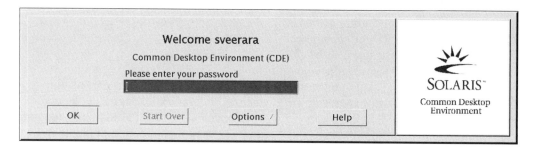

After you enter your username and password correctly, the Solaris logo will be displayed while CDE loads its desktop. On a SPARCstation 20, CDE can take up to two minutes to load. On newer systems such as Ultra 1, Ultra 2, and Ultra 10, CDE usually takes about 15 to 30 seconds to load. Once CDE has finished loading, you will be presented with the CDE desktop. This desktop has many similarities to the Motif desktop, so if you are familiar with Motif Window Manager (MWM), the CDE desktop will appear very familiar. The main difference will be the Front Panel, shown here:

## Using the Front Panel

The Front Panel provides you with pop-up program menus, a *virtual workspace manager*, and a *trashcan* to dispose of files (similar to the approach taken by Windows and by the Mac OS), along with access to a file manager, a mail reader, printing tools, and the online help system. It also provides buttons for logging out and locking the display.

**The Graphical Workspace Manager**    In the center of the Front Panel are four large buttons, usually labeled One, Two, Three, and Four. These buttons constitute the main pieces of the Graphical Workspace Manager (GWM), which is responsible for controlling the virtual workspaces. Each virtual workspace can be thought of as a separate desktop in which windows can be opened and programs can be run. By using virtual workspaces, you can have many windows open without cluttering your main workspace.

Also contained in the GWM are two smaller buttons and a "busy light." The busy light blinks when CDE is trying to run a program or is busy with some task. The two smaller buttons provide a central location for logging out and locking the console. To log out of CDE, just click the button labeled EXIT. To lock the display, click the button with the lock icon. Locking your display prevents unauthorized use of your system when you are away from it and have not logged out.

The four large buttons in the GWM correspond to the four virtual workspaces that CDE starts by default. Clicking one of these buttons will cause the display to switch to the corresponding virtual workspace. To add or delete a virtual workspace, click in the center of the Front Panel with the middle or right mouse button. You will be presented with a pop-up menu for adding and deleting virtual workspaces. To rename a virtual workspace, click on it using the middle or left mouse button. The current name of the workspace will become highlighted, allowing you to enter a new one.

 *Running multiple virtual workspaces impacts system performance. You may want to evaluate your own needs and determine the optimal number of virtual workspaces for your systems.*

**Front Panel Features**    In addition to the GWM, several other icons in the Front Panel afford access to important CDE tools. Some of these icons also feature pop-up menus that allow additional programs and features to be accessed.

The left-most icon in the Front Panel is an analog clock. You can instantly tell what time it is without having to issue the **date** command in a terminal session, or having to run a program like **xclock**. By placing a clock in the Front Panel, the CDE designers increased the amount of screen space you have available. (Programs like **xclock** display the time in a separate window and in some cases can take up a significant portion of your screen area.) Next to the clock icon is the calendar icon. The calendar icon displays the current date. If you click the calendar icon, the CDE Calendar Manager will appear. Calendar Manager is a sophisticated appointment manager that allows the user to manage appointments and to-do lists in a variety of formats. It also allows you to share your schedule with other CDE users.

To the right of the calendar icon is the icon for File Manager, an interface for manipulating files and running programs that is similar to the Mac Finder and Microsoft Windows Explorer. As File Manager is a very important tool that may come in for a great deal of use in a typical session, I'll save more discussion of it for later in this section, in the discussion of CDE Tools. The icon next to File Manager is the icon for the CDE terminal, **dtterm**. This terminal is far more advanced than the traditional **xterm**, which gave you the ability to run a shell inside a window, but not much more. (For users familiar with Microsoft Windows, **xterm** is similar to the DOS command interpreter, *command.com* or *cmd.exe*.) Many features such as resetting the terminal or changing fonts were difficult to access in **xterm**. The CDE terminal, **dtterm**, provides all of **xterm**'s functionality along with a simple menu interface to the more advanced features.

Just above the terminal icon, you will see a small upward-pointing arrow. Clicking this arrow produces a pop-up menu (called a *subpanel*) from which you can access additional CDE tools, including a graphical text editor and an icon editor. The subpanel can be customized to launch user-specific programs such as **xterm**. The last icon on the left-hand side of the GWM is the mailer icon. The CDE mailer provides a powerful mail client that supports templates, mail folders, searches, mailing lists, and MIME attachments.

On the right-hand side of GWM panel is the printer control. In addition to letting you manipulate and monitor the printing queue on a particular printer, this tool supports drag-and-drop printing of documents from File Manager. Next to this icon is the Style Manager icon. Style Manager allows you to customize the various aspects of the CDE interface on the fly. It simplifies tasks such as setting the desktop background, window colors, and mouse response time. I cover Style Manager in detail later in this chapter, in the section "Customizing CDE."

To the right of the Style Manager icon is the Application Manager icon. Application Manager, using the File Manager interface, enables you to launch programs by clicking on them, much as in the Mac OS and in Microsoft Windows. Next to this icon is the Help System icon for searching and viewing the CDE help system, which is extensive. All of the help topics are set up as books in a hierarchical structure, which makes locating the correct material very easy. Moreover, most of the help pages include hyperlinks for browsing related materials quickly.

At the far right of the Front Panel is the Trashcan icon. Users can discard files and applications by dragging them from File Manager or Application Manager and dropping them onto the Trashcan icon. This method of disposing of files is very similar to that used by MS Windows and the Mac OS. Items in the trash are deleted only when the user requests it. Thus accidentally trashed files can be recovered simply—by dragging them out of the trash.

## Logging into CDE (Behind the Scenes)

When the X Window System was first introduced, in order to use it you had to log in to the console of the machine, make sure your environment was correct, and then issue the X Window System startup command. This meant that every user needed to maintain several configuration files for the X Window System and the windowing system. The configuration files told the X Window System what it should do when it started running. In the case of windowing systems like Motif or OpenLook, the configuration files were also required in order for the windowing system to function correctly.

The X Window System graphical environment provides the user with great flexibility in terms of configuration. Often, many startup files are involved; some of these are specific to the X Window System and the window manager. For example, people who use the Motif Window Manager can customize the .xinitrc and .mwmrc files in their home directory. In this case, the .xinitrc file is read by the **xinit** (X Initialization) program utility while the .mwmrc file is read by **mwm** (Motif Windows Manager). To add to the problems, different windows manager programs can be deployed per the user's preference. Each windows manager utilize different system configuration files. To complicate things further, sometimes there will be a configuration file for each X application as well. Because of the high degree of configurability offered by X, every user's desktop looks and behaves differently. In such an environment, troubleshooting the user's desktop is a tedious and time-consuming task for system administrators. With the arrival of the CDE platform and its universal vendor acceptance, the users' graphical environments have a much more consistent look and feel.

For example, if you were using Motif's Window Manager, **mwm**, you needed at least two configuration files. The first one, named .xinitrc or .Xclients, controlled the startup of the X Window System. In this file you had to issue the commands required to start **mwm** correctly. The second one, called .mwmrc, was used to configure **mwm** to suit your needs. Normally these configuration files were used by the X Window System startup program **xinit** or **startx**. Since everyone customized the X Window System to their needs, each and every problem they might encounter in starting and using the X Window System would require administrative help. This translated to an enormous workload for system administrators, since each new user configuration potentially entailed systemwide changes. Additionally, the system administrators had to maintain site-specific stub scripts that had to be included in the home directory of each user in order to allow them to use the X Window System.

CDE removes this extra workload by automatically handling the details of starting the X Window System and providing a common base environment. CDE starts when a UNIX system boots; its login program, called **dtlogin**, handles all the details of starting the X Window System. When you access the login screen of a machine running CDE, X Window System is already running, so you do not have to do anything extra to access the X Window System. This is an asset to both users and system administrators, since users no longer have to maintain the X Window System configuration files, and system administrators can rely on basic CDE functionality to be present for all users without extra work on their part.

Normally, when you log in to CDE it restores your system to the environment that was running when you last logged out. While you are using CDE, it keeps track of the applications that you run in the current session, such as a terminal window or a web browser. When you exit CDE, it saves the state of your environment in this current session in order to restore it at your next login. Most of the time this is desirable, but occasionally you will need to log in without having your last session restored. CDE accommodates this by allowing you to choose a different session before logging in. When you log in on the console of a system you will have four different sessions available:

- Standard CDE Session
- Open Windows Session
- User's Last Desktop
- Failsafe (Command Line)

The different sessions available on the Solaris 8 version of CDE are shown here:

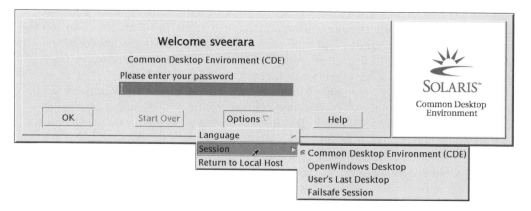

The default session, selected here, logs you in to the CDE desktop that was running when you last logged out. The Open Windows session logs you in to the Open Windows desktop used in Solaris 2.4 and earlier systems. This desktop is provided as a convenience for those users who prefer the Open Windows desktop to CDE. The Failsafe session presents you with a single terminal window without any windowing system. It is mainly used to fix configuration problems with CDE. The Command Line session is used when an X Window System environment is not required, usually before shutdowns or reboots of the machine. The "Command Line" login session is only available when logging in on the

console. If you use a remote X server, such as Reflection X on Windows or MacX on the
Mac OS, this option will not be available.

## dtterm

In CDE it is possible to accomplish common tasks without using the UNIX command
line, but in order to access the vast majority of UNIX programs, you will need to use
the command line. (By common tasks I mean such activities as running programs and
editing files.) In CDE you can access the command line using a terminal emulator called
**dtterm**. A terminal emulator makes it seem, at least to your UNIX machine, that you
are logged in using a text-only terminal. The terminal emulator usually runs a shell
that you use to interact with UNIX. If you are familiar with Windows, **dtterm** and
other terminal emulators are similar to the DOS shell or cmd.exe, which allow you
to run several instances of DOS concurrently. For those readers who are familiar with
the X Window System, the **dtterm** program is intended as a replacement for **xterm**. It
provides the same type of terminal environment as **xterm** but adds several improvements
that make it easier to use and customize. The standard **dtterm** window is shown here:

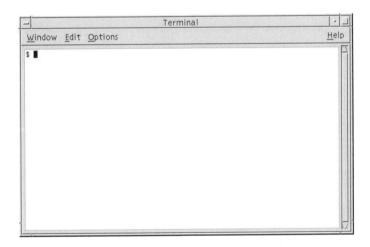

Many new CDE users who are familiar with Windows or the Mac OS often note
that the **dtterm** looks just like a **telnet** window. This was one of the major goals of the CDE
design team. They wanted to provide a more intuitive look and feel to the traditional UNIX
tools. By preserving the power of **xterm**, the CDE design team kept older UNIX users
happy but also allowed new users who were not familiar with UNIX to get acquainted
with the environment using a familiar GUI.

Usually **dtterm** is accessed from the Front Panel by clicking its icon, but it can also be launched from the command line, as follows:

```
$ dtterm &
```

Ensure that the PATH environment variable contains /usr/dt/bin, or else you may receive a "command not found" error message.

 **Note** *Normally all of the CDE programs, including **dtterm**, are located in the directory /usr/dt/bin. By adding this directory to your PATH environment variable you will be able to execute **dtterm** and all the other CDE programs without having to specify their complete path.*

## The dtterm Menus

Every **dtterm** window has the following four menus: Windows, Edit, Options, and Help.

The Window menu has two items, New and Close, that allow for a new **dtterm** to be created or for the existing **dtterm** to be closed.

The Edit menu also has two items, Copy and Paste, for copying and pasting text from one window to another. The Edit menu in **dtterm** was designed to allow users to copy and paste text reliably without having to worry about special mouse configurations on systems without a three-button mouse. Normally, UNIX workstations that run the X Window System are equipped with a three-button mouse. If you highlight text using the left mouse button, the X Window System automatically copies that text for you, and you can then use the center mouse button to paste the text into another program. Although three-button mice are common on most UNIX workstations, more and more people are using UNIX on PCs and laptops that do not come equipped with three-button mice, so the Edit menu makes the operations available in a place that most PC users would expect to find them.

The Options menu is for customizing the appearance and behavior of **dtterm**. Its menu items are described briefly in the following list:

- ■ **Menu Bar**   The Options > Menu Bar item allows the menu bar to be hidden. This is useful for maximizing terminal space when running **dtterm** on a small monitor. The menu bar can be restored by using the pop-up menu that appears when you click inside the **dtterm** window with the second mouse button.

- ■ **Scroll Bar**   The Options > Scroll Bar item toggles the state of the scroll bar. If the scroll bar is showing, selecting this item will hide it. If the scroll bar is hidden, selecting this item will cause it to be displayed.

■ **Global**    The Options > Global item brings up the Global Options window:

You can use this window to customize the Cursor, Color, Scroll Behavior, and Bell sounds of every **dtterm** from that point onward, in this session and subsequent ones. Click the Help button to bring up the help page for the window. It contains detailed information about all of the available options. After you select a set of options, click the OK button to apply the changes; then all of your chosen settings will be applied each time **dtterm** is launched. To preview the settings on the current window, click the Apply button. To reset **dtterm** to the default settings, click the Reset button.

■ **Terminal**    The Options > Terminal item brings up the Terminal Options window:

You can use this window to modify keyboard and screen controls. In most cases the defaults function quite well. In order for some programs and shell scripts to function properly, however, you may need to change the Newline Sequence setting to Return/ Line Feed. A description of each item is available in the online help.

- **Window Size**   The Options > Window Size item displays a submenu for choosing between two terminal sizes, 80 x 24 and 132 x 24. This menu is very useful when viewing files with long lines. It is also useful when running **dtterm** remotely on a Windows or Mac OS system where X server, such as Reflection X on Windows or MacX on MacOS, does not allow windows to be resized.

- **Font Size**   The Options > Font Size item also displays a submenu offering different font sizes, between 8-point and 24-point, for the terminal output. The default for most systems is usually either 10- or 12-point.

- **Reset**   The last item in the Options menu, Reset, can be helpful for recovering from terminal configuration problems. It has a submenu with the items Soft Reset and Hard Reset. Performing a soft reset means that the terminal characteristics are reset. This is useful when control characters that may exist in a file or in the output of a program have corrupted the terminal display. In some cases, however, resetting the terminal characteristics is not enough to recover the display. The hard reset is provided for those instances. It causes **dtterm** to reinitialize itself, which usually can correct almost all problems. Usually the soft reset is preferred to the hard reset, since a hard reset tends to lose command history information in some shells.

Finally, the Help menu, as described earlier in the chapter, affords quick and intuitive assistance in the form of hierarchical, hyperlinked help pages explaining the use and purpose of the various parts of **dtterm**. The Help menu allows you to access tutorial the man page and other reference material, such as keyboard configuration, about **dtterm**.

## Command-Line and X-Resource Features in dtterm

In addition to menu-based customization, **dtterm** also supports numerous command-line options and X-Resource settings. X-Resources are used by the X Window System to determine different attributes or properties of a window. Some common window properties that are controlled by X-Resources are the size of a window, the font to use in the window, and the title bar that should be displayed. Normally, X-Resources can be configured in the ~/.Xdefaults file.

Table 3-1 lists the common **dtterm** command-line options.

Let us take a look at a few examples. The following command starts a **dtterm** and runs the given **rsh** command in it:

```
$ dtterm -e rsh soda
```

| Option | Purpose |
|---|---|
| –bg or –background | Specifies the background color for **dtterm**. |
| –fg or –foreground | Specifies the foreground color for **dtterm**. This is the color the text will be displayed in. |
| –fn or –font | Specifies the font for the terminal. |
| –geometry | Specifies the onscreen size of the terminal. |
| –title | Specifies the string that **dtterm** displays for new windows. |
| +sb or –sb | Specifies whether or not the scroll bar should be displayed. |
| –e | Specifies an executable program and its arguments invoked as a subprocess when **dtterm** is started. The –e option should always be the last one. |

**Table 3-1.**   *Command-line Options for dtterm*

The following command will start a **dtterm** with a black background, a yellow foreground, and a scroll bar:

```
$ dtterm -bg black -fg yellow -sb &
```

# Customizing CDE

The two main methods of customizing CDE are to use the Style Manager or to create new CDE actions. Using the Style Manager, you can customize several CDE attributes, including the window color, the font size, and the background image that is displayed. By creating new actions, you can add icons to the Front Panel that allow you to access additional programs such as web browsers.

## Using the Style Manager

The Style Manager allows you to customize each of the following properties of the CDE environment:

- Color
- Font

- Backdrop
- Keyboard
- Mouse
- Beep
- Screen
- Window
- Startup

Usually the Style Manager is launched when its Front Panel icon is clicked, but it can also be launched from the command line, as follows:

```
$ dtstyle &
```

Once the Style Manager loads, it displays its main window, which contains several icons corresponding to the properties just listed:

Clicking the Color icon displays the Color Palette Manager. The Color Palette Manager allows you to choose from over 30 predefined color schemes. You can also add, delete, and modify color schemes and test them on the fly. The Font icon gives you access to the Font Manager, which allows you to choose the default font for terminal output, window decorations, and icon text.

The Backdrop icon launches the Backdrop Manager. This manager allows you to choose one of 26 backdrops for each virtual console. It also allows you to deactivate backdrops by choosing the No Backdrops option. Several UNIX programs, including **xsetroot, xv,** and **Esetroot**, allow you to manually set the background of your desktop to a particular color or picture. Since CDE handles setting the background by default, the No Backdrops option is provided for users who prefer to set the background on their own.

The Screen button is used to configure the delay for the screen saver. It also allows you to pick one of several predefined screen savers. The screen saver can be activated either by leaving the machine idle for the given delay or by clicking the lock icon in the Front Panel.

The buttons for Mouse, Keyboard, and Beep allow you to set various attributes including the key repeat rate, the mouse threshold, and the keyboard beep. If you are familiar with Microsoft Windows or the Mac OS, note that these buttons allow you to change your mouse, keyboard, and sound settings much as you would using the Mouse, Keyboard, and Sound Control Panels. The Window button allows for configuring the behavior of windows, such as auto-raise or click-to-raise. It also allows you to enable the icon box for storing icons. This feature will be familiar to **mwm** users. Normally CDE stores the icons of running programs on the desktop. If the icon box is enabled, CDE will store the icons for running programs in this window, freeing up desktop space.

 *The last button, Startup, controls the startup behavior of CDE. Usually the behavior is to restore the last session, or to restore a baseline session called the Home Session. This behavior can be changed using the Startup Manager.*

## Creating and Installing New Actions

To get the most out of the Front Panel, most users add their own commands to it. In CDE terminology, commands that are accessible from the Front Panel are called *actions*. An action is basically an icon located in the Front Panel that allows you to execute a command by clicking on it. It is similar to a Shortcut in Windows or an Alias in MacOS. Most actions are grouped together in the pop-up menus (called subpanels) that can be accessed by clicking on the small arrow located above one of the main icons in the Front Panel. In this section we will cover adding *subpanels* to group commands and creating new actions for your favorite commands.

Normally, the Front Panel contains only a few subpanels. Most users add additional subpanels in order to group programs or actions together. To add a subpanel, first decide where you want it to appear in the Front Panel, then right-click the icon directly below that location. For example, if you want to add a subpanel above the clock icon, click on the clock with the right mouse button. A small menu with three items will be presented. In this menu, choose the Add Subpanel option. This will create a small arrow above the control, along with the subpanel. A newly created subpanel will contain an item labeled Install Icon. You'll be using this item to install actions into the subpanel.

**Creating an Action**    In CDE the programs that you launch from the Front Panel are referred to as *actions*. You can add actions to the Front Panel by using the Create Action program. This program is located in the Desktop Apps folder of the Application Launcher, or it can be launched from the command line as follows:

```
$ dtcreate &
```

When the program finishes loading, the Create Action window is displayed:

As an example of creating a new action, let's create an action for **xterm** and install it. The same process can be used to create and install actions for any program or command. The steps are:

1. Enter the name the action should be given in the text field labeled Action Name (Icon Label):. This name can be anything you want. It does not have to be the same as the name of the program that will be executed. For example, for **xterm** I entered **XTerm**.

2. Enter the command for this action in the text field labeled Command When Action Is Opened (Double-clicked):. This must be the exact command to run. Including the full path to a program is recommended, since the Front Panel may or may not have the same search path as your shells. For **xterm** I entered **/usr/opewin/bin/xterm**. This tells CDE to look for the program **xterm** in the directory */usr/opewin/bin*. (Depending on your setup, however, the **xterm** program may be located in a different directory.)

3. Enter the help text for this action in the text area labeled Help Text For Action Icon. If you do not want any help text to be displayed, just leave this area blank.

4. Choose the type of window for the action by selecting one of the choices in the drop-down menu labeled Window Type:. In most instances the default works fine.

5. Select Save from the File menu and save the action.

At this point you will be prompted for a location where the action should be saved. You can save the action anywhere you want, but the normal locations to store actions are:

- In your home directory.
- In a special directory, *.dt/appmanager*, located in your home directory. (Normally this would be something like */home/ranga/.dt/appmanager*.)

**Installing an Action**    Once you have created an action, you can install it in a submenu using the following steps:

1. Use the arrow above the **dtterm** icon to display the Personal Applications subpanel.
2. Using the File Manager (**dtfile**), go to the directory containing your actions. In my case the actions were saved in my home directory.
3. Click the icon for the action and drag it onto the Install Icon item in the Personal Applications subpanel.

The action will be installed in this subpanel. Clicking it will launch the specified program.

# The Solaris File System Layout

The layout of the Solaris file system is similar to that of other UNIX versions, with some minor differences and additions that administrators need to be familiar with. In this section I will give you a general idea of the file system layout so that you will be able to easily search for and locate files and programs that may be important to administering your system. This section covers the following four major areas of the Solaris directory tree:

- Device directories
- Program directories
- Configuration directories
- Directories for temporary or variable files

## Device Directories

The directories that contain files related to devices are /dev and /devices. Historically all of the device files on UNIX systems were stored in /dev, but in Solaris 8 the devices file are stored in /devices using a directory tree that matches the device tree used by the Solaris 8 boot system. The /dev directory in Solaris 8 now contains a set of links from the files in /devices to mimic the older UNIX device names. For example, consider the entry for the system console /dev/console:

```
$ ls -l /dev/console
lrwxrwxrwx   1 root      root           30 Nov 25  1998
 /dev/console -> ../devices/pseudo/cn@0:console
```

As you can see, the actual console device is in the /devices directory. The same is true for devices like hard disks. For example, the hard disk /dev/dsk/c0t3d0s0 is actually a link to the following file:

```
/devices/iommu@f,e0000000/sbus@f,e0001000/espdma@f,400000/esp@f,800000/sd@3,0:a
```

Some of the important subdirectories in /dev are listed in Table 3-2.

The device files in the /dev and /devices directories are explained in greater detail in Chapter 7.

## Removable Media Directories

In addition to the /dev and /devices directories, if your system has removable media such as a CD-ROM drive or a floppy drive, your directory tree will contain the directory

| Directory | Purpose of Files |
|---|---|
| /dev/cua | Accessing devices connected to the serial ports of your workstation. These files are used by the **tip** and **cu** commands. |
| /dev/dsk | Accessing the file systems on your hard drives. These files are used by the **mount** command. |
| /dev/fd | Accessing a particular file descriptor, such as Standard Input (STDIN) and Standard Output (STDOUT). These files are used by most programs, including the shell. |
| /dev/pts | Allowing logins on pseudoterminals. These are used when logging into a system via **telnet**, remote shell (**rlogin** and **rsh**), or secure shell (**slogin** and **ssh**). The secure shell, a freely available program, is covered in Chapter 16. |
| /dev/rdsk | Accessing the raw media of your hard drives. These files are used by the **fsck** command. |

**Table 3-2.**    *Important Directories in /dev*

/cdrom or /floppy (or both, of course). When you insert a CD-ROM or a floppy disk with a supported format, it will be automatically mounted on the appropriate directory so that you can access it immediately. This convention has been extended by many Solaris administrators to include the popular Iomega Jaz and Zip drives. Thus, on systems equipped with these drives, you will often see the directories /jaz and /zip in addition to the standard /cdrom or /floppy directories. Removable media is covered in greater detail in Chapter 7.

# Program Directories

In Solaris 8, programs are stored in one of two main locations: /usr or /opt. The programs stored in /usr are programs that are required by most users, and in some cases are required for the system to boot and run correctly. The programs in /opt are usually *optional* software packages that are needed only by particular users of a system. Usually the programs installed in /opt are extremely specialized, such as network management, mathematical modeling, or CAD/CAM applications. In addition, some of the prepackaged freeware tools available for Solaris are installed in /opt.

As mentioned, the programs stored in /usr are those that are required by *users*. These include both end users and system administrators. (In other versions of UNIX, some of the programs required by users are stored in /bin, while programs required by system administrators are stored in /sbin.) In Solaris 8, all of the end user programs are stored in /usr/bin, and programs used by system administrators are normally stored in /usr/sbin. For compatibility reasons, there are two links (/bin and /sbin) in the root directory that point to /usr/bin and /usr/sbin.

In addition to /usr/bin and /usr/sbin, the main directories that contain most of the programs required by users, there are several other important directories in /usr that a system administrator should be familiar with. These are listed in Table 3-3.

| Directory | Contents |
|---|---|
| /usr/ccs | Programs and libraries that are used for compiling and building programs. The standard build programs **make**, **ld**, and **yacc** are stored in /usr/ccs/bin. |
| /usr/dt | The CDE configuration files, binaries, and libraries. The CDE applications, like **dtterm**, are located in /usr/dt/bin. |
| /usr/include | The C language header files for the libraries that are installed on your system. |

**Table 3-3.**    *Important Directories in /usr*

| Directory | Contents |
|---|---|
| /usr/java | The Java Development Kit and Java Runtime. On newer versions of Solaris this may be a link to the directory /usr/java1.1 or /usr/java1.2. |
| /usr/lib | The libraries used by programs on your system. Usually /lib is a link to this directory. |
| /usr/openwin | The libraries and programs for the X Window System and OpenLook. In Solaris 8, /usr/X links to the /usr/openwin directory. |
| /usr/platform | Programs and libraries that are intended for a particular type of hardware. For example, this directory contains subdirectories for machines of type sun4m (Super SPARC-based workstations) and sun4u (UltraSPARC-based workstations). |
| /usr/sbin/static | Statically linked versions of critical commands. The programs in this directory are useful when trying to recover a system whose /usr/lib directory has been deleted or damaged. |
| /usr/share/man | The manual pages for your system. |
| /usr/ucb | The SunOS/BSD compatibility commands. |
| /usr/xpg4 | A standard set of programs that adhere to the X/Open XPG4 standard. |

**Table 3-3.**   *Important Directories in /usr* (continued)

## Configuration Directories

In Solaris 8 almost all of the system boot and runtime configuration files are stored in the directory /etc. In addition to containing the configuration files for the system, /etc also contains the boot and shutdown scripts used to start processes when the system reaches a particular run level. The system startup and shutdown procedure is discussed in greater detail in Chapter 4.

Table 3-4 lists some of the important files stored in /etc. Each of these files, and many other important configuration files stored in /etc, will be discussed in much greater detail as they become relevant throughout this book. Similarly, Table 3-5 lists some of the important directories to be found in /etc.

| File | Contents |
| --- | --- |
| /etc/auto_* | The /etc/auto_direct, /etc/auto_home, and /etc/ auto_master files. These are used by the automounter to allow you to access NFS volumes without having to mount them manually. |
| /etc/format.dat | The device descriptions for all the hard drives and removable media types that are supported under Solaris |
| /etc/group | A list of the valid groups on your system. |
| /etc/hostname.* | The hostname for your system. Usually the file is named something like /etc/hostname.le0 or /etc/hostname.hme0. |
| /etc/inetd.conf | The list of network services your system responds to. On most Solaris systems this file is a link to the file /etc/ network/inetd.conf. |
| /etc/issue | The login banner displayed by the system before you log in. |
| /etc/motd | The Message of the Day file. Contains a set of messages displayed to all users when they log in. It is normally used for announcing administrative policy or system maintenance schedules. |
| /etc/mnttab | The list of currently mounted file systems. |
| /etc/nodename | The name of your system, as displayed with the command **uname –n**. |
| /etc/nsswitch.conf | The name service and NIS/NIS+ configuration information. |
| /etc/pam.conf | The Pluggable Authentication Modules (PAM) framework configuration information. |
| /etc/passwd | The password database for your systems. Contains all of the user information about valid local users. (The actual passwords for users are stored in the file /etc/shadow.) |
| /etc/profile | The default configuration file for the Bourne shell (**/bin/sh**), and the Korn shell (**/bin/ksh**). |
| /etc/resolv.conf | The information used by your system to translate hostnames into IP addresses. |

**Table 3-4.**    *Commonly Accessed Configuration Files in /etc*

| | |
|---|---|
| /etc/services | A list of well-known ports for network applications. |
| /etc/shadow | The passwords for all the local users of your system. (This file is readable only by root.) |
| /etc/shells | A list of all the "approved" shells on your system. It is used by the FTP server to ensure that users with invalid shells do not access your system. |
| /etc/syslog.conf | The syslogd daemon's configuration file. (The syslogd daemon is used to log significant events or errors that occur on your system.) |
| /etc/system | The configuration parameters for the Solaris kernel. |
| /etc/termcap | The parameters describing the different types of terminals supported under Solaris. |
| /etc/vfstab | The default descriptions for each file system on your machine. |

**Table 3-4.** *Commonly Accessed Configuration Files in /etc (continued)*

| Directory | Contents |
|---|---|
| /etc/cron.d | The configuration files for the **cron** command (discussed in Chapter 5). Some system administrators also use this directory to store scripts executed by **cron**. |
| /etc/default | The configuration files that control the default behavior of the system. For example, the file /etc/default/login controls the behavior of the login command. |
| /etc/dfs | The configuration files used by the Network File System (NFS) server. |
| /etc/inet | Configuration files related to the network. |

**Table 3-5.** *Important Directories in /etc*

| Directory | Contents |
|---|---|
| /etc/init.d | The startup and shutdown scripts for the system. |
| /etc/rc*.d | The /etc/rc0.d through /etc/rc3.d and the /etc/rcS.d directories contain links to files in the /etc/init.d directory. These links control the processes that are started and stopped as the system boots or is shut down. On some systems, administrators may have added the directories /etc/rc4.d through /etc/rc6.d. |
| /etc/lp | The printer configuration files. |

**Table 3-5.** *Important Directories in /etc* (continued)

## Directories for Temporary or Variable Files

The two main directories for temporary and variable files are /tmp and /var. Usually, /tmp contains temporary files that are required by the system while it is running. This includes named pipes and special device files used by some programs like database engines. The /var directory contains those files whose contents are variable and change often, but need to remain intact after reboot.

In Solaris the contents of the /tmp directory are stored partly in system memory (RAM) and partly on disk using a special type of file system called *tmpfs*. The tmpfs file system is discussed in greater detail in Chapter 8. One of the big advantages of the tmpfs file system is that compiling and executing programs from a tmpfs-based directory, such as /tmp, is extremely fast; because the files are already in memory, you don't have to wait for the hard disk to retrieve them.

 *A side effect of tmpfs is that every time a Solaris system reboots, the files contained in /tmp will be erased. If you have any temporary files that are extremely important (like core dumps or log files), make sure that you put them in /var/tmp instead of in /tmp.*

The /var directory is used to store files whose content changes frequently. Some common examples are log files, printer spool files, mail spool files, and software package files. The main directories located in /var are listed in Table 3-6.

| Directory | Contents |
|---|---|
| /var/adm | The system logging and accounting files. One of the important files in this directory is /var/adm/messages, which contains the system messages. It is often used by administrators to diagnose problems with hardware and software configuration. |
| /var/cron | Log files for **cron**. |
| /var/mail | Directory where users' mail is kept. On most systems there is a symbolic link from /var/mail to /usr/mail. |
| /var/nis | NIS+ databases. |
| /var/preserve | Backup files for **vi** and **ex**. |
| /var/sadm | Databases maintained by the software package management utilities. To get a complete manifest of the contents of all the software packages installed on your system, check the file /var/sadm/install/contents. |
| /var/sadm/pkgs | The removal/backup information for software packages installed on your system. |
| /var/spool | Root directory for files used in printer spooling, mail delivery, **cron**, and **at**. |

**Table 3-6.**   *The Main Directories in /var*

# Summary

In this chapter we covered the Common Desktop Environment and the layout of the Solaris file system. These topics will help you to start using and administrating your system effectively. In the CDE section I showed you how to how to log in, use the Front Panel, and use the advanced features of **dtterm**, the new terminal emulator included in CDE. We also looked at customizing the look of CDE via the Style Manager, along with creating new actions for use in the Front Panel. In the second section of this chapter we looked at the main directories and files on your Solaris system. The tables in this section will help you to navigate the directory tree and find the programs and configuration files that you need to use.

# How to Find Out More

The following books are good sources of information on CDE:

CDE Documentation Group. *Common Desktop Environment 1.0 User's Guide.* (Addison-Wesley, 1995.)

Fernandez, Charles. *Configuring CDE: The Common Desktop Environment.* (Prentice Hall, 1996.)

Several excellent online resources are available for getting more information about CDE. Please refer to one of the following web sites for more information:

The AIX Common Desktop Environment:
**http://dept.physics.upenn.edu/~anthonyc/aCDE.html**

The CDE FAQ:
**http://www.lib.ox.ac.uk/internet/news/faq/archive/cde-cose-faq.html**

The
# Complete
# Reference

Solaris 8

# Chapter 4

# System Startup and Shutdown

olaris 2.x uses a flexible boot process based on the System V Release 4.0
specification for UNIX systems, making it easier to create and customize startup
and shutdown procedures that are consistent across sites and systems. This is
in contrast to the simpler BSD-style boot process used by Solaris 1.x, which lacked
a differentiated organization of startup scripts corresponding to distinct system
states. The aim of this chapter is to introduce readers to the basic terminology and
initialization elements that play an important role in bringing a Solaris system to
single and multiuser runlevels or init states, which are mutually exclusive modes
of operation. Transitions between init states are managed by the **init** process. After
reading this chapter, Solaris 2.x administrators should feel confident in tailoring the
startup and shutdown of their own systems, and should have a clear understanding
of the boot sequence dependencies when upgrading legacy Solaris 1.x systems.

In many respects, Solaris startup and shutdown is similar to many other systems.
However, it is important to recognize and appreciate the distinguishing features of the
Solaris operating system from other servers. One of the outstanding facilities for SPARC
hardware is the firmware monitoring system, known as OpenBoot, which is responsible
for key prebooting tasks:

- Starting the Solaris operating system by typing:

```
ok boot
```

at the OpenBoot prompt, which boots the Solaris kernel (on Solaris x86, the boot
command must be issued through the Primary Boot Subsystem menu)

  - Setting system configuration parameters, such as the boot device, which could
    be one of the hard disks (specified by a full device pathname), another host on
    the network, or a CD-ROM
  - Watching network traffic by issuing the command:

```
ok watch-net
```

at the OpenBoot prompt

  - Performing simple diagnostic tests on system devices (for example, testing the
    termination status of a SCSI bus or the Power-On Self Test POST tests)

Rather than just being a simple operating system loader, like the LILO Linux Loader
supplied with many Linux distributions, OpenBoot also permits programs written in
the stack-based Forth programming language to be written, loaded, and run before
booting commences. This is very useful for customizing servers in large organizations,
where a corporate logo must be displayed on boot, rather than the default Sun logo.

This task can be achieved by creating a Forth array with the appropriate pixel values, and executing the **oem-logo** command. Variables can also be set postboot during single and multiuser init states by using the **eeprom** command as superuser.

For example, **eeprom** can be used to change the amount of RAM self-tested at boot to 64M:

```
server# eeprom selftest-#megs=64
```

On Solaris x86 systems, the firmware does not directly support this kind of **eeprom** functionality: Every PC manufacturer has a different BIOS system, making it difficult. Instead, storage is simulated by variables set in the bootenv.rc file.

To view the OpenBoot release information for your firmware, use the command:

```
ok banner
SPARCstation 10, Type 5 Keyboard
ROM Rev. 2.4, 64 MB memory installed, Serial #6745644
Ethernet address 6:3:10:a:cc:4a HostID 5767686
```

If the prompt for OpenBoot is not **ok** (for example, it is displayed as **>**), then simply type **n** to return to the **ok** prompt:

```
>
n
ok
```

A second distinguishing feature of the Solaris operating system is the aim of maximized up-time, through efficient kernel design and the user application model. In some non-Solaris server environments, the system must be rebooted every time a new application is installed. Alternatively, a kernel rebuild might be required to change a configuration. Fortunately, rebooting is rarely required for Solaris systems, as applications are logically isolated from system configuration options, and many system-level configuration options can be set in a superuser shell. For example, many TCP/IP options can be set dynamically using the command:

```
server# ndd /dev/tcp
```

In some newer hardware configurations, it is not even necessary to reboot to install new hardware. These are the kinds of benefits that will be a welcome relief to new Solaris administrators.

# The System V Boot Process

Upon booting from OpenBoot, Solaris has several different modes of operation, known as "runlevels" or "init states," so called because the **init** command is often used to change runlevels, although **init**-wrapper scripts (such as shutdown) are also used. These init states can be single or multiuser, often serve a different administrative purpose, and are mutually exclusive (in other words, a system can only ever be in one init state). Typically, a Solaris system designed to stay up indefinitely will cycle through a predefined series of steps in order to start all the software daemons necessary for the provision of basic system services, primary user services, and optional application services. These services are often only provided when a Solaris system operates in a multiuser run state, with services being initialized by run control (**rc**) shell scripts. Usually, one run control script is created to start each system, user, or application service. Fortunately, many of these scripts are created automatically for administrators during the Solaris installation process. However, if you intend to install third-party software (such as a database server), it will be necessary to create your own run control scripts in the /etc/init.d directory to start up these services automatically at boot time. This process is fully described later in this chapter.

If the system needs to be powered off for any reason (for example, a scheduled power outage), or switched into a special maintenance mode to perform diagnostic tests, there is also a cycle of iterating through a predefined series of run control scripts to kill services and preserve user data. It is essential that this sequence of events is preserved so that data integrity is maintained. For example, operating a database server typically involves communication between a server-side data-writing process and a daemon listener process, which accepts new requests for storing information. If the daemon process is not stopped prior to the data-writing process, it could accept data from network clients and store it in a cache when the database has already been closed. This could lead to the database being shut down in an inconsistent state, potentially resulting in data corruption and/or record loss. This process is demonstrated in Figure 4-1. It is essential that Solaris administrators apply their knowledge of shell scripting to rigorously managing system shutdowns as well as startups using run control scripts.

There are three kinds of boots administrators should be aware of. In addition to a normal reboot, which is initiated by the command:

```
server# shutdown
```

from a superuser shell, a reconfiguration boot involves reconstructing device information in the /dev and /devices directories, and a recovery boot involves saving and analyzing crash dump files if a system does not respond to commands issued on the console. A reconfiguration boot is commonly undertaken in older SPARC systems when new hard disks are added to the system, although this may not be necessary

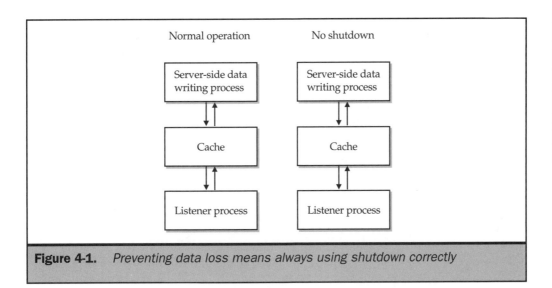

**Figure 4-1.**    *Preventing data loss means always using shutdown correctly*

with newer systems, such as the E450, which have hot-swapping facilities. This kind of boot can be initiated by typing:

```
server# boot -r
at the OpenBoot monitor prompt, or by issuing the command:
server# touch /reconfigure
```

prior to issuing a **shutdown** command from a superuser shell. A recovery boot is a rare event on a Solaris system, although hardware failures, kernel module crashes, and incorrect kernel parameters can sometimes result in a hung system. A stack trace is usually provided if a system crash occurs, which can provide vital clues to tracking the source of any system problems using the kernel debugger (**kadb**).

# Runlevels

Although Solaris has eight init states, only five are commonly encountered by administrators during normal operations. These include:

- **runlevel S**   A single user init state used for administrative tasks and the repair of corrupted file systems, using the command:

  ```
  server# /usr/sbin/fsck
  ```

- **runlevel 2**   The init state changes to multiuser mode for the first time, with the exception of NFS exported network resources.
- **runlevel 3**   All users can log in, and all system and NFS network resources are available.
- **runlevel 6**   Halts the operating system and initiates a reboot.
- **runlevel 0**   The operating system is shut down, ensuring it is safe to power down.

In older SPARC systems, it is necessary to bring the system down to runlevel 0 to install new hardware, such as disk drives, peripheral devices, and memory modules. However, newer systems, such as the E450, are able to continue to operate in multiuser init states while disks are "hot swapped" into special drive bays. This means these machines may not have a need to enter runlevel 6. Furthermore, up-times of many months are not uncommon.

It is easy to identify a system's runlevel interactively for single-user init levels 0 and S and multiuser init state 3. Runlevel S displays the default prompt for a Bourne shell:

```
#
```

Runlevel 0 displays the default OpenBoot prompt:

```
ok
```

Runlevel 3 displays the banner:

```
server console login:
```

To check a system's current runlevel from a script, use the command:

```
server# who -r
```

The output from the **who** command can be piped through a filter to execute other commands depending on the current runlevel. For example, if a database application required that NFS volumes be made available on the local server, a quick check of the runlevel in the database initialization script could exit if the runlevel was not 3:

```
#!/bin/sh
# Determine run-level
set '/usr/bin/who -r'
# Check third argument for current run-level
if [ $3 != "3" ]
then
```

```
      echo 'Error: NFS services are not available under run level 3.'
echo 'NFS Volumes must be available to run this application.'
exit
fi
# else execute database initialization here
```

The complete set of runlevels, with their respective run control script directories, is displayed in Table 4-1.

## Boot Phases

For most systems, the default runlevel is init state 3, which permits multiple user logins with all daemons running, including exported network research services (NFS). However, to reach this state from the OpenBoot monitor, it is necessary to cycle through a sequence of predefined init state transitions, from single-user (1, S) to multiuser (2, 3) runlevels. This sequence of transition events is shown in Figure 4-2. In this section, we will examine the system activities associated with each of these runlevels.

| Runlevel | Description | User Status | Run Control Script Directory |
|---|---|---|---|
| 0 | Hardware maintenance mode | Console access | /etc/rc0.d |
| 1 | Administrative state; only root file system is available | Single-user | /etc/rc1.d |
| 2 | First multiuser state; NFS resources unavailable | Multiuser | /etc/rc2.d |
| 3 | NFS resources available | Multiuser | /etc/rc3.d |
| 4 | User-defined state | Not specified | N/A |
| 5 | Power-down firmware state | Console access | /etc/rc5.d |
| 6 | Operating system halted | Single-user | /etc/rc6.d |
| S | Administrative tasks and repair of corrupted file systems | Console access | /etc/rcS.d |

**Table 4-1.**   *Solaris Runlevels and Their Functions*

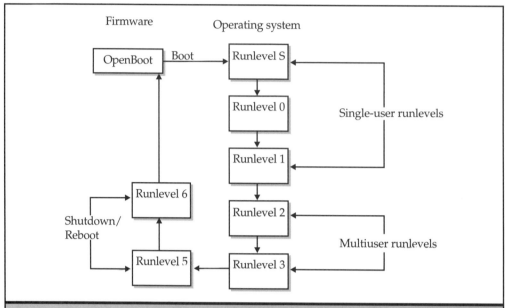

**Figure 4-2.**   *Boot sequence from OpenBoot, through single and multiuser runlevels*

The Solaris software environment provides a detailed series of run control (**rc**) scripts to control runlevel changes. We will examine each of the control scripts in turn, and highlight the improvements and innovations from the old BSD-style Solaris 1.x control scripts. Each runlevel has an associated **rc** script located in the /sbin directory, which is also symbolically linked into the /etc directory: **rc0**, **rc1**, **rc2**, **rc3**, **rc5**, **rc6**, and **rcS**. /sbin/rc0 is responsible for:

- Executing all scripts in /etc/rc0.d, if the directory exists
- Terminating all system services and active processes, initially using /usr/sbin/killall and /usr/sbin/killall 9 for stubborn processes
- Syncing all mounted file systems, using /sbin/sync
- Unmounting all mounted file systems, using /sbin/umountall

/sbin/rc5 and /sbin/rc6 are just symbolic links to /sbin/rc0, and do not need to be maintained separately. /sbin/rc1 is responsible for executing all scripts in the /etc/rc1.d directory, if it exists. This terminates all system services and active processes, initially using /usr/sbin/killall and /usr/sbin/killall 9 for stubborn processes. The differences between /etc/rc0 and /etc/rc1 are that the latter brings up the system into single-user mode after shutting down all processes in multiuser mode and does not unmount any file systems.

In runlevel 2 state, /sbin/rc2 executes all scripts in the /etc/rc2.d directory, bringing the system into its first multiuser state. Thus, all local file systems listed in /etc/vfstab are mounted, disk quotas and file system logging are switched on if configured, temporary editor files are saved, the /tmp directory is cleared, system accounting is enabled, and many network services are initialized. These services are described in more detail in Table 4-2.

In runlevel 3 state, /sbin/rc3 executes all scripts in the /etc/rc3.d directory, bringing the system into its final multiuser state. These services are mainly concerned with shared network resources, such as NFS, but Solstice Enterprise Agents and other SNMP-based systems may also be started here. /sbin/rcS executes all scripts in the /sbin/rcS.d directory to bring the system up to the single-user runlevel. A minimal network configuration is established if a network can be found, otherwise an interface error is reported. Essential system file systems (such as /, /usr and /proc) are mounted if they are available, and the system name is set.

Under Solaris 1.x, there were two main BSD-style control scripts: /etc/rc and /etc/rc.local. Typically, vendor-provided daemons were initialized from /etc/rc, and customized and locally installed daemons were executed from /etc/rc.local. For example, /etc/rc was responsible for mounting file systems, enabling quotas, adding swap space, and starting the Internet superdaemon (**inetd**). Alternatively, /etc/rc.local was responsible for later innovations, such as web servers and authentication services, as well as printer drivers. A general rule of thumb when upgrading legacy systems from Solaris 1.x to Solaris 2.x is to cross-check all the required services in /etc/rc, and ensure that they are enabled in either /etc/rc1.d or /etc/rc2.d. Add any local customizations from /etc/rc.local to a System V style startup script in /etc/rc2.d. Alternatively, shared network resource scripts can be added to /etc/rc3.d. Many Solaris 1.x applications will run in binary compatibility mode under Solaris 2.x, but your software vendor should be contacted for the latest versions of third-party software.

To the superuser on the console, the transition between runlevels is virtually invisible. Most daemons, whether starting in a single-user or multiuser init state, display a status message when starting up, which is echoed to the console. A sample console display during booting will look something like:

```
ok boot
Resetting ...
SPARCstation 10 (1 X 390Z50), Keyboard Present
ROM Rev. 2.4, 64 MB memory installed, Serial #6745644
Ethernet address 6:3:10:a:cc:4a HostID 5767686
Boot device: /iommu/sbus/espdma@f,400000/esp@f,800000/sd@1,0
File and args:
SunOS Release 5.8 Version generic [UNIX(R) System V Release 4.0]
Copyright (c) 1983-1997, Sun Microsystems, Inc.
configuring network interfaces: le0.
Hostname: server
The system is coming up. Please wait.
add net default: gateway 10.16.27.1
NIS domainname is subdomain.mydomain.com
```

```
starting rpc services: rpcbind keyserv ypbind done.
Setting netmask of le0 to 255.255.0.0
Setting default interface for multicast: add net 224.0.0.0: gateway server
syslog service starting.
Print services started.
volume management starting.
Starting Apache webserver...done.
The system is ready.
server console login:
```

When booting into single-user mode, there will obviously be fewer messages displayed on the console, as multiuser init state processes are not started. The single-user runlevel messages will appear as something like:

```
ok boot -s
SunOS Release 5.8 Version [UNIX(R) System V Release 4.0]
Copyright (c) 1983-1997, Sun Microsystems, Inc.
configuring network interfaces: le0.
Hostname: server
INIT: SINGLE USER MODE
Type Ctrl-d to proceed with normal startup,
(or give root password for system maintenance):
```

At this point, the password for the superuser account should be entered (it will not be echoed to the display). Assuming that the correct password is entered, the display will then proceed with another banner and a Bourne shell prompt:

```
Sun Microsystems Inc. SunOS 5.6 May 1997
#
```

After maintenance is complete, simply exit the shell by using CTRL + d, and the system will then proceed with a normal multiuser boot.

## init

The /sbin/init daemon is responsible for process control initialization and is a key component of the booting process. Although it is not significant in many day-to-day operations after booting, its configuration for special purposes can be confusing for first-time users. In this section, we will examine the initialization of **init** using the /etc/inittab file and explain in detail what each entry means. The primary function of **init** is to spawn processes, usually daemon processes, from configuration information specified in the file /etc/inittab in ASCII format. Process spawning always takes place in a specific software context, which is determined by the current runlevel.

After booting the kernel from the OpenBoot monitor, **init** reads the system environment variables stored in /etc/default/init (for example, the time zone variable **TZ**), and sets them for the current runlevel. **init** then reads the /etc/inittab file (described more completely in the next section), setting the init level specified in that file by the **initdefault** entry. In most multiuser systems, this entry will correspond to runlevel 3, and the entry will look like:

```
is:3:initdefault:
```

If the file /etc/inittab does not exist during booting, the superuser will be asked to manually enter the desired runlevel for the system. If this event ever occurs unexpectedly for a multiuser system, it is a good strategy to enter single-user mode (by typing **s**) to perform maintenance on the /etc/inittab file. Another potential problem (which is discussed later) is if /etc/inittab does contain an empty **rstate** value in the **initdefault** entry: The system will go to firmware and continuously reboot! If this occurs, exit from the operating system into the OpenBoot monitor by holding down the "STOP" key, and pressing **A**. PLEASE NOTE: The key combination is case-sensitive; STOP+ "A" will not work! It must be STOP+"a" PW. You can now boot directly into single-user mode and add an appropriate **rstate** entry to the /etc/inittab file. There are safeguards built into **init**, however. If the system discovers that any entry in /etc/inittab is respawning rapidly (more than five times per minute), **init** assumes that a typographical error has been made in the entry, and a warning message is printed on the system console. **init** will then not respawn the affected entry until at least five minutes have elapsed since the problem was identified.

After entering a multiuser runlevel for the first time since booting from the OpenBoot monitor, **init** reads any appropriate **boot** and **bootwait** entries in /etc/inittab. This provides for basic initialization of the operating system, such as mounting file systems, which are generally performed before users are allowed to operate on the system.

In order to spawn processes specified in /etc/inittab, **init** reads each entry and determines the process requirements for the commands to be executed. For example, for entries that must be respawned in the future, a child process is created using **fork()**. After reading all entries and spawning all processes, **init** simply waits until it receives a signal to change the system's init state (this explains why **init** is always visible in the process list). /etc/inittab is always reread at this point to ensure that any modifications to its specified behavior are used. In addition, **init** can be initialized at any time by passing a special parameter to force rereading of /etc/inittab:

```
server# init q
```

When **init** receives a valid request to change runlevels, a warning signal is sent to all affected processes and waits five seconds before forcibly terminating any processes that do not behave well and exit by sending a kill signal. Affected processes are those that will be invalid under the target init state (for example, when going from multiuser to single-user mode, daemons started in multiuser mode will be invalid). Since five seconds may not be sufficient to shut down an entire database server and close all open files, it is best to make sure such activities precede any change of state that affects the main applications running on your system (for example, by executing the appropriate command in /etc/init.d with the **stop** parameter).

/sbin/init can only be executed by a superuser, as changes in the system's init state executed by a normal user could have serious consequences (one example would be using **init** to power down a live server). Thus, it is always wise to ensure that file permissions are correctly set on the /sbin/init binary.

## inittab

/etc/inittab is frequently referenced by the **init** process, and controls process dispatching by **init**. It contains:

- The specification for the default runlevel, which is init state 3 on most multiuser systems
- A list of processes to monitor and actions related to their termination
- A list of actions to be executed when a new init state is entered

The /etc/inittab file consists of text entries of the form:

```
id:rstate:action:process
```

where **id** is a unique identifier for the **iniitab** entry. The runlevels to which the action applies is specified by **rstate**, and **action** indicates how the command identified by **process** is to be executed. Any legal Bourne shell command syntax is acceptable here. It is possible to specify more than one **rstate** to which an action applies. A sample /etc/inittab file looks like:

```
ap::sysinit:/sbin/autopush -f /etc/iu.apap::sysinit:/sbin/soconfig -f /etc/sock2path
fs::sysinit:/sbin/rcS    >/dev/console 2<>/dev/console </dev/console
s:3:initdefault:
3:s1234:powerfail:/usr/sbin/shutdown -y -i5 -g0 >/dev/console 2<>/dev/console
s0:0:wait:/sbin/rc0    >/dev/console 2<>/dev/console </dev/console
s1:1:wait:/usr/sbin/shutdown -y -iS -g0    >/dev/console 2<>/dev/console </dev/console
s2:23:wait:/sbin/rc2    >/dev/console 2<>/dev/console </dev/console
s3:3:wait:/sbin/rc3    >/dev/console 2<>/dev/console </dev/console
```

```
s5:5:wait:/sbin/rc5     >/dev/console 2<>/dev/console </dev/console
s6:6:wait:/sbin/rc6     >/dev/console 2<>/dev/console </dev/console
fw:0:wait:/sbin/uadmin 2 0     >/dev/console 2<>/dev/console </dev/console
of:5:wait:/sbin/uadmin 2 6     >/dev/console 2<>/dev/console </dev/console
rb:6:wait:/sbin/uadmin 2 1     >/dev/console 2<>/dev/console </dev/console
sc:234:respawn:/usr/lib/saf/sac -t 300
co:234:respawn:/usr/lib/saf/ttymon -g -h -p "'uname -n' console login: " -T vt100
-d /dev/console -l console -m ldterm,ttcompat
```

This /etc/inittab file only contains entries for the actions **sysinit**, **respawn**, **initdefault**, **wait**, and **powerfail**. These are the common actions found on most systems. However, Solaris provides a wide variety of actions that may be useful in special situations, such as when **powerwait** is more appropriate than **powerfail**. Potential actions are identified by any one of the following:

- **initdefault**   This is a mandatory entry found on all systems, which is used to configure the default runlevel for the system. This is specified by the highest init state specified in the **rstate** field. If this field is empty, **init** interprets the **rstate** as the highest possible runlevel (runlevel 6), which will force a continuous reboot of the system. In addition, if the entry is missing, the administrator must supply one manually on the console for booting to proceed.

- **sysinit**   This entry is provided as a safeguard for asking which runlevel is required at boot time if the **initdefault** entry is missing. Only devices required to ask the question are affected.

- **boot**   This entry is only parsed at boot time and is mainly used for initialization following a full reboot of the system after power down.

- **off**   This entry ensures that a process is terminated upon entering a particular runlevel. A warning signal is sent, followed by a kill signal, again with a five-second interval.

- **once**   This entry is similar to **boot**, but more flexible, in that the named process runs only once and is not respawned.

- **ondemand**   This entry is similar to the **respawn** action.

- **powerfail**   Runs the process associated with the entry when a power-fail signal is received.

- **powerwait**   Similar to **powerfail**, except that **init** waits until the process terminates before further processing entries in /etc/inittab. This is especially useful for enforcing sequential shutdown of services that are prioritized.

- **bootwait**   This entry is parsed only on the first occasion that the transition from single-user to multiuser runlevels occurs following a system boot.

■ **wait** This entry starts a process and waits for its completion on entering the specified runlevel. However, the entry is ignored if /etc/inittab is reread during the same runlevel.

■ **respawn** This entry ensures that if a process that should be running is not, it should be respawned.

The /etc/inittab file follows conventions for text layout used by the Bourne shell: A long entry can be continued on the following line by using a backslash "\", and comments can only be inserted into the process field by using a hash character "#". There is a limitation of 512 characters for each entry imposed on /etc/inittab; however, there is no limit on the number of entries that may be inserted.

## Control Scripts/Directories

Each runlevel has a corresponding control script denoted rc*n*, where *n* is the runlevel. These scripts reside in /sbin and are executed upon entering each runlevel. After they have been executed, the set of secondary scripts that reside in the directory rc*n*.d are exccuted. For example, upon entering the multiuser init state 2, the /sbin/rc2 script is executed, which in turn executes all the scripts that reside in the directory /etc/rc2.d. These scripts are either kill scripts, starting with the letter K, or startup scripts, starting with the letter S. Kill scripts have precedence over startup scripts. In addition to distinguishing scripts on the basis of K or S, scripts are also numbered, ensuring that execution is sequential in nature. This is important for high-level applications, such as application servers, which rely on the prior execution of network daemons and database servers.

To illustrate this process further, the typical startup scripts found in /etc/rc2.d in Solaris 2.x with a default installation are shown in Table 4-2, and the typical kill scripts found in /etc/rc0.d in Solaris 2.x are shown in Table 4-3.

| Script | Description |
| --- | --- |
| S05RMTMPFILES | Removes temporary files in the /tmp directory. Unlike Solaris 1.x, *all* files, including directory structures, are removed. |

**Table 4-2.** *Typical Multiuser Startup Scripts Under Solaris 2.x*

| Script | Description |
|---|---|
| S20sysetup | Establishes system setup requirements, and checks /var/crash to determine whether the system is recovering from a crash. |
| S21perf | Enables system accounting using /usr/lib/sa/sadc and /var/adm/sa/sa. |
| S30sysid.net | Executes /usr/sbin/sysidnet, /usr/sbin/sysidconfig, and /sbin/ifconfig, which are responsible for configuring network services. |
| S69inet | Initiates second phase of TCP/IP configuration, following on from the basic services established during single-user mode (**rcS**). Setting up IP routing (if /etc/defaultrouter exists), performing TCP/IP parameter tuning (using **ndd**), and setting the NIS domain-name (if required), are all performed here. |
| S70uucp | Initializes the UNIX-to-UNIX copy program (UUCP) by removing locks and other unnecessary files. |
| S71sysid.sys | Executes /usr/sbin/sysidsys and /usr/sbin/sysidroot. |
| S72autoinstall | Script to execute JumpStart installation if appropriate. |
| S72inetsvc | Final network configuration using /usr/sbin/ifconfig after NIS/NIS+ have been initialized. Also initializes Internet Domain Name Service (DNS) if appropriate. |
| S80PRESERVE | Preserves editing files by executing /usr/lib/expreserve. |
| S91leoconfig | Configuration for ZX graphics cards (if installed). |
| S92rtvc-config | Configuration for SunVideo cards (if installed). |
| S92volmgt | Starts volume management for removable media using /usr/sbin/vold. |

**Table 4-2.**    *Typical Multiuser Startup Scripts Under Solaris 2.x* (continued)

| Script | Description |
|---|---|
| K00ANNOUNCE | Announces that "System services are now being stopped." |
| K10dtlogin | Initializes tasks for the Common Desktop Environment (CDE), including killing the dtlogin process. |
| K20lp | Stops printing services using /usr/lib/lpshut. |
| K22acct | Terminates process accounting using /usr/lib/acct/shutacct. |
| K42audit | Kills the auditing daemon (/usr/sbin/audit). |
| K47asppp | Stops the asynchronous PPP daemon (/usr/sbin/aspppd). |
| K50utmpd | Kills the utmp daemon (/usr/lib/utmpd). |
| K55syslog | Terminates the system logging service (/usr/sbin/syslogd). |
| K57sendmail | Halts the sendmail mail service (/usr/lib/sendmail). |
| K66nfs.server | Kills all processes required for the NFS server (/usr/lib/nfs/nfsd). |
| K69autofs | Stops the automounter (/usr/sbin/automount). |
| K70cron | Terminates the cron daemon (/usr/bin/cron). |
| K75nfs.client | Disables client NFS. |
| K76nscd | Kills the name service cache daemon (/usr/sbin/nscd). |
| K85rpc | Disables remote procedure call (rpc) services (/usr/sbin/rpcbind). |

**Table 4-3.** *Typical Single-User Kill Scripts Under Solaris 2.x*

Each of the scripts in rc*n*.d directories are typically symbolic links from their real entries in the /etc/init.d directory.

# /etc/init.d

For a multiuser system, the most important control scripts reside in the /etc/rc2.d and /etc/rc3.d directories, which are responsible for enabling multiuser services and NFS network resource sharing, respectively. A basic script for starting up a web server looks like this:

```
#!/bin/sh
# Sample webserver startup script
# Should be placed in /etc/rc2.d/S99webserver
case "$1" in
    'start')
            echo "Starting webserver...\c"
            if [ -f /usr/local/sbin/webserver ]; then
                    /usr/local/sbin/webserver start
            fi
            echo ""
            ;;
    'stop')
      echo "Stopping webserver...\c"
            if [ -f /usr/local/sbin/webserver ]; then
                  /usr/local/sbin/webserver stop
            fi
            echo ""
    ;;
    *)
            echo "Usage: /etc/rc2.d/S99webserver { start | stop }"
            ;;
    esac
```

This file should be created by root (with the group sys) and placed in the file
/etc/rc2.d/S99webserver, and it should have executable permissions:

```
server# chmod 0744 /etc/rc2.d/S99webserver
server# chgrp sys /etc/rc2.d/S99webserver
```

When called with the argument **start** (represented in the script by "$1"), the script
prints a status message that the web server daemon is starting and proceeds to execute
the command if the web server binary exists. The script can also act as a kill script,
since it has a provision to be called with a **stop** argument. Of course, a more complete
script would provide more elaborate status information if the web server binary did
not exist, and may further process any output from the web server by using a pipe (for
example, mailing error messages to the superuser).

One of the advantages of the flexible boot system is that these scripts can be executed
to start and stop specific daemons without changing the init state. For example, if a web
site was going to be updated, and the web server needed to be switched off for a few
minutes, the command:

```
server# /etc/rc2.d/S99webserver stop
```

would halt the web server process, but would not force the system back into a single-user state. The web server could be restarted after all content was uploaded by typing the command:

```
server# /etc/rc2.d/S99webserver start
```

In order to conform to System V standards, it is actually more appropriate to create all the run control scripts in the /etc/init.d directory and then create symbolic links back to the appropriate rc2.d and rc3.d directories. This means all scripts executed by init through different runlevels are centrally located and can be easily maintained. With the web server example, a file could be created in /etc/init.d with a descriptive filename:

```
server# vi /etc/init.d/webserver
```

After adding the appropriate contents, the file could be saved, and the appropriate symbolic link could be created using the symbolic link command **ln**:

```
server# ln -s /etc/init.d/webserver /etc/rc2.d/S99webserver
```

Using this convention, kill and startup scripts for each service can literally coexist in the same script, with the ability to process a **start** argument for startup scripts, and a **stop** argument for kill scripts. In this example, you would also need to create a symbolic link to /etc/init.d/webserver for K99webserver.

## Changing Runlevels

In order to manually change runlevels, the desired init state is used as an argument to /sbin/init. For example, to bring the system down to a single-user mode for maintenance, the following command can be used:

```
server#  init s
INIT: New run level: S
The system is coming down for administration. Please wait.
Print services stopped.
syslogd: going down on signal 15
Killing user processes: done.
INIT: SINGLE USER MODE
Type Ctrl-d to proceed with normal startup,
(or give root password for system maintenance):
Entering System Maintenance Mode ...
```

However, to shut down the system, it is more common to use one of the shutdown methods outlined in the following section.

# System Shutdown

The system is most easily shut down by using the new /usr/sbin/shutdown command (not the old BSD-style /usr/ucb/shutdown command discussed later). This command is issued with the form:

```
server# shutdown -i run-level -g grace-period -y
```

where run-level is an **init** state different from the default **init** state **S** (that is, one of the runlevels **0**, **1**, **2**, **5**, or **6**). However, most administrators will typically be interested in using **shutdown** with respect to the reboot or power down runlevels. The grace period is the number of seconds before the shutdown process is initiated. On single-user machines, the superuser will easily know who is logged in and what processes need to be terminated gracefully. However, on a multiuser machine, it is more useful to warn users in advance of a power down or reboot. If the change of **init** state is to proceed without user intervention, it is useful to include the **-y** flag at the end of the **shutdown** command, otherwise the message:

```
Do you want to continue? (y or n):
```

will be displayed, and **y** must be entered in order for the shutdown to proceed. The default grace-period on Solaris is 60 seconds, so if the administrators wanted to reboot with two minutes' warning given to all users, without user intervention, the command would be:

```
server# shutdown -i 5 -g 120 -y
```

The system will periodically display a message warning all users of the imminent init state change:

```
Shutdown started. Mon Jan 10 10:22:00 EST 2000
Broadcast Message from root (console) on server Mon Jan 10 10:22:00...
The system server will be shut down in 2 minutes
```

The system then reboots without user intervention and does not enter the OpenBoot monitor. If commands need to be issued using the monitor (for instance, an **init** state of 0 is desired), the following command can be used:

```
# shutdown -i0 -g180 -y
Shutdown started. Mon Jan 10 11:15:00 EST 2000
Broadcast Message from root (console) on server Mon Jan 10 11:15:00...
The system will be shut down in 3 minutes
```

```
        .
        .
        .
INIT: New run level: 0
The system is coming down. Please wait.
        .
        .
        .
The system is down.
syncing file systems... [1] [2] [3] done
Program terminated
Type help for more information
ok
```

There are many ways to warn users in advance of a shutdown. One way is to edit the "message of the day" file (/etc/motd) to contain a warning that the server will be down and/or rebooted for a specific time. This message will be displayed every time a user successfully logs in with an interactive shell. The following message gives the date and time of the shutdown, expected duration, and a contact address for inquiries:

```
System server will be shut down at 5 p.m. 2/1/2000.
Expected downtime: 1 hour.
E-mail root@system for further details.
```

At least 24 hours notice is usually required for users on a large system, as long jobs need to be rescheduled. In practice, many administrators will only shut down or reboot outside business hours to minimize inconvenience—however, power failure and hardware problems can necessitate unexpected downtime.

This method works well in advance, but since many users are continuously logged in from remote terminals, they won't always read the new message of the day. An alternative approach is to use the "write all" command (**wall**), which sends a message to all terminals of all logged-in users. This command can be sent manually at hourly intervals prior to shutdown, or a cron job could be established to perform this task automatically. An example command would be:

```
server# wall
System server will be shut down at 5 p.m. 1/10/2000.
Expected downtime: 1 hour.
E-mail root@system for further details.
^d
```

After sending the **wall** message, a final check of logged-in users prior to shutdown can be performed using the **who** command:

```
server# who
root  console     Jan 10 10:15
pwatters    pts/0 Jan 10 10:15          (client)
```

A message can be sent to the user pwatters on pts/0 directly to notify him of the imminent shutdown:

```
server# write pwatters
Dear pwatters,
Please log out immediately as the system server is going down.
If you do not log out now, your unsaved work may be lost.
Yours sincerely,
System Administrator (root@system)
^d
```

Depending on the status of the user, it may also be fruitful to request a talk session by using the command:

```
server# talk pwatters
```

If all these strategies fail to convince the user pwatters to log out, there is nothing left to do but proceed with the shutdown.

## Using shutdown or init

As outlined above, the correct System V approach to shutting down a system involves running /usr/sbin/shutdown, which is a wrapper script that executes **init** to change the system's runlevel. To bring the system down to runlevel 0, the /sbin/rc0 script executes all kill scripts in the /etc/rc0.d directory, which ensures that databases and other applications that need to be halted in a specific way (for example, to flush caches and save state information) can be notified of the shutdown. This can be a very slow and time-consuming process, depending on how the kill script is written. In the next section, we look at the traditional approach of generating a process list and sending a signal to stop the target process. However, if there are many processes to be identified and signaled in this way, halting using the System V approach can be very slow indeed.

If you are sure there are no services or applications on your system that need to be halted gracefully, it is possible to use the BSD-style **shutdown** program, which is available on Solaris 2.x as /usr/ucb/shutdown. This command results in a kill signal being sent by **init** to all multiuser processes, which is much faster than the System V equivalent. A similar command is provided by the **halt** command, which also does not execute any scripts in /etc/rc0.d, but which does synchronize disk data by using the **sync** command. However, it should be emphasized that these approaches should only be adopted where there is no risk of data loss.

It is also possible to speed up shutdown by using **init** directly instead of the wrapper program **shutdown**. This does not issue warnings to logged-in users, which is acceptable for a single-user workstation, but is probably unwise for servers.

## Kill Scripts

Under System V, kill scripts follow the same convention as startup scripts, in that a **stop** argument is passed to the script to indicate that a kill rather than a startup is required, in which case a **start** argument would be passed. A common approach to killing off processes is to find them by name in the process list. The following script kills the asynchronous PPP daemon, which is the link manager for the asynchronous data link protocol. This daemon is started using **aspppd**—thus, the script generates a process list that is piped through a **grep** to identify any entries containing **aspppd**, and the process number is extracted using **awk**. This value is assigned to a variable (**$procid**), which is then used by the **kill** command to terminate the appropriate process:

```
procid=`ps -e | grep aspppd | awk '{print $1}'`
if test -n "$procid"
then
            kill $procid
fi
```

Alternatively, **sed** could be used to match the process name:

```
procid=`/usr/bin/ps -e |
    /usr/bin/grep aspppd |
    /usr/bin/sed -e 's/^  *//' -e 's/ .*//''
```

When multiple processes are to be terminated using a single script (for example, when the NFS server terminates), a shell function (**killprocid()**) can be written, which takes an argument and searches for it in the process list, terminating the named process if it exists:

```
killprocid() {
procid=`/usr/bin/ps -e |
        /usr/bin/grep -w $1 |
```

```
        /usr/bin/sed -e 's/^  *//' -e 's/ .*//''
  [ "$procid" != "" ] && kill $procid
}
```

Individual processes can then be terminated using the same function:

```
killproc nfsd
killproc mountd
killproc rpc.boot
killproc in.rarpd
killproc rpld
```

There are two problems with these approaches to process termination. First, there is an ambiguity problem in that different daemons and applications can be identified by the same name. For example, a system may be running the Apache web server, which is identified by the process name **httpd**, as well as a web server from another vendor (such as NCSA), which is also identified by **httpd**. If a script was written to kill the Apache web server, but the first process identified actually belonged to the NCSA web server, the NCSA web server process would be terminated. One solution to this problem is to ensure that all applications are launched with a unique name or from a wrapper script with a unique name. The second problem is that for a system with even a moderately heavy process load (for example, 500 active processes), executing the **ps** command to kill each process is going to generate a large CPU overhead, leading to excessively slow shutdown times. Alternative solutions to this problem are provided in the previous section.

## Summary

In this chapter, we have examined different methods for starting up and shutting down a Solaris server, and discussed advanced configuration of initialization files to start up local services such as databases, applications, and web servers. Although Solaris 1.x administrators may find the notation and layout of these startup scripts difficult to interpret, by working through the examples provided, you should be able to better appreciate that increased functionality accompanies the complexity associated with System V. If you experience difficulty in understanding shell scripts, there are many good books available on Bourne shell script programming. Although newer scripting languages such as Perl are easier to use than Bourne shell, Bourne shell is still the reference shell and should be used to write all startup and shutdown scripts, even though Solaris 8 now comes installed with Perl.

## How to Find Out More

An excellent guide to the booting process and the OpenBoot monitor can be found in the article "Questions and Answers on OpenBoot," by Steve Leung, in Sun World:

http://www.sunworld.com/swol-10-1995/swol-10-openboot.html

For information on dual-booting Solaris and other operating systems, such as Linux, see Sun's own instructions at:

http://www.sun.com/software/linux/docs/dual_boot.html

# Chapter 5

## Process Management

P rocesses lie at the heart of modern multiuser operating systems and provide the capability to run multiple applications and services concurrently on top of the kernel. In user terms, process management is a central feature of using a single login shell to start and stop multiple jobs running concurrently, often suspending their execution while waiting for input. Solaris 8 provides many tools for process management, which changed significantly during the transition from Solaris 1.x. In this chapter, we will highlight the new process management tools and command formats. We will discuss the innovative /proc file systems and the associated tools that allow administrators to deal with zombie processes. This chapter will also talk about automating tasks and the scheduling facility.

## Processes

One of the appealing characteristics of Solaris and other UNIX-like systems is that applications can execute (or spawn) other applications—after all, user shells are nothing more than applications themselves. A shell can spawn another shell or application, which can spawn another shell or application, and so on. Instances of applications, such as the **sendmail** mail transport agent or the **telnet** remote access application, can be uniquely identified as individual processes and are associated with a unique process identifier (PID), which is an integer.

You may be wondering why process identifiers are not content-addressable—that is, why the **sendmail** process cannot be just identified as "sendmail." Such a scheme would be quite sensible if it were impossible to execute multiple, independent instances of the same application (such as MacOS). However, Solaris allows the same user or different users to concurrently execute the same application independently, meaning that an independent identifier is required for each process. This means that each PID is related to a user's identifier (UID) and to that user's group identifier (GID). The UID in this case can either be the real UID of the user who executed the process or the effective UID, if the file executed is setuid. Similarly, the GID in this case can either be the real GID of the user who executed the process belongs to or the effective GID, if the file executed is setgid. When an application can be executed as setuid and setgid, other users can execute such a program as the user who owns the file. This means that setting a file as setgid for root can be dangerous in some situations, although necessary in others.

An application, such as a shell, can spawn another application by using the system call **system()** in a C program. This is expensive performance-wise, because a new shell process is spawned in addition to the target application. However, an alternative is to use the **fork()** system call, which spawns child processes directly, with the application executed using **exec()**. Each child process is linked back to its parent process: If the parent process exits, the parent process automatically reverts to PID 1, which exits when the system is shut down or rebooted.

In this section, we look at ways to determine which processes are currently running on your system, and how to examine process lists and tables to determine what system resources are being used by specific processes.

# Listing Processes

The main command used to list commands is **ps**, which is highly configurable, and
has many command-line options. These options and the command format changed
substantially from Solaris 1.x to Solaris 2.x. The former used BSD-style options, like **ps
aux**, while the latter uses System V-style parameters, like **ps -eaf**. However, **ps** takes a
snapshot of the current process list. Many administrators find they need to interactively
monitor processes on systems that have a high load so they can kill processes that are
consuming too much memory, or at least assign them a lower execution priority. One
popular process-monitoring tool is **top**, which is described later in this chapter. As
shown in Figure 5-1, the CDE has its own graphical "process finder," which also lists
currently active processes. It is possible to list processes here by PID, name, owner,
percentage of CPU time consumed, physical memory used, virtual memory used, date
started, parent PID, and the actual command executed. This does not provide as much
information as **top**, but it is a useful tool within the CDE.

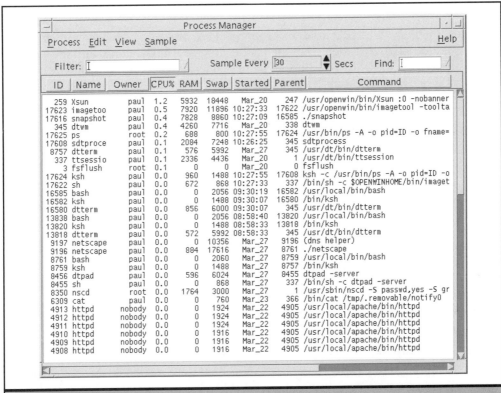

**Figure 5-1.**   *CDE's graphical process finder*

## ps

**ps** lists all currently active processes on the local system. By default, **ps** just prints the processes belonging to the user who issues the **ps** command:

```
client% ps
PID TTY       TIME CMD
 29081 pts/8   0:00 ksh
```

The columns in the default **ps** list are the process identifier (PID), the terminal from which the command was executed (TTY), the CPU time consumed by the process (TIME), and the actual command that was executed (CMD), including any command-line options passed to the program. Alternatively, if you would like more information about the current user's processes, you can add the **-f** parameter:

```
bash-2.03$ ps -f
     UID     PID   PPID  C STIME    TTY      TIME CMD
     pwatters 29081 29079  0 10:40:30 pts/8    0:00 /bin/ksh
```

Again, the PID, TTY, CPU time, and command are displayed. However, the UID is also displayed (UID), as is the PID of the parent process (PPID), along with the starting time of the process (STIME). In addition, there is a deprecated column (C), which used to display processor utilization. To obtain the maximum detail possible, you can also use the **-l** (long) option—and long it certainly is, as shown in this example:

```
bash-2.03$ ps -l
 F S   UID   PID  PPID  C PRI NI     ADDR     SZ    WCHAN TTY      TIME CMD
 8 S  6049 29081 29079  0  51 20 e11b4830   372 e11b489c pts/8    0:00 ksh
 8 R  6049 29085 29081  0  51 20 e101b0d0   512          pts/8    0:00 bash
Here, we can see:
```

- Flags (F) associated with the processes
- State (S) of the processes (29081 is sleeping "S," 29085 is running "R")
- Process identifier (29081 and 29085)
- Parent process identifier (29079 and 29081)
- Processor utilization (deprecated)
- Process priority (PRI), which is 51
- Nice value (NI), which is 20
- Memory address (ADDR), which is expressed in hexadecimal format (e11b4830 and e101b0d0)
- Size (SZ) in kilobytes, which is 372K and 512K

- Memory address for sleeping process events (WCHAN), which is e11b489c for PID 29081
- CPU time used (TIME)
- Command executed (CMD)

If you're a system administrator, you're probably not interested in the status of just your own processes, but rather, of all or some of the processes actively running on the system. There are many ways to do this. One is to generate a process list using the **-A** or **-e** option; either of these lists information for all processes currently running on the machine:

```
server# ps -A
   PID TTY       TIME CMD
     0 ?         0:00 sched
     1 ?         0:01 init
     2 ?         0:01 pageout
     3 ?         9:49 fsflush
   258 ?         0:00 ttymon
   108 ?         0:00 rpcbind
   255 ?         0:00 sac
    60 ?         0:00 devfseve
    62 ?         0:00 devfsadm
   157 ?         0:03 automount
   110 ?         0:01 keyserv
   112 ?         0:04 nis_cache
   165 ?         0:00 syslogd
```

Again, the default display of PID, TTY, CPU time, and command is generated. The processes listed relate to the scheduler, **init**, the system logging facility, the NIS cache, and several other standard applications and services. It is good practice to become familiar with the main processes on your system and the relative CPU times they usually consume. This can be very useful when troubleshooting or when evaluating security. One of the nice features of **ps** is the ability to combine multiple flags to print out a more elaborate process list. For example, we can combine the **-A** option (all processes) with the **-f** option (full details) to produce a process list with full details. Here are the full details for the same process list:

```
server# ps -Af
     UID   PID  PPID  C    STIME TTY       TIME CMD
    root     0     0  0   Mar 20 ?         0:00 sched
    root     1     0  0   Mar 20 ?         0:01 /etc/init -
    root     2     0  0   Mar 20 ?         0:01 pageout
    root     3     0  0   Mar 20 ?         9:51 fsflush
    root   258   255  0   Mar 20 ?         0:00 /usr/lib/saf/ttymon
    root   108     1  0   Mar 20 ?         0:00 /usr/sbin/rpcbind
```

```
root   255   1   0   Mar 20  ?      0:00 /usr/lib/saf/sac -t 300
root    60   1   0   Mar 20  ?      0:00 /usr/lib/devfsadm/devfseventd
root    62   1   0   Mar 20  ?      0:00 /usr/lib/devfsadm/devfsadmd
root   157   1   0   Mar 20  ?      0:03 /usr/lib/autofs/automountd
root   110   1   0   Mar 20  ?      0:01 /usr/sbin/keyserv
root   112   1   0   Mar 20  ?      0:05 /usr/sbin/nis_cachemgr
root   165   1   0   Mar 20  ?      0:00 /usr/sbin/syslogd
```

Another common use for **ps** is to print process information in a format suitable for the scheduler:

```
client% ps -c
   PID  CLS PRI TTY       TIME CMD
 29081   TS  48 pts/8     0:00 ksh
 29085   TS  48 pts/8     0:00 bash
```

This can be useful when used in conjunction with the **priocntl** command, which displays the parameters used for process scheduling. This allows administrators, in particular, to determine the process classes currently available on the system, or to set the class of a specific process to interactive or time-sharing. You can obtain a list of all supported classes by passing the **-l** parameter to **priocntl**:

```
server# priocntl -l
CONFIGURED CLASSES
==================
SYS (System Class)
TS (Time Sharing)
        Configured TS User Priority Range: -60 through 60
IA (Interactive)
        Configured IA User Priority Range: -60 through 60
```

You can combine this with a **-f** full display flag to **ps -c** in order to obtain more information:

```
client% ps -cf
     UID   PID  PPID CLS PRI    STIME TTY      TIME CMD
    paul 29081 29079  TS  48 10:40:30 pts/8    0:00 /bin/ksh
    paul 29085 29081  TS  48 10:40:51 pts/8    0:00 /usr/local/bin/bash
If you want to obtain information about processes being executed by a
particular group of users, this can be specified on the command line by
using the -g option, followed by the GID of the target group. In this
example, we print out all processes from users in group 0:
client% ps -g 0
   PID TTY       TIME CMD
```

```
0 ?          0:00 sched
1 ?          0:01 init
2 ?          0:01 pageout
3 ?          9:51 fsflush
```

Another common configuration option used with **ps** is **-j**, which displays the session identifier (SID) and the process group identifier (PGID), as shown here:

```
bash-2.03$ ps -j
   PID  PGID    SID TTY       TIME CMD
 29081 29081 29081 pts/8     0:00 ksh
 29085 29085 29081 pts/8     0:00 bash
```

Finally, you can print out the status of light-weight processes (LWP) in your system. These are virtual CPU or execution resources, which are designed to make the best use of available CPU resources based on their priority and scheduling class. Here is an example:

```
client% ps -L
   PID  LWP TTY      LTIME CMD
 29081    1 pts/8     0:00 ksh
 29085    1 pts/8     0:00 bash
```

Table 5-1 summarizes the main options for **ps**.

## top

If you're an administrator, you probably want to keep an eye on all processes running on a system, particularly if it's in production use. This is because programs that have bugs can consume large amounts of CPU time, preventing operational applications from carrying out their duties efficiently. Monitoring the process list semiconstantly is necessary, especially if performance begins to suffer on a system. Although you could keep typing **ps -eaf** every five minutes or so, a much more efficient method is to use the **top** program to interactively monitor the processes in your system and its vital statistics, such as CPU activity states, real and virtual memory status, and the load average. In addition, **top** displays the details of the leading processes that consume the greatest amount of CPU time during each sampling period. The display of **top** can be customized to include any number of these leading processes at any one time, but displaying the top 10 or 20 is usually sufficient to keep an eye on rogue processes. The latest version of **top** can always be downloaded from **ftp://ftp.groupsys.com/pub/top**.

   **top** reads the /proc file system to generate its process statistics. This usually means that **top** runs as a set-uid process, unless you remove the read and execute permissions

| Option | Description |
|--------|-------------|
| -a | Lists most frequently requested processes |
| -A, -e | Lists all processes |
| -c | Lists processes in scheduler format |
| -d | Lists all processes |
| -f | Prints comprehensive process information |
| -g | Prints process information on a group basis for a single group |
| -G | Prints process information on a group basis for a list of groups |
| -j | Includes SID and PGID in printout |
| -l | Prints complete process information |
| -L | Displays LWP details |
| -p | Lists process details for list of specified process |
| -P | Lists the CPU ID to which a process is bound |
| -s | Lists session leaders |
| -t | Lists all processes associated with a specific terminal |
| -u | Lists all processes for a specific user |

**Table 5-1.** *Main Options for Listing Processes with ps*

for non-root users, and run it only as root. Paradoxically, this may be just as dangerous, because any errors in **top** may impact the system at large if executed by the root user. Again, setuid processes are dangerous, and you should evaluate whether the trade-off between accessibility and security is worthwhile in this case.

One of the main problems with **top** and Solaris is that they are very sensitive to changes in architecture and/or operating system version. This is particularly the case if the GNU **gcc** compiler is used to build **top**, as it has its own set of include files. These must exactly match the version of the current operating system, otherwise, **top** will not work properly. The CPU state percentages may be wrong, indicating that processes are consuming all CPU time when the system is actually idle. The solution is to rebuild **gcc** so it generates header files appropriate for your current operating system version.

Let's examine a printout from **top**:

```
last pid: 16630;  load averages:  0.17,  0.08,  0.06              09:33:29
72 processes:  71 sleeping, 1 on cpu
CPU states: 87.6% idle,  4.8% user,  7.5% kernel,  0.1% iowait,  0.0% SWAP
Memory: 128M real, 3188K free, 72M SWAP in use, 172M SWAP free
```

This summary tells us that the system has 72 processes, with only one running actively and 71 sleeping. The system was 87.6 percent idle in the previous sampling epoch, and there was very little swapping or iowait activity, ensuring fast performance. The load average for the previous 1, 5, and 15 minutes was 0.17, 0.08, and 0.06 respectively—this is not a machine that is taxed by its workload. The last PID to be issued to an application—16630—is also displayed.

```
  PID USERNAME THR PRI NICE  SIZE   RES STATE   TIME   CPU COMMAND
  259 root        1  59    0   18M 4044K sleep 58:49  1.40% Xsun
16630  pwatters    1  59    0 1956K 1536K cpu     0:00  1.19% top
  345 pwatters 8  33    0 7704K 4372K sleep   0:21  0.83% dtwm
16580 pwatters 1  59    0 5984K 2608K sleep   0:00  0.24% dtterm
 9196 pwatters 1  48    0   17M 1164K sleep   0:28  0.01% netscape
13818 pwatters 1  59    0 5992K  872K sleep   0:01  0.00% dtterm
  338 pwatters 1  48    0 7508K   0K sleep   0:04  0.00% dtsession
  112 pwatters 3  59    0 1808K  732K sleep   0:03  0.00% nis_cachemgr
  157 pwatters 5  58    0 2576K  576K sleep   0:02  0.00% automountd
  422 pwatters 1  48    0 4096K  672K sleep   0:01  0.00% textedit
 2295 pwatters 1  48    0 7168K   0K sleep   0:01  0.00% dtfile
 8350 root       10  51    0 3000K 2028K sleep   0:01  0.00% nscd
 8757 pwatters 1  59    0 5992K 1340K sleep   0:01  0.00% dtterm
 4910 nobody     1   0    0 1916K   0K sleep   0:00  0.00% httpd
  366 pwatters 1  28    0 1500K   0K sleep   0:00  0.00% sdtvolcheck
```

The **top** listing proper shows a lot of information about each process running on the system, including the PID, the user who owns the process, the nice value, the size of the application, the amount resident in memory, its current state (active or sleeping), the CPU time consumed, and the command name. For example, the Apache web server runs as the **httpd** process (PID=4910), by the user nobody, and is 1916K in size.

Now, if we execute an application that requires a lot of CPU power, we will be able to monitor the impact on the system as a whole by examining the changes in the processes displayed by **top**. If we execute the command:

```
client% find . -name apache -print
```

the impact on the process distribution is immediately apparent:

```
last pid: 16631;  load averages:  0.10,  0.07,  0.06                    09:34:08
73 processes:  71 sleeping, 1 running, 1 on cpu
CPU states:  2.2% idle,  0.6% user, 11.6% kernel, 85.6% iowait,  0.0% SWAP
Memory: 128M real, 1896K free, 72M SWAP in use, 172M SWAP free
```

This summary tells us that the system now has 73 processes, with only one running actively, one on the CPU, and 71 sleeping. The new process is the **find** command, which is actively running. The system is now only 2.2 percent idle, a large increase on the previous sampling epoch. There is still no swapping activity, but iowait activity has risen to 85.6 percent, slowing system performance. The load average for the previous 1, 5, and 15 minutes was 0.10, 0.07, and 0.06 respectively. On the average, this machine is still not taxed by its workload, and wouldn't be unless the load averages grew to greater than one. The last PID to be issued to an application—16631—is also displayed, in this case, again referring to the **find** command.

```
  PID USERNAME THR PRI NICE  SIZE    RES STATE   TIME    CPU COMMAND
16631 pwatters 1  54    0   788K   668K run     0:00   1.10% find
  259 root        1  59    0    18M  4288K sleep  58:49   0.74% Xsun
16630 pwatters 1  59    0  1956K  1536K cpu     0:00   0.50% top
 9196 pwatters 1  48    0    17M  3584K sleep   0:28   0.13% netscape
 8456 pwatters 1  59    0  5984K    0K sleep    0:00   0.12% dtpad
  345 pwatters 8  59    0  7708K    0K sleep    0:21   0.11% dtwm
16580 pwatters 1  59    0  5992K  2748K sleep   0:00   0.11% dtterm
13838 pwatters 1  38    0  2056K   652K sleep   0:00   0.06% bash
13818 pwatters 1  59    0  5992K  1884K sleep   0:01   0.06% dtterm
  112 root        3  59    0  1808K   732K sleep   0:03   0.02% nis_cachemgr
  337 pwatters 4  59    0  4004K    0K sleep    0:00   0.01% ttsession
  338 pwatters 1  48    0  7508K    0K sleep    0:04   0.00% dtsession
  157 root        5  58    0  2576K   604K sleep   0:02   0.00% automountd
 2295 pwatters 1  48    0  7168K    0K sleep    0:01   0.00% dtfile
  422 pwatters 1  48    0  4096K    0K sleep    0:01   0.00% textedit
```

**find** now uses 1.1 percent of CPU power, which is the highest of any active process (that is, in the "run" state) on the system. It uses 788K of RAM, less than most other processes—however, most other processes are in the "sleep" state and do not occupy much resident memory.

## truss

If you've identified a process that appears to be having problems, and you suspect an application bug, it's not just a matter of going back to the source to debug the program or making an educated guess about what's going wrong. In fact, one of the great features of Solaris is the ability to trace system calls for every process running on the system. This means that if a program is hanging, for example, because it can't find its initialization file, the failed system call revealed by using **truss** would display this information. **truss** prints out each system call, line by line, as it is executed by the system. The syntax is rather like a C program, making it easy for C programmers to interpret the output. The arguments are displayed by retrieving information from the appropriate headers, and any file information is also displayed.

As an example, let's look at the output from the **cat** command, which we can use to display the contents of the /etc/resolv.conf, which is used by the Domain Name Service to identify domains and nameservers (further described in Chapter 13). Let's look at the operations involved in running this application:

```
server# truss cat /etc/resolv.conf
execve("/usr/bin/cat", 0xEFFFF740, 0xEFFFF74C)  argc = 2
open("/dev/zero", O_RDONLY)                    = 3
mmap(0x00000000, 8192, PROT_READ|PROT_WRITE|PROT_EXEC, MAP_PRIVATE, 3, 0) = 0xEF7B0000
open("/usr/lib/libc.so.1", O_RDONLY)           = 4
fstat(4, 0xEFFFF2DC)                           = 0
mmap(0x00000000, 8192, PROT_READ|PROT_EXEC, MAP_PRIVATE, 4, 0) = 0xEF7A0000
mmap(0x00000000, 704512, PROT_READ|PROT_EXEC, MAP_PRIVATE, 4, 0) = 0xEF680000
munmap(0xEF714000, 57344)
            = 0
mmap(0xEF722000, 28368, PROT_READ|PROT_WRITE|PROT_EXEC, MAP_PRIVATE|MAP_FIXED, 4, 598016) =
0xEF722000
mmap(0xEF72A000, 2528, PROT_READ|PROT_WRITE|PROT_EXEC, MAP_PRIVATE|MAP_FIXED, 3, 0) = 0xEF72A000
close(4)                                       = 0
open("/usr/lib/libdl.so.1", O_RDONLY)          = 4
fstat(4, 0xEFFFF2DC)                           = 0
mmap(0xEF7A0000, 8192, PROT_READ|PROT_EXEC, MAP_PRIVATE|MAP_FIXED, 4, 0) = 0xEF7A0000
close(4)                                       = 0
open("/usr/platform/SUNW,Ultra-2/lib/libc_psr.so.1", O_RDONLY) = 4
fstat(4, 0xEFFFF0BC)                           = 0
mmap(0x00000000, 8192, PROT_READ|PROT_EXEC, MAP_PRIVATE, 4, 0) = 0xEF790000
mmap(0x00000000, 16384, PROT_READ|PROT_EXEC, MAP_PRIVATE, 4, 0) = 0xEF780000
close(4)                                       = 0
close(3)                                       = 0
munmap(0xEF790000, 8192)                       = 0
fstat64(1, 0xEFFFF648)                         = 0
open64("resolv.conf", O_RDONLY)                = 3
fstat64(3, 0xEFFFF5B0)                         = 0
llseek(3, 0, SEEK_CUR)                         = 0
mmap64(0x00000000, 98, PROT_READ, MAP_SHARED, 3, 0) = 0xEF790000
read(3, " d", 1)                               = 1
memcntl(0xEF790000, 98, MC_ADVISE, 0x0002, 0, 0) = 0
domain paulwatters.com
nameserver 192.56.67.16
nameserver 192.56.67.32
nameserver 192.56.68.16
```

```
write(1, "d o m a i n   p a u l w a t t e r s .".., 98)      = 98
llseek(3, 98, SEEK_SET)                           = 98
munmap(0xEF790000, 98)                            = 0
llseek(3, 0, SEEK_CUR)                            = 98
close(3)                                          = 0
close(1)                                          = 0
llseek(0, 0, SEEK_CUR)                            = 57655
_exit(0)
```

First, **cat** is called using **execve()**, with two arguments (that is, the application name, **cat**, and the file to be displayed, /etc/resolv.conf). The arguments to execve include the name of the application (/usr/bin/cat), a pointer to the argument list (0xEFFFF740), and a pointer to the environment (0xEFFFF74C). Next, library files such as /usr/lib/libc.so.1 are read. Memory operations (such as **mmap()**) are performed continuously. The resolv.conf is opened as read-only, after which the contents are literally printed to standard output and the file is closed. **truss** can be used in this way to trace the system calls for any process running on your system.

## Getting Detailed Process Information

Now that we have examined what processes are, we will look at some special features of processes as implemented in Solaris. One of the most innovative characteristics of processes under Solaris is the process file system (PROCFS), which is mounted as the /proc file system. Images of all currently active processes are stored by their PID in the /proc file system. Let's look at an example. First, we identify a process—in this example, the current Korn shell for the user pwatters:

```
server# ps -eaf | grep pwatters
 pwatters 310   291  0   Mar 20 ?          0:04 /usr/openwin/bin/Xsun :0 -nobanne
r -auth /var/dt/A:0-nsayKa
 pwatters 11959 11934  0 09:21:42 pts/1    0:00 grep pwatters
 pwatters 11934 11932  1 09:20:50 pts/1    0:00 -ksh
```

Now that we have a target PID (11934), we can change to the /proc/11934 directory, and we will be able to view the image of this process:

```
server# cd /proc/11934
server# ls -l
total 3497
-rw-------   1 pwatters   other    1769472 Mar 30 09:20 as
-r--------   1 pwatters   other        152 Mar 30 09:20 auxv
-r--------   1 pwatters   other         32 Mar 30 09:20 cred
```

```
--w-------    1 pwatters     other          0 Mar 30 09:20 ctl
lr-x------    1 pwatters     other          0 Mar 30 09:20 cwd ->
dr-x------    2 pwatters     other       1184 Mar 30 09:20 fd
-r--r--r--    1 pwatters     other        120 Mar 30 09:20 lpsinfo
-r--------    1 pwatters     other        912 Mar 30 09:20 lstatus
-r--r--r--    1 pwatters     other        536 Mar 30 09:20 lusage
dr-xr-xr-x    3 pwatters     other         48 Mar 30 09:20 lwp
-r--------    1 pwatters     other       2016 Mar 30 09:20 map
dr-x------    2 pwatters     other        544 Mar 30 09:20 object
-r--------    1 pwatters     other       2552 Mar 30 09:20 pagedata
-r--r--r--    1 pwatters     other        336 Mar 30 09:20 psinfo
-r--------    1 pwatters     other       2016 Mar 30 09:20 rmap
lr-x------    1 pwatters     other          0 Mar 30 09:20 root ->
-r--------    1 pwatters     other       1440 Mar 30 09:20 sigact
-r--------    1 pwatters     other       1232 Mar 30 09:20 status
-r--r--r--    1 pwatters     other        256 Mar 30 09:20 usage
-r--------    1 pwatters     other          0 Mar 30 09:20 watch
-r--------    1 pwatters     other       3192 Mar 30 09:20 xmap
```

Each of the directories with the name associated with the PID contains additional subdirectories, which contain state information and related control functions. In addition, a watchpoint facility is provided that is responsible for controlling memory access. There are a series of **proc** tools that interpret the information contained in the /proc subdirectories, which display the characteristics of each process. These are detailed in the next section.

## proc tools

The **proc** tools are designed to operate on data contained within the /proc file system. Each utility takes a PID as its argument and performs operations associated with the PID. For example, the **pflags** command prints the flags and data model details for the PID in question. For the Korn shell example above, we can easily print out this status information:

```
server# /usr/proc/bin/pflags 29081
29081:  /bin/ksh
        data model = _ILP32  flags = PR_ORPHAN
  /1:   flags = PR_PCINVAL|PR_ASLEEP [ waitid(0x7,0x0,0x804714c,0x7) ]
```

We can also print the credential information for this process, including the effective and real UID and GID of the process owner, by using the **pcred** command:

```
bash-2.03$ /usr/proc/bin/pcred 29081
29081:  e/r/suid=100  e/r/sgid=10
```

Here, both the effective and the real UID is 100 (user pwatters), and the effective and real GID is 10 (group staff). To examine the address space map of the target process, we can use the **pmap** command and all the libraries it requires to execute:

```
server# /usr/proc/bin/pmap 29081
29081:  /bin/ksh
08046000       8K read/write/exec      [ stack ]
08048000     160K read/exec            /usr/bin/ksh
08070000       8K read/write/exec      /usr/bin/ksh
08072000      28K read/write/exec      [ heap ]
DFAB4000      16K read/exec            /usr/lib/locale/en_AU/en_AU.so.2
DFAB8000       8K read/write/exec      /usr/lib/locale/en_AU/en_AU.so.2
DFABB000       4K read/write/exec      [ anon ]
DFABD000      12K read/exec            /usr/lib/libmp.so.2
DFAC0000       4K read/write/exec      /usr/lib/libmp.so.2
DFAC4000     552K read/exec            /usr/lib/libc.so.1
DFB4E000      24K read/write/exec      /usr/lib/libc.so.1
DFB54000       8K read/write/exec      [ anon ]
DFB57000     444K read/exec            /usr/lib/libnsl.so.1
DFBC6000      20K read/write/exec      /usr/lib/libnsl.so.1
DFBCB000      32K read/write/exec      [ anon ]
DFBD4000      32K read/exec            /usr/lib/libsocket.so.1
DFBDC000       8K read/write/exec      /usr/lib/libsocket.so.1
DFBDF000       4K read/exec            /usr/lib/libdl.so.1
DFBE1000       4K read/write/exec      [ anon ]
DFBE3000     100K read/exec            /usr/lib/ld.so.1
DFBFC000      12K read/write/exec      /usr/lib/ld.so.1
 total      1488K
```

It's always surprising to see how many libraries are loaded when an application is executed, especially something as complicated as a shell, leading to a total of 1488K memory used. You can obtain a list of the dynamic libraries linked to each process by using the **pldd** command:

```
server# /usr/proc/bin/pldd 29081
29081:  /bin/ksh
/usr/lib/libsocket.so.1
/usr/lib/libnsl.so.1
/usr/lib/libc.so.1
/usr/lib/libdl.so.1
/usr/lib/libmp.so.2
/usr/lib/locale/en_AU/en_AU.so.2
```

Signals are the way in which processes communicate with each other, and they can also be used from shells to communicate with spawned processes (usually to suspend or kill them). We examine signals in detail in section three of this chapter. However, by using the **psig** command, it is possible to list the signals associated with each process:

```
bash-2.03$ /usr/proc/bin/psig 29081
29081:  /bin/ksh
HUP     caught  RESTART
INT     caught  RESTART
QUIT    ignored
ILL     caught  RESTART
TRAP    caught  RESTART
ABRT    caught  RESTART
EMT     caught  RESTART
FPE     caught  RESTART
KILL    default
BUS     caught  RESTART
SEGV    default
SYS     caught  RESTART
PIPE    caught  RESTART
ALRM    caught  RESTART
TERM    ignored
USR1    caught  RESTART
USR2    caught  RESTART
CLD     default NOCLDSTOP
PWR     default
WINCH   default
URG     default
POLL    default
STOP    default
TSTP    ignored
CONT    default
TTIN    ignored
TTOU    ignored
VTALRM  default
PROF    default
XCPU    caught  RESTART
XFSZ    ignored
WAITING default
LWP     default
FREEZE  default
THAW    default
CANCEL  default
LOST    default
RTMIN   default
RTMIN+1 default
RTMIN+2 default
```

```
RTMIN+3 defaut
RTMAX-3 default
RTMAX-2 default
RTMAX-1 default
RTMAX   default
```

It is also possible to print a hexadecimal format stack trace for the LWP in each process by using the **pstack** command. This can be useful in the same way that the **truss** command was used:

```
bash-2.03$ /usr/proc/bin/pstack 29081
29081:  /bin/ksh
 dfaf5347 waitid   (7, 0, 804714c, 7)
 dfb0d9db _waitpid (ffffffff, 8047224, 4) + 63
 dfb40617 waitpid  (ffffffff, 8047224, 4) + 1f
 0805b792 job_wait (719d) + 1ae
 08064be8 sh_exec  (8077270, 14) + af0
 0805e3a1 ???????? ()
 0805decd main     (1, 8047624, 804762c) + 705
  0804fa78 ???????? ()
```

Perhaps the most commonly used **proc** tool is the **pfiles** command, which displays all the open files for each process. This is very useful for determining operational dependencies between data files and applications:

```
bash-2.03$ /usr/proc/bin/pfiles 29081
29081:  /bin/ksh
  Current rlimit: 64 file descriptors
   0: S_IFCHR mode:0620 dev:102,0 ino:319009 uid:6049 gid:7 rdev:24,8
      O_RDWR|O_LARGEFILE
   1: S_IFCHR mode:0620 dev:102,0 ino:319009 uid:6049 gid:7 rdev:24,8
      O_RDWR|O_LARGEFILE
   2: S_IFCHR mode:0620 dev:102,0 ino:319009 uid:6049 gid:7 rdev:24,8
      O_RDWR|O_LARGEFILE
  63: S_IFREG mode:0600 dev:174,2 ino:990890 uid:6049 gid:1 size:3210
      O_RDWR|O_APPEND|O_LARGEFILE FD_CLOEXEC
```

In addition, it is possible to obtain the current working directory of the target process by using the **pwdx** command:

```
bash-2.03$ /usr/proc/bin/pwdx 29081
29081:  /home/paul
```

If you need to examine the process tree for all parent and child processes containing the target PID, this can be achieved by using the **ptree** command. This is very useful for determining dependencies between processes that are not apparent by consulting the process list:

```
bash-2.03$ /usr/proc/bin/ptree 29081
247   /usr/dt/bin/dtlogin -daemon
  28950 /usr/dt/bin/dtlogin -daemon
    28972 /bin/ksh /usr/dt/bin/Xsession
      29012 /usr/dt/bin/sdt_shell -c        unset DT;      DISPLAY=lion:0;
        29015 ksh -c         unset DT;       DISPLAY=lion:0;        /usr/dt/bin/dt
          29026 /usr/dt/bin/dtsession
            29032 dtwm
              29079 /usr/dt/bin/dtterm
                29081 /bin/ksh
                  29085 /usr/local/bin/bash
                    29230 /usr/proc/bin/ptree 29081
```

Here, **ptree** has been executed from the Bourne Again Shell (bash), which was started from the Korn shell (ksh), spawned from the **dtterm** terminal window, which was spawned from the **dtwm** window manager, and so on. Although many of these **proc** tools will seem obscure, they are often very useful when trying to debug process-related application errors, especially in large applications like database management systems.

# lsof

**lsof** stands for "list open files," and it lists information about files that are currently opened by the active processes running on Solaris. It is not included in the Solaris distribution; however, the current version can always be downloaded from **ftp://vic.cc.purdue.edu/pub/tools/unix/lsof**. What can you use **lsof** for? Well, that largely depends on how many problems you encounter that relate to processes and files. Often, administrators are interested in knowing which processes are currently using a target file or files from a particular directory. This can occur when a file is locked by one application, for example, but is required by another application (again, a database system's data files are one example where this might happen, if two database instances attempt to write to the files at once). If you know the path to a file of interest, you can use **lsof** to determine which processes are using files in that directory. Let's examine the processes that are using files in the /tmp file system:

```
bash-2.03$ lsof /tmp
COMMAND    PID USER      FD    TYPE DEVICE SIZE/OFF    NODE NAME
```

```
ssion      338 pwatters  txt   VREG   0,1   271596 471638794 /tmp (SWAP)
(unknown)  345 pwatters  txt   VREG   0,1   271596 471638794 /tmp (SWAP)
le        2295 pwatters  txt   VREG   0,1   271596 471638794 /tmp (SWAP)
le        2299 pwatters  txt   VREG   0,1   271596 471638794 /tmp (SWAP)
```

Obviously, there's a bug in the routines that obtain the command name (the first four characters are missing!), but since the PID is correct, this is enough information to identify the four applications currently using files in /tmp. For example, **dtsession** (PID 338) manages the CDE session for the user pwatters, and is using a temporary text file in the /tmp directory.

Another common problem **lsof** is used for, with respect to the /tmp file system, is the identification of processes that continue to write to unlinked files—thus space is being consumed, but it may appear that no files are growing any larger! This confusing activity can be traced back to a process by using **lsof**. However, rather than directly using **lsof** on the /tmp directory, examine the root directory ("/") on which /tmp is mounted. After finding the process that is writing to an open file, the process can be killed. If the size of a file is changing across several different sampling epochs (for example, by running the command once a minute), you've probably found the culprit:

```
server# lsof /
COMMAND     PID     USER  FD   TYPE DEVICE SIZE/OFF   NODE NAME
(unknown)     1     root  txt  VREG  102,0   446144 118299 / (/dev/dsk/c0d0s0)
(unknown)     1     root  txt  VREG  102,0     4372 293504 / (/dev/dsk/c0d0s0)
(unknown)     1     root  txt  VREG  102,0   173272 293503 / (/dev/dsk/c0d0s0)
sadm         62     root  txt  VREG  102,0   954804 101535 / (/dev/dsk/c0d0s0)
sadm         62     root  txt  VREG  102,0   165948 101569 / (/dev/dsk/c0d0s0)
sadm         62     root  txt  VREG  102,0    16132 100766 / (/dev/dsk/c0d0s0)
sadm         62     root  txt  VREG  102,0     8772 100765 / (/dev/dsk/c0d0s0)
sadm         62     root  txt  VREG  102,0   142652 101571 / (/dev/dsk/c0d0s0)
```

One of the restrictions on mounting a file system is that you can't unmount that file system if files are open on it. The reason for this is that if files are open on a file system, and it is dismounted, any changes made to the file may not be saved, resulting in data loss. Looking at a process list may not always reveal which processes are opening which files. This can be very frustrating if Solaris refuses to unmount a file system because there are open files. Again, **lsof** can be used to identify the processes that are opening files on a specific file system.

The first step is to consult the output of the **df** command to obtain the names of currently mounted file systems:

```
bash-2.03$ df -k
Filesystem              kbytes     used    avail capacity  Mounted on
/proc                        0        0        0     0%    /proc
/dev/dsk/c0d0s0        2510214   929292  1530718    38%    /
fd                           0        0        0     0%    /dev/fd
/dev/dsk/c0d0s3       5347552   183471  5110606     4%    /usr/local
swap                    185524    12120   173404     7%    /tmp
```

If you want to unmount the /dev/dsk/c0d0s3 file system, but you are prevented from doing so because of open files, you can obtain a list of all open files under /usr/local by using the command:

```
bash-2.03$ lsof /dev/dsk/c0d0s3
COMMAND     PID      USER    FD   TYPE DEVICE SIZE/OFF   NODE NAME
gres        423 pwatters   txt   VREG  102,3 1747168 457895 /usr/local (/dev/dsk/c0d0s3)
d          4905      root   txt   VREG  102,3  333692  56455 /usr/local (/dev/dsk/c0d0s3)
d          4906    nobody   txt   VREG  102,3  333692  56455 /usr/local (/dev/dsk/c0d0s3)
d          4907    nobody   txt   VREG  102,3  333692  56455 /usr/local (/dev/dsk/c0d0s3)
d          4908    nobody   txt   VREG  102,3  333692  56455 /usr/local (/dev/dsk/c0d0s3)
d          4909    nobody   txt   VREG  102,3  333692  56455 /usr/local (/dev/dsk/c0d0s3)
d          4910    nobody   txt   VREG  102,3  333692  56455 /usr/local (/dev/dsk/c0d0s3)
d          4911    nobody   txt   VREG  102,3  333692  56455 /usr/local (/dev/dsk/c0d0s3)
d          4912    nobody   txt   VREG  102,3  333692  56455 /usr/local (/dev/dsk/c0d0s3)
d          4913    nobody   txt   VREG  102,3  333692  56455 /usr/local (/dev/dsk/c0d0s3)
```

Obviously, all these processes will need to stop using the open files before the file system can be unmounted. If you're not sure where a particular command is running from, or on which file system its data files are stored, you can also use **lsof** to check open files by passing the PID on the command line. First, you need to identify a PID by using the **ps** command:

```
client% ps -eaf | grep apache
  nobody 4911 4905  0   Mar 22 ?         0:00 /usr/local/apache/bin/httpd
  nobody 4910 4905  0   Mar 22 ?         0:00 /usr/local/apache/bin/httpd
  nobody 4912 4905  0   Mar 22 ?         0:00 /usr/local/apache/bin/httpd
```

```
nobody  4905     1  0   Mar 22 ?      0:00 /usr/local/apache/bin/httpd
nobody  4907  4905  0   Mar 22 ?      0:00 /usr/local/apache/bin/httpd
nobody  4908  4905  0   Mar 22 ?      0:00 /usr/local/apache/bin/httpd
nobody  4913  4905  0   Mar 22 ?      0:00 /usr/local/apache/bin/httpd
nobody  4909  4905  0   Mar 22 ?      0:00 /usr/local/apache/bin/httpd
nobody  4906  4905  0   Mar 22 ?      0:00 /usr/local/apache/bin/httpd
```

Let's examine the process 4905 for **apache**, and see what files are currently being opened by it:

```
client% lsof -p 4905
COMMAND  PID  USER   FD    TYPE DEVICE  SIZE/OFF      NODE NAME
d        4905 nobody txt   VREG 102,3   333692  56455 /usr/local (/dev/dsk/c0d0s3)
d        4905 nobody txt   VREG 102,0    17388 100789 / (/dev/dsk/c0d0s0)
d        4905 nobody txt   VREG 102,0   954804 101535 / (/dev/dsk/c0d0s0)
d        4905 nobody txt   VREG 102,0   693900 101573 / (/dev/dsk/c0d0s0)
d        4905 nobody txt   VREG 102,0    52988 100807 / (/dev/dsk/c0d0s0)
d        4905 nobody txt   VREG 102,0     4396 100752 / (/dev/dsk/c0d0s0)
d        4905 nobody txt   VREG 102,0   175736 100804 / (/dev/dsk/c0d0s0)
```

**apache** obviously has a number of open files!

# Sending Signals

Since all processes are identifiable by a single PID, it can be used to manage that process by means of a signal. Signals can be sent to other processes in C programs using the **signal()** function, or can be sent directly from the shell. Solaris supports a number of standard signal types that can be used as a means of interprocess communication. A common use for signals is to manage user applications launched from a shell. A "suspend" signal can be sent to an application running in the foreground by pressing CTRL-Z at any time. To actually run this application in the background in C-shell, for example, you need to type **bg**. A unique background job number is then assigned to the job, and typing **fg** *n*, where *n* is that number, brings the process back to the foreground. You can run as many applications as you like in the background. In this example, we run **httpd** in the foreground, which is process number 123. When we press CTRL-Z, the process is suspended, and when we type **bg**, it is assigned the background process number 1. We can then execute other commands, such as **ls**, while **httpd** runs in the background. When we then type **fg**, the process is brought into the foreground again.

```
client 1% httpd
^z
Suspended
client 2% bg
[1] httpd&
client 3% ls
httpd.conf    access.conf      srm.conf
client 4% fg
```

The **kill** command is also useful. **kill** is used to send signals directly to any process on the system. It is usually called with two parameters: the signal type and the PID. For example, if you have made changes to the configuration file for the Internet superdaemon, you must send a signal to the daemon to tell it to reread its configuration file. Note that you don't need to restart the daemon itself—this is one of the advantages of a process-based operating system that facilitates interprocess communication. If **inetd** had the PID 167, typing:

```
server# kill -1 167
```

would force **inetd** to reread its configuration file and update its internal settings. The **-1** parameter stands for the SIGHUP signal, which means "signal hang up." However, imagine a situation where you want to switch off **inetd** temporarily to perform a security check. You can send a "kill" signal to the process by using the **-9** parameter (the SIGKILL signal):

```
server# kill -1 167
```

Although SIGHUP and SIGKILL are the most commonly used signals in the shell, there are several others used by programmers, which are defined in the signal.h header file. There is also another potential consequence of sending a signal to a process: Instead of hanging up or being killed, it could exit and dump a core file, which is a memory image of the process to which the message was sent. This is very useful for debugging, although too many core files will quickly fill up your file system! Table 5-2 shows the most commonly used signals, as originally defined in UNIX version 7.

| Signal | Code | Action | Description |
|--------|------|--------|-------------|
| SIGHUP | 1 | Exit | Hang up |
| SIGINT | 2 | Exit | Interrupt |
| SIGQUIT | 3 | Core | Quit |
| SIGILL | 4 | Core | Illegal instruction |
| SIGTRAP | 5 | Core | Trace |
| SIGABRT | 6 | Core | Abort |
| SIGEMT | 7 | Core | Emulation trap |
| SIGFPE | 8 | Core | Arithmetic exception |
| SIGKILL | 9 | Exit | Killed |
| SIGBUS | 10 | Core | Bus error |
| SIGSEGV | 11 | Core | Segmentation fault |
| SIGSYS | 12 | Core | Bad system call |
| SIGPIPE | 13 | Exit | Broken pipe |
| SIGALRM | 14 | Exit | Alarm clock |
| SIGTERM | 15 | Exit | Terminate |

**Table 5-2.**   *Commonly Used Signals*

Alternatively, for the Solaris version you are using (including Solaris 8), you can obtain
a list of available signals to the **kill** command by passing the **-l** option:

```
client% kill -l
 HUP INT QUIT ILL TRAP ABRT EMT FPE KILL BUS SEGV SYS PIPE ALRM TERM USR1 USR2
CLD PWR WINCH URG POLL STOP TSTP CONT TTIN TTOU VTALRM PROF XCPU XFSZ WAITING
LWP FREEZE THAW RTMIN RTMIN+1 RTMIN+2 RTMIN+3 RTMAX-3 RTMAX-2 RTMAX-1 RTMAX
```

# Automating Jobs

Many system administration tasks need to be performed on a regular basis. For example, log files for various applications need to be archived nightly and a new log file created. Often a short script is created to perform this, by following these steps:

1. Kill the daemon affected, using the **kill** command.

2. Compress the logfile, using the **gzip** or **compress** command.

3. Change the log filename to include a timestamp so it can be distinguished from other logfiles, by using the **time** command.

4. Move it to an archive directory, using the **mv** command.

5. Create a new logfile by using the **touch** command.

6. Restart the daemon by calling the appropriate /etc/init.d script.

Instead of the administrator having to execute these commands interactively at midnight, they can be scheduled to run daily using the **cron** scheduling command. Alternatively, if a job needs to be run only once at a particular time—for example, bringing a new web site online at 7 A.M. one particular morning, the **at** scheduler can be used. In this section, we look at the advantages and disadvantages of each scheduling method.

## Using *at*

You can schedule a single system event for execution at a specified time by using the **at** command. The jobs are specified by files in /var/spool/cron/atjobs, and configuration is managed by the file /etc/cron.d/at.deny. The job can be a single command or can refer to a script that contains a set of commands. Let's imagine you wanted to start up **sendmail** at a particular time. This could be because maintenance of the network infrastructure is scheduled to occur until 8:30 A.M. tomorrow, but you really don't feel like logging in early and starting up **sendmail** (you've switched it off completely during the outage to prevent users from filling the queue). Let's add a job to the queue, which is scheduled to run at 8:40 A.M., giving the network guys a 10-minute window:

```
client% at 0840
at> /usr/lib/sendmail -bd
at> <EOT>
```

```
commands will be executed using /bin/ksh
job 954715200.a at Mon Apr  3 08:40:00 2000
```

After submitting a job using **at**, you can make sure the job is properly scheduled by checking to see whether an **atjob** has been created:

```
client% cd /var/spool/cron/atjobs
client% ls -l
total 8
-r-Sr--r--   1 paul      other        3701 Apr  3 08:35 954715200.a
```

The file exists, which is a good start. Let's check that it contains the appropriate commands to run the job:

```
bash-2.03$ cat 954715200.a
: at job
: jobname: stdin
: notify by mail: no
export PWD; PWD='/home/paul'
export _; _='/usr/bin/at'
cd /home/paul
umask 22
ulimit unlimited
/usr/lib/sendmail -bd
```

This looks good. After 8:40 A.M. next morning, the command should have executed at the appropriate time, and some output should have been generated and sent to you as a mail message. Let's see what the message contains:

```
From paul Sat Apr  1 08:40:00 2000
Date: Sat Apr  1 2000 08:40:00 +1000 (EST)
From: paul <paul>
To: paul
Subject: Output from "at" job
Your "at" job on tango
"/var/spool/cron/atjobs/954715200.a"
produced the following output:
/bin/ksh[5]: sendmail: 501 Permission denied
```

Oops! You forgot to submit the job as root: Normal users don't have permission to start **sendmail** in the background daemon mode. You would need to submit this job as root to be successful.

## Scheduling with *cron*

An **at** job executes only once at a particular time. However, **cron** is much more flexible because you can schedule system events to execute repetitively, at regular intervals, by using the **crontab** command. Each user on the system can have a **crontab**, which allows them to schedule multiple events to occur at multiple times on multiple dates. The jobs are specified by files in /var/spool/cron/cronjobs, and configuration is managed by the files /etc/cron.d/cron.allow and /etc/cron.d/cron.deny.

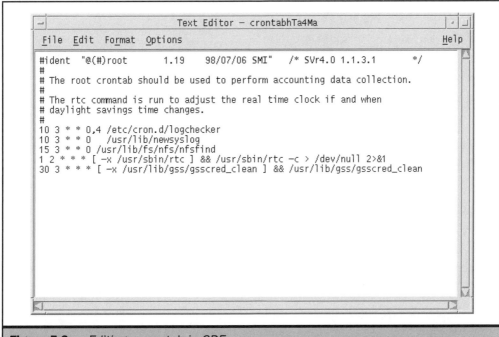

**Figure 5-2.**   *Editing a crontab in CDE*

To check your own **crontab**, you can use the **crontab -l** command:

```
server# crontab -l root
10 3 * * 0,4 /etc/cron.d/logchecker
10 3 * * 0   /usr/lib/newsyslog
15 3 * * 0 /usr/lib/fs/nfs/nfsfind
1 2 * * * [ -x /usr/sbin/rtc ] && /usr/sbin/rtc -c > /dev/null 2>&1
30 3 * * * [ -x /usr/lib/gss/gsscred_clean ] && /usr/lib/gss/gsscred_clean
```

This is the standard **crontab** generated by Solaris for root, which performs tasks such as checking if the **cron** logfile is approaching the system limit at 3:10 A.M. on Sundays and Thursdays, creating a new system log at 3:10 A.M. only on Sundays, and reconciling time differences at 2:01 A.M. every day of the year.

The six fields in the **crontab** stand for:

- Minutes, in the range 0–59
- Hours, in the range 0–23
- Days of the month, in the range 1–31
- Months of the year, in the range 1–12
- Days of the week, in the range 0–6, starting with Sundays
- The command to execute

If you want to add or delete an entry from your **crontab**, you can use the **crontab -e** command, as shown in Figure 5-2. This will start up your default editor (**vi** on the command line, **textedit** in CDE), and you can make changes interactively. After saving your job, you then need to run **crontab** by itself to make the changes.

## Summary

In this chapter, we have examined the most commonly used process and scheduling management tools under Solaris. Processes are at the very core of multiuser systems. For users to make the best of the Solaris environment—by managing jobs with **kill** and the **proc** tools, and scheduling their own regular jobs with **cron**—they need to understand how processes are represented and executed. In the following chapters, all the applications we examine, such as **sendmail**, **telnet**, and **ftp**, and services like NIS+, are all process based, making this chapter critical reading for all Solaris users.

## How to Find Out More

An excellent introduction to process management can be found in *Advanced Topics in UNIX*, by Ronald J. Leach, published by John Wiley & Sons.

The Complete Reference

Solaris 8

# Part II

## System Maintenance

# The Complete Reference

Solaris 8

# Chapter 6

## User and Software Administration

wo basic and ongoing duties that are the responsibilities of the Solaris 8 system administrator are user administration and software administration. User administration consists of adding, updating, and deleting user accounts, and it includes managing users' passwords. Software administration consists of adding, patching, upgrading, and removing software packages.

In this chapter, I will show you the basic commands needed in user and software administration. I'll also cover the databases that are typically used for user administration, and I'll discuss in detail the topic of password management. As for software administration, I will cover the concept of packages, and present the commands used to manage packages. At the end of the chapter, we'll examine the use of patches, as well as the commands used install and remove them.

# User Administration

Systems provide services such as email, news, and web access to its users. To gain access to the system and its various services, files, and other resources, the system requires the users to connect and identify themselves to the system before obtaining access to the service. This section focuses on how to add, modify, and delete user accounts from a Solaris system. Then we will examine the *shadow* password security mechanism that Solaris uses to ensure password security for local users. By the end of this section, you will be able to efficiently maintain user accounts on your systems.

## The User Database

In Solaris 8 all the information about the users of a system is stored in the user database file, which is named, confusingly, /etc/passwd. I say "confusingly" because, even though the file*name* includes the word "passwd," the file itself does not contain any passwords. (It used to, in earlier versions of Solaris. However, Solaris now stores user passwords in a separate file, /etc/shadow, discussed later in this section.)

The file /etc/passwd contains several single-line entries, called *user records* (one record per user), that have the following format:

*username:x:uid:gid:comment:home-dir:login-shell*

- The first field holds the user's name, which must be between one and eight alphanumeric characters. (Most sites use a minimum of three characters.)

- The second field always contains the letter x, which is merely a placeholder or a user's password. This field is included only for reasons of backward compatibility: Originally UNIX systems stored the user's encrypted password in this field, but Solaris and other versions of UNIX have since opted to store passwords in the /etc/shadow file instead, for greater security.

- The third field contains the user's user identification number (referred to as the *UID*). This ID is used for determining file, directory, and process ownership.

- The fourth field contains the group identification number (referred to as the *GID*) of the user's primary group. The group ID is used to determine if a user has access rights to files, directories, and processes owned by other users. The UNIX notion of groups of users is covered in greater detail later in this section.

- The fifth field, which is called the *comment* field, normally holds the full name of the user. This field is sometimes referred to as the GECOS or GCOS field in recognition of the operating system from which it was borrowed.

- The sixth field holds the home directory of the user.

- The seventh field holds the user's login shell, which is invoked when the user logs in. Some of the common shells are /bin/sh, /bin/ksh, and /bin/csh. Other shells you may encounter include /bin/bash and /bin/tcsh.

For example, my user record looks like this:

```
ranga:x:500:100:Sriranga Veeraraghavan:/home/ranga:/bin/bash
```

User records can be added to /etc/passwd using the **useradd** command. User records for existing users can be modified using the **usermod** command. User records can be deleted using the **userdel** command. These commands are discussed in detail later in this section.

## Usernames

A user's *username* is the symbolic name that the system uses to identify a user. For human users who log in to a system, usernames should normally be three to eight characters long. For small sites with fewer than 50 users, you can assign usernames based on a user's first name, last name, or initials. Another option for small sites is to allow users to choose a username on their own.

Most larger sites implement a policy where usernames are determined by taking the first letter of the user's first name and appending the user's last name. Using this scheme the user *James Kirk* would be given the username *jkirk*. In this scheme it is possible of course to end up with two or more users who would be allotted the same username. In most cases, you can resolve such a conflict by using the first character of the user's first name and the first character of the user's middle name before appending the user's last name. For example, if you have two users with the names *John Adams* and *John Quincy Adams*, you can give *John Adams* the username *jadams* and *John Quincy Adams* the username *jqadams*.

## Passwords

A user's password is required for authentication during the login procedure. When UNIX was first developed, a user's encrypted password was stored in the second field of a user's record in /etc/passwd. Because many programs need to access the information stored in this file, it was made to be readable by all users on a system.

Unfortunately this meant that malicious users could easily read the /etc/passwd file and attempt to decrypt the passwords (usually, the password for root would be the most important one to crack). In order to ensure that malicious users on a system do not have access to the encrypted passwords, Solaris stores the user passwords in the file /etc/shadow, which is readable only by root.

Each entry in /etc/shadow has the following format:

*username:password:lastchg:min:max:warn:inactive:expire:flag*

- The first field holds the user's *username* as it appears in /etc/passwd.

- The second field holds the user's *password* in the form of a 13-character encrypted string. When a user logs in, the password that they enter is encrypted and compared with this string. If the two match, the user is permitted to log in. If this field contains the string "NP" or "*LK*", it indicates that the login is either not permitted or locked. If this field is empty, then there is no password required for this user to log in (leaving the field empty is not recommended).

- The third field holds the date on which the password was *last changed* by the user. The date is stored as the number of days between January 1, 1970, and the date that the password was last modified.

- The fourth field holds the *minimum* number of days required between password changes. If you leave this field blank, then the user will not be forced to change their password periodically (leaving this field blank is not recommended).

- The fifth field holds the *maximum* number of days the password is valid. If you leave this field blank, the user's password is valid forever. (Leaving this field blank is not recommended.)

- The sixth field holds the number of days before a password expires that the user is *warned* of the upcoming expiration of that password.

- The seventh field holds the number of days of *inactivity* you'll allow the user. If you leave this field blank, it means any period of inactivity is acceptable.

- The eighth field holds the absolute date that specifies when the user may no longer log in. This date is consider the *expiration* date for the login. This field is for user accounts that allow for temporary or guest users to access a system for a short period of time (for example, customer support representatives who require access to your system).

- The ninth field, *flag*, is not unused.

Except for the password field, the information in /etc/shadow is manipulated using the **usermod** command. A user's password can be assigned or changed by the root user account (also known as the super user) by means of the **passwd** command. Individual users may also use the **passwd** command to change their own password only. Both the **passwd** and the **usermod** commands are discussed later in this section.

## User IDs

The *user ID* (commonly referred to as the *UID*) is the unique number assigned to a user that the system uses to distinguish between different users. On Solaris 8 systems UIDs can have a value from 0 to 2,147,483,647. Solaris 8 reserves the UIDs between 0 and 100 and between 60,000 and 65,535 for system use as described in Table 6-1. For interoperability with older Sun operating systems and other versions of UNIX, it is recommended that you assign UIDs between 100 and 60,000 for normal users.

The default Solaris 8 installation contains many built-in accounts. Several of these built-in users are also referred to as the psuedo users. These are typically users who do not log in and are required for process or daemon programs and file ownership reasons so that the operating system can function normally. Daemon programs refer to continually running system processes that either provide a service or are essential to the functioning of the operating system. Some of the significant pseudo users vis à vis system maintenance are given in Table 6-2, along with their UIDs.

| Note | *At most large sites, the UIDs between 100 and 500 are also treated as reserved. Usually, the UIDs in this range are assigned to pseudo users required for special daemon programs, like database servers or web servers. Another commonly reserved UID on Solaris is the anonymous FTP user, ftp, which is normally given the UID 10,000 or 30,000.* |

| UID | Description |
|-----|-------------|
| 0 | Reserved for **root** (superuser). |
| 1–10 | Reserved for daemons and system maintenance pseudo users. |
| 11–99 | Reserved for daemons; for example, the printer daemon. |
| 60001 | Reserved for the user **nobody**, which has the lowest access privileges. When **root** accesses files on a NFS drive, the permissions of **nobody** are used on the remote system. |
| 60002 | Reserved for the user **noaccess** (similar to nobody). |
| 65534 | Reserved for the user **nobody4**. This is used for compatibility with older SunOS 4.x systems. |

**Table 6-1.** *Reserved UIDs on Solaris*

| Username | UID | Description |
|----------|-----|-------------|
| daemon | 1 | Used by system server processes |
| bin | 2 | Owner of user-executable files |
| sys | 3 | Owner of system configuration files |
| adm | 4 | Owner of system accounting files and log files |
| uucp | 5 | Used by the *UNIX-to-UNIX Copy* process (*UUCP*) |
| nuucp | 9 | Used by the *UNIX-to-UNIX Copy* process (*UUCP*) |
| lp | 71 | Used by the *line printer* (*lp*) process |

**Table 6-2.**    *Solaris Pseudo Users*

## Displaying All Users

To list all users, run the **logins** command as the root user. The output will be similar to the following:

```
# logins
root           0      other     1      Super-User
smtp           0      root      0      Mail Daemon User
daemon         1      other     1
bin            2      bin       2
sys            3      sys       3
adm            4      adm       4      Admin
uucp           5      uucp      5      uucp Admin
nuucp          9      nuucp     9      uucp Admin
listen        37      adm       4      Network Admin
lp            71      lp        8      Line Printer Admin
ranga        500      users   100      Sriranga
Veeraraghavan
nobody     60001      nobody 60001     Nobody
noaccess   60002      noaccess 60002   No Access User
nobody4    65534      nogroup 65534    SunOS 4.x Nobody
```

The output displays the user name, UID, primary group name, GID, and the GECOS field.

*You can also cat the /etc/passwd file to obtain user listing. However, it is not formatted as the output from the logins command.*

## Displaying Logged-in Users

To check for only those users who are logged in, you can use either the **w**, the **who**, or the **finger** command. The **w** command gives you a summary of the system information along with a list of the current users of the system:

```
$ w
11:25pm  up 36 day(s),  6:01,  8 users,  load average: 0.01, 0.00, 0.01
User      tty            login@  idle   JCPU   PCPU  what
phox      pts/2          4:26pm  6:06                 -tcsh
sveerara  pts/7          Tue 1pm 34:01  32:04    14  -bash
bbong     pts/0          22Jun99 3days  202:55        rsh nm-build2-nt
lgroth    pts/6          Fri 9am 7days     6          bash
```

From the output, you can tell when a particular user logged in, how long they have been idle, their CPU usage, and the command that they are currently running. If you are just interested in the login information about a single user, you can invoke the **w** command, which takes the following form:

```
$ w username
```

Here, *username* is that of the user you are interested in. For example, the following command would display login information about the user sveerara:

```
$ w sveerara
User      tty            login@  idle   JCPU   PCPU  what
sveerara  pts/7          29Jun99 2days  83:09    21  -bash
sveerara  pts/1          9Jul99  9days     1         -ksh
```

The one piece of information that the **w** command does not provide is the name of the system from which a user has logged in. This information is provided by the **who** command:

```
$ who
phox      pts/2          Jul  1 16:26      (phox-spare4.cisco.com)
sveerara  pts/7          Jun 29 13:05      (srv-ultra.cisco.com)
bbong     pts/0          Jun 22 17:47      (bbong-ss20.cisco.com)
lgroth    pts/6          Jun 25 09:56      (lgroth-ultra.cisco.com)
```

You can see in the last column the remote host or console port that a user has logged in from. Unlike the **w** command, the **who** command does not let you check on the login information about a particular user. Fortunately the **finger** command combines the features of both the **w** and the **who** commands. In its basic form it lists information about the current logins:

```
$ finger
Login        Name        TTY      Idle   When       Where
sveerara     Sriranga    pts/7    1d Tue 13:05      srv-ultra.cisco.com
bbong        Budianto    pts/0    1d Tue 17:47      bbong-ss20.cisco.com
vnatu        Vaibhav     pts/8    2d Mon 11:55      vnatu-ultra.cisco.com
```

To use **finger** to check on the login information about a particular user, you can use the following syntax:

```
$ finger -s username
```

Here, *username* is that of the user you are interested in. The following command would display login information about the user sveerara:

```
$ finger -s sveerara
Login        Name     TTY      Idle      When       Where
sveerara Sriranga    pts/7    1d Tue 13:05      srv-ultra.cisco.com
sveerara Sriranga    pts/1    8d Fri 15:40      bfiresto-ss20.cisco.com
```

You can use the **-s** option with **finger** to summarize information about a user's logins. Without it, **finger** will display a detailed listing about the user. For example, for the user sveerara, the detailed output might look like the following:

```
$ finger sveerara
Login name: sveerara                    In real life: Sriranga Veeraraghavan
Directory: /users/sveerara             Shell: /usr/bin/ksh
On since Jun 29 13:05:42 on pts/7 from srv-ultra.cisco.com
1 day 20 hours Idle Time
No unread mail
Project: c, java, perl, sh spoken here
No Plan.
```

You can also use the **finger** command to check which users are logged on to a remote system:

```
$ finger @host
```

Here, *host* is the hostname of the system you want to check. For example, the following command will list the users at **host soda.berkeley.edu**:

```
$ finger @soda.berkeley.edu
[soda.CSUA.Berkeley.EDU]
Login     Name                     TTY   Idle   Login Time    Office   Phone
aaron     Aaron Smith              w0    1:26   Sat    10:25           (650)  335
aaron     Aaron Smith              *wi     1d   Jul  1 17:03           (650)  335
alanc     Alan Coopersmith         w+   17:40   Sat    11:37
...
```

As you can see from the output, **finger** first lists the system name that it is connecting to, and then it lists the users on that system. The output will vary between different remote systems, depending on the version of UNIX they are running.

If you just want to check for a particular user on a remote system, you can use the following form for the summary information:

```
$ finger -s username@host
```

For more detailed information, use this form:

```
$ finger username@host
```

Here, *username* is that of the user you want to gather information about, and *host* is the remote hostname.

For example, the following command would print the summary information for the user sveerara on the host naan:

```
[naan.cisco.com]
Login      Name       TTY      Idle    When     Where
sveerara   Sriranga   pts/3      31  Sun 12:11  kanchi.cisco.com
```

*The finger commands output is a result of the response from the "fingerd" on the queried server. Finger has some serious security implications. If you do not have a good reason to run finger, disable it in the /etc/inetd.conf file by placing a "#" before the line that lists finger or just deleting the line itself and then sending a HUP signal to the inetd process.*

## Switching Users

There are times when you want to assume the role of another user. For example, you may want to become the root user to perform administration-level tasks. The "Switch User" command **su** comes in handy. You can use the **su** command to switch to a different user:

```
$ su username
```

The *username* argument is optional and specifies the user that you wish to become; entering the command all by itself implies that you will be switching over to the root user. For example, the following entry would switch to the user ranga:

```
$ su ranga
Password:
```

If you are switching to another user from the root user, you will not be prompted for the password. For all other users you will need to know the password of the user in order for the **su** command to succeed. Once you enter the correct password at the prompt, your UID will be switched to that of the username you've specified. To restore your standard UID, just type the **exit** command at the prompt.

When you use the simple form of the **su** command, you still retain the same environment; only your UID and shell will be changed to that of the user you've specified. To assume the same environment as the user, you can execute the **su** command:

```
$ su - username
```

Again, *username* here is that of the user you want to become.

## The Root User

If you do not specify a user with the **su** command, it assumes that you want to become the root user. For example, the following command will switch your UID to that of root, and also give you root's environment:

```
$ su -
```

This command is the same as the following command:

```
$ su - root
```

Once you enter a password for the root user, you will be presented with the hash character prompt:

```
#
```

Whenever this prompt is displayed, you will need to exercise extreme caution. The root user is the most powerful user on the system, and has the ability to change any files, to start and stop any processes, and to shut down the system. In short, root has the ability to change any part of the system's configuration, so you need to be extra careful with every command you execute while you are the root user. A typing mistake as a normal user is generally benign, but a typing mistake by root can disable the entire system beyond recovery.

To ensure that you use the root account safely, keep these rules in mind:

- Keep the root prompt set to the hash character, "#". This will help you to remember that you have complete control of the system.

- Restrict access to the root account. Make sure that only those users who need to perform system maintenance have access to the root account. Normal users shouldn't have the root password for your system.

- Restrain yourself from using the root account for tasks other than system administration. When you need to perform a system administration task, become root by using the **su** command to perform the administration tasks and then **exit** immediately.

- Change the root password often. By keeping the same password for extended periods of time, you make the root account vulnerable to attack. Password security is discussed later in this chapter.

## Group IDs

The *group ID* (commonly referred to as the *GID*) is the numerical ID used by the system to identify groups of users. All versions of UNIX allow users to be placed into groups that have special access privileges to certain files, directories, and processes. Some of the common reasons for creating and using groups are:

- To allow members of an administrative group to make minor changes to some system files or processes.

- To reflect the structure of an organization. For example, users who work in a particular department or geographical region or who have a special business function can be placed into groups to reflect this.

- To permit only particular groups within a software development environment to have access to source files. Normally members of only one or two software development groups are permitted to access source files for modification; members of other development groups are permitted readonly access.

The GIDs for all the groups on a system are stored in the /etc/group file. This file uses the following format:

*groupname:password:gid:user-list*

- The first field, *groupname*, stores the name of the group. The *groupname* can be from one to eight alphanumeric characters.

- The second field, *password*, is obsolete and is maintained only for compatibility with older scripts and programs. This field is almost always left blank on Solaris systems.

- The third field, *gid*, stores the group's unique numerical ID. The maximum GID supported by Solaris is 2,137,483,647, but it is recommended that only GIDs less than 60,000 should be used for interoperability with older versions of SunOS and other versions of UNIX.

- The fourth field, *user-list*, contains the comma-separated list of users in the group. Users do not need to be specified in the user list for their default group (given in /etc/passwd).

The /etc/group file is normally modified using the **groupadd**, **groupmod**, and **groupdel** commands discussed in the next section.

## Listing Group Membership

If you want to list the group membership for a particular user, you can use the **groups** command:

$ groups *username*

Here, *username* is that of the user whose group membership you want to list. For example, the following command would list the group membership of the user ranga:

```
$ groups ranga
users
```

## Switching Between Groups

When you log in, your group is automatically set to the default group listed in the /etc/passwd file. If you need to change your group at a later time, you can use the **newgrp** command:

$ newgrp *groupname*

Here, *groupname* is the name of the group you want to change to. For example, the following command would switch to the group named "staff":

```
$ newgrp staff
```

In order for this command to succeed, you need to be a member of the group that you specify. If you are not, you will receive an error message similar to the following:

```
newgrp: Sorry
```

# Managing the User Database

In this section we will cover the commands that are used to manage the user database /etc/passwd and its related files /etc/shadow and /etc/group. A brief description of the contents of these files is given in Table 6-3. The main user management commands are **useradd** (adds a user), **usermod** (modifies the information concerning a user's account), and **userdel** (deletes a user's account from the system). The group management commands are **groupadd** (adds a group), **groupmod** (modifies a group), and **groupdel** (deletes a group). Finally, the **passwd** command is used for maintaining the passwords for users.

## Managing User Accounts

User management consists of adding new users, modifying user information for existing users, and deleting old user accounts. Depending on your organization, you may or may not need to perform user management tasks frequently. At universities, user management tasks are heaviest at the beginning and end of semesters and quarters. At corporations, user management tasks may be required year-round.

## Adding User Accounts

Use the **useradd** command to add a user to the system. It creates the appropriate entries in both /etc/passwd and /etc/shadow with standard defaults. The basic syntax is as follows:

```
# useradd username
```

| File | Description |
|------|-------------|
| /etc/passwd | The main user database file, often referred to (erroneously) as the password file. It holds entries for each of the users on a system, but does not contain their passwords. |
| /etc/shadow | The shadow password file. It stores the encrypted passwords for all of the users on a system. For security reasons, its contents can only be accessed by root. |
| /etc/group | The group file. It stores the list of all the groups on the system and the users associated with those groups. |

**Table 6-3.**   *User Database Files*

Here, *username* is the login name of the user. The **useradd** command can only be run by the root user, as illustrated by the hash character prompt. As an example of using **useradd**, the following command adds the user jkirk:

```
# useradd jkirk
```

If the user jkirk was already defined in the user database then you will see the following error message.

```
UX: useradd: ERROR: jkirk is already in use. Choose another.
```

We can confirm that the user jkirk was added correctly by entering the following code:

```
# grep jkirk /etc/passwd /etc/shadow
/etc/passwd:jkirk:x:10001:1::/home/jkirk:/bin/sh
/etc/shadow:jkirk:*LK*:::::::
```

As you can see, an entry for jkirk was added to both /etc/passwd and /etc/shadow. The newly created user is given the next available UID, in this case 10001. Depending on your system, this value may be different. Also, newly created users are automatically assigned a GID of 1, corresponding to the group named other. The default home directory is always /home/*username* (in this case /home/jkirk), and the default shell is always /bin/sh. The record in /etc/shadow creates the user with a locked password (indicated by *LK*) in order to prevent logins until such time as you explicitly assign the user a password.

In addition to its basic mode, **useradd** supports several options, listed in Table 6-4, that allow you to specify the information about a user directly. You can use these options individually or combine them to suit your needs.

As an example of using these options, the following command adds the user jkirk and explicitly specifies most of his user information:

```
# useradd -c 'James Tiberius Kirk' -d /users/jkirk -m -u 937 jkirk
```

Once a user has been added to the system, you still need to assign him or her a password before they can log in and starting using the account. When a user is initially added to the system, their password is set to the special password *LK*, indicating that the account is locked. Assigning and managing passwords is covered in the section, "Managing Passwords."

| Use... | To Specify... |
|---|---|
| **-c** *comment* | The GECOS comment for a user. You must use quotes if the comment includes spaces. |
| **-d** *pathname* | The pathname of the home directory. |
| **-m** | Use this to create the home directory of the user if it does not already exist. You'll usually use this option in conjunction with the -d *pathname* option. |
| **-g** *groupname*<br>**-g** *gid* | The default groupname or GID for the user. |
| **-e** *expire* | The date on which the account will no longer be valid. You'll usually use this option when creating temporary accounts. |
| **-f** *inactive* | The maximum inactivity period (in days) you'll permit for the user. Normally you'll use this option when creating temporary accounts. |
| **-u** *uid* | The UID to use for this user. |
| **-s** *shell* | The login shell for the user. |

**Table 6-4.**   *Options for useradd*

## Modifying User Accounts

The **usermod** command allows you to change the attributes of users on your system. You can change the username, UID, GID, the expiration date, the inactivity period, the shell, and the path to the home directory of a user. The basic syntax is as follows:

```
# usermod options username
```

Here, *options* are one or more of the options described in Table 6-5 and *username* is that of the user whose attributes you wish to change.

As an example of using these options, the following command modifies the home directory and the user ID for the user jkirk:

```
# usermod -u 176 -g captains -d /home/enterprise/jkirk -m jkirk
```

| Use... | To Specify... |
|---|---|
| **-c** *comment* | A GECOS comment for a user. You must use quotes if the comment includes spaces. |
| **-e** *expire* | The date on which the account will no longer be valid. This option is normally used when creating temporary accounts. |
| **-f** *inactive* | The maximum inactivity period (in days) for the user. This option is normally used when creating temporary accounts. |
| **-d** *pathname* | The *pathname* of the new home directory. |
| **-g** *groupname*<br>**-g** *gid* | The new default *groupname* or *GID* for the user. |
| **-m** | Use this to move the user's home directory to the new directory that you specified with the **-d** option. |
| **-l** *newname* | A new name for the user. This option changes the *username* for the user to *newname*. |
| **-s** *shell* | The login *shell* for the user |
| **-u** *uid* | A new UID for the user. The UID associated with the user's home directory is not modified; thus a user will be able to access their home directory until the UID for the directory is changed. |

**Table 6-5.** *Options for usermod*

## Deleting User Accounts

To delete a user's account, you can use the **userdel** command:

```
# userdel username
```

Here, *username* is that of the user you want to remove. For example, the following command would remove the user jkirk from the system:

```
# userdel jkirk
```

By default, **userdel** does not delete the home directory of the user you specify. In order to delete the home directory at the same time the user is removed from the system, you can include the **-r** option with **userdel**, as follows:

```
# userdel -r username
```

For example, the following command would remove the user jkirk from the system, along with his home directory:

```
# userdel -r jkirk
```

## Managing Passwords

Password management is a responsibility that you'll have to undertake whenever you add a new user, or when you have to change the password for a user who has forgotten his password. You can manage passwords using the **passwd** command. To change the password for the current user, you can enter the command in its simplest form, as shown here:

```
$ passwd
```

To change the password for a different user, you can use the **passwd** command:

```
# passwd username
```

For example, to specify the password for the newly created user jkirk, you would enter the following:

```
# passwd jkirk
```

You will be prompted to enter the user's password twice:

```
New password:

Re-enter new password:
```

If the two passwords entered are not identical then you will get the following error message:

```
passwd(SYSTEM): They don't match; try again.
```

Or, you will be notified that the change has been successfully applied:

```
passwd (SYSTEM): passwd successfully changed for jkirk
```

When specifying a user's password, make sure that the password you use is not the same as your own password or the password for the root account. In most cases, you will want to use a default password and then force the user to change it when they log in for the first time. Choose a default password randomly, or have it randomly generated—and be sure to change it every few weeks.

## Forcing Password Changes

You can force a user to change their password upon the next login by using the **-f** option with **passwd**, as follows:

```
# passwd -f username
```

Here, *username* is that of the user for whom you want to force a password change. For example, the following command would force the user jkirk to change his password at the next login:

```
# passwd -f jkirk
```

The **-f** option to **passwd** is also useful when a user forgets his password: You can set the password to a default, and the user will be forced to change it (in other words, he will be given the opportunity to start using a new one of his own choosing) upon login.

## Periodically Changing Passwords

One of the biggest problems in password management is convincing users to create and use passwords that are secure. Most users tend to pick passwords that they can remember easily. Some common passwords include:

- Names of spouses, children, parents, or pets
- Birthdays of spouses, children, parents, or pets
- Common phrases, such as abc123, trustno1, mypass

The biggest problem with such passwords is that they are easy for hackers to break. Once a hacker breaks a user's password, the hacker will be able to gain authorized access to your system, because they will appear to be a legitimate user. There are many different solutions for ensuring password security, but most of them are intrusive to users. The standard method for ensuring password security in Solaris 8, however, is designed to be unintrusive to users, while still preventing hackers from exploiting broken passwords.

Solaris 8 uses an aging scheme based on password expiration after a certain period of time. Whenever a user changes their password, the date on which the change was made is recorded in /etc/shadow (in the *lastchg* field). Also recorded in /etc/shadow is the number of days the password is valid (in the *max* field). When a user logs in, the current date is compared to the last changed date plus the value in the *max* field. If the current date is greater than this value, the user is forced to change their password. You can set this value using the **-x** option with the **passwd** command, as follows:

```
# passwd -x days username
```

Here, *days* is the maximum number of days the password is valid and *username* is the name of the user you want this change applied to. For example, the following command would specify that the password for user jkirk remain valid for 30 days:

```
# passwd -x 30 jkirk
```

Once this command is executed, the user jkirk will be prompted to change his password during the login process 30 days after his last password change. The system will not allow the user to log in until he provides a password that is different in at least three characters from the old password.

It is also possible to set the default maximum age (in weeks) for all accounts on your system by editing the file /etc/default/passwd. Simply change the following line in this file to equal the maximum number of weeks for which you want a password to be valid:

```
MAXWEEKS=
```

A standard period of time for password expiration is about 30 days, or four weeks. Most users will find this time period unintrusive. Also, it minimizes the amount of time that user passwords are vulnerable to hackers. (Sites within a secure corporate intranet may find it less burdensome to use a longer period, for example from 60 to 90 days.)

In order to make sure that your users are prepared to change their passwords, it is possible to warn them of an upcoming password expiration by using the **-w** option with the password command, as follows:

```
# passwd -w days username
```

Here, *days* is the number of days before the password expires that the system begins to warn the user (the warning is given each time the user logs in during the warning period), and *username,* as usual, is that of the user you wish to warn. For example, the following command would enable the warning for the user jkirk three days before the password expired:

```
# passwd -w 3 jkirk
```

Normally, three to five days of warnings should give the user enough time to choose a new password.

A common problem with any password expiration is that some users will change their password during login and then change it back immediately after login. This practice defeats the purpose of password expiration. You can prevent this by setting the minimum valid time for a password using the **-n** option with the **passwd** command, as follows:

```
# passwd -n min username
```

Here, *min* is the minimum number of days a user has to wait before changing their password; *username* as usual is the username of the user to whom you wish to apply this change. For example, the following command would set the minimum waiting period to two days for the user jkirk:

```
# passwd -n 2 jkirk
```

**Note**  *A standard waiting period is between one and three days. After this amount of time, most users will just stick with their new password rather than keep trying to change their password.*

## Locking Passwords

By locking passwords, you can prevent unauthorized users from accessing the system without having to delete them from the system. Here are some situations in which you may need to deny user access:

■ A user changes from one project to another, thus they no longer need access to your system.

■ A user leaves your company or university, thus they should not be allowed to access your systems.

■ A user has been abusing their access privileges, thus management/administration feels that their system access should be denied as a reprimand.

The **-l** option to the **passwd** command allows you to lock a password. Its syntax is as follows:

```
# passwd -l username
```

Here, *username* is that of the user whose access you wish to deny. For example, the following command would lock the password for the user jkirk:

```
# password -l jkirk
```

Once the password for the user jkirk is locked, all login attempts by jkirk will fail.

## Managing Groups

Group management is similar to user management and consists of adding groups, modifying existing groups, and deleting old groups. Most administrators do not perform these tasks frequently, since Solaris 8 comes with almost all of the groups that are required for running the system. The only group you will need to add to a new Solaris installation is the staff group with a GID of 10. This group is required for compatibility with some older BSD-based tools and programs.

If you are administering a small site, you should also add the group users. By making this group the default group for all the users on your system, it is easy for them to share files. At large sites, a single users group will not be sufficient, and you may need to add groups based on their roles at your site.

### Adding Groups

To add a group to your system, you can use the **groupadd** command. Here is its basic syntax:

```
# groupadd -g gid groupname
```

Here, *gid* is the GID of the group you want to add, and *groupname* is the name of the group. For example, to add the group staff with GID 10, you would enter the following:

```
# groupadd -g 10 staff
```

### Modifying Groups

To change the name of a group on your system, you can use the **groupmod** command, as follows:

```
# groupmod -n newname oldname
```

Here, *newname* is the new name you want the group to have, and *oldname* is the current name of the group. For example, the following command will change the name of the "staff" group to "admins":

```
# groupmod -n admins staff
```

The **groupmod** command can also be used to change the GID of a group. It takes this form:

# groupmod -g *gid groupname*

Here, *gid* is the new GID for the group, and *groupname* is the name of the group. For example, the following command would change the GID for the "staff" group to 12:

```
# groupmod -g 12 staff
```

You can change the GID and the name of the group at the same time by combining the options to groupmod as follows:

# groupmod -g *gid* -n *newname oldname*

Here, *gid* is the new GID you want to assign for the group, *newname* is the new name of the group, and *oldname* is the current name of the group. For example, the following command would change both the GID and the name of the "staff" group:

```
# groupmod -g 12 -n admins staff
```

## Adding Users to Groups

Once you have created a group, you can add users to it using the command **usermod**. This command has two forms: The first form allows you to add groups by name, and the second form allows you to add groups by GID. The syntax for the two forms are:

# usermod -G *groupname1,...,groupnameX username*
# usermod -G *gid1,...,gidX username*

Here, *groupname1,...,groupnameX* are the groupnames; *gid1,...,gidX* are the GIDs to which you want to add the user *username*. For example, if you wanted to add the user jkirk to the two groups "captains" and "crew," you would use this command:

```
# usermod -G captains,crew jkirk
```

The groups that you are trying to add the user to must already exist in order for the **usermod** operation to work correctly.

## Deleting a Group

To delete a group, you can use the **groupdel** command. Its syntax is:

# groupdel *groupname*

Here, *groupname* is the name of the group you want to delete. For example, to delete the "staff" group, you would enter the following:

```
# groupdel staff
```

# Software Administration

One of the most innovative features in Solaris is the software package system that allows administrators to easily install, patch, upgrade, and remove software from a system. Almost all software for Solaris is available in package format, starting with the operating system, its patches, and upgrades. Most of the popular freeware packages are also available in package form for Solaris 2.5 and later from the Sun Freeware web site:

**http://www.sunfreeware.com**

Most of the packages at this site are in GNU Zip (GZIP) format, so to be able to use them you will also need to download and install the GZIP package, as described later in this section.

The first half of this section concentrates on the commands used to manage software packages; the second half covers the commands used to manage patches.

## Managing Software Packages

The main tasks involved in package management are adding packages with the **pkgadd** command, checking on the status of installed packages with the **pkginfo** and **pkgchk** commands, and removing packages with the **pkgrm** command. Each of these commands deal with *package instances* (usually referred to as simply *packages*), each of which consists of three different sets of files:

- The actual files for the software you are trying to install
- A set of scripts that are used (a) to configure your system once the software package has been added, and (b) to unconfigure your system once the software package has been removed
- A set of control files that allow Solaris to track the integrity of the package once it is installed

Package instances are available in two different formats: the directory format and the package stream format. Packages in the directory format are stored in a set of directories that mirror the directory structure for the package after installation. The packages delivered by Sun and other software vendors are usually in directory format.

Packages in the package stream are stored and delivered as a single file that you can add directly. The packages available from the Sun Freeware site are normally delivered in package stream format. For an administrator, the major difference between the two is in the syntax used to add the packages.

## Adding Packages

To add a software package to your system, you can use the **pkgadd** command. For packages in the directory format, you can use the following syntax:

# pkgadd -d *dir pkginst*

Here, *dir* is the directory where the package instance is stored, and *pkginst* is the name of the package instance you wish to add. For example, to add a package named CSCOcam stored in the directory /tmp, you would enter the following:

```
# pkgadd -d /tmp CSCOcam
```

The system would then return a prompt similar to this one:

```
The following packages are available:
  1  CSCOcam      Client Application Manager
                  SPARC
Select package(s) you wish to process (or 'all' to process
all packages). (default: all) [?,??,q]:
```

If you pressed RETURN or ENTER, **pkgadd** would proceed to install the package on your system.

For packages that use the directory format, you can determine the name of the package based on the name of the top-level directory of the package. In this case, the name of the package is CSCOcam. As you can see, the prompt from **pkgadd** also contains this name.

To add a package stored in the package stream format, you can use the following syntax:

# pkgadd -d *pkginst*

Here, *pkginst* is the name of the package instance you wish to add. As an example of adding a package, you can add the GZIP package from the Sun Freeware site by making this entry:

```
# pkgadd gzip-1.2.4-sol26-SPARC-local
```

To determine the name of a package in package stream format, you will have to look at the information stored in the prompt produced by **pkgadd** when the package is being added:

```
The following packages are available:
  1  FSFgzip     gzip
                  (Solaris2.6beta) 1.2.4
Select package(s) you wish to process (or 'all' to process
all packages). (default: all) [?,??,q]:
```

As you can see, the name of the package we are adding is FSFgzip.

## Package Naming Conventions

Although the only actual restriction on the name of a package is that the name must not be longer than eight characters, there is an "unofficial" naming convention for packages that implements additional, suggested restrictions. The convention is slightly different for packages created by corporations and packages created at universities or public research institutes.

- For packages created by corporations, the naming convention consists of using the four-letter stock symbol of the corporation followed by the package name. The four-letter stock symbol is normally given in upper case. For example, packages shipped by Sun start with SUNW and packages shipped by Cisco Systems start with CSCO. Many more examples of package names are given later in this chapter.

- For packages created at universities and research institutes, the package name consists of a three- or four-letter abbreviation followed by the package name. The university abbreviation is usually given in uppercase letters. For example, packages created at the University of California at Berkeley start with the letters UCB. Some of the other common abbreviations are given in Table 6-6.

In addition to these abbreviations, you will frequently see the abbreviations GNU and FSF. The GNU project (GNU stands for "GNU is Not UNIX") and the Free Software Foundation (FSF) are dedicated to providing powerful and free tools for UNIX and UNIX-like systems. Some of the major packages from GNU and FSF are the GNU C Compiler (GCC), Emacs, and PERL.

SYSTEM MAINTENANCE

| Abbreviation | University or Research Institution |
|---|---|
| UCD | University of California at Davis |
| MIT | Massachusetts Institute of Technology |
| CIT | California Institute of Technology (CalTech) |
| LLL | Lawrence Livermore Labs |
| LBL | Lawrence Berkeley Labs |
| NARC | Nasa Ames Research Center |

**Table 6-6.**    *University Abbreviations Commonly Found in Package Names*

## Resolving Conflicts

As the package is added to your system, you may be asked questions regarding the installation directory or conflicts on your system. For example, when adding the GZIP package, you might see the following messages:

```
The following files are already installed on the system and are being
used by another package:
* /usr/local/bin <attribute change only>
* /usr/local/info <attribute change only>

* - conflict with a file which does not belong to any package.

Do you want to install these conflicting files [y,n,?,q]
```

In most cases, the error messages will be about file ownership differences or permissions differences, and you can choose to install the conflicting files without causing any problems to your system. Sometimes you will encounter a situation where a file such as a shared library is common between an installed package and the package you are trying to install. In such a case, you should quit the installation by typing **q** at the prompt and then determine if it is safe to add the package by gathering more information about the conflicting files from the vendor or creator of the package.

## Getting Information about Install Packages

Once you have a package installed, you can get more information about it and all the other installed packages on your system by using the **pkginfo** command.

In its simplest form, it lists the type, name, and a brief description about every installed package:

```
$ pkginfo
system          AXILvplr        Axil platform links
system          AXILvplu        Axil usr/platform links
application FSFgzip             gzip
system          PFUaga          AG-10 Device Driver
system          PFUagacf        AG-10 System Software(Usr)
...
```

The first column lists the type of the package, the second lists the name of the package, and the third lists a brief description of the package. The type of a package is usually either *application* or *system*. Normally only operating system packages and vendor-specific device drivers are system packages; all other packages are considered application packages.

**Checking Individual Packages**    To determine whether or not a particular package is installed on your system, you can specify the name of the package as an argument to **pkginfo**:

$ pkginfo *pkginst*

Here, *pkginst* is the name of the package that you are interested in. For example, the following command would list the information for the package FSFgzip:

```
$ pkginfo FSFgzip
```

If the package is currently installed, you will receive a message similar to the following:

```
application FSFgzip             gzip
```

If you've specified the name of a package that is not installed, as in this example,

```
$ pkginfo banana
```

then an error message similar to the following will be displayed:

```
ERROR: information for "banana" was not found
```

SYSTEM MAINTENANCE

When you are not sure about the name of a particular package, you can use **grep** to filter the output of **pkginfo** in order to look for packages whose name matches a particular pattern:

$ pkginfo | grep *str*

Here, *str* is the string you want to match in the name or in the description of the package. For example, the following command would look for all packages that contain the word Java in their name or description:

```
$ pkginfo | grep Java
system      SUNWdthj        HotJava Browser for Solaris
system      SUNWjvdem       JavaVM demo programs
system      SUNWjvdev       JavaVM developers package, includes javac, javah, and javap
system      SUNWjvjit       Java JIT compiler
system      SUNWjvman       JavaVM man pages
system      SUNWjvrt        JavaVM run time environment
```

## Quiet Mode

If you are writing a script that needs to check for the presence of certain packages, you can use the **-q** option and check the return code of **pkginfo**:

$ pkginfo -q *pkginst*

Here, *pkginst* is the name of the package that you are interested in. If the package is installed, **pkginfo** will exit with an exit code of 0 stored in the **$?** shell variable; otherwise it will exit with an exit code of 1. For example, the following command sequence would determine whether the package "banana" is installed:

```
$ pkginfo -q banana
$ echo $?
1
```

Since **$?** is set to 1, the package banana is not installed.

## Detailed Package Information

The **pkginfo** command also provides detailed information about installed packages when the **-l** option is specified:

$ pkginfo -l *pkginst*

Here, *pkginst* is the name of the package you want to get detailed information about. For example, the following command would print out detailed information about the SUNWjvdev package:

```
$ pkginfo SUNWjvdev
PKGINST:  SUNWjvdev
     NAME:  JavaVM developers package, includes javac, javah, and javap
 CATEGORY:  system
     ARCH:  sparc
  VERSION:  1.1.7,REV=1999.01.15.10.50
  BASEDIR:  /usr
   VENDOR:  Sun Microsystems, Inc.
     DESC:  JavaVM developers packages, includes javac, javah, and javap
   PSTAMP:  javavm990205151252
 INSTDATE:  Feb 21 1999 13:37
  HOTLINE:  Please contact your local service provider
   STATUS:  completely installed
    FILES:     778 installed pathnames
                 8 shared pathnames
                36 directories
                21 executables
             26628 blocks used (approx)
```

## Listing the Files in a Package

Once a package is installed it is not easy to list the individual files and directories contained in the package. A common method is to look through the "master list" of all installed files to see if it lists all the files that are contained in a particular package. This master list is stored in the file /var/sadm/install/contents. Each entry in the contents file has the following format:

*path type class perms owner group size checksum instdate pkginst*

- ■ *path*  The pathname to the file
- ■ *type*  The file's type. Normally this is f for plain files, d for directories, s for symbolic links, and v for volatile files. Volatile files are plain files whose size is subject to change.
- ■ *class*  The installation class to which the file belongs. Normally this is none.
- ■ *perms*  The permissions for the file or directory.
- ■ *owner*  The symbolic name of the owner of the file or directory.
- ■ *group*  The symbolic name of the group of the file or directory.
- ■ *size*  The size of the file in bytes.
- ■ *checksum*  The cyclic redundancy check (CRC) for the file.
- ■ *instdate*  The UNIX date (time in seconds since 0:00 1 Jan 1970) at which the file or directory was installed.
- ■ *pkginst*  The name of the package in which the file is contained.

To list all of the entries in a particular package, you would use a command similar to the following:

awk '$NF ~/*pkginst*/ { print ; }' /var/sadm/install/contents

Here, *pkginst* is the name of the package whose contents you want to list. For example, the following command would list the contents of the FSFgzip package:

```
awk '$NF ~/FSFgzip/ { print ; }'  /var/sadm/install/contents
```

## Checking Package Integrity

One of the greatest benefits of packages is that you can always check the integrity of an installed package to make sure that its contents have not changed since installation. If you receive a complaint that a particular piece of software is not working correctly, you can use the **pkgchk** command to ensure that the contents of the package have not been altered since it was installed. This command will tell you if any of the following problems pertain:

- The permissions of files or directories have changed.
- The size of a file or the checksum of a file has changed. This could indicate that someone has altered the file or that it has been overwritten.
- A file or directory is no longer present.

The basic syntax for checking a package is:

$ pkgchk *pkginst*

Here, *pkginst* is the name of the package whose contents you want to check. For example, the following command would check the contents of the FSFgzip package:

```
$ pkgchk FSFgzip
```

If this command produces any output, you will want to make sure that the files or directories in question have not been altered.

## Fixing Problems

If a file in FSFgzip package has a problem, you might see output from **pkgchk** similar to the following:

```
ERROR: /usr/local/man/man1/znew.1
    permissions <0644> expected <0666> actual
```

In this case package check reports that there is a problem with the permissions for a particular file. It is possible for pkgchk to fix this problem when invoked with the **-f** option:

> # pkgchk -f *pkginst*

Here, *pkginst* is the name of the package whose contents you want to check. For example, the following command would resolve the permission problem with the FSFgzip package:

```
# pkgchk -f FSFgzip
```

You can also use the **-f** option to fix owner and group problems.

## Ignoring Volatile Files

Many software packages include configuration files or data files that are expected to change over time. Such files are normally marked as *volatile* in the contents file, and by default **pkgchk** reports errors for all files contained in a package, but the size of a volatile file will usually be different than its size when it was installed, so you usually want to ignore them when checking a package. To have **pkgchk** ignore such files when it checks a package, use the **-n** option, as follows:

> $ pkgchk -n *pkginst*

Here, *pkginst* is the name of the package whose contents you want to check. For example, the following command would check the FSFgzip package and ignore any volatile files contained in the package:

```
$ pkgchk -n FSFgzip
```

**Note** *The **-n** option and the **-f** option are usually used together for checking a package, because you normally want to ignore volatile files and fix any problems that are encountered with the file attributes.*

## Removing Packages

There are several reasons for removing packages that you have installed on a system. In the case of many product upgrades, you will have to remove the existing package or packages that make up the product before you can install the newer version. This is the case for the Java Development Kit on Solaris 8; you have to remove the older version of the JDK before you can upgrade it. Another common reason for removing packages is related to demo software or licensing issues. Once a license expires, you may have to remove those packages that make up that software package.

The basic syntax for removing a package is:

# pkgrm *pkginst*

Here, *pkginst* is the name of the package you want to remove. As explained earlier in this section, you can use the **pkginfo** command in order to obtain the names of all the installed packages on your system. For example, you would use the following command to remove the FSFgzip package:

```
# pkgrm FSFgzip
```

This would produce a prompt similar to the following:

```
The following package is currently installed:
   FSFgzip          gzip
                    (Solaris2.6beta) 1.2.4
Do you want to remove this package?
```

You would press ENTER to remove the package from your system.

### Removing Multiple Packages

If you want to remove several packages at once, use the following syntax:

```
# pkgrm pkginst …
```

Here *pkginst … specifies* the names of the packages you want to remove.  For example, to remove the packages FSFgzip and GNUless from your system, you would enter the following:

```
# pkgrm FSFgzip GNUless
```

You will then be prompted to confirm the removal of each package.

## Managing Patches

Regardless of how well-tested an operating system release is, there are bound to be bugs in some of its programs and scripts. In order to fix these problems, you will need to apply patches to your system. Most patches simply replace one or two files. For example, a patch might replace a program like **ksh** (the Korn Shell) if a flaw is discovered in the version of that program that was released with the operating system. Occasionally, patches insert new files rather than replacing existing ones.

The two main types of problems that patches are used to correct are software bugs and security problems.

- Software bugs are the result of programming mistakes in the software. Sometimes these can be simple problems where a program fails to honor an option covered in its man page. Often bugs are more complex problems, where programs tend to crash under heavy system load or under relatively uncommon circumstances.

- Security problems are not necessarily bugs in the software programs; rather, they are weaknesses in the software that might be exploited by malicious users to gain unauthorized access to your system. Security problems can also be used by hackers to initiate denial of service (DOS) attacks against your system. Denial of service attacks can crash your systems or render them unusable; in either case your legitimate users will lose the ability to access your system.

## Patch Types

In order to keep a system running smoothly, you will need to periodically apply the latest patches to it. Patches for Solaris 8 are available from the following URL:

**http://sunsolve.sun.com**

There are two main types of patches available from this site: "point" patches and "cluster" patches. Point patches are patches that are targeted at fixing a single problem, and in general replace or add very few files to your system. Cluster patches are collections of point patches, released as a group.

## Point Patches

Point patches are normally designated with a the following format:

*patchnum-patchver*

Here, *patchnumber* is the number of the patch, and *patchver* is its version. For example, the patch 103738-02 corresponds to the second revision of the patch 103738.

You will occasionally see the term "jumbo" or "mega" patch used to refer to a collection of point patches. These are simply point patches that are intended to replace or modify a large number of files. The other common type of point patch is a "recommended" patch. Sun uses this term to refer to patches that fix problems most likely to be encountered by all users.

On most systems, you should only apply the point patches that are categorized as security fixes or "recommended" patches. Since patches are quick fixes for flawed code, regardless of the number of tests a patch is run through, they will not be tested in the same thorough manner as an operating system release. Sometimes the limited testing can miss problems that result in side effects and new bugs. By installing patches only for problems that you are actually experiencing, you can reduce your risk of introducing new bugs along with the patches.

## Cluster Patches

Periodically Sun incorporates a set of security fixes and "recommended" patches into a "cluster" patch. A cluster patch is simply a repackage of a set of patches, to facilitate download and installation. Cluster patches normally come with a single installation script to install all of the patches in the "cluster" in the proper order. In general, cluster patches undergo more testing than point patches, so it is less risky to install them once they're made available than to install the point patches individually when they first come out.

## Installing Point Patches

If you are having a problem for which Sun has released a point patch, you can download the patch from **http://sunsolve.sun.com**, and then use the **patchadd** command to install it:

```
# patchadd pathname
```

Here, *pathname* is the full pathname to the patch. For example, if you have downloaded the patch 105757-01 in the /tmp directory, you can enter the following:

```
# patchadd /tmp/105757-01
```

If you've downloaded several patches into a single directory, you can add them all at the same time by using the following syntax:

```
# patchadd -M dir patch_id ...
```

Here, *dir* is the pathname to the directory where the patches are located and *patch_id* ... are the patches you want to install. For example, the following command will install patches 105757-01 and 105755-03 (which are stored in the directory /tmp):

```
# patchadd -M /tmp 105757-01 105755-03
```

## Listing Installed Patches

To list installed patches, you can use the **showrev** command, as follows:

```
$ showrev -p
```

This will produce a listing of all the patches that are installed, in a manner similar to the following:

```
Patch: 105757-01 Obsoletes:  Requires:  Incompatibles:  Packages: SUNWcsu
Patch: 105755-03 Obsoletes:  Requires:  Incompatibles:  Packages: SUNWcsu
Patch: 105746-01 Obsoletes:  Requires:  Incompatibles:  Packages: SUNWcs
Patch: 105621-09 Obsoletes: 105686-02, 105845-01, 106064-01, 106075-01 Requires:
Incompatibles:  Packages: SUNWcsu, SUNWcsr, SUNWarc, SUNWhea, SUNWnisu
...
```

Each line in the output includes five headings:

- **Patch**   Identifies the number and version of the patch.
- **Obsoletes**   Lists the number and version of any patches that this particular patch renders obsolete.
- **Requires**   Lists the number and version of any patches that are required in order for this patch to function correctly.
- **Incompatibles**   Lists the number and version of any patches that are incompatible with this patch.
- **Packages**   Lists the packages that are affected by this patch.

**Listing Information about a Single Patch**   If you need to check if a particular patch is installed, you can filter the output of the **showrev** command by making an entry similar to the following:

$ showrev -p | awk '$2 ~ /^*patchnum*/ { print; }'

Here, *patchnum* is the number of the patch you are interested in. Instead of *patchnum*, you could also specify a particular version of a patch by using the *patchnum-patchver* format:

$ showrev -p | awk '$2 ~ /^*patchnum-patchver*$/ { print; }'

For example, the following command will print out the information for patch 105797, version 5:

```
$ showrev -p | awk '$2 ~ /^105797-05$/ { print; }'
Patch: 105797-05 Obsoletes:  Requires:  Incompatibles:  Packages: SUNWcsr
```

If you receive no output from this command, the patch in question is not installed on your system.

## Removing Patches

In some instances a patch that has been released to fix one problem can result in unexpected additional problems. For example, the Solaris 2.6 patch 106292-03 can cause one or two of the Solaris packaging tools to break. In the case of this patch it is better to remove it and wait for a newer version. To remove a patch from your system, you can use the **patchrm** command:

    # patchrm *patch*

Here, *patch* is the name of the patch you want to remove, in *patchnum-patchver* format. For example, the following command would remove the patch 106292-03:

```
# patchrm 106292-03
```

If you attempt to remove a patch that has not been installed on your system, you will receive a message similar to the following:

```
Checking installed packages and patches...
Patch 106292-03 has not been applied to this system.
patchrm is terminating.
```

## Installing Cluster Patches

The process of installing a cluster patch is more complicated than installing a point patch. One aspect of installing cluster patches—issuing the installation commands—is quite easy, because the cluster patch combines the installation of several point patches with a single installation script. However, another aspect of the process—planning system downtime—is somewhat complicated.

## Planning System Downtime

Most cluster patches include fixes to the Solaris kernel along with fixes to regular utilities. In order for the kernel fixes to take effect, you will need to reboot the system. Additionally, cluster patches take between two and six hours to install. Since most systems are used heavily during major portions of the week and/or provide services that users may depend on around the clock, you will need to schedule downtime for your system in order to install the patches, and let users know when the system will be unavailable. Most system administrators notify their users a week in advance of any scheduled downtime, and also give them reminders one or two days before the system is downed. If at all possible, you should schedule downtime on what is considered a weekend for your company or organization (or even a company holiday, if the typical weekend sees regular user activity). You should plan for about eight hours of downtime, which will give you ample time to patch the system and test it out before putting it back into service.

## Downloading and Expanding a Cluster Patch

Cluster patches are available from SunSolve via the Solaris patch home page, located at the following URL:

**http://sunsolve.Sun.COM/pub-cgi/show.pl?target=patches/patch-access**

This page allows you to download the cluster patch that is appropriate for your version of Solaris. The cluster patch will be downloaded as a single compressed file. The filename will look something like this:

_version_\_Recommended.tar.Z

Here, _version_ is the version of Solaris you are running. For example, the Solaris 2.6 cluster patch is named 2.6_Recommended.tar.Z. As of this writing, no patch clusters have been released for Solaris 8.

The size of the cluster patch varies between the different versions of Solaris, from 11 MB for Solaris 7 to 45 MB for Solaris 2.5.1. Make sure that you download the cluster patch into a directory that has sufficient space to store the compressed file and its uncompressed contents. You can make sure of this by using the **df** command:

$ df -k _dir_

Here, _dir_ is the directory you will be downloading the patch into. For example, the following command would check the /var/tmp directory:

```
$ df -k /var/tmp
Filesystem          kbytes    used    avail capacity  Mounted on
/dev/dsk/c0t3d0s1   123455    96842   14268    88%    /var
```

From the number listed in the avail column, we can see that this directory has about 13 MB free (the output values for **df** are in kilobytes). The **df** command is discussed in greater detail in Chapter 9.

Once you have downloaded the cluster patch, you can extract its contents as follows:

$ cd _dir_ && zcat _version_\_Recommended.tar.Z | tar -xvf -

Here, _dir_ is the directory into which you've downloaded the cluster patch, and _version_ is the version of Solaris you are running. For example, the following command will extract the contents of the cluster patch for Solaris 2.6 (assuming that it has been downloaded into the directory /var/tmp):

```
$ cd /var/tmp && zcat 2.6_Recommended.tar.Z | tar -xvf -
```

Every file in the patch will be listed on your screen as it is extracted.

Once the cluster patch has been expanded, a directory named *version*_Recommended will be created. Its contents will be similar to the following:

```
$ ls 2.6_Recommended
./                  105464-01/       105703-08/       106226-01/
../                 105490-07/       105720-06/       106235-02/
105181-12/          105552-02/       105741-05/       106242-02/
105210-18/          105558-03/       105755-07/       106257-04/
105216-03/          105562-03/       105786-07/       106271-05/
105284-23/          105566-06/       105797-05/       106301-01/
105356-07/          105568-12/       105800-05/       106439-02/
105357-02/          105580-09/       105837-02/       106448-01/
105375-09/          105600-07/       105926-01/       106828-01/
105379-05/          105615-04/       106040-10/       CLUSTER_README
105393-07/          105621-09/       106049-01/       copyright
105395-03/          105642-05/       106125-06/       install_cluster*
105401-20/          105665-03/       106193-03/       patch_order
105407-01/          105669-04/       106222-01/
```

## Installing the Cluster Patch

There are two steps to installing a cluster patch. The first step is to read the CLUSTER_README file. This file contains an overview of the installation process along with a description of the individual patches contained within the cluster patch. Make sure that you read the CLUSTER_README and understand how the cluster patch will update your system. By understanding the effects of the cluster patch before you install it, you will avoid most of the problems associated with patching. As the saying goes, "When all else fails, read the directions!"

Once you have read the CLUSTER_README, you can make the following entry to start the cluster patch installation:

```
# ./install_cluster
```

This assumes that you are in the cluster patch directory where the **install_cluster** script is located. Once the script starts, you will be presented with this prompt:

```
Patch cluster install script for Solaris 2.6 Recommended

*WARNING* SYSTEMS WITH LIMITED DISK SPACE SHOULD *NOT* INSTALL PATCHES:

With or without using the save option, the patch installation process
will still require some amount of disk space for installation and
administrative tasks in the /, /usr, /var, or /opt partitions where
patches are typically installed. The exact amount of space will
```

SYSTEM MAINTENANCE

```
depend on the machine's architecture, software packages already
installed, and the difference in the patched objects size. To be
safe, it is not recommended that a patch cluster be installed on a
system with less than 4 MBytes of available space in each of these
partitions. Running out of disk space during installation may result
in only partially loaded patches. Check and be sure adequate disk space
is available before continuing.

Are you ready to continue with install? [y/n]:
```

This example shows the initial output for the Solaris 2.6 cluster patch. The output will vary for other versions. To continue installing the patch, type *Y* at the prompt. This will start the installation process. The output will be similar to the following:

```
Sufficient save space exists, continuing...
Installing patches located in /var/tmp/2.6_Recommended
Using patch_order file for patch installation sequence
Installing 106125-06...
Installing 106828-01...
...
```

Each patch will be listed as it is installed.

Occasionally you may see a message similar to the following:

```
Installation of 105395-03 failed. Return code 2.
```

If you receive any messages similar to this, check the cluster patch installation log after the installation completes. The path to this file is displayed at the end of the installation by the **install_cluster** script. Usually, these error messages reflect the fact that you've already installed either that same patch or a more recent one.

## Summary

In this chapter, we examined user administration and software administration in Solaris. First we covered the different databases used in user administration, and then we looked at the topic of password management. For user management, we covered each of the commands required to add, update, and remove users and their passwords from your system. In the latter part of this chapter we covered software administration, starting with the concept of packages and extending into the commands used to manage them. Finally, we looked at patches and the commands used to install and remove them.

# How to Find Out More

If you are interested in user and password management, you can get more information by consulting one of the following resources:

Kimery, Sam. *Sunsoft Solaris 2.\* User's Guide.* (OnWord Press, 1994)

Calkins, Bill. *Solaris 2.6 Administrator Certification Training Guide, Part 1.* (Macmillan Technical Publishing, 1999.)

Rosen, Kenneth H.; Rosinski, Richard R.; Farber James M.; Host, Douglas A. *UNIX System V Release 4: An Introduction.* (Osborne/McGraw-Hill, 1996.)

For more information about software packages, consult the following web site:

**http://www.sunfreeware.com/pkgadd.html**

This page has a detailed description of packages and the tools for creating and maintaining packages. It also has links to other sites that discuss software packaging on Solaris.

For additional information about patches, you can consult the SunSolve homepage at

**http://www.sunsolve.com**

The SunSolve site has all of the information about point and cluster patches, including detailed README files for every patch. Also featured on the SunSolve site are several articles that describe Solaris patches in greater detail.

An excellent article entitled "A Patch-Work" covering Solaris patching is available from the Sun World web site; to access it directly, use the following URLs:

**http://www.sunworld.com/swol-02-1999/swol-02-supersys.html** (Part 1)

**http://www.sunworld.com/swol-03-1999/swol-03-supersys.html** (Part 2)

Patches are also available on the SunSolve CD-ROM that Sun periodically ships to its customers. If you would like to subscribe to the SunSolve CD-ROM, please contact your Sun sales representative. If you do not have a sales representative, you can contact Sun directly using this URL:

**http://www.sun.com/service/contacting/sales.html**

The
# Complete
Reference

Solaris 8

# Chapter 7

## Managing Devices

One of the most important and challenging roles of a system administrator is device management. Devices, in this context, can be defined as both physical and logical entities that together constitute a hardware system. Although some operating systems hide device configuration details from all users (even administrators!) in proprietary, binary formats, Solaris device configuration is easy to use, with configuration information stored in special files known as device files. In addition to providing the technical background on how device files operate and how device drivers can be installed, this chapter provides practical advice on installing standard devices, such as new hard drives, as well as more modern media, such as CD-Rs and Zip disks.

Solaris 8 now supports the dynamic reconfiguration of many system devices on some SPARC platforms, particularly in the medium-level server range (such as E450) and above. This allows administrators to remove faulty hardware components and replace them without having to power down a system and perform a reconfiguration boot, which is necessary for older systems. This is particularly significant for systems that have high redundancy of system components to guarantee uptime under all but the most critical of circumstances.

## Device Files

Device files are special files that represent devices in the Solaris operating system and are located in the /dev directory and its subdirectories (such as /dev/dsk). The /devices directory is a tree that completely characterizes the hardware layout of the system in the file system namespace. Although it may seem initially confusing that there are separate directories for devices and for system hardware, the difference between the two systems will become apparent in the discussion that follows. Solaris refers to both physical and logical devices in three separate ways: with physical device names, as physical device files, and with logical device names. Physical device names are easily identified as they are long strings that provide all details relevant to the physical installation of the device. Every physical device has a physical name: For example, an SBUS could have the name /sbus@1f,0, and a disk device might have the name /sbus@1f,0/SUNW,fas@2,8800000/sd@1,0. Physical device names are usually displayed at boot time and when using selected applications that access hardware directly, such as **format**.

On the other hand, physical device files, which are located in the /devices directory, are comprised of an instance name that is an abbreviation for a physical device name, which can be interpreted by the kernel. For example, the SBUS /sbus@1f,0 might be referred to as "sbus", and a device disk /sbus@1f,0/SUNW,fas@2,8800000/sd@1,0 might be referred to as "sd1". The mapping of instance names to physical devices is not hard-wired. The /etc/path_to_inst file always contains these details, keeping them consistent between boots. For an Ultra 2, this file looks like:

```
"/sbus@1f,0" 0 "sbus"
"/sbus@1f,0/sbusmem@2,0" 2 "sbusmem"
"/sbus@1f,0/sbusmem@3,0" 3 "sbusmem"
"/sbus@1f,0/sbusmem@0,0" 0 "sbusmem"
"/sbus@1f,0/sbusmem@1,0" 1 "sbusmem"
"/sbus@1f,0/SUNW,fas@2,8800000" 1 "fas"
"/sbus@1f,0/SUNW,fas@2,8800000/ses@f,0" 1 "ses"
"/sbus@1f,0/SUNW,fas@2,8800000/sd@1,0" 16 "sd"
"/sbus@1f,0/SUNW,fas@2,8800000/sd@0,0" 15 "sd"
"/sbus@1f,0/SUNW,fas@2,8800000/sd@3,0" 18 "sd"
"/sbus@1f,0/SUNW,fas@2,8800000/sd@2,0" 17 "sd"
"/sbus@1f,0/SUNW,fas@2,8800000/sd@5,0" 20 "sd"
"/sbus@1f,0/SUNW,fas@2,8800000/sd@4,0" 19 "sd"
"/sbus@1f,0/SUNW,fas@2,8800000/sd@6,0" 21 "sd"
"/sbus@1f,0/SUNW,fas@2,8800000/sd@9,0" 23 "sd"
"/sbus@1f,0/SUNW,fas@2,8800000/sd@8,0" 22 "sd"
"/sbus@1f,0/SUNW,fas@2,8800000/sd@a,0" 24 "sd"
"/sbus@1f,0/SUNW,fas@2,8800000/st@1,0" 8 "st"
"/sbus@1f,0/SUNW,fas@2,8800000/st@0,0" 7 "st"
"/sbus@1f,0/SUNW,fas@2,8800000/sd@c,0" 26 "sd"
"/sbus@1f,0/SUNW,fas@2,8800000/st@3,0" 10 "st"
"/sbus@1f,0/SUNW,fas@2,8800000/sd@b,0" 25 "sd"
"/sbus@1f,0/SUNW,fas@2,8800000/st@2,0" 9 "st"
"/sbus@1f,0/SUNW,fas@2,8800000/sd@e,0" 28 "sd"
"/sbus@1f,0/SUNW,fas@2,8800000/st@5,0" 12 "st"
"/sbus@1f,0/SUNW,fas@2,8800000/sd@d,0" 27 "sd"
"/sbus@1f,0/SUNW,fas@2,8800000/st@4,0" 11 "st"
"/sbus@1f,0/SUNW,fas@2,8800000/sd@f,0" 29 "sd"
"/sbus@1f,0/SUNW,fas@2,8800000/st@6,0" 13 "st"
"/sbus@1f,0/SUNW,fas@2,8800000/ses@0,0" 25 "ses"
"/sbus@1f,0/SUNW,fas@2,8800000/ses@1,0" 26 "ses"
"/sbus@1f,0/SUNW,fas@2,8800000/ses@2,0" 27 "ses"
"/sbus@1f,0/SUNW,fas@2,8800000/ses@3,0" 28 "ses"
"/sbus@1f,0/SUNW,fas@2,8800000/ses@4,0" 29 "ses"
"/sbus@1f,0/SUNW,fas@2,8800000/ses@5,0" 30 "ses"
"/sbus@1f,0/SUNW,fas@2,8800000/ses@6,0" 31 "ses"
"/sbus@1f,0/SUNW,fas@2,8800000/ses@7,0" 32 "ses"
"/sbus@1f,0/SUNW,fas@2,8800000/ses@8,0" 33 "ses"
"/sbus@1f,0/SUNW,fas@2,8800000/ses@9,0" 34 "ses"
"/sbus@1f,0/SUNW,fas@2,8800000/ses@a,0" 35 "ses"
"/sbus@1f,0/SUNW,fas@2,8800000/ses@b,0" 36 "ses"
"/sbus@1f,0/SUNW,fas@2,8800000/ses@c,0" 37 "ses"
```

```
"/sbus@1f,0/SUNW,fas@2,8800000/ses@d,0" 38 "ses"
"/sbus@1f,0/SUNW,fas@2,8800000/ses@e,0" 39 "ses"
"/sbus@1f,0/SUNW,CS4231@d,c000000" 0 "audiocs"
"/sbus@1f,0/dma@0,81000" 0 "dma"
"/sbus@1f,0/dma@0,81000/esp@0,80000" 0 "esp"
"/sbus@1f,0/dma@0,81000/esp@0,80000/sd@0,0" 30 "sd"
"/sbus@1f,0/dma@0,81000/esp@0,80000/sd@1,0" 31 "sd"
"/sbus@1f,0/dma@0,81000/esp@0,80000/sd@2,0" 32 "sd"
"/sbus@1f,0/dma@0,81000/esp@0,80000/sd@3,0" 33 "sd"
"/sbus@1f,0/dma@0,81000/esp@0,80000/sd@4,0" 34 "sd"
"/sbus@1f,0/dma@0,81000/esp@0,80000/sd@5,0" 35 "sd"
"/sbus@1f,0/dma@0,81000/esp@0,80000/sd@6,0" 36 "sd"
"/sbus@1f,0/dma@0,81000/esp@0,80000/st@0,0" 14 "st"
"/sbus@1f,0/dma@0,81000/esp@0,80000/st@1,0" 15 "st"
"/sbus@1f,0/dma@0,81000/esp@0,80000/st@2,0" 16 "st"
"/sbus@1f,0/dma@0,81000/esp@0,80000/st@3,0" 17 "st"
"/sbus@1f,0/dma@0,81000/esp@0,80000/st@4,0" 18 "st"
"/sbus@1f,0/dma@0,81000/esp@0,80000/st@5,0" 19 "st"
"/sbus@1f,0/dma@0,81000/esp@0,80000/st@6,0" 20 "st"
"/sbus@1f,0/dma@0,81000/esp@0,80000/ses@0,0" 2 "ses"
"/sbus@1f,0/dma@0,81000/esp@0,80000/ses@1,0" 3 "ses"
"/sbus@1f,0/dma@0,81000/esp@0,80000/ses@2,0" 4 "ses"
"/sbus@1f,0/dma@0,81000/esp@0,80000/ses@3,0" 5 "ses"
"/sbus@1f,0/dma@0,81000/esp@0,80000/ses@4,0" 6 "ses"
"/sbus@1f,0/dma@0,81000/esp@0,80000/ses@5,0" 7 "ses"
"/sbus@1f,0/dma@0,81000/esp@0,80000/ses@6,0" 8 "ses"
"/sbus@1f,0/dma@0,81000/esp@0,80000/ses@7,0" 9 "ses"
"/sbus@1f,0/SUNW,fas@e,8800000" 0 "fas"
"/sbus@1f,0/SUNW,fas@e,8800000/ses@f,0" 0 "ses"
"/sbus@1f,0/SUNW,fas@e,8800000/sd@f,0" 14 "sd"
"/sbus@1f,0/SUNW,fas@e,8800000/st@6,0" 6 "st"
"/sbus@1f,0/SUNW,fas@e,8800000/sd@d,0" 12 "sd"
"/sbus@1f,0/SUNW,fas@e,8800000/st@4,0" 4 "st"
"/sbus@1f,0/SUNW,fas@e,8800000/sd@e,0" 13 "sd"
"/sbus@1f,0/SUNW,fas@e,8800000/st@5,0" 5 "st"
"/sbus@1f,0/SUNW,fas@e,8800000/sd@b,0" 10 "sd"
"/sbus@1f,0/SUNW,fas@e,8800000/st@2,0" 2 "st"
"/sbus@1f,0/SUNW,fas@e,8800000/sd@c,0" 11 "sd"
"/sbus@1f,0/SUNW,fas@e,8800000/st@3,0" 3 "st"
"/sbus@1f,0/SUNW,fas@e,8800000/st@0,0" 0 "st"
"/sbus@1f,0/SUNW,fas@e,8800000/sd@a,0" 9 "sd"
"/sbus@1f,0/SUNW,fas@e,8800000/st@1,0" 1 "st"
"/sbus@1f,0/SUNW,fas@e,8800000/sd@6,0" 6 "sd"
```

```
"/sbus@1f,0/SUNW,fas@e,8800000/sd@4,0" 4 "sd"
"/sbus@1f,0/SUNW,fas@e,8800000/sd@5,0" 5 "sd"
"/sbus@1f,0/SUNW,fas@e,8800000/sd@2,0" 2 "sd"
"/sbus@1f,0/SUNW,fas@e,8800000/sd@3,0" 3 "sd"
"/sbus@1f,0/SUNW,fas@e,8800000/sd@0,0" 0 "sd"
"/sbus@1f,0/SUNW,fas@e,8800000/sd@1,0" 1 "sd"
"/sbus@1f,0/SUNW,fas@e,8800000/sd@8,0" 7 "sd"
"/sbus@1f,0/SUNW,fas@e,8800000/sd@9,0" 8 "sd"
"/sbus@1f,0/SUNW,fas@e,8800000/ses@0,0" 10 "ses"
"/sbus@1f,0/SUNW,fas@e,8800000/ses@1,0" 11 "ses"
"/sbus@1f,0/SUNW,fas@e,8800000/ses@2,0" 12 "ses"
"/sbus@1f,0/SUNW,fas@e,8800000/ses@3,0" 13 "ses"
"/sbus@1f,0/SUNW,fas@e,8800000/ses@4,0" 14 "ses"
"/sbus@1f,0/SUNW,fas@e,8800000/ses@5,0" 15 "ses"
"/sbus@1f,0/SUNW,fas@e,8800000/ses@6,0" 16 "ses"
"/sbus@1f,0/SUNW,fas@e,8800000/ses@7,0" 17 "ses"
"/sbus@1f,0/SUNW,fas@e,8800000/ses@8,0" 18 "ses"
"/sbus@1f,0/SUNW,fas@e,8800000/ses@9,0" 19 "ses"
"/sbus@1f,0/SUNW,fas@e,8800000/ses@a,0" 20 "ses"
"/sbus@1f,0/SUNW,fas@e,8800000/ses@b,0" 21 "ses"
"/sbus@1f,0/SUNW,fas@e,8800000/ses@c,0" 22 "ses"
"/sbus@1f,0/SUNW,fas@e,8800000/ses@d,0" 23 "ses"
"/sbus@1f,0/SUNW,fas@e,8800000/ses@e,0" 24 "ses"
"/sbus@1f,0/sbusmem@f,0" 15 "sbusmem"
"/sbus@1f,0/sbusmem@d,0" 13 "sbusmem"
"/sbus@1f,0/sbusmem@e,0" 14 "sbusmem"
"/sbus@1f,0/cgthree@1,0" 0 "cgthree"
"/sbus@1f,0/SUNW,hme@e,8c00000" 0 "hme"
"/sbus@1f,0/zs@f,1000000" 1 "zs"
"/sbus@1f,0/zs@f,1100000" 0 "zs"
"/sbus@1f,0/SUNW,bpp@e,c800000" 0 "bpp"
"/sbus@1f,0/lebuffer@0,40000" 0 "lebuffer"
"/sbus@1f,0/lebuffer@0,40000/le@0,60000" 0 "le"
"/sbus@1f,0/SUNW,hme@2,8c00000" 1 "hme"
"/sbus@1f,0/SUNW,fdtwo@f,1400000" 0 "fd"
"/options" 0 "options"
"/pseudo" 0 "pseudo"
```

In addition to physical devices, Solaris also needs to refer to logical devices. For example, physical disks may be divided into many different slices, so the physical disk device will need to be referred to using a logical name. Logical device files in the /dev directory are symbolically linked to physical device names in the /devices directory. Most user applications will refer to logical device names.

# /dev and /devices

A typical listing of the /dev directory has numerous entries that look like:

| | | | | | |
|---|---|---|---|---|---|
| arp | ptys0 | ptyyb | rsd3a | sd3e | ttyu2 |
| audio | ptys1 | ptyyc | rsd3b | sd3f | ttyu3 |
| audioctl | ptys2 | ptyyd | rsd3c | sd3g | ttyu4 |
| bd.off | ptys3 | ptyye | rsd3d | sd3h | ttyu5 |
| be | ptys4 | ptyyf | rsd3e | skip_key | ttyu6 |
| bpp0 | ptys5 | ptyz0 | rsd3f | sound/ | ttyu7 |
| cgthree0 | ptys6 | ptyz1 | rsd3g | sp | ttyu8 |
| conslog | ptys7 | ptyz2 | rsd3h | sr0 | ttyu9 |
| console | ptys8 | ptyz3 | rsr0 | stderr | ttyua |
| cua/ | ptys9 | ptyz4 | rst11 | stdin | ttyub |
| dsk/ | ptysa | ptyz5 | rst12 | stdout | ttyuc |
| dtremote | ptysb | ptyz6 | rst13 | SWAP/ | ttyud |
| dump | ptysc | ptyz7 | rst19 | syscon | ttyue |
| es/ | ptysd | ptyz8 | rst20 | systty | ttyuf |
| fb0 | ptyse | ptyz9 | rst21 | tcp | ttyv0 |
| fbs/ | ptysf | ptyza | rst27 | term/ | ttyv1 |
| fd/ | ptyt0 | ptyzb | rst28 | ticlts | ttyv2 |
| hme | ptyt1 | ptyzc | rst29 | ticots | ttyv3 |
| icmp | ptyt2 | ptyzd | rst35 | ticotsord | ttyv4 |
| ie | ptyt3 | ptyze | rst4 | tnfctl | ttyv5 |
| ip | ptyt4 | ptyzf | rst5 | tnfmap | ttyv6 |
| ipd | ptyt5 | pump | rts | tod | ttyv7 |
| ipdcm | ptyt6 | qe | sad/ | tty | ttyv8 |
| ipdptp | ptyt7 | random| | sd0a | ttya | ttyv9 |
| isdn/ | ptyt8 | rawip | sd0b | ttyb | ttyva |
| kbd | ptyt9 | rdsk/ | sd0c | ttyp0 | ttyvb |
| kmem | ptyta | rmt/ | sd0d | ttyp1 | ttyvc |
| kstat | ptytb | rsd0a | sd0e | ttyp2 | ttyvd |
| ksyms | ptytc | rsd0b | sd0f | ttyp3 | ttyve |
| le | ptytd | rsd0c | sd0g | ttyp4 | ttyvf |
| llc1 | ptyte | rsd0d | sd0h | ttyp5 | ttyw0 |
| lockstat | ptytf | rsd0e | sd15a | ttyp6 | ttyw1 |
| log | ptyu0 | rsd0f | sd15b | ttyp7 | ttyw2 |
| logindmux | ptyu1 | rsd0g | sd15c | ttyp8 | ttyw3 |
| md/ | ptyu2 | rsd0h | sd15d | ttyp9 | ttyw4 |
| mem | ptyu3 | rsd15a | sd15e | ttypa | ttyw5 |

| | | | | | |
|---|---|---|---|---|---|
| mouse | ptyu4 | rsd15b | sd15f | ttypb | ttyw6 |
| nrst11 | ptyu5 | rsd15c | sd15g | ttypc | ttyw7 |
| nrst12 | ptyu6 | rsd15d | sd15h | ttypd | ttyw8 |
| nrst13 | ptyu7 | rsd15e | sd16a | ttype | ttyw9 |
| nrst19 | ptyu8 | rsd15f | sd16b | ttypf | ttywa |
| nrst20 | ptyu9 | rsd15g | sd16c | ttyq0 | ttywb |
| nrst21 | ptyua | rsd15h | sd16d | ttyq1 | ttywc |
| nrst27 | ptyub | rsd16a | sd16e | ttyq2 | ttywd |
| nrst28 | ptyuc | rsd16b | sd16f | ttyq3 | ttywe |
| nrst29 | ptyud | rsd16c | sd16g | ttyq4 | ttywf |
| nrst35 | ptyue | rsd16d | sd16h | ttyq5 | ttyx0 |
| nrst4 | ptyuf | rsd16e | sd17a | ttyq6 | ttyx1 |
| nrst5 | ptyv0 | rsd16f | sd17b | ttyq7 | ttyx2 |
| nukk | ptyv1 | rsd16g | sd17c | ttyq8 | ttyx3 |
| null | ptyv2 | rsd16h | sd17d | ttyq9 | ttyx4 |
| openprom | ptyv3 | rsd17a | sd17e | ttyqa | ttyx5 |
| pcmcia/ | ptyv4 | rsd17b | sd17f | ttyqb | ttyx6 |
| pm | ptyv5 | rsd17c | sd17g | ttyqc | ttyx7 |
| printers/ | ptyv6 | rsd17d | sd17h | ttyqd | ttyx8 |
| profile | ptyv7 | rsd17e | sd1a | ttyqe | ttyx9 |
| ptmajor | ptyv8 | rsd17f | sd1b | ttyqf | ttyxa |
| ptmx | ptyv9 | rsd17g | sd1c | ttyr0 | ttyxb |
| pts/ | ptyva | rsd17h | sd1d | ttyr1 | ttyxc |
| ptyp0 | ptyvb | rsd1a | sd1e | ttyr2 | ttyxd |
| ptyp1 | ptyvc | rsd1b | sd1f | ttyr3 | ttyxe |
| ptyp2 | ptyvd | rsd1c | sd1g | ttyr4 | ttyxf |
| ptyp3 | ptyve | rsd1d | sd1h | ttyr5 | ttyy0 |
| ptyp4 | ptyvf | rsd1e | sd2a | ttyr6 | ttyy1 |
| ptyp5 | ptyw0 | rsd1f | sd2b | ttyr7 | ttyy2 |
| ptyp6 | ptyw1 | rsd1g | sd2c | ttyr8 | ttyy3 |
| ptyp7 | ptyw2 | rsd1h | sd2d | ttyr9 | ttyy4 |
| ptyp8 | ptyw3 | rsd2a | sd2e | ttyra | ttyy5 |
| ptyp9 | ptyw4 | rsd2b | sd2f | ttyrb | ttyy6 |
| ptypa | ptyw5 | rsd2c | sd2g | ttyrc | ttyy7 |
| ptypb | ptyw6 | rsd2d | sd2h | ttyrd | ttyy8 |
| ptypc | ptyw7 | rsd2e | sd30a | ttyre | ttyy9 |
| ptypd | ptyw8 | rsd2f | sd30b | ttyrf | ttyya |
| ptype | ptyw9 | rsd2g | sd30c | ttys0 | ttyyb |
| ptypf | ptywa | rsd2h | sd30d | ttys1 | ttyyc |
| ptyq0 | ptywb | rsd30a | sd30e | ttys2 | ttyyd |

| | | | | | |
|---|---|---|---|---|---|
| ptyq1 | ptywc | rsd30b | sd30f | ttys3 | ttyye |
| ptyq2 | ptywd | rsd30c | sd30g | ttys4 | ttyyf |
| ptyq3 | ptywe | rsd30d | sd30h | ttys5 | ttyz0 |
| ptyq4 | ptywf | rsd30e | sd31a | ttys6 | ttyz1 |
| ptyq5 | ptyx0 | rsd30f | sd31b | ttys7 | ttyz2 |
| ptyq6 | ptyx1 | rsd30g | sd31c | ttys8 | ttyz3 |
| ptyq7 | ptyx2 | rsd30h | sd31d | ttys9 | ttyz4 |
| ptyq8 | ptyx3 | rsd31a | sd31e | ttysa | ttyz5 |
| ptyq9 | ptyx4 | rsd31b | sd31f | ttysb | ttyz6 |
| ptyqa | ptyx5 | rsd31c | sd31g | ttysc | ttyz7 |
| ptyqb | ptyx6 | rsd31d | sd31h | ttysd | ttyz8 |
| ptyqc | ptyx7 | rsd31e | sd32a | ttyse | ttyz9 |
| ptyqd | ptyx8 | rsd31f | sd32b | ttysf | ttyza |
| ptyqe | ptyx9 | rsd31g | sd32c | ttyt0 | ttyzb |
| ptyqf | ptyxa | rsd31h | sd32d | ttyt1 | ttyzc |
| ptyr0 | ptyxb | rsd32a | sd32c | ttyt2 | ttyzd |
| ptyr1 | ptyxc | rsd32b | sd32f | ttyt3 | ttyze |
| ptyr2 | ptyxd | rsd32c | sd32g | ttyt4 | ttyzf |
| ptyr3 | ptyxe | rsd32d | sd32h | ttyt5 | udp |
| ptyr4 | ptyxf | rsd32e | sd33a | ttyt6 | volctl |
| ptyr5 | ptyy0 | rsd32f | sd33b | ttyt7 | vvod |
| ptyr6 | ptyy1 | rsd32g | sd33c | ttyt8 | winlock |
| ptyr7 | ptyy2 | rsd32h | sd33d | ttyt9 | wscons |
| ptyr8 | ptyy3 | rsd33a | sd33e | ttyta | zero |
| ptyr9 | ptyy4 | rsd33b | sd33f | ttytb | zsh |
| ptyra | ptyy5 | rsd33c | sd33g | ttytc | zsh0 |
| ptyrb | ptyy6 | rsd33d | sd33h | ttytd | zsh1 |
| ptyrc | ptyy7 | rsd33e | sd3a | ttyte | |
| ptyrd | ptyy8 | rsd33f | sd3b | ttytf | |
| ptyre | ptyy9 | rsd33g | sd3c | ttyu0 | |
| ptyrf | ptyya | rsd33h | sd3d | ttyu1 | |

Many of these device filenames are self-explanatory:

■ /dev/console represents the console device. Error and status messages are usually written to the console by daemons and applications using the syslog service (described in Chapter 16). /dev/console typically corresponds to the monitor in text mode; however, the console is also represented logically in windowing systems, such as OpenWindows, where the command:

```
server% cmdtool -C
```

brings up a console window.

- /dev/hme is the network interface device file.
- /dev/dsk contains device files for disk slices.
- /dev/tty*n* and /dev/pty*n* are the *n* terminal and *n* pseudo terminal devices attached to the system.
- /dev/null is the end point of discarded output; many applications pipe their output.

The drvconfig command creates the /devices directory tree, which is a logical representation of the physical layout of devices attached to the system, and pseudo drivers. drvconfig is executed automatically after a reconfiguration boot. It reads file permission information for new nodes in the tree from /etc/minor_perm, which contains entries like:

```
sd:* 0666 httpd staff
```

where **sd** is the node name for a disk device, **0666** is the default file permission, **httpd** is the owner, and **staff** is the group.

## Storage Devices

Solaris supports many different kinds of mass-storage devices, including SCSI hard drives (and IDE drives on the x86 platform), reading and writing standards and rewritable CD-ROMs, Iomega Zip and Jaz drives, tape drives, and floppy disks. Hard drives are the most common kinds of storage devices found on a Solaris system, ranging from individual drives used to create system and user file systems to highly redundant, server-based RAID systems. These RAID configurations can comprise a set of internal disks, managed through software (such as DiskSuite), or high-speed, external arrays, like the A1000, which include dedicated RAM for write-caching. Since disk writing is one of the slowest operations in any modern server system, this greatly increases overall operational speed.

Hard drives have faced stiff competition in recent years, with new media such as Iomega's Zip and Jaz drives providing removable media for both random and sequential file access. This makes them ideal media for archival backups, competing with the traditional magnetic tape drives. The latter have largely been replaced in modern systems by the digital DAT tape system, which has high reliability and data throughput rates (especially the DDS-3 standard).

In this section, we will look at the issues surrounding the installation and configuration of storage devices for Solaris, providing practical advice for installing a wide range of hardware.

## Hard Drives

When formatted for operation with the Solaris operating system, hard disks are logically divided into one or more "slices" (or partitions), on which a single file system resides. File systems contain sets of files, which are hierarchically organized around a number of directories. The Solaris system contains a number of predefined directories that often form the top level of a file system hierarchy. Many of these directories lie one level below the root directory, often denoted by "/", which exists on the primary system disk of any Solaris system. In addition to a primary disk, many Solaris systems will have additional disks that provide storage space for user and daemon files. Each file system has a mount point that is usually created in the top level of the root file system. For example, the /export file system is obviously mounted in the top level of "/ ". The mount point is created by using the **mkdir** command:

```
server# mkdir /export
```

In contrast, the /export/home file system, which usually holds the home directories of users and user files, is mounted in the top level of the /export file system. Thus, the mount point is created by using the command:

```
server# mkdir /export/home
```

A single logical file system can be created on a single slice, but cannot exist on more than one slice unless there is an extra level of abstraction between the logical and physical file systems (for example, a virtual disk is created using DiskSuite, which spans many physical disks). A physical disk can also contain more than one slice. On SPARC architecture systems, there are eight slices that can be used, numbered 0 through 7. On Intel architecture systems, however, there are 10 available slices, numbered 0 through 9.

The actual assignment of logical file systems to physical slices is a matter of discretion for the individual administrator, and although there are customary assignments recommended by Sun and other hardware vendors, it is possible that a specific site policy or an application's requirements necessitate the development of a local policy. For example, database servers often make quite specific requirements about the allocation of disk slices to improve performance. However, with modern high-performance RAID systems, these recommendations are often redundant. Since many organizations will have many different kinds of systems deployed, it is useful to maintain compatibility between systems as much as possible.

Figure 7-1 shows the typical file system layout for a SPARC architecture system following customary disk slice allocations. Slice 0 holds the root partition, and slice 1

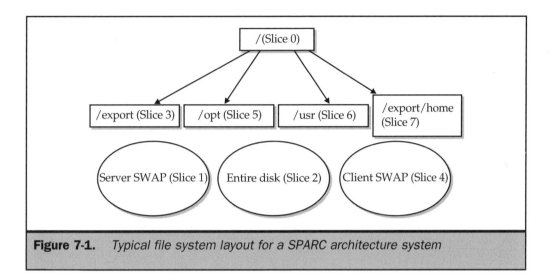

**Figure 7-1.**    *Typical file system layout for a SPARC architecture system*

is allocated to SWAP space. For systems with changing virtual memory requirements, it might be better to use a SWAP file on the file system rather than allocate an entire slice for SWAP. Slice 2 often refers to the entire disk, and /export on slice 3 traditionally holds older versions of the operating system, which are used by client systems with lower performance (for example, Classic or LX systems, which use the trivial FTP daemon, **tftpd**, to download their operating system upon boot). These systems may also use slice 4 as exported SWAP space. Export may also be used for file sharing using the networked file system, NFS. Slice 5 holds the /opt file system, which is the default location under Solaris 8 for local packages installed using the **pkgadd** command. Under earlier versions of Solaris, the /usr/local file system held local packages, and this convention is still used by many sites. The system package file system /usr is usually located on slice 6, and /export/home usually contains user home directories on slice 7. Again, earlier systems located user home directories under /home, but since this is used the **automounter** program in Solaris 8, some contention can be expected.

Figure 7-2 shows the typical file system layout for an Intel architecture system following customary disk slice allocations. Slice 0 again holds the root partition, and slice 1 is also allocated to SWAP space. Slice 2 continues to refer to the entire disk, /export on slice 3 again holds older versions of the operating system, which are used by client systems, and slice 4 contains exported SWAP space for these clients. The local package file system /opt is still located on slice 5, and the system package file system /usr is again located on slice 6. Slice 7 contains the user home directories on /export/home. However, the two extra slices serve very different purposes: Boot information for Solaris is located on slice 8, and is known as the boot slice, and slice 9 provides space for alternative disk blocks, and is known as the alternative slice.

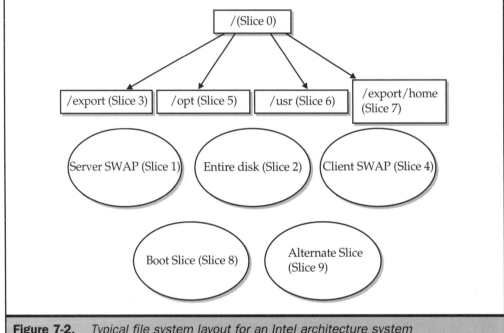

**Figure 7-2.**    *Typical file system layout for an Intel architecture system*

## CD-ROMs

A popular format of read-only mass storage on many servers is the compact disc read-only memory (CD-ROM). Although earlier releases of Solaris worked best with Sun-branded CD-ROM drives, as of Solaris 2.6 the operating system fully supports all SCSI-2 CD-ROMs. For systems running older versions of Solaris, it may still be possible to use a third-party drive, but the drive must support 512 byte sectors (the Sun standard). A second Sun default to be aware of is that CD-ROMs must usually have the SCSI target ID of 6, although this limitation has again been overcome in later releases of the kernel. However, a number of third-party applications with "auto detect" functions may still expect to see the CD-ROM drive at SCSI ID 6.

A number of different CD formats are also supported with the **mount** command that is used to attach CDs to the file system. It is common to use the mount point /cdrom for the primary CD-ROM device in Solaris systems, although it is possible to use a different mount point for mounting the device by using a command-line argument to **mount**.

## Zip and Jaz Drives

There are two ways to install Zip and Jaz drives: by treating the drive as a SCSI disk, in which case format data needs to be added to the system to recognize it, or by using Andy Polyakov's ziptool, which will format and manage protection modes supported by Zip 100 and Jaz 1GB/2GB drives. Both of these techniques will only support SCSI and not parallel port drives.

Treating the Zip 100 SCSI drive or the Jaz 1G drive as a normal SCSI device is the easiest approach, as there is built-in Solaris support for these SCSI devices. However, only standard, non-write-protected disks can be used. The steps for installation are similar for both the Zip and Jaz drives:

1. Set the SCSI ID switch to any ID that is not reserved.

2. Attach the Zip or Jaz Drive to your SCSI adapter or chain, and make sure it has power.

3. Create a device entry in /etc/format.dat by editing the file and inserting the following for a Zip drive:

```
disk_type="Zip 100"\
                        :ctlr=SCSI\
                        :ncyl=2406:acyl=2:pcyl=2408:nhead=2\
                        :nsect=40:rpm=3600:bpt=20480\
            partition="Zip 100"\
                        :disk="Zip 100":ctlr=SCSI\
                        :2=0,192480
                        :2=0,1159168
```

For a Jaz drive, enter the following information in /etc/format.dat:

```
disk_type="Jaz 1GB"\
                        :ctlr=SCSI\
                        :ncyl=1018:acyl=2:pcyl=1020:nhead=64\
                        :nsect=32:rpm=3600:bpt=16384
            partition="Jaz 1GB"\
                        :disk="Jaz 1GB":ctlr=SCSI\
                        :2=0,2084864
```

4. Perform a reconfiguration boot by typing:

```
ok boot -r
```

at the OpenBoot prompt, or by using these commands from a superuser shell:

```
server# touch /reconfigure
server# sync; sync; init 6
```

The drive should now be visible to the system. To actually use the drive to mount a volume, insert a Zip or Jaz disk into the drive prior to booting the system. After booting, run the format program:

```
server# format
```

Assuming that the **sd** number for your drive is 3, select this **sd** as the disk to be formatted. Create the appropriate partition using the **partition** option, and following the instructions given below for creating disk slices. Create an appropriate label for the volume, and quit the **format** program. Next, create a new file system on the drive by using the **newfs** command, for example:

```
server# newfs -v /dev/sd3c
```

After creating the file system, you can mount it by typing:

```
server# mount /dev/sd3c /mount_point
```

where **/mount_point** is something self-documenting (such as /zip or /jazz). This needs to be created before mounting by typing:

```
server# mkdir /zip
```

or:

```
server# mkdir /jazz
```

An alternative and more flexible approach is to use the ziptool program, which is available at **http://fy.chalmers.se/~appro/ziptool.html**. Ziptool supports all Zip and Jaz drive protection modes, and permits unconditional low-level formatting of protected disks, disk labeling, and volume management for Solaris 2.6 and greater. The program has to be executed with root privileges regardless of the access permissions set on SCSI disk device driver's entries in /devices. Consequently, if you want to let all users use it, it has to be installed as set-root-uid:

```
server# /usr/ucb/install -m 04755 -o root ziptool /usr/local/bin
```

However, you should note that running setuid programs has security implications. After downloading and unpacking the sources, the program can be compiled by:

```
server# gcc -o ziptool ziptool.c -lvolmgt
```

Of course, you will need to ensure that the path to libvolmgt.a is in your LD_ LIBRARY_PATH (usually /lib):

```
ziptool device command
```

where **device** must be the full name of a raw SCSI disk file, such as /dev/rsdk/c0t5d0s2, and **command** is one or more of:

- **rw**  Unlocks the Zip disk temporarily.
- **RW**  Unlocks the Zip disk permanently.
- **ro**  Puts the Zip disk into read-only mode.
- **RO**  Puts the Zip disk into a read-only mode that is password protected.
- **WR(*)**  Protects the disk by restricting reading and writing unless a password is entered.
- **eject**  Ejects the current Zip disk.
- **noeject**  Stops the Zip disk from being ejected.

Further information on installing Jaz and Zip drives can be found on the Iomega support web site:

**http://www.iomega.com/support/documents/4019.htmlhttp://www.iomega.com/support/documents/2019.html**

## Tape Drives

Solaris supports a wide variety of magnetic tapes using the remote magtape (**rmt**) protocol. Tapes are generally used as backup devices rather than as interactive storage devices. What they lack in availability, they definitely make up for in storage capacity. Many digital audio tape (DAT) drives have capacities of 24G, making it easy to perform a complete backup of many server systems on a single tape. This removes the need for late-night monitoring by operations staff to insert new tapes when full, as many administrators will have experienced in the past.

Device files for tape drives are found in the /dev/rmt directory. They are numbered sequentially from 0, so default drives will generally be available as /dev/rmt/0.

To back up to a remote drive, use the command **ufsdump**, which is an incremental file system dumping program. For example, to create a full backup of the /dev/rdsk/c0t1d0s1 file system to the tape system /dev/rmt/0, simply use the command:

```
example# ufsdump 0 /dev/rmt/0 /dev/rdsk/c0t1d0s1
```

This command specifies a level 0 (complete) dump of the file system, specifying the target drive and data source as /dev/rmt/0 and /dev/rdsk/c0t1d0s1, respectively.

## Floppy Disks

Floppy disk drives are usually standard on both SPARC and Intel architecture systems. In addition, using the Volume Manager, detecting and mounting floppy disks is straightforward. Insert the target disk into the drive, and use the command:

```
server# volcheck
```

This will check all volumes that are managed by volume management and will mount any valid file system that is found. The mount point for the floppy drive is determined by the settings in /etc/vfstab:

```
fd                           -                              /dev/fd
fd        -      no          -
```

Refer to the section on entering disk information into the virtual file system database for more details on configuring the /etc/vfstab file. A very useful feature of **volcheck** is to automatically check for new volumes, for example:

```
server# volcheck -i 60 -t 3600 /dev/diskette0 &
```

works in the background to check every minute if there is a floppy in the drive. However, this polling only takes place for one hour unless renewed.

# Serial Devices

Like any modern server system, Solaris supports the connection of simple external devices through both a serial (RS-232-C or RS-423) and parallel port. The two most common uses for serial devices on a SPARC system are connecting a VT-100 terminal or equivalent to operate as the system console if no graphics device is installed, and as a modem, enabling dial-up Internet access using the Point-to-Point Protocol (PPP). The former is a common practice in many server rooms, where the expense of a monitor and video card can be eliminated by using a VT-100 terminal as the console, as many SPARC machines require a display device to boot at all. On x86 systems, there are many more devices available that often only have drivers available for other operating systems. Sun and other third-party hardware vendors are slowly making releases available for these devices through the Solaris Developer Connection. If you need to obtain an updated copy of the Solaris Device Configuration Assistant, and any updated device drivers for supported external devices, these are currently available for download at **http://soldc.sun.com/support/drivers/boot.html**.

Unlike the other applications reviewed in this chapter for device configuration, Solaris has a graphical user interface (GUI) for serial device configuration, provided through the **admintool** program. **admintool** is generally used for system administration tasks such as adding users and groups. However, it also has facilities for configuring parallel devices such as printers and serial devices such as modems. It contains templates for configuring standard modem and terminal devices, and supports multiple ports (see Figure 7-3).

Central to the idea of providing services through serial ports is the port monitor, which continuously monitors the serial ports for requests to log in. The port monitor doesn't process the communication parameters directly, but accepts requests and passes them to the operating system. Newer releases of Solaris use the **ttymon** port monitor, which allows multiple concurrent **getty** requests from serial devices.

To configure the port for a terminal, start up **admintool**, and enter the user mode, which can be Basic, More, or Expert. Basic setup will be useful for most circumstances. **admintool** allows the configuration of most parameters for the port, including the baud rate for communications, default terminal type, flow control, and carrier detection. The values entered here should match those on the matching VT-100 terminal. Once the settings have been saved, it is possible to check the validity of the settings by using the **pmadm** command:

```
server# pmadm -l -s ttyb
```

Modem access can be configured to be inbound-only, outbound-only, or bidirectional, which allows traffic in both directions, using a similar scheme. To test the modem, use the **tip** command:

```
server# tip hardwire
```

**Figure 7-3.** *Managing serial devices using admintool*

**hardwire** should be defined /etc/remote. If the message:

```
connected
```

appears on your terminal, you've passed the first test. For Hayes-compatible modems, try to issue a command string like:

```
ATE1V1
```

If you see **ok**, the modem is communicating as expected and can now be configured to run PPP. More information about PPP and Solaris can be found at **ftp://cs.anu.edu.au/ pub/software/ppp**.

## Checking for Devices

Obtaining a listing of devices attached to a Solaris system is the best way to begin examining this important issue. In Solaris 8, obtaining system configuration information, including device information, can be made easy by using the print configuration (**prtconf**) command:

```
server% prtconf
```

on any SPARC or Intel architecture system. On an Ultra 5 workstation, the system configuration looks like:

```
SUNW,Ultra-5_10
    packages (driver not attached)
        terminal-emulator (driver not attached)
        deblocker (driver not attached)
        obp-tftp (driver not attached)
        disk-label (driver not attached)
        SUNW,builtin-drivers (driver not attached)
        sun-keyboard (driver not attached)
        ufs-file-system (driver not attached)
    chosen (driver not attached)
    openprom (driver not attached)
        client-services (driver not attached)
    options, instance #0
    aliases (driver not attached)
```

```
memory (driver not attached)
virtual-memory (driver not attached)
pci, instance #0
    pci, instance #0
        ebus, instance #0
            auxio (driver not attached)
            power (driver not attached)
            SUNW,pll (driver not attached)
            se, instance #0
            su, instance #0
            su, instance #1
            ecpp (driver not attached)
            fdthree (driver not attached)
            eeprom (driver not attached)
            flashprom (driver not attached)
            SUNW,CS4231, instance #0
        network, instance #0
        SUNW,m64B, instance #0
        ide, instance #0
            disk (driver not attached)
            cdrom (driver not attached)
            dad, instance #0
            atapicd, instance #2
    pci, instance #1
        pci, instance #0
            pci108e,1000 (driver not attached)
            SUNW,hme, instance #1
            SUNW,isptwo, instance #0
                sd (driver not attached)
                st (driver not attached)
SUNW,UltraSPARC-IIi (driver not attached)
pseudo, instance #0
```

Never panic about the message that a driver is "not attached" to a particular device. Since device drivers are only loaded on demand in Solaris, only those devices that are actively being used will have their drivers loaded. When a device is no longer being used, the device driver is unloaded from memory. This is a very efficient memory management strategy that optimizes the use of physical RAM by deallocating memory for devices when they are no longer required. In the case of the Ultra 5, we can see that devices such as the PCI bus and the IDE disk drives have attached device drivers and were being used while prtconf was running.

For an x86 system, the devices found are quite different:

```
System Configuration: Sun Microsystems i86pc
Memory size: 128 Megabytes
System Peripherals (Software Nodes):
i86pc
    +boot (driver not attached)
        memory (driver not attached)
    aliases (driver not attached)
    chosen (driver not attached)
    i86pc-memory (driver not attached)
    i86pc-mmu (driver not attached)
    openprom (driver not attached)
    options, instance #0
    packages (driver not attached)
    delayed-writes (driver not attached)
    itu-props (driver not attached)
    isa, instance #0
        motherboard (driver not attached)
        asy, instance #0
        lp (driver not attached)
        asy, instance #1
        fdc, instance #0
            fd, instance #0
            fd, instance #1 (driver not attached)
        kd (driver not attached)
        bios (driver not attached)
        bios (driver not attached)
        pnpCTL,0041 (driver not attached)
        pnpCTL,7002 (driver not attached)
        kd, instance #0
        chanmux, instance #0
    pci, instance #0
        pci8086,1237 (driver not attached)
        pci8086,7000 (driver not attached)
        pci-ide, instance #0
            ata, instance #0
                cmdk, instance #0
                sd, instance #1
        pci10ec,8029 (driver not attached)
        pci5333,8901 (driver not attached)
```

```
used-resources (driver not attached)
objmgr, instance #0
pseudo, instance #0
```

# At Boot Time

The OpenBoot monitor has the ability to diagnose hardware errors on system devices before booting the kernel. This can be particularly useful for identifying bus connectivity issues such as unterminated SCSI chains, and some basic functional issues such as whether or not devices are responding. Issuing the command:

```
ok reset
```

will also force a self-test of the system.

Just after booting, it is useful to review the system boot messages, which can be retrieved by using the **dmesg** command. This displays a list of all devices that were successfully attached at boot time and also displays any error messages that were detected. Let's look at the **dmesg** output for a SPARC Ultra architecture system:

```
server# dmesg
Jan 17 13:06
cpu0: SUNW,UltraSPARC-IIi (upaid 0 impl 0x12 ver 0x12 clock 270 MHz)
SunOS Release 5.8 Version Generic_103640-19 [UNIX(R) System V Release
4.0]
Copyright (c) 1983-1996, Sun Microsystems, Inc.
mem = 131072K (0x8000000)
avail mem = 127852544
Ethernet address = 8:0:20:90:b3:23
root nexus = Sun Ultra 5/10 UPA/PCI (UltraSPARC-IIi 270MHz)
pci0 at root: UPA 0x1f 0x0
PCI-device: pci@1,1, simba #0
PCI-device: pci@1, simba #1
dad0 at pci1095,6460 target 0 lun 0
dad0 is /pci@1f,0/pci@1,1/ide@3/dad@0,0
        <Seagate Medalist 34342A cyl 8892 alt 2 hd 15 sec 63>
root on /pci@1f,0/pci@1,1/ide@3/disk@0,0:a fstype ufs
su0 at ebus0: offset 14,3083f8
su0 is /pci@1f,0/pci@1,1/ebus@1/su@14,3083f8
su1 at ebus0: offset 14,3062f8
su1 is /pci@1f,0/pci@1,1/ebus@1/su@14,3062f8
keyboard is </pci@1f,0/pci@1,1/ebus@1/su@14,3083f8> major <37> minor <0>
```

```
mouse is </pci@1f,0/pci@1,1/ebus@1/su@14,3062f8> major <37> minor <1>
stdin is </pci@1f,0/pci@1,1/ebus@1/su@14,3083f8> major <37> minor <0>
SUNW,m64B0 is /pci@1f,0/pci@1,1/SUNW,m64B@2
m64#0: 1280x1024, 2M mappable, rev 4754.9a
stdout is </pci@1f,0/pci@1,1/SUNW,m64B@2> major <8> minor <0>
boot cpu (0) initialization complete - online
se0 at ebus0: offset 14,400000
se0 is /pci@1f,0/pci@1,1/ebus@1/se@14,400000
SUNW,hme0: CheerIO 2.0 (Rev Id = c1) Found
SUNW,hme0 is /pci@1f,0/pci@1,1/network@1,1
SUNW,hme1: Local Ethernet address = 8:0:20:93:b0:65
pci1011,240: SUNW,hme1
SUNW,hme1 is /pci@1f,0/pci@1/pci@1/SUNW,hme@0,1
dump on /dev/dsk/c0t0d0s1 size 131328K
SUNW,hme0: Using Internal Transceiver
SUNW,hme0: 10 Mbps half-duplex Link Up
pcmcia: no PCMCIA adapters found
```

**dmesg** first performs a memory test, sets the Ethernet address for the network
interface, and then initializes the PCI bus. An IDE disk is recognized and mapped into
a physical device, and the appropriate partitions are activated. The standard input
devices (keyboard and mouse) are activated, and the boot sequence is largely complete.
However, the output is slightly different for the x86 system:

```
Jan 17 08:32
SunOS Release 5.8 Version Generic [UNIX(R) System V Release 4.0]
Copyright (c) 1983-1998, Sun Microsystems, Inc.
mem = 130688K (0x7fa0000)
avail mem = 114434048
root nexus = i86pc
isa0 at root
pci0 at root: space 0 offset 0
        IDE device at targ 0, lun 0 lastlun 0x0
        model ST310230A, stat 50, err 0
                cfg 0xc5a, cyl 16383, hd 16, sec/trk 63
                mult1 0x8010, mult2 0x110, dwcap 0x0, cap 0x2f00
                piomode 0x200, dmamode 0x200, advpiomode 0x3
                minpio 240, minpioflow 120
                valid 0x7, dwdma 0x407, majver 0x1e
ata_set_feature: (0x66,0x0) failed
        ATAPI device at targ 1, lun 0 lastlun 0x0
```

```
        model CD-912E/ATK, stat 50, err 0
                cfg 0x85a0, cyl 0, hd 0, sec/trk 0
                mult1 0x0, mult2 0x0, dwcap 0x0, cap 0xb00
                piomode 0x200, dmamode 0x200, advpiomode 0x1
                minpio 209, minpioflow 180
                valid 0x2, dwdma 0x203, majver 0x0
PCI-device: ata@0, ata0
ata0 is /pci@0,0/pci-ide@7,1/ata@0
Disk0:  <Vendor 'Gen-ATA ' Product 'ST310230A          '>
cmdk0 at ata0 target 0 lun 0
cmdk0 is /pci@0,0/pci-ide@7,1/ata@0/cmdk@0,0
root on /pci@0,0/pci-ide@7,1/ide@0/cmdk@0,0:a fstype ufs
ISA-device: asy0
asy0 is /isa/asy@1,3f8
ISA-device: asy1
asy1 is /isa/asy@1,2f8
Number of console virtual screens = 13
cpu 0 initialization complete - online
dump on /dev/dsk/c0d0s3 size 156 MB
```

## While the System Is Up

If you are working remotely on a server system, and you are unsure of the system architecture, the command:

```
server# arch -k uname -m does the same
```

returns **sun4u** on the Ultra 5 system, but **sun4m** on a SPARC 10 system. For a complete view of a system's device configuration, you may also wish to try the **sysdef** command, which displays more detailed information concerning pseudo devices, kernel loadable modules, and parameters. Here's the **sysdef** output for an x86 server:

```
server# sysdef
# sysdef
*
* Hostid
*
  0ae61183
*
* i86pc Configuration
*
```

```
*
* Devices
*
+boot (driver not attached)
        memory (driver not attached)
aliases (driver not attached)
chosen (driver not attached)
i86pc-memory (driver not attached)
i86pc-mmu (driver not attached)
openprom (driver not attached)
options, instance #0
packages (driver not attached)
delayed-writes (driver not attached)
itu-props (driver not attached)
isa, instance #0
        motherboard (driver not attached)
        asy, instance #0
        lp (driver not attached)
        asy, instance #1
        fdc, instance #0
                fd, instance #0
                fd, instance #1 (driver not attached)
        kd (driver not attached)
        bios (driver not attached)
        bios (driver not attached)
        pnpCTL,0041 (driver not attached)
        pnpCTL,7002 (driver not attached)
        kd, instance #0
        chanmux, instance #0
pci, instance #0
        pci8086,1237 (driver not attached)
        pci8086,7000 (driver not attached)
        pci-ide, instance #0
                ata, instance #0
                        cmdk, instance #0
                        sd, instance #1
        pci10ec,8029 (driver not attached)
        pci5333,8901 (driver not attached)
used-resources (driver not attached)
objmgr, instance #0
pseudo, instance #0
        clone, instance #0
        ip, instance #0
```

```
        tcp, instance #0
        udp, instance #0
        log, instance #0
        sad, instance #0
        iwscn, instance #0
        mm, instance #0
        tl, instance #0
        cn, instance #0
        openeepr, instance #0
        kstat, instance #0
        pm, instance #0
        sy, instance #0
        vol, instance #0
        xsvc, instance #0
        ptm, instance #0
        pts, instance #0
        devinfo, instance #0
        ksyms, instance #0
*
* Loadable Objects
*
* Loadable Object Path = /platform/i86pc/kernel
*
drv/eisa
drv/isa
drv/mc
drv/openeepr
drv/pci
drv/rootnex
mach/uppc
misc/bootdev
misc/emul_80387
misc/pci_autoconfig
mmu/mmu32
unix
drv/aha
drv/asy
drv/chanmux
drv/cnft
drv/elx
drv/fd
drv/fdc
drv/kd
```

```
drv/kdmouse
drv/logi
drv/lp
drv/mlx
drv/msm
drv/smartii
drv/smc
drv/tr
misc/mse
drv/eha
drv/ata
drv/dpt
drv/mscsi
drv/pci-ide
drv/sbpro
drv/mcis
strmod/ansi
strmod/char
strmod/emap
strmod/vuid2ps2
strmod/vuid3ps2
strmod/vuidkd
strmod/vuidm3p
strmod/vuidm4p
strmod/vuidm5p
*
* Loadable Object Path = /kernel
*
strmod/hwc
exec/coffexec
misc/kgssapi
misc/cis
misc/cs
misc/pcalloc
misc/pcmcia
misc/dadk
misc/gda
misc/sccd_audio
misc/scdk
misc/snlb
misc/strategy
misc/sysinit
misc/rpcsec_gss
```

```
drv/arp
        hard link:   strmod/arp
drv/clone
drv/cn
drv/devinfo
drv/i2o_bs
drv/i2o_scsi
drv/icmp
drv/ip
drv/iwscn
drv/llc1
drv/log
drv/mm
drv/options
drv/pci_to_i2o
drv/profile
drv/pseudo
drv/ptc
drv/ptsl
drv/rts
drv/sad
drv/st
drv/sy
drv/tcp
drv/tl
drv/udp
drv/wc
fs/cachefs
fs/fifofs
fs/hsfs
fs/lofs
fs/nfs
        hard link:   sys/nfs
fs/procfs
fs/sockfs
fs/specfs
fs/tmpfs
fs/ufs
sched/TS
sched/TS_DPTBL
sys/c2audit
sys/doorfs
sys/inst_sync
```

```
sys/kaio
sys/msgsys
sys/pipe
sys/pset
sys/semsys
sys/shmsys
drv/pci_pci
drv/adp
drv/aic
drv/blogic
drv/chs
drv/corvette
drv/cpqncr
drv/csa
drv/dnet
drv/eepro
drv/elxl
drv/esa
drv/flashpt
drv/iee
drv/ieef
drv/iprb
drv/mega
drv/mtok
drv/ncrs
drv/nee
drv/nei
drv/nfe
drv/p9000
drv/p9100
drv/pcn
drv/pcscsi
drv/pe
drv/sd
drv/smce
drv/smceu
drv/smcf
drv/spwr
drv/trantor
drv/xsvc
mach/ast
mach/compaq
```

```
mach/corollary
mach/pcplusmp
mach/syspro
mach/tpf
mach/wysemp
fs/autofs
drv/pcic
drv/pcs
drv/pem
drv/ra
drv/pcelx
drv/pcmem
drv/pcram
drv/pcser
drv/cmdk
drv/objmgr
drv/pcata
exec/elfexec
exec/intpexec
genunix
misc/consconfig
misc/des
misc/gld
misc/i2o_msg
misc/ipc
misc/klmmod
misc/klmops
misc/krtld
misc/md5
misc/nfs_dlboot
misc/nfssrv
misc/rpcsec
misc/scsi
misc/seg_drv
misc/seg_mapdev
misc/strplumb
misc/swapgeneric
misc/tlimod
misc/ufs_log
strmod/bufmod
strmod/connld
strmod/dedump
```

```
strmod/ldterm
strmod/pckt
strmod/pfmod
strmod/pipemod
strmod/ptem
strmod/redirmod
strmod/rpcmod
        hard link:  sys/rpcmod
strmod/timod
strmod/tirdwr
strmod/ttcompat
*
* Loadable Object Path = /usr/kernel
*
exec/javaexec
fs/fdfs
fs/namefs
fs/pcfs
fs/s5fs
misc/diaudio
strmod/eucu8
strmod/u8euc
strmod/u8koi8
strmod/u8lat1
strmod/u8lat2
strmod/rlmod
strmod/telmod
sched/IA
sched/RT
sched/RT_DPTBL
sys/sysacct
drv/audiocs
drv/dump
drv/kstat
drv/ksyms
drv/lockstat
drv/logindmux
drv/ptm
drv/pts
drv/winlock
drv/pm
```

```
drv/tnf
drv/vol
*
* System Configuration
*
  SWAP files
SWAPfile            dev  swaplo blocks   free
/dev/dsk/c0d0s3    102,3      8 321288 321288
```

The key sections in the **sysdef** output are details of all devices, such as the PCI bus, and pseudo devices for each loadable object path (including /kernel and /usr/kernel). Loadable objects are also identified, along with SWAP and virtual memory settings. Although the output may seem verbose, the information provided for each device can prove to be very useful in tracking down hardware errors or missing loadable objects.

# Adding Devices

In many cases, adding new devices to a Solaris system is straightforward, as most devices connect to the SCSI bus, which is a standard interface. The steps involved are usually preparing the system for a reconfiguration boot, powering down the system, connecting the hardware device and noting the SCSI device number, powering on the system, and using the **format** command if necessary to create a file system. In this section, we examine the procedure for adding disks to both SPARC and Intel architecture machines, and highlight potential problems that may occur.

## Hard Disks

Hard disk installation and configuration on Solaris is often more complicated than other UNIX systems. However, this complexity is necessary to support the sophisticated hardware operations typically undertaken by Solaris systems. For example, Linux refers to hard disks using a simple BSD-style scheme: /dev/hd$n$ are the IDE hard disks on a system, and /dev/sd$n$ are the SCSI hard disks on a system, where $n$ refers to the hard disk number. A system with two IDE hard disks and two SCSI hard disks will therefore have the following device files configured:

```
/dev/hda
/dev/hdb
/dev/sda
/dev/sdb
```

Partitions created on each drive are also sequentially numbered; if /dev/hda is the boot disk, it may contain several partitions on the disk, reflecting the basic UNIX system directories:

```
/dev/hda1 (/ partition)
/dev/hda2 (/usr)
/dev/hda3 (/var)
/dev/hda4 (swap)
```

Instead of simply referring to the disk type, disk number, and partition number, the device filename for each partition (slice) on a Solaris disk contains four identifiers: controller (c), target (t), disk (d), and slice (s). Thus, the device file:

```
/dev/dsk/c0t3d0s0
```

identifies slice 0 of disk 0, controller 0 at SCSI target ID 3. To complicate matters further, disk device files exist in both the /dev/dsk and /dev/rdsk directories, which correspond to block device and raw device entries, respectively. Raw and block devices refer to the same physical partition, but are used in different contexts. Using raw devices only allows operations of small amounts of data, whereas a buffer can be used with a block device to increase the data read size. It is not always clear whether to use a block or raw device interface. However, low-level system commands (like the **fsck** command, which performs disk maintenance) typically use raw device interfaces, whereas commands that operate on the entire disk (such as **df**, which reports disk usage) will most likely use block devices.

To install a new hard drive on a Solaris system, just follow these steps:

1. Prepare the system for a reconfiguration boot by issuing the command:

   ```
   server# touch /reconfigure
   ```

2. Synchronize disk data, and power down the system using the commands:

   ```
   server# sync; sync; sync; shutdown
   ```

3. Switch off power to the system, and attach the new hard disk to the external SCSI chain, or install it internally into an appropriate disk bay.

4. Check that the SCSI device ID does not conflict with any existing SCSI devices. If a conflict exists, simply change the ID using the switch.

5. Power up the system, and use the boot command to load the kernel, if the OpenBoot monitor appears:

   ```
   ok boot
   ```

The next step, assuming you have decided which partitions you want to create on your drive using the information supplied previously, is to run the **format** program.

In addition to creating slices, **format** also displays information about existing disks and slices and can be used to repair a faulty disk. When **format** is invoked without a command-line argument:

```
server# format
```

it displays the current disks, and asks the administrator to enter the number of the disk to format. Selecting a disk for formatting at this point is nondestructive, so even if you make a mistake, you can always exit the **format** program without damaging data. For example, on a SPARC-20 system with three 1.05G SCSI disks, **format** opens with the screen:

```
Searching for disks...done
AVAILABLE DISK SELECTIONS:
0. c0t1d0 <SUN1.05 cyl 2036 alt 2 hd 14 sec 72>
/iommu@f,e0000000/sbus@f,e0001000/espdma@f,400000/esp@f,800000/
sd@1,0
1. c0t2d0 <SUN1.05 cyl 2036 alt 2 hd 14 sec 72>
/iommu@f,e0000000/sbus@f,e0001000/espdma@f,400000/esp@f,800000/
sd@2,0
2. c0t3d0 <SUN1.05 cyl 2036 alt 2 hd 14 sec 72>
/iommu@f,e0000000/sbus@f,e0001000/espdma@f,400000/esp@f,800000/
sd@3,0
Specify disk (enter its number):
```

It is also possible to pass a command-line option to **format** comprising the disk (or disks) to be formatted, for example:

```
# format /dev/rdsk/c0t2d0
```

After selecting the appropriate disk, the message:

```
[disk formatted]
```

will appear if the disk has previously been formatted. This is an important message, as it is a common mistake to misidentify a target disk from the available selection of both formatted and unformatted disks. The menu looks like:

```
FORMAT MENU:
        disk      - select a disk
        type      - select (define) a disk type
```

```
        partition  - select (define) a partition table
        current    - describe the current disk
        format     - format and analyze the disk
        fdisk      - run the fdisk program
        repair     - repair a defective sector
        show       - translate a disk address
        label      - write label to the disk
        analyze    - surface analysis
        defect     - defect list management
        backup     - search for backup labels
        verify     - read and display labels
        save       - save new disk/partition definitions
        volname    - set 8-character volume name
        !<cmd>     - execute <cmd>, then return
        quit
format>
```

If the disk has not been formatted, the first step is to prepare the disk to accommodate slices and file systems by formatting the disk. Do this by issuing the **format** command:

```
format> format
Ready to format. Formatting cannot be interrupted
and takes 15 minutes (estimated). Continue? yes
```

The purpose of formatting is to identify defective blocks and mark them as bad, and generally to verify that the disk is operational from a hardware perspective. Once this has been completed, new slices can be created and sized by using the **partition** option at the main menu:

```
format> partition
```

In this case, we want to create a new slice 5 on disk 0 at target 3, which will be used to store user files when mounted as /export/home, and corresponding to block device /dev/dsk/c0t3d0s5. After determining the maximum amount of space available, enter that size in gigabytes (in this case, 1.05G) when requested to do so by the **format** program for slice 5 (enter 0 for the other slices). If the disk is not labeled, you will also be prompted to enter a label containing details of the disk's current slices, which is useful for recovering data. This is an important step, as the operating system will not be able to find any newly created slices unless the volume is labeled. To view the disk label, use the **prtvtoc** command. Here's the output from the primary drive in an x86 system:

```
# prtvtoc /dev/dsk/c0d0s2
* /dev/dsk/c0d0s2 partition map
*
* Dimensions:
*     512 bytes/sector
*      63 sectors/track
*     255 tracks/cylinder
*   16065 sectors/cylinder
*    1020 cylinders
*    1018 accessible cylinders
*
* Flags:
*   1: unmountable
*  10: read-only
*
*                          First     Sector    Last
* Partition  Tag  Flags    Sector    Count     Sector   Mount Directory
        0     2    00       48195     160650    208844   /
        1     7    00      208845      64260    273104   /var
        2     5    00           0   16354170  16354169
        3     3    01      273105     321300    594404
        6     4    00      594405    1317330   1911734   /usr
        7     8    00     1911735   14442435  16354169   /export/home
        8     1    01           0      16065      16064
        9     9    01       16065      32130      48194
```

The disk label contains a full partition table, which can be printed for each disk using the **print** command:

```
format> print
```

For our 1.05G disk, the partition table will look like:

```
Part Tag Flag Cylinders Size Blocks
0 root wm 0 0 (0/0/0) 0
1 swap wu 0 0 (0/0/0) 0
```

```
2 backup wm 0 - 3732 (3732/0/0) 2089920
3 unassigned wm 0 0 (0/0/0) 0
4 unassigned wm 0 0 (0/0/0) 0
5 home wm 0 - 3732 1075MB (3732/0/0) 2089920
6 usr wm 0 0 (0/0/0) 0
7 unassigned wm 0 0 (0/0/0) 0
```

After saving the changes to the disk's partition table, exit the **format** program, and create a new UFS file system on the target slice using the **newfs** command:

```
server# newfs /dev/rdsk/c0t3d0s5
```

After a new file system is constructed, it is ready to be mounted. First a mount point is created:

```
server# mkdir /export/home
```

followed by the appropriate mount command:

```
server# mount /dev/dsk/c0t3d0s5 /export/home
```

At this point, the disk is available to the system for the current session. However, if you want the disk to be available after reboot, it is necessary to create an entry in the virtual file systems table, which is created from /etc/vfstab file. An entry like:

```
/dev/dsk/c0t3d0s5 /dev/rdsk/c0t3d0s5 /export/home ufs 2 yes -
```

contains details of the slice's block and raw devices, the mount point, the file system type, instructions for **fsck**, and most importantly, a flag to force mount at boot.

For an x86 system, the output of **format** looks slightly different, given the differences in the way that devices are denoted:

```
AVAILABLE DISK SELECTIONS:
       0. c0d0 <DEFAULT cyl 1018 alt 2 hd 255 sec 63>
          /pci@0,0/pci-ide@7,1/ata@0/cmdk@0,0
Specify disk (enter its number):
```

The partition table is similar to that for the SPARC architecture systems:

```
partition> print
Current partition table (original):
Total disk cylinders available: 1018 + 2 (reserved cylinders)

Part        Tag    Flag     Cylinders        Size          Blocks
  0        root    wm       3 -    12       78.44MB    (10/0/0)       160650
  1         var    wm      13 -    16       31.38MB    (4/0/0)         64260
  2      backup    wm       0 -  1017        7.80GB    (1018/0/0)   16354170
  3        SWAP    wu      17 -    36      156.88MB    (20/0/0)       321300
  4  unassigned    wm       0                    0    (0/0/0)             0
  5  unassigned    wm       0                    0    (0/0/0)             0
  6         usr    wm      37 -   118      643.23MB    (82/0/0)      1317330
  7        home    wm     119 -  1017        6.89GB    (899/0/0)    14442435
  8        boot    wu       0 -     0        7.84MB    (1/0/0)         16065
  9  alternates    wu       1 -     2       15.69MB    (2/0/0)         32130
```

# CD-ROMs

CD-ROMs are supported directly by the operating system in SPARC architectures and do not require any special configuration other than the usual process of initializing the system for a reconfiguration reboot, powering down the system, attaching the CD-ROM device to the SCSI bus, and powering on the system. It is not necessary to use **format** or **newfs** to read the files on the CD-ROM, nor is it usually necessary to manually mount the file system, as the volume manager (**vold**) is usually enabled on server systems. **vold** is covered in detail in Chapter 8.

A common problem for Solaris x86 users is that there are few tested and supported CD-ROM brands for installing the operating system (although most fully compliant ATA/ATAPI CD-ROMs should work). The older Sound Blaster IDE interface for CD-ROMs does not appear to be suitable, although support may be included in a later release (the Alternate Status register is apparently not implemented on the main integrated circuit for the controller board). It is always best to check the current Hardware Compatibility List (HCL).

# CD-Rs and CD-RWs

Solaris supports both readable and writable CDs. In addition to the CD-R (CD-Readable) format, Solaris also supports CD-RW (CD-ReWritable), previously known as CD-Erasable. It is a new optical disc specification created by the industry organization OSTA (**http://www.osta.org/**). You can hook up many SCSI CD-R and CD-RW devices to a SPARC system to SCSI device ID 6, and they will function as normal CD-ROM drives. Although the technical ability to support any SCSI-based device is a given for the operating system, a potentially limiting factor for nonstandard hardware is finding software to adequately support it. Luckily, there are many different open source and commercial editions of CD-recording software available for the Solaris platform. To obtain support for both Solaris 1.x and 2.x, the best application is **cdrecord**, by Jörg Schilling, which can be downloaded from **ftp://ftp.fokus.gmd.de/pub/unix/cdrecord/**. It is freeware and makes use of the real-time scheduler in later versions of Solaris 2. **cdrecord** also compiles on the Solaris-x86 platform and can create both music and data discs. It has a rather clunky command-line interface; however, it has more features than many of the commercial systems, including the following options:

- **-dummy**   The ability to simulate a recording for test purposes.
- **-multi**   Using a single CD for multiple recording sessions.
- **-fix**   Manually fixing the disk, if you want to view data from an open session on a normal CD-ROM.
- **-speed**   Setting the recording speed factor.

If you prefer a commercial system, GEAR for UNIX is also available (**http://www.gearcdr.com/html/products/gear/unix/index.html**), as well as Creative Digital Research's CDR Publisher (**http://www.cdr1.com/**), which is available through Sun's Catalyst program.

# Summary

In Solaris, devices are represented by files that are visible to all users, which makes it easier to understand how physical devices are mapped into logical devices by the operating system. The sophisticated methods Solaris uses to refer to both physical and logical devices can seem daunting at first, especially if you are used to referring to disk drives as "C:" or "D:". But the extra work is worth the effort when setting up server systems like the E450, which may have 20 or more internal disks, combined with fast, external storage in the form of an A1000 RAID system. Keeping track of the many different kinds of storage and devices can be made easier by learning the basics of device nomenclature as outlined in this chapter.

# How to Find Out More

For updated device drivers for Solaris x86 systems, see the resource center at **http://soldc.sun.com/support/drivers/boot.html**. Alternatively, for more information on the CD-recording process, check out Andy McFadden's CD-ROM FAQ.

# Chapter 8

# Basic File System
# Management

A file system provides a convenient method for organizing and storing files. The primary file system on Solaris is the UNIX File System (UFS), which was developed in the early 1980s and derives from the BSD environment. A file system is the interface that the user interacts with through the operating system. The file systems are defined on partitions. Partitions themselves are defined on disks. It is only when the partitions get defined on disks that file systems can be defined.

In this chapter we will first look at the structure of a hard disk and describe the "classical" strategy for storing files and directories on disk and the UFS improvements to that strategy. Once we have examined the basic concepts of UFS, we will cover the Virtual File System Interface, which abstracts the UNIX file system concepts to allow Solaris machines to access distributed file systems and file systems from operating systems like DOS. The second section of this chapter describes the process of formatting, partitioning, and creating a UFS file system, while the third section covers the commands used to enable access to a file system.

# File System Basics

File systems are software programs that allow you to efficiently organize data on a *hard disk* or other physical media. A hard disk is made out of one or more magnetic disks, called *platters*, which rotate around a central shaft. Each platter contains millions of magnetic particles, whose magnetic field determines whether or not any information is stored there. For each platter there is a movable arm that extends from the outer edge of the disk to the central shaft. At the end of each arm is a read-and-write head that can access any point on the disk surface. All of the arms are connected together so that they move in unison.

Each platter contains a set of *blocks* or *sectors*, which are used to store data. The blocks are organized into circular rings called *tracks*. Tracks on different platters that are located at the same distance from the edge of their respective disk platter are referred to as a *cylinder*. Since all the tracks of a cylinder are accessed by the read-and-write heads of the hard drive simultaneously, the delay for accessing data stored on different platters but in the same cylinder can be quite a bit smaller than if the data was located in different cylinders. The basic structure of a hard drive is illustrated in Figure 8-1.

## Special Disk Blocks

A file system treats the whole set of physical disk blocks as a linear string of data, where each block can be accessed by knowing its address. Although most of the blocks in a disk are used for data, some of the blocks have special purposes. The disk partition for UFS file system is represented in Figure 8-2. The partition consists of cylinder groups, which are a number of contiguous cylinders on a disk. During the discussion on boot blocks you will find a reference to inodes. Inodes are simply Information nodes that provide detailed information on files such as their owner, size, etc. The beginning of the disk contains the boot block containing the necessary information to bring the UNIX system into operation.

SYSTEM MAINTENANCE

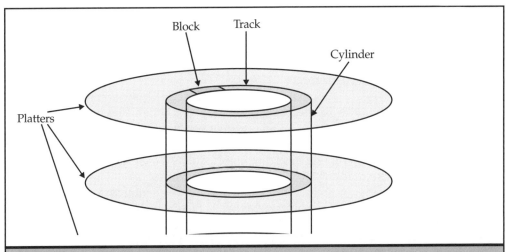

**Figure 8-1.**    *Basic hard drive structure*

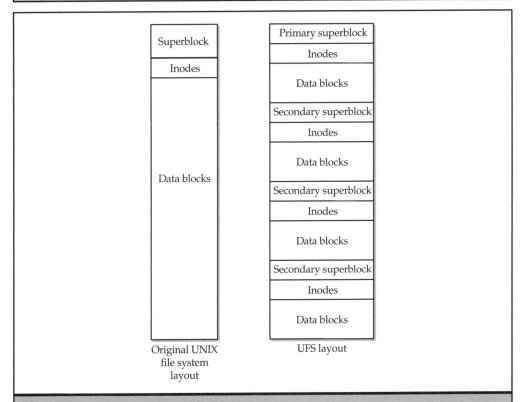

**Figure 8-2.**    *Layout of the UNIX file system*

If the file system is not bootable then the boot block is left unused. In UFS following the boot block is a sequence of repeating blocks throughout the disk partition. This repeating block consists of the following:

Superblock: The superblock contains information about the disk geometry and a list of free-blocks and inodes (Information nodes). Because of the importance of this block, multiple copies of the superblock are maintained for file system integrity. The information contained in the superblock is static.

Cylinder group summary block: The cylinder group block keeps a summary of the following: the size of the file system; the number of inodes and data blocks; pointers to the last block, fragment, and inode used; the number of available fragments; the used inode map; and the free inode map.

Inode table: Defines the inodes for the cylinder group. Inodes are assigned one per file. Each Inode Block consists of ownership, timestamps (creation, modification, access), size, number of hard links, and location of data block information for that file.

Data block: The data block contains data pertaining to files. The physical size of the data block depends on the way the file system was created. UFS makes an attempt to place data blocks within a cylinder group.

## The Superblock

The superblock contains information about the file system as a whole. Specifically, it contains information about:

- the size of the file system
- the number of free blocks, the list of free blocks, and the index for the next one
- the number of free inodes, the size of the inode list, and the index for the next one

Originally the list of free blocks was stored as a linked list, but over time the linked list proved to have poor performance. UFS replaced the linked list with a bitmap (a large array of integers, where each entry can have the value 0 or 1). In order to locate a set of free blocks, the system looks for a consecutive number of blocks that are marked as unallocated (free). For example, if 0 indicates allocated and 1 indicates free, the following bitmap describes a disk that that has its first six blocks allocated and the last two blocks free:

```
00000011
```

On a real disk the bitmap will be much larger, since it stores information for every block on the disk.

Another improvement in UFS over the original UNIX file system is the replication of the primary superblock at several different points in the disk. In the original UNIX file systems, if a disk crash damaged the first or second blocks of a disk, all the data on the disk was lost. UFS eliminates this possibility by storing copies of the superblock at several different points on the disk. The superblock located in the first or second sector of the disk is called the *primary superblock,* while the duplicate superblocks are called *secondary superblocks.* Even if the primary superblock is damaged by a disk crash, it is possible to recover a UFS disk by using any secondary superblock.

The secondary superblocks are stored one per cylinder group and placed at a varying offset from the beginning of a cylinder group in order to safeguard against a crash that could destroy the superblock data. The offsets for the secondary superblocks are calculated based on the location of the superblock in the previous cylinder group: Each secondary superblock is placed one track further from the beginning of the cylinder group than the superblock in the preceding cylinder group. This scheme allows UFS to ensure that information will not be lost due to corruption of a single track, cylinder, or platter. The exact locations of the secondary superblocks on a hard drive are determined when you create a UFS file system using the **newfs** command as explained later in this chapter.

## Inodes

Following the superblock is a set of blocks called inodes that contain information about the files and directories stored in the data blocks. The primary contents of an inode are a set of pointers to the locations of the file's data blocks on disk. For this reason, inodes are involved in every action performed on a file or directory. When a file or directory is opened, closed, read, or written, its inode is accessed. Depending on the size of a file, its data might be reached through pointers to *direct* blocks or *indirect* blocks. Direct blocks are pointers to actual data blocks, whereas indirect blocks are pointers to a block containing pointers to data blocks. UFS supports triple indirect blocks for supporting extremely large files. Double indirect blocks (two pointers) are basically a pointer that points to another block that in turn points to the data block. Similarly, a triple indirect block consists of three pointers. Figure 8-3 illustrates the structure of an inode and the direct and indirect blocks.

In addition to the pointers to the data blocks, the inode contains the following information about files and directories:

- mode and type
- owner and group
- size in bytes
- last accessed and modified times

Some of the information about a file, such as its permissions, owner, and group, can be modified by such tools as **chmod, chown,** and **chgrp**. Other information, like a file's type and its size in bytes, is controlled by the file system and cannot be modified directly. The one piece of information that is not stored in an inode is the *name* of the file or directory. This information is stored in the data blocks of the directory in which the file or directory is located.

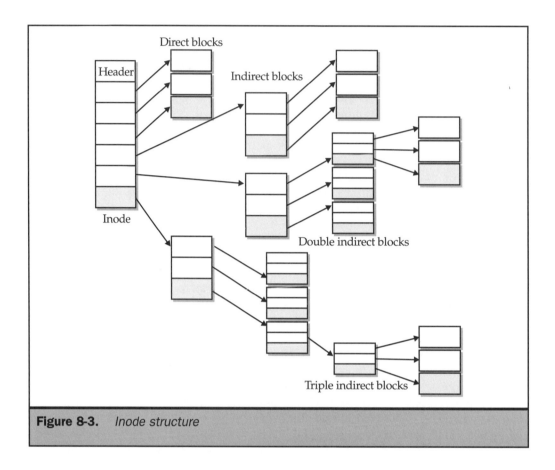

**Figure 8-3.**   *Inode structure*

# The Virtual File System Interface

Until the early version of Solaris, SunOS primarily supported UFS and the Network File System (NFS). There were some add-ons for accessing floppy disks formatted for use on DOS systems. To add a new type of file system required extensive modifications to the kernel and related system utilities. In an effort to simplify this process, Solaris introduced the concept of the Virtual File System Interface (VFS). VFS is based on the virtual inode, referred to as *vnode*, which abstracts the operations that can be performed by the kernel on an inode. In VFS, every time a file is opened, closed, read, or written, the vnode for the file is accessed instead of its inode. This layer of abstraction allows for different file systems to be written as modules that the kernel can access without having to know any details about the file system's implementation. In addition to UFS and NFS, the most common file systems that were implemented using VFS are the High Sierra File System (HSFS), PC File System (PCFS), proc File System, and the tmp File System.

## High Sierra File System (HSFS)

The High Sierra File System (HSFS) is the standard file system used for accessing CD-ROMs under Solaris. It is based on the ISO 9660 standard that defines a common data interchange format for CD-ROMs. CD-ROMs formatted using the ISO 9660 specification can be read by all UNIX, Macintosh, DOS, and Windows systems. In addition to implementing the ISO 9660 standard, HSFS incorporates two UNIX-specific extensions called High Sierra and Rock-Ridge, which will be covered shortly.

Files on a High Sierra or ISO 9660 CD-ROM have names in the following form:

*filename.ext;version*

Here *filename* and the optional *.ext* make up the name of the file. Both *filename* and *ext* can consist in a sequence of uppercase alphanumeric characters and _ (underscore) characters. The *version* consists of a sequence of digits that represents the version number of the file. The *filename* is limited to 28 characters, while *ext* is limited to three characters; that allows up to 32 characters in all for a full filename, dot, and extension. When the name of a file is listed, HSFS converts all the uppercase characters in *filename* and *ext* to lowercase, and discards the ; character and *version*. If HSFS finds more than one version of a file, it allows access only to the file with the highest *version*.

All of the files on a High Sierra or ISO 9660 CD-ROM are mapped to have a UID of 0, a GID of 3, and a file mode of 555. This allows all the files on a High Sierra or ISO 9660 CD-ROM to be read and executed by all users on the system. Also, High Sierra and ISO 9660 CD-ROMs only support regular files and directories. These limitations do not apply to CD-ROMs that use the Rock-Ridge extensions.

Rock-Ridge is a set of extensions to the High Sierra and ISO 9660 standards that allow CD-ROMs to support the full range of UNIX file information. CD-ROMs formatted with Rock-Ridge extensions can have file and directory names that contain any character supported under UFS. Also, the filenames are case sensitive, and may contain any combination of upper and lowercase characters. Filename lengths can be as long as those under UFS. On Rock-Ridge CD-ROMs, files and directories can have any permission supported under UFS. The write permissions on files are ignored, due to the read-only nature of CD-ROMs. Rock-Ridge CD-ROMS can support regular files, directories, symbolic links, and device nodes such as block and character files.

## PC File System (PCFS)

The PC File System (PCFS) allows for read and write access to DOS-formatted file systems. PCFS allows you to access a DOS file system under Solaris and manipulate it using standard UNIX commands like **ls**, **mv**, **touch**, and **mkdir**.

Files and directories created using PCFS have to comply with either the DOS short-filename convention or the Windows 95 long-filename convention. The DOS short-filename convention allows for files whose filename has the form:

*FILENAME.EXT*

where *FILENAME* consists of one to eight uppercase characters, and the optional *EXT* consists of one to three uppercase characters. The Windows 95 long-filename convention is similar to standard UFS filenames in that a filename can consist of up to 255 characters. The convention supports all the upper and lowercase letters, spaces (except for leading spaces), and the following characters:

+ = [ ] . - _ ,

PCFS displays filenames exactly as they are stored on the media, which means that DOS short names show up as all uppercase and Windows 95 long filenames retain their case. The only exception is that searches for filenames are not case sensitive, thus the file HELLO.TXT and Hello.txt will be treated as the same file during a search.

## proc File System

The proc File System on Solaris was borrowed from the experimental operating system Plan 9 developed by AT&T. When some engineers who had worked on Plan 9 joined the Solaris development team, they created the proc File System and a set of associated tools, which are stored in /usr/proc/bin. Before the proc File System was developed, programs like **ps** or **top** that need to access kernel state had to be recompiled for each version of Solaris. The proc File System avoids this problem by providing all programs with a uniform interface into the kernel via a special file system mounted on the directory /proc.

The following listing shows a small subset of the directories in /proc:

```
$ /bin/ls -l /proc/
total 62
dr-x--x--x   5 root      root           736 Jun 10 17:02 0
dr-x--x--x   5 root      root           736 Jun 10 17:02 1
dr-x--x--x   5 root      root           736 Jun 10 17:03 114
dr-x--x--x   5 root      root           736 Jun 10 17:03 116
dr-x--x--x   5 root      root           736 Jun 10 17:03 142
dr-x--x--x   5 root      root           736 Jun 10 17:03 147
```

Each name of each directory in /proc corresponds to an active process ID. The owner of the directory is the UID of the process, while the group of the directory is the GID of the process. This allows only the owner of a process (and root) to have access to a process's information. Each process directory contains the following files and directories.

```
./          cred        lpsinfo     map         rmap        usage
../         ctl         lstatus     object/     root@       watch
as          cwd@        lusage      pagedata    sigact      xmap
auxv        fd/         lwp/        psinfo      status
```

Some of the important per-process files are explained in Table 8-1. For a full description of all of these files please consult the proc(4) manpage using the command:

```
$ man -s 4 proc
```

The proc File System and the proc tools are covered in greater detail in Chapter 5.

## The Memory Based File System (tmpfs)

The Memory Based File System, called tmpfs, is a file system that combines all of the available physical and virtual memory into a single file system. Most Solaris systems contain a single tmpfs file system mounted on /tmp. Files and directories located in a tmpfs file system will be lost if the system is rebooted, because the files are contained partially in system memory that does not maintain data across reboots. The tmpfs was

| File/Directory | Description |
|---|---|
| as | Contains the address-space image of the process. |
| psinfo | Contains information about the process needed by the **ps** command. |
| cred | Contains a description of the permissions associated with the process. |
| sigact | Contains an array that describes the signal handlers associated with the process. |
| cwd | A symbolic link to the process's current working directory. |
| fd | A directory containing references to the open files of the process. |
| root | A symbolic link to the process's root directory. This can be different from the system root directory if the process or one of its ancestors has executed **chroot** command. |

**Table 8-1.**   *Important Per-Process Files and Directories*

designed to provide high performance for processes that create a large number of short-lived files, with the main target being large compilations.

One of the important caveats with the tmpfs is that the memory used to store files in tmpfs is the same memory that is used when commands are executed. This means that storing large files on the tmpfs file system mounted on /tmp can affect the amount of memory that is available for programs. Similarly, programs requiring large amounts of memory will reduce the amount of space available in a tmpfs file system. Another constraint with tmpfs is that the maximum number of files that can be present in a tmpfs file system is determined from the amount of physical memory on the system; it is not affected by the amount of virtual memory (SWAP space) that is configured.

The process of formatting a disk and partitioning it for a tmpfs file system is the same process detailed in this chapter. The only difference is that a tmpfs file system is added and deleted using the **SWAP** command.

# Creating File Systems

Now that we have looked at the basic types of file systems available in Solaris, we will examine the process of formatting a hard drive and creating a UFS file system. When you install Solaris, the installer takes care of this process for you. You will need to create a new file system only when you are adding a new hard drive to your system.

The first step in creating a file system is to determine the device of the hard drive on which you want to create the file system. Once you know this device, you can use the **format** command to format the disk. On Solaris x86, the **fdisk** command is used instead of the **format** command. After formatting the disk, the **newfs** command is used to create the UFS file system. In this section we will walk through each of these steps in order to illustrate the process of creating a new UFS file system.

## Determining a Hard Drive's Device

The first step in creating a new UFS file system is to determine the device on which the file system needs to be created. In Solaris 8 a hard disk can by accessed by referring to its *physical* device pathname or its *logical* device pathname. The physical device pathname represents the full device pathname as used by the boot system and the kernel. The logical device pathname is the pathname normally used by administrators to reference a device. We will look at the physical pathnames briefly in this section, but the rest of this chapter will use the logical device pathnames.

### Physical Device Pathnames

The device files corresponding to a hard drive's physical device pathname are located in the /devices directory and look similar to the following example.

```
/devices/iommu@f,e0000000/sbus@f,e0001000/espdma@f,400000/esp@f,800000/sd@3,0:a
```

The individual directories in this pathname have the following significance:

- The directory iommu@f,e0000000 represents the I/O Memory Management Unit.
- The directory sbus@f,e0001000 represents the sbus controller. If you have a PCI or ISA bus in your workstation, then the physical device pathnames will use either pci or isa, respectively, in place of sbus.
- The directory espdma@f,400000 represents the DMA controller.
- The directory esp@f,800000 represents the host adapter, which is the IDE or SCSI controller.
- The last entry in the pathname, sd@3,0:a, is the actual device file for the hard disk. In this case we are looking at the device file for the SCSI hard disk (sd) with the SCSI ID of 3 (@3), logical unit number (LUN) of 0 and the "a" partition (:a). For stand-alone disks the Logical Unit Number is always 0. However, in storage arrays the LUN number can be 0 or higher. Consulting the vendor documentation will provide you with more information about the LUN. Partitions are numbered from *a* thru *h* corresponding to 0 through 7 partition numbers. Partitions are discussed later in the chapter.

In some cases you will see the last entry in the physical device pathname with the suffix *raw*. This suffix identifies the raw device, which is the actual media rather than the file system that resides on the media. The raw device is used by programs, such as **fsck**, that are used to maintain file systems. Raw devices and file system maintenance are covered in the next chapter, "Advanced File System Management." A complete discussion of the physical device pathnames is given in Chapter 7.

## Logical Device Pathnames

Logical device pathnames are the common pathnames used by administrators to refer to devices. The logical device pathnames consist of a set of symbolic links in the /dev directory. For hard disks, there are links from the /dev/dsk and /dev/rdsk directories to the appropriate physical device pathname in /devices. The symbolic links in /dev/dsk refer to the file system located on the disk, while the symbolic links in /dev/rdsk refer to the raw device.

A logical device file for a hard drive on Solaris 8 uses a form similar to the following:

/dev/dsk/c[*C*]t[*T*]d[*D*]s[*S*]

Here *C* corresponds to the controller the disk is connected to, *T* corresponds to the target number of the disk, *D* corresponds to the disk number (normally 0 for SCSI disks), and *S* corresponds to the partition number (between 0 and 7). For example, the logical device file, /dev/dsk/c0t3d0s1, refers to the first partition of the disk on controller 0 with a SCSI ID of 3.

The target number of a disk, t[*T*], is available for SCSI disks only and corresponds to the SCSI ID of the disk. The logical device files for IDE disks use the following form:

/dev/dsk/c[*C*]d[*D*]s[*S*]

Here *C* corresponds to the controller the disk is connected to, *D* corresponds to the disk number, and *S* corresponds to the partition number. The disk number, d[*D*], is 0 for the master drive and 1 for the slave drive.

## Partitions

Partitions are a method of dividing a large disk into separate "subdisks" that are limited to a particular size. Normally, you want to partition a disk into smaller subdisks to prevent a particular program or user from filling your disk with large useless files. All disks in Solaris have eight partitions ranging from 0 to 7. Of these eight, partition 2 is special, because it allows for access to the entire disk. The other seven partitions can be of any size smaller than the total size of your disk. On disks with a single large partition, the other partitions (with the exception of partition 2 as noted above) have a size of 0.

# Formatting and Partitioning

Under Solaris 8 the **format** command is used to format and partition disks. The easiest way to use the **format** command is to invoke it interactively as root:

```
# format
```

When **format** starts, it presents you with a list of all the hard drives on the system that can be formatted and partitioned:

```
AVAILABLE DISK SELECTIONS:
       0. c0t3d0 <Andataco Quantum LPS1080S cyl 2895 alt 2 hd 8 sec 91>
          /sbus@1,f8000000/esp@0,800000/sd@3,0
Specify disk (enter its number):
```

In this case a single SCSI hard disk with SCSI ID 3 was found. When more than one disk is available for formatting, each disk is listed in order of its device entry:

```
AVAILABLE DISK SELECTIONS:
       0. c0d0
```

```
            /isa/ata@1f0,0/cmdk@0,0
      1. c0d1
            /isa/ata@1f0,0/cmdk@1,0
Specify disk (enter its number):
```

Here two IDE disks on the first IDE controller were found to be available for formatting.

The listing produced by **format** makes it easier for you to format hard drives, since you do not have to know the device name of the disk you want to format ahead of time. It is also safer, since you can always exit at this stage if you ran the **format** command by mistake. One thing to keep in mind is that the list presented by **format** consists of all hard drives on your system, including those that contain mounted file systems, so you need to be careful about selecting the correct hard drive. If you make a mistake and select the wrong disk, you can type CTRL+C to abort **format**. No changes will be made to your system.

In the following example, we will assume that the following disk was selected for formatting:

```
c0t3d0 <Andataco Quantium LPS1080S cyl 2895 alt 2 hd 8 sec 91>
        /sbus@1,f8000000/esp@0,800000/sd@3,0
```

## The format Main Menu
Once a disk is selected as the target for the **format** command, the main menu is presented:

```
FORMAT MENU:
        disk       - select a disk
        type       - select (define) a disk type
        partition  - select (define) a partition table
        current    - describe the current disk
        format     - format and analyze the disk
        repair     - repair a defective sector
        label      - write label to the disk
        analyze    - surface analysis
        defect     - defect list management
        backup     - search for backup labels
        verify     - read and display labels
        save       - save new disk/partition definitions
        inquiry    - show vendor, product and revision
        volname    - set 8-character volume name
        !<cmd>     - execute <cmd>, then return
        quit
format>
```

If you made a mistake and selected the wrong disk, you can use the **disk** option from this menu to select another disk. This option presents you with a listing of all the disks available. If you need to format more than one disk you can use the **disk** option to switch between disks.

**Changing the Hard Drive's Parameters**   The **type** option to the **format** command allows you to explicitly specify information about your hard drive. Normally **format** determines information about a hard drive based on entries in the file /etc/format.dat, but sometimes the parameters it selects may not be optimal (or even correct). For example, **format** determined that the hard drive with SCSI ID 3 has the following properties:

```
Andataco Quantum LPS1080S cyl 2895 alt 2 hd 8 sec 91
```

If the manual or the manufacturer's documentation for the hard drive states that the disk has parameters different from what **format** reports, you should use the **type** option to specify the correct values.

 *If you're planning to use the **type** option to the **format** command, make sure that you have the complete specification or manual for your hard drive, which should be available from your hard drive vendor's web site.*

When you select the **type** option you will be presented with a menu similar to the following (some of the entries have been omitted for brevity):

```
format> type

AVAILABLE DRIVE TYPES:
        0. Auto configure
        1. Quantum ProDrive 105s
...
       16. Other
Specify disk type (enter its number):
```

To change the parameters for a drive, select the last option (in this case 16) corresponding to **other**. At this point you will be prompted to enter the correct values for different hard drive parameters. The first parameter you are asked for is the number of data cylinders:

```
Enter number of data cylinders:
```

Normally, the number of data cylinders in Solaris is equal to the number of physical cylinders in the hard drive minus two. This is because Solaris uses two cylinders, called *alternate cylinders*, for remapping bad blocks. You can specify a smaller number of data cylinders if you want to have more than two alternate cylinders.

The next two questions ask you for the number of alternate cylinders and the number of physical cylinders. Both questions come with default values. However, the number of alternate cylinders determines the answer to the "Enter number of data cylinders:" question. If you wish to choose a different number of alternate cylinders, compute the number of data cylinders as follows:

Data cylinders = Physical cylinders—Alternate cylinders

Unless you want to use more than two alternate cylinders, you should select the defaults:

```
Enter the number of alternate cylinders[2]:
Enter the number of physical cylinders[2895]:
```

The next question asks you about the number of heads in your hard drive:

```
Enter the number of heads:
```

You will need to have the hard drive's manual in order to answer this question. Once you have entered the number of heads, you should select the default for the next question:

```
Enter the physical number of heads[default]:
```

Next you will be asked about the number of data sectors per track:

```
Enter the number of data sectors/track:
```

Again, you will need to have the hard drive's manual in order to answer this question. Once you have entered this question, you should select the default for the next question:

```
Enter the number of physical sectors/track[default]:
```

The last question you need to answer with a nondefault value is the following:

```
Enter the rpm of the drive[3600]:
```

Normally this is a value such as 3600, 5400, 7200, or 10000, but you will need the hard disk's manual to enter the correct value. Entering the wrong value will still allow your hard drive to function correctly, but it may not be as efficient as possible.

For the following questions, you should select the default by simply pressing ENTER:

```
Enter format time[default]:
Enter cylinder skew[default]:
Enter track skew[default]:
Enter tracks per zone[default]:
Enter alternate tracks[default]:
Enter alternate sectors[default]:
Enter cache control[default]:
Enter prefetch threshold[default]:
Enter minimum prefetch[default]:
Enter maximum prefetch[default]:
```

Finally, the last question asks you for the name of the disk:

```
Enter the disk type name (remember quotes):
```

This is the name under which the disk will show up in the menu of the **type** command. Normally you should enter the disk's model number here:

```
Enter the disk type name (remember quotes): "Quantum LPS1080S"
```

**Formatting a Disk**   When you select a disk from the initial list presented by **format**, you may see a message similar to the following:

```
[disk formatted]
```

This indicates that the disk you have selected has already been formatted. If you see such a message on a SPARC-based workstation, you can skip directly to partitioning the hard drive. Otherwise you should select the **format** option to format the disk:

```
format> format
Ready to format.  Formatting cannot be interrupted
and takes 17 minutes (estimated). Continue?
```

You should type yes at this prompt to format the disk. This will display the starting time of the format, and then will proceed to format and verify your disk.

```
Beginning format. The current time is Fri May 21 16:07:19 1999

Formatting...
done

Verifying media...
        pass 0 - pattern = 0xc6dec6de
    1966/8/48
...
```

After several verification passes, you will be returned to the main menu of **format**. On an x86-based workstation, you should use the **fdisk** menu option instead:

```
format> fdisk
The recommended default partitioning for your disk is:
  a 100% "SOLARIS System" partition.

To select this, please type "y".  To partition your disk
differently, type "n" and the "fdisk" program will let you
select other partitions.
```

Normally you should type **y**, since the partition command allows you to partition your hard drive after formatting it. Once **fdisk** completes you will see the following message:

```
WARNING: Solaris fdisk partition changed - Please relabel the disk
```

To label the disk, select the **label** option from the **format** main menu:

```
format> label
Ready to label disk, continue?
```

Enter **yes** at this prompt to label the disk. It is necessary to label the disk before partitioning it.

**Partitioning a Disk**    Once a disk is formatted it needs to be partitioned for use. The partition scheme for a disk largely depends on what you will be using the disk for. If you are going to be using the disk for storing user home directories or as a partition for serving files, you can make a single large partition for the entire disk. If you are running a web server and an ftp server, you may want to create two separate partitions, one for each server. Solaris allows you to define up to seven partitions, so you can implement any partitioning scheme you want.

To partition a disk, select the **partition** option from the **format** main menu. You will be presented with the partition menu, which allows you to modify each partition manually, select a predefined partition table, or modify a predefined partition table:

```
format> partition
PARTITION MENU:
        0       - change '0' partition
        1       - change '1' partition
        2       - change '2' partition
        3       - change '3' partition
        4       - change '4' partition
        5       - change '5' partition
        6       - change '6' partition
        7       - change '7' partition
        select - select a predefined table
        modify - modify a predefined partition table
        name    - name the current table
        print   - display the current table
        label   - write partition map and label to the disk
        !<cmd> - execute <cmd>, then return
        quit
partition>
```

The preferred method of partitioning a disk is to use the **modify** option. This option presents several predefined partition tables that you can change to suit your needs. This option also gives you the flexibility of allocating space to each partition without having to select each partition individually. Selecting **modify** presents the following menu:

```
partition> modify
Select partitioning base:
        0. Current partition table (unnamed)
        1. All Free Hog
Choose base (enter number)[0]?
```

You should select the All Free Hog method, which provides the easiest method for allocating free space. Basically this method prompts you for the sizes of all the partitions except partition 2 and the "free hog" partition. It then allocates the remaining space to the "free hog" partition. Partition 2 is normally called the "backup" partition and refers to the entire disk. It is used by the **fsck** command to repair problems encountered after a disk crash. If you were to choose this partition as your "free hog" partition, it is possible that a disk crash might render your disk unrecoverable. For this reason you should pick a partition other than 2 for the "free hog" partition.

The first question you are asked when creating a new partition table is:

```
Free Hog Partition[6]?
```

You can choose any partition you want for the "free hog" partition, but the standard Solaris practice is to pick the default, 6. Once you have selected the "free hog" partition, you will be prompted for the sizes of the other six partitions:

```
Enter size of partition '0' [0b, 0k, 0.00mb]:
```

You can enter the sizes that you want in bytes, kilobytes, or megabytes. Most administrators prefer to use megabytes since the numbers are smaller and easier to keep track of. If you do not want to specify a size for a particular partition just accept the default of 0 (by pressing ENTER).

As an example, we will partition this hard drive to have a 100-megabyte partition as partition 7 and a "free hog" partition as partition 6. The responses to the prompts are as follows:

```
Enter size of partition '0' [0b, 0k, 0.00mb]:
Enter size of partition '1' [0b, 0k, 0.00mb]:
Enter size of partition '3' [0b, 0k, 0.00mb]:
Enter size of partition '4' [0b, 0k, 0.00mb]:
Enter size of partition '5' [0b, 0k, 0.00mb]:
Enter size of partition '7' [0b, 0k, 0.00mb]: 100mb
```

Notice that we are not prompted for the size of partition 2, which is used by Solaris to address the entire disk. Also, we are not prompted for the size of partition 6, which we chose earlier to be the "free hog" partition, since its size is determined dynamically.

After partitioning the disk, we need to check that the partition table has been updated correctly. For this, we use the **print** option:

```
partition> print
Total disk cylinders available: 2895 + 2 (reserved cylinders)
```

| Part | Tag | Flag | Cylinders | Size | Blocks | |
|------|------|------|-----------|------|--------|---|
| 0 | root | wm | 0 | 0 | (0/0/0) | 0 |
| 1 | SWAP | wm | 0 | 0 | (0/0/0) | 0 |
| 2 | backup | wm | 0 - 2894 | 1.00GB | (2895/0/0) | 2107560 |
| 3 | unassigned | wm | 0 | 0 | (0/0/0) | 0 |
| 4 | unassigned | wm | 0 | 0 | (0/0/0) | 0 |
| 5 | unassigned | wm | 0 | 0 | (0/0/0) | 0 |

```
6 unassigned    wm     0 - 2329      828.24MB    (2330/0/0) 1696240
7 unassigned    wm     2612 - 2893   100.24MB    (282/0/0)   205296
```

As you can see, partition 6, the "free hog" partition, was given the size 828.24 megabytes, which is the total size of the disk minus the space allotted for partition 7. You may notice that the space taken by partitions 6 and 7 together does not equal the total size of the disk, as shown for partition 2. This is because the size of partition 2 reflects the unformatted capacity of the disk, whereas the sizes for partitions 6 and 7 reflect the formatted capacity. The unformatted capacity is always much larger than the formatted capacity. This size discrepancy is partially due to the two alternate cylinders used by Solaris for remapping bad blocks.

Once you have confirmed that the partition table is configured correctly, you need to write the table to the disk using the **label** option:

```
partition> label
Ready to label disk, continue?
```

Answer **yes** to the question and the partition table will be written to the disk. Once this command completes, you can then type **quit** to return to the **format** main menu:

```
partition> quit
format>
```

**Saving the Partition Map**   You can save the partition map you just entered using the **save** command of the **format** main menu. Unlike the **label** command, which writes the defined partition map to the disk, the **save** command saves the partition map as a file anywhere on your file system. This command prompts you for a filename as follows:

```
format> save
Saving new partition definition
Enter file name["./format.dat"]:
```

You can enter either a relative or absolute path at the prompt. Once this information has been saved you will be presented with the **format** prompt. The file that was created by this command contains a "partition" entry similar to the following:

```
partition = "original" \
        : disk = "SUN2.1G" : ctlr = SCSI \
        : 2 =  0, 4154160 : 3 =  0, 1311760 : 6 =  863, 2842400
```

You can include this "partition" entry in the master format data file, /etc/format.dat, which contains the master list of disk drives and partition types that the **format** command can use to automatically configure new hard drives. Once the "partition" entry created by the **save** command is added to /etc/format.dat, you will be able to access it as an additional partition type in the menu presented by the **select** command within the partition menu:

```
partition> select
        0. SUN2.1G
        1. original
```

**Exiting from Format**    To exit from format and return to the shell, type **quit** at the main prompt:

```
format> quit
```

## Creating a New UFS File System

Once a disk has been formatted and partitioned, a new UFS file system needs to be created on each of the partitions before you can use the disk. To create a new file system, we will use the **newfs** command. Its basic syntax is:

# newfs *device*

Here *device* is the logical device pathname on which you want the file system created. In the case of the previous example, we will need to create two file systems, one for partition 6 and one for partition 7. To create a UFS file system on partition 6 on the SCSI disk with SCSI ID 3, we can use the command:

```
# newfs /dev/dsk/c0t3d0s6
```

**Note**    *Here we are using the regular logical device rather than the raw logical device. Only file system maintenance utilities like **fsck** use the raw logical device.*

The output from **newfs** will be similar to the following:

```
/dev/rdsk/c0t3d0s6: 1696240 sectors in 2329 cylinders of 19 tracks, 110 sectors
        828.24MB in 48 cyl groups (48 c/g, 17.23MB/g, 144 i/g)
superblock backups (for fsck -F ufs -o b=#) at:
 32, 100464, 200896, 301328, 401760, 502192, 602624, 703056, 803488, 903920,
 1004352, 1104784, 1205216, 1305648, 1406080, 1506512, 1606944, 1707376,
 ...
```

Each of the numbers above that follow the line:

```
superblock backups (for fsck -F ufs -o b=#) at:
```

are locations of alternate superblocks. You should make a hard copy of the output from **newfs** and store it in a safe location, preferably in a different room than the hard drive.

*The reason to have a hard copy of this output is that a disk crash of the different file system where you stored a "soft" copy could render it impossible to recover this file system. The reason to store the hard copy in a different location than the hard disk is that anything that causes physical damage to the disk, such as water damage or fire, could also damage your hard copy if it was stored in the same location.*

The command to create a file system for partition 7 is similar to the previous example:

```
newfs /dev/dsk/c0t3d0s7
```

Once you have created the file systems, you can mount them using the **mount** command, as explained in the next section.

## Options for newfs

The two main options used in conjunction with **newfs** are the **-m** and **-o** options. The **-m** option allows you to modify the amount of reserved space on the file system. The **-o** option allows you to specify whether the system should optimize the file system for space or for allocation time.

**Tuning Reserved Space**    Every UFS disk has some amount of *reserved space* that is off limits to normal users. Reserved space is a part of the disk that can only be accessed by root. As discussed earlier in the chapter, this prevents normal users from filling up an essential disk and rendering it inaccessible. Once the nonreserved portion of a disk is full, only root can write files to the disk. By default the amount of reserved space on a disk is 10 percent, which allows for good disk performance even when the disk is mostly full. For disks smaller than 2 gigabytes this is a good default. For larger disks, however, this can amount to a large amount of space that is inaccessible to normal users. For example, on an 8-gigabyte disk, almost 800 megabytes will be reserved. On disks that are used to store user data, such as home directories, you may want to reduce the amount of reserved space; to do this use the **-m** option of **newfs**:

    # newfs -m *percent device*

Here *percent* is the percentage of the disk you want to mark as reserved space, and *device* is the logical device pathname on which you want the file system created. For example, the following command creates a new file system with 5 percent reserved space on partition 7 of the SCSI disk that has ID 3:

```
# newfs -m 5 /dev/dsk/c0t3d0s7
```

**Optimizing for Space Versus Time**   When **newfs** creates a file system it is tuned to use *space* efficiently on a disk. With normal settings the file system will have very little *fragmentation*, a term that describes the number of free blocks that are not contiguous. Low fragmentation means most of the free blocks are not trapped between large sets of allocated blocks. While this allows for blocks on disk to be allocated easily when they are required, it also means that a significant amount of *time* is required for allocating or freeing blocks on the disk. For systems like web servers or FTP servers, the speed at which a file (especially its disk blocks) can be read is often more important than the level of fragmentation of the disk. For workstations and NFS servers with user data, usually the amount of free space available is more important than the speed of data access.

You can tune the performance of a particular file system at creation time with the **-o** option of **newfs** as follows:

```
# newfs -o option device
```

Here *option* is either space or time, and *device* is the logical device pathname on which you want the file system created. For example, the following command creates a new file system optimized for time on partition 7 of the SCSI disk with ID 3:

```
# newfs -o time /dev/dsk/c0t3d0s7
```

# Mounting and Unmounting File Systems

In order to use a newly created file system you need to mount it as part of your directory tree. Since all files in UNIX are in a single directory tree, the mount operation makes it look like the contents of the new file system are the contents of an existing directory. In this section we will look at the commands **mount** and **umount**, which are used to mount and unmount file systems.

To mount a file system stored on a new hard drive, you first need to perform the steps outlined in the previous section. If you haven't performed these steps yet, please refer back to those instructions. Briefly those steps were:

1. Format the disk.

2. Create partitions on the disk.

3. Create the appropriate file systems on the partitions.

For disks that already contain file systems, you can use the **mount** and **umount** commands described in this section.

# Mounting a File System

The general syntax for mounting a file system is:

# mount *device directory*

Here *device* is the regular (not raw) logical device pathname you want to mount, and *directory* is the directory you want to overlay with the file system contained on the given *device*. For example, the following command mounts the file system stored on /dev/dsk/c0t3d0s6 on the directory /www:

```
# mount /dev/dsk/c0t3d0s6 /www
```

In this case this logical device pathname contains the UFS file system that was created using **newfs** in the previous example. Note that although in this example we are using a newly created file system, you can use **mount** to mount any logical device pathname that contains a file system supported by Solaris 8.

There are three important points that you need to remember when mounting a file system. The first is that the destination directory must exist before the mount can take place. For example, if the directory /www did not exist, **mount** would issue the following error message:

```
mount: mount point /www does not exist
```

The second important point is that **mount** overlays the directory that was specified with the contents of the file system that was just mounted. For example, let's say that the /www directory had the following contents before the mount command was issued:

```
./           bin/        htdocs/      jrun/      man/
../          cgi-bin/    icons/       libexec/   proxy/
RCS/         conf/       include/     logs/      servlets/
```

After the mount command those files would no longer be visible. Instead only the files in the mounted file system would be seen. In this case, since the mounted file system was newly created we have only the following entries:

```
./            ../         lost+found/
```

The lost+found directory is used by the **fsck** command to place recovered files from a crashed disk. This directory is explained in greater detail in Chapter 8.

The third point is that a mount operation will not succeed if a destination directory is in use.

This restriction prevents data in the destination directory from being corrupted. If one or more processes on your system are using the destination directory you will receive an error message from **mount**. For example, consider the following commands:

```
# cd /www ; mount /dev/dsk/c0t1d0s3 /www
```

The first command changes the working directory to /www and the second command attempts to mount partition 3 of the SCSI disk with ID 1 on this directory. This command will fail since the directory /www is busy (it is the working directory of the current shell). The error message will be similar to the following:

```
mount: /dev/dsk/c0t1d0s3 is already mounted, /www is busy,
        or the allowable number of mount points has been exceeded
```

A short script that allows you to determine which processes are using a particular directory is given later in this chapter. Using this script you can either kill processes that are using a particular directory (or any of its subdirectories), or you can speak to the owner(s) of the processes and ask them to terminate the processes. The latter approach is favored, if you have the time to contact the owner(s).

## Options for mount

In addition to simply mounting devices, it is possible to specify options to **mount** by using the **-o** flag. For example, the following command mounts the third partition of the SCSI hard drive that has SCSI ID 4 on the directory /usr/archive, as read-only:

```
# mount -o ro /dev/dsk/c0t4d0s3 /usr/archive
```

Normally the **ro**, read-only, option is used for CD-ROMs, but sometimes you may need to use it while restoring files from a removable disks, such as a Jaz or Zip drive. This option is also used for security on NFS file systems, described in Chapter 7.

To specify more than one option, you can list them, separated by commas. For example:

```
# mount -o ro,intr /dev/dsk/c0t4d0s3 /usr/archive
```

The **ro** option mounts the listed partition as read-only, and the **intr** option allows for users to kill commands that hang while waiting on the device execution of binaries from the partition once it is mounted. The **intr** option may be useful when mounting an extremely slow device, such as a Zip disk.

Table 8-2 lists some of the common options to **mount** that are available for UFS file systems. These options can be specified to the mount command on the command line as well as in its configuration file, /etc/vfstab.

| Option | Description |
|--------|-------------|
| nosuid | Prevents the set-user-identifier or set-group-identifier bits to take effect. |
| remount | Indicates to **mount** that it should attempt to remount an already-mounted file system. This is commonly used to change the mount flags for a file system, especially to change a read-only file system to read-write. |
| ro | Mounts a file system as read-only. |
| rw | Mounts a file system as read-write. |
| intr | Allows processes that are waiting on the file system to be killed. |
| nointr | Prevents the termination of processes that are waiting on the file system. |

**Table 8-2.** *Mount Options*

## mount -a

The **-a** flag indicates to **mount** that it should mount all the file systems that it knows about. In the case where no device or mount point is given, this information is obtained from **mount**'s configuration file. This configuration file is discussed in a subsequent section. Usually the command:

```
# mount -a
```

is never given directly by an administrator; rather, it is issued by the /etc/init.d/ MOUNTFSYS script during the system startup. An equivalent of this command is the /usr/sbin/mountall command.

## mount -F

The **-F** flag indicates to the **mount** command the type of file system that the target device has on it. Although on Solaris 8 **mount** can automatically detect the file system type of hard drives, floppy disks, and CD-ROMs, you may still need to use the **-F** option for mounting some PCFS drives.

For example, to mount a PCFS disk with the regular logical device pathname /dev/dsk/c0d1, you should use the command:

```
# mount -F pcfs /dev/dsk/c0d1 /mnt/d
```

Mounting a PCFS floppy disk depends on what version of Solaris you're using. In older versions of Solaris you need to use the following command to mount a PCFS floppy disk:

```
# mount -F pcfs /dev/diskette /floppy
```

In newer versions of Solaris (2.5 and higher), this is handled automatically by the Volume Manager, as covered later in this chapter.

## Listing Mounted File Systems

The **mount** command can list all of the mounted file systems in three separate formats. The default format is as follows:

> *dir* on *device options* on *date*

Here *dir* is the directory where the file system is mounted, *device* is the path to the device where the file system is located, *options* are the mount options used for mounting the file system, and *date* is the date when the file system was mounted. To get the default format you can just type the **mount** command without any arguments:

```
$ mount
/ on /dev/dsk/c0t3d0s0 read/write/setuid/largefiles on Thu Jun 10 17:03:23 1999
/proc on /proc read/write/setuid on Thu Jun 10 17:03:23 1999
/dev/fd on fd read/write/setuid on Thu Jun 10 17:03:23 1999
/var on /dev/dsk/c0t3d0s1 read/write/setuid/largefiles on Thu Jun 10 17:03:23 1999
/export on /dev/dsk/c0t3d0s5 setuid/read/write/largefiles on Thu Jun 10 17:03:24 1999
/tmp on SWAP read/write on Thu Jun 10 17:03:24 1999
```

The second format is a terse listing; it's available using the **-p** option:

```
$ mount -p
/dev/dsk/c0t3d0s0 - / ufs - no rw,suid,largefiles
/proc - /proc proc - no rw,suid
fd - /dev/fd fd - no rw,suid
/dev/dsk/c0t3d0s1 - /var ufs - no rw,suid,largefiles
/dev/dsk/c0t3d0s5 - /export ufs - no suid,rw,largefiles
SWAP - /tmp tmpfs - no
```

The third format is a verbose listing, available by using the **-v** option. It is similar to the default format, but it adds information about the type of file system:

```
$ mount -v
/dev/dsk/c0t3d0s0 on / type ufs read/write/setuid/largefiles on Fri Jul 23 10:52:48 1999
```

```
/proc on /proc type proc read/write/setuid on Fri Jul 23 10:52:48 1999
fd on /dev/fd type fd read/write/setuid on Fri Jul 23 10:52:48 1999
/dev/dsk/c0t3d0s1 on /var type ufs read/write/setuid/largefiles on Fri Jul 23 10:52:48 1999
/dev/dsk/c0t3d0s5 on /export type ufs setuid/read/write/largefiles on Fri Jul 23 10:52:50 1999
SWAP on /tmp type tmpfs read/write on Fri Jul 23 10:52:50 1999
```

## Unmounting File Systems

A file system is unmounted using the **umount** command. The general syntax has two forms:

> # umount *directory*

> # umount *device*

In the first form **umount** will attempt to unmount the file system that is mounted on the specified directory. In the second form **umount** will attempt to unmount the file system that is located on the specified device, where *device* is a regular logical device pathname. Normally the first form is preferred by administrators because it is easier to know the directory you want to unmount. The second form is required on systems where more than one logical device pathname can be mounted on the single directory.

As an example, the following command:

```
umount /www
```

unmounts the file system that was mounted on /www. A side effect of the unmount operation is that the contents of the directory structure that existed before the mount are made accessible.

### Unmounting Busy Directories

If the directory used as a mount point—or any subdirectory in the mounted file system—is in use by a user or a process, **umount** will not allow the file system to be unmounted. This restriction prevents the corruption of data on the file system. For example, if the directory /www were in use, **umount** would produce the following error:

```
umount: /dev/dsk/c0t3d0s6: device busy
```

In this case most administrators use one of the process management tools described in Chapter 5, such as **lsof**, to find the process ID of the process that is using the file system. Once the process ID of this process has been found, terminating it with the **kill** command will allow you to unmount the file system. A script that facilitates this task is as follows:

```
#!/bin/sh
# find process using directory (fpud)

if [ "$1" = "-all" ] ; then
    MYDIR=/
elif [ -d "$1" ] ; then
    MYDIR=`(cd $i && /bin/pwd)`
else
    echo "USAGE: `basename $0` [dir]" ; exit 1
fi

for i in `find /proc -depth -name cwd -print 2>/dev/null` ;
do
    ( cd $i && DIR=`/bin/pwd` ;
        PID=`dirname $i | sed -e 's/\/proc\///'` ;
        printf "%-32s %16d\n" "$DIR" "$PID"; ) 2>/dev/null | grep "$MYDIR"
done
exit 0
```

The syntax for this script is:

$ fpud *directory*

Here *directory* is the pathname to the directory you are interested in. This assumes that the name of the script is **fpud**. The output of the script is similar to the following:

```
$ fpud /user/ranga
/users/ranga/bin                        1589
/users/ranga                            1434
```

The first column lists the name of the directory, while the second lists the process ID. If you want to get a listing of a process not owned by the current user, you will need to be root when you execute the script. Notice that subdirectories of the directory that you requested are also listed in the output. These directories are listed in the output because if a subdirectory of a given directory is busy, then you will not be able to unmount that directory.

This script also accepts the **-all** option, which lists the working directory for each process on your system:

```
$ fpud -all
```

Once you know the process ID that is using a particular directory, you can kill that process using the **kill** command.

# Mount Configuration Files

Both the **mount** and **umount** commands use the configuration file /etc/vfstab, which lists all the partitions that need to be mounted at boot time along with the directory where they are to be mounted. This file also allows you to specify the mount options for a file system. Furthermore, it allows you to mount a file system by specifying its directory rather than its logical device pathname.

The file /etc/vfstab is divided into several columns with information about the file systems being used by the various partitions.

```
#   1          2            3        4        5        6        7
# device     device      mount     FS      fsck    mount    mount
# to mount   to fsck     point     type    pass    at boot  options
```

- The first column contains the logical device pathname to the device that contains the file system.

- The second column contains the raw logical device pathname that is used by the fsck program to verify the state of the file system at boot time.

- The third column contains the *mount point*, or directory where the file system is to be mounted.

- The fourth column contains the file system type (this is usually UFS or PCFS).

- The fifth column contains an integer describing the behavior of fsck during boot. If this column contains a 1, then the system will not boot until fsck declares that the file system is stable. If this column contains a -, fsck will not be run on the file system during system boot.

- The sixth column is used to indicate the file system that should be mounted at boot time. If this column contains the word "yes" then the file system will be mounted at system boot.

- The last column contains the mount options that should be used when mounting the file system.

As an example, a short /etc/vfstab follows.

```
fd        -       /dev/fd fd       -       no       -
/proc     -       /proc   proc     -       no       -
/dev/dsk/c0t3d0s3         -        -       SWAP     -       no       -
/dev/dsk/c0t3d0s0         /dev/rdsk/c0t3d0s0       /       ufs     1   no -
/dev/dsk/c0t3d0s1         /dev/rdsk/c0t3d0s1       /var    ufs     1   no -
SWAP      -       /tmp    tmpfs    -       yes      -
```

### SWAP and proc File Systems

As you can see from this example, /etc/vfstab contains several entries that do not completely adhere to the format explained earlier. The first entry, fd, corresponds to the file descriptors used by all programs for Standard Input (STDIN), Standard Output (STDOUT), and Standard Error (STDERR). The other two entries, SWAP and proc, correspond to the proc File System and tmp File System that were described earlier in this chapter. Both of these file systems are automatically mounted at system boot time and you should not have to mount or unmount these file systems by hand.

## Volume Management

In most versions of UNIX, you have to manually mount CD-ROMs and floppy disks using the **mount** command and the correct logical device pathname. In Solaris you do not have to do this, as a process known as *volume manager* takes care of mounting CD-ROMs and floppy disks for you.

The volume manager consists of a single program called **vold** (volume daemon), which waits for insertions of floppies and CDs. When it detects that a floppy disk or a CD-ROM has been inserted, it invokes a second program called **rmmount** (removable media mounter) to mount the disk. The **vold** is also responsible for handling eject requests for CD-ROM and floppy disks.

### Checking for Volume Management

Normally volume management is started at runlevel 2 by the script /etc/rc2.d/ S92volmgt, but in some cases it may not be running after startup. You can check if volume management is running by using the command:

```
$ /bin/ps -ef | grep vold | grep -v grep
```

This should produce output similar to the following:

```
root    245     1  0   Jun 10 ?            0:00 /usr/sbin/vold
```

This output indicates that volume management is running. If you do not get any output, volume management is not running on your system. Make sure that the script

/etc/init.d/volmgt is present on your system and that the link /etc/rc2.d/ S92volmgt points to it. Then you can start volume management manually using the command:

```
# /etc/init.d/volmgt start
```

## Volume Management Tips

On older SPARC-based workstations, you may have to run the command **volcheck** after inserting a floppy disk, since on those machines the floppy drive doesn't tell Solaris that a floppy was inserted. On most systems this is not required for CD-ROMs, but on some older x86-based workstations, you may need to run the **volcheck** command in order for CD-ROMs to be mounted.

One of the nice features of volume management is that it allows you to configure audio CDs to auto-play when they are inserted into the CD-ROM drive. Most system administrators use a GUI program called **workman** that allows you to listen to audio CDs. The homepage for workman is located at:

**http://www.midwinter.com/workman**

You can configure volume management to automatically play CDs in **workman** by adding the following line to the "removable media mounter" configuration file, /etc/rmmount.conf:

```
action cdrom action_workman.so /usr/openwin/bin/workman
```

The line above should be added before the line:

```
action cdrom action_filemgr.so
```

The "removable media mounter," /usr/sbin/rmmount, is automatically executed by **vold** whenever a CD-ROM or floppy is inserted, so you do not have to start or stop any processes after making changes to the file /etc/rmmount.conf.

You can also use **vold** to automatically mount Jaz and Zip disks by adding the following line to the file /etc/vold.conf:

```
use rmscsi drive /dev/rdsk/c*s2 dev_rmscsi.so rmscsi%d
```

In Solaris 2.6 and higher, you just need to uncomment this line; on older versions you will need to add it.

## Ejecting Disks

Ejecting floppy disks, CD-ROMs, and other removable media is extremely easy with volume management. The basic syntax is:

# eject *drive*

Here *drive* is floppy, cdrom, or rmscsi. Thus, to eject a floppy disk you would use the command:

```
# eject floppy
```

To eject either a Jaz or Zip disk use the command:

```
# eject rmscsi
```

If **eject** is unable to unmount the disk, it will issue an error message similar to the following:

```
/vol/dev/rdsk/c0t6d0/sol_7_x86: Device busy
```

In this case you need to determine which process is using the device and terminate that process.

## Summary

In this chapter we have covered the basics of file system maintenance. First we looked at the basic structure of a file system and introduced the concept of a superblock and an inode and their relation to UFS, the standard Solaris file system. Then we explained the Solaris extension of an inode called a vnode, which allows for Solaris to access file systems of many different types. The key file systems that we highlighted were the High Sierra File System for CD-ROMs, the PC File System for DOS and Windows 95 disks, the proc File System, and the tmp File System.

In the second section of this chapter we explained the process used for creating a new UFS file system, starting with determining the logical device pathname. We also covered the **format** command, which is used to format and partition disks, and the **newfs** command, which creates a UFS file system. The final section of this chapter was devoted to introducing the **mount** and **umount** commands used to mount and unmount file systems. We looked at some of the common options to **mount** and showed you how to use the mount configuration file /etc/vfstab. Finally we looked at the volume manager, which allows you to automatically mount and eject floppy disks, CD-ROMs, and other removable media.

## How to Find Out More

The best sources of information about creating and maintaining file systems on Solaris are available on-line.

One of the best sources of information is the sun-managers-faq located at:

**ftp://ftp.cs.toronto.edu/pub/jdd/sun-managers/faq**

Section 5 of the FAQ is devoted to SCSI drives and their configuration.

A good source of information about disk and tape drives, including excellent Solaris-specific information, is located on the Stokely Consulting home page, at:

**http://www.stokely.com/unix.sysadm.resources/disk.printing.html**

In particular there are several links devoted to removable devices.

Some of the books that cover the topic of Solaris file systems in greater detail are:

Wong, Brian L. *Configuration and Capacity Planning for Solaris Servers.* (Prentice Hall, 1997.)

Calkins, Bill. *Solaris 2.6 Administrator Certification Training Guide.* (Macmillan Technical Publishing, 1999.)

Freeland, Curt; McKay, Dwight; and Parkinson, Kent. *Solaris 2.X for Managers and Administrators.* (OnWord Press, 1997.)

# The Complete Reference

Solaris 8

# Chapter 9

## Advanced File System Management

Once you have your file systems up and running, you need to monitor them for problems. In addition, in many commercial operations it will be necessary to account for and control the CPU time, connect time, and disk space usage for individual applications and users. In this chapter, we will present strategies for monitoring disk problems and limiting their impact by implementing quotas. We will also examine how to recover from disk crashes using **fsck**. Finally, we will investigate the implementation of system accounting and auditing procedures using the **/usr/lib/acct/runacct** and **/usr/lib/acct/prdaily** programs.

# Monitoring Usage/Quotas

Resource management is one of the administrator's key responsibilities, particularly where the availability of a service is the organization's primary source of income (or recognition). For example, if an application server requires 10 megabytes of free disk space for internal caching of objects retrieved from a database, then performance on the client side will suffer if this space is not available because a user decided to dump his collection of MP3 music files onto the system hard drive. If external users cannot access a service because of internal resource allocation problems, they are unlikely to continue using your service. There is also a possibility that a rogue user (or competitor) may attempt to disrupt your service by attempting any number of well-known exploits to reduce your provision of service to clients. In this section, we will examine resource management strategies that are flexible enough to meet the needs of casual users, but that limit the potential for accidental or malicious resource misuse.

## Monitoring Usage

The most commonly used command for monitoring disk space usage is **/usr/bin/df**, which by default displays the number of free blocks and files on all currently mounted volumes. Alternatively, many administrators create an alias for **df** in their shell initialization script like **df -k** (by creating an entry in ~/.cshrc for the C-shell), which displays the amount of free disk space in kilobytes. The basic output for **df** for a SPARC system looks like this:

**server# df**

```
Filesystem           kbytes     used   avail capacity  Mounted on
/dev/dsk/c0t0d0s0    245911    30754  190566    14%    /
/dev/dsk/c0t0d0s4   1015679   430787  523952    46%    /usr
/proc                     0        0       0     0%    /proc
fd                        0        0       0     0%    /dev/fd
/dev/dsk/c0t0d0s3    492871   226184  217400    51%    /var
```

```
/dev/md/dsk/d1           4119256 3599121   478943    89%     /opt
SWAP                      256000    43480   212520    17%     /tmp
/dev/dsk/c0t2d0s3        4119256 3684920   393144    91%     /disks/vol1
/dev/md/dsk/d0          17398449 12889927 4334538    75%
/disks/vol2
/dev/md/dsk/d3           6162349 5990984   109742    99%     /disks/vol3
/dev/dsk/c1t1d0s0       8574909 5868862  1848557    77%     /disks/vol4
/dev/dsk/c2t3d0s2       1820189 1551628   177552    90%     /disks/vol5
/dev/dsk/c1t2d0s0       4124422 3548988   575434    87%     /disks/vol6
/dev/dsk/c2t2d0s3       8737664 8281113   456551    95%     /disks/vol7
/dev/md/dsk/d2          8181953 6803556  1296578    84%     /disks/vol8
client:/disks/junior_developers
                        4124560 3469376   613944    85%

/disks/junior_developers
```

For an Intel system, the output is similar, although disk slices have a different naming convention (as outlined in Chapter 7):

**server# df**

```
Filesystem                kbytes      used     avail capacity  Mounted on
/proc                          0         0         0      0%   /proc
/dev/dsk/c0d0s0            73684     22104     44212     34%   /
/dev/dsk/c0d0s6           618904    401877    161326     72%   /usr
fd                             0         0         0      0%   /dev/fd
/dev/dsk/c0d0s1            29905      4388     22527     17%   /var
/dev/dsk/c0d0s7          7111598         9   7040474      1%   /export/home
SWAP                      222516       272    222244      1%   /tmp
/vol/dev/diskette0/unnamed_floppy
                           1423       131      1292     10%
/floppy/unnamed_floppy
```

**df** has a number of command-line options that can be used to customize the collection and display of information. For example:

**server# df -a**

prints usage data for all file systems, even those that have the "ignore" option set in their entries in /etc/mnttab. (These file systems are covered in more detail in Chapter 8.) The results of this procedure are shown in the following output:

```
Filesystem                kbytes     used    avail  capacity  Mounted on
/dev/dsk/c0t0d0s0         245911    30754   190566    14%     /
/dev/dsk/c0t0d0s4        1015679   430787   523952    46%     /usr
/proc                         0        0        0     0%      /proc
fd                            0        0        0     0%      /dev/fd
/dev/dsk/c0t0d0s3        492871   226185   217399    51%      /var
/dev/md/dsk/d1          4119256  3599121   478943    89%      /opt
SWAP                     256000    43480   212520    17%      /tmp
/dev/dsk/c0t2d0s3       4119256  3684920   393144    91%      /disks/vol1
/dev/md/dsk/d0         17398449 12889927  4334538    75%      /disks/vol2
/dev/md/dsk/d3         6162349  5990984   109742    99%      /disks/vol3
/dev/dsk/c1t1d0s0      8574909  5868862  1848557    77%      /disks/vol4
/dev/dsk/c2t3d0s2      1820189  1551628   177552    90%      /disks/vol5
/dev/dsk/c1t2d0s0      4124422  3548988   575434    87%      /disks/vol6
auto_direct           4124560  3469376   613944    85%      /disks/www
auto_direct                 0        0        0     0%       /disks/ftp
server:vold(pid329)         0        0        0     0%       /vol
/dev/dsk/c2t2d0s3      8737664  8281113   456551    95%      /disks/vol7
/dev/md/dsk/d2         8181953  6803556  1296578    84%      /disks/vol8
client:/disks/junior_developers
                      4124560  3469376   613944    85%      /disks/junior_developers
```

The actual contents of /etc/mnttab can be displayed with the following command:

**server# cat /etc/mnttab**

```
/dev/dsk/c0t0d0s0        /        ufs       rw,suid,dev=800000,largefiles    944543087
/dev/dsk/c0t0d0s4        /usr     ufs       rw,suid,dev=800004,largefiles    944543087
/proc   /proc   proc    rw,suid,dev=29c0000    944543087
fd      /dev/fd fd      rw,suid,dev=2a80000    944543087
/dev/dsk/c0t0d0s3        /var     ufs       rw,suid,dev=800003,largefiles    944543087
/dev/md/dsk/d1   /opt    ufs     suid,rw,largefiles,dev=1540001   944543105
SWAP    /tmp    tmpfs   ,dev=1 944543105
/dev/dsk/c0t2d0s3        /disks/vol1ufs     suid,rw,largefiles,dev=800013    944543105
/dev/md/dsk/d0   /disks/vol2   ufs      nosuid,rw,largefiles,quota,dev=1540000 944543105
/dev/md/dsk/d3   /disks/vol3   ufs      nosuid,rw,largefiles,dev=1540003  944543106
/dev/dsk/c1t1d0s0        /disks/vol4 ufs    nosuid,rw,largefiles,dev=800080 944543105
/dev/dsk/c2t3d0s2        /disks/vol5   ufs     nosuid,rw,largefiles,dev=80010a 44543106
/dev/dsk/c1t2d0s0        /disks/vol6 ufs     suid,rw,largefiles,dev=800088    944543106
auto_direct      /disks/www         autofs ignore,direct,nosuid,dev=2c00001   944543181
auto_direct      /disks/ftp autofs  ignore,direct,nosuid,dev=2c00002         944543181
server:vold(pid329)      /vol    nfs       ignore,noquota,dev=2bc0002        944543192
/dev/dsk/c2t2d0s3        /disks/vol7 ufs     nosuid,rw,largefiles,dev=800103 944548661
/dev/md/dsk/d2   /disks/vol8 ufs     nosuid,rw,largefiles,quota,dev=1540002  944553321
client:/disks/junior_developers   /disks/junior_developers        nfs      nosuid,dev=2bc0040
944604066
```

To avoid delays in printing resource information on NFS-mounted volumes, it is also possible to check just local file systems using the following command:

**server# df -l**

```
Filesystem            kbytes     used   avail capacity  Mounted on
/dev/dsk/c0t0d0s0     245911    30754  190566    14%    /
/dev/dsk/c0t0d0s4    1015679   430787  523952    46%    /usr
/proc                      0        0       0     0%    /proc
fd                         0        0       0     0%    /dev/fd
/dev/dsk/c0t0d0s3     492871   226184  217400    51%    /var
/dev/md/dsk/d1       4119256  3599121  478943    89%    /opt
SWAP                  256000    43488  212512    17%    /tmp
/dev/dsk/c0t2d0s3    4119256  3684920  393144    91%    /disks/vol1
/dev/md/dsk/d0      17398449 12889901 4334564    75%    /disks/vol2
/dev/md/dsk/d3       6162349  5990984  109742    99%    /disks/vol3
/dev/dsk/c1t1d0s0    8574909  5868862 1848557    77%    /disks/vol4
/dev/dsk/c2t3d0s2    1820189  1551628  177552    90%    /disks/vol5
/dev/dsk/c1t2d0s0    4124422  3548988  575434    87%    /disks/vol6
/dev/dsk/c2t2d0s3    8737664  8281113  456551    95%    /disks/vol7
/dev/md/dsk/d2       8181953  6803556 1296578    84%    /disks/vol8
```

A block device can be specified on the command line, and its individual usage measured. For example, here's how to measure a slice on controller 1:

**server# df /dev/dsk/c1d0d2**

```
Filesystem            kbytes     used   avail capacity  Mounted on
/dev/dsk/c1t1d0s0    8574909  5868862 1848557    77%    /disks/vol4
```

Users can also check the status of the disks holding their individual user directories and files by using **df**. For example, the following command:

**server# df /staff/pwatters**

will display the disk space usage for the disk on which the home directory exists for user pwatters:

```
Filesystem            kbytes     used   avail capacity  Mounted on
/dev/md/dsk/d0      17398449 12889146 4335319    75%    /disks/vol2
```

The command:

**server# df /tmp/mbox.pwatters**

checks the size of the partition on which the temporary mailbox for the user pwatters was created by the **elm** mail-reading program:

```
Filesystem        kbytes    used   avail capacity  Mounted on
SWAP              256000   45392  210608    18%     /tmp
```

This is a good thing to check if you intend to send a lot of mail messages!

For auditing purposes, many sites generate a **df** report at midnight, or during a change of administrator shifts, so that a snapshot of the system can be recorded. In addition, if disk space is becoming an issue, and extra volumes need to be justified in a systems budget, it is useful to be able to estimate how rapidly disk space is being consumed by users. Using the **cron** utility, it is possible to set up and schedule a script using **crontab** to check disk space at different time periods, and to mail this information to the administrator (or even post it to a web site, if system administration is centrally managed).

A simple script to monitor disk space usage and mail the results to the system administrator (root@server) looks like this:

```
#!/bin/csh -f
df | mailx -s "Disk Space Usage" root@server
```

As an example, if this script were named /usr/local/bin/monitor_usage.csh, and executable permissions were set for the nobody user, then the following **crontab** entry could be created for the nobody user to run at midnight every night of the week:

```
0 0 * * * /usr/local/bin/monitor_usage.csh
```

Alternatively, the script could be made more general, so that users could specify another user who would be mailed:

```
#!/bin/csh -f
df | mailx -s "Disk Space Usage" $1
```

The **crontab** entry would then look like this:

```
0 0 * * * /usr/local/bin/monitor_usage.csh remote_user@client
```

The results of the disk usage report would now be sent to the user remote_user@client instead of root@server.

Further information on the **cron** utility and submitting **cron** jobs is provided in Chapter 5.

Another way of obtaining disk space usage information with more directory-by-directory detail is by using the **/usr/bin/du** command. This command prints the sum of the sizes of every file in the current directory, and performs the same task recursively for any subdirectories. The size is calculated by adding together all of the file sizes in the directory, where the size for each file is rounded up to the next 512-byte block. For example, taking a **du** of the /etc directory looks like this:

**server# cd /etc**
**server# du**

```
14        ./default
7         ./cron.d
6         ./dfs
8         ./dhcp
201       ./fs/hsfs
681       ./fs/nfs
1         ./fs/proc
209       ./fs/ufs
1093      ./fs
26        ./inet
127       ./init.d
339       ./lib
37        ./mail
4         ./net/ticlts
4         ./net/ticots
4         ./net/ticotsord
13        ./net
3         ./opt/SUNWleo/bin
4         ./opt/SUNWleo
92        ./opt/licenses/from-zoul
118       ./opt/licenses
13        ./opt/SUNWmd
1         ./opt/SUNWimap/license_dir
2         ./opt/SUNWimap
1         ./opt/SUNWicg
32        ./opt/totalnet/httpd/conf
33        ./opt/totalnet/httpd
37        ./opt/totalnet
7         ./opt/ssh
2         ./opt/SUNWneo
13        ./opt/SUNWsymon
198       ./opt
```

```
3          ./rc0.d
2          ./rc1.d
13         ./rc2.d14       ./rc3.d
5          ./rcS.d
3          ./saf/zsmon
6          ./saf
2          ./security/audit/localhost
3          ./security/audit
1          ./security/dev
18         ./security/lib
1          ./security/spool
53         ./security
5          ./skel
1          ./tm
2          ./acct
32         ./uucp
2          ./fn
1          ./openwin/devdata/profiles
2          ./openwin/devdata
3          ./openwin
9          ./lp/alerts
1          ./lp/classes
15         ./lp/fd
1          ./lp/forms
1          ./lp/interfaces
1          ./lp/printers
1          ./lp/pwheels
36         ./lp
2          ./dmi/ciagent
3          ./dmi/conf
6          ./dmi
42         ./snmp/conf
43         ./snmp
7          ./http
2          ./ski
2          ./totalnet
2429       .
```

Thus, /etc and all its subdirectories contain a total of 2,429 kilobytes of data. Of course, this kind of output is fairly verbose, and probably not much use in its current form. If we were only interested in *recording* the directory sizes, to collect data for auditing and usage analysis, we could write a short Perl script to collect the data for us, as follows:

```perl
#!/usr/local/bin/perl
# directorysize.pl: reads in directory size for current directory
and prints
# results to standard output
@du = `du`;
for (@du)
{
($sizes,$directories)=split /\s+/, $_;
print "$sizes\n";
}
```

If this script were saved as directorysize.pl, in the /usr/local/bin/directory, and the executable permissions were set, it would produce a list of directory sizes as output, like the following:

**server# cd /etc**
**server# /usr/local/bin/directorysize.pl**

```
28
14
12
16
402
1362
2
418
2186
52
254
678
74
8
8
8
26
6
8
184
236
```

26
2
4
2
64
66
74
14
4
26
396
6
4
26
28
10
6
12
4
6
2
36
2
106
10
2
4
64
4
2
4
6
18
2
30
2
2
2
2
72
4
6

```
12
84
86
14
4
4
4832
```

Since we are interested in usage management, we might want to modify our script to display the total amount of space occupied by a directory and its subdirectories, as well as the average amount of space occupied. The latter is very important when evaluating caching or investigating load balancing issues:

```perl
#!/usr/local/bin/perl
# directorysize.pl: reads in directory size for current directory
and prints
# the sum and average disk space used to standard output
$sum=0;
$count=0;
@ps = `du -o`;
for (@ps)
{
($sizes,$directories)=split /\s+/, $_;
$sum=$sum+$sizes;
$count=$count+1;
}
print "Total Space: $sum K\n";
print "Average Space: $count K\n";
```

Note that we used **du -o** as the command so that the space occupied by subdirectories is not added to the total for the top-level directory. The output from the command for /etc now looks like:

**server# cd /etc**
**server# /usr/local/bin/directorysize.pl**

```
Total Space: 4832 K
Average Space: 70 K
```

Again, a **cron** job could be set up to mail this information to an administrator at midnight every night. To do this, first create a new shell script to call our Perl script, which is made more flexible by passing the directory to be measured, and the user to which the mail will be sent, as arguments:

```
#!/bin/csh -f
cd $1
/usr/local/bin/directorysize.pl | mailx -s "Directory Space Usage" $2
```

If you save this script to /usr/local/bin/checkdirectoryusage.csh, and set the executable permission, you could then schedule a disk space check of a cache file system. A second command could be included that sends a report for the /disks/junior_developers file system, that is remotely mounted from client, to the team leader on server:

```
0 0 * * * /usr/local/bin/checkdirectoryusage.csh /cache squid@server
1 0 * * * /usr/local/bin/checkdirectoryusage.csh /disks/junior_developers
team_leader@server
```

| Note | *It should be emphasized that tools may already be available on Solaris to perform some of these tasks more directly. For example, **server% du -s** will return the sum of directory sizes automatically. However, the purpose of this section has been to demonstrate how to customize and develop your own scripts for file system management.* |

## Implementing Quotas

Although the kinds of scripts that were presented in the preceding section are useful for monitoring disk use and collecting data for performance measurement purposes, they are not suitable for policy enforcement. Fortunately, Solaris provides a number of tools to enforce policies on disk and resource usage, based around the idea of quotas, or a prespecified allocation of disk space for each user and file system. Thus, a single user can have disk space allocated on different slices, and file systems can have quotas either enabled or disabled (they are disabled by default). Although many organizations disable disk quotas for fear of reducing productivity by placing unnecessary restrictions on the development staff, there are often some very good reasons for implementing quotas on specific slices. For example, if an open file area, like an anonymous FTP incoming directory, is located on the same partition as normal user data, a denial-of-service attack could be initiated by a rogue user who decides to fill the incoming directory with a large files, until all free space is consumed. Alternatively, a CGI application that writes data to a user's home directory (for example, a guestbook) can also fall victim to a denial-of-service attack: A malicious script could be written to enter a million fake entries into the address book, thereby filling the partition to capacity. The result in both of these cases is loss of service, and loss of system control. It is therefore important that networked systems have appropriate checks and balances in place to ensure that such situations are avoided.

Quotas are also critical to ensure fair resource sharing among developers. Otherwise, a developer who decides to back up his PC drive to his home directory on a server, completely filling the partition, could thereby prevent other users from writing data.

In addition to security concerns, enforcing quotas is also optimal from an administrative point of view: It forces users to rationalize their own storage requirements so that material that is not being used can be moved off-line or deleted. This saves administrators from having to make such decisions for users (who may be dismayed at the results if the administrator has to move things in a hurry!).

One simple policy is to enforce disk quotas on all public file systems that have network access. It is easy to increase quotas for all users; therefore the policy can be flexible. In addition, quotas can be "hard" or "soft": Hard quotas strictly enforce incursions into unallocated territory, while soft quotas provide a buffer for temporary violations of a quota, and the users are given warning before enforcement begins. Depending on the security level at which your organization operates (for example, C2 standards for military organizations), a quota policy may already be available for you to implement.

A total limit on the amount of disk space available to users can be specified using quotas for each user individually. Let's take the user pwatters on server as an example. We may allot this user, a Java developer, a quota of 10 megabytes for development work on the /staff file system. To set up this quota, we need to undertake the following steps:

1. Edit the /etc/vfstab file as root and add the **rq** flag to the mount options field for the /staff file system. This enables quotas for the file system.

2. Change directory to /staff and create a file called quotas.

3. Set permissions on /staff/quotas to be read and written for root only.

4. Edit user quotas for user pwatters on file system /staff by using the **edquota** command, and enter the number of inodes and 1KB blocks that will be available to user pwatters. For example, enter the following:

   fs /staff blocks (soft = 10000, hard = 11000) inodes (soft = 0, hard = 0)

5. Check the settings that have been created by using the **quota** command.

6. Enable the quota for user pwatters by using the **quotaon** command.

These steps can be implemented by entering the following:

```
server# vi /etc/vfstab
server# cd /staff
server# touch quotas
server# chmod u+rw quotas
server# edquota pwatters
server# quota –v pwatters
server# quotaon /staff
```

When we verify the quotas using **quota -v**,

server# quota -v pwatters

the output should look like the following:

```
Disk quotas for pwatters (uid 1001):
Filesystem      usage  quota  limit    timeleft  files  quota  limit    timeleft
/staff             0  10000  11000                   0      0      0
```

You can see we entered a soft limit of 10 megabytes and a hard limit of 11 megabytes for user pwatters. If halfway through the development project this user requests more space, the quota could be adjusted by using the **edquota** command again. To check quotas for all users, use the **repquota** command:

**server# repquota /staff**

```
Block limits
User             used    soft    hard
jsmith      --    2048    4096    8192
pwatters    --     131   10000   20000
qjones      --   65536   90000  100000
llee        --    4096    8192   10000
```

If a user attempts to exceed his or her quota during an interactive session, then unless you've set up a warning to be issued under those circumstances, the first indication that the user will have will often come in the form of a "file system full" or "write failed" message. After checking the amount of free space on the partition where their home disk is located, many users are at a loss to explain why they can no longer edit files or send email!

# Fixing Problems Using fsck

**/usr/sbin/fsck** is a file-system checking and repair program commonly found on Solaris and other UNIX platforms. It is usually executed by the superuser while the system is in a single-user init state (for example, after entering runlevel S), but can also be performed on individual volumes during multi-user runlevels. However, there is one golden rule for using **fsck**: *Never, ever apply fsck to a mounted file system.* To do so could leave the file system in an inconsistent state and cause a kernel panic, at which point it would be best to head for the backup tape locker! Any fixes to potential problems on a mounted file system could end up creating more damage than the original problem. In this section, we will examine the output of **fsck**, as well as look at some examples of common problems, and investigate how **fsck** repairs corrupt and inconsistent disk data.

Although Solaris 7 and 8 still retain **fsck**, it is really only necessary for Solaris 2.6 and prior releases. This is because logging is now provided for UNIX file systems (UFS). Thus, before any changes are made to a file system, details of the change are recorded in a log prior to their physical application. While this consumes some extra CPU and disk overhead (approximately 1 percent of disk space is required on each volume with logging enabled), it does ensure that the file system is never left in an inconsistent state. In addition, boot time is reduced, because **fsck** does not need to be executed.

Why do inconsistencies occur in the first place? In theory, they shouldn't, but there are three common reasons:

- Switching off a Solaris server without powering down first.
- Halting a system without synchronizing disk data (therefore, always use **sync** before shutting down using **halt**).
- Defective hardware (such as damaged disk blocks and heads, which may have been caused by moving the system and/or power surges).

These problems manifest themselves in corruption to the internal set of tables that every UNIX file system keeps to manage free disk blocks and inodes. Corruption of these tables leads to blocks that are actually free being reported as already allocated, and, conversely, some blocks that are actually occupied by a program being reported as being free. This is obviously problematic for mission-critical data, and is a good advertisement for RAID storage (or at least, reliable backups).

## The Phases of fsck

The first step to running **fsck** is to enable file-system checking to occur during boot. To do this, it is necessary to specify an integer value in the *fsck* field in the virtual file system configuration file /etc/vfstab. Entering a **1** in this field ensures sequential fsck checking, while entering **2** does not ensure sequential checking, as in the following example:

```
#device device mount FS fsck mount mount
#to mount to fsck point type pass at boot options
#
/dev/dsk/c1t2d1s3 /dev/rdsk/c1t2d1s3 /usr ufs 2 yes -/
-
```

After being enabled for a particular file system, **fsck** can be executed. **fsck** checks the integrity of several different features of the file system. Most significant is the superblock, which stores summary information for the volume. Since the superblock is the most modified item on the file system, being written and rewritten every time data is changed on a disk, it is the most commonly corrupted feature. Checks on the superblock include the following:

- A check of the file system size, which obviously must be greater than the size computed from the number of blocks identified in the superblock.

- The total number of inodes, which must be less than the maximum number of inodes.

- A tally of reported free blocks and inodes.

If any of these values are identified as corrupt by **fsck**, the superuser can select one of the many superblock backups that were created during initial file-system creation as a replacement for the current superblock. We will examine superblock corruption and how to fix it in the next section. In addition to superblock, the number and status of cylinder group blocks, inodes, indirect blocks, and data blocks are also checked. Since free blocks are located by maps stored in the cylinder group, **fsck** verifies that all the blocks marked as free are not actually being used by any files—if they are, files could be corrupted. If all blocks are correctly accounted for, **fsck** determines whether the number of free blocks plus the number of used blocks equals the total number of blocks in the file system. If **fsck** detects any incongruity, the maps of unallocated blocks are rebuilt, although there is obviously a risk of data loss whenever there is a disagreement over the actual state of the file system. **fsck** always uses the actual count of inodes and/or blocks if the superblock information is wrong, and replaces the incorrect value if this is verified by the superuser. We will revisit this issue in the next section.

When inodes are examined by **fsck** the process is sequential in nature, and aims to identify inconsistencies in format and type, link count, duplicate blocks, bad block numbers, and inode size. Inodes should always be in one of three states: allocated (being used by a file), unallocated (not being used by a file), and partially allocated, meaning that during an allocation or unallocation procedure, data has been left behind that should have been deleted, or completed. Alternatively, partial allocation could result from a physical hardware failure. In both of these cases, **fsck** will attempt to clear the inode.

The link count is the number of directory entries that are linked to a particular inode. **fsck** always checks that the number of directory entries listed is correct by examining the entire directory structure, beginning with the root directory, and tallying the number of links for every inode. Clearly, the stored link count and the actual link count should agree; however, the stored link count can occasionally be different from the actual link count. This could result from a disk not being synchronized before a shutdown, for example—while changes to the file system may have been saved, the link count will not have been correctly updated. If the stored count is not zero, but the actual count is zero, then disconnected files are placed in the lost+found directory found in the top level of the file system concerned. In other cases, the actual count replaces the stored count.

An *indirect block* is a pointer to a list of every block claimed by an inode. **fsck** checks every block number against a list of allocated blocks; if it discovers that two inodes claim the same block number, that block number is added to a list of duplicate block numbers. The administrator may be asked to choose which inode is correct—obviously this can be a difficult decision, and usually it means it is time to verify files against backups. **fsck** also checks the integrity of the actual block numbers, because these can also become corrupt—a block number should always lie in the interval between the number of the first data block and the number of the last data block. If a bad block number is detected, the inode is cleared.

Directories are also checked for integrity by **fsck**. Directory entries are equivalent to file entries on the file system, except they have a different mode value in the inode. **fsck** checks for the following problems in performing its check of the validity of directory data blocks: unallocated nodes associated with inode numbers; inode numbers exceeding the maximum number of inodes for a particular file system; incorrect inode numbers for the standard directory entries that are represented by a single dot " . " and by a pair of dots " . . "; and directories actually being accidentally disconnected from the file system. We will examine some of these errors, and how they are rectified, in the next section.

**fsck** examines each disk volume in five distinct stages, performing all of the checks discussed above: phase 1, in which blocks and sizes are checked; phase 2, where pathnames are verified; phase 3, where connectivity is examined; phase 4, where an investigation of reference counts is undertaken; and phase 5, where the actual cylinder groups are checked.

## fsck Examples

In this section, we will examine a full run of **fsck**, outlining the most common problems and how they are rectified; in addition, we'll present some examples of less commonly encountered problems. On a SPARC 20 system, **fsck** for the / file system looks like this:

```
** /dev/rdsk/c0d0s0
** Currently Mounted on /
** Phase 1 - Check Blocks and Sizes
** Phase 2 - Check Pathnames
** Phase 3 - Check Connectivity
** Phase 4 - Check Reference Counts
** Phase 5 - Check Cyl groups
FREE BLK COUNT(S) WRONG IN SUPERBLK
SALVAGE?
```

Clearly, the actual block count and the block count recorded in the superblock are at odds with each other. At this point, **fsck** requires superuser permission to install the actual block count in the superblock; the administrator indicates Yes by pressing _Y_. The scan continues with the /usr partition:

```
1731 files, 22100 used, 51584 free (24 frags, 6445 blocks,  0.0% fragmentation)
** /dev/rdsk/c0d0s6
** Currently Mounted on /usr
** Phase 1 - Check Blocks and Sizes
** Phase 2 - Check Pathnames
** Phase 3 - Check Connectivity
** Phase 4 - Check Reference Counts
** Phase 5 - Check Cyl groups

FILE SYSTEM STATE IN SUPERBLOCK IS WRONG; FIX?
```

In this case, the file system state in the superblock records is incorrect, and again, the administrator is required to give consent for it to be repaired. The scan then continues with the /var and /export/home partitions:

```
26266 files, 401877 used, 217027 free (283 frags, 27093 blocks,  0.0% fragmentation)
** /dev/rdsk/c0d0s1
** Currently Mounted on /var
** Phase 1 - Check Blocks and Sizes
** Phase 2 - Check Pathnames
** Phase 3 - Check Connectivity
** Phase 4 - Check Reference Counts
** Phase 5 - Check Cyl groups
1581 files, 4360 used, 25545 free (41 frags, 3188 blocks,  0.1% fragmentation)
** /dev/rdsk/c0d0s7
** Currently Mounted on /export/home
** Phase 1 - Check Blocks and Sizes
** Phase 2 - Check Pathnames
** Phase 3 - Check Connectivity
** Phase 4 - Check Reference Counts
** Phase 5 - Check Cyl groups
2 files, 9 used, 7111589 free (13 frags, 888947 blocks,  0.0% fragmentation)
```

Obviously, the /var partition and /export/home have passed examination by **fsck** and are intact. However, the fact that the / and /usr file systems were in an inconsistent state suggests that the file systems were not unmounted cleanly, perhaps during the last reboot. Fortunately, the superblock itself was intact. You will not always be so fortunate. In the following example, the superblock of /dev/dsk/c0t0d0s2 has a bad _magic number_, indicating that it is damaged beyond repair:

**server# fsck /dev/dsk/c0t0d0s2**

```
BAD SUPERBLOCK: MAGIC NUMBER WRONG
 USE ALTERNATE SUPERBLOCK TO SUPPLY NEEDED INFORMATION
eg. fsck [-F ufs] -o b=# [special ...]
where # is the alternate super block. SEE fsck_ufs(1M).
```

In that case, you need to specify one of the alternative superblocks that were created by the **newfs** command. When a file system is created, there is a message printed about the creation of superblock backups:

```
superblock backups (for fsck -b #) at:
32, 5264, 10496, 15728, 20960, 26192, 31424, 36656, 41888,
47120, 52352, 57584, 62816, 68048, 73280, 78512, 82976, 88208,
93440, 98672, 103904, 109136, 114368, 119600, 124832, 130064,
135296, 140528, 145760, 150992, 156224, 161456.
```

In the example above, you may need to specify one of these alternative superblocks so that the disk contents are once again readable. If you didn't record the superblock backups during the creation of the file system, you can easily retrieve them by using **newfs** (and using **-N** to prevent the creation of a new file system):

**server# newfs -Nv /dev/dsk/c0t0d0s2**

Once you have determined an appropriate superblock replacement number (for example, 32), use **fsck** again to replace the older superblock with the new one:

**server# fsck -o b=32 /dev/dsk/c0t0d0s2**

Disks that have physical hardware errors often report being unable to read inodes beyond a particular point. For example, the following error message:

```
Error reading block 31821 (Attempt to read from filesystem
resulted in short read) while doing inode scan. Ignore error
<y> ?
```

stops the user from continuing with the fsck scan. This would probably be a good time to replace the disk rather than attempting any corrective action. Never be tempted to ignore these errors, hoping for the best. You will ultimately have to take responsibility for lost and damaged data, and users will be particularly unforgiving if they discover that you had advance warning of a problem.

Here is an example of what can happen if there is a link count problem:

**server # fsck /**

```
** /dev/rdsk/c0t1d0s0
** Currently Mounted on /
** Phase 1 - Check Blocks and Sizes
** Phase 2 - Check Pathnames
** Phase 3 - Check Connectivity
** Phase 4 - Check Reference Counts
LINK COUNT DIR I=4  OWNER=root MODE=40700
SIZE=4096 MTIME=Nov  1 11:56 1999  COUNT 2 SHOULD BE 4
ADJUST? y
```

If the adjustment does not fix the error, use **find** to track down the problem file, and delete it, as follows:

server# find / -mount -inum 4 -ls

It should be in the lost+found directory for the partition in question (in this case, /lost+found).

As outlined above, you can also have the problem of having duplicate inodes, as shown here:

```
** Phase 1 - Check Blocks and Sizes
  314415 DUP I=5009
  345504 DUP I=12011
  345505 DUP I=12011
  854711 DUP I=91040
  856134 DUP I=93474
  856135 DUP I=93474
```

The problem of duplicate inodes, often found in Solaris 2.5 and 2.6, does not usually occur in Solaris 7. Therefore, if you're running an earlier version of Solaris, an upgrade may correct the problem.

# System Accounting

Solaris provides a centralized auditing service that is known as *system accounting*. This service is very useful for accounting for the various tasks that your system may be involved in, as it can be used to monitor resource usage, troubleshoot system failures, isolate bottlenecks in the system, and assist in system security. In addition, system accounting acts as a real accounting service, and can be used for billing in the commercial world. In this section, we will review the major components of system accounting, including several applications and scripts that are responsible for preparing daily reports on connections, process and disk load, and usage statements for users. Once the appropriate script in /etc/init.d has been enabled, system accounting does not typically involve administrator intervention.

SYSTEM MAINTENANCE

## Collecting Data

Collecting data for accounting is simple: Create a startup script (/etc/rc2.d/S22acct) in order to begin collecting data soon after the system enters multi-user mode, and optionally, create a kill script (/etc/rc0.d/K22acct) to turn off data collection cleanly before the system shuts down. As per standard System V practice, you should create a single script in **/etc/init.d** (e.g., /etc/init.d/accounting) and link it symbolically to both of those filenames, thus ensuring that both a start and a stop parameter can be interpreted by the script. (See Chapter 4 for examples.) When accounting is enabled, details of processes, storage, and user activity are recorded in specially created log files, which are then processed daily by the **/usr/lib/acct/runacct** program. The output from **runacct** is also processed by **/usr/lib/acct/prdaily** (which generates the reports described in the next section). There is also a separate monthly billing program called **/usr/lib/acct/monacct**, which is executed monthly, and generates accounts for individual users.

The accounting file startup and shutdown script should look like this:

```
parameter=$1
case $parameter in
'start')
     echo "Initializing process accounting"
        /usr/lib/acct/startup
        ;;
'stop')
        echo "Halting process accounting"
        /usr/lib/acct/shutacct
        ;;
esac
```

When called with the start parameter, this script executes another script, /usr/lib/acct/startup, which is responsible for executing the **/usr/lib/acct/acctwtmp** program, which sets up record-writing utilities in the /var/adm/wtmp file. It then starts a script called turnacct, which is called with the name of the file in which the kernel records the process accounting details. (Usually that file is named /var/adm/pacct.) Finally, the startup section of the script removes all the temporary files associated with previous accounting activities.

## Generating Reports

Once data collection has been enabled, generating reports is a simple matter of setting up a **cron** job for a nonprivileged user (usually adm), typically at a time of low system load. In the following example, accounting runs are performed at 6 A.M.:

```
0 6 * * * /usr/lib/acct/runacct 2> /var/adm/acct/nite/fd2log
```

The file /var/adm/acct/nite/fd2log contains a log of the accounting run. A typical entry might look like this:

```
cat: cannot open /var/adm/acct/nite/statefile
```

This indicates that either the statefile does not exist or has incorrect permissions for a nonprivleged user like adm. This should be corrected as soon as possible. You might also see a message about the holidays file:

```
***UPDATE /etc/acct/holidays WITH NEW HOLIDAYS***
```

If we examine /etc/acct/holidays, here's what we find:

```
1/1             New Years Day
1/2             Concession Day
1/26            Australia Day
4/10            Good Friday
4/13            Easter Monday
4/14            Easter Tuesday
4/25            Anzac Day
6/8             Queen's Birthday
10/5            Labour Day
12/25           Christmas
12/26           Boxing Day
12/29           Concession Day
12/30           Concession Day
12/31           Concession Day
```

All holidays listed can be localized to a specific geographic location (in this example, Australian holidays are shown). Holidays affect the way that both prime time and non-prime time hours are processed in the accounting system, as all holidays are counted as non-prime time. Thus, only holidays that are intended to be counted as non-prime should be recorded as such in the holidays file.

A typical command summary (cms) statement is shown in Table 9-1. Once you know what each column in this report represents, it becomes obvious that in this example, reading, sending, and receiving mail are the main uses of this server, on a daily basis at least, while the **runacct** command, which actually performs the accounting, was one of the least used programs! Here is an explanation of the columns in the preceding report:

■ **CMND NAME**   Shows the command as executed. This can lead to some ambiguity, as different commands could have the same filename. In addition, any shell or Perl scripts executed would be displayed under the shell and Perl interpreter respectively, rather than showing up as a process on their own.

| CMND NAME | NUMBER CMNDS | TOTAL KCOREMIN | TOTAL CPU-MIN | TOTAL REAL-MIN | MEAN SIZE-K | MEAN CPU-MIN | HOG FACTOR | CHARS TRNSFRD | BLOCKS READ |
|---|---|---|---|---|---|---|---|---|---|
| TOTALS | 1034 | 1843.03 | 0.46 | 546.88 | 4049.14 | 0.00 | 0.00 | 107141376 | 982 |
| pine | 5 | 1426.41 | 0.11 | 177.47 | 13477.87 | 0.02 | 0.00 | 72782400 | 237 |
| sendmail | 171 | 176.44 | 0.09 | 4.73 | 1873.71 | 0.00 | 0.02 | 14895311 | 306 |
| sh | 107 | 31.15 | 0.04 | 0.29 | 881.70 | 0.00 | 0.12 | 58380 | 0 |
| uudemon | 114 | 27.91 | 0.02 | 0.10 | 1154.92 | 0.00 | 0.24 | 67765 | 8 |
| in.ftpd | 1 | 23.20 | 0.02 | 0.69 | 1435.05 | 0.02 | 0.02 | 6442528 | 7 |
| mail.loc | 13 | 19.69 | 0.02 | 0.06 | 1193.21 | 0.00 | 0.27 | 11973498 | 57 |
| tcsh | 4 | 13.61 | 0.01 | 179.98 | 1361.33 | 0.00 | 0.00 | 153040 | 1 |
| uuxqt | 48 | 11.01 | 0.01 | 0.08 | 1159.30 | 0.00 | 0.13 | 35568 | 0 |
| uusched | 48 | 10.99 | 0.01 | 0.09 | 1014.52 | 0.00 | 0.13 | 36096 | 180 |
| popper | 9 | 7.84 | 0.01 | 1.55 | 1205.74 | 0.00 | 0.00 | 155107 | 32 |
| sed | 58 | 7.63 | 0.01 | 0.02 | 618.38 | 0.00 | 0.58 | 44907 | 2 |
| date | 34 | 7.26 | 0.01 | 0.01 | 821.74 | 0.00 | 0.72 | 26348 | 1 |
| rm | 36 | 5.68 | 0.01 | 0.02 | 681.44 | 0.00 | 0.45 | 0 | 8 |
| acctcms | 4 | 4.92 | 0.01 | 0.01 | 953.03 | 0.00 | 0.97 | 125984 | 1 |
| in.telne | 4 | 4.85 | 0.00 | 180.03 | 1076.74 | 0.00 | 0.00 | 55744 | 0 |
| cp | 42 | 4.47 | 0.01 | 0.02 | 525.65 | 0.00 | 0.36 | 14434 | 60 |
| ckpacct | 24 | 4.23 | 0.00 | 0.09 | 907.14 | 0.00 | 0.05 | 49200 | 0 |
| awk | 26 | 4.01 | 0.01 | 0.02 | 616.82 | 0.00 | 0.36 | 950 | 0 |
| chmod | 37 | 3.69 | 0.01 | 0.01 | 553.60 | 0.00 | 0.55 | 0 | 0 |
| cat | 22 | 3.58 | 0.00 | 0.01 | 825.54 | 0.00 | 0.55 | 1540 | 2 |
| acctprc | 1 | 2.98 | 0.00 | 0.00 | 744.00 | 0.00 | 0.96 | 46152 | 0 |

**Table 9-1.** *Command Summary Statement*

- **NUMBER CMNDS**   Displays the number of times that the command named under **CMND NAME** was executed during the accounting period.

- **TOTAL KCOREMIN**   Shows the cumulative sum of memory segments (in kilobytes) used by the process identified under **CMND NAME** per minute of execution time.

- **TOTAL CPU-MIN**   Prints the accumulated processing time for the program named under **CMND NAME**.

- **TOTAL REAL-MIN**   Shows the actual time in minutes that the program named in **CMND NAME** consumed during the accounting period.

- **MEAN SIZE-K**   Indicates the average of the cumulative sum of consumed memory segments (**TOTAL KCOREMIN**) over the set of invocations denoted by **NUMBER CMDS**.

- **MEAN CPU-MIN**   The average CPU time computed from the quotient of **NUMBER CMDS** divided by **TOTAL CPU-MIN**.

- **HOG FACTOR**   The amount of CPU time divided by actual elapsed time. This ratio indicates the degree to which a system is available compared to its use. The hog factor is often used as a metric to determine overall load levels for a system, and is useful for planning upgrades and expansion.

- **CHARS TRNSFD**   Displays the sum of the characters transferred by system calls.

- **BLOCKS READ**   Shows the number of physical block reads and writes that the program named under **CMND NAME** accounted for.

Often, the values of these parameters are confusing: For example, let's compare the characteristics of **pine**, which is a mail client, and **sendmail**, which is a mail transport agent. **pine** was only executed five times, but accounted for 1426.41 KCOREMIN, while **sendmail** was executed 171 times with a KCOREMIN of 176.44. The explanation for this apparent anomaly is that users probably log in once in the morning, and leave their **pine** mail client running all day. The users sent an average of 34.2 messages during this day, many of which contained attachments, thus accounting for the high CPU overhead.

When examined over a number of days, accounting figures provide a useful means of understanding how processes are making use of the system's resources. When examined in isolation, however, they can sometimes misrepresent the dominant processes that the machine is used for. This is a well-known aspect of statistical sampling: Before you can make any valid generalizations about a phenomenon, your observations must be repeated and sampled randomly. Thus, it is useful to compare the day-to-day variation of a system's resource use with the monthly figures that are generated by **/usr/lib/acct/monacct**. Table 9-2 compares these daily values with the previous month's values generated by **monacct**.

SYSTEM MAINTENANCE

| COMMAND NAME | NUMBER CMNDS | TOTAL KCOREMIN | TOTAL CPU-MIN | TOTAL REAL-MIN | MEAN SIZE-K | MEAN CPU-MIN | HOG FACTOR | CHARS TRNSFRD | BLOCKS READ |
|---|---|---|---|---|---|---|---|---|---|
| TOTALS | 513833 | 529119.94 | 262.83 | 632612.94 | 2013.17 | 0.00 | 0.00 | 895961208 | 138299 |
| nscp | 1538 | 163985.79 | 6.77 | 59865.58 | 2423.18 | 0.00 | 0.00 | 4744854 | 720 |
| Installp | 110508 | 58676.62 | 33.65 | 197.77 | 1743.57 | 0.00 | 0.17 | 27303024 | 139 |
| Sed | 122726 | 45704.45 | 40.87 | 98.07 | 1118.16 | 0.00 | 0.42 | 20044188 | 171 |
| Pine | 165 | 43839.27 | 3.88 | 1594.97 | 11304.12 | 0.02 | 0.00 | 1578316160 | 4675 |
| Project | 13 | 37654.92 | 22.76 | 22.79 | 1654.41 | 1.75 | 1.00 | 6187332 | 106 |
| ll-ar | 4 | 24347.44 | 26.49 | 50.37 | 919.24 | 6.62 | 0.53 | 201642 | 5 |
| nawk | 75544 | 21678.96 | 24.46 | 40.21 | 886.40 | 0.00 | 0.61 | 61351684 | 135 |
| predict | 289 | 16808.70 | 13.59 | 13.74 | 1236.66 | 0.05 | 0.99 | 38996306 | 293 |
| Sqpe | 17 | 15078.86 | 4.15 | 10.30 | 3636.67 | 0.24 | 0.40 | 90547712 | 889 |
| Grep | 71963 | 13042.15 | 18.69 | 26.47 | 697.69 | 0.00 | 0.71 | 377825714 | 3 |
| Pkgparam | 24578 | 11360.71 | 9.11 | 9.68 | 1246.38 | 0.00 | 0.94 | 102325648 | 0 |
| false_ne | 7 | 10399.85 | 2.12 | 2.13 | 4899.81 | 0.30 | 1.00 | 212530 | 5 |
| pkgremov | 89 | 10073.67 | 8.95 | 22.70 | 1125.88 | 0.10 | 0.39 | 1129787392 | 18845 |
| pkginsta | 125 | 7163.67 | 4.75 | 38.21 | 1508.46 | 0.04 | 0.12 | 1912983552 | 4077 |
| tee | 8622 | 3237.38 | 2.03 | 2.30 | 1592.24 | 0.00 | 0.88 | 2134692 | 0 |
| ls | 8825 | 3133.31 | 2.59 | 3.31 | 1209.06 | 0.00 | 0.78 | 2038136 | 215 |

**Table 9-2.** *Variation Comparison Of A System's Resource Use With The Monthly Figures Generated by /usr/lib/acct/monacct*

As we can see, the individual day's figures are misleading: In fact, spread over a whole month, the **netscape** program tended to use more resources than the **pine** mail client, being invoked 1,538 times, and using 163985.79 KCOREMIN, compared to 165 invocations and 43839.27 KCOREMIN for **pine**. Clearly, it is very useful to examine monthly averages for a more reliable, strategic overview of system activity, while daily summaries are useful for making tactical decisions about active processes.

## Charging Fees

In the previous section, we looked at the output for **monacct**, which is the monthly accounting program. To enable **monacct**, a **cron** job needs to be created for the adm account, which is similar to the entry for the **runacct** command in the previous section:

```
0 5 1 * * /usr/lib/acct/monacct
```

In addition to computing per-process statistics, **monacct** also computes usage information on a per-user basis, which can be used to bill customers according to the number of CPU minutes they used. Table 9-3 examines user reports for the same month that was reviewed in the previous section:

Of the nonsystem users, obviously pwatters is going to have a large bill this month, with 65 prime CPU minutes consumed. Billing could also proceed on the basis of KCOREMINS utilized; pwatters, in this case, used 104572 KCOREMINS. How an organization bills its users is probably already well established, but even if users are not billed for cash payment, examining how the system is used is very valuable for planning expansion and for identifying rogue processes that reduce the availability of a system for legitimate processes.

 # Summary

In this chapter, we examined advanced methods for file system management and usage monitoring, which could be used for both system maintenance purposes and for forming the basis for billing users. In addition to developing user-based policies, we also examined how these could be effectively enforced using hard and soft disk quotas.

# How to Find Out More

For more information regarding the tuning of systems based on accounting data and other measurements, see the following:

Cockroft, Adrian; and Pettit, Richard. *Sun Performance and Tuning*.
(Sun Microsystems Press, 1998.)

| UID | LOGIN NAME | CPU (MINS) PRIME | CPU (MINS) NPRIME | KCORE-MINS PRIME | KCORE-MINS NPRIME | CONNECT (MINS) PRIME | CONNECT (MINS) NPRIME | # DISK BLOCKS | # OF PROCS | # OF SESS | # DISK SAMPLES | FEE |
|---|---|---|---|---|---|---|---|---|---|---|---|---|
| TOTAL | 233 | 30 | 363969 | 158762 | 1061 | 1005 | 11830502 | 513833 | 134 | 45 | 0 | |
| 0 | root | 157 | 4 | 180984 | 3881 | 546 | 0 | 1858608 | 444602 | 3 | 3 | 0 |
| 1 | daemon | 0 | 0 | 0 | 0 | 0 | 0 | 6 | 0 | 0 | 3 | 0 |
| 2 | bin | 0 | 0 | 0 | 0 | 0 | 0 | 5759280 | 0 | 0 | 3 | 0 |
| 3 | sys | 0 | 0 | 114 | 89 | 0 | 0 | 18 | 51 | 0 | 3 | 0 |
| 4 | adm | 1 | 7 | 618 | 4856 | 0 | 0 | 15136 | 20005 | 0 | 3 | 0 |
| 5 | uucp | 1 | 4 | 1371 | 3557 | 0 | 0 | 5088 | 22036 | 0 | 3 | 0 |
| 10 | pwatters | 65 | 6 | 104572 | 15758 | 197 | 88 | 2026666 | 1842 | 68 | 3 | 0 |
| 12 | llee | 0 | 0 | 0 | 0 | 0 | 0 | 12 | 0 | 0 | 3 | 0 |
| 71 | lp | 0 | 0 | 0 | 26 | 0 | 0 | 13822 | 134 | 0 | 3 | 0 |
| 108 | jsmith | 0 | 0 | 0 | 0 | 0 | 0 | 318 | 0 | 0 | 3 | 0 |
| 436 | dbrown | 0 | 0 | 0 | 0 | 0 | 0 | 48 | 0 | 0 | 3 | 0 |
| 1001 | bjones | 0 | 0 | 16 | 9 | 0 | 2 | 78 | 21 | 2 | 3 | 0 |
| 1002 | ledwards | 0 | 0 | 130 | 21 | 0 | 0 | 34 | 102 | 0 | 3 | 0 |
| 1003 | tgonzale | 0 | 0 | 0 | 0 | 0 | 0 | 40896 | 0 | 0 | 3 | 0 |
| 1012 | ljung | 5 | 10 | 74282 | 130564 | 318 | 915 | 2110492 | 3521 | 61 | 3 | 0 |
| 60001 | nobody | 3 | 0 | 1883 | 0 | 0 | 0 | 0 | 21519 | 0 | 0 | 0 |

**Table 9-3.**   *monacct Also Computes Usage Information on a Per-User Basis*

# The Complete Reference

Solaris 8

# Chapter 10

## Backups

Software and hardware failures are an unfortunate fact of life in the IT industry. These incidents often cause a sense of panic in organizations, especially when data is lost or corrupted during a peak service period. A system crash or a disk failure should not be a cause for alarm. The administrator should be well armed and well prepared to, first, determine the cause of the problem; second, rectify any hardware faults; and third, restore any lost data by using a recovery procedure. Solaris provides a wide variety of backup and restore software that can be used in conjunction with any number of media, for example, magnetic and digital audio tapes, writable CD-ROMs, Zip drives, and intentionally redundant hard drives. In this chapter, we will examine the development and implementation of backup and recovery procedures with Solaris, and review some popular freeware and commercial backup and recovery tools (also referred to as backup and restore tools).

## Understanding Backups

In most organizations that use Solaris server systems, the data that is stored in user files and database tables is quite valuable, if not vital, to the organization or its users. In addition, many organizations provide services that rely on server uptime and information availability in order to manage the business, generate income, and maintain or enhance the organization's reputation. On a small scale, a departmental server might provide file serving, authentication services, and print access for a handful or several hundred employees. If the server hard disk crashes, the affected users won't be able to read their mail or retrieve their files and are going to be very angry at 9 A.M. if system data cannot be restored in a timely fashion. On a larger scale, if a major business-to-consumer web site, like Amazon.com, or a business-to-business hub, like Office.com, experiences any downtime, every minute that the system is unavailable costs the organization money in lost sales, frustrated consumers, and reduced customer confidence. Just as much as commercial sites, government web sites that provide valuable advice to government, business, and consumers (for example the Government Accounting Office's site, **http://www.gao.gov**) are expected to be available continuously. Moreover, in all of the types of situations mentioned here, it is not enough just to ensure that an organization's service is highly available; it is at least as important that the restored data that it provides after an outage needs to be *valid*. Validity is why backups need to be taken seriously and regularly.

In this section, we will examine the background and rationale for providing a reliable backup and restore service that will in turn ensure a high level of service provision, even in the event of hardware failure.

### Why Do You Need Backups?

The primary demand we make of a backup and recovery service is that it rapidly restore a malfunctioning system to a functional state. The relationship between time of restoration and user satisfaction is inverse, as shown in Figure 10-1: The longer a restore takes, the faster users will become angry; conversely, the rapid restoration of service will give users confidence in the service they are using. For this reason, many sites require "full dump" backups of the entire file system at one moment in time (a "snapshot") *and* incremental backups of their complete file systems each night.

The second requirement we place on a backup and recovery service is that it ensures data integrity. It is not sufficient just to restore some data and hope that it's "close enough" to the original; it is essential that all restored data can actually be used by applications, as if no break in service had occurred. This is particularly important for database applications, which may have several different kinds of files associated with them—table indexes, data files, and rollback segments must all be synchronized if the database is to operate correctly, and user data must be consistent with the internal structure and table ownership rights. If files are simply backed up onto disk while the database is open, those files can be restored, true, but that doesn't necessarily mean that the database system will be able to use the files. It is essential to understand the restoration and data integrity requirements for all key applications on your system, and identify any risks that might be presented by data corruption. A comprehensive backup and restore plan should include provision for regular cold and warm dumps of databases to a file system that is itself regularly backed up. A cold database dump can be taken when the database server is offline; a warm database dump can be taken while the database server is still running.

A third requirement for a backup and restore service is flexibility. Data should be recorded and compressed on media that can potentially be read on a different machine, using a different operating system. In addition, using alternative media for concurrent backups is also useful for ensuring availability in case of hardware failure of a backup device. For example, you may use a DDS-3 DAT tape drive as your main backup device for nightly incremental backups, but you may also decide to burn a CD-R every

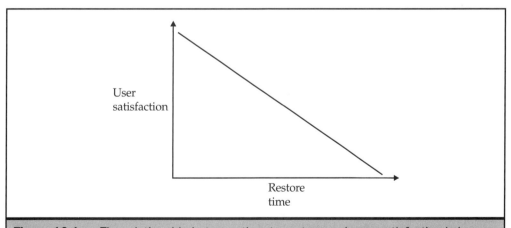

**Figure 10-1.**    *The relationship between time to restore and user satisfaction is inverse*

week with a full dump of the database. If your server should be affected by a power surge, and the DAT drive is damaged, and a replacement would take one week to arrive, then the CD-R dump can be used as a fallback, even though it may not be completely up to date.

# Determining a Backup Strategy

Typical backup and restore strategies employ two related methods for recording data to any medium: full and incremental dumps. A full dump involves copying an entire file system or set of file systems to a backup medium. Historically, large file systems have taken a long time to back up because of slow tape speeds and poor I/O performance, and the incremental method was developed to address the problem of slow backups. An incremental dump is an iterative method that involves performing a baseline dump on a regular basis (usually once every week), and then performing a further dump every night of those files that have changed since the previous full dump. Although this approach can require the maintenance of complex lists of files and file sizes, in most cases it reduces the overall time to back up a file system, because on most file systems only a small proportion of the total number of files changes from week to week. This reduces the overall load on the backup server, and incidentally improves tape performance by minimizing friction on drive heads. However, using incremental backups can increase the time to restore a system, as up to seven backup tapes must be processed in order to restore data files fully. (Seven tapes are required so that a single tape can be assigned to each day.) Many sites even use a combination of incremental and full daily dumps on multiple media to ensure that full restores can be performed rapidly, and to ensure redundant recording of key data.

After deciding on an incremental or full dump (or combination) backup strategy, it is important to plan how backups can be integrated into an existing network. There are four possible configurations that can be considered, as illustrated in the following figures.

The simplest approach is to attach a single backup device to each server, so that it acts as its own backup host. One such configuration is shown in Figure 10-2.

The first approach is appealing because it allows data to be backed up and restored using the same device, without any requirement for network connectivity. However, it does not provide for redundancy through the use of multiple backup devices. This can be provided for by including multiple backup devices for a single host. This configuration is shown in Figure 10-3.

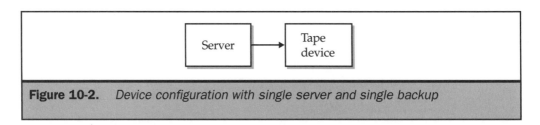

**Figure 10-2.** *Device configuration with single server and single backup*

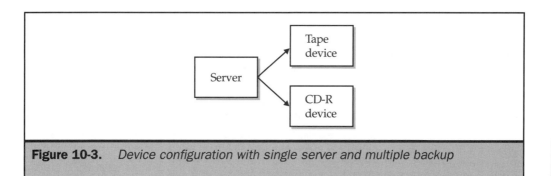

**Figure 10-3.** *Device configuration with single server and multiple backup*

The cost of maintaining single or multiple backup devices for each server in an organization can be very high. In order to reduce costs, many organizations have moved to centralize the management and storage of data for entire departments or sites on a single server. This approach is detailed in Figure 10-4, in which multiple client machines have their local hard drives backed up to a central Solaris server. As shown in the figure, the central backup server can also be attached to multiple backup devices, providing different levels of redundancy for data of greater or lesser relative significance. For example, although most data from user PCs might not require double or triple redundancy, financial records might well deserve such extra protection. The freeware software product AMANDA, reviewed later in this chapter, is ideal for backing up multiple clients through a single backup server, with or without multiple backup devices.

There is also an increasing trend toward developing "storage area networks" (SANs), where backup management and data storage are distributed across multiple backup hosts and multiple devices. Thus, a client's data could potentially be stored on many different

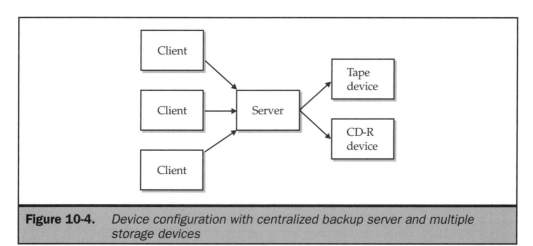

**Figure 10-4.** *Device configuration with centralized backup server and multiple storage devices*

backup servers, and management of that data could be performed from a remote manager running on the client. This configuration is shown in Figure 10-5. For example, there is a Veritas client for Windows called Backup Exec, which can connect to many different Solaris servers through an SMB service, such as SAMBA, backing up data to multiple media. Other server-side packages, such as Legato Networker, offer distributed management of all backup services. Both of these products will be reviewed later in this chapter. New to the game is Sun's own Java-based Jiro technology, which implements the proposed Federated Management Architecture (FMA) standard. FMA is one proposal for implementing distributed storage across networks in a standard way and is receiving support from major hardware manufacturers like Hitachi, Quantum, Veritas, and Fujitsu for future integration with their products. More information on Jiro and FMA can be found at **http://www.jiro.com/**.

# Selecting Backup Media

The main media currently in use for backup and restoration are tapes, disk drives, Zip and Jaz drives, and recordable or rewritable CDs. The backup medium you select should be chosen to best meet the triple requirements of rapid restoration, data integrity, and flexibility. Reliability must also be considered, as well as capacity and data size. For example, while tapes are generally considered very reliable for bulk storage, tape drives are much slower than a hard drive. On the other hand, a

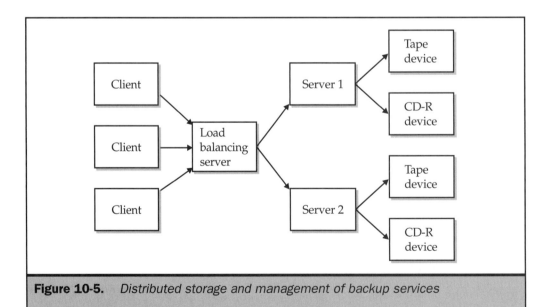

**Figure 10-5.** *Distributed storage and management of backup services*

20-gigabyte tape is much cheaper than an equivalent-capacity hard drive, so the cost of any backup solutions must be weighed against the value of the data being stored. It can be just as important to consider the size of the data being backed up, and how often the data on a hard disk changes. These factors affect how large the tapes will need to be to store incremental dumps. For more information on choosing a bulk storage device, see the FAQ for the USENET forum comp.arch.storage at the following site:

**http://alumni.caltech.edu/~rdv/comp-arch-storage/FAQ-1.html**

# Tape Drives

Solaris supports many tape drives, from Archive's old "Quarter Inch Cartridge" QIC 150 (with a maximum 250-MB capacity) to modern digital audio tape (DAT) and digital linear tape (DLT) systems. The QIC 150 is a low-end drive that takes a two-reel cassette; it was widely used in many early Sun workstations. DAT tapes for DDS-2 drives have a capacity of 4 to 8 GB, while tapes for the newer DDS-3 standard have 12 to 24 GB capacity, depending on compression ratios. DDS-2 drives can typically record between 400 and 800 KB per second, again depending upon compression ratios. The transition from analog to digital encoding methods has increased the performance and reliability of tape-based backup methods, and they are still the most commonly used methods today. Digital linear tape drives are becoming more popular in the enterprise because of their very large storage capacities. For example, a Compaq 1624 DLT drive can store between 35 and 70 GB, depending upon the compression, which is much more than the DAT drives can do. They also feature much higher transfer rates, between 1.25 and 2.5 MB per second. Of course, DLT drives are more expensive than DAT drives, just as DAT drives have always been more costly than a QIC. Admittedly, though, a QIC is generally much too small to be useful for most systems today.

# Hard Drives

Since hard drives have the fastest seek times of all backup media, they are often used to store archives of user files, copied from client drives using an SMB service. In addition, hard drives form the basis of so-called RAID systems (*redundant array of inexpensive disks*). An array of disk drives can work together as a single, logical storage device, collectively acting as a single storage system, and by virtue of its built-in redundancy can withstand the loss of one or more of its constituent devices. For example, depending on the "level" of RAID protection, if a single drive in the array is damaged by a power surge, then your system may be able to continue its functions with a minimum of administrator interference and no impact on functionality, until the drive is replaced. Many systems now support hot-swapping of drives, so that the faulty drive could be removed and replaced without shutting down the system.

You may be wondering why, if RAID is easily available, anybody would consider still using backups. The answer is that entire RAID arrays are just as vulnerable to power surges as a single drive; in the event of a full hardware failure, all your data could still be lost unless it is stored safely off-site, on a tape or CD-ROM. To circumvent concurrent drive corruption at the end of a disk's life, many administrators not only use drives of equivalent capacities from different manufacturers, but they are perennially buying new drives "to add to the mix," as it were, in order to maintain an array of drives of different vintages (i.e., at least one of the drives is always newer than the others and will supposedly have a longer life). Many administrators seek *used* drives to add to their otherwise newer arrays in order to maintain the differences in age. These ploys greatly lessen the chances that two or more drives would fail at the same time from age or use.

RAID has many protection levels, which are numbered starting from zero; RAID levels 0 and 1 are the most commonly used. RAID level 0 involves "parallelizing" data transfer between disks, spreading data across multiple drives and thereby improving overall data transmission rates. This technique is known as *striping*. While RAID level 0 has the ability to write multiple disks concurrently, it does not support redundancy, which is provided with RAID level 1. This level makes an identical copy of a primary disk onto a secondary disk. This kind of *mirroring* provides complete redundancy: If the primary disk fails, the secondary disk is able to provide all the data that was contained on the primary disk until the primary disk is replaced. Because striping and mirroring consume large amounts of disk space, the cost of maintaining the actual data is rather high on a per megabyte basis. Higher RAID levels use heuristic techniques in attempt to provide similar functionality while reducing the overall cost. For example, RAID level 4 stores parity information only and uses only a single drive, rather than an array, which reduces the overall amount of disk space required, but is more risky than RAID level 1. For the latest developments in RAID technology, see the following web site: **http://www.raid.org/**.

| Tip | *Software RAID solutions typically support both striping and mirroring. This speeds up data writing and makes provision for the transfer of control from the primary disk to the secondary disk in the event of a primary disk failure. In addition, many software solutions support different RAID levels on different partitions on a disk, which may also be useful in reducing the overall amount of disk space required to store data safely. For example, while users might require access to a fast partition using RAID level 0, there may be another partition that is dedicated to a financial database, which requires mirroring (thus RAID level 1). Sun's **DiskSuite** product is currently one of the most popular software RAID solutions.* |
|---|---|

Custom hardware configurations involving RAID are also proving popular, because of the minimal administrative overhead involved with installing and configuring such systems. While not exactly "plug and play," external RAID arrays, such as the StorEdge A1000, have many individual disks that can be used to implement both mirroring and striping, and can manage data transfer rates of up to 40 MB per second. Banks of fast-caching memory, up to 80 MB, are available in some RAID configurations to speed up disk writes by temporarily storing them in RAM before writing them to one or more disks in the array. A RAID array using this RAM technique is significantly faster than a normal disk drive.

## Zip/Jaz Disks

Portable, magnetic storage media like Zip and Jaz drives, discussed in Chapter 7, can be useful as a backup medium. Only the SCSI interfaces for Zip and Jaz are fully supported under Solaris, but it may be possible to use ATAPI interfaces on Solaris x86. At this writing, USB and parallel-port interfaces are also not supported under Solaris. Zip drives come in two storage capacities: the standard 100MB drive, and the expanded 250MB drive, which is backward compatible with the 100MB drive. Admittedly, a 100 or 250MB drive is not going to get you very far with backups, even though Zip drives have relatively fast write speeds compared with tape drives. Zip drives are most useful for dumps of database tables or user files that need to be interchanged with PCs and other client systems.

Jaz drives offer several improvements over Zip technology, the most distinguishing characteristic being their increased storage capacity. Jaz drives also come in two flavors: the standard 1GB drive, and a newer 2GB version, which is backward compatible with the standard drive. The Jaz drive is also much faster than the Zip drive, with reported average seek times of around 10 ms. This makes Jaz drives comparable in speed to many IDE hard drives, and provides the flexibility of easily sharing data between server and client systems.

Zip drive technology has improved in recent years. However, early versions of the 100M suffered from a problem known as the "click of death," where a drive would fail to read or write while a number of repetitive clicks were heard from inside the drive. This problem has disappeared with newer models, and users should feel confident in using Zip as a storage medium. For a history of the "click of death" problem, see Steve Gibson's page:

> **http://grc.com/clickdeath.htm**

Further discussion of Zip and Jaz drives can be found on the **alt.iomega.zip.jazz** USENET forum.

## CD-Rs and CD-RWs

CD recording and CD rewriting devices, discussed in Chapter 7, are rapidly gaining momentum as desktop backup systems. They are cheap, fast, and, in the case of CD-RW, reusable. In backup systems, CD-R and CD-RW devices serve two separate purposes, respectively: Because CD-RW disks can be reused, they are very useful for day-to-day backup operations; CD-R disks, on the other hand, are more useful for archiving and auditing purposes.

For example, many organizations outsource their development projects to third-party contractors. In such situations, it is useful for both the contractor and the client to have an archival copy of what has been developed in case there is some later disagreement concerning developmental goals and milestones. Also, contracts involved with government organizations may require regular snapshots to satisfy auditing requirements. Since CD-R is a write-once, read-only technology, it is best suited to these purposes related to preserving evidence of how something stood at a specific point in time. Otherwise, CD-R is wasteful as a normal backup medium: Its write-once limitation means the disk is trash as soon as the next full dump is performed. CD-RWs are much better for backup purposes: They can be rewritten hundreds of times to keep them up-to-date, and with over 600 MB of storage, they are competitive with Zip drives for storage and much cheaper per unit than Jaz drives.

# Performing Backup and Restore

Backup and restore software falls into three categories:

- Standard Solaris tools, like **tar**, **dd**, **cpio**, **ufsdump**, and **ufsrestore**, which are quite adequate for backing up single machines, even with multiple backup devices
- Centralized backup tools, like AMANDA and Legato Networker, which are useful for backing up multiple machines through a single backup server
- Distributed backup tools, like Veritas NetBackup, which are capable of managing storage remotely for multiple machines

## Standard Solaris Tools

In this section, we will examine the standard Solaris backup and restore tools that are generally used for single machines with one or two backup devices.

In addition to backing up and recovering from data loss, the standard Solaris backup and restore tools are often useful for normal users to manage their own accounts on the server. For example, users can create "tape archives" using the **tar** command, whose output can be written to a single disk file. This is a standard way of distributing source trees in the Solaris and broader UNIX community. Users can also use the **dd** command to make copies of disks and tapes.

It is also possible to back up database files in combination with standard Solaris tools. For example, Oracle server is supplied with an **exp** utility, which can be used to perform a dump of the database while it is still running:

```
exp system/manager FULL=Y
```

where system is the username for an administrator with DBA privileges, and manager is the password. This will create a file called expat.dmp, which can then be scheduled to be backed up every night using a **cron** job like:

```
0 3 * * * exp system/manager FULL=Y
```

Although some sites prefer to perform full dumps every night, this involves transferring an entire file system to a backup medium. That entails a small system overhead if the file system is only a few megabytes, but a large overhead for, say, a database with a tablespace of 50 gigabytes. The latter would place a great strain on a backup server, especially if it was also used for other purposes. Thus, it might be more appropriate to perform an incremental dump, which only records data that has changed. Incremental dumps will be discussed in the section on **ufsdump**.

## Using tar

The **tar** command is used to create a tape archive, or to extract the files contained in a tape archive. Although **tar** was originally conceived with a tape device in mind, in fact, any device can hold a **tar** file, including a normal disk file system. This is why users have adopted **tar** as their standard archiving utility, even though it does not perform compression like the Zip tools for PCs. Tape archives are easy to transport between systems using FTP or secure-copy in binary transfer mode, and are the standard means of exchanging data between Solaris systems.

As an example, let's create a tar file of the /opt/totalnet package. First, check the potential size of the tape archive by using the **du** command:

**server% cd /opt/totalnet**

**server% du**

```
4395      ./bin
367       ./lib/charset
744       ./lib/drv
434       ./lib/pcbin
777       ./lib/tds
5731      ./lib
5373      ./sbin
145       ./man/man1
135       ./man/man1m
281       ./man
53        ./docs/images
56        ./docs
15837     .
```

The estimated size of the archive in this example is therefore 15,387 blocks. This could also have been achieved by using the command **du -s**, which just computes the size without printing the details of directory sizes. To create a tape archive in the /tmp directory for the whole package, including subdirectories, execute the following command:

**server# tar cvf /tmp/totalnet.tar \***

```
a bin/ 0K
a bin/atattr 54K
a bin/atconvert 58K
a bin/atkprobe 27K
a bin/csr.tn 6K
a bin/ddpinfo 10K
a bin/desk 17K
a bin/ipxprobe 35K
a bin/m2u 4K
a bin/maccp 3K
a bin/macfsck 3K
a bin/macmd 3K
a bin/macmv 3K
a bin/macrd 3K
a bin/macrm 3K
a bin/nbmessage 141K
a bin/nbq 33K
a bin/nbucheck 8K
a bin/ncget 65K
a bin/ncprint 66K
a bin/ncput 65K
a bin/nctime 32K
a bin/nwmessage 239K
a bin/nwq 26K
a bin/pfinfo 70K
a bin/ruattr 122K
a bin/rucopy 129K
a bin/rudel 121K
a bin/rudir 121K
a bin/ruhelp 9K
a bin/u2m 4K
a bin/rumd 120K
a bin/rumessage 192K
a bin/ruprint 124K
```

```
a bin/rurd 120K
a bin/ruren 121K
```

To extract the tar file's contents to disks, execute the following commands:

**server# cd /tmp**

**server# tar xvf totalnet.tar**

```
x bin, 0 bytes, 0 tape blocks
x bin/atattr, 54676 bytes, 107 tape blocks
x bin/atconvert, 58972 bytes, 116 tape blocks
x bin/atkprobe, 27524 bytes, 54 tape blocks
x bin/csr.tn, 5422 bytes, 11 tape blocks
x bin/ddpinfo, 9800 bytes, 20 tape blocks
x bin/desk, 16456 bytes, 33 tape blocks
x bin/ipxprobe, 35284 bytes, 69 tape blocks
x bin/m2u, 3125 bytes, 7 tape blocks
x bin/maccp, 2882 bytes, 6 tape blocks
x bin/macfsck, 2592 bytes, 6 tape blocks
x bin/macmd, 2255 bytes, 5 tape blocks
x bin/macmv, 2866 bytes, 6 tape blocks
x bin/macrd, 2633 bytes, 6 tape blocks
x bin/macrm, 2509 bytes, 5 tape blocks
x bin/nbmessage, 143796 bytes, 281 tape blocks
x bin/nbq, 33068 bytes, 65 tape blocks
x bin/nbucheck, 7572 bytes, 15 tape blocks
x bin/ncget, 66532 bytes, 130 tape blocks
x bin/ncprint, 67204 bytes, 132 tape blocks
x bin/ncput, 65868 bytes, 129 tape blocks
x bin/nctime, 32596 bytes, 64 tape blocks
x bin/nwmessage, 244076 bytes, 477 tape blocks
x bin/nwq, 26076 bytes, 51 tape blocks
x bin/pfinfo, 71192 bytes, 140 tape blocks
x bin/ruattr, 123988 bytes, 243 tape blocks
x bin/rucopy, 131636 bytes, 258 tape blocks
x bin/rudel, 122940 bytes, 241 tape blocks
x bin/rudir, 123220 bytes, 241 tape blocks
x bin/ruhelp, 8356 bytes, 17 tape blocks
x bin/u2m, 3140 bytes, 7 tape blocks
x bin/rumd, 122572 bytes, 240 tape blocks
```

```
x bin/rumessage, 195772 bytes, 383 tape blocks
x bin/ruprint, 126532 bytes, 248 tape blocks
x bin/rurd, 122572 bytes, 240 tape blocks
x bin/ruren, 123484 bytes, 242 tape blocks
```

In Solaris, tape archives are not compressed by default. To compress the archives, you can use normal Solaris **compress**:

**server% compress file.tar**

This will create a compressed file called file.tar.Z. Alternatively, the GNU **gzip** utility often achieves better compression ratios than standard **compress**, so it's a good idea to download it and install it. When executed, it creates a file call file.tar.gz:

**server% gzip file.tar**

Although Solaris does come with **tar** installed, we advise downloading, compiling, and installing GNU **tar** because of the increased functionality that it includes with respect to compression. To create a compressed tape archive file.tar.gz using this version of **tar**, use the **z** flag in addition to the normal **cvf** flags:

**server% tar zcvf file.tar \***

## Using cpio

**cpio** is used for copying file archives, and is much more flexible than **tar** because a **cpio** archive can span multiple volumes. This command can be used in three different modes:

- Copy-in, executed with **cpio -i**, extracts files from standard input, from a stream created by **cat** or similar.
- Copy-out, denoted by **cpio -o**, obtains a list of files from standard input, and creates an archive from these files, including their path name.
- Copy-pass, performed by **cpio -p**, is equivalent to copy-out mode, except that no archive is actually created.

The basic idea behind **cpio** for archiving is to generate a list of files to be archived, print it to standard output, and then pipe it through **cpio** in copy-out mode. For example, to archive all of the text files in one's home directory and store them in an archive called myarchive in the /staff/pwatters directory, use the command:

**server% find . -name '\*.txt' -print | cpio -oc > /staff/pwatters/myarchive**

Recording headers in ASCII is portable between operating systems, and is achieved by using the **-c** option. When the command completes, the number of blocks required to store the files is reported:

```
8048 blocks
```

The files themselves are stored in text format, with an identifying header, which we can examine with **cat** or **head**:

### server% head myarchive

```
0707010009298a00008180000011fc0000005400000001380bb9b600001e9b00000055000000
00000000000000000000000001f00000003Directory/file.txtThe quick brown fox
jumps over the lazy dog.
```

Since recording headers in ASCII is portable, files can be extracted from the archive by using the **cat** command:

### server% cat myarchive | cpio -icd "*"

This extracts all files and directories as required (specified by using the **-d** option). It is just as easy to extract a single file: To extract Directory/file.txt, for example, we use the command:

### server% cat myarchive | cpio -ic "Directory/file.txt"

If you are copying files directly to tape, it is important to use the same blocking factor (block size) when you retrieve or copy files from the tape to the hard disk as you did when you copied files from the hard disk to the tape. You *can* specify a particular blocking factor by using the **-B** directive, but even if you don't and use the defaults instead, there should be no problems.

## Using dd

**dd** is a program that copies raw disk or tape slices block-by-block to other disk or tape slices: It is like **cp** for slices. It is often used for backing up disk slices to other disk slices and/or to a tape drive, and for copying tapes. To use **dd**, it is necessary to specify an input file **if** and an output file **of**, and a block size. For example, to copy the root partition "/" on /dev/rdsk/c1t0d0s0 to /dev/rdsk/c1t4d0s0, you can use the command:

```
server# dd if=/dev/rdsk/c1t0d0s0 of=/dev/rdsk/c1t4d0s0 bs=128k
```

(To actually make the new partition bootable, you will also need to use the **installboot** command after **dd**.)

Another use for **dd** is backing up tape data from one tape to another tape. This is particularly useful for re-creating archival backup tapes that may be aging. For example, to copy from tape drive 0 (/devrmt/0) to tape drive 2 (/dev/rmt/2), use the command:

```
server# dd if=/dev/rmt/0h  of=/dev/rmt/1h
```

It is also possible to copy the contents of a floppy drive by redirecting the contents of the floppy disk and piping it through **dd**:

```
server# dd < /floppy/floppy0 > /tmp/floppy.disk
```

## Using ufsdump and ufsrestore

**ufsdump** and **ufsrestore** are standard backup and restore applications for UNIX file systems. **ufsdump** is often set to run from **cron** jobs late at night to minimize load on server systems. **ufsdump** can be run on a mounted file system; however, it may be wise to unmount it first, perform a file system check (using **fsck**), remount it, and then perform the backup. **ufsrestore** is normally run in single-user mode after a system crash.

The key concept in planning a ufsdump is the *dump level* of any particular backup. The dump level determines whether or not **ufsdump** performs a full or incremental dump. A full dump is represented by a dump level of zero, while the numbers one through nine can be arbitrarily assigned to incremental dump levels. The only restriction on the assignment of dump level numbers for incremental backups is their numerical relationship to each other: A high number should be used for normal daily incremental dumps, followed once a week by a lower number that specifies that the process should be restarted. This approach uses the same set of tapes for all files, regardless of the day they were recorded on. For example, Monday through Saturday would have a dump level of 9, while Sunday would have a dump level of 1. After cycling through incremental backups during the weekdays and Saturday, the process starts again on Sunday.

Some organizations like to keep the work of certain days separate from other days in a single tape. This makes it easier to recover work from an incremental dump where speed is important, and/or where it is expected that there will be a call for backups from a particular day. For example, someone may wish to retrieve a version of a file that was edited on a Wednesday and the following Thursday, but they want the version just prior to the latest (i.e., Wednesday). The Wednesday tape can then be used in conjunction with **ufsdump** to retrieve the file. A weekly full dump is scheduled to occur on Sunday, when there are few people using the system. Thus, Sunday would have a dump level of 0, followed by Monday, Tuesday, Wednesday, Thursday, and Friday with dump levels of 5, 6, 7, 8, and 9 respectively. To signal the end of a backup cycle, Saturday then has a lower dump level than Monday, which could be one of 1, 2, 3, or 4.

Prior to beginning a ufsdump, it is often useful to estimate the size of a dump, in order to determine how many tapes will be required. This estimate can be obtained by dividing the size of the partition by the capacity of the tape. For example how many tapes would be required to back up the /dev/rdsk/c0t0d0s4 file system use:

**server# ufsdump S /dev/rdsk/c0t0d0s4**

```
50765536
```

The approximately 49 megabytes on the drive will therefore easily fit onto a QIC, DAT, or DLT tape.

To perform a full dump of a x86 partition (/dev/rdsk/c0d0s0) at level 0, we can use the following approach:

**# ufsdump 0cu /dev/rmt/0 /dev/rdsk/c0d0s0**

```
DUMP: Writing 63 Kilobyte records
DUMP: Date of this level 0 dump: Mon Feb 03 13:26:33 1997
DUMP: Date of last level 0 dump: the epoch
DUMP: Dumping /dev/rdsk/c0d0s0 (solaris:/) to /dev/rmt/0.
DUMP: Mapping (Pass I) [regular files]
DUMP: Mapping (Pass II) [directories]
DUMP: Estimated 46998 blocks (22.95MB).
DUMP: Dumping (Pass III) [directories]
DUMP: Dumping (Pass IV) [regular files]
DUMP: 46996 blocks (22.95MB) on 1 volume at 1167 KB/sec
DUMP: DUMP IS DONE
DUMP: Level 0 dump on Mon Feb 03 13:26:33 1997
```

The parameters passed to **ufsdump** include 0 (dump level), **c** (cartridge: blocking factor 126), and **u** (updates the dump record /etc/dumpdates). The dump record is used by **ufsdump** and **ufsrestore** to track the last dump of each individual file system:

**server# cat /etc/dumpdates**

```
/dev/rdsk/c0t0d0s0          0 Wed Feb  2 20:23:31 2000
/dev/md/rdsk/d0             0 Tue Feb  1 20:23:31 2000
/dev/md/rdsk/d2             0 Tue Feb  1 22:19:19 2000
/dev/md/rdsk/d3             0 Wed Feb  2 22:55:16 2000
/dev/rdsk/c0t0d0s3          0 Wed Feb  2 20:29:21 2000
```

```
/dev/md/rdsk/d1            0 Wed Feb  2 21:20:04 2000
/dev/rdsk/c0t0d0s4         0 Wed Feb  2 20:24:56 2000
/dev/rdsk/c2t3d0s2         0 Wed Feb  2 20:57:34 2000
/dev/rdsk/c0t2d0s3         0 Wed Feb  2 20:32:00 2000
/dev/rdsk/c1t1d0s0         0 Wed Feb  2 21:46:23 2000
/dev/rdsk/c0t0d0s0         3 Fri Feb  4 01:10:03 2000
/dev/rdsk/c0t0d0s3         3 Fri Feb  4 01:10:12 2000
```

**ufsdump** is very flexible because it can be used in conjunction with **rsh** (remote shell) and remote access authorization files (.rhosts and /etc/hosts.equiv) to remotely log in to another server and dump the files to one of the remote server's backup devices. However, the problem with this approach is that using .rhosts leaves the host system vulnerable to attack: If an intruder gains access to the client, he can then remotely log in to a remote backup server without a username and password. The severity of the issue is compounded by the fact that a backup server that serves many clients has access to most of that client's information in the form of tape archives. Thus, a concerted attack on a single client, leading to an unchallenged remote login to a backup server, can greatly expose an organization's data. The problems associated with remote access and authorization are covered in depth in Chapter 16.

A tool called **Secure Shell** (**SSH**) can be used to overcome the need for using the remote commands. By combining **SSH** and **ufsdump**, it is possible to create a full dump of a file system from a client, transfer it securely to the backup server, and then copy it to the backup server's remote devices:

**client# ufsdump 0f - / | ssh server "dd of=/dev/rmt/0 bs=24b conv=sync"**

A handy trick often used by administrators is to use **ufsdump** to move directories across file systems. A ufsdump is performed for a particular file system, which is then piped through **ufsrestore** to a different destination directory. For example, to move existing staff files to a larger file system, use the following sequence of commands:

**server# mkdir /newstaff**

**server# cd /staff**

**server# ufsdump 0f - /dev/rdsk/c0t0d0s2 | (cd /newstaff; ufsrestore xf -)**

Users of **ufsdump** should be aware of a buffer overflow vulnerability that exists in some versions of **ufsdump** supplied with Solaris 2.6 and Solaris 7. Under some conditions, rogue local users could exploit this vulnerability to obtain root access. A patch is available from SunSolve (**http://www.sunsolve.com**), and a full explanation of the problem can be found at **http://www.securityfocus.com/bid/680**.

After backing up data using **ufsdump**, it easy to restore the same data using the **ufsrestore** program. To extract data from a tape volume on /dev/rmt/0, use the following command:

### # ufsrestore xf /dev/rmt/0

```
You have not read any volumes yet.
Unless you know which volume your file(s) are on you should start
with the last volume and work towards the first.
Specify next volume #: 1
set owner/mode for '.'? [yn]
```

If you reply **y**, then **ufsrestore** extracts all of the files on that volume. However, you can also list the table of contents of the volume to standard output if you are not sure of the contents of a particular tape:

### # ufsrestore tf /dev/rmt/0

```
1        ./openwin/devdata/profiles
2        ./openwin/devdata
3        ./openwin
9        ./lp/alerts
1        ./lp/classes
15       ./lp/fd
1        ./lp/forms
1        ./lp/interfaces
1        ./lp/printers
1        ./lp/pwheels
36       ./lp
2        ./dmi/ciagent
3        ./dmi/conf
6        ./dmi
42       ./snmp/conf
```

**ufsrestore** also supports an interactive mode, which has online help to assist you in finding the correct volume to restore from:

### # ufsrestore i

### ufsrestore > help

```
Available commands are:
        ls [arg] - list directory
```

```
          cd arg - change directory
          pwd - print current directory
          add [arg] - add 'arg' to list of files to be extracted
          delete [arg] - delete 'arg' from list of files to be extracted
          extract - extract requested files
          setmodes - set modes of requested directories
          quit - immediately exit program
          what - list dump header information
          verbose - toggle verbose flag (useful with ''ls'')
          help or '?' - print this list
If no 'arg' is supplied, the current directory is used
ufsrestore >
```

# Centralized and Distributed Tools

If you want to use anything other than the standard UNIX backup tools, there are many freeware and commercial packages that are available, depending on what facilities you require. For example, AMANDA is a freeware program that will centralize the storage and control for backup and restore of remote machines. However, it does not support distributed storage, which the two commercial vendors (Veritas and Legato) specialize in. Veritas Software and Legato Systems are far and away the leading vendors in the automated enterprise-wide backup and restore application arena.

## AMANDA

**AMANDA**, the Advanced Maryland Automatic Network Disk Archiver, is a backup system that follows the centralized backup server for multiple clients scheme that we examined in Figure 10-4. It can back up client drives from any operating system that supports SMB, including Solaris, Linux, and NT clients. Although AMANDA was designed to operate with a single tape drive, it can be configured to use multiple tape drives and other backup devices. One advantage of AMANDA over other backup systems is that it provides management of native Solaris backup and restore commands: This means that AMANDA backup files are really **tar** files that can be manually extracted and viewed without using the AMANDA system if it is not available for some reason. This is particularly significant for full dumps that must be restored to a "green fields" server that does not yet have AMANDA installed. AMANDA can be downloaded from **http://www.amanda.org**, and the FAQ is available at

> **http://www.ic.unicamp.br/~oliva/snapshots/amanda/FAQ**

The AMANDA approach to backups is different from a solution based around **cron**-scheduling of **tar** commands: It has an efficient scheduling and storage management system, which involves spooling both incremental and full dumps to a holding disk on the backup server. The data is not written directly to the backup device, so that there is a better logical separation between the preparing of backup files and the actual recording process. This separation is particularly important when using CD-R technology because of the buffer overrun problem: If data is not made available to the CD-R device quickly enough, then it fails to write a track, and the disk is wasted because data cannot be rewritten to it. If the backup file is prepared in advance on the holding disk, then most of the overhead involved in copying the backup file to the backup device is removed.

The other advantage AMANDA has is its efficient scheduling of dumps to the backup device. Performing a nightly incremental dump followed by a Sunday night full dump is very wasteful because in many organizations only a few files may have changed on the server. While this approach is standard among many backup programs, AMANDA introduces the concept of a "dump cycle," which minimizes the total number of dumps by estimating the time taken to dump any particular file. It attempts to balance total backup times across different days based on past performance of a particular device.

Unfortunately, it is not possible to set up AMANDA in the traditional way, whereby a full dump is performed on weekends and incremental dumps are performed each weeknight. So, while the dump cycle approach is very efficient, it may initially seem very confusing to many administrators, and it may be inappropriate for organizations that have a strict policy regarding backup scheduling. In addition, AMANDA has a further limitation: It cannot back up a file system that is bigger than the size of a single backup medium. That means that for large disks (18 GB and upwards), AMANDA may only be used with the latest DAT and DLT tapes, and not QIC tapes or CD-R technology. While small drives and partitions can be backed up using these devices, it is obviously a limitation for organizations with large data-handling requirements.

## Legato Networker

Legato's **Networker** storage management product is quite different from AMANDA. It is a commercial product, but it is often supplied with database server packages like Oracle. It is similar to AMANDA in that it prefers centralized over distributed control of all backup resources (in contrast to Veritas, which is reviewed below). However, multiple backup servers *can* exist; the only condition is that they be controlled by a central backup server. This approach is outlined in Figure 10-4. Networker is well known for its ability to back up from and restore to different clients, even those running different operating systems. This can be very useful when upgrading client operating systems—for example, migrating from Linux to Solaris, since a complete reinstall of user packages and files is not necessary (they can simply be retrieved from a central Networker server).

To make it easy for Windows and other PC users to integrate neatly within an enterprise server environment, Legato also supplies an NT client, which is shown in Figure 10-6.

More information about Legato products can be obtained from **http://www.legato.com/**.

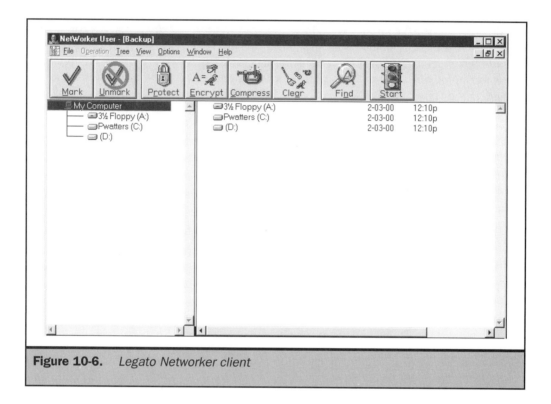

**Figure 10-6.**    *Legato Networker client*

## Veritas NetBackup

While AMANDA is focused on a single backup server providing services to many clients, Veritas provides a distributed backup management system, known as NetBackup, which can be used to process terabytes of data from many different clients across many different backup servers and multiple devices. This is similar to the approach outlined in Figure 10-5, and is aimed at maximizing the utilization of existing resources, such as tape drives and CD-R devices, no matter where they are located on a corporate intranet, or even across the Internet. In addition, NetBackup aims to provide the greatest amount of choice for clients, who can seamlessly manage their own backups across multiple hosts and devices.

NetBackup also includes support for many server-side database systems, such as Oracle, dispensing with the need for performing separate warm dumps to backed-up files. NetBackup uses a set of storage rules on the server side to determine how files and data sources of various types are managed. These can be configured by network administrators remotely from any client that has access to the backup servers. Veritas, like Legato, supplies several clients that make it easier for PC clients to operate within a larger storage management framework. Backup Exec is the Veritas Windows NT client that can be used to back up local files to a remote server running NetBackup. Figure 10-7 shows the easy-to-use interface for the Backup Exec client.

In an approach that is similar to the use of RAID, NetBackup backup devices can be used concurrently to transparently store data from different clients through multiplexing: There is a logical separation between the clients, and the particular strengths and weaknesses of any one server. In addition, load can be balanced much more evenly across backup devices without concern for the capacity of any one particular drive. Thus, unlike AMANDA, it is quite easy to back up a single large partition using NetBackup.

Further information about NetBackup can be found at **http://www.veritas.com/**.

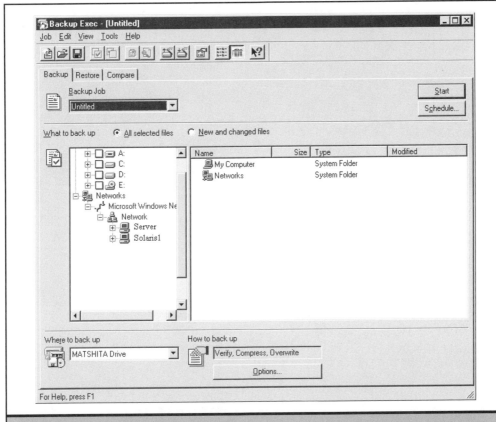

**Figure 10-7.**    *Legato Networker client*

## Summary

In this chapter, we have examined basic approaches to backup and restore operations that are suitable for most systems that act as their own backup server. In addition, we have reviewed more sophisticated centralized and distributed solutions, both commercial and freeware, for reducing the overall cost of backups while making better use of existing hardware, even if devices are attached to remote systems. Many sites will combine RAID technologies with backups to ensure data integrity.

## How to Find Out More

An excellent reference work that deals with backup for Solaris is the following (especially Chapter 7):

Preston, W. Curtis. *UNIX Backup and Recovery*. (O'Reilly, 1999.)

# The Complete Reference

Solaris 8

# Part III

## Basic Network Administration

The
Complete
Reference

Solaris 8

# Chapter 11

## Networking Basics

In the last decade, computer networks have become an integral part of all major computing environments. In addition to providing basic file and print services, networks are being used to provide extensive services ranging from electronic mail to web-based productivity tools. The changes in computing brought about by networking are immense. Before networks became commonplace, even the simple task of sharing a file with a friend was complicated: First you had to copy the file onto a floppy disk and then give that floppy to your friend. If your computer ran a different operating system than that of your friend, you needed to find a disk format that both of you could use for sharing files. If you made any changes to the file after you'd distributed a copy of it to your friend, then you needed to make another copy or make sure that your friend updated her copy. For a single file, the chores of copying and updating were minor annoyances, but for large sets of files, the process could easily become a nightmare. The problems associated with sharing resources such as printers and modems were much worse than the problems of file sharing. Often, using a printer meant getting access to a special system connected to the printer, and you would need to arrange for access hours or days in advance.

The networks have solved these and many other problems. By interconnecting computers you can easily share all types of resources, making it possible to work much more efficiently. For example, to share a file with a friend in a network environment, you just need to tell your friend the path to the file on your system. By allowing access to the original file, you never need to worry about keeping multiple copies synchronized. For printer and modem sharing, the advantages are even greater: Everyone can access these resources as long as they are connected to the network. The task of installing, configuring, and maintaining networks that can meet increasing user demands is an extremely challenging task. In this chapter we will cover the basic concepts that are required to understand and, hopefully, maintain networks based on Solaris systems. The first part of this chapter is an overview of basic networking concepts. The second section contains an overview of the startup process for networking on Solaris, along with a tour of the basic network debugging tools that are available on Solaris.

# TCP/IP Overview

In 1969, the United States Department of Defense's Advanced Research Projects Agency (ARPA) started developing a wide area packet-switched network called ARPANET. This network was designed to allow government scientists and engineers to share expensive computing resources. One of the major goals of ARPA was to design a set of robust protocols that could maintain connectivity between hosts despite problems such as broken cables, faulty hardware, or corrupt and lost data. The DOD wanted to develop a network that could keep military sites connected despite heavy damage to individual sections of the network.

An additional goal of ARPANET was to develop a set of standards that were "cross platform." At the time computers were rare and expensive systems, and the computers at one government facility were usually different from the computers at a separate facility. In order to accommodate computers of varying hardware configurations and operating systems, the protocols developed by ARPA for ARPANET were designed to be easy to implement on all kinds of systems. The main products of ARPANET were the Transmission Control Protocol and the Internet Protocol (TCP/IP). These protocols allow you to easily build networks that interconnect hybrid platforms. The largest example of this type of network is the Internet, which interconnects millions of computers around the world.

# The TCP/IP Suite Architecture

The TCP/IP communications suite was designed to be highly modular. Previous networking suites like IBM's Systems Network Architecture (SNA) or Digital Equipment Corporation's Digital Network Architecture (DNA) were single monolithic solutions that integrated every aspect of intercommunication between systems. TCP/IP designers used a different model, dividing the process of intercommunication into several independent *layers*, each of which can be developed and maintained separately from the others. The standard model for describing this layered approach to networking is the United States Department of Defense (DOD) model.

The DOD model consists of four separate layers: the Application, Transport, Network, and Link layers. Each layer is responsible for a different aspect of data communication. The Application layer is responsible for providing a simple application-to-application communication mechanism. The Transport layer is responsible for communicating data reliably between applications running on hosts across the network. The Network layer is responsible for determining the best route that data packets should follow to reach their destination. The Link layer is where media access and transmission mechanisms take place.

Each layer in the DOD model provides a specific set of services to other layers and encapsulates the services of the layer below in order to provide a simpler interface for the layer above it. As an example, consider the Network layer. This layer uses the services of the Link layer to provide an interface to the network for the Transport layer. The layers intercommunicate by exchanging *service primitives* via a set of predefined addresses called *service access points* or *ports*.

## Layers and Protocols

When a system sends information to a remote system, the information passes down through the layers on the local system and passes up through the layers on the remote system. Each layer in the stack thinks that it is communicating directly with its peer on the remote system. For example, the Application layer on one system always thinks that it is communicating with the Application layer on a remote system. Information is passed from one layer to a layer below it in *information units* (also called *service data units*). Information units contain a layer-specific source and destination address followed by a data block. The source and destination addresses are always at the beginning or head of an information unit, and together make up the section called the *header*. When an information unit is passed from one layer to the layer below it, the lower layer adds its own header to the information unit. The new header contains the layer-specific source and the destination addresses. When the remote system receives information from the local system, it passes it up through the layers. When a layer receives an information unit from a layer below it, it strips off the layer-specific header (containing the source and destination addresses) and passes the data to the layer above it. When the top layer of the remote system receives the data, it interprets the data.

The manner in which the data is interpreted depends on the *protocol* that was used to exchange the data. A *protocol* is simply a set of rules that specify how information will be exchanged for providing a particular service. Normally, protocols are implemented as two separate processes: a *client* process and a *server* process. The client process runs on the local system and asks for a particular service from a remote system on the network. The process that runs on the remote system and answers requests for a particular service is called the server. In UNIX, server processes are sometimes referred to as daemons because they are normally executed in the background like other UNIX daemons such as **cron** or **at**. The client program for a given protocol usually has the same name as the protocol. For example, the client for the File Transfer Protocol (FTP) is called **ftp**. Daemon programs have names of the form *protocol*d or in.*protocol*d, where *protocol* is the name of the protocol the daemon implements. As an example, the name of the daemon that implements the server process of the File Transfer Protocol is **in.ftpd**. Figure 11-1 shows the layers in the TCP/IP protocol architecture.

## The Application Layer

The first layer in the DOD model is the Application layer. Most of the protocols you may be familiar with are located at this layer. Some of these common protocols are Telnet (terminal emulation), FTP (file transfer), HTTP (hypertext transfer), SMTP (simple mail transfer), and NFS (network file system).

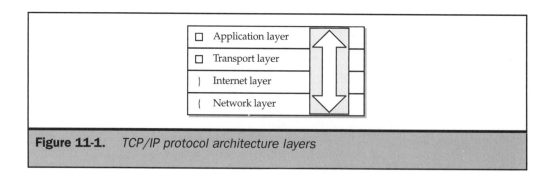

**Figure 11-1.**    *TCP/IP protocol architecture layers*

The Telnet protocol allows you to create a virtual terminal connection with a remote system that acts like a direct connection to a terminal on the remote system. In order to connect to a remote system using the Telnet protocol, you can simply execute the **telnet** command with the name of the remote host:

```
$ telnet host
```

The Telnet protocol is discussed in greater detail in Chapter 16.

FTP, which stands for File Transfer Protocol, was one of the first protocols to be created as part of the ARPANET project. It allows you to connect to a remote system in order to copy files to the system (upload) or to copy files from the system (download). To initiate an FTP session with a remote system you can use the **ftp** command with the name of the remote host:

```
$ ftp host
```

The FTP protocol is covered in Chapter 20.

HTTP, the HyperText Transfer Protocol, forms the basis for the World Wide Web. It is one of the newest protocols on the Internet and has been widely adopted. Usually a program called a browser, such as Netscape's Navigator, is used to request web pages from a server that understands HTTP. This protocol is discussed in Chapter 21.

Most of the email transfers on the Internet are handled by the Simple Mail Transfer Protocol, SMTP. In general, email transfers have a different type of priority than other protocols. When you send an email message, you are usually concerned that it eventually arrives; it is not essential that messages are received by the remote system the minute you send them. Servers that run SMTP take care of storing, formatting, and forwarding email messages correctly. SMTP is covered in detail in Chapter 19.

The Network File System (NFS) was developed by Sun to allow files to be shared seamlessly across the network. With NFS you can make a directory tree on a remote system appear to be part of your local directory tree. When programs access files stored in an NFS directory, the network request for the file is handled automatically. NFS is covered in greater detail in Chapter 17.

# The Transport Layer

The Transport layer (also called the host-to-host layer) is responsible for creating and maintaining network connections. Once a connection is created the Transport layer guarantees the integrity of the data exchanged across the network. The two main transport protocols at this layer are the Transmission Control Protocol (TCP) and the User Datagram Protocol (UDP). These two protocols represent the two major types of network communications: *connection-oriented* communication and *connection-less* communication. TCP is a connection-oriented protocol that guarantees delivery of packets, and UDP, a connection-less protocol, does not have a guarantee of delivery. The TCP and UDP protocols are covered in detail later in this section.

In connection-oriented communications, a logical connection is created between the two systems that need to exchange data. Once this connection is in place, data is transmitted. Every time data is received, it is acknowledged so that the sender knows that the data was received correctly. If the sender does not receive an acknowledgement, it will keep retransmitting until it is successful. This guarantees that the data will eventually be delivered to the remote system. Since connection-oriented communications maintain information about the state of packets that have been transmitted, protocols that use this method of communicating are referred to as *stateful protocols*.

Connection-less communications are exactly the opposite; they do not use a logical connection to exchange data. Rather, they simply send data to the remote system and hope that it arrives correctly. Whether or not data arrives correctly is left up to the "best effort" of the network. In most cases the data will be delivered correctly. Even if the data arrives correctly, there is no acknowledgement to the sender from the recipient regarding the data. Connection-less communication tends to be faster and cheaper (in terms of system resources) because it does not have the overhead associated with the creation and maintenance of a logical connection. In connection-less communication, the state of the packets that have been transmitted is not maintained anywhere; every communication is separate and independent. For this reason, connection-less protocols are called *stateless protocols*.

# Internet Layer

The Internet layer is responsible for providing the transport, routing, fragmentation, and reassembly of UDP datagrams and TCP *segments* from the Transport layer. A TCP segment is the smallest allowed group of TCP data. The two main protocols in this layer are the Internet Protocol (IP) and the Internet Control Message Protocol (ICMP).

The Internet Protocol (IP) is the backbone of the TCP/IP protocol suite. Each TCP segment and UDP datagram is transferred across the network in the form of IP datagrams. Although it is responsible for transferring all TCP and UDP-based communications, IP is a stateless connection-less datagram delivery service between hosts on the network. It is similar to UDP in that it makes no guarantee that datagrams will be delivered correctly or in sequence. It is possible for IP datagrams to never arrive at their intended destination. IP places the burden of reliability on protocols, such as TCP, at higher layers.

In order to exchange IP datagrams correctly between different hosts on the network, IP stipulates that every system has an *IP address* that uniquely identifies it. A system's IP address is like a phone number; it allows you to connect to that system from anywhere within the network, provided you know the correct number. On the Internet, IP addresses are assigned by the Network Information Center, InterNIC. If you are connecting to the Internet via an Internet service provider (ISP), then your IP addresses are supplied from the pool of addresses that InterNIC has allotted to your ISP. When the Internet layer receives a TCP segment or a UDP datagram from the Transport layer, it adds the source and destination IP addresses as part of the IP header. The format of an IP address is discussed in detail later in this chapter.

The second major protocol at the Internet layer is the Internet Control Message Protocol (ICMP). It is used to communicate error messages and other network conditions between different systems connected to the network. ICMP defines several different message types that allow systems to exchange network information efficiently. Two of the most common uses for ICMP are checking if hosts are available and obtaining routing information. The different message types of ICMP are covered later in this chapter.

# Network Access Layer

The Network Access layer, also known as the Link layer, is the last layer in the DOD model. It is responsible for converting the data from the Network layer into a form that can be transmitted over the physical media that connect a system to the network (via the system's network interface card, or NIC). The form the data will be converted to depends on the type of physical media. Most systems usually contain a single NIC, but some systems that need to operate on several different networks can contain two or more. Such systems are normally referred to as multi-homed systems.

Every NIC has a hardware or physical address associated with it. This address is normally referred to as the Media Access Control (MAC) address, and it is usually a unique 48-bit number hard-coded on the NIC. (Some vendors provide the ability to administratively assign MAC addresses to NICs.) When the Link layer receives an IP datagram from the Network layer, it adds a header that contains the source and destination MAC address for the two systems that are exchanging data.

The main protocol implemented at this level is the Address Resolution Protocol (ARP), which handles mapping the IP address of a system to the physical or hardware address of its NIC. ARP is a simple protocol that consists of two types of messages: the "Who is" message and the "I am" message. When the Link layer needs to send data to a system whose MAC address is unknown, it issues a "Who is" message. For example, if system A did not know the MAC address of system B, system A would issue the ARP message "Who is B." When system B receives this message it will respond with the message "I am B; my MAC address is *xx-xx-xx-xx-xx-xx*." The ARP mapping is covered in greater detail in the debugging section later in this chapter.

There are several different types of physical media supported under Solaris. The most popular physical media types have been standardized by the Institute of Electrical and Electronics Engineers (IEEE) and other standards bodies. There are four predominant types of physical media in networks today. These are Ethernet, Token Ring, Fiber Distributed Data Interface (FDDI), and Asynchronous Transfer Mode (ATM).

## Ethernet

Ethernet is covered in the IEEE 802.3 standard and is one of the most common physical media in use today. It is based on a broadcast-based bus system and offers fast connectivity at relatively low cost. It allows multiple hosts to share the same physical media for transmitting. In addition, since Ethernet is bus-based, any single host can be removed from the bus without affecting the overall network.

The transmission protocol used by Ethernet is called Carrier Sense Multiple Access with Collision Detection (CSMA/CD). When a system wants to transmit data, it listens for a carrier to see if any other systems are transmitting. The system waits until no other systems are transmitting and then sends its data. If it turns out that two systems hear that the way is clear and decide to transmit at the same time, the resulting collision is detected by both systems. In this case both systems back off for a random amount of time before attempting to retransmit. As the number of systems on an Ethernet increases, the frequency of collisions will increase as well. Since collisions require retransmission, this increase in the number of systems reduces the effective speed of the network.

Ethernet supports five different speeds: 2 megabits/sec, 5 megabits/sec, 10 megabits/sec, 100 megabits/sec, and 1,000 megabits/sec. These are referred to as 10BASE-2, 10BASE-5, 10BASE-T, 100BASE-T, and 1000BASE-FX respectively. 1000BASE-FX (also called Gigabit Ethernet) is a new technology and is mostly restricted to large servers. Most new deployments for workstation use 100BASE-T (also called Fast Ethernet), while deployments from the late 1980s and early 1990s use 10BASE-T. 10BASE-2 and 10BASE-5 were popular in the late 1970s and early 1980s but are rarely encountered today.

## Token Ring

Token Ring was originally developed by IBM and was later standardized under the IEEE 802.5 standard. It was designed to provide a guaranteed access speed for all hosts connected to the network. As its name implies, in Token Ring all hosts are connected together to form a logical ring. A single token (a specially marked frame) is available in this ring, and only the host that has the token can transmit. This scheme eliminates collisions and guarantees that every host can transmit at the maximum possible speed supported by the ring. Although the ring guarantees collision-free transmissions, it does not provide for any contingency in the case that the ring is broken.

There are two standard speeds for Token Ring networks: 4 megabits/sec and 16 megabits/sec. In the late 1980s and early 1990s Token Ring networks were popular because they could achieve higher data rates than Ethernet networks. The introduction of Fast Ethernet and Gigabit Ethernet in recent years has removed the speed advantage of Token Ring over Ethernet. Today very few sites are actively deploying Token Ring, and most sites using Token Ring are converting to Fast Ethernet.

## Fiber Distributed Data Interface

The Fiber Distributed Data Interface (FDDI) can be considered as an enhanced version of Token Ring that uses fiber optic cabling to allow for transmission speeds of up to 100 megabits/sec. In addition to speed, FDDI offers extra redundancy in its ring structure. Normally FDDI uses two separate rings: one for transmitting and one for receiving. If either ring is cut, FDDI is self healing and will fall back to the other ring for both transmitting and receiving. The major drawback with FDDI is the cost. Both the fiber optic cabling and the NICs for FDDI are quite expensive. This expense has kept FDDI restricted to high-end server systems.

## Asynchronous Transfer Mode

Asynchronous Transfer Mode (ATM) is a new technology that started to gain popularity in the mid 1990s. It is based on the simple idea that all information should be transmitted in small fixed-size frames called *cells*. ATM cells are 53 bytes long, containing 5 bytes for a header and 48 bytes for data. Networks built around ATM are connection-oriented. In ATM a connection is first created between the two systems that want to communicate. Once a connection is established, every cell that is exchanged between the hosts uses the exact same path. This allows ATM connections to easily handle both constant-rate traffic, like audio and video, and variable-rate traffic, like data. The major attraction to ATM is in fact its ability to handle audio and video on demand for hundreds of simultaneous users.

By concentrating on transmitting extremely small amounts of information, ATM networks can offer extremely high speeds. The two standard speeds are 155 megabits/sec and 655 megabits/sec. Currently ATM does not handle speeds in the range of Gigabit Ethernet, but its other features still make it one of the most promising Link layer technologies.

# IP Addresses

Every device in a TCP/IP network has a unique address, called an IP address, which describes its location in the network. This address is similar to a postal address in that it describes the location of something by using a scheme that progresses from general to specific. IP addresses consist of two parts: the network address and the node address. Whereas the network address is common to all hosts and devices that are on the same physical network, the node address is unique to a single host on that network. The network address and the node address in an IP address are completely independent of the MAC address of a system. You can change both parts as required. For this reason, TCP/IP addresses are described as symbolic.

An IP address is 32 bits (4 bytes) long. The number of bits corresponding to the node and network parts vary based on the IP address class to which an address belongs. The possible IP address classes are A, B, C, D, and E.

To make address administration easier, you can specify IP addresses by using a notation known as the *dotted decimal notation*. This type of notation treats the 32-bit IP address as four separate sets of bytes. Each byte is represented by its decimal equivalent; thus, values range between 0 and 255. For example, an IP address in this format is 10.8.11.2.

## Address Classes

As mentioned above, the five IP address classes are A, B, C, D, and E. Each of these address classes divides the number of addresses available for networks and nodes slightly differently. For example, Class A addresses allow for a small number of networks with a large number of hosts, while Class C addresses allow for a large number of networks with a small number of hosts.

The first byte of a Class A address is used to designate the network address. This allows the remaining 3 bytes to be used for identifying hosts on the network. Each Class A network is capable of accommodating millions of hosts. There are 127 Class A networks, with addresses ranging from 0.0.0.0 to 127.255.255.255. One of these networks, the 10.0.0.0 network, is reserved for private use. This means that you will never encounter a host on the Internet with a network address of 10.0.0.0.

In addition to the 10.0.0.0 network, there are two other special Class A networks: 0.0.0.0 and 127.0.0.0. The 0.0.0.0 network always refers to the local network a system is connected to. The 127.0.0.0 network always refers to the *loopback network*, which is used to send IP datagrams to the local machine in exactly the same way other machines on the network are addressed. Normally the address 127.0.0.1 is designated as the local host, but you can use any other address in the 127.0.0.0 network for the same purpose. For example, 127.6.5.4 also designates the local host.

Class B addresses use the first and second bytes for the network address, leaving the last 2 bytes free for identifying hosts. There are 65,535 Class B networks, with addresses ranging from 128.0.0.0 to 191.255.255.255. Each of these networks is capable of accommodating thousands of hosts.

Class C addresses use the first 3 bytes to identify the network, leaving only the last byte available for hosts. Class C networks are the smallest of all classes, as each can accommodate only 254 hosts. However, with 3 bytes reserved to identify the network, millions of Class C networks can be defined. Class C addresses range from 192.0.0.0 to 223.255.255.255.

Class D and Class E addresses do not describe a network of hosts. A Class D address is a set of multicast addresses that identifies a group of computers running a distributed application on the network. Class D addresses range from 224.0.0.0 to 239.255.255.255. Class E addresses are currently unused and are considered reserved for future purposes. Class E addresses range from 240.0.0.0 to 247.255.255.255.

## Subnets

Although a Class B network can accommodate thousands of nodes and a Class A network can accommodate millions of nodes, in practice it is not possible to put all of these hosts on the same network. Some of the main problems are limitations in the physical media (for example, 10BASE-T Ethernet imposes a limit of 1,024 nodes per network), congestion problems due to large amounts of traffic, and large geographic separations. Thus, even if the maximum number of nodes supported by the underlying physical media is adequate for your purposes, the traffic and geographic range may militate against connecting the maximum number, and you would therefore have to break the network into smaller, subnetworks (*subnets*).

> **Tip**  *Besides being necessitated by limitations imposed by the type of physical media connecting your network, subnets may be required if you expect that your network's applications will be causing network congestion by generating a large amount of traffic. Also, subnets make it much easier to manage organizations that have branch offices across the nation or around the world: If each branch office has a separate network; you can simply connect the branch subnets together to form an intranet.*

To break your network into subnets, TCP/IP allows you to extend the network ID portion beyond its default boundary by using a *subnet mask*. A subnet mask is just a 32-bit number that is applied to an IP address in order to identify the network and node addresses. The dotted decimal notation used for subnet masks is the same as the notation used for IP addresses. The subnet masks for the different IP address classes are given in Table 11-1.

As an example, you can extend the network address portion of a Class B address by reserving the third byte for your subnet network addresses, that is, by setting the subnet mask to 255.255.255.0. This subnet mask is the same as a Class C address.

# Network Transport Protocols

The three main transport protocols that we cover in this section are TCP, UDP, and ICMP. The first two, TCP and UDP, operate at the Transport layer, while ICMP operates at the Network layer.

## TCP

The Transmission Control Protocol (TCP) implements reliable connection-oriented communications for any applications that can use it. The reliability of TCP stems from four key features. First, TCP breaks application data into small chunks, called *segments*, which can be easily transmitted. By breaking a large message into smaller messages, TCP

BASIC NETWORK ADMINISTRATION

| Address Class | Subnet Mask |
|---|---|
| A | 255.0.0.0 |
| B | 255.255.0.0 |
| C | 255.255.255.0 |

**Table 11-1.**   *Subnet Masks for Standard IP Address Classes*

minimizes the amount of data that needs to be retransmitted when a failure occurs. The second feature is acknowledgements. When TCP receives a segment, it sends an acknowledgement in order to inform the remote system that the segment was received. The third feature TCP uses for reliability is timers. Every time a segment is transmitted, TCP starts a timer that waits for the remote system to acknowledge the receipt of the segment. If an acknowledgement is not received before the timer expires, TCP will retransmit the segment. The final features, TCP uses for reliability are packet checksums. If a packet with a bad checksum is received, it is immediately discarded by TCP.

When the Transport layer receives a packet that uses TCP from the Application layer, a TCP header is appended to the packet. Figure 11-2 displays the TCP header and its format. Among other things, there are three important pieces of information in the TCP header: the source and destination ports (also called service access points), the sequence number, and the acknowledgement number. The source port is the port that will be used by the remote system to communicate with the local system. When a remote system needs to respond to a message, it will specify the source port on the messages it received as the destination port for its message. The destination port number determines which process on the remote system will receive the data. Normally a daemon process needs to be listening for incoming messages on this port in order for TCP communications to work correctly. On Solaris, the TCP ports and the associated service names are defined in the /etc/services file. The ports for several well-known TCP-based protocols are given in Table 11-2. The sequence number of the packet is used by TCP to ensure that applications receive data in the same order it was sent. Since TCP rides on an unreliable transport mechanism, it is possible for TCP segments to arrive out of order; the sequence number allows for TCP segments to be reassembled in the correct order. The acknowledgement

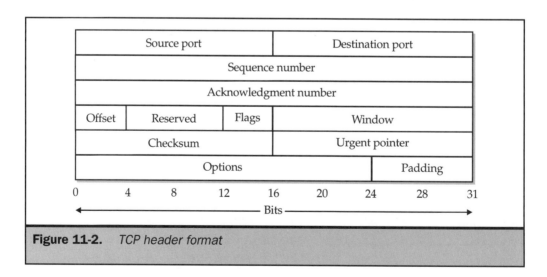

**Figure 11-2.** *TCP header format*

| Port | Service Name | Description |
|---|---|---|
| 7 | echo | Similar to the **echo** command, it echoes every segment you send it. |
| 13 | daytime | Allows remote user to determine the current time from your system's perspective. |
| 21 | ftp | Used for the control channel of the File Transfer Protocol (FTP). This protocol is discussed in Chapter 21. |
| 22 | ssh | Used by the secure shell command, **ssh**, for encrypted communications with remote systems. The **ssh** command is covered in Chapter 16. |
| 23 | telnet | Used by the Telnet protocol for terminal access to remote systems. This protocol is covered in Chapter 16. |
| 25 | smtp | Used by mail transfer programs such as **sendmail** (covered in Chapter 19). |
| 514 | shell | Used by the remote shell command, **rsh**, to allow users from remote systems to execute commands on your system. The **rsh** command is covered in Chapter 16. |

**Table 11-2.**   *Port Numbers for Well-Known TCP-Based Applications*

number is used by TCP to determine the next segment to transmit. This allows for a system to selectively ask for the most recent corrupted packet, which removes the need for large numbers of packet retransmissions.

**Checking for TCP-Based Protocols**   You can easily verify if a remote system is running the daemon process for a particular protocol using the **telnet** command (discussed in detail in Chapter 16) in the following form:

```
$ telnet host port
```

Here *host* is the hostname or IP address of the remote system, and *port* is the port number on which the daemon should be listening for connections. As discussed earlier in this chapter, the port numbers for most TCP-based protocols are available in the file

/etc/services. For example, if we were interested in verifying that the HTTP daemon was running on the system blue, the following command could be used:

**$ telnet blue 80**

If you receive a message similar to the following it usually means that the daemon is running correctly:

```
Trying 10.8.11.2...
Connected to blue.bosland.us.
Escape character is '^]'.
```

On the other hand, if you receive a message similar to the following:

```
Trying 10.8.11.2...
telnet: Unable to connect to remote host: Connection refused
```

it means that the daemon you are interested in is not listening for connections or that your connection to the remote system is experiencing problems. You can use the **ping** command discussed later in this chapter to test your connection.

## UDP

User Datagram Protocol (UDP) is a simple connectionless, unreliable transport protocol. It directly transmits the data that an application wants to write, and with very little overhead. Figure 11-3 displays the UDP message format. UDP only adds the source and destination port numbers along with the checksum information for the packet. The source and destination port numbers have the same function as with TCP. The checksum in UDP packets is also quite similar to the TCP checksum: When a UDP packet with a bad checksum is received, the packet is automatically discarded.

UDP is normally used by protocols that are concerned with the size of data being exchanged. Some transactional services that involve exchanging small amounts of data use UDP for faster performance, especially when all of the data that needs to be sent fits

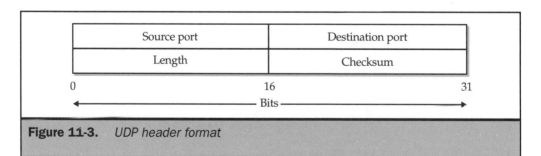

**Figure 11-3.**    *UDP header format*

into a single packet transmitted by UDP. For applications designed to recover from errors, retransmitting a lost or damaged datagram incurs less overhead than is involved in establishing and releasing a TCP connection. One major limitation with UDP is that the maximum packet size is 64 kilobytes of data per packet. Any protocol that uses it needs to be able to segment its data correctly.

## Standard Protocols

A complete list of the TCP and UDP ports for well-known protocols is stored in the file /etc/services. The entries in this file have the following format:

```
name        port/transport              aliases        # comments
```

Here *name* is the name of the protocol, port is the *port* number that is used by the protocol, *transport* is the protocol's transport mechanism (either tcp or udp), *aliases* are other names that the protocol is known by, and *comments* are short descriptions of the protocol. Both aliases and comments are optional. As an example, consider the following line for the remote shell protocol:

```
shell          514/tcp         cmd              # no passwords used
```

We can tell from this entry that this protocol is called shell and has an alias cmd. We also know that it uses port 514 with TCP as its transport.

The TCP ports under 1024 are considered reserved and are allotted only to established or *standard* protocols. Each standard protocol in the TCP/IP must be an "open" protocol, which means that documentation about the inner workings of the protocol must be available for everyone; the specification of a protocol is not under the control of any single individual or corporation. Before a protocol can be accepted as standard it must be extensively reviewed and documented in a Request for Comments (RFC) memo. The RFCs for all the standard protocols are public documents that are freely available on the Internet. Here are two popular sites for obtaining RFCs:

**http://www.rfc-editor.org/rfc.html**

**ftp://ftpeng.cisco.com/fred/rfc-index/rfc.html**

Throughout this book you will see references to the RFC documents that contain the description and formal specification of various TCP/IP protocols. Normally RFCs are referenced as RFC *xxxx*, where *xxxx* refers to the number of the document. For example, RFC 959 is the document specifying the File Transfer Protocol.

## ICMP

The Internet Control Message Protocol (ICMP) is used by systems to communicate their current status and the status of the network from their perspective. ICMP is based on raw IP datagrams that contain a special body identifing the ICMP message type. There are 15 distinct types of ICMP messages broken into to two general categories: error messages and informational messages.

ICMP error messages are used to communicate problems in the networks like destination unreachable, transit time exceeded, and parameter problems with IP datagrams. The ICMP informational messages are used to communicate network status such as the presence of new routers and the reduction or redirection of traffic. The most common ICMP informational messages are ICMP echo request, ICMP echo reply, ICMP timestamp request, and ICMP timestamp reply.

The ICMP echo request and ICMP echo reply are used by the **ping** command, discussed later in this chapter, to determine whether a particular system is on the network. If we consider two systems, A and B, the test works as follows:

1. System A sends an ICMP echo request to system B.

2. When System B receives the ICMP echo request, it responds with an ICMP echo response.

If the ICMP echo request from system A never reaches system B, then A will wait for a certain timeout period before reporting that the destination was unreachable. In some cases A may receive an ICMP error message from an intermediate system that processed the IP datagram destined for B. Some of the common ICMP error messages received in this scenario are network unreachable, host unreachable, destination network unknown, or destination host unknown.

The ICMP timestamp request and ICMP timestamp reply messages are similar to the ICMP echo request and ICMP echo reply messages, in that one system sends a request and expects to receive a response. The main difference is that the ICMP timestamp reply message contains information about what the remote system thinks the time is in milliseconds since midnight. By exchanging these messages, systems on the network can synchronize their system clocks to within milliseconds. This synchronization is important for many time-critical applications, where clock skew can cause problems if one system appears to be in the future with respect to other systems. Note that the ICMP timestamp packets are not meant to provide a comprehensive time synchronization solution. A separate protocol called the Network Time Protocol (NTP) is better suited for this purpose. NTP is provided as part of the SUNWntpr and SUNWntpu packages. A detailed discussion of NTP is beyond the scope of this book.

# TCP/IP Startup and Debugging

In this section we will look at the startup procedure for TCP/IP on Solaris and we'll also examine the Internet "super server," **inetd**, which controls most of the TCP/IP services available under Solaris. The last part of this section covers the standard network debugging tools, **arp**, **ping**, and **snoop**.

# TCP/IP Startup

TCP/IP startup on Solaris occurs when the system is brought to runlevel 2. When the system leaves runlevel 2 and enters multiuser mode, all of the basic initialization for network services is complete. Most of the daemons corresponding to the network services available on Solaris are not automatically started; instead Solaris uses a single "super-server" daemon, called **inetd**, that listens for network connections.

When the system enters runlevel 2, three separate scripts are executed in order to activate TCP/IP services:

- **/etc/init.d/rootusr**   This script configures all of the TCP/IP interfaces and services that are required to enable other network-related system resources.

- **/etc/init.d/inetinit**   This script configures the Network Information Service (covered in Chapter 15) and the route discovery daemon, **in.routed**, and also enables packet forwarding if the system has more than one NIC.

- **/etc/init.d/inetsvc**   This script concludes the TCP/IP startup process by verifying the configuration of the network interfaces, starting the domain name service (DNS) if necessary, and finally starting the Internet super server, **inetd**.

## The Internet "Super Server," inetd

In Solaris, network services such as Telnet server and FTP server are started only when a request is made for their services. The **inetd** daemon listens for requests on behalf of most of the network services and starts the appropriate service when a request is made. Since it controls most of the network services, **inetd** is known as the Internet "super server," or master Internet daemon. On most systems, using **inetd** allows for more efficient utilization of system resources because it avoids the overhead of running dozens of servers that just listen for incoming connections.

When **inetd** starts, it reads its configuration file, /etc/inetd.conf, to determine which network services it will be managing. The standard services managed by **inetd** are given in Table 11-3.

The format of the inetd.conf file is:

```
name   socket proto flags user path args
```

The definition of the individual fields are as follows:

- **name**   The name of the service—for example, telnet or ftp. This name must have a corresponding entry in /etc/services in order for **inetd** to be able to listen for connections on its behalf.

- **socket**   Either stream or datagram, depending on the transport protocol. TCP-based services like ftp and telnet use stream sockets. UDP-based services like SNMP use datagram sockets.

| Service | Description |
|---------|-------------|
| ftp | Responsible for responding to user requests involving file transfers. The ftp service is covered in detail in Chapter 20. |
| telnet | Responsible for providing terminal emulation services. Telnet is covered in detail in Chapter 16. |
| rsh | Handles the Berkeley remote shell protocol and allows users from remote systems to execute commands on your system. It is covered in detail in Chapter 16. |
| login | Handles the Berkeley remote login protocol. It is covered in Chapter 16. |
| finger | Allows remote users of the **finger** command to check information about users of your system. The **finger** command was covered in Chapter 6. |
| echo | Supported over both UDP and TCP, and returns whatever it is sent, hence the name echo. |
| discard | Simply discards whatever it is sent. |
| daytime | Returns the current time. |

**Table 11-3.**   *Some of the Standard Services Managed by inetd*

- **proto**   The name of the transport protocol. Usually this is udp or tcp.
- **flags**   Either wait or nowait. Most TCP servers use the flag nowait since they can relinquish their network resources once they are finished with a session. UDP servers use the flag wait since they rely on timeouts to determine when a session has concluded.
- **user**   The user ID that should be used to invoke the server. This field is designed to accommodate servers that need access to privileged system information and thus need to be run as root.
- **path**   The pathname to the server binary.
- **args**   The arguments that the server should be invoked with.

As an example, the entry for the ftp server looks like the following:

```
ftp  stream  tcp  nowait  root   /usr/sbin/in.ftpd   in.ftpd -l
```

From this entry we can tell that the ftp server is located at /usr/sbin/in.ftpd, uses TCP as its transport, and runs as root.

**Restarting inetd**    From time to time you will need to add or delete a service from the /etc/inetd.conf file. You may also need to modify the parameters or location of a service that is already managed by **inetd**. To disable a service, you just need to insert the # character in front of the service configuration entry. This causes the entry to be treated as a comment and will thus be ignored by **inetd**. To reenable the service, simply remove the # character. Modifying a managed service mainly involves changing the arguments passed to the program responsible for that service.

Once you have made any changes to the configuration file of **inetd**, you need to restart it in order to for your changes to take effect. To restart **inetd**, you need to first determine its process ID and then you need to send it the HUP signal. To determine the process ID of **inetd**, you can use the following command:

**$ /bin/ps -ef | grep inetd**

root   140   1 0   Aug 08 ?       0:00 /usr/sbin/inetd -s

ranga   2306  2257  0 08:51:50 pts/0   0:00 grep inetd

In the output, you need to look for the line that contains the process name /usr/sbin/inetd. In this case it is the first line of the output. The second column contains the process ID, in this case 140. To send the HUP signal to this process you can use the **kill** command:

```
# kill -HUP pid
```

Here *pid* is the process ID you obtained from the output of the **ps** command. In the case of the previous example, we can use the following command:

**# kill -HUP 140**

# Debugging Tools for Networks

There are three main debugging tools for networking problems. These tools are the **arp**, **ping**, and **snoop** commands. The **arp** command allows you to view the current mappings of IP addresses to MAC addresses in order to ensure that Link level communications are proceeding correctly. The **ping** command allows you to check the connectivity between different hosts. The **snoop** command is the most powerful of all: It allows you to view every packet as it appears on the network. In this section we will look at each of these commands in turn.

## Displaying the ARP Table

Every system stores a mapping of IP addresses to Media Access Control (MAC) addresses in a table called the *Address Resolution Protocol cache*, or simply the *ARP cache*. This table is periodically updated by the Address Resolution Protocol (ARP). The updates are based on the presence or absence of a particular MAC address in the broadcast traffic. For this reason ARP is usually associated with Ethernet networks, but it is also available on Token Ring and FDDI networks. When an address that is not present in the ARP cache is requested by the system, ARP creates a message requesting the mapping and broadcasts it on the network. If a response is received, the new mapping is added to the ARP table and any pending messages to the remote host are transmitted. ARP will broadcast four messages before reporting a failure.

You can view all of the entries in the ARP cache on your system using the **arp** command as follows:

> $ **arp -a**

The output will be similar to the following:

```
Net to Media Table
Device    IP Address              Mask            Flags   Phys Addr
------    ------------------      ---------------  -----   ---------------
be0       blue.bosland.us         255.255.255.255          00:20:af:d7:04:c2
be0       green.bosland.us        255.255.255.255          08:00:07:9e:75:da
be0       yellow                  255.255.255.255  SP      08:00:20:7b:3d:99
be0       BASE-ADDRESS.MCAST.NET  240.0.0.0        SM      01:00:5e:00:00:00
```

The first column contains the interface that was used to learn the MAC address. In this example, all of the entries were obtained from the be0 Ethernet interface. (Interfaces are covered in greater detail in the next chapter.) The second and third columns contain the hostname and network mask of the system corresponding to the MAC address. The IP address is printed in the second column if the hostname is not resolvable. Please see Chapter 13 for more information on hostnames.

The fourth column contains a set of flags that indicate the state of the entry. There are four possible flags: S, P, M, and U. The S flag indicates that the entry was not obtained via ARP, but was added manually. Usually only the entries for multicast addresses and the local machine will have the S flag set. The P flag indicates that the entry will be *published* by the system. When an ARP broadcast for this address is received by the system, it will respond to the ARP request with the MAC address stored in the ARP cache. This process is called publishing the ARP entry. Usually the P flag is only set for the entry corresponding to the local machine. The U flag indicates that the entry is *unresolved*. The U flag is normally set for entries while an ARP request is still pending. The M flag is used for multicast addresses only.

The fifth column contains the actual MAC address corresponding to the host given in the second column.

If you are interested in looking for all of the ARP entries that share a similar type of Ethernet card or are within a particular domain, you can combine the **arp** command with the **grep** command as follows:

```
$ arp -a | grep param
```

Here *param* is the parameter you are interested in looking for in the output. For example, the following command prints out all of the ARP cache entries for hosts in the bosland.us domain:

### $ arp -a | grep bosland.us

```
be0     blue.bosland.us     255.255.255.255     00:20:af:d7:04:c2
be0     green.bosland.us    255.255.255.255     08:00:07:9e:75:da
be0     nummi.bosland.us    255.255.255.255     00:05:02:88:c2:35
```

Just as **arp** resolves IP addresses to MAC addresses, the Reverse Address Resolution Protocol (RARP) does the opposite. RARP is used by machines at boot time to discover their IP addresses. RARP is particularly useful during jumpstart installations and with diskless clients. The **in.rarpd** daemon runs on the server side and waits for RARP requests to arrive. The **in.rarpd** daemon utilizes the /etc/ethers and the /etc/hosts databases to map the Ethernet addresses to the corresponding IP addresses. Diskless clients or jumpstart machines submit their RARP broadcast requests for an IP address to the network. At such time the requesting machine must be defined in both the /etc/ethers and the /etc/hosts databases for **in.rarpd** to respond.

**Displaying the Entry for a Single Host**    By default, **arp** displays the contents of the entire ARP cache on your system. If you are only interested in the ARP cache entry for a particular host, you can display it using the following version of the command:

```
$ arp host
```

Here *host* is either the IP address or the hostname of the host you are interested in. For example, the following command retrieves the ARP cache entry for the host blue:

**$ arp blue**

```
blue (10.8.11.2) at 0:20:af:d7:4:c2
```

If the host blue did not have an entry in the ARP cache you would have received an error message similar to the following:

```
blue (10.8.11.2) -- no entry
```

**Adding and Deleting Entries**   Normally, adding and deleting entries from the ARP cache is handled by ARP, but on occasion you may need to do it yourself. You'll more often have reason to delete bad entries than to add entries, but most system administrators do not need to do either task on a regular basis. To add an entry into the ARP cache you can use the **arp** command as follows:

```
# arp -s host mac type
```

Here *host* is the hostname or IP address of the system you are adding, *mac* is the MAC address of that system, and *type* is an optional flag that indicates what ARP should do with this address. The two main types are pub and temp, where pub indicates that the entry should be published by ARP, and temp indicates that entry is temporary and ARP can delete the entry as part of its normal process. As an example, the following command adds a temporary ARP entry for the host with the IP address 10.8.11.4 to the ARP cache:

**# arp -s 10.8.11.4 00:40:05:43:34:6F temp**

You will need to know the MAC address of the system you are adding to the ARP cache before you execute this command. The next chapter describes the **ifconfig** command, which you can use to determine the MAC address of a UNIX system. For other types of systems, please consult the vendor's networking documentation.

Once you have added an entry you can verify whether it was added correctly by specifying the address, as shown here:

**$ arp 10.8.11.4**

```
10.8.11.4 (10.8.11.4) at 0:40:5:43:34:6f
```

To delete an entry you can use the following version of the command:

```
# arp -d host
```

Here *host* is the hostname or IP address of the system you are deleting. For example, the following command deletes the entry for the host with the IP address 10.8.11.4:

**# arp -d 10.8.11.4**

```
10.8.11.4 (10.8.11.4) deleted
```

You can verify whether the ARP cache entry was deleted correctly by specifying the address, as shown here:

**$ arp 10.8.11.4**

```
10.8.11.4 (10.8.11.4) -- no entry
```

## Testing Reachability

You can test the reachability of a remote system using the **ping** command. This command was written by Mike Muuss and derives its name from the sonar operation used to locate objects underwater. The sonar version sends out a sound in the water and waits for the reflection from objects in the water. The UNIX version sends an ICMP echo request to the host and waits for an ICMP echo reply to be returned. When you run the **ping** command, your system acts as a client for ICMP echo responses from the remote system, which acts as a server of ICMP echo responses. Since it is usually impossible to connect to a host that you cannot contact using **ping**, most system administrators start debugging networking problems using it.

The simplest test for reachability using the **ping** command is as follows:

```
$ ping host
```

Here *host* is the hostname or IP address of the host you want to contact. For example, the following command tests the connectivity between the current system and the host blue:

**$ ping blue**

```
blue.bosland.us is alive
```

When a host is unreachable the **ping** command appears to hang due to the ICMP timeout it uses. Until the timeout expires it keeps listening for a response, but you will eventually be notified that the host is unreachable. In this example, the output indicates that the host doc.bosland.us is unreachable:

**$ ping doc**

```
no answer from doc.bosland.us
```

The default timeout is 20 seconds, but you can specify a different timeout as follows:

```
$ ping host timeout
```

Here *host* is the hostname or IP address of the host you want to contact and *timeout* is the timeout in seconds. If you are trying to contact hosts that are extremely slow you may need to increase the timeout in order for your system to receive a response. For example, the following **ping** command sets the timeout to 30 seconds when trying to contact doc:

**$ ping doc 30**

If you try several different timeout values and you still cannot contact the remote system, try to **ping** several other systems to determine where the problem may lie. The next chapter discusses the **traceroute** program that will help you to make an accurate determination of where networking problems may be occurring.

**Debugging Problems of Intermittent Reachability**   One of the most common problems in networks is intermittent reachability. In most cases there are long periods of good connectivity intermixed with a few intermittent instances of unreachability. In order to debug such a problem, you need to keep trying to **ping** a host repeatedly. You can do this using the **-s** option of the **ping** command:

```
$ ping -s host
```

Here *host* is the hostname or IP address of the host you want to contact. In this mode, **ping** sends an ICMP echo request message to the remote system every second. The ICMP echo responses are printed as they are received from the remote system. For example, the following command will repeatedly **ping** the host blue:

**$ ping -s blue**

```
PING blue.bosland.us: 56 data bytes
```

```
64 bytes from blue.bosland.us (10.8.11.2): icmp_seq=0. time=1. ms
64 bytes from blue.bosland.us (10.8.11.2): icmp_seq=1. time=0. ms
64 bytes from blue.bosland.us (10.8.11.2): icmp_seq=2. time=0. ms
^C
----blue.bosland.us PING Statistics----
3 packets transmitted, 3 packets received, 0% packet loss
round-trip (ms)  min/avg/max = 0/0/1
```

The format of each ICMP echo response is as follows:

```
size from host (ip): icmp_seq=seqnum. time=delay. ms
```

Here *size* is the size of the response, in bytes (normally 64 bytes), *host* is the hostname of the remote system, and *ip* is the IP address of the remote system. The *seqnum* is the ICMP sequence number contained in the ICMP echo response received by the **ping** command. Each time **ping** sends an ICMP echo request it places a sequence number into the request. When the remote system returns an ICMP echo response, it places the same sequence number into the response. If you see that responses are being received out of order, it may mean that there are routing problems in the network. The **traceroute** command discussed in the next chapter will help you debug those types of problems.

Finally, the *delay* is the number of milliseconds that it took for the ICMP echo response from the server to reach the **ping** command. You can use the delay to estimate the type of connection to the network the remote system has. For local area networks (LANs), usually the delays are between 0 and 20 milliseconds. Most sites on the Internet will usually have delays between 20 and 100 milliseconds, depending on your proximity to the site. Remote systems connected to the network via a modem or serial link often have much larger delays, in the range of 1,000 to 1,500 milliseconds.

As the previous output illustrates, pressing CTRL-C will exit the program. This causes the summary information to be printed at the bottom of the output, including the percent of packets lost over the network. If you try to contact a host that is unreachable, the **ping** command will print out an initial message and then appear to hang until you press CTRL-C to terminate it. For example, assuming the host doc was unreachable, the output would look similar to the following:

**$ ping -s doc**

```
PING doc.bosland.us: 56 data bytes
^C
----doc.bosland.us PING Statistics----
2 packets transmitted, 0 packets received, 100% packet loss
```

BASIC NETWORK
ADMINISTRATION

By default the **-s** option configures the **ping** command to send out an ICMP echo request every second. You can increase the time interval with the **-I** option:

```
$ ping -s -I interval host
```

Here *interval* is the number of seconds that **ping** should wait between ICMP echo request transmissions, and *host* is the hostname or IP address of the remote system you are trying to contact. For example, the following command sets the interval to two seconds:

**$ ping -s -I 2 blue**

```
PING blue.bosland.us: 56 data bytes
64 bytes from blue.bosland.us (10.8.11.2): icmp_seq=0. time=1. ms
64 bytes from blue.bosland.us (10.8.11.2): icmp_seq=1. time=0. ms
64 bytes from blue.bosland.us (10.8.11.2): icmp_seq=2. time=0. ms
^C
----blue.bosland.us PING Statistics----
3 packets transmitted, 3 packets received, 0% packet loss
round-trip (ms)  min/avg/max = 0/0/1
```

The only difference in the output will be in the speed with which the ICMP echo responses are printed to the screen.

**Debugging Protocol Reachability Problems**   Occasionally you will find remote systems that are reachable by **ping** are unreachable by higher-level services such as Telnet or FTP. In order to debug this problem you first need to verify that the remote system is reachable for large packets. In this section we'll explore how to do that. After verifying that you can send large packets to the remote system, you can use the **telnet** command to test whether the protocol is running on the remote system, as covered earlier in this chapter.

Normally the **ping** command sends only small packets to the remote system, so even heavily congested networks and heavily loaded systems can respond to such a request. However, in congested or heavy load situations larger packets may not reach the remote system or may be dropped by the remote system. You can test this using the **ping** command as follows:

```
$ ping -s host size
```

Here *host* is the hostname or IP address of the remote system and *size* is the size in bytes of the packet you want to send. For example, the following command sends a 4-kilobyte packet to the host blue:

**$ ping -s blue 4096**

```
PING blue.bosland.us: 4096 data bytes
4104 bytes from blue.bosland.us (10.8.11.2): icmp_seq=0. time=4. ms
4104 bytes from blue.bosland.us (10.8.11.2): icmp_seq=1. time=3. ms
^C
----blue.bosland.us PING Statistics----
2 packets transmitted, 2 packets received, 0% packet loss
round-trip (ms)  min/avg/max = 3/3/4
```

As you can see, the delay per packet has increased since the example preceding this one. This is due to the amount of time required to send the larger packet through the network and the additional processing time for a larger packet. For remote systems, where the delay is in the range of 500 to 1,000 milliseconds for ordinary pings, you may need to use the **-I** option to increase the amount of time between transmissions.

In this example, we tested the connectivity using 4,096-byte packets. This is a common number to use, since most of the traffic on a network uses packets of approximately this size. Some of the common packet sizes to try when testing whether a remote system is receiving large packets are 512 bytes, 1,024 bytes, 4,092 bytes, and 8,096 bytes. The 1,024-byte packets are commonly used in Ethernet networks since this size closely approximates the size of an Ethernet frame.

When testing with different packet sizes it is possible to specify the number of packets that should be sent to the remote system, by using the following version of the **ping** command:

```
$ ping -s host size count
```

Here _host_ is the hostname or IP address of the remote system, _size_ is the size in bytes of the packet you want to send, and _count_ is the number of packets you want to send. For example, the following command sends three 1,024-byte packets to the host blue:

**$ ping -s blue 1024 3**

```
PING blue.bosland.us: 1024 data bytes
1032 bytes from blue.bosland.us (10.8.11.2): icmp_seq=0. time=2. ms
1032 bytes from blue.bosland.us (10.8.11.2): icmp_seq=1. time=1. ms
1032 bytes from blue.bosland.us (10.8.11.2): icmp_seq=2. time=1. ms

----blue.bosland.us PING Statistics----
3 packets transmitted, 3 packets received, 0% packet loss
round-trip (ms)  min/avg/max = 1/1/2
```

BASIC NETWORK
ADMINISTRATION

When you specify the number of packets **ping** should send, it will exit and print out the summary after it has finished transmitting that number of packets. You do not have to quit the program by pressing CTRL-C. This feature is extremely useful for hosts that are unreachable, as is the case shown here:

**$ ping -s doc 1024 3**

```
PING doc.bosland.us: 1024 data bytes

----doc.bosland.us PING Statistics----
3 packets transmitted, 0 packets received, 100% packet loss
```

In this case the host doc was unreachable, and the output indicates that all three packets transmitted were lost. If you want to specify a number of packets, with the default packet size for **ping**, just specify the packet size as 56 bytes:

```
$ ping -s host 56 count
```

Here *host* is the hostname or IP address of the remote system and *count* is the number of packets you want to send.

## Viewing Packets Directly

One of the most powerful tools for debugging networking problems is a program called **snoop**. This utility prints out every packet that appears on the local network and allows you to see exactly what is transmitted and received by different protocols. It also allows you to view only those packets sent from or destined for a particular host. When you are debugging problems with connectivity or protocols, **snoop** provides an easy way of capturing the communication "on the wire" for analysis.

The simplest form of **snoop** is the summary mode, which displays summary information about all UDP, ICMP, and higher-level TCP-based protocol packets that were received on your system. Summary mode is invoked as follows:

**# snoop**

The **snoop** command must be run as root since it requires the network interface to be set in "promiscuous mode." Setting the network interface in promiscuous mode allows the **snoop** command to view all of the network traffic addressed to the interface, including monocasts and broadcasts. The following shows an example of the output from the **snoop** command:

```
Using device /dev/be (promiscuous mode)
green.bosland.us -> yellow        TELNET C port=2058
       yellow -> green.bosland.us TELNET R port=2058 /dev/be (promiscuous
green.bosland.us -> yellow        TELNET C port=2058
```

```
       yellow -> green.bosland.us TELNET R port=2058
yellow -> blue.bosland.us TCP D=2049 S=970 Fin Ack=2523351011 Seq=1258353367 Len=0 Win=8760
blue.bosland.us -> yellow       TCP D=970 S=2049      Ack=1258353368 Seq=2523351011 Len=0 Win=8703
```

If left to itself, the **snoop** command will produce output to your screen forever; to terminate it, just press CTRL-C. If you prefer that the **snoop** command terminate itself after capturing a certain number of packets, you can specify the **-c** option as follows:

```
# snoop -c count
```

Here *count* is the number of packets you want captured. As an example, the following **snoop** command will automatically terminate after capturing 10 packets:

**# snoop -c 10**

*The **-c** option can be combined with all the other options discussed later in this section.*

Each of the lines in the output of **snoop** has a format similar to the following:

```
source -> destination    protocol data
```

Here *source* is the hostname or IP address of the source of packet, *destination* is the hostname or IP address of the destination of the packets, *protocol* is the protocol used for this packet, and *data* is protocol-specific information stored in the packet. As an example, consider the following output line from **snoop**:

```
green.bosland.us -> yellow       TELNET C port=2058
```

You can tell that this packet was generated by the Telnet protocol and originated at the host green.bosland.us, with its ultimate destination set to the host yellow. Since this packet was generated by the Telnet protocol, the data displayed is specific to that protocol. In this case the data contains the destination port on the host yellow.

**Verbose Mode**   In most cases the summary information will give you a good idea of the frequency and type of packets interchanged by the different hosts on the network. Sometimes you will want to get more information about the packet headers at lower layers, such as the IP or TCP layers. There are two different modes that list this information: the verbose mode and the verbose-summary mode. The verbose mode contains an extremely detailed breakdown of the packet contents for each of the layers. The output can span dozens of lines per packet and often is hard to read in real time; therefore the best use of this form is when capturing the output of **snoop** to a file. The verbose-summary mode is much more succinct and prints out a single summary line for each layer, and so is much easier to read in real time.

To invoke **snoop** in verbose mode, you need to specify the **-v** option, as shown here:

# **snoop -v**

The output for each packet is divided into three or four separate sections, depending on the type of packet. The first two sections are normally ETHER and IP. The ETHER section contains information specific to Ethernet, such as the arrival time, the source and destination MAC addresses, and the packet size. The IP section contains IP-specific information such as header and body sizes, the source and destination IP addresses, and the IP header options. The third and fourth sections vary according to the type of packet:

- For TCP packets the third section is TCP and the fourth section is protocol-specific. The TCP section contains TCP-specific information such as the source and destination ports. The protocol-specific section normally contains a few lines of the protocol-specific packet headers.

- For UDP packets the third section in the verbose output is UDP. It normally contains source and destination port information along with information about the length and checksum of the UDP packet.

- For ICMP packets the third section is ICMP. The ICMP section contains information about the type of ICMP request and the checksum for the packet.

Each output line for a particular layer is labeled starting with the name of that layer:

```
LAYER:   data
```

Here *LAYER* is the name of the layer and *data* is some of the information, stored in the packet, which is specific to that layer. For example, an output line for TCP will look like the following:

```
TCP:   Source port = 23
```

In this case the data informs you about the source port for this TCP packet.

You can tell where each section of a particular layer starts based on two lines in the following format:

```
LAYER: ----- LAYER Header -----
LAYER:
```

Of course, *LAYER* is the name of the layer the information corresponds to. For example, the header lines for the IP section will look like the following:

```
IP:    ----- IP Header -----
IP:
```

The following is an example of the complete verbose mode output for a single ICMP echo request packet:

```
ETHER:   ----- Ether Header -----
ETHER:
ETHER:   Packet 19 arrived at 19:28:10.35
ETHER:   Packet size = 98 bytes
ETHER:   Destination = 8:0:20:7b:3d:99, Sun
ETHER:   Source      = 0:20:af:d7:4:c2,
ETHER:   Ethertype = 0800 (IP)
ETHER:
IP:    ----- IP Header -----
IP:
IP:    Version = 4
IP:    Header length = 20 bytes
IP:    Type of service = 0x00
IP:          xxx. .... = 0 (precedence)
IP:          ...0 .... = normal delay
IP:          .... 0... = normal throughput
IP:          .... .0.. = normal reliability
IP:    Total length = 84 bytes
IP:    Identification = 33725
IP:    Flags = 0x0
IP:          .0.. .... = may fragment
IP:          ..0. .... = last fragment
IP:    Fragment offset = 0 bytes
IP:    Time to live = 64 seconds/hops
IP:    Protocol = 1 (ICMP)
IP:    Header checksum = cccc
IP:    Source address = 10.8.11.2, blue.bosland.us
IP:    Destination address = 10.8.11.14, yellow
IP:    No options
IP:
ICMP:   ----- ICMP Header -----
```

```
ICMP:
ICMP:   Type = 8  (Echo request)
ICMP:   Code = 0
ICMP:   Checksum = 8027
ICMP:
```

The output of **snoop**'s verbose mode is quite easy to filter with the **grep** command. When you are debugging a problem, normally you need to look at each layer independently in order to isolate the layer at which the problem is occurring. Some of the common problems include Ethernet frames directed to the wrong MAC address, and incorrect destination IP address. In order to display the information for a particular layer you can use a command similar to the following:

```
# snoop -v | grep 'LAYER:'
```

Here *LAYER* is the layer you are interested in. For example, the following command filters all of the information except for the messages relevant to the IP layer:

**# snoop -v | grep 'IP:'**

If you want to display all the information except the information for a particular layer, say TCP, for example, you can use the **grep -v** command instead:

```
# snoop -v | grep -v 'LAYER:'
```

For example, the following command filters all of the TCP related information:

**# snoop -v | grep -v 'TCP:'**

If you want to view only the information for certain layers you can use the **egrep** command instead of the **grep** command:

```
# snoop -v | egrep 'LAYER1:|LAYER2:'
```

Here *LAYER1* and *LAYER2* are the layers you are interested in. For example, the following command filters out all information not related to IP or TCP:

**# snoop -v | egrep 'IP:|TCP:'**

Similar to the **grep -v** command, the **egrep -v** command can be used to filter out information related to certain layers:

```
# snoop -v | egrep -v 'LAYER1:|LAYER2:'
```

Here *LAYER1* and *LAYER2* are the layers you are *not* interested in. For example, the following command filters out all information related to IP or TCP:

> **# snoop -v | egrep -v 'IP:|TCP:'**

**Verbose-Summary Mode**    The verbose-summary mode presents most of the same information as the verbose mode but in a shorter format. To invoke **snoop** in verbose-summary mode you need to use the **-V** option:

> **# snoop -V**

In the verbose-summary mode the output for each layer is summarized in a single line. For TCP packets the output for a single packet contains four lines: one line for Ethernet, one line for IP, one line for TCP, and one line for the higher-level TCP protocol. For UDP and ICMP packets the output for a single packet consists of three lines: one line for Ethernet, one line for IP, and one line for UDP or ICMP depending on the packet's type. As an example, the output for a single TCP packet produced by Telnet looks like the following:

```
green.bosland.us -> yellow   ETHER Type=0800 (IP), size = 60 bytes
green.bosland.us -> yellow   IP   D=10.8.11.14 S=10.8.11.7 LEN=40, ID=15014
green.bosland.us -> yellow   TCP  D=23 S=2058     Ack=1092431497 Seq=4059795981 Len=0 Win=16616
green.bosland.us -> yellow   TELNET C port=2058
```

As you can see from the output each line has the following format:

```
source -> destination  LAYER data
```

Here *source* is the hostname of the host producing the packet, *destination* is the host that is the packet's ultimate destination, *LAYER* is the layer that the information corresponds to, and *data* is the information that is specific to a particular layer. For the ETHER layer, *data* is usually the type of the frame and its size. For the IP layer, *data* contains the source and destination IP addresses of the packet along with the length and the ID of the packet. For TCP and UDP layers, *data* contains the source and destination ports. For the ICMP layer, *data* contains the type of the ICMP packet.

As with the verbose mode, it is easy to filter the output of the verbose-summary mode with the **grep** or **egrep** commands. To view the information for a particular layer, you can use a command similar to the following:

```
# snoop -V | grep ' LAYER '
```

BASIC NETWORK ADMINISTRATION

For example, the following command prints out only the TCP-related information for every TCP packet:

**# snoop -V | grep ' TCP '**

The output will look similar to the following:

```
green.bosland.us -> yellow       TCP D=23 S=2058    Ack=1092858010 Seq=4059796178 Len=0 Win=16616
     yellow -> green.bosland.us TCP D=2058 S=23    Ack=4059796178 Seq=1092858010 Len=101 Win=9112
```

**Capturing snoop Output**    Usually when you are debugging a networking problem, it is very hard to determine from the real-time output of **snoop** what the problem is. Normally you need to dump the output to a file and then analyze the contents of the file. There are two methods for capturing the output of **snoop** to a file. The first method is to use standard shell redirection, and the second method is to use the **-o** option of **snoop**. Standard shell redirection captures the output of snoop in the same form as it is printed on the screen, while the **-o** option captures the raw contents of the packets. Shell redirection is the most commonly used method for capturing the output of **snoop**, but there may be some cases where you will want to view the actual contents of packets. One of the most common uses for the **-o** option is for debugging problems with files being incompletely transferred via FTP or HTTP. By capturing the output of **snoop** you can determine where the files are being truncated.

To capture the output of **snoop** to a file using shell redirection, you can use the following form:

```
# snoop options > file 2>&1
```

Here *options* are any of the options for the **snoop** command discussed in this section, and *file* is the pathname of the file you want the output saved in. As an example, the following command saves the verbose-summary mode output of **snoop** into the file /tmp/snoop.out:

**# snoop -V > /tmp/snoop.out 2>&1**

To terminate the capture of output, just press CTRL-C. You can then view the file using the **cat** or **more** commands. If you want to view the output on the screen while it is being captured, you can use the **tee** command in conjunction with the **snoop** command as follows:

```
# snoop options 2>&1 | tee file
```

Again, *options* are any of the options for the **snoop** command discussed in this section, and *file* is the pathname of the file you want the output saved in. As an

example, the following command saves the output of **snoop** into the file
/tmp/snoop.out while also displaying it to the screen:

> # **snoop 2>&1 | tee /tmp/snoop.out**

As mentioned above, the second method for capturing the output of **snoop** to a file
is to use the **-o** option:

```
# snoop -o file
```

where *file* is the pathname of the file you want the output saved in. As an example, the
following command saves the contents of the packets read by your system in the file
/tmp/snoop.out:

> # **snoop -o /tmp/snoop.out**

While the command is running it displays a count of the number of packets it is
writing to screen, as illustrated here:

```
Using device /dev/be (promiscuous mode)
15
```

To terminate the capture of packets, just press CTRL-C. Once the capture is
completed, you can view the resulting file using the **snoop** command again, only this
time the **-i** option must be used. The output of the command can be directed to a test
file, say /tmp/snoop.txt, as follows:

> # **snoop -i /tmp/snoop.out > /tmp/snoop.txt**

**Capturing Parts of Packets** In addition to capturing the contents of every packet
into a file, it is possible to use **snoop** to capture only a certain part of a packet using the
**-x** option:

```
# snoop option -x start,finish
```

Here *option* is either the **-v** or **-V** mode options and *start* and *finish* are the locations in
bytes of where **snoop** should start and finish printing the contents of a packet. If *finish*
is not specified, then **snoop** will print the contents of the entire packet from the *start*
position to the end of the packet. To display the entire packet, you can specify *start*
as 0 and omit *finish*:

> # **snoop -x 0**

To list the first 512 bytes of the packet in verbose-summary mode, you could use the command:

**# snoop -V -x 0,512**

At the end of the mode-specific output for a packet (that is, either the verbose mode output or the verbose-summary mode output), the **-x** option appends the contents of the selected bytes in two main sets of columns. The first main set of columns contains hexadecimal representation of the packet, while the second set of columns contains the ASCII representation. The output for a single packet will look similar to the following:

```
green.bosland.us -> yellow          TELNET C port=2058

    0: 0800 207b 3d99 0800 079e 75da 0800 4500     .. {=.....u...E.
   16: 0028 52ea 0000 ff06 3ec1 0a08 0b07 0a08     .(R.....>.......
   32: 0b0e 080a 0017 f1fb 94ca 4126 be09 5010     ..........A&..P.
   48: 40e8 b6b0 0000 0000 0000 0000               @..........
```

**Advanced Filtering**    The most powerful feature of the **snoop** command is its filtering capability, which allows you to selectively direct or deal with the output for a single host, the source or destination hostname, network addresses, or protocol type. The basic syntax for creating a filter expression is as follows:

```
# snoop options expression
```

Here *options* are any of the options discussed earlier in this chapter, and *expression* is an expression of a sort that can be recognized and acted upon by **snoop**. The simplest such expression is one that simply lists the hostnames or IP addresses for systems to which you want to apply your filtering. The syntax is as follows:

```
# snoop options host1 … hostN
```

Again, *options* are any of the options discussed earlier in this chapter and *host1 ... hostN* are the hosts you are interested in. For example, the following command will produce verbose-summary output for any packets destined for or coming from the hosts green and blue:

**# snoop -V green blue**

```
green.bosland.us -> blue.bosland.us TELNET C port=2059 p
blue.bosland.us -> green.bosland.us TELNET R port=2059 p
```

The second type of filter is one that filters on the protocol type:

```
# snoop type
```

Here *type* is the protocol type parameter, either **tcp**, **udp**, or **icmp**. To filter all packets except TCP packets you can use the **tcp** parameter as follows:

**# snoop tcp**

This command will output the summary information for only TCP-based packets. To output information for ICMP packets, use the **icmp** operator instead of the **tcp** operator. Similarly, to output information for UDP-based packets, use the **udp** parameter instead of the **tcp** operator.

The main **snoop** parameters are those that require additional arguments. These parameters are described in Table 11-4.

As an illustration of how to use these parameters, consider the following problem. You observe that a certain client is having trouble accessing web pages from your web server. In order to debug this problem you need to look at all the TCP packets going from your web server to the client system on port 80. (Port 80 is the standard port of the HTTP protocol used for serving web pages. It is discussed in greater detail in

| Parameter | Outputs Information for ... |
|---|---|
| **host** *hostname* | Packets that are either coming from or going to the specified *hostname*. The *hostname* can also be the system's IP address. |
| **net** *network* | Packets that are either coming from or going to the network whose network number is specified by *network*. |
| **port** *num* | Packets that are either destined to or coming from the TCP or UDP port number specified by *num*. |
| **from** *host* | Packets that are coming from the specified *host*. The argument *host* can be either the system's hostname or IP address. The **src** parameter can be used as an alias for this parameter. |
| **to** *host* | Packets that are going to the specified *host*. The argument *host* can be either the system's hostname or IP address. The **dst** parameter can be used as an alias for this parameter. |

**Table 11-4.**   *snoop Parameters*

Chapter 21.) To look for these packets you need to construct a **snoop** expression. The first step is to ask **snoop** to display only those packets that are TCP based:

# snoop tcp

Next we need to narrow down the output to only those TCP packets that have their source or destination port set to 80:

# snoop tcp port 80

Now we need to narrow down the output to contain only that traffic from your web server (we assume here that it is called www):

# snoop tcp port 80 from www

If you specified www without the **from** parameter, the output would include information about packets destined for port 80 on the system www in addition to packets from port 80. The final step is to specify the destination of the packet using the **to** parameter. For a client named banana we could use the following command:

# snoop tcp port 80 from www to banana

Finally, by using the output from one of the verbose modes you could see if the client was receiving complete information from the server.

# Summary

In this chapter we looked at the overall structure of the TCP/IP protocol suite, which is used by Solaris as its standard networking infrastructure. We examined each of the layers in the suite and covered some of the basic features of the different protocols that operate at each layer. In the second section we looked at the startup of TCP/IP on Solaris along with the setup of the Internet "super server," **inetd**. The second section concluded with an overview of the network debugging tools **arp**, **ping**, and **snoop**. The next chapter will extend the information covered in this chapter to included detailed configuration information about interfaces and routing.

# How to Find Out More

If you are interested in finding out more information about TCP/IP networking, there are many excellent sources of information both in print and on the web. A good starting point is the RFCs that detail the different standard protocols on the Internet. You can obtain copies of all of the RFCs from the following sites:

http://www.rfc-editor.org/rfc.html

**ftp://ftpeng.cisco.com/fred/rfc-index/rfc.html**

The definitive references for TCP/IP networks available in printed format are written by Andrew Tanenbaum and Richard Stevens:

Stevens, Richard. *TCP/IP Illustrated Volumes 1–3.* (Addison-Wesley Longman, 1994.)

Stevens, Richard. *UNIX Network Programming Volumes 1 and 2.* (Prentice Hall, 1998.)

Tanenbaum, Andrew S. *Computer Networks.* (Prentice Hall, 1996.)

Tanenbaum's *Computer Networks* textbook contains an excellent overview of all different types of networking technologies from the Physical layer to the Application layer. Richard Stevens has two excellent series of books, *TCP/IP Illustrated* and *UNIX Network Programming*, which cover every aspect of TCP/IP administration and programming on UNIX systems.

# Chapter 12

## Routing

C ommunication between different machines, through the transmission of data packets, can only take place through the process of *routing*. Routing involves finding a path between two hosts. It doesn't matter whether they exist on the same network or are separated by thousands of miles and hundreds of intermediate hosts; in both cases the basic principles are the same. However, for security reasons, many sites on the Internet have installed *packet filters*, which deny certain packet transmissions on a host basis or port basis. In this chapter, we will examine static and dynamic methods for configuring routes between hosts, and examine the mechanisms of IP filtering and firewalls.

# Network Interfaces

Solaris supports many different kinds of network interfaces for local area and wide area transmission. Ethernet and FDDI are commonly used for creating networks of two or more systems at a single site through a LAN, and T1 and X.25 lines (and most recently, ATM—Asynchronous Transfer Mode networks) are used for high-speed, wide-area connections. Network interfaces are connected by hubs and routers: A hub is a device that can interconnect many devices so that they can be channeled directly to a central router for wide-area connection. For example, each physical floor of a building may have a hub, and each of these hubs then connects to a single hub that serves for the whole building. This hub *may be* connected to an Internet Service Provider (ISP) through a router (in this example we'll call it router.company.com), and a dedicated ISDN service. A general rule of thumb for connecting routable networks is not to have more than three levels of connection between a server and a router, otherwise, the number of errors increases dramatically. Figure 12-1 shows a possible Class C network configuration for such a building. Class A, B, and C networks are explained in Chapter 11.

The configuration pictured in Figure 12-1 is fine if a single company (we'll use the name company.com) owns and occupies this building, and both the company and the building use the same ISP. However, let's imagine that company.com downsizes and leases the second floor to a government department, department.gov. The government department wants to make use of the existing ISP arrangements, and is happy to share the cost of the ISDN connection. However, they want to logically isolate their network from that of company.com for security purposes: They intend to install a packet filter on their own router, which explicitly denies or allows packets to cross into the government department's network.

This logical separation can be easily achieved by separating the existing network into two subnets, allowing the government department to install their own router, and connecting the two networks through that router. Traffic to the ISP can still flow through the existing connection, even though the hosts on the second floor are now separated from the router. Routing solves the problem of determining a network path between the department and the ISP. More generally, routing allows one host to find a path to any other host on the Internet. Figure 12-2 shows the revised configuration for this building, incorporating the changes required by the government department, forming two Class C networks whose routers are connected to each other.

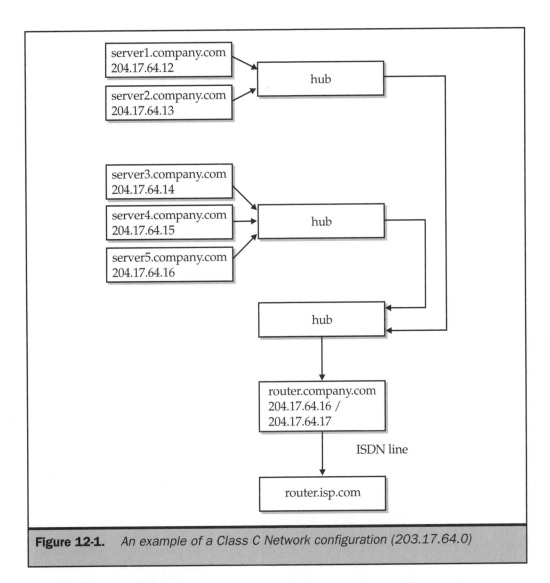

**Figure 12-1.** *An example of a Class C Network configuration (203.17.64.0)*

From a network perspective, a host must either be a router or a host. A router can be a Solaris server that performs other functions (for example, a DNS server or an NIS server); it can also be a dedicated, hardware-based system supplied by another manufacturer (for example, Cisco or Ascend). In this chapter, we will examine ways of setting up and configuring a Solaris host to be a router, although it may be that your organization prefers to use a dedicated system for routing.

The basic function of a router, as displayed in Figures 12-1 and 12-2, is to pass information from one network to another. In the examples, information is passed from one Class C network to another, and also to the router of an ISP. The ISP's router then connects with many other ISPs' routers, eventually giving global coverage. The

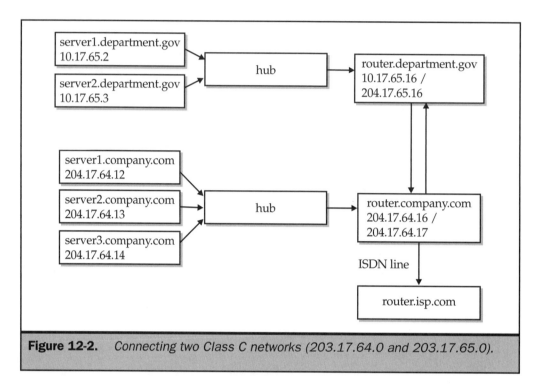

**Figure 12-2.** *Connecting two Class C networks (203.17.64.0 and 203.17.65.0).*

information passed between networks is contained in discrete packets, and since the router passes this information along, it follows that any router along the route can potentially make a copy of the data and save it to a local disk. This is the source of many security-related problems on the Internet, since usernames and passwords are also transmitted as packets, and can be intercepted by any intermediate router between client and server. Solutions to this problem are covered in Chapter 16, "Remote Access."

To be a router, a system must have multiple physical network interfaces. This is distinct from a system having one or more virtual interfaces defined for a single physical interface card. Thus, the router for company.com in the preceding examples has the interfaces 204.17.64.16 and 204.17.64.17. The first interface accepts traffic from the internal network and passes it to the second interface, while the second interface accepts traffic from the other routers and passes it to the internal network, or to other routers as appropriate. Having two network interfaces allows data to be passed through the machine and exchanged across different networks. In the example above, the company.com router was able to exchange information between the department.gov router and the ISP's router. Thus, many routers can be interconnected to form networks in which packets can be passed from a source to a destination host transparently.

Since the department.gov router serves as a packet-filtering firewall, it is likely that the network has a nonroutable, internal structure, which is not directly accessible to the external network, but *is* visible from the router (on the 10.17.65.0 network). Thus, a rogue user from company.com will be able to "see" the external interface for the department.gov router, but will not be able to see the internal interface, or any of the hosts beyond, unless she manages to break into the router through the external interface. This adds a second layer of protection against intrusion. A packet filter can then be used to explicitly deny connections to machines in the internal network, except for very specific system or network services. For example, a departmental mail server may reside on server1.department.gov, and external machines will ultimately need access to the sendmail ports on this server. This can be achieved by *port forwarding*, or the ability of the router to map a port on its external interface to a port on a machine on the internal network. For example, a web server on server1.department.gov:80 could be accessed from the external network by connecting to router.department.gov:8080 if the mapping were enabled. These techniques can achieve the necessary logical isolation between external users and actual network configuration and can be useful for security planning. Packet filtering, port forwarding, and nonroutable networks are discussed later in the chapter.

A machine with more than one network interface might or might not be configured to act as a router; if it isn't, it is referred to a *multi-homed host*. Multi-homing can be useful for performing such functions as load balancing, and directly serving different Class C networks, without passing information between them.

In order to configure routing, it is necessary to enable the appropriate network interfaces. In this chapter, we will assume that an Ethernet network is being used; thus, each system that acts as a router must have at least two Ethernet interfaces installed. Solaris supports multiple Ethernet interfaces to be installed on a single machine. These are usually designated by files with names such as:

/etc/hostname.hme*n*

or, for older machines:

/etc/hostname.le*n*

where *n* is the interface number. Interface files contain a single IP address, or fully qualified domain name, with the primary network interface being designated with an interface number of zero. Thus, the primary interface of a machine called server would be defined by the file /etc/server.hme0, which might contain the IP address 203.17.64.28, or the fully qualified domain name external.server.com. A secondary network interface, connected to a different subnet, might be defined in the file /etc/server.hme1. In this case, the file might contain the IP address 10.17.65.28, or internal.server.com. Note that it is preferable to use fully qualified domain names to IP addresses, because the former is an absolute addressing scheme, while the latter may be dynamically allocated using DHCP, or a similar protocol. This setup is commonly used in organizations that have a provision for a failure of the primary network interface, or to enable load balancing of server requests across multiple subnets (for example, for an intranet web server processing HTTP requests). A system with a second network interface can act either as a router or as a multi-homed host. Hostnames and IP addresses are locally administered through a naming service, which is usually the Domain Name Service (DNS) for companies connected to the Internet, and the Network Information Service (NIS/NIS+) for companies with large internal networks that require administrative functions beyond what DNS provides, including centralized authentication. Chapter 13 covers how to set up and maintain a DNS server, and Chapter 15 presents NIS and NIS+ in detail.

> **Tip**    *It is quite possible to assign different IP addresses to the same network interface, which can be useful for hosting "virtual" domains that require their own IP address, rather than relying on application-level support for multi-homing (for example, when using the Apache web server). Simply create a new /etc/hostname.hmeX:Y file for each IP address required, where X represents the physical device interface, and Y represents the virtual interface number.*

In the examples presented above, each of the routers had two interfaces: one for the internal network and one for the external Internet. The subnet mask used by each of these interfaces must also be defined in /etc/netmasks. This is particularly important if the interfaces lie on different subnets, or if they serve different network classes. In addition, it might also be appropriate to assign a fully qualified domain name to each of the interfaces, although this will depend on the purpose to which each interface is assigned. For the system router.department.gov, there will be two hostname files created in the /etc directory. The /etc/hostname.hme0 file will contain the entry 10.17.65.16, while the /etc/hostname.hme0 file will contain the entry 204.17.65.16.

When installing a system as a router, it is necessary to determine which network interface to use as the external interface for passing information between networks. This interface must be defined in the file /etc/defaultrouter, by including that interface's IP address. This address can be matched to a hostname if appropriate. For example, the internal and external interfaces for router.department.gov will be defined in /etc/hosts as:

```
127.0.0.1        localhost       loghost
10.17.65.16      internal
204.17.65.16     router          router.department.gov
```

If the server is to be multi-homed instead of being a router, ensure that /etc/defaultrouter does not exist, and create an /etc/notrouter file:

**server# rm /etc/defaultrouter**

**server# touch /etc/notrouter**

For both routing and multi-homed hosts, the status of all network interfaces can be checked by using the **netstat -i** command:

**router# netstat -I**

```
Name Mtu  Net/Dest     Address          Ipkts    Ierrs  Opkts    Oerrs Collis Queue
lo0  8232 loopback     localhost        199875   0      199875   0     0      0
hme0 1500 203.17.65.0  department.gov   16970779 623190 19543549 0     0      0
hme1 1500 10.17.65.0   internal.gov     68674644 54543  65673376 0     0      0
```

In this example, *Mtu* is the maximum transfer rate, which is much higher for the loopback address than the network interface (as would be expected), and the number of *Ipkts* (inbound packets) and *Opkts* (outbound packets) is equivalent for lo0 (as one would hope). The loopback interface significantly increases the efficiency of a host that transmits packets to itself: In this example, there is an almost sixfold difference between the Mtu for the lo0 interface and either of the standard network interfaces. The primary network interface hme0 is connected to the 203.17.65.0 network, and has transmitted a large number of packets in and out since booting (16,970,779 and 19,543,549, respectively). There have been a number of inbound errors (623,190), but no outbound errors or collisions. Examining how these figures change over time can indicate potential problems in network topology that may need to be addressed. For example, if you are testing a web server and it doesn't appear to be working, the *Ipkts* count can reveal whether or not the connections are actually being made: If the counter does not increase as expected, it may indicate an intermediate hardware failure (for example, a dead hub). Another example of intermittent hardware failure might be revealed by a large number of inbound packets (representing requests), but only a small number of outbound packets. In the following example, there are 1,000,847 inbound packets, but only 30,159 outbound packets since boot. Since it is unlikely in most situations that a 33-to-1 imbalance exists in the ratio of inbound to outbound packets, the hme0 network interface should be checked. There are also many collisions being experienced by the hme0 interface. Collisions between packets render them useless, and the figure reported here indicates a significant loss of bandwidth. If the interface is working as expected, it can also be worthwhile to investigate other causes, for example, problems arising from such software factors as incorrect configuration of a packet filter:

**server# netstat -I**

```
Name  Mtu   Net/Dest     Address      Ipkts  Ierrs Opkts  Oerrs Collis Queue
lo0   8232  loopback     localhost    7513   0     7513   0     0      0
hme0  1500  204.17.64.0  1000847 5    30159  0     3979   0
```

**netstat -s** also allows these per-interface statistics to be viewed on a per-protocol basis, which can be very useful in determining potential problems with routing, especially if the router is packet filtering. The following example shows output from the **netstat -s** command, which displays the per-protocol statistics for the UDP, TCP, and ICMP protocols:

**router# netstat -s**

The output from **netstat -s** begins with the UDP statistics, including the number of datagrams received, and the number transmitted. The In/Out ratio is fairly even at 1.09, and the networking appears to be working well: There were no detected UDP errors (that is, udpInErrors = 0), as you can see in the following:

```
UDP
        udpInDatagrams     =502856    udpInErrors      =      0
        udpOutDatagrams    =459357
```

The TCP statistics (below) are more mixed: There were 324 tcpAttemptFails, but given that there were 33,786 tcpActiveOpens at the time **netstat** was run, this is quite reasonable. The ratio of tcpInInorderSegs to tcpInUnorderSegs (in other words, received in order versus not received in order) was 229 to 1, which is not uncommon.

```
TCP     tcpRtoAlgorithm    =        4    tcpRtoMin           =      200
        tcpRtoMax          =240000       tcpMaxConn          =       -1
        tcpActiveOpens     =  33786      tcpPassiveOpens     =  12296
        tcpAttemptFails    =    324      tcpEstabResets      =    909
        tcpCurrEstab       =    384      tcpOutSegs          =19158723
        tcpOutDataSegs     =13666668     tcpOutDataBytes     =981537148
        tcpRetransSegs     =  33038      tcpRetransBytes     =41629885
        tcpOutAck          =5490764      tcpOutAckDelayed    =462511
        tcpOutUrg          =     51      tcpOutWinUpdate     =    456
        tcpOutWinProbe     =    290      tcpOutControl       =  92218
        tcpOutRsts         =   1455      tcpOutFastRetrans   =  18954
        tcpInSegs          =15617893
        tcpInAckSegs       =9161810      tcpInAckBytes       =981315052
        tcpInDupAck        =4559921      tcpInAckUnsent      =      0
        tcpInInorderSegs   =5741788      tcpInInorderBytes   =1120389303
        tcpInUnorderSegs   =  25045      tcpInUnorderBytes   =16972517
        tcpInDupSegs       =4390218      tcpInDupBytes       =4889714
        tcpInPartDupSegs   =    375      tcpInPartDupBytes   =130424
        tcpInPastWinSegs   =     17      tcpInPastWinBytes   =1808990872
        tcpInWinProbe      =    162      tcpInWinUpdate      =    270
        tcpInClosed        =    313      tcpRttNoUpdate      =  28077
        tcpRttUpdate       =9096791      tcpTimRetrans       =  18098
        tcpTimRetransDrop  =     26      tcpTimKeepalive     =    509
        tcpTimKeepaliveProbe=    76      tcpTimKeepaliveDrop =      1
        tcpListenDrop      =      0      tcpListenDropQ0     =      0
        tcpHalfOpenDrop    =      0
```

There are some IP errors but they were quite minor: There were eight ipInHdrErrors but only one ipInCksumErrs, and two udpInCksumErrs.

| IP | ipForwarding | = | 2 | ipDefaultTTL | = | 255 |
|----|----|----|----|----|----|----|
| | ipInReceives | = | 16081438 | ipInHdrErrors | = | 8 |
| | ipInAddrErrors | = | 0 | ipInCksumErrs | = | 1 |
| | ipForwDatagrams | = | 0 | ipForwProhibits | = | 2 |
| | ipInUnknownProtos | = | 274 | ipInDiscards | = | 0 |
| | ipInDelivers | = | 16146712 | ipOutRequests | = | 19560145 |
| | ipOutDiscards | = | 0 | ipOutNoRoutes | = | 0 |
| | ipReasmTimeout | = | 60 | ipReasmReqds | = | 0 |
| | ipReasmOKs | = | 0 | ipReasmFails | = | 0 |
| | ipReasmDuplicates | = | 0 | ipReasmPartDups | = | 0 |
| | ipFragOKs | = | 7780 | ipFragFails | = | 0 |
| | ipFragCreates | = | 40837 | ipRoutingDiscards | = | 0 |
| | tcpInErrs | = | 291 | udpNoPorts | = | 144065 |
| | udpInCksumErrs | = | 2 | udpInOverflows | = | 0 |
| | rawipInOverflows | = | 0 | | | |

On the ICMP front (shown below), icmpOutErrors and icmpInErrors are both zero, but there were 2,113 icmpOutDestUnreachs, indicating that at some point a network connection was not able to be made when requested. This can be checked with the **traceroute** utility described later in this chapter. It also is often useful to run a **cron** job to extract these figures to a file, and then to write a Perl script to compare the values of concern, rather than relying on the printout itself. This is because it is possible that errors could be masked by integers being "wrapped around" and starting at zero on the printout, after they reach values which are greater than the maximum available for a machine's architecture. However, this should not be a problem for the new 64-bit kernels available with Solaris 7 and 8.

| ICMP | icmpInMsgs | = | 17469 | icmpInErrors | = | 0 |
|----|----|----|----|----|----|----|
| | icmpInCksumErrs | = | 0 | icmpInUnknowns | = | 0 |
| | icmpInDestUnreachs | = | 2343 | icmpInTimeExcds | = | 26 |
| | icmpInParmProbs | = | 0 | icmpInSrcQuenchs | = | 0 |
| | icmpInRedirects | = | 19 | icmpInBadRedirects | = | 19 |
| | icmpInEchos | = | 9580 | icmpInEchoReps | = | 5226 |
| | icmpInTimestamps | = | 0 | icmpInTimestampReps | = | 0 |
| | icmpInAddrMasks | = | 0 | icmpInAddrMaskReps | = | 0 |
| | icmpInFragNeeded | = | 0 | icmpOutMsgs | = | 11693 |
| | icmpOutDrops | = | 140883 | icmpOutErrors | = | 0 |
| | icmpOutDestUnreachs | = | 2113 | icmpOutTimeExcds | = | 0 |
| | icmpOutParmProbs | = | 0 | icmpOutSrcQuenchs | = | 0 |

**BASIC NETWORK ADMINISTRATION**

```
icmpOutRedirects    =      0      icmpOutEchos         =       0
icmpOutEchoReps     =   9580      icmpOutTimestamps    =       0
icmpOutTimestampReps=      0      icmpOutAddrMasks     =       0
icmpOutAddrMaskReps =      0      icmpOutFragNeeded    =       0
icmpInOverflows     =      0
```

# Viewing Your Interfaces

The **ifconfig** command is responsible for configuring each network interface at boot time. **ifconfig** can also be used to check the status of active network interfaces by passing the **-a** parameter:

**router# ifconfig -a**

```
lo0: flags=849<UP,LOOPBACK,RUNNING,MULTICAST> mtu 8232
        inct 127.0.0.1 netmask ff000000
hme0: flags=863<UP,BROADCAST,NOTRAILERS,RUNNING,MULTICAST> mtu 1500
        inet 10.17.65.16 netmask ffffff00 broadcast 10.17.65.255
hme1: flags=863<UP,BROADCAST,NOTRAILERS,RUNNING,MULTICAST> mtu 1500
        inet 204.17.65.16 netmask ffffff00 broadcast 204.17.65.255
```

In this case, the primary interface hme0 is running on the internal network, while the secondary interface hme1 is visible to the external network. The netmask for a Class C network is used on both interfaces, while both have a distinct broadcast address. This ensures that information broadcast on the internal network is not visible to the external network. There are several parameters shown with **ifconfig -a**, including those specifying whether or not the interface is UP or DOWN (in other words, active or inactive). In the following example, the interface has not been enabled at boot time:

**server# ifconfig hme1**

```
hme1: flags=863<DOWN,BROADCAST,NOTRAILERS,RUNNING,MULTICAST> mtu 1500
        inet 204.17.64.16 netmask ffffff00 broadcast 204.17.64.255
```

If the /etc/ethers database has been updated by the administrator to include details of the Ethernet addresses of hosts on the local network, then there is also an entry displayed about the corresponding interface when using **ifconfig**:

**server# cat /etc/ethers**

```
8:0:19:7:f2:a1 server
server# ifconfig hme1
hme1: flags=863<UP,BROADCAST,NOTRAILERS,RUNNING,MULTICAST> mtu 1500
        inet 204.17.128.16 netmask ffffff00 broadcast 204.17.128.255
ether 8:0:19:7:f2:a1
```

In detecting problems with a routing network interface it can also be useful to examine the address resolution protocol results for the local area network. This will determine whether or not the interface is visible to its clients:

**server# arp -a**

```
Net to Media Table
Device  IP Address               Mask            Flags  Phys Addr
------  --------------------  ---------------  -----  --------------
hme0    server1.company.com 255.255.255.255          00:c0:ff:19:48:d8
hme0    server2.company.com 255.255.255.255          c2:d4:78:00:15:56
hme0    server3.company.com 255.255.255.255          87:b3:9a:c2:e9:ea
```

# Modifying Interface Parameters

There are two methods for modifying network interface parameters:

- The **ifconfig** command can be used to modify operational parameters, and to bring an interface on-line ("up") or shut it down ("down").

- *Or* one can use **ndd** to set parameters for TCP/IP transmission that will affect all network interfaces.

In this section, we will examine both of these methods, and how they may be used to manage interfaces and improve performance.

It is sometimes necessary to shut down and start up a network interface in order to upgrade drivers or install patches affecting network service. To shut down a network interface, one can use the following command sequence:

**server# ifconfig hme1 down**

**server# ifconfig hme1**

```
hme1: flags=863<DOWN,BROADCAST,NOTRAILERS,RUNNING,MULTICAST> mtu 1500
        inet 204.17.64.16 netmask ffffff00 broadcast 204.17.64.255
```

It also possible to bring this interface back "up" by using **ifconfig**:

**server# ifconfig hme1 up**

**server# ifconfig hme1**

```
hme1: flags=863<UP,BROADCAST,NOTRAILERS,RUNNING,MULTICAST> mtu 1500
        inet 204.17.64.16 netmask ffffff00 broadcast 204.17.64.255
```

**ndd** is used to set parameters for network protocols, including TCP, IP, UDP, and ARP. For example, ndd can be used to modify the parameters associated with IP forwarding and routing. Let's look at the set of configurable parameters for TCP transmission:

**server# ndd /dev/tcp \?**

```
?                               (read only)
tcp_close_wait_interval         (read and write)
tcp_conn_req_max_q              (read and write)
tcp_conn_req_max_q0             (read and write)
tcp_conn_req_min                (read and write)
tcp_conn_grace_period           (read and write)
tcp_cwnd_max                    (read and write)
tcp_debug                       (read and write)
tcp_smallest_nonpriv_port       (read and write)
tcp_ip_abort_cinterval          (read and write)
tcp_ip_abort_linterval          (read and write)
tcp_ip_abort_interval           (read and write)
tcp_ip_notify_cinterval         (read and write)
tcp_ip_notify_interval          (read and write)
tcp_ip_ttl                      (read and write)
tcp_keepalive_interval          (read and write)
tcp_maxpsz_multiplier           (read and write)
tcp_mss_def                     (read and write)
tcp_mss_max                     (read and write)
tcp_mss_min                     (read and write)
tcp_naglim_def                  (read and write)
tcp_rexmit_interval_initial     (read and write)
tcp_rexmit_interval_max         (read and write)
tcp_rexmit_interval_min         (read and write)
tcp_wroff_xtra                  (read and write)
tcp_deferred_ack_interval       (read and write)
tcp_snd_lowat_fraction          (read and write)
tcp_sth_rcv_hiwat               (read and write)
```

```
tcp_sth_rcv_lowat              (read and write)
tcp_dupack_fast_retransmit     (read and write)
tcp_ignore_path_mtu            (read and write)
tcp_rcv_push_wait              (read and write)
tcp_smallest_anon_port         (read and write)
tcp_largest_anon_port          (read and write)
tcp_xmit_hiwat                 (read and write)
tcp_xmit_lowat                 (read and write)
tcp_recv_hiwat                 (read and write)
tcp_recv_hiwat_minmss          (read and write)
tcp_fin_wait_2_flush_interval  (read and write)
tcp_co_min                     (read and write)
tcp_max_buf                    (read and write)
tcp_zero_win_probesize         (read and write)
tcp_strong_iss                 (read and write)
tcp_rtt_updates                (read and write)
tcp_wscale_always              (read and write)
tcp_tstamp_always              (read and write)
tcp_tstamp_if_wscale           (read and write)
tcp_rexmit_interval_extra      (read and write)
tcp_deferred_acks_max          (read and write)
tcp_slow_start_after_idle      (read and write)
tcp_slow_start_initial         (read and write)
tcp_co_timer_interval          (read and write)
tcp_extra_priv_ports           (read only)
tcp_extra_priv_ports_add       (write only)
tcp_extra_priv_ports_del       (write only)
tcp_status                     (read only)
tcp_bind_hash                  (read only)
tcp_listen_hash                (read only)
tcp_conn_hash                  (read only)
tcp_queue_hash                 (read only)
tcp_host_param                 (read and write)
tcp_1948_phrase                (write only)
```

Parameters can also be set specifically for IP as well as TCP. For example, if the parameter **ip_forwarding** has a value of 2 (the default), it will only perform routing when two or more interfaces are active. However, if this parameter is set to 0, then ip_forwarding will never be performed (that is, it will ensure that routing is ignored, and thus that multi-homing is active). This can be set by using the following command:

**server# ndd -set /dev/ip ip_forwarding 0**

Administrators should be aware that modifying **ndd** parameters for a specific purpose could interfere with other TCP services provided by the server. Proceed with caution!

To ensure that this configuration is preserved from boot to boot, it is possible to edit the networking startup file /etc/rc2.d/S69inet and add this line to any others that configure the network interfaces. Alternatively, it may be wiser to create a separate startup file (for example, /etc/rc2.d/S69spNet) that contains the nondefault settings, so that these changes can be easily reversed by typing:

server# /etc/rc2.d/S69spNet stop

server# /etc/rc2.d/S69inet start

It may be necessary to set several of these parameters in a production environment to ensure optimal performance, especially when application servers and web servers are in use. For example, when a web server makes a request to port 80 using TCP, a connection is opened and closed. However, the connection is kept open for a default time of two minutes to ensure that all packets are correctly received. For a system with a large number of clients, this can lead to a bottleneck of stale TCP connections, which can have a significant impact on the performance of the web server. Fortunately, the parameter that controls this behavior (**tcp_close_wait_interval**) can be set to something more sensible (like 30 seconds) using **ndd**:

server# ndd -set /dev/tcp tcp_close_wait_interval 30000

However, administrators should be aware that altering this parameter will affect all TCP services, so while a web server might perform optimally with **tcp_close_wait_interval** equal to 30 seconds, a database listener that handles large datasets may require a much wider time window. The best way to determine optimal values is to perform experiments with low, moderate, and peak levels of traffic for both the web server and the database listener to determine a value that will provide reasonable performance for both applications. (It is also important to check SunSolve for the latest patches and updates for recently discovered kernel bugs.)

# IP Routing

Now that we have discussed how to install, configure, and tune network interfaces, we shall turn our attention to setting up routing by explaining how packets are transferred, hosts to routers, and exchanged between routers. We will also examine how to troubleshoot routing problems with **traceroute**, and introduce the different routing protocols that are currently being used on the Internet.

There are two kinds of routing: static and dynamic. Static routing is common in simple networks with only a few hosts and networks interconnected. Dynamic routing is more suitable for large networks, where the routes between networks cannot be readily specified. Let's look at a couple of examples that will make it clear why static routing is difficult to maintain on large networks. If your organizational network has only two routers connecting three networks, then the number of routes that need to be installed if you're doing it statically is four (i.e., the square of the number of routers). In contrast, for a building with five routers, the number of routes that need to be specified if you're doing it statically is 25. If a static router configuration changes, then all of the static configuration files on all of the routers need to be changed (i.e., there is no mechanism for the "discovery" of routes). Alternatively, if a static router fails because of a hardware fault, then packets may not be able to be correctly routed. Dynamic routing solves all of these problems, but requires more processing overhead on each router. There are two related dynamic routing daemons—**in.rdisc** and **in.routed**, the router discovery daemon and the route daemon respectively—whose configuration will be discussed at length in this section.

## Overview of Packet Delivery

Before we examine the differences between static and dynamic routing in detail, let's take a step back and consider how information is passed between two systems, whether the exchange is host-host, host-router, or router-router. All information is exchanged in the form of discrete packets, which is the smallest unit of information that is transmitted between hosts using TCP/IP. A packet contains both a header and a message component, as shown in Figure 12-3. In order to deliver packets from one host to another host successfully, each packet contains information in the header, which is similar in purpose to an envelope. Among many other fields, the header contains the address of the destination machine and the address of the source machine. The message section of the packet contains the actual data to be transferred. (Actually, in TCP transmission the header is allowed to include message information inserted by the source machine. This is

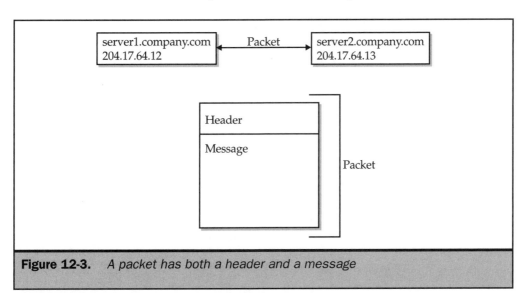

**Figure 12-3.** *A packet has both a header and a message*

referred to as *data encapsulation*.) In normal TCP transmission mode, only 64 kilobytes of data can be transferred in a single session, unless *large window support* is enabled, in which case, up to 1 gigabyte of data may be transmitted. The action of passing a packet is referred to as a *hop*, so routing involves enabling packets to "hop" from a source host to any arbitrary host on the Internet.

**Note** *Although packets are often transferred on the Transport Layer using the Transmission Control Protocol (TCP), which guarantees the delivery of packets, some applications use User Datagram Protocol (UDP) instead, which cannot guarantee the continuity of a connection.*

In order for packets to be delivered correctly between two hosts, all intermediate routers must be able to determine where the packets have come from and where they must be delivered to. This can be achieved by referring to a host by using its IP address (for example, 203.16.42.58) or its fully qualified domain name (for example, server.company.com). Although it is also possible to refer to a machine by its Ethernet (hardware) address, it is often preferred in TCP/IP to use a logical rather than a physical representation of a machine's network interface card.

Sending a packet across a network makes full use of all network layers. For example, if a **telnet** session is to be established between two machines, the Application Layer protocol specifies how the message and header are to be constructed, information that is then passed to the Transport Layer protocol. For a **telnet** session, the Transport Layer protocol is TCP, which proceeds with encapsulation of the packet's data, which is split into segments. The data is divided according to the size of the TCP window allowed by the system. Each segment has a header and a checksum; the checksum is used by the destination host to determine whether a received packet is likely to be free of corruption. When a segment is due to be transmitted from the source host, a three-way handshake occurs between source and destination: A SYN segment is sent to the destination host requesting a connection, and an acknowledgement (ACK) is returned to the source when the destination host is ready to receive. When the ACK is received by the source host, its receipt is acknowledged back to the destination, and transmission proceeds with data being passed to the IP Layer, where segments are realized as *IP datagrams*. IP also adds a header to the segment, and passes it to the Physical Networking Layer for transport. A common method of enacting a "denial of service" attack on a remote host involves sending many SYN requests to a remote host while refusing to complete the "three-way handshake." Solaris now limits the maximum number of connections with incomplete handshakes to reduce the impact of the problem. When a packet finally arrives at the destination host, it travels through the TCP/IP protocol stack in the reverse order from that which it took on the sender (just like a deck of cards that has been dealt onto a playing table, and retrieved from the top of the pack).

When packets need to be passed through several hosts to reach their ultimate destination, the method of passing data from source to destination is the same—but the next hop along the route needs to be determined somehow. The path that a packet takes across the network depends on the IP address of the destination host as specified in the packet header. If the destination host is on the local network, it can be delivered immediately, without intervention of a separate router. For example, a source host 204.12.60.24 on the Class C network 204.12.60.0 can pass a packet directly to a destination 204.12.60.32. However, once a packet needs to be delivered beyond the local network, the process becomes more complicated. The packet is passed to the router on the local network (which may be defined in /etc/defaultrouter), and a router table is consulted. The router table contains a list of the hosts on the local network and other routers to which the router has a connection. For example, the router for the 204.12.60.0 network might be 204.12.60.64. Thus, a packet from 204.12.60.24 would be passed to 204.12.60.64 if the destination host was not on the 204.12.60.0 network. The router 204.12.60.64 may have a second interface 204.12.61.64 that connects the 204.12.60.0 and 204.12.59.0 networks. If the destination host was 204.12.59.28, the packet could now be delivered directly to the host because the router bridges the two networks. However, if the packet is not deliverable to a host on the 204.12.59.0 network, then it must be passed to another router defined in the current router's tables.

## traceroute

If the process of finding a route is difficult to conceptualize, Solaris provides the **traceroute** tool to display literally the route taken by a packet between two hosts. The **traceroute** utility measures the time taken to reach each intermediate host from source to destination. If an intermediate host cannot be reached in a specified time period (usually this is specified in the *ttl* "time to live" field), an error message is reported. A maximum number of hops (usually 30) is specified to prevent **traceroute** from looping infinitely if an operational route cannot be found. **traceroute** is also very useful for determining network points of failure due to misconfiguration and hardware problems. Here is an example of a traceroute between a host on the AT&T network and a host on the Sun network:

**client% traceroute www.sun.com**

```
Tracing route to wwwseast.usec.sun.com [192.9.49.30]
over a maximum of 30 hops:
  1   184 ms   142 ms   138 ms   202.10.4.131
  2   147 ms   144 ms   138 ms   202.10.4.129
  3   150 ms   142 ms   144 ms   202.10.1.73
  4   150 ms   144 ms   141 ms   atm11-0-0-11.ia4.optus.net.au [202.139.32.17]
  5   148 ms   143 ms   139 ms   202.139.1.197
  6   490 ms   489 ms   474 ms   hssi9-0-0.sf1.optus.net.au [192.65.89.246]
  7   526 ms   480 ms   485 ms   g-sfd-br-02-f12-0.gn.cwix.net [207.124.109.57]
  8   494 ms   482 ms   485 ms   core7-hssi6-0-0.SanFrancisco.cw.net [204.70.10.9]
  9   483 ms   489 ms   484 ms   corerouter2.SanFrancisco.cw.net [204.70.9.132]
 10   557 ms   552 ms   561 ms   xcore3.Boston.cw.net [204.70.150.81]
```

```
11   566 ms   572 ms   554 ms   sun-micro-system.Boston.cw.net [204.70.179.102]
12   577 ms   574 ms   558 ms   wwwseast.usec.sun.com [192.9.49.30]
Trace complete.
```

## Static Routes

On hosts, routing information can be extracted in two ways:

- by building a full routing table, exactly as it does on a router
- *or* by creating a minimal kernel table, containing a single default route for each available router (in other words, static routing)

The most common static route is from a host to a local router, as specified in the /etc/defaultrouter file. For example, for the host 204.12.60.24 the entry in /etc/defaultrouter might be:

```
204.12.60.64
```

This places a single route in the local routing table. Responsibility for determining the next hop for the message is then passed to the router. Static routes can also be added for servers using **in.routed** by defining them in the /etc/gateways file. When using static routing, routing tables in the kernel are defined when the system boots and do not normally change, unless modified by using the **route** or **ifconfig** command. When a local network has a single gateway to the rest of the Internet, static routing is the most appropriate choice.

## Routing Protocols

The Routing Information Protocol (RIP) and the Router Discovery Protocol (RDISC) are some of the standard routing protocols for TCP/IP networks, and Solaris supports both. RIP is implemented by **in.routed**, the routing daemon, and is usually configured to start during multiuser-mode startup. The route daemon always populates the routing table with a route to every reachable network, but whether or not it advertises its routing availability to other systems is optional.

Hosts use the RDISC daemon (**in.rdisc**) to collect information about routing availability from routers. RDISC should run on both routers and hosts. **in.rdisc** typically creates a default route for each router that responds to requests. This route is central to the ability of RDISC-enabled hosts to dynamically adjust to network changes. Routers that only run **in.routed** cannot be discovered by RDISC-enabled hosts. For hosts running both **in.rdisc** and **in.routed**, the latter will operate until an RDISC-enabled router is discovered on the network, in which case, RDISC will take over routing.

# The Kernel Routing Table

The routing table maintains an index of routes to networks and routers that are available to the local host. Routes can be determined dynamically by using RDISC for example, or can be added manually by using **route** or **ifconfig**. These commands are normally used at boot time to initialize network services. There are three kinds of routes:

- *Host routes* map a path from the local host to another host on the local network.

- *Network routes* allow packets to be transferred from the local hosts to other hosts on the local network.

- *Default routes* pass the task of finding a route to a router. Both RIP and RDISC daemons can use default routes.

Dynamic routing often causes changes in the routing table after booting, when a minimal routing table is configured by **ifconfig** by initializing each network interface, since the daemons manage changes in the network configuration and router availability.

## Viewing the Routing Table (netstat -r)

The command **netstat -r** shows the current routing table. Routes are always specified as a connection between the local server and a remote machine via some kind of gateway. The output from the **netstat -r** command contains several different flags: Flag **U** indicates that the route between the destination and gateway is up, while flag **G** shows that the route passes through a gateway. Flag **H** indicates that the route connects to a host, while the **D** flag signifies that the route was dynamically created using a redirect. Besides the *Flags* column, there are three other columns shown in the routing table: *Ref* indicates the number of concurrent routes occupying the same link layer; *Use* indicates the number of packets transmitted along the route, on the interface identified in the *Interface* column.

The following example shows an example server (server.company.com) that has four routes: The first is for the loopback address (lo0), which is up and is connected through a host, and the second route is for the local Class C network (204.16.64.0), through the gateway gateway.company.com., which is also up. The third route is the special multicast route, which is also up, while the fourth route is the default route, pointing to the local network router, which is also up.

**bash-2.01$ netstat -r**

```
Routing Table:
  Destination           Gateway             Flags  Ref   Use   Interface
------------------    -------------------   -----  ----- ------ ---------
  127.0.0.1             localhost            UH     0     877   lo0
```

```
204.17.64.0            gateway.company.com  U    3    85  hme0
BASE-ADDRESS.MCAST.NET host.company.com     U    3     0  hme0
default                router.company.com   UG   0   303
```

# Manipulating the Routing Table (Using route)

The **route** command is used to manipulate the routing tables manually. If dynamic routing is working correctly, it should not normally be necessary to do this. However, if static routing is being used, or the RDISC daemon does not discover any routes, it may be necessary to add routes manually. In addition, it may also be necessary to delete routes explicitly for security purposes. You should be aware, though, that except for interface changes, the routing daemon might not respond to any modifications that were enacted manually to the routing table. It is best to shut down the routing daemon first before making changes, and then restart it after all changes have been initiated.

## Adding Host Routes

To add a direct route to another host, the **route** command is used with the following syntax:

```
route add -host destination_ip local_ip -interface interface
```

Thus, if we wanted to add a route between the local host (for example, 204.12.17.1) and a host on a neighbouring Class C network (204.12.16.100), for the primary interface hme0 we would use the command:

**route add -host 204.12.16.100 204.12.17.1 -interface hme0**

## Adding Network Routes

To add a direct route to another network, the **route** command is used with the following syntax:

```
route add -net destination_network_ip local_ip -netmask mask
```

If we wanted to add a route between the local host (for example, 204.12.17.1) and the network for the host we specified above (i.e., the 204.12.16.0 network), for the Class C netmask (255.255.255.0), we would use the command:

**route add -net 204.12.16.0 204.12.17.1 -netmask 255.255.255.0**

## Adding a Default Route

To add a default route, the **route** command can be used with the following syntax:

```
route add default hostname -interface interface
```

For example, to add a default route to a local router (204.54.56.1) for a secondary interface hme1, you can use the command:

**route add default 204.54.56.1 -interface hme1**

# Dynamic Routing

In this section, we will look more closely at the RDISC dynamic routing protocol. A prerequisite for dynamic routing to operate is that the /etc/defaultrouter file should be empty.

## in.routed

**in.routed** is the network routing daemon, and is responsible for dynamically managing entries in the kernel routing tables, as described above. It is usually started from a line in the networking startup file (/etc/rc2.d/S69inet) during multiuser boot using the command:

**/usr/sbin/in.routed -q**

The routing daemon uses port 520 to route packets and to establish which interfaces are currently up and which are down. **in.routed** listens for requests for packets and for known routes from remote hosts. This supplies the hosts on a network with the information they need for determining how many hops to a host. When it is initialized, the routing daemon checks both of the gateways specified in /etc/gateways.

It is also possible to run the routing daemon in a special memory-saving mode that retains only the default routes in the routing table. This can be enabled by initializing **in.routed** with the **-S** parameter instead of the **-q** parameter. While this approach may leave a system at the mercy of a faulty router, it does save memory and reduces the number of active routes in the lists that **in.routed** is required to periodically update.

## in.rdisc

The RDISC daemon uses the ICMP router discovery protocol, and is usually executed on both hosts and routers at boot time, at which time routers broadcast their availability and hosts start listening for available routers. Routers broadcast their availability using the 224.0.0.1 multicast address. Routers that share a network with a host are selected first as the default route, if one is found. Another approach is for the host to send out a broadcast on the 224.0.0.2 multicast address to solicit any available routers. In either case, if a router is available, it will accept packet forwarding requests from the host concerned.

# IP Filtering/Firewalls

After going to all the trouble of making routing easy to use and semiautomated with the dynamic routing protocols, there are some situations that require that the smooth transfer of packets from one host to another via a router be prevented. This is usually because of security concerns about data that is contained on hosts on a particular network. For example, Windows networks broadcast all kinds of information about workgroups and domains that is visible to any computer that can connect through the network's router. If the network's router prevents a computer on another network from listening to this information, it can still be broadcast internally and not be visible to the outside world. Fortunately, this kind of "packet filtering" is selective: Only specific ports are blocked at the router level, and they can also be blocked in whichever direction the administrator chooses. For example, a database listener operating on a router could accept connections from machines internal to the network while being blocked from accessing machines external to the network. For large organizations that have direct connections to the Internet, setting up a corporate firewall at the router level has become a priority in order to protect sensitive data while providing employees with the access to the Internet that they require. In this section, we examine the basics of packet filtering, and review the installation and configuration of the popular IPFilter package for Solaris.

# What Is IP Filtering?

IP filtering involves the selective restriction and permission of access to TCP and UDP ports on a system. IP filtering is commonly used for two purposes: to secure a network from attacks and intrusion from rogue users on outside hosts, and to prevent the broadcast and transmission of unauthorized data from an internal network to the rest of the Internet. In the former case, an attacker may attempt to gain entry to your system by using an application like **telnet**, or may try to insert or retrieve data from a database by connecting to a database listener and issuing SQL commands from a client application. Both of these scenarios are common enough to motivate many sites to restrict all incoming traffic to their networks, except on a very small number of specific ports. Commonly allowed ports include:

- Secure shell (ssh) on port 22
- Secure copy (scp) on port 24
- Mail server (sendmail) on port 25
- WWW server (apache) on port 80

This may seem like a very minimal list to many administrators, but the fact is that almost every UNIX daemon has been discovered to suffer from "buffer overflow" problems in recent years, leaving systems open to exploitation. A rule of thumb is to only allow services that users definitely need to be productive, and that have been approved by management. Some users might argue that allowing the **finger** service is useful, but it also gives away a lot of information about home directories and valid usernames that can be exploited by rogue users. Although Solaris restricts ports less than 1024 for the superuser and system accounts, all ports above 1024 are available for users to engage in unauthorized activities—for which your company may be held responsible. For example, a user might run a web server or ftp server on port 8080 to distribute pirate software; if a software manufacturer discovers this operation, they will most likely sue your company rather than the individual involved. Blocking access to all ports unless they are specifically required or sanctioned limits these kinds of problems.

Firewalls are able to restrict both incoming traffic and outgoing traffic because a firewall may also act as a router; and you may recall that routers always have at least two network interfaces. One good reason to consider blocking outgoing network traffic on some ports is that users might otherwise engage in leisure activities, such as playing networked adventure games and using chat rooms, when they should be working. Since you don't really want to be the policeman "patrolling" the system for violators, it is best just to restrict any access in the first place to avoid problems down the road. It's also possible to use a firewall to accept or deny connections based on an IP address: Obviously, a machine making a connection from the external network, but pretending to have an address from inside the network (this is known as "IP spoofing"), should be identified and its attempts rejected. Figure 12-4 summarizes the functions of a router that acts as a packet filtering "firewall." In this figure, permitted ports are shown with the label "OK," while denied ports are shown with "NO." All connections for sendmail (25) are accepted, as are ssh connections. However, external connections to a database listener are rejected (port 1521), and a machine on the external side spoofing an internal network IP address has all its connections rejected.

# The IP Filter Package

IPFilter, a kernel-loadable module that is attached at boot time, is a popular freeware packet filtering package for Solaris. Kernel loading makes IPFilter very secure because it cannot be tampered with by user applications. However, as we will see below, there are also problems with this approach because if the modules are unstable, then loading them into the kernel can cause the Solaris system to crash.

The IPFilter distribution is available from the following site:

**http://coombs.anu.edu.au/~avalon/**

### Configuring and Using IPFilter

The first step in creating an IPFilter configuration file is to consult with users and managers to determine a list of acceptable services. Many companies will already have an acceptable-use policy that will govern which ports should be available, and

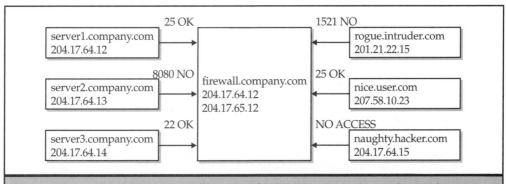

**Figure 12-4.**   *Basic firewall configuration for blocking incoming and outgoing ports*

what permissions should be given for user-initiated services. After a list of ingoing and outgoing port requirements is determined, it is best to write a rule that, firstly, denies all packets, and then to write rules following that that explicitly allow the services you have identified. Remember to enable allowed services in both directions as needed: For example, it is usually necessary for users to both receive and send electronic mail, so an inbound and outbound rule needs to be included for sendmail (port 25).

IPFilter rules are processed in the order that they are specified in the configuration file. Every rule is processed, which means that more general rules (like blocking all connections) should precede specific rules (like allowing bidirectional sendmail connections) in the configuration file. If you have a very complicated configuration, it is also possible to specify that processing terminate at any point in the file if a certain condition is met by using the keyword **quick** (yes, that's quick, not quit). Other important keywords include **block**, **to**, and **from** to construct rules for limiting packet transmission. The **block** command blocks packets from a particular source to a particular destination; the **from** command specifies the source of these packets; and the **to** command specifies the destination of these packets. The following example prevents any packets from the Class B network 178.222.0.0:

> **block in quick from 178.222.0.0/16 to any**

The **pass** command allows packets to pass the firewall. For example, the rule:

> **pass in all**

allows all packets to pass. Since routers by definition have more than two interfaces, it is also possible to specify a network interface to which a specific rule applies. For example, the following rule

> **block in quick on hme2 all**

prevents all transmissions on the **hme2** interface. An interface specification can be mixed with a normal rule so that one interface accepts traffic from one Class C network (178.222.1.0), but another interface may accept traffic only from a different Class C network (178.221.2.0), as specified here:

> **block in quick on hme2 from 178.222.1.0/24 to any**

> **block in quick on hme1 from 178.222.2.0/24 to any**

All of our IPFilter examples so far have focused on inbound traffic using the **in** command. As we mentioned earlier, it is also possible to restrict outbound traffic in the same way by using the **out** command. The following example prevents traffic from the internal, nonroutable network (10.222.1.0) to pass through:

> **block out quick on hme0 from 10.222.1.0/24 to any**

That rule would only be applied to organizations that didn't want their employees using the Internet. Perhaps it could be combined with a **cron** job that would reconfigure the firewall to allow access during lunch time and after work.

It is also possible to limit particular protocols so that TCP applications (like **SSH**) would be allowed, but UDP applications (like some streamed audio applications) would be banned by specifying **proto udp** in the rule:

> **block in quick on hme0 proto udp from 10.222.1.0/24 to any**

The most complicated rule comes in the form of a port-by-port specification of what is allowed and disallowed on a protocol-by-protocol basis. For example, the following rule blocks all web server requests from the internal network from reaching their destination:

> **block in quick on hme0 proto tcp from any to 10.222.1.0/24 port = 80**

This would allow telnet and ftp connections to proceed freely, as TCP is only restricted on port 80.

## Problems with IP Filtering

Although IP filtering technology is very comprehensive, and is very useful in placing very specific restrictions on network transmission, there are some drawbacks with configuring firewalls in general, and IPFilter in particular. Since firewall configuration involves writing rules, the syntax of the commonly used rule languages is often difficult to understand; thus, packet filters can be difficult to configure correctly. Once you've created a configuration, there is also no testbed provided for determining whether or not your configuration is satisfactory. Also, there may be contention between one or more rules that is incorrectly resolved. There are also bugs in packet filtering packages. This means that administrators should not rely solely on a filtering package to protect their network. (Other measures, like disabling unrequired services in /etc/services, and commenting out all unwanted daemons in /etc/inetd.conf, go a long way toward protecting a system.)

In particular, bugs in IPFilter can be more serious than bugs in other packages because IPFilter is a kernel-loadable module; thus, instead of an application-level filtering program crashing and dumping core, IPFilter will sometimes crash the kernel and cause a panic. Be aware that some versions of IPFilter will cause panics on Solaris kernels, while others work happily. The output from a crash looks like the following:

```
BAD TRAP: cpu=1 type=0x31 rp=0x3b103003 addr=0xe1 mmu_fsr=0x0
BAD TRAP occurred in module "ipf" due to an illegal access to a user
address.
sched: trap type = 0x31
addr=0x1e
pid=0, pc=0x60bc8607, sp=0x33ba0300, tstate=0x1e02f000, context=0x0
```

```
g1-g7: 1c, 13578104, 0, 0, 0, 0, 333e8000
Begin traceback... sp = 3033ba00
Called from 1005cb74, fp=30033c20, args=0 60760b14 20 10418440 0 0
Called from 1005cc90, fp=30033c80, args=60098aa0 600992c0 60098ac0
40000000 60099328 8c2421a
Called from 10026a48, fp=30033ce0, args=60098aa0 60098ab4 10418440
10418440 d 0
Called from 1005cc48, fp=0, args=60098aa0 0 0 0 0 0
```

This kind of problem is always a risk when installing kernel-loadable modules. Fortunately, Solaris does provide some tools to determine which modules are at fault. To examine the cause of the IPFilter problem, the following steps can be followed:

1. Create the system crash directory, and enable the **savecore** facility in the system startup file (/etc/init.d/sysetup).

2. Wait for a crash, and then let the system reboot.

3. Enter the crash directory and analyze the crash file with the iscda.sh script available from SunSolve, at the following site:

   **http://sunsolve1.sun.com.au/sunsolve/us/iscda.html**

4. Identify the command that caused the kernel panic. If it is an IPFilter command, download and test the most recent version.

## Summary

Routing is a complex but important topic in the Internet world. Administrators will often be asked to investigate why a host or network is unreachable, and you may also be faced with a "green fields" operation, where it is your responsibility to ensure connectivity as well as network security. In this chapter, we have covered the basics of static and dynamic routing, but we haven't covered commercial alternatives to the existing routing daemons (for example, **gated** is a heterogeneous daemon that performs the functions of other dynamic routing daemons through a single program). In addition, many commercial packages exist for the management of firewalls and packet filtering systems, and large organizations should investigate these packages as alternatives to the solutions discussed above.

## How to Find Out More

There is a very active discussion group on IPFilter, with searchable archives available, at **http://false.net/ipfilter**. There is also a firewall mailing list that is good for more general discussion of firewall-related issues, and the contents are available at **www.greatcircle.com/firewalls/**. If you are more interested in commercial firewall products, check out the comparisons at **www.fortified.com/fwcklist.html/**.

# The Complete Reference

Solaris 8

# Chapter 13

## The Domain Name Service

When your local system needs to communicate with a remote system, it uses the remote system's IP address. Computers are completely happy using IP addresses to communicate, but for humans it is much easier to work with names. It is much easier to type **www.yahoo.com** in your web browser than to type its IP address, **204.71.200.74**.

The mechanism that translates the name of a system into its IP address is the Domain Name Service (DNS). DNS is a distributed database in which every site's mappings of IP addresses to hostnames are kept. Within an organization DNS also plays a crucial role in hostname-to-IP resolution for all IP-based service. Each site that chooses to provide its services to the world may provide the host name to IP address mapping for those systems. Most Internet sites such as yahoo.com provide a mapping for its servers to facilitate access to its servers and services by name.

In order to allow remote uses to use a name instead of an IP address to access the systems within your site, you need to set up a DNS database and a DNS server for your site. All of the accesses to the DNS database for your site are handled by your DNS server (also known as a *name server*). There are several different DNS servers available, but the most common DNS server on the Internet is part of the Berkeley Internet Name Domain (BIND) software package. BIND was developed at the University of California at Berkeley, and is now maintained by the Internet Software Consortium (ISC). The two most common major versions of BIND are version 4 and version 8, with version 8 being the most recent. Solaris 7 includes major version 8 of BIND, while Solaris 2.5 and 2.6 included major version 4 of BIND. This chapter covers the setup and configuration of name servers on both versions.

The first half of this chapter offers an overview of DNS. The second half covers the configuration of DNS clients and servers. The final section shows you how to test DNS using the debugging utility **nslookup**.

# An Overview of DNS

DNS was developed in response to some of the problems encountered in the early days of ARPANET and the Internet. In order to understand the motivations for its design, we need to look briefly at the history of the Internet, which began in the late '60s as an experimental wide-area computer network funded by the Department of Defense's Advanced Research Projects Agency (ARPA).

## A Brief History of the Internet

In the beginning, the Internet was called the ARPANET and it was intended to allow government scientists and engineers to share the government's limited computing resources. Only government users were allowed to access the handful of computers connected to ARPANET, and it remained that way until the early '80s, when two major networking developments led to a huge expansion of the ARPANET. The first major development was the Transmission Control Protocol and the Internet Protocol (TCP/IP), which standardized the communications protocol used by computers on the ARPANET. The second major development was the inclusion of TCP/IP into UC Berkeley's version of UNIX known as BSD. Since BSD was available to other universities at minimal cost, almost every university in America got a copy of BSD and connected to the ARPANET.

In the span of only a few years, thousands of computers were connected to a network that had been designed to handle only a few dozen computers. Since many of the computers were simultaneously connected to the ARPANET and their own university networks, it was decided that the ARPANET would serve as the backbone of the entire network called the Internet. In 1988, the Defense Department decided that the ARPANET project had continued long enough and stopped funding the project. At this point the National Science Foundation (NSF) took over and supported the Internet. Their support ended in 1995, when private companies including BBNPlanet, MCI, and Sprint took over the backbone.

## The HOSTS.TXT File

When ARPANET was first designed, every computer on the network had a file called HOSTS.TXT. This file contained all the information about every host on the network, including the hostname-to-IP address mapping. Since there were so few computers on the network at that time, the file was small and could be easily maintained. It was the responsibility of SRI-NIC located at the Stanford Research Institute in Menlo Park, California, to maintain the contents of HOSTS.TXT for all the computers on the ARPANET. When BSD systems began connecting to the ARPANET, the HOSTS.TXT file was adapted to support UNIX and was renamed to /etc/hosts.

When administrators needed to make changes to this file, they emailed their requests to SRI-NIC. All of the requests would be consolidated together about once or twice a week and a new version of HOSTS.TXT would be posted by SRI-NIC. Administrators had to periodically obtain a new copy of this file in order to keep their sites up to date. As the number of computers on the Internet started to increase into the thousands and hundreds of thousands, administering and distributing HOSTS.TXT became a major problem. Every time a new host was added, a change had to be made to the central version, and every other host on ARPANET had to get the new version of this file. As a single, centrally administered information repository, HOSTS.TXT entailed a high maintenance overhead.

In order to alleviate the problems and high maintenance associated with the HOSTS.TXT approach, SRI-NIC designed a replacement system based on a distributed database built on a hierarchical domain structure. The new system, the Domain Name Service (DNS) database, requires that every computer on the Internet be part of a *domain*, and that each domain have a *name server* that maintains a database of the hosts for that domain. ARPANET switched to the DNS system in September 1984 and it has been the standard method for accessing hostname-to-IP address mappings ever since.

## BIND

The reference implementation of the DNS name server is the Berkeley Internet Name Domain (BIND) package. It is bundled with all major versions of UNIX, including Solaris.

BIND was developed at the University of California at Berkeley as a graduate student project under a grant from the US Defense Advanced Research Projects Administration (DARPA). The original BIND development team included Douglas Terry, Mark Painter, David Riggle, and Songnian Zhou. Until version 4.8.3, BIND was maintained by members of this team via the Computer Systems Research Group (CSRG) at UC Berkeley.

In 1985, BIND development and maintenance moved to the Digital Equipment Corporation (DEC, now Compaq Computer Corporation), and BIND versions 4.9 and 4.9.1 were released by DEC. In 1987, Paul Vixie became the primary caretaker, architect, and programmer for BIND. The next major version of BIND, 4.9.2, was sponsored by Paul's company Vixie Enterprises. After the release of version 4.9.2, Paul turned over developed maintenance of BIND to the Internet Software Consortium (ISC). In May 1997 ISC released a major upgrade to BIND as version 8.0. It contained main new features and security enhancements along with support for DHCP based clients. The most recent version of BIND as of this writing is 8.1.2.

In this chapter, as well as in most other references, you will find BIND versions 4.x.x referred to as BIND 4 and BIND versions 8.x.x referred to as BIND 8.

# The Domain Structure in DNS

Domains in DNS are used to create a hierarchical tree structure similar to the UNIX file system. DNS is based on a single root domain, represented by the single period "." at the top of its tree. The root domain is similar to the root directory "/" of the UNIX file system. The root domain is the starting point in DNS name space: At the time of this writing there are 13 name servers (some of these have names like a.root-servers.net., b.rootservers.net., c.rootservers.net) that are geographically distributed and can answer queries. These servers are maintained by SRI-NIC.

Underneath the root domain are several *top-level* domains and their subdomains. These are equivalent to subdirectories under the root directory. Each system within a domain is called a *host*.

**Top-Level Domains**    Top-level domains are those domains that are located directly under the root domain. There are two types of top-level domains, *organizational* and *geographical*. The organizational top-level domains are used to identify machines belonging to a particular type of organization within the United States. The geographical domains are used to identify machines that are located within a particular country. Table 13-1 lists the top-level organizational domains.

In addition to the current top-level domains, there are several domains based on geography. These would include most countries, and states of the United States. Some

| Domain | Description | Example |
|---|---|---|
| .com | Commercial organizations and businesses | cisco.com |
| .edu | Educational organizations, normally universities | berkeley.edu |
| .gov | Government (US) organizations | nasa.gov |
| .mil | Military (US) organizations | navy.mil |
| .net | Network organizations and ISPs | bbnplanet.net |
| .org | Nonprofit organizations | pbs.org |
| .arpa | Use for inverse address lookups | sri-nir.apra |

**Table 13-1.**   *Organizational Top-Level Domains*

of these geographic domains may decide on their own subdomain structure underneath their geographical domain in order to make it easy for users to identify specific types of organizations within their country. A complete list of the geographical domains can be found at **http://www.iana.org/domain-names.html**.

There are several proposals for additional top-level domains, in order to better differentiate the types of services that are provided by the sites within a domain. For example, the .com domain was originally intended only for sites belonging to corporations, but with the proliferation of the Internet, noncommercial sites such as *your-name*.com have become commonplace. The new proposed domains would help to differentiate personal sites and informational sites from commerce sites. Some of the proposed domains are also intended to allow parents to restrict children from inappropriate content. Currently, however, there is no consensus on the new top-level domains. Some of the more popular proposed domains are listed in Table 13-2.

**Subdomains**   When a domain has so many hosts it starts to become confusing. A subdomain can be created to associate hosts that are related in some manner, like by physical location or business function. This is similar to the creation of subdirectories; if a particular directory contains too many files, you can create a subdirectory and move related files into it in order to keep your file system well organized.

New subdomains can be created at any time without informing any of the domains higher in the DNS tree. The relationship between a domain and its subdomain can be thought of as a parent-and-child relationship. When a parent creates a subdomain, it delegates authority for that subdomain to the child's name server. The parent knows

| Proposed Domain | Description | Examples |
|---|---|---|
| .arts | Cultural- or arts-oriented organizations | Museums or theater companies |
| .firm | Incorporated businesses or trade organizations | Corporations, such as Cisco Systems and IBM, and other business-related sites, such as NASDAQ and the New York Stock Exchange |
| .rec | Sites devoted to recreation and entertainment | Online gaming or movie and radio sites |
| .info | Sites providing information services | Search engines or databases |
| .nom | Personal or individual sites | Your personal web page |
| .store | Online retailers | Bookstores and online superstores |

**Table 13-2.**   *Proposed Additional Top-Level Domains*

only the address of the child's name server; it does not know about any of the systems located in the child's subdomain.

You may hear subdomains referred to as *zones*. A zone is simply the piece of the naming tree that is under the administrative control of a particular name server. Figure 13-1 illustrates zones and their relation to subdomains. Here, the bosland.us domain has three subdomains: rem.bosland.us, eng.bosland.us, and fin.bosland.us. The eng.bosland.us and fin.bosland.us subdomains are each handled by a different name server, so they are in separate zones. The name server for bosland.us and rem.bosland.us are the same system, they are in a single zone.

**Fully Qualified Names**   Each domain within the DNS tree has a *fully qualified domain name* (FQDN). A domain's FQDN is similar to the absolute pathname for a directory in the UNIX directory tree. To identify the FQDN for a particular domain, we start by first getting the name of the current domain, then adding the name of the parent domain, and then adding the name of the grandparent's domain, and so on until we reach the root of the tree.

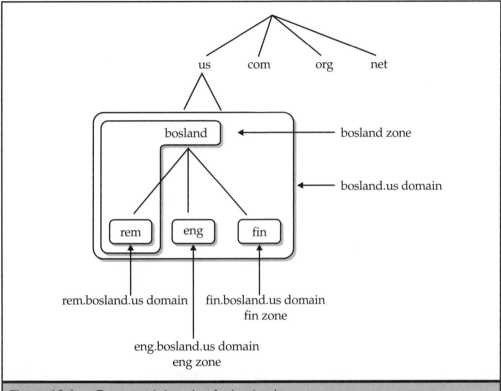

**Figure 13-1.**    *Zones and domains for bosland.us*

BASIC NETWORK
ADMINISTRATION

> **Note**   *An example of a fully qualified domain name is csua.berkeley.edu., which corresponds to the Computer Science Undergraduates Association at UC Berkeley. From the FQDN we can tell that csua is a subdomain of the berkeley domain, which is itself a subdomain of the .edu top-level domain. Notice the last ".” after edu in the example: It is used to represent the root domain, indicating that this is a FQDN.*

The counterpart of FQDN for hosts within a domain is the *fully qualified host name* (FQHN). A host's FQHN is similar to the absolute pathname for a file in the UNIX directory tree. To obtain the FQHN for a host, simply add the hostname for the system to the FQDN for the host's domain. For example, the FQHN for the system **www** within the **csua.berkeley.edu**. domain is **www.csua.berkeley.edu**.

**DNS Naming Rules**    DNS is fairly flexible about the names that can be given to hosts and domains, but it does have a few restrictions in order to make the system robust and scalable. The main restriction is that domain and host names must contain only lowercase letters (uppercase are automatically converted to lowercase), the hyphen character "-", and numerals. The other restrictions are that:

- The maximum number of characters in a domain or host name is 63.
- The maximum number of characters in an FQDN is 255.
- The maximum number of subdomains is 127.

The restrictions are designed to limit the DNS tree to about 5 or 6 levels, thereby ensuring that name lookups are reasonably fast.

# DNS Queries

DNS is based on a query-and-response process called *name resolution*, since it resolves the hostname of a system down to its IP address. When a DNS client (called a *stub resolver*) wants to determine the IP address for a host, for example **www.yahoo.com**, it sends a resolution request to its DNS server (called a *name server*) requesting the IP address for that host. That name server then communicates with other name servers in order to determine the information requested by the client. The advantage of this design is that no single name server needs to know all of the information about a domain. When a name server does not know the address of a host, it just needs to refer the resolver to a different name server that might be able to determine the address.

Figure 13-2 illustrates the process used by a DNS client to resolve the hostname **www.yahoo.com** to its IP address. First our client queries our name server for **www.yahoo.com**. Our name server then issues a query to the root name server for **www.yahoo.com**. The root name server does not know the IP address, but it does know the IP address for the .com name server and responds with that IP address. This is called a *referral*, since our name server is being referred to another name server. Our name server takes this IP address and issues a query to the .com name server for **www.yahoo.com**. The .com web server doesn't know the IP address, but it knows the IP address for the yahoo.com name server, so it returns this IP address to our name server. Our name server then queries the name server for yahoo.com for **www.yahoo.com**. This name server knows the IP address of **www.yahoo.com**, so it returns it to our name server. Our name server takes this response and returns it to our client.

All of the queries and responses shown in Figure 13-2 are transmitted using UDP datagrams. These transmissions requests are sent and received by the DNS server on port 53. In /etc/services, this port is listed as reserved for the service "domain," and the name server uses this service name to determine the UDP port on which to send and receive DNS queries and responses.

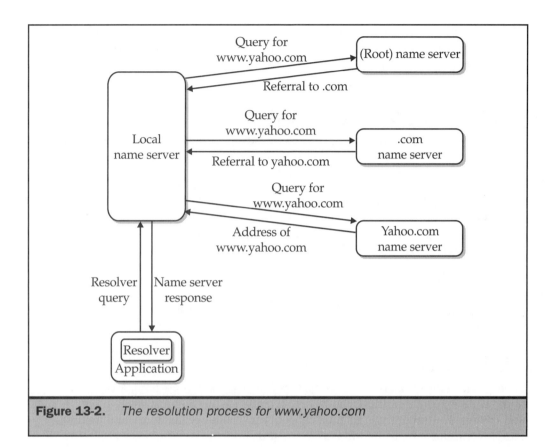

**Figure 13-2.**   *The resolution process for www.yahoo.com*

## Recursive and Iterative Queries

In our example, you probably noticed that it was only our name server that kept trying to resolve **www.yahoo.com**; the other name servers just referred our name server to other name servers. That's because there are two types of requests being made in the previous example. The first query in the example, in which the stub resolver (DNS client) queries its name server (DNS server), is known as a *recursive* request. A name server that receives this type of request has to respond with either the correct IP address or an error message, because DNS clients are not capable of dealing with referrals to other name servers. Therefore, the name server that receives the request has to recursively ask other servers for the IP address it is interested in until it receives a proper response, which it then passes to the DNS client.

The requests made by the client's name server to other name servers are known as *iterative* requests. An iterative request requires the receiver to respond with the closest matching address rather than the exact IP address. The name of the iterative request comes from the fact that it concludes after a single iteration. For example, when our name server contacted the root name server for the IP address **www.yahoo.com**, the response it received matched only the .com portion of the address.

# Configuring DNS Clients

There are two parts to configuring DNS, configuring a system to use DNS for resolving names and configuring the DNS server in order for other systems to access the DNS information for your site. Almost every system needs to be configured to be a DNS client, so we will cover that topic first. Later in this chapter we will examine the different types of DNS servers and show you how to configure each one.

In order to configure a Solaris 8 system to use DNS you need to modify two files, the name resolution configuration file, /etc/resolv.conf, and the network services configuration file, /etc/nsswitch.conf. The network services configuration file specifies the different methods that the *stub resolver* should use to determine the name of a host while the name resolution configuration is used to configure the *stub resolver* on your system. The stub resolver is a shared library that allows applications to access DNS information.

## The Name Resolution Configuration File

There are four *directives*, or commands, that can be placed in the name resolution configuration file, /etc/resolv.conf. These commands are **domain**, **nameserver**, **search**, and **sortlist**. This section covers the syntax of each of these directives, and includes a sample configuration file that illustrates their use.

### The domain Directive

The domain directive allows you to specify your current domain. Its syntax is as follows:

domain *domainname*

Here, *domainname* is your default domain. The default domain is appended to any non-FQHN (fully qualified hostnames) that are queried by an application. For example, if you specified the following directive

```
domain bosland.us
```

then any queries for hosts (**ftp**, **www**, etc.) would be translated into the appropriate FQHN, such as **ftp.bosland.us** or **www.bosland.us**, before being passed to a DNS server for resolution.

## The nameserver Directive

The **nameserver** directive allows you to specify a name server for your domain. Its syntax is as follows:

nameserver *address*

Here, *address* is the IP address of the name server. You cannot specify an alphabetical name for the name server since the stub resolver has no way of determining the IP address of the name server. You will need to obtain the IP address of the name server for your domain from your network administrator or your ISP. If you are responsible for the name server for your domain, you can add its IP address once you have configured a name server using the instructions given later in this chapter.

As an example, if the name server for the bosland domain has the address 10.0.0.2, the **nameserver** directive would be specified as follows:

```
nameserver 10.0.0.2
```

You can specify up to three instances of the **nameserver** directive in order to provide redundancy for name resolution. The name servers are queried in the order that they are listed. If the first one does not respond, the second one is queried, and so on. If you do not specify this directive at all then the stub resolver assumes that the local system is the name server and uses the IP address of 127.0.0.1.

## The search Directive

The **search** directive allows you to specify any additional domains in which you want to automatically search for hosts. The syntax for this directive is as follows:

search *domainlist*

Here, *domainlist* is a space-separated list of up to six domains you want to query. The search directive is useful when you want to access systems within other subdomains of your site's main domain. For example, if your system was in the domain bosland.us, the following **search** directive would allow you to access hosts in the eng.bosland.us subdomain without having to specify an FQHN:

```
search bosland.us eng.bosland.us
```

## The sortlist Directive

The **sortlist** directive allows you to specify the networks the stub resolver should prefer if it receives multiple addresses in response to a query. Normally this directive is used on systems that are connected to several networks. For example, consider a server that is connected to two networks, 10.0.0.0 and 192.168.0.0. If each of these networks has a separate name server, then it is possible for a query to generate two different responses. Since the stub resolver picks the first response, sometimes you may get an unexpected address for a particular host. The **sortlist** directive allows you to specify the preferred order for responses. It is specified as follows:

sortlist *network1 ... networkN*

Here, *network1 ... networkN* are network addresses listed in the order in which responses should be preferred. In the case of a server connected to the 10.0.0.0 network and 192.168.0.0 network, you could specify the following sortlist if you always want to prefer responses originating from the 192.168.0.0 over those from 10.0.0.0:

```
sortlist 192.168.0.0 10.0.0.0
```

If one of the networks you are connected to is subnetted, you can specify the network address and the subnet address using the following syntax:

*network/subnet*

Here, network is the network address and subnet is the subnet mask. For example, if your system was connected to the 192.168.0.0 network and the 10.8.0.0 network (subnet mask 255.255.0.0), you could specify the following sortlist directive that preferred 192.168.0.0 over 10.8.0.0:

```
sortlist 192.168.0.0 10.8.0.0/255.255.0.0
```

## Comments

It is also possible to add comments to /etc/resolv.conf by starting a line with the ";" character (a semicolon). If a semicolon is encountered at the beginning of any line, all the characters after it will be ignored. As an example, the following line is ignored:

```
; /etc/resolv.conf for ftp.bosland.us
```

The stub resolver also ignores any blank lines in the file.

## Sample /etc/resolv.conf

The following is an example of a complete name-resolution configuration file /etc/resolv.conf:

```
; /etc/resolv.conf for ftp.bosland.us

domain bosland.us
```

```
; name servers for bosland.us and eng.bosland.us
nameserver 10.0.0.2
nameserver 10.0.0.3

; search list, first look in bosland.us then in eng.bosland.us
search bosland.us eng.bosland.us
```

This configuration file specifies to the stub resolver that:

- The default domain is bosland.us.
- The name servers that this system will try are 10.0.0.2 and 10.0.0.3.
- The resolver will attempt to resolve non–fully qualified names in either the bosland.us domain or the eng.bosland.us domain.

## The Network Services Configuration File

By default Solaris systems are not configured to use DNS. You can enable the stub resolver to use DNS by modifying the network services configuration file, /etc/nsswitch.conf. To enable DNS, edit the following line:

```
hosts:        files
```

to read

```
hosts:        files dns
```

This change specifies that if the resolver cannot find an IP address to hostname mapping in the /etc/hosts file it should query the name server(s) listed in /etc/resolv.conf. Although DNS is the preferred means of name resolution, the /etc/hosts file is still found on most machines because it can significantly reduce the time required to look up frequently accessed IP addresses.

### The /etc/hosts file

The /etc/hosts file should be used to map IP addresses to hostnames for a small number of important and frequently accessed hosts in your local domain. Since it is hard to keep updating this file on several machines, you should list only those hostnames that change infrequently: the localhost (the localhost entry maps to the 127.0.0.1 IP address and is used when a service on the server wants to communicate with the server itself), NFS servers, and possibly your NIS/NIS+ server (if you use either of these services). All other hosts should be accessed using DNS.

The format of entries in /etc/hosts is as follows:

*address hostname hostalias1 ... hostaliasN*

Here, *address* is the IP address of the host with the name *hostname*, and *hostalias1* ...
*hostaliasN* are aliases for the host. The *hostalias* fields are optional. Also, any lines
starting with the hash character, "#", are treated as comments and ignored.

As an example, the following entry maps the address 10.0.0.2 to the
hostname kanchi:

```
10.0.0.2 kanchi
```

If the host kanchi had the aliases **www** and **ftp**, the following entry could be specified:

```
10.0.0.2 kanchi www ftp
```

Here is an example of a complete /etc/hosts file:

```
# host table
127.0.0.1       localhost
10.0.0.7        badri    loghost
10.0.0.2        kanchi              # user accounts nfs server
```

Notice that only three entries are present. The first entry is for the default localhost
IP address, the second is for the system's IP address, and the third is for the nfs server
used by the system. Depending on your site, you may need to add a few more entries
to /etc/hosts, but make sure to keep the number of hosts that are listed in this file at a
minimum. This will make is easier for you to maintain the file and keep it
synchronized on your systems.

# Configuring DNS Servers

In this part of the chapter we will examine the different types of DNS servers and show
you how to configure each one.

You can configure your system to act as one of three different types of name
servers: master, slave, and hint. A master (previously known as primary) name server
is the most *authoritative* of the three; it is considered to have the most up-to-date
records for all the hosts in its zone. In DNS the term authoritative means that a
response from the name server is consider to be absolutely correct. The slave
(previously known as secondary) server receives its updates from the master name
server. The slave is a replica of the master name server and it depends on the master to
receive the zone data. The slave lists masters that it can contact to update its copy of the

zone. A hint (previously known as caching) name server just contains a list of root name servers to resolve queries that it receives. The hint name server is not authoritative for any domain. When a query is made to a hint server for the first time, it forwards the query to an authoritative server. When the authoritative server answers the query, the hint server copies that entry to its local cache and returns it to the resolver that asked for the address. The hint server then responds to any further queries for that host using the IP address in its cache—that is, until the entry expires. The concept of expiration is discussed in greater detail later in this chapter.

Depending on the setup of your site, you might not need to configure your own name server. Here are some situations with different name server requirements:

- If you are simply connecting to an existing network, there may be a name server already configured for that network; if that's the case, you won't have to configure your own.

- If you are setting up a new department or a new group within an existing department, you will need to set up at least a caching name server to reduce the load on your site's master name server.

- If you are setting up a new site or a new subdomain within an existing site, you will want to configure a master and possibly a slave name server.

It is also possible that you may be in an environment where you need to configure a single name server to be master for one domain, slave for another, and acting as a caching name server. There is nothing within DNS that prevents you from doing this; a single name server can have multiple roles.

## The master Servers

A master name server responds to queries with authoritative answers for the zone in which it is located. The database file from which the master name server returns its authoritative answers is called the *zone database file*. This file contains the hostnames and their corresponding IP addresses for the hosts within the server's zone. Information in the zone database file is stored in the form of *resource records*. These records define various attributes about the database file along with the hostname and IP address information stored in the database. The significant resource records are covered later in this chapter.

In addition to returning authoritative answers for hosts within its domain, a master name server has two other features. First, a master name server can query (if so configured) other name servers and maintain a cache of their responses. This cache reduces the time needed to resolve frequently accessed hostnames. Second, a master name server's zone database can delegate responsibility for subdomains to other name servers.

In order to change the information for a domain controlled by a master name server, the zone database file on the master name server must be changed. This file contains a serial number that must be incremented each time the database is altered in order to ensure that slave name servers will correctly obtain the changes.

*Failing to increment the serial number is the single most common mistake that inexperienced DNS administrators make. Using a consistent serial numbering scheme such as one described under "The Start of Authority (SOA) Resource Record" will assist in the process of incrementing the serial number.*

## The slave Servers

Slave name servers are backup name servers for the master name server. If the master name server crashes or becomes inaccessible, the slave name server will be able to return authoritative answers based on its database. Most domains have at least one slave server for redundancy purposes. The slave name servers can also query other name servers and store a cache of responses in order to speed up responses to frequently accessed hostnames.

A slave name server's zone database is the replica of the database of the master name server. The slave name server periodically synchronizes with the database on the master to update the zone information. This synchronization is based on comparing the serial number of the master name server's zone database to that of the slave name server's zone database. If the serial number of the master is larger than that of the slave's, the slave name server performs what is referred to as *zone transfer*: the procedure used by the slave name server for obtaining a new copy of the zone database from the master name server.

## The Hint Server

Hint name servers do not contain any authoritative information. They simply forward queries to other name servers and cache the answer for a certain period of time. When a resolver queries a hint name server, that server returns the answer it has stored in its cache instead of forwarding the query to another name server. Since the information returned by the hint name server is always second-hand information, all responses from a such a name server are classified as nonauthoritative. Hint name servers are generally used to reduce DNS traffic within large domains.

## The Name Server Configuration Files

You can run master, slave, or the hint name servers on Solaris 8 by properly configuring the name server daemon /usr/sbin/in.named. Configuration of the name server involves two steps. The first step is to create the name server configuration file. The second step is to create the zone database containing information about your domain.

Earlier versions of Solaris used the BIND 4 version of the name server and its configuration stored in the file /etc/named.boot. In Solaris 8, which includes BIND 8, the name server configuration file is stored in /etc/named.conf. Since the syntax of each of these files is quite different, I will cover them here separately.

The name server configuration file is used to specify the files that make up the zone database for your domain. The zone database is simply a set of files that include all of the information about the hostnames and IP addresses of systems in your domain. A domain needs a minimum of four files for a complete zone database: db.*domain,* db.*network*, db.127.0.0, and db.cache.

- The db.*domain* file contains a mapping of hostnames to IP addresses for a given *domain.* As an example, the file db.bosland will contain the mapping of hostnames to IP address for the bosland.us domain.

- The db.*network* file contains the mapping of IP addresses to hostnames for a particular *network.* As an example, the file db.10.0.0 will contain the mapping of IP addresses to hostnames for the 10.0.0.0 network.

- The db.127.0.0 contains a mapping of IP addresses to hostnames for the localhost network.

- The db.cache contains an initial list of hostname-to-IP address mappings for a name server that performs caching functions. Normally the db.cache file is a copy of the list of root name servers available from **ftp://ftp.rs.internic.net/domain/named.root**.

This section concentrates on setting up the name server configuration file, while the next section examines the format and content of the zone database files.

## The Name Server Configuration File (Solaris 2.6 and Earlier)

Solaris 2.6 and earlier versions of Solaris include BIND 4. The name server configuration file in BIND 4 is located in /etc/named.boot. This file has a simple format: Each line contains a directive, followed by a space-separated list of arguments to the directive. The main directives are **directory**, **primary**, **secondary**, and **cache**.

The format of the directory directive is as follows:

directory *dir*

Here, *dir* specifies the directory in which the files for the zone database are stored. Some common values for *dir* are /etc/named and /var/named. As an example, the following **directory** directive specifies that the zone database be stored in /var/named:

```
directory /var/named
```

The **primary** directive specifies that the name servers should act as a primary name server for a particular domain. The format of this directive is:

primary *domain file*

Here, *domain* is the name of the domain for which the server acts as a primary name server, and *file* is the pathname to the zone database file that contains information for the specified *domain*. The pathname for *file* should be a pathname that is relative to the directory specified by the **directory** directive. As an example, the following **primary** directive specifies that the name server should act as the primary name server for the bosland.us domain:

```
primary          bosland.us          db.bosland
```

The **secondary** directive specifies that the name server should act as a secondary name server for a particular domain. The format of this directive is:

secondary *domain address file*

Here, *domain* is the name of the domain for which the server acts as a secondary name server, *address* is the IP address of the primary name server for the domain, and *file* is the pathname to the zone database file that contains information for the specified *domain*. The pathname for *file* should be a pathname that is relative to the directory specified by the **directory** directive. As an example, the following **secondary** directive specifies that the name server should act as the secondary name server for the bosland.us domain:

```
secondary bosland.us 10.0.0.2 db.bosland
```

This example assumes that the IP address of the primary name server for the bosland.us domain is 10.0.0.2.

The **cache** directive specifies that the name server should act as a caching name server for a particular domain (usually the root domain, "."). The format of the **cache** directive is similar to that of the **primary** directive:

cache *domain file*

Here, *domain* is the domain for which the name server should cache the responses to queries, and *file* is a pathname to the database file that contains the initial list of hosts for the cache. The pathname for *file* should be a pathname that is relative to the directory specified by the **directory** directive. As an example, the following **cache** directive configures the server to cache all response in the root domain, ".":

```
cache            .                    db.cache
```

The complete /etc/named.boot for a the primary name server for the bosland.us domain might look like the following.

```
directory /var/named
primary          bosland.us                  db.bosland
primary          0.0.10.in-addr.arpa         db.10.0.0.0
primary          0.0.127.in-addr.arpa        db.127.0.0.0
cache            .                           db.cache
```

The /etc/named.boot for a secondary name server in the bosland.us domain might look like the following:

```
directory /var/named
secondary        bosland.us              10.0.0.2    db.bosland
secondary        0.0.10.in-addr.arpa     10.0.0.2    db.10.0.0.0
secondary        0.0.127.in-addr.arpa    10.0.0.2    db.127.0.0.0
cache            .                                   db.cache
```

This example assumes that 10.0.0.2 is the address of the primary name server for the domain. Another important detail to notice about the previous examples is the reverse network address that is used for the db.*network* file. These files use the special domain .in-addr.arpa. that is reserved for reverse name resolution. Reverse name resolution is the process by which servers can convert an IP address to a hostname. You may have also noticed that the reverse network address for the 10.0.0.0 network is listed as 0.0.10. This illustrates another DNS convention: The last digit of a network is not listed in the reverse form.

**Note**    *In the previous example, the secondary name server is named as a secondary for the localhost network, 127.0.0.0. This is done for ease of administration, since the* **secondary** *directive causes the initial database file for this network to be downloaded automatically by the name server. You can make the secondary name server a primary for the localhost network, but in that case you will have to install the db.127.0.0.0 file manually on the secondary server.*

To configure a caching-only name server you only need two directives in the /etc/named.boot file:

```
directory /var/named
cache            .                                   db.cache
```

## The Name Server Configuration File (Solaris 8)

Solaris 8 includes BIND 8, whose name server configuration file is located at /etc/named.conf. This file has a format that offers greater flexibility and many more options for configuring a name server than the format for the /etc/named.boot file used by BIND 4.

A complete discussion of the options available in the BIND 8 configuration file is beyond the scope of this chapter, so we will concentrate on the most commonly used options. For a more detailed discussion of the available options, you can consult either the man page of in.named, or the online configuration guide, which is located at **http://www.isc.org/view.cgi?/products/BIND/docs/config/index.phtml**. The basic format for directives in the /etc/named.conf is as follows:

```
directive {
    parameter1;
    ...
    parameterN;
};
```

Here, *directive* is the directive you want to enable, and *parameter1 … parameterN* are the parameters to that directive. The parameters are given one per line, and each must end with a semicolon. The directives that we will be concentrating on are the **options** directive and the **zone** dircctive.

Two of the most common parameters for the **options** directive are the **directory** parameter and the **pid-file** parameter. The **directory** parameter specifies the pathname to the directory where the zone database files are stored. The **pid-file** parameter specifies the location of the file containing the process ID of the name server while it is running. In Solaris 2.6 and earlier this file was always stored in /var/tmp/named.pid, but in Solaris 8 you can configure the location.

The format for the **directory** parameter is as follows:

directory *"pathname"*;

Here, *pathname* is the pathname to the zone database. As an example, the following directory parameter specifies that the zone database be stored in /var/named:

```
directory "/var/named";
```

The format of the **pid-file** parameter is similar to that of the **directory** parameter:

pid-file *"pathname"*;

Here, *pathname* is the pathname to the file containing the process ID of the name server while it is running. The following example specifies that the PID file should be stored in /etc/named.pid for compatibility with earlier versions of Solaris:

```
pid-file "/etc/namcd.pid";
```

If you have to maintain a name server on earlier versions of Solaris, using a common path to the PID file will make the process of manually starting and stopping the name server simpler.

The complete **options** directive looks like the following:

```
options {
     directory "/var/named";
     pid-file  "/etc/named.pid";
};
```

The **zone** directive has several important parameters based on the type of name service it is configuring for a particular domain. I will cover only those parameters related to configuring a master, slave, and hint name server for a domain, as these are most likely the tasks you will encounter.

The **zone** directive's equivalent to the **primary** directive from /etc/named.boot has the following format:

zone *"domain"* in {
    type master;
    file *"pathname"*;
};

Here, *domain* is the FQDN of the domain for which the server will act as a master name server and *pathname* is the pathname to the file containing the database for the specified *domain*. The specified *pathname* should be a pathname that is relative to the directory specified in the **directory** parameter of the **options** directive. The following **zone** directive specifies that the name server should act as the master for the bosland.us domain:

```
zone "bosland.us" in {
     type master;
     file "db.bosland";
};
```

The **type** parameter of this particular **zone** directive configures a master name server for the specified domain.

The **zone** directive's equivalent to the **secondary** directive from /etc/named.boot has the following format:

zone *"domain"* in {
    type slave;
    file *"pathname"*;
    masters { *address;* };
};

Here, *domain* is the FQDN of the domain for which the server will act as a slave name server, *pathname* is the pathname to the file containing the database for the specified *domain*, and *address* is the IP address of the master name server. The specified *pathname* should be a pathname that is relative to the directory specified in the **directory** parameter of the **options** directive. The following **zone** directive specifies that the name server should act as the slave name server for the bosland.us domain:

```
zone "bosland.us" in {
    type slave;
    file "db.bosland";
    masters { 10.0.0.2; };
};
```

This example assumes that the IP address of the master name server for the bosland.us domain is 10.0.0.2.

The **zone** directive's equivalent to the **cache** directive from /etc/named.boot has the following format:

zone *"domain"* in {
   type hint;
   file *"pathname"*;
};

Here, *domain* is the FQDN of the domain for which the server will cache address (usually the root domain, "."), and *pathname* is the pathname to the file containing the initial list of addresses that should be added to the cache. As an example, the following zone directive enables caching for the root domain:

```
zone "." in {
    type hint;
    file "db.cache";
};
```

The complete /etc/named.conf for a master name server in the bosland.us domain might look like the following:

```
options {
    directory "/var/named";
    pid-file  "/etc/named.pid";
};

zone "bosland.us" in {
    type master;
    file "db.bosland";
```

```
};

zone "0.0.10.in-addr.arpa" in {
     type master;
     file "db.10.0.0.0";
};

zone "0.0.127.in-addr.arpa" in {
     type master;
     file "db.127.0.0.0";
};

zone "." in {
     type hint;
     file "db.cache";
};
```

The complete /etc/named.conf for a slave name server in the bosland.us domain might look like the following:

```
options {
     directory "/var/named";
     pid-file  "/etc/named.pid";
};

zone "bosland.us" in {
     type slave;
     file "db.bosland";
     masters { 10.0.0.2; };
};

zone "0.0.10.in-addr.arpa" in {
     type slave;
     file "db.10.0.0.0";
     masters { 10.0.0.2; };
};

zone "0.0.127.in-addr.arpa" in {
     type slave;
     file "db.127.0.0.0";
     masters { 10.0.0.2; }
```

```
};

zone "." in {
    type hint;
    file "db.cache";
};
```

As before, this example assumes that 10.0.0.2 is the address of the master name server for the domain. Another important detail to notice about the previous examples is the reverse network address that is used for the db.*network* file. They use the same convention as the /etc/named.boot file, with the special domain .in-addr.arpa, and the reverse network address for the 10.0.0.0 network is listed as 0.0.10.

The /etc/named.conf for a caching or hint name server may look like the following:

```
options {
    directory "/var/named";
    pid-file  "/var/tmp/named.pid";
};

zone "." in {
    type hint;
    file "db.cache";
};
```

# The Zone Database and Resource Records

As explained earlier in the chapter, the zone database is a set of text files that contain information about the machines in a domain, in a format known as *resource records*. These records are simply a method of representing the mapping between a host and its IP address. Information about hosts within a domain can be added or removed from the zone database by adding or deleting resource records in the zone database file located on a master name server. The four main files that make up a zone database—the db.*domain,* db.*network,* db.127.0.0.0, and db.cache files—were introduced in the previous section. In this section I will cover the contents of these files and, as an example, I will present a set of sample files for the bosland.us domain.

Within each database file there are three main sections: the Start of Authority section (SOA) section, the name server section (NS), and the database section. Each of these sections consists of one or more resource records. Most resource records can have one of the following formats:

[TTL] *class type data*
*class* [TTL] *type data*

The TTL field stands for "Time-to-Live" and is a decimal number that indicates to the name server how often the record needs to be updated. This can vary from a few minutes to a several days. The TTL field is optional; if it is omitted a default of three hours is used. The *class* field indicates which class of data the record belongs to. Currently only the IN class, corresponding to Internet data, is used. The two other classes—CH, corresponding to ChaosNet, and HS, corresponding to Hesiod—are obsolete and no longer used. (HS was meant to be a replacement for NIS but it was abandoned after the introduction of NIS+.)

The *type* field indicates what kind of record you are dealing with. The *data* field holds the parameters required by that type of resource record. The eight main *type*s are given in Table 13-2. The data fields are discussed in greater detail in the sections that cover each of these types.

Some resource records, such as the SOA record, require a preceding data field as well as a trailing data field. Usually the first data field is a domain name or a host name. The format of these resource records is:

*data1 class type data2*

| Type | Name | Description |
|------|------|-------------|
| A | Address record | Defines a mapping of a hostname to an IP address |
| CNAME | Canonical Name | Defines an alias for a hostname |
| MX | Mail exchanger | Designates a host as a mail exchanger |
| NS | Name Server record | Specifies the IP address for a name server in the domain |
| PTR | Pointer record | Defines a reverse mapping of an IP address to a hostname |
| RP | Responsible Person record | Specifies the email address of the person responsible for a particular system |
| SOA | Start of Authority record | Defines a domain for the information stored within a database file |
| TXT | Text record | Freeform text string that describes a particular host |

**Table 13-3.** *The Main Types of Resource Records*

Here, *data1* is the first set of data and *class* is the records class (usually IN for Internet). The *type* field defines the type of the record and the *data2* field holds the parameters required by that *type* of resource record.

In addition to resource records, the database files can contain comments, which are indicated by starting the line with a semicolon. Any text after the semicolon is treated as a comment and is ignored. Blank lines are also ignored.

The Start of Authority (SOA) section of a database file contains a single SOA record that defines the domain that the information contained in the database file applies to. The Name Server (NS) section of the database files contains one or more NS records that define the name servers for the domain defined by the SOA record. The third and final section of a database file contains all of the resource records with information about the hosts in the zone. There are three main types of records encountered in this section: PTR records, A records, and CNAME records. The db.*network* contains mostly PTR records; in the db.*domain* file we will encounter A and CNAME records.

## The Start of Authority (SOA) Resource Record

The Start of Authority (SOA) resource record is located at the top of each file in the zone database. There is only one SOA record per file in the zone database, and it makes up the first section of the file, the SOA section. The SOA record indicates that the name server with this database file is the best source of information about the domain.

The format of an SOA record is as follows:

*[zone] IN SOA origin contact (serial refresh retry expire minimum)*

Here, *zone* identifies the name of the zone, *IN* identifies the Internet class, and *SOA* identifies the type of record. The remaining fields in the syntax are listed here:

| Field | Description |
|---|---|
| origin | The master name server for this domain. |
| contact | This defines the email address of the individual responsible for maintaining this domain. |
| serial | This specifies a numeric value, which is used by the slave server to refresh its copy of the zone database. This number increases as new versions of the zone database are created. |
| refresh | Defines the polling interval in seconds. This is the period after which the slave server will check with the master for changes in the zone database. A transfer takes place only after the serial of the master is higher than that of the slave. |
| retry | Defines a retry interval in seconds. If the zone transfer fails then the slave server will retry after this many seconds have elapsed. |

| Field | Description |
|-------|-------------|
| expire | Define the duration in seconds for which the slave server will retain zone data without requesting a zone refresh from the master. |
| minimum | Defines the time to live(ttl) to the zonal resource records. This applies to those records that do not have ttl explicitly defined. |

Here is a sample SOA record for the **bosland.us** domain:

```
bosland.us. IN SOA kanchi.bosland.us. root.kanchi.bosland.us. (
        1998102301      ; Serial
        10800           ; Refresh after 3 hours
        3600            ; Retry after 1 hour
        604800          ; Expire after 1 week
        86400 )         ; Minimum TTL of 1 day
```

Here you can determine that the file containing this record holds information for the bosland.us. domain, and that the master name server for the domain is the host **kanchi.bosland.us.**.

Notice that the email address of the administrator is root.kanchi.bosland.us. (notice the trailing period) instead of root@kanchi.bosland.us. (also with the trailing period). The difference is the use of a period instead of the @ sign. This is important because the @ character has a special significance in the database files: It corresponds to the default domain, or *origin*, specified in the name server's configuration file, covered later in this chapter. Any time you use the @ symbol it is replaced with the origin. In order to avoid conflicts, therefore, the email address of the administrator is specified in the format *user.host* instead of *user@host*.

The origin is also appended to any names that are not fully qualified. For example, if this record omitted the trailing period after kanchi.bosland.us, DNS would think that the master name server for the bosland.us. domain is really a host named kanchi.bosland.us.bosland.us. For this reason it is important to always remember the trailing period after hostnames.

The five parameters used by the SOA record are specified within parentheses. They are *serial number, refresh interval, retry interval, expire,* and *minimum TTL.* Slave name servers refer to these parameters in order keep their copy of the zone database up to date.

The first parameter, *serial number,* is used for revision control of the database file. The serial number should be incremented each time a change is made to the database file so that the slave servers can obtain a copy of the update file via a zone transfer. The most common scheme for the serial number is to use the current date, in the form *YYYYMMDDxx,* where *YYYY* is the four-digit year (2000), *MM* is the two-digit month

(07 for July), *DD* is the two-digit day (04 for the fourth), and *xx* is the revision done that day (10 for the tenth revision). This allows for up to 100 revisions per day. At some sites, three digits are used for the revision instead of two, allowing for up to 1000 revisions per day. In most cases two digits should be enough. In the previous example, the serial number for the SOA record was 1998102301, indicating that it was last updated on October 23, 1998.

> **Tip**   *If for some reason you have to decrement the serial number on the master name server, you will need to shut down all of your slave name servers and remove their database files in order for the new serial number to take effect on the slave name servers. When the slave name servers restart, they will automatically obtain new copies of the database files with the new serial number. The process of shutting down and restarting a name server is covered later in this chapter.*

The second parameter, *refresh*, defines the rate (in seconds) at which the slave name servers should compare the serial number of their SOA record with the corresponding record on the master name server. Normally the refresh rate is set between one and three hours to minimize traffic on the network.

The third parameter, *retry*, is related to the refresh rate. It indicates the number of seconds the slave name server should wait before attempting to contact the master for a refresh if the first refresh attempt failed. Normally this parameter is set between 30 to 90 minutes. This allows ample time for a master name server reboot.

The fourth parameter, *expire*, controls the maximum number of retries the slave name server will try before refusing to service requests. By combining a long *retry* with an *expire* parameter, if the master name server is overloaded when the slave name server first tries to refresh the record, the slave name server will not overwhelm the master with retries.

The last parameter, *minimum TTL*, specifies the amount of time (in seconds) that name servers querying this record will be allowed to cache responses. This value defines the default for all resource records contained in the same file as the SOA record, but it can be overridden on an individual basis using the TTL field on a particular resource record.

## The Name Server (NS) Resource Record

The Name Server (NS) resource record specifies the authoritative name servers for the domain defined by the SOA record. The NS records follow the SOA record and there can be multiple NS records per database. The format of an NS record is:

*domain* IN NS *name server*

Here, *domain* is the FQDN of the local domain and *name server* is the FQHN of the name server. As an example, the following NS records define two name servers for the bosland.us domain.

```
bosland.us. IN NS kanchi.bosland.us.
bosland.us. IN NS ns1.bosland.us.
```

Optionally you can press the tab key or space bar instead of the FQDN for *domain* as shown below:

```
IN NS kanchi.bosland.us.
IN NS ns1.bosland.us.
```

This specifies that the domain defined for the SOA record should be applied to the NS record as well.

If you have one or more slave name servers for your domain, you have to specify the names of each of the slave name servers using the NS record. In the previous example, ns1.bosland.us might be the slave name server for the bosland.us domain. You will also need to add an Address (A) record, discussed shortly, to the zone database for each of the name servers.

The NS record also allows you to create a subdomain and delegate responsibility for that domain to a different system. To create a subdomain, simply specify the name of the subdomain and the FQHN of the name server for that domain. For example, the following NS record creates the subdomain eng within the bosland.us domain and specifies that the name server for that system is ns1.eng.bosland.us:

```
eng.bosland.us. IN NS ns1.eng.bosland.us.
```

You will need to create an Address (A) record for the host ns1.eng.bosland.us in the same zone database file in order for responsibility for the subdomain to be properly delegated to this host.

## Address (A) and Canonical Name (CNAME) Resource Records

The Address (A) resource record provides a mapping from hostnames to IP addresses. There should be an A record for each machine that needs to have a resolvable hostname within DNS. The format of an A record is:

*hostname* IN A *address*

Here, *hostname* is the FQHN of a host and *address* is the IP address for that host. For example, the hostname record for the host kanchi in the bosland.us domain might like the following:

```
kanchi.bosland.us.              IN A    10.0.0.2
```

Optionally you can specify just the hostname and omit the domain name:

```
kanchi              IN A    10.0.0.2
```

Since only the hostname is specified, the domain name from the SOA record in the file will be applied to construct the FQHN, in this case kanchi.bosland.us..

The Canonical Name (CNAME) resource record makes it possible to create aliases for particular hosts. This is useful for giving common names to large servers. If the host kanchi ran the web server for the bosland.us domain, it would be easier for outside user to access it as **www.bosland.us** instead of **kanchi.bosland.us**. The CNAME record makes this possible. The format of a CNAME record is similar to that of an A record:

> *alias* IN CNAME *hostname*

Here, *alias* is the FQHN for the alias you want to provide for the host specified by *hostname* (also a FQHN). For example, the following CNAME record aliases kanchi.bosland.us to **www.bosland.us**:

```
www.bosland.us.     IN CNAME     kanchi.bosland.us.
```

Optionally you can omit the domain name from both alias and host. The domain name specified by the SOA record will be used if the domain name is omitted.

Notice that the CNAME record does not define an IP address for the host. The CNAME record just points to another resource record that should be used to determine the IP address of the host. In order to use a CNAME record correctly, the host you are creating an alias for must have an A record.

One of the biggest advantages provided by the CNAME record is that you do not have to move the IP addresses of key systems when it is time to upgrade them. For example, let's say that the current web server for your domain is an old SPARCstation 2, and you want to upgrade the web server to an UltraSPARC 60. Without CNAME records you would have to reconfigure the IP address on the old web server before you could add the new one. Depending on other factors this could mean down time of several hours to several days, during which your web site will be inaccessible. If you have a CNAME record defined, you can add your new web server and change the CNAME record to point to it all without any downtime.

## The Mail Exchanger (MX) record

The Mail Exchanger (MX) record enables you to specify the name of the host in your domain that is responsible for receiving mail from the outside. This record is used by sendmail (the mail transfer process) to determine the machine from which to send and receive mail. The format of an MX record is:

> *domain* IN MX *priority hostname*

Here, *domain* is the FQDN of the domain, *priority* is a metric used by sendmail, and *hostname* is the hostname of the system in your domain that is responsible for receiving mail. As an example, the following MX record specifies that mail.bosland.us is the mail exchanger for the bosland.us domain:

```
bosland.us.            IN MX  10        mail.bosland.us.
```

The MX record is similar to the CNAME record, in that it does not define the IP address of the mail exchanger, just its hostname. You will need to have a separate A record for the host in order for mail transfers to work correctly.

If you have multiple MX records, **sendmail** will first communicate with the mail exchanger with the lowest priority number. If that fails, **sendmail** will try the mail exchanger with the next lowest priority, and so on. For example, if there were two mail exchangers in the bosland.us domain:

```
bosland.us.            IN MX  10        mail-1.bosland.us.
bosland.us.            IN MX  20        mail-2.bosland.us.
```

the mail exchanger mail-1.bosland.us would be used before mail-2.bosland.us for exchanging mail. If mail-1 was inaccessible, then mail-2 would be used.

## The Responsible Person (RP) and Text (TXT) Resource Records

The Responsible Person (RP) and Text (TXT) resource records are used to provide contact and host information about your domain in a form that can be accessed via DNS queries. TXT records are freeform text entries that allow you to specify any information you want about a particular host. Usually you would use these records to give location or contact information for that host. The RP record allows you to specify the email address of the person who is responsible for a particular host.

The format of a TXT record is:

*hostname* IN TXT *"information"*

Here, *hostname* is the FQHN of the host the TXT record applies to, and *information* is a string that contains any description you want to note about the host. If it contains any spaces, the informational string has to use double quotes. As an example, the following TXT record gives some additional information about the host mail.bosland.us:

```
mail.bosland.us.            IN TXT  "Location: SJ BLG1 Floor 2 Rack 3"
```

You can specify multiple TXT records for the same host by skipping directly to the IN TXT *"information"* portion of the line for each new TXT record. You do this by pressing the TAB key or the space bar at the beginning of each new line instead of entering the hostname, as illustrated here:

```
mail.bosland.us.        IN TXT  "Location: SJ BLG1 Floor 2 Rack 3"
                        IN TXT  "Contact: Sriranga V. <ranga@kanchi>"
```

In this example, we specified the contact email address in a TXT record (for the purpose of clarity we have lined up the IN on the second line below the IN on the first line, and it is perfectly all right to do so). There is no requirement that the TXT records contain a contact address. If you want to specify a contact for a particular machine, use the RP record, whose format is as follows:

*hostname1* IN RP *email hostname2*

Here, *hostname1* is the FQHN for the host the RP record applies to, *email* is the email address (in *user.host* format) of the administrator of that machine, and *hostname2* is the FQHN of a host that contains additional TXT records describing the responsible person. You can replace *hostname2* with a period, ".", if you don't want to create TXT records with additional information. As an example, the following RP record specifies that root@kanchi.bosland.us is the responsible person for the host mail.bosland.us:

```
mail.bosland.us.        IN RP  ranga.kanchi.bosland.us.  .
```

## The Pointer (PTR) Resource Record

The Pointer or PTR records are used for *reverse address resolution*. Reverse address resolution is the process by which a name server converts an IP address into a hostname. In order to support reverse address resolution, SRI-NIC created a special domain known as in-addr.arpa., which holds the name space for inverse address mappings. PTR records use this domain to map IP addresses to hostnames. PTR records are normally used in the db.*network* or the db.127.0.0 files. The format of a PTR record is:

*reverseaddr*.in-addr.arpa. IN PTR *hostname*

Here, *reverseaddr* is the IP address, in reverse order, of the host specified by *hostname*. As an example, the following PTR record allows for the IP address 10.0.0.2 to be reverse resolved to the hostname kanchi.bosland.us.:

```
2.0.0.10.in-addr.arpa. IN PTR          kanchi.bosland.us.
```

As you can see, the IP address for kanchi, 10.0.0.2, is present in reverse order, 2.0.0.10. In order for IP-address-to-hostname resolution to work properly, the IP address of the host needs to be in reverse order, as shown in this example. Many Internet servers attempt to do a reverse address resolution of a hostname based on your IP address. If this fails, they normally deny access. For this reason, when you create a db.*network* file you will need to ensure that you have entered an inverse mapping for all of your hosts.

## Sample Zone Database Files

Creating the zone database files is an easy process once you know what resource records are and what the format for each resource record is. All you have to do is to create the db.*domain*, db.*network*, and db.127.0.0.0 database files in the directory you choose to store your zone database in. In order to create the db.cache file, you can simply ftp the file

**ftp://ftp.rs.internic.net/domain/named.root**

and rename it to db.cache. For the other files, you can refer to the examples in this section and tailor the records to suit your needs.

### The db.domain File for bosland.us

The db.*domain* file for the bosland.us domain is called db.bosland. As mentioned previously, this file maps the hostnames in the bosland.us domain to their IP address. This mapping is done with a list of A records, one per host in the domain. The file also lists the master and slave name servers for the domain.

```
bosland.us. IN SOA kanchi.bosland.us. root.kanchi.bosland.us. (
        1998102301      ; Serial
        10800           ; Refresh after 3 hours
        3600            ; Retry after 1 hour
        604800          ; Expire after 1 week
        86400 )         ; Minimum TTL of 1 day

; Name Servers
bosland.us. IN NS kanchi.bosland.us.
            IN NS ns1.bosland.us.

; Host Addresses
localhost.bosland.us.          IN A    127.0.0.1
kanchi.bosland.us.             IN A    10.0.0.2
melkote.bosland.us.            IN A    10.0.0.3
madhura.bosland.us.            IN A    10.0.0.4
kashi.bosland.us.              IN A    10.0.0.5
udupi.bosland.us.              IN A    10.0.0.6
badri.bosland.us.              IN A    10.0.0.7
kaveri.bosland.us.             IN A    10.0.0.8
```

BASIC NETWORK
ADMINISTRATION

```
yamuna.bosland.us.            IN A    10.0.0.9
ns1.bosland.us.               IN A    10.0.0.10

; Aliases
www.bosland.us.       IN CNAME        kanchi.bosland.us.
ftp.bosland.us.       IN CNAME        kanchi.bosland.us.
```

To add a host from the bosland.us domain, add an A record for it into the section that starts with the comment:

```
; Host Addresses
```

To delete a host from the domain, delete its A record from the same section.

## The db.network File for bosland.us

The db.*network* file for the bosland.us domain is called db.10.0.0, since all of the hosts in the bosland network are on the 10.0.0.0 network. As mentioned previously, this file maps the IP address for hosts in the bosland.us domain to their hostnames, allowing reverse name lookups (required by some servers) to return the correct information. This mapping is done with a list of PTR records, one per host in the domain. The file also lists the reverse records for the master and slave name servers for the domain.

If your domain has multiple networks, for example 192.168.0.0 and 10.0.0.0, you will need to create two db.*network* files, one for each network. For these two networks you would need to create the files db.192.168.0.0 and db.10.0.0.0:

```
0.0.10.in-addr.arpa. IN SOA kanchi.bosland.us.
root.kanchi.bosland.us. (
        1998102301        ; Serial
        10800             ; Refresh after 3 hours
        3600              ; Retry after 1 hour
        604800            ; Expire after 1 week
        86400 )           ; Minimum TTL of 1 day

; Name Servers
0.0.10.in-addr.arpa.              IN NS    kanchi.bosland.us.
                                  IN NS    ns1.bosland.us.


; PTR records for reverse resolution
2.0.0.10.in-addr.arpa.            IN PTR   kanchi.bosland.us.
3.0.0.10.in-addr.arpa.            IN PTR   melkote.bosland.us.
```

```
4.0.0.10.in-addr.arpa.          IN PTR   madhura.bosland.us.
5.0.0.10.in-addr.arpa.          IN PTR   kashi.bosland.us.
6.0.0.10.in-addr.arpa.          IN PTR   udupi.bosland.us.
7.0.0.10.in-addr.arpa.          IN PTR   badri.bosland.us.
8.0.0.10.in-addr.arpa.          IN PTR   kaveri.bosland.us.
9.0.0.10.in-addr.arpa.          IN PTR   yamuna.bosland.us.
10.0.0.10.in-addr.arpa.         IN PTR   ns1.bosland.us.
```

Similar to the db.*domain* file, if you need to add a host or remove a host, simply add or delete the appropriate PTR record in the section labeled:

```
; PTR records for reverse resolution
```

One important detail to notice about this file is the reverse network address that is used for the SOA and NS resource records. While the domain for the reverse network is the same as for PTR records (.in-addr.arpa.), the reverse network does not use the same convention. The reverse network address for the 10.0.0.0 network is listed as 0.0.10 in both the SOA and NS records. These records use the same convention as the **primary** and **secondary** directives in the /etc/named.boot and the **zone** directive in the /etc/named.conf, and the last digit of a network is not listed in the reverse form.

> **Note**    *If the IP addresses for your domain are controlled by your Internet Service Provider (ISP) rather than your corporation or university, you may not be able to configure your name server as a master name server for the .in-addr.arpa. domain, since the Authoritative name server for the .in-addr.arpa.domain is really your ISP. Although you should not have to create a db.network file in this case, you will still have to provide your ISP with the appropriate information so that they can properly update their db.network file for your domain.*

## The db.127.0.0.0 File

Each of your name servers needs a db.*network* file for the loopback or localhost network, 127.0.0.0. This network is used by the system when it generates network traffic destined for itself. You need to include this file as part of the zone database in order for reverse address resolution to work correctly on the loopback network. The file is quite short, and you can tailor it for your domain by replacing the *name server* and *administrator* data fields in the SOA record and the *name server* data field in the NS record.

```
0.0.127.in-addr.arpa. IN SOA kanchi.bosland.us. root.kanchi.bosland.us. (
        1997100204      ; Serial
        10800           ; Refresh after 3 hours
```

```
3600              ; Retry after 1 hour
        604800            ; Expire after 1 week
        86400 )           ; Minimum TTL of 1 day

; Name servers
0.0.127.in-addr.arpa.    IN NS        kanchi.bosland.us.
                         IN NS        ns1.bosland.us.

; PTR records for reverse resolution
1.0.0.127.in-addr.arpa. IN PTR        localhost.
```

# Starting and Stopping the Name Server

In Solaris 8, the name server is located at /usr/sbin/in.named. It is started automatically by the script /etc/rc2.d/S72inetsvc when the system reaches runlevel 2 and a /etc/named.conf file exists, so you do not have to do any extra work to integrate the name server into the systems startup and shutdown procedures.

You should never have to stop the running name server, but in case you want to terminate its process you should try the following command (assuming that the Solaris 8 named process id file is /etc/named.pid):

```
# kill 'cat /etc/named.pid'
```

If you have stopped the name server manually, you can restart it by re-executing it as follows:

```
# /etc/sbin/in.named
```

## Restarting the Name Server

If you make changes to the zone database while the name server is running, you will have to restart before it will recognize the changes. You can restart the name server by sending its process a Hangup (HUP) signal as follows:

```
# kill -HUP 'cat /etc/named.pid'
```

Recall that the file /etc/named.pid stores the process ID of the name server while it is running. If you are using Solaris 8, this command assumes that you have configured the name server to use the file /etc/namcd.pid via the **pid-file** parameter to the **options** directive in the name server configuration file, /etc/named.conf. On Solaris 2.6 and earlier, /etc/named.pid is the default location for this file.

## Checking to See If the Name Server Is Running

You can check if the server is running in two ways. The first method is to use the following **kill** command:

```
$ kill -0 'cat /etc/named.pid '
```

If you receive no output from the command, this means the name server is running correctly. If on the other hand this command returns output similar to the following:

```
kill: (23980) - No such pid
```

it means that the name server is not running. You can determine the reason by examining the contents of /var/adm/messages. The messages from the name server will look similar to the following:

```
Jul 13 08:55:03 badri named[23980]: starting.  named 4.9.4-P1
Jul 13 08:55:03 badri named[23980]: /etc/named.boot: No such file or directory
```

In this case the name server did not start because the /etc/named.boot file that configures the name server was not present.

The second method for checking whether or not the name server is running is to use the following command:

```
$ /bin/ps -ef | grep named | grep -v grep
```

If this command returns output similar to the following:

```
root        250  0.0  0.6  1392    848  ?  S   Jun 10   0:46 in.named
```

it means that the name server is running. If you receive no output or if the output does not contain any listing for the in.named process, you will need to consult the file /var/adm/messages in order to determine the problem.

# Testing Your Name Server

Once your name server has been configured and is running you need to test it to ensure that it is functioning correctly. There are several tools are available for testing and querying a name server, but the most widely used one is named **nslookup**. This section focuses on basic and advanced queries for testing your name server with **nslookup**.

## Simple Queries with nslookup

The **nslookup** command is an interactive tool that allows you to query name servers. The simplest method for using it is as follows:

$ nslookup *hostname*

Here, *hostname* is the hostname you want to look up. The hostname you specify does not have to be fully qualified. To test your name server look up a name stored in the zone database on your server. As an example, in the bosland.us domain a query for the host badri returns:

```
$ nslookup badri
Server:    kanchi.bosland.us
Address:   10.0.0.2

Name:      badri.bosland.us
Address:   10.0.0.7
```

As you can see from the output, the name and IP address of the name server that was used to resolve your query as well as the name and address of the host you queried are displayed. In this case we see that the address for the host badri is 10.0.0.7. The **nslookup** command always returns the name server that it used for performing the query before it lists the output of the query. In this case the name server kanchi, 10.0.0.2, was used.

If you enter a hostname that is not resolvable you will receive output similar to the following:

```
$ nslookup nosuchhost.bosland.us
Server:    kanchi.bosland.us
Address:   10.0.0.2

*** kanchi.bosland.us can't find nosuchhost.bosland.us: Non-existent host/domain
```

As you can see, the output indicates that either the host does not exist or that you did not specify the domain correctly.

*In order for this command to work correctly you will need to have your system's /etc/resolv.conf configured to point to your name server, as explained earlier in this chapter.*

## Advanced Queries with nslookup

The **nslookup** command has its own "shell" for performing advanced queries such as looking up a particular type of resource record. To perform advanced queries, simply enter **nslookup** on the command line.

```
$ nslookup
Default Server:  kanchi.bosland.us
Address:  10.0.0.2

>
```

The ">" character is the **nslookup** prompt. From this prompt you can query for particular types of resource records. To quit **nslookup**, can type the command **exit** or press CTRL+D.

To query an A record for a particular host, you can just type its hostname. For example, the following query returns the A record for the host badri in the bosland.us domain:

```
> badri
Server:  kanchi.bosland.us
Address:  10.0.0.2

Name:    badri.bosland.us
Address:  10.0.0.7
```

To query a different type of record you need to use the **set** command, as follows:

> set q=*record*

Here *record* is the type of record you want to query. All of the record types covered in this chapter are supported by this command. Once you have issued a **set** command, all of the queries you perform will retrieve records of that record type. For example, to query the SOA record for the bosland.us domain you could issue the following:

```
>set q=soa
> bosland.us
Server:  kanchi.bosland.us
Address:  10.0.0.2

bosland.us
        origin = kanchi.bosland.us
        mail addr = root.kanchi.bosland.us
        serial = 1998102301
        refresh = 10800 (3 hours)
        retry   = 3600 (1 hour)
        expire  = 604800 (7 days)
        minimum ttl = 86400 (1 day)
bosland.us      name server = kanchi.bosland.us
kanchi.bosland.us       internet address = 10.0.0.2
```

BASIC NETWORK
ADMINISTRATION

To restore the default behavior of nslookup (querying A records) execute the command:

```
> set q=a
```

If you want to test a different name server than the default name server specified in /etc/resolv.conf, then change the name server that nslookup uses by means of this server command:

> server *address*

Here, *address* is the IP address of the alternate server. For example, you could use the following command to switch the name server from kanchi.bosland.us to ns1.bosland.us:

```
> server 10.0.0.10
```

All subsequent queries would use the name server 10.0.0.10 instead of the default.
The other useful command within nslookup is this ls command that lists all of the hosts in a particular domain:

> ls *domain*

Here, *domain* is the domain for which you are interested in listing the hosts. For example, the following command lists all of the hosts in the bosland.us domain:

```
> ls bosland.us
```

The output will be similar to the following:

```
badri                          10.0.0.7
bosland.us.                    server = kanchi.bosland.us
kanchi                         10.0.0.2
kashi                          10.0.0.5
...
```

For domains with a large number of hosts the output will probably scroll off the screen. You can capture the output using the redirection operator ">" as follows:

> ls *domain* > *file*

Here, *domain* is the domain you are interested in querying hosts for and *file* is the absolute path to the file you want the output stored in. For example, the following command stores the output in the file /tmp/bosland.hosts:

```
> ls bosland.us > /tmp/bosland.hosts
```

While the command is running, you will see output similar to the following:

```
[kanchi.bosland.us]
##
Received 12 answers (12 records).
```

The hash mark, "#", is used as a status indicator that the file is being written. The number of hash marks will vary based on the number of records received. Once the file has been written, you can display it using the **view** command:

> view *file*

Here, *file* is the absolute path to the file in which the output was stored. For example, the following command views the file /tmp/bosland.hosts that was created by the previous query:

```
> view /tmp/bosland.hosts
```

# Securing Your DNS Server

There are two different techniques for securing your DNS server. The first is to restrict responses, and the second is to restrict zone transfers. To completely secure your DNS server you need to use both techniques, but in most cases simply restricting zone transfers to your slave servers will be sufficient.

## Restricting Responses

You can restrict the hosts that your name server will respond to by adding one or more special secure_zone-domain TXT records into your db.*domain* file. The secure_zone is a special domain that lets you define an access list of the network addresses allowed to query your name servers. If you include one or more secure_zone-domain TXT records in your db.*domain* file, only those networks listed in these records will be able to access information about your network; any clients from other hosts will be refused.

The secure_zone-domain TXT record has the following format:

secure_zone   IN   TXT   *"address:mask"*

Here, *address* is a network address from which you want to allow queries, and *mask* is the network mask for that network. To specify a single host IP address you can use the following format instead:

secure_zone   IN   TXT   "*address*:H"

Here, *address* is the IP address of the host from which you want to allow queries.

As an example, you could use the following secure_zone-domain TXT records in the db.bosland file to restrict queries to the bosland.us domain to the 10.0.0.0 network:

```
secure_zone    IN    TXT "10.0.0.0:255.0.0.0"
secure_zone    IN    TXT "127.0.0.1:H"
```

The second secure_zone-domain TXT record is required in order for DNS queries originating from DNS clients on the name server to be serviced correctly.

## Restricting Zone Transfers

Restricting zone transfers is more important than restricting queries, since a zone transfer contains all of the information about your zone. A malicious system masquerading as a slave name server for your domain could steal your entire zone database via an illicit zone transfer. If you simply restrict queries, it is like putting bars on your windows but leaving the front door wide open.

The method for restricting zone transfers is slightly different between BIND 4 and BIND 8, but the concept is similar: You specify the list of IP addresses that are allowed to initiate zone transfers with your name server. In BIND 4 the restriction is global to all files in the zone database, while in BIND 8 the restriction can differ from one zone directive to another.

In BIND 4 (Solaris 2.6 and earlier) you can restrict zone transfers of your zone database using the **xfrnets** directive in the name server configuration file, /etc/named.boot. The syntax of this directive is as follows:

xfrnets *address1*&255.255.255.255 ... *addressN*&255.255.255.255

Here, *address1 ... addressN* are the IP addresses of systems that are allowed to initiate a zone transfer from your system. Only those systems whose IP addresses are listed in the arguments to this directive will be allowed to initiate a zone transfer; attempts by other hosts will be refused. Normally you want to use only the IP addresses of your master and slave name servers. As an example, the following xfrnets directive restricts zone transfers for the bosland.us domain to the IP addresses 10.0.0.10 (ns1.bosland.us):

```
xfrnets 10.0.0.10&255.255.255.255
```

If you want to be less restrictive (which is not recommended), you can restrict zone transfers to a network rather than an IP address by using the general form of the xfrnets directive:

xfrnets *address1&mask1 ... addressN&maskN*

Here, *address1&mask1 ... addressN&maskN* are the network address and network mask for networks from which hosts are allowed to initiate a zone transfer with your system. For example, the following **xfrnets** directive allows any host on the 10.0.0.0 network to initiate a zone transfer:

```
xfrnets 10.0.0.0&255.0.0.0
```

In BIND 8, you need to use specify an **allow-transfer** parameter for each **zone** directive in the name server configuration file, /etc/named.conf. The syntax for this parameter is similar to that of the **xfrnets** directive:

allow-transfer { *address1 ... addressN* };

Here, *address1 ... addressN* are either the IP addresses or network addresses from which you want to allow zone transfers. As an example, the following **allow-transfers** parameter in the **zone** directive for bosland.us restricts transfers for the bosland.us domain to the slave name server 10.0.0.10 (ns1.bosland.us):

```
zone "bosland.us" in {
    type master;
    file "db.bosland";
    allow-transfer {10.0.0.10};
};
```

Unlike the **xfrnets** directive, **allow-transfer** is a parameter of the **zone** directive, which means that you need to specify it for every **zone** directive in order to restrict zone transfers.

# Summary

In this chapter we examined the Domain Name Service (DNS). First we looked at the history behind the creation of DNS, and then we examined its structure and organization. The second part of the chapter was devoted to the configuration of DNS under Solaris 8. This section first covered the configuration of DNS clients, mainly involving the /etc/resolv.conf file. The section also illustrated the configuration of

DNS servers in detail, starting with an explanation of the different types of servers and continuing with an examination of procedures for setting up each of these servers. The final part of the second section examined the **nslookup** command for testing your name server.

# How to Find Out More

There are several excellent sources of information about DNS. The first is the reference book that covers the BIND software package used by Solaris:

Albitz, Paul; and Liu, Cricket. *DNS and BIND*. (O'Reilly and Associates, 1992.)

A second source is the BIND home page, which contains an overview of the DNS software as well as configuration examples and detailed descriptions of the zone database files and other DNS configuration files. The BIND home page is located at:

**http://www.isc.org/view.cgi?/products/BIND/index.phtml**

Another source of information about BIND and DNS is the FAQ for the usenet newsgroup comp.protocols.tcp-ip.domains. The latest version of the FAQ is located at:

**http://www.intac.com/~cdp/cptd-faq/**

If you want general information about DNS, you can also try the DNS Resources Directory, located at:

**http://www.dns.net/dnsrd/**

**Programs**   In addition to the standard **nslookup** command, there are two other programs freely available on the Internet that can help you debug problems with DNS. The first program, called dig (not covered in this chapter), is an advanced version of **nslookup**. The output from this command is highly customizable, making it a good choice for writing shell scripts that need to query a name server. It is available from:

**ftp://ftp.isi.edu/pub/dig.2.0.tar.Z**

The second program, called **dnswalk** (also not covered in this chapter), is useful for validating and isolating problems with your DNS database. It inspects the records in your DNS database and generates warnings or errors when it finds inconsistencies. The home page for **dnswalk** is located at:

**http://www.visi.com/~barr/dnswalk/**

The
# Complete
# Reference

Solaris 8

# Chapter 14

## The Dynamic Host
## Configuration Protocol

W hen the Internet was first being developed there were very few computers, and most of them were large and immobile. At that time, IP addresses were plentiful and could be allotted easily. Often when a machine was allotted an IP address it would stick with the same address until it was decommissioned. Since computers could not easily be moved from one network to another, this scheme of allotting computers a static IP address "for life" worked well. With the turn to laptop and palmtop computers, this scheme became inadequate.

Today many computers move from one network to another on a daily basis. If you had to manually reconfigure the IP address on a laptop or palmtop every time it moved from one room to another it would severely limit the computer's usefulness. Fortunately, there is a protocol called the Dynamic Host Configuration Protocol (DHCP) that allows for computers to determine their IP address and default gateway along with other networking parameters from a central server on a network.

In this chapter we will first look at the DHCP protocol, and then we'll see how to configure a Solaris server to act as a DHCP server for your network. Finally I'll cover setting up a Solaris machine as a DHCP client.

## What Is DHCP?

DHCP was created by the Dynamic Host Configuration Working Group of the Internet Engineering Task Force (IETF). It was designed to enable individual computers on an IP network to extract their configurations from a central DHCP server on a network. Although the DHCP server is primarily used by the individual computers (DHCP clients) to configure their IP addresses, in addition, the server also transmits the information necessary for configuring other related network parameters, such as the subnet mask, default router, and Domain Name System (DNS) server. The DHCP server will answer requests from any DHCP client, but, interestingly, it does not have to *store* any information about a particular client machine. This reduces the work involved in administering a large network.

DHCP is based on the Bootstrap Protocol (BOOTP), which is used for configuring diskless workstations and network computers. It maintains some backward compatibility with BOOTP. The main difference is that while BOOTP was designed for manual configuration of the host information in a server database, DHCP allows for dynamic allocation of network addresses and configurations to newly attached hosts. DHCP also allows for recovery and reallocation of network addresses through a leasing mechanism. In some aspects DHCP is also similar to the Reverse Address Resolution Protocol (RARP), which is used by Sun to allow workstations to determine their IP addresses dynamically at boot time. The main differences between DHCP and RARP are:

- RARP doesn't allow the server to communicate any other network parameters; DHCP does.

- RARP servers can only serve a single network, whereas DHCP and BOOTP requests and responses can be routed across networks.

# How DHCP Works

Every DHCP server is responsible for a pool of IP addresses in a particular network. This pool of addresses is referred to as the *scope* of the DHCP server. The DHCP server configures a client by exchanging DHCP packets, or *messages*, with the client. When a DHCP server receives a request from a client, it looks for the first available address in its pool and returns it to the client. The exact process is as follows:

1. The DHCP client broadcasts a DHCPDISCOVER message on its local network.

2. When a DHCP server receives the DHCPDISCOVER message it responds with a DHCPOFFER message containing IP address configuration information. (If the network has more than one DHCP server, each server can send a DHCPOFFER message to the client.)

3. Upon receiving one or more DHCPOFFER messages, the DHCP client broadcasts a DHCPREQUEST message indicating which DHCP server's offer the client has selected. Only the server selected by the client will continue configuring the client.

4. The DHCP server selected by the client will send a DHCPACK message that contains the same configuration information as in its DHCPOFFER message. If the server is unable to satisfy the client's DHCPREQUEST message, the server responds with a DHCPNAK message. This can occur if the client was too slow in transmitting its DHCPREQUEST.

   ■ If the client receives a DHCPNAK message, it restarts the configuration process.

5. When the client receives the DHCPACK message with the configuration parameters it checks the parameters to make sure the address is not being used.

   ■ If the address is available, the client machine configures its IP address as specified by the DHCPACK message. If multiple DHCPACK messages are received, then the client chooses the first one that matches the DHCPOFFER message it received.

   ■ If the address specified in the DHCPACK is in use, the client waits at least 10 seconds and then sends a DHCPDECLINE message to the server, restarting the configuration process.

6. When the client is finished with the IP address it sends a DHCPRELEASE message to the DHCP server. Once the server receives this message, it marks the IP address as available for other clients.

The messages used in this process are summarized in Table 14-1, which lists them in the sequence in which they are normally sent.

## DHCP Leases

In the DHCPOFFER and DHCPACK messages the DHCP server specifies the time period, called the *lease*, for which the IP address is valid. After the lease expires, the

BASIC NETWORK ADMINISTRATION

| Message Name | From | To | Purpose |
|---|---|---|---|
| DHCPDISCOVER | Client | All servers | Broadcast to locate available servers. |
| DHCPOFFER | Server | Client | Response to DHCPDISCOVER, with offer of configuration parameters. |
| DHCPREQUEST | Client | All servers | Acceptance of the parameters from one server. Implicitly declines offers from all other servers. |
| DHCPACK | Server | Client | Confirmation of offered configuration parameters. |
| DHCPNAK | Server | Client | Refusal of the client's acceptance. |
| DHCPDECLINE | Client | Server | Alert that the offered network address is already in use. |
| DHCPRELEASE | Client | Server | Relinquishment of the address. |

**Table 14-1.**  *DHCP Messages*

DHCP server can reclaim the address and allot it to another client. In order for the client to retain the IP address allotted to it, it must *renew* the lease. The renewal process is based on three times:

- *T0*, the lease expiration time
- *T1*, the renewal start time, approximately (0.5 * *T0*)
- *T2*, the renewal timeout, approximately (0.875 * *T0*)

As an example, if a client was granted a lease on an IP address for four days, the client would start the renewal process after it has used the IP address for about two days. The actual values for *T1* and *T2* are generated by applying a random factor to the results of the products given above. This random factor prevents any problems that might be caused by synchronization in renewal times between several DHCP clients and a single DHCP server. The renewal process used by the DHCP clients is as follows:

1. At time *T1*, the DHCP client sends a DHCPREQUEST message specifying its current IP address to the DHCP server. The DHCPREQUEST message is sent only to the DHCP server; it is not broadcast to the network.

2. When the DHCP server receives this message, it responds to the client with a DHCPACK message containing the same IP address that was specified in the client's DHCPREQUEST message. If the server is unable to allot the same IP address, it will not respond.

3. The DHCP client waits until time *T2* for a DHCPACK message from the server.

- If the DHCPACK message arrives, the client resets its lease expiration time to the length of the new lease contained in the DHCPACK message.

- If the DHCPACK message does not arrive from the DHCP server by time *T2*, the client restarts the renewal process by sending another DHCPREQUEST message to the server. It also recalculates *T1* and *T2* based on the time remaining until *T0*.

4. If the DHCP client does not receive a DHCPACK message by the time the lease expires at *T0*, it will send a DHCPRELEASE message and restart the entire DHCP address acquisition process.

## Allocation Types

In response to a DHCPREQUEST the DHCP server has three different mechanisms for allocating an IP address to the client:

- Automatic Allocation
- Dynamic Allocation
- Manual Allocation

DHCP servers use automatic allocation to assign *permanent* IP addresses to clients. A permanent IP address allotted to a client by a DHCP server does not have a lease expiration; it is permanently useable by the client.

In order to allot IP addresses that have a fixed lease, DHCP servers use dynamic allocation. If the server allots an IP address to a DHCP client using dynamic allocation, the client must renew the lease for that address as explained earlier, or risk losing the addresses. Most DHCP servers use dynamic allocation since it allows an IP address to be automatically reused when a client releases it.

Manually allocated IP addresses are assigned by the network administrator, and the DHCP server simply transmits this information to the client.

# DHCP Limitations

Although DHCP is perfectly suited for a dynamic computing environment where IP address configuration needs to be fast and transparent, it does have two major limitations that you should be aware of:

- There is no easy way for clients to request a specific hostname.
- There is no easy way to have fallback DHCP servers.

By keeping these limitations in mind, deploying and managing DHCP will be much easier for you.

## Hostnames

The DHCP server is responsible for assigning IP addresses only; it does not control the hostname of your machine. Once a machine is assigned an IP address by the DHCP server, that machine's hostname is determined by the DNS record corresponding to that IP address. Consider the following setup:

- A DHCP server whose scope is the address range 10.0.0.2 to 10.0.0.250.
- The DNS entries for addresses in this range are of the form dhcp-$n$, where $n$ is the last number of the IP address (thus dhcp-10 corresponds to IP addresses 10.0.0.10).

If a DHCP client obtains the IP address 10.0.0.3 from the DHCP server, its hostname will be dhcp-3, and the DHCP client cannot easily request that it be given a different name. This is a problem for mobile UNIX systems that need to have a single hostname. Currently there are several systems in development that address this problem, but none of them have reached widespread deployment. Most of the work has been concentrated on developing a DNS server that cooperates with a DHCP server in assigning hostnames.

### Fallback Servers

Normally fallback DHCP servers are handled by having two or more servers with nonoverlapping scopes. If one server is down, clients can lease an address from the other servers. This system works in networks where there are slightly fewer DHCP clients than there are IP addresses. For example, say that you have two DHCP servers responsible for 32 IP addresses each. If one of these servers goes down then the other server can only handle up to 32 DHCP requests before refusing clients.

Ideally you would want both DHCP servers to share the same scope so that even if one of the servers was down, the remaining servers could still handle DHCP requests for *all* of the addresses in the available pool. Currently you cannot implement this, because a mechanism to share the DHCP scope information between the DHCP servers does not exist. The Dynamic Host Configuration (DHC) Working Group of the Internet Engineering Task Force (IETF) is working on adding this functionality into DHCP. To overcome this limitation the DHCP allocable IP pool can be distributed between several DHCP servers in such a way that there is no overlap.

## Configuring a DHCP Server

Configuring a Solaris system to act as a DHCP server for your network is a three-step process. First you need to decide which blocks of IP addresses on your network should be allotted to DHCP. The second step is to configure one or more DHCP servers to handle this block, using the **dhcpconfig** command. The third step is to integrate the DHCP *daemon* into the boot process so that it automatically starts every time your system boots.

# Allocating IP Address Blocks

When allocating IP address blocks for DHCP, you need to decide how many IP addresses on your network will be used for DHCP and how these addresses should be divided between your DHCP servers. In order to make a good decision you need to determine the following:

- The number of machines that require static IP addresses
- The average number of temporary hosts on your network

The number of machines that require static IP addresses will help you determine the number of IP addresses available for DHCP. The average number of temporary hosts will help you determine the number of DHCP servers that you need to configure.

## Static IP Addresses

Normally machines that require static IP addresses are UNIX servers, UNIX workstations, routers, and switches. If you have Windows NT, Novell NetWare, or MacOS servers on your network, they should also be given static IP addresses. Most other machines (usually referred to as *desktops* or *workstations*) on your network can be configured to use DHCP.

As an example, let's consider the network 10.1.1.0 (netmask 255.255.255.0), which has a total of 254 useable IP addresses. One of the machines on the network will be the router, so there are 253 addresses left over for other systems. If you have a switch, it will require an IP address, leaving 252 addresses for other systems. If most of the machines on this network are servers, then you would want to reserve only 25 percent or less of the addresses for DHCP. If only half of the machines were servers, then you would want to reserve about 50 percent of the addresses for DHCP. On networks where very few of the hosts are servers, you can reserve up to 75 percent of addresses for DHCP.

As an example, if the 10.1.1.0 network is evenly distributed between servers and desktops (about 120 machines of each type), you could allot half of the addresses, about 120, for DHCP.

## Temporary Hosts

The average number of temporary hosts, such as laptops, on your network will determine how many DHCP servers you will need to configure. On networks that have DHCP clients, you should have at least two DHCP servers. Networks with many temporary hosts will need three or more servers in order to balance the load and provide redundancy in case one of the servers becomes unavailable.

The average number of temporary hosts is hard to determine accurately; most of the time you will need to make estimates or educated guesses based on the type. You can start with the number of desktop systems on your network and fill in from there.

BASIC NETWORK
ADMINISTRATION

For example, if most of the machines on a network are Windows desktop machines or MacOS-based workstations then the number of temporary hosts will be low. Most desktop systems are started once in the morning and are perhaps rebooted once or twice during the day. These systems will request an IP address from the DHCP server at most a few times each day (i.e., each time the system is rebooted). This translates to a light load for the DHCP server, which means that two DHCP servers will be adequate. If one of the servers crashes or becomes unreachable, the other server can easily handle the incoming requests for DHCP clients.

In a network where most users have laptops that are frequently moved between offices or conference rooms, DHCP servers will receive requests throughout the day. If 50 percent or more of the machines on a network are laptops, you will want to configure at least three or four DHCP servers. In this type of network, you need as much redundancy as possible. If one DHCP server out of four fails, it should not have a huge impact on DHCP clients. By increasing the number of DHCP servers, you can minimize the effect of a single failure.

In the network 10.1.1.0, let's suppose that most of the 120 DHCP clients are laptops. Further, we assume that of the 120 laptop clients, we can expect that a maximum of 100 laptops connect to the network at any given time. Therefore, we configure four DHCP servers dhcp-a, dhcp-b, dhcp-c, and dhcp-d. A possible configuration of their scopes could be:

- dhcp-a with address 10.1.1.2 has a scope of 10.1.1.8 to 10.1.1.32 containing 25 IP addresses.

- dhcp-b with address 10.1.1.3 has a scope of 10.1.1.33 to 10.1.1.52 containing 20 IP addresses.

- dhcp-c with address 10.1.1.4 has a scope of 10.1.1.53 to 10.1.1.82 containing 30 IP addresses.

- dhcp-d with address 10.1.1.5 has a scope of 10.1.1.83 to 10.1.1.107 containing 25 IP addresses.

 *The use of four servers in this example is for illustration purposes only. You can configure as many servers as you wish.*

## Using dhcpconfig

Once you have decided how to partition your network's IP addresses, you can begin to configure a DHCP server on your Solaris system, using this command as the root user:

```
# /usr/sbin/dhcpconfig
```

This will present you with the following menu:

```
***           DHCP Configuration              ***

Would you like to:

        1) Configure DHCP Service
        2) Configure BOOTP Relay Agent
        3) Unconfigure DHCP or Relay Service
        4) Exit


Choice:
```

Here you need to enter the number corresponding to the task you want to perform. The first option starts an interactive program that leads you through the DHCP server installation. The second option, to configure a BOOTP Relay Agent, is normally used when your server has to forward DHCP requests to another server. The third option will unconfigure an existing DHCP server. If you don't have any DHCP servers configured, this choice does nothing. Selecting the fourth option exits the **dhcpconfig** program.

## Using dhcpconfig to Configure the DHCP Service

In this example we will look at configuring a DHCP server from the previous section: dhcp-a (10.1.1.2), which has a scope of 10.1.1.8 to 10.1.1.32. The configuration process creates all of the required files on your system to support the DHCP server daemon **in.dhcpd**.

To begin configuring the DHCP server, select option 1 by typing **1** at the prompt. You will then be asked the the following question:

```
Would you like to stop the DHCP service? (recommended) ([Y]/N):
```

By answering **Y** here, any running DHCP server daemon will be stopped. Stopping the DHCP server daemon is a good idea, since making changes to its configuration while it is running can cause problems for DHCP clients that are attempting to request IP addresses from the server.

Once the DHCP server daemon has stopped, the actual configuration procedure starts. This procedure is divided into a several parts, with one or two questions in each. The parts are:

- Configuring the DHCP Database
- Configuring the DHCP Server Options
- Initializing the dhcptab
- Enabling DHCP on your local network
- Configuring DHCP for remote networks

The following sections walk you through each of these steps.

**Configuring DHCP Database**   The first part in the configuration procedure configures the DHCP database. The first question in this part asks you to give the location of the DHCP database. The DHCP database, or *datastore*, is the file that is used by the DHCP server to determine which IP addresses are in its scope. You will be prompted as follows:

```
###     DHCP Service Configuration      ###
###     Configure DHCP Database Type and  Location      ###
Enter datastore (files or nisplus) [nisplus]:
```

Normally you want to store this information on the DHCP server itself, so type **files** and press return. If your site already has DHCP set up to use databases that are controlled by NIS+ you can enter **nisplus** here. (You will need to know the path to the datastore in NIS+ to configure the server correctly.)

If you selected files, you will be asked to select a location for the DHCP database:

```
Enter absolute path to datastore directory [/var/dhcp]:
```

In most cases the default location of /var/dhcp is adequate, but you can pick any location you want. Other common locations include /etc/config/dhcp and /etc/dhcp/db. Once you decide which directory to use, enter its full path at the prompt.

**Configuring DHCP Server Options**   The second part of the configuration procedure configures the DHCP server daemon's options. The first question in this part is:

```
###     DHCP server daemon option setup ###
Would you like to specify nondefault daemon options (Y/[N]):
```

You can skip the other questions in this step by selecting **N**, but in most cases you should select **Y** and configure some of the options on the server. The first option you can configure is the amount of time a DHCPOFFER is good for:

```
How long (in seconds) should the DHCP server keep outstanding OFFERs? [10]:
```

The default is 10 seconds, but if your network has many DHCP clients or older, slower machines acting as DHCP clients, you should increase this time to about 20 seconds.

The second option you can configure is the interval at which the DHCP server rereads its configuration file:

```
How often (in minutes) should the DHCP server rescan the dhcptab? [Never]:
```

The default of **Never** is common for most UNIX server processes; they read their configuration file when they are started. If you need to have a server process reread its configuration file, usually you need to restart it or send it a HUP signal using the **kill** command. If you are comfortable with the standard behavior of daemons, then you can leave the default for this option. If you want the server to reread its configuration automatically, you should specify a time in minutes here. If you are going to be changing the configuration frequently, say once an hour, specify 60 or 90 here. If you are going to be changing the configuration once a week or less, then specify something like 1440 or larger here.

The third question in this section is:

```
Do you want to enable BOOTP compatibility mode? (Y/[N]):
```

Unless you have to support diskless clients on your network, answer **N** here. BOOTP is the predecessor to DHCP, so there is no need to use it for configuring IP addresses. If you are going to be configuring JumpStart on the same system, BOOTP will be configured by the JumpStart process.

**Initializing the dhcptab**    The third configuration part gathers the information required to initialize the dhcptab file. This file contains information about the scope of the server. This file also includes information about the duration of the lease for IP addresses that the server grants via dynamic allocation.

The first question gathers the lease duration in days:

```
###     Initialize dhcptab table     ###
Enter default DHCP lease policy (in days) [3]:
```

Once the DHCP lease runs out, the DHCP client has to renew the lease from the server. If your network has many temporary hosts (many laptops), then you may want to set this value to one or two days instead of the default of three days. By lowering the lease period the DHCP server can reclaim IP addresses with a greater frequency. This is useful for networks where most of the hosts are temporary. However, if most of the hosts on your network are Windows or MacOS workstations that are rebooted only once every few days, a short lease period can burden your network with DHCP renewal requests from these workstations to the DHCP server. In this scenario you should set the lease period to a larger value such as five days.

The second question in this part allows you to configure the DHCP server to allow clients to negotiate their lease period:

```
Do you want to allow clients to renegotiate their leases? ([Y]/N):
```

This option allows clients to ask the DHCP server for extended leases that are larger than the default lease time that you specified. Allowing clients that may be active for extended periods of time to request longer lease times will reduce the amount of DHCP renewal traffic on your network, so you should answer **Y** here.

**Enabling DHCP**   After initializing the dhcptab you will be asked if you want to configure DHCP on your network:

```
###     Select Networks For BOOTP/DHCP Support  ###
Enable DHCP/BOOTP support of networks you select? ([Y]/N):
```

Answer **Y** to this question to continue configuring DHCP. You will then be asked if you want to configure DHCP on your local network, in this case 10.1.1.0:

```
###     Configure Local Networks       ###
Configure BOOTP/DHCP on local LAN network: 10.1.1.0? ([Y]/N):
```

If you answer **Y**, you will be asked if you want to add hostnames for these DHCP hosts into the file /etc/hosts:

```
Do you want hostnames generated and inserted in the files hosts table? (Y/[N]):n
```

If your network uses DNS or NIS/NIS+, answer **N** to this question. You or your site's DNS administrator will have to add the hostnames for DHCP hosts to your DNS database as explained in Chapter 13. If you are using NIS/NIS+ to maintain the hosts file, you will need to add the hostnames for the DHCP hosts to the NIS/NIS+ hosts map.

When you are adding hostnames into DNS or NIS/NIS+ for your DHCP hosts, you can choose any hostnames, but in general it is good to stick to a common scheme that identifies these hosts as different from hosts that use static IP addresses. Two common hostname schemes are:

- dhcp-*n*, where *n* is the last number in the IP address. For example, a DHCP host with the IP address 10.1.1.18 would have the hostname dhcp-18.

- dhcp-*loc-n*, where *loc* is the building or floor where the machine is currently located, and *n* is the last number in the IP address. For example a DHCP host with the IP address 10.1.1.18 located in the building Cory may have the hostname dhcp-cory-18.

**Note**   *At some sites the word temp or mobile is used instead of dhcp in the hostname schemes.*

The third and fourth questions in this part ask for the starting IP address and the number of hosts you want to configure for this DHCP server:

```
Enter starting IP address [10.1.1.0]: 10.1.1.3
Enter the number of clients you want to add (x < 255): 25
```

In this case, we are configuring the first dhcp server, dhcp-a, on our 10.1.1.0 network, so we use the starting IP address 10.1.1.3 as described in the previous section. Since this server is responsible for the addresses 10.1.1.3 to 10.1.1.32, we specify 25 as the number of clients to add.

Before **dhcpconfig** configures the DHCP server to support these IP addresses, you will be asked one final question:

```
Disable (ping) verification of 10.0.0.0 address(es)? (Y/[N]):
```

What if someone has statically assigned (knowingly or unknowingly) an IP address from your DHCP server address pool. Surely, it will result in an IP address conflict causing grief to both the statically assigned and the DHCP assigned hosts. This question suggests that the server can check if the IP address that is about to be issued is already in use. If you answer **Y** here, the server will assume that all of the IP addresses in the block that you specified are available to be given out to new clients. You can answer **Y** here if you are absolutely sure that this is the case. Doing so will disable the IP address verification process. Normally, though, you want to answer **N**, because you do not want the server to give out IP addresses that are already in use.

Once you answer this question, you will be presented with a status update. After the configuration completes, the following message will be presented:

```
Configured 25 entries for network: 10.1.1.0.
```

At this point your DHCP server daemon will be completely configured to serve DHCP clients on your local network.

**Configuring Remote Networks**    The DHCP protocol was designed to handle requests across networks, which allows you to set up a set of DHCP servers on one network and use DHCP relays to send and receive DHCP requests from clients on different networks. The final step in the DHCP server configuration is to configure support for remote networks:

```
###     Configure Remote Networks     ###
Would you like to configure BOOTP/DHCP service on remote networks? ([Y]/N):
Enter Network Address of remote network, or <RETURN> if finished:
```

Regardless of how you answer the first question, you will be asked for the network address of a remote network. If you do not want to configure remote network support just press RETURN or ENTER. Otherwise, enter the address of the network you want to configure. For example, to configure DHCP for the network we've been following so far in our example, just enter **10.1.2.0**.

Once you have entered the address of a remote network you will be asked the following question:

```
Do clients access this remote network via LAN or PPP connection? ([L]/P):
```

If clients on this network use dialup modems to connect to the network, you will need to enter **P** at the prompt; otherwise enter **L** at the prompt.

The second question in this part is:

```
Do you want hostnames generated and inserted in the files hosts table? (Y/[N]):
```

As mentioned earlier, if your site uses DNS or NIS/NIS+ you should answer **N** here and update your DNS server's database or your NIS/NIS+ maps.

The third question asks you to configure the default router (also referred to as the default gateway) for hosts on the remote network:

```
Enter Router (From client's perspective), or <RETURN> if finished.
IP address:
```

You will need to determine the IP address of the default router on the remote network and enter it here. Usually this means consulting the network administrator or checking the configuration of a system on the remote network. You can enter as many IP addresses as you want, but normally you should only need to enter one. When you are finished entering IP addresses, press RETURN or ENTER at the following prompt:

```
IP address:
```

The fourth question in this part is optional, and asks you for the MTU (maximum transfer unit) of the remote network:

```
Optional: Enter Remote Network's MTU (e.g. Ethernet == 1500):
```

If you know the physical layer used for the remote network, you can enter a value here. For example, if the 10.1.2.0 network was based on Ethernet, you could specify 1500 here. If you are unsure, leave this question blank.

The rest of the questions for the remote network are the same as for your local network. When you've finished the configuration for a remote network you will be returned to the following prompt:

```
Enter Network Address of remote network, or <RETURN> if finished:
```

You can enter the network address for another network here, or press RETURN or ENTER to be returned to the main menu.

In addition to configuring your DHCP server for a remote network, you will need to configure a DHCP relay agent on that remote network. This procedure is outlined in the next section.

## Finishing the Configuration

Once you have finished configuring DHCP on all of your networks, you will be asked to restart the DHCP service:

```
Would you like to restart the DHCP service? (recommended) ([Y]/N):
```

You should answer **Y** to this question. If you answer **N**, the DHCP server will not be started; thus, DHCP clients will not be able to obtain IP addresses. You could answer **N** here and start the DHCP service manually, by issuing the following command as the root user:

```
# /etc/init.d/dhcp start
```

Once you have answered the restart question, you will be presented with the starting menu; select option 4 to exit **dhcpconfig**.

## Using dhcpconfig to Configure a DHCP Relay Agent

If you configured your DHCP server daemon to support a remote network, you will have to configure a DHCP relay agent on that remote network in order for your server to receive DHCP requests from the DHCP clients on that network. A DHCP relay agent serves as an "agent" on a network to fulfill DHCP requests for clients on that network. This may be necessary in environments where system administrators have decided to centralize DHCP administration. Therefore, in an enterprise network environment, a single server may act as the DHCP server while other networks contain DHCP relay agents. In this manner on a remote network, the DHCP relay agent is able to fulfill the IP address requests for clients of that network. Figure 14-1 displays this configuration. The relay agent acts as a proxy, exchanging DHCP messages between the network where the DHCP server is located and the clients on the remote network. A common practice is to run a DHCP relay agent on the router that connects the two networks. However, this depends on your router policy, network topology, and the type of router you are using. Depending on the router's vendor, the configuration of the DHCP relay agent will vary. An alternative is to configure a Solaris server as the DHCP relay agent.

To configure a Solaris system to act as a relay agent, select option 2 from the **dhcpconfig** main menu, as shown on the following page.

BASIC NETWORK ADMINISTRATION

```
***              DHCP Configuration               ***

Would you like to:

        1) Configure DHCP Service
        2) Configure BOOTP Relay Agent
        3) Unconfigure DHCP or Relay Service
        4) Exit

Choice:
```

You will first be asked if you want to stop the DHCP daemon:

```
Would you like to stop the DHCP service? (recommended) ([Y]/N):
```

You should stop this service for the reasons explained earlier in this chapter. Once the DHCP server daemon has been stopped, you will enter the DHCP relay agent configuration:

```
###     BOOTP Relay Agent Configuration ###
Enter destination BOOTP/DHCP servers. Type '.' when finished.
IP address or Hostname:
```

You can enter as many IP addresses or hostnames for DHCP servers as you like. For example, if you were on the 10.1.2.0 network and you wanted to forward requests

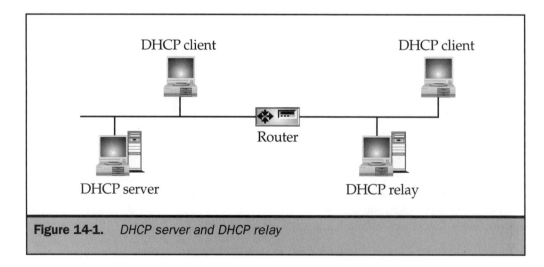

**Figure 14-1.** *DHCP server and DHCP relay*

to the DHCP servers dhcp-a, dhcp-b, dhcp-c, and dhcp-d located on the 10.1.1.0 network you could enter the hostnames. Depending on the hostname resolution you may choose to enter either the host name or the IP address. For illustration purposes only, we have entered both the hostname and IP addresses:

```
IP address or Hostname: dhcp-a
IP address or Hostname: 10.1.1.3
IP address or Hostname: dhcp-c
IP address or Hostname: 10.1.1.5
IP address or Hostname:.
```

When you are finished, type a single period at the "IP address or Hostname:" prompt. This completes the DHCP relay agent configuration. You will then be asked if the DHCP server daemon should be restarted:

```
Would you like to restart the DHCP service? (recommended) ([Y]/N):
```

Answer **Y** here to have the DHCP relay agent started on the system.

**Security Concerns with DHCP Relay Agents**    DHCP servers and clients are susceptible to a "Denial of Service" attack from malicious clients. It is possible for a malicious client to request all the available DHCP IP addresses on a network without ever releasing any of the IP addresses it was granted. From the DHCP server's perspective, all of the IP addresses in its scope would then be in use; as a result it will refuse to grant IP addresses to legitimate DHCP clients on your network. Your legitimate clients will thus be without network access until the malicious client is found and shut down. Another possibility is for malicious clients to request several addresses and then overload the server with renewal requests. If the DHCP server becomes overloaded with renewal requests, it will not be able to handle requests from legitimate DHCP clients.

Denial of Service attacks are not particularly dangerous on a local network. Since the malicious client has to be directly connected to the network for an extended period of time, you or your network administrator can easily track down the client and shut it down. If the DHCP servers on your network receive requests via a DHCP relay agent, however, it may not be possible to track down the malicious client. Because the malicious client can be connected to any network on which a DHCP relay agent is configured, attacks on your network can easily occur from unsecured networks or from networks beyond your administrative control.

Although these types of attacks are possible, they have not been seen in large network environments. Most universities and corporations that use DHCP and DHCP relay agents have not encountered DHCP outages due to such attacks. Most of the problems encountered in DHCP networks have been caused by bugs in DHCP clients from the operating system vendors rather than from malicious clients designed to attack your network. For additional protection against the possibility of intentional Denial of Service attacks, be sure to locate your network behind a firewall.

## Using dhcpconfig to Unconfigure the DHCP Service

If you wish to disable the DHCP server, you can use the **dhcpconfig** command to do this by selecting option 3 from the main menu:

```
***            DHCP Configuration            ***

Would you like to:

        1) Configure DHCP Service
        2) Configure BOOTP Relay Agent
        3) Unconfigure DHCP or Relay Service
        4) Exit

Choice:
```

You will be presented with the following message and prompt:

```
###             WARNING WARNING WARNING        ###
Unconfigure will delete the following tables in the current
resource (files):

        1) dhcptab.
        2) ALL dhcp-network tables.

It will also stop the DHCP service and remove /etc/default/dhcp.
If you are sharing the DHCP service tables either via NISplus or file
sharing among multiple DHCP servers, those servers will be unable to
service requests after these tables are removed.

Note that any hosts table entries which have been added will need to
be manually removed.

Are you SURE you want to unconfigure the DHCP service? (Y/[N]):
```

Type **Y** and press RETURN or ENTER in order to unconfigure the DHCP service. You will see messages similar to the following on your screen:

```
Removing: dhcptab...
Removing: 10_1_1_0...
```

Once the process is complete you will be presented with the DHCP Configuration menu. DHCP will be unconfigured at this point. (You can then reconfigure DHCP to meet your new requirements by rerunning **dhcpconfig**.) If you are finished, select option 4 to exit.

## Automatically Starting and Stopping the DHCP Server

By default the DHCP server is not started during system boot on Solaris. To enable this, you need to link the script /etc/init.d/dhcp into the appropriate system boot directories—in this case rc3.d for system startup and rc2.d for system shutdown.

To have the DHCP server start automatically at system boot, execute the following commands as the root user:

```
# cd /etc/rc3.d
# ln -s ../init.d/dhcp S31dhcp
```

This will create a link that will automatically start the DHCP server when your system reaches runlevel 3 (normally during system boot).

You can execute the following commands as the root user to have the DHCP server automatically stop during system shutdown:

```
# cd /etc/rc2.d
# ln -s ../init.d/dhcp K69dhcp
```

This link will shutdown the DHCP when your system reaches runlevel 2 (normally during reboots).

# Configuring the DHCP Client

Configuring the DHCP client on Solaris is a simple two-step process. The first step is to manually configure your interface for DHCP. The second step is to integrate this configuration with the system boot.

## Manually Configuring the DHCP Client

Before you configure an interface for DHCP, use the **ifconfig** to list the available interface.

```
$ ifconfig -a
```

If you see an output that looks like the following example.

```
lo0: flags=849<UP,LOOPBACK,RUNNING,MULTICAST> mtu 8232
        inet 127.0.0.1 netmask ff000000
```

then it is quite possible that your network Interface is not "plumbed." Sun defines plumbing an interface as follows:

"Open the device associated with the physical interface name and set up the streams needed for TCP/IP to use the device."

In other words, the process of plumbing an Interface makes the Interface available for operation. A more normal output would look like this:

```
lo0: flags=849<UP,LOOPBACK,RUNNING,MULTICAST> mtu 8232
        inet 127.0.0.1 netmask ff000000
le0: flags=863<UP,BROADCAST,NOTRAILERS,RUNNING,MULTICAST> mtu 1500
        inet 10.8.11.14 netmask ff000000 broadcast 10.255.255.255
        ether 8:0:20:7b:3d:99
```

The le0 interface (in this case the second entry corresponding to le0) is already configured for using a static IP address. You can unconfigure this interface and proceed to configure DHCP on the interface. To unconfigure this interface you can use the **ifconfig** command as follows:

# ifconfig unplumb *interface*

For example, to unconfigure the le0 interface you could use this command:

```
# ifconfig unplumb le0
```

If you have a 100M bit Ethernet interface you will need to use hme0 or be0 instead of le0. If your 100Mbit Ethernet interface is on your motherboard, as in the Sun Ultra series, you should use hme0. If your 100Mbit Ethernet is on an external card, you should use be0. To determine the types of Ethernet interfaces available, you can use the following command sequence:

```
$ prtconf | egrep 'le[ ,]|be[ ,]|qe[ ,]|hme[ ,]|qfe[ ,]'
```

The output will be similar to one of the following:

```
hme (driver not attached)
```

or

```
le, instance #0
```

The "(driver not attached)" next to the interface name suggests that the interface is not plumbed. In this case you will need to use the **ifconfig** command to plumb the interface as follows:

```
# ifconfig plumb hme0
```

## Preparing Your Interface

In order to inform the kernel about your interface you will need to use the following command:

# ifconfig plumb *interface*

Here you should replace *interface* with the name of your interface. For example, to configure the le0 interface you could use this command:

```
# ifconfig plumb le0
```

After informing the kernel about your interface, check the status of the interface with the following command:

```
$ ifconfig -a
```

This displays information along the lines mentioned in the previous section:

```
lo0: flags=849<UP,LOOPBACK,RUNNING,MULTICAST> mtu 8232
        inet 127.0.0.1 netmask ff000000
le0: flags=842<BROADCAST,RUNNING,MULTICAST> mtu 1500
        inet 0.0.0.0 netmask 0
        ether 8:0:20:7b:3d:99
```

## Enabling DHCP on an Interface

To enable DHCP on an interface you can use the following command:

# ifconfig *interface* dhcp

For example, to configure the le0 interface for DHCP you could use this command:

```
# ifconfig le0 dhcp
```

When this command returns, your interface will be configured for DHCP. If you receive an error message regarding a timeout, you will need to check the status of the DHCP server process on the DHCP server; use the following command to do so.

```
$ /bin/ps -ef | grep dhcp | grep -v grep
```

If this command does not produce any output you will need to start the DHCP server as follows:

```
# /etc/init.d/dhcp start
```

## Checking the Interface Status

Once your interface is correctly configured for DHCP, you can check its status using the following command:

```
$ ifconfig -a
lo0: flags=849<UP,LOOPBACK,RUNNING,MULTICAST> mtu 8232
        inet 127.0.0.1 netmask ff000000
le0: flags=4843<UP,BROADCAST,RUNNING,MULTICAST,DHCP> mtu 1500
        inet 10.1.1.15 netmask ff000000 broadcast 10.1.1.255
        ether 8:0:20:7b:3d:99
```

As you can see, the IP address for this interface has been configured as 10.1.1.15.

You can also get the status of the interface using the following command, which will give you information of a different sort concerning the DHCP address that your system has been allotted:

$ ifconfig *interface* dhcp status

For example, to check on the status of the le0 interface you could use this command:

```
$ ifconfig le0 dhcp status
Interface  Status      Sent Received  Rejects
le0        BOUND         2      2        0
           (Began,Expires,Renew) = (05/10/1999 16:43, 05/10/1999 18:43, 05/10/1999 17:43)
```

As you can see, this command gives you information in additional categories, including:

■ The time at which the IP address was issued by the server

■ The date on which the address will expire

■ The date on which the address was last renewed

# Automatically Configuring DHCP at Boot

To automatically configure DHCP on an interface at boot time you need to create the following files:

/etc/hostname.*interface*
/etc/dhcp.*interface*

You can create these files using the command:

# touch /etc/hostname.*name* /etc/dhcp.*name*

For example, if you are using the interface le0, you could issue this command:

```
# touch /etc/hostname.le0 /etc/dhcp.le0
```

Having done so, when you reboot your system you should see the following message, indicating that DHCP has been successfully configured on your interface. For example, if the interface le0 is configured for DHCP, you should see the following message:

```
starting DHCP on primary interface le0
```

## Summary

In this chapter we examined the Dynamic Host Configuration Protocol, which allows a DHCP server to automatically assign IP addresses to DHCP clients. First we looked at the process used by the DHCP client to obtain an IP address from the DHCP server. Then we covered the configuration of the DHCP server, starting with deciding on the number of addresses to reserve for DHCP and concluding with an example of using the **dhcpconfig** command to configure the DHCP server. In the last section of this chapter we looked at configuring a Solaris system as a DHCP client.

## How to Find Out More

If you are interested in more information about DHCP, please consult the following book:

Kercheval, Berry. *DHCP: A Guide to Dynamic TCP/IP Network Configuration.* (Prentice Hall, 1999.)

Another excellent source of information about DHCP is the DHCP home page located at the following URL:

**http://www.dhcp.org**

For information about DHCP extensions such as Dynamic DNS please consult the following web site:

**http://www.oceanwave.com/technical-resources/unix-admin/dns-nis.html**

For more information about configuring the Solaris DHCP server consult the online Sun Answerbook covering Network Administration, using the following URL:

**http://docs.sun.com:80/ab2/coll.47.4/NETCOM/@Ab2PageView/35648?**

If you are interested in alternative implementation of the DHCP server or client, you can try out the Internet Software Consortium (ISC)'s DHCP implementation. They are available for free from the following site:

**http://www.isc.org/dhcp.html**

The ISC's implementation of the DHCP client and server is intended to be the reference implementation for all platforms and strictly adheres to the description of DHCP as given in the RFC.

The RFCs regarding DHCP and the related BOOTP and RARP protocols are:

- **RFC 2131** DHCP
- **RFC 951** BOOTP
- **RFC 903** RARP

The
Complete
Reference

Solaris 8

# Chapter 15

## Network Information Service (NIS+)

In Chapter 13, we looked at the domain name service (DNS) which allows hosts around the Internet to be easily and consistently identified by user-friendly names rather than computer-friendly IP addresses. However, while DNS is a very common network information service, it is not the only kind of service available. NIS, the original Network Information Service, was supported by Solaris 1.x, and NIS+, which is an improved version of NIS, has been supported by all versions of Solaris since version 2 (including Solaris 8). In this chapter we'll focus on this improved version.

NIS+ is a centralized repository of information about hosts, networks, services, and protocols on a local-area network. This information is physically stored in a set of maps that are intended to replace the network configuration files usually stored in a server's /etc directory. The set of all maps on an NIS+ network, known collectively as a *namespace*, can keep track of very large networks (of up to 10,000 hosts) where responsibilities are delegated to local servers. NIS+ improved upon the standard NIS by enhancing authentication processes and introducing a sophisticated resource authorization scheme. These improvements have permitted NIS+ namespaces to span public networks like the Internet with little risk of data loss or interception. (Regarding that risk, however, note that NIS+ relies on the relatively weak DES encryption algorithm.)

In this chapter, we will examine the process of setting up an NIS+ server, and highlight the differences between NIS+ and NIS—and also the differences between NIS+ and naming services like DNS, which will be useful because many administrators may choose to run DNS alongside NIS+ for reasons which will become clear as you read the chapter. In addition, we will review the role and configuration of primary and slave servers, and walk through the installation of NIS+ using the script method.

## Overview of NIS+

NIS+ is a Solaris network information service whose primary focus is the management of users, hosts, networks, services, and protocols. NIS+ does not replace DNS, which is still required for host addressing and identification; rather, it gives networks more than DNS can provide on its own: As a centralized repository of shared network information, NIS+ can be used to manage large networks more effectively. However, because it has some overlap with DNS, and because of the extra administrative burden involved in installing and configuring NIS+ primary and slave servers, many organizations choose not to use NIS+. It should be pointed out, however, that NIS+ can be relatively easy to configure if you use the NIS+ scripts to install and configure namespaces, instead of using NIS+ commands directly.

**Note**   *NIS+ namespaces can be constructed to parallel the host designations assigned through DNS. This is done to simplify operations and to make the integration of both services more seamless.*

NIS revolved around the idea of *maps*: generally a database with two columns, of which one was a primary key that is used to retrieve an associated value. This associative nature made the storage and retrieval of mail, passwords, and group and Ethernet information fast for small networks, but rapidly became difficult to manage (not to mention slow) for large networks. NIS+, in contrast, uses tables, which store such information as server addresses, timezones, and network services. Sixteen tables are defined by the system. In this section, we will examine the most commonly used types of NIS maps and NIS+ tables, but before we get into those topics we will first present a conceptual overview of how NIS+ could be used to better manage an organization's network data.

## How NIS+ Can Improve Your Management of Network Data

Let's imagine that we're setting up a Solaris network for an imaginary college called Panther College, which has a DNS domain of panther.edu. Panther has two teaching divisions: an undergraduate school (undergrad.panther.edu) and a graduate school (graduate.panther.edu). The domain panther.edu has a Class C network (192.12.1.0), as do each of the undergraduate (192.12.2.0) and graduate schools (192.12.3.0). Each of these networks can have over 250 hosts each, which more than adequately covers the staff members in both teaching divisions. To support DNS, there may be a campuswide DNS server ns.panther.edu at 192.12.1.16, while the undergrad.panther.edu network has its own DNS server at ns.undergrad.panther.edu (192.12.1.16), and ns.graduate.panther.edu (192.12.2.16), as shown in Figure 15-1. This is a fairly standard setup for a medium-sized network like a college campus. Keep in mind that DNS domains and NIS+ can be logically separate, and may have no relationship with each other, even though many sites choose to maintain compatibility between them.

The NIS+ domains for Panther College can exactly mirror the DNS configuration, as shown in Figure 15-2. However, some differences in naming are immediately apparent. While DNS uses lowercase names by convention, and does not terminate

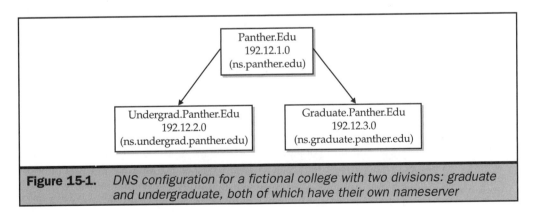

**Figure 15-1.** *DNS configuration for a fictional college with two divisions: graduate and undergraduate, both of which have their own nameserver*

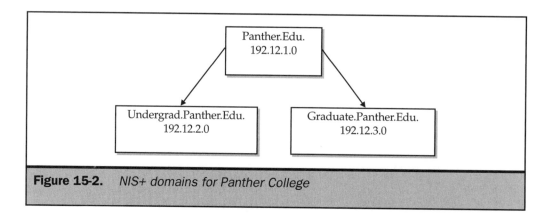

**Figure 15-2.** *NIS+ domains for Panther College*

names with a period, the NIS+ convention is to name each element in a domain with an initial capital letter, and to terminate each name with a period.

In addition, the second-level domain identified in DNS as panther.edu would be the "root domain" in an NIS+ network, and the third-level domains undergrad.panther.edu and graduate.panther.edu would be described as "nonroot domains." Each of these domains would be associated with a server, and the existing DNS servers would double up as NIS+ servers. In fact, in normal NIS+ usage, *each* of the three domains at Panther College would require two servers: a master server and at least one replica or slave server. This ensures that if the master server is disrupted or experiences hardware failure, then there is always a replica server that holds copies of network service information. The expanded NIS+ domains for Panther College, with a master and slave server each (called Master and Replica), are shown in Figure 15-3.

In addition to domains and servers, NIS+ also services clients. Each client is associated with a specific server and domain. For example, a client in the chemistry lab in the graduate school (Curie.Graduate.Panther.Edu.) would be served by Master.Graduate.Panther.Edu., and would be part of the Graduate.Panther.Edu. domain. Alternatively, a history professor in the undergraduate school with a computer named FDR.Undergrad.Panther.Edu would be served by Master.Undergrad.Panther.Edu., and would be part of the Undergrad.Panther.Edu. domain. Figure 15-4 shows the hierarchy of control for the FDR.Undergrad.Panther.Edu. client. When each client is installed, a directory cache is created, which enables the client to locate other hosts and services via the appropriate server.

So far, we have mentioned only one of the many kinds of namespace components: the domain. Many other components exist in the namespace, among them group objects, directory objects, and table objects. We will examine these important features of the namespace in the following sections. In addition, we will present the specific configuration of NIS maps and NIS+ tables.

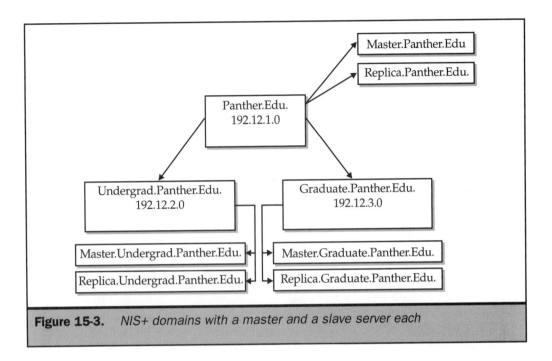

**Figure 15-3.**    *NIS+ domains with a master and a slave server each*

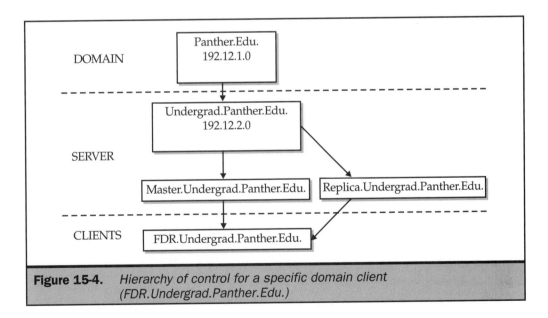

**Figure 15-4.**    *Hierarchy of control for a specific domain client (FDR.Undergrad.Panther.Edu.)*

> ### Note
> *It is worth mentioning at this point that one of the main reasons that organizations choose to implement NIS+ is the improved security that accompanies the system. For example, NIS+ tables are not directly editable, unlike their normal Solaris counterparts in the /etc directory. Requests to change or even access information in the namespace can only take place once a user has been authenticated. In addition to authentication, each user must be authorized to access a particular resource. This doubly protects sensitive and organizational data in a networked environment. The main authentication exchange takes place when either a user presents his or her credentials, or a host presents its credentials, in the form of an unencrypted LOCAL form, or a more secure, DES-encrypted exchange. The former is used for testing, while the latter is always used for deployment. After authentication, authorization for the requested resource is checked. Access rights can always be examined by using the **niscat** command, which is discussed later in this chapter.*

## NIS Maps

As we mentioned above, NIS used a series of maps to encode data about the network structure. Many of these are in a form that can be accessed through an address key (having a "byaddr" suffix), or through a name (with a "byname" suffix). Whenever a client needs to find information about a particular host, service, group, network, or netgroup, it can be retrieved by consulting the appropriate map as defined in the namespace. The main system maps are listed below.

- **bootparams**   Contains a list of diskless clients for a domain.
- **ethers.byaddr**   Contains a list of the Ethernet addresses of all hosts in the domain, and their hostnames.
- **ethers.byname**   Contains a list of the hostnames of all hosts in the domain, and their Ethernet addresses.
- **group.bygid**   Contains a list of groups that are indexed by group ID (gid).
- **group.byname**   Contains a list of groups that are indexed by group name.
- **hosts.byaddr**   Contains a list of the addresses of all hosts in the domain, and their hostnames.
- **hosts.byname**   Contains a list of the hostnames of all hosts in the domain, and their addresses.
- **mail.aliases**   Contains a list of mail aliases within the namespace, indexed by name.
- **mail.byaddr**   Contains a list of mail aliases within the namespace, indexed by address.
- **netgroup**   Contains netgroup information, indexed by group name.
- **netgroup.byhost**   Contains netgroup information, indexed by hostname.
- **netgroup.byuser**   Contains netgroup information, indexed by username.

■ **netid.byname**   Contains the netname of hosts and users.

■ **netmasks.byaddr**   Defines the netmasks defined in the domain namespace.

■ **networks.byaddr**   Defines the networks in the domain namespace, sorted by address.

■ **networks.byname**   Defines the networks in the domain namespace, sorted by name.

■ **passwd.byname**   Defines the password database, sorted by username.

■ **passwd.byuid**   Defines the password database, sorted by user ID.

■ **protocols.byname**   Defines the network protocols used in the domain, sorted by name.

■ **protocols.bynumber**   Defines the network protocols used in the domain, sorted by number.

■ **publickey.byname**   Contains public keys for RPC.

■ **rpc.bynumber**   Contains RPC details indexed by number.

■ **services.byname**   Defines all available Internet services by name.

■ **ypservers**   Contains a list of all NIS servers available.

As you can see, there are many similarities in name and function between the NIS maps and the /etc system files they are intended to replace. However, both the /etc files and NIS maps perform poorly under heavy loads, when the number of hosts defined in a specific namespace exceeds the hundreds. In such cases, it is much more appropriate to bypass NIS and /etc, and move directly to an NIS+ installation, where a single table (such as Ethers) replaces the dual lookup system used by NIS (such as ethers.byname and ethers.byaddr).

## NIS+ Tables

Namespace information in NIS+ is stored in tables, which are based on a centralized administration model that allows particular functions to be delegated to specific servers. NIS+ is similar to DNS in that it arranges hosts and resources hierarchically into domains, it has inbuilt redundancy with master and slave servers, and it can store much more information about a network than just the names and locations of its hosts. Since each host in a domain has many different characteristics and user details, requiring those details to be recorded and stored centrally entails updating them frequently, which can be time consuming and often gives rise to such issues as contention in the recording of user and host data. However, NIS+ namespaces can be updated incrementally, as changes occur, so that the entire database does not need to be updated all at one time. Changes entered into a master domain server can be propagated through time to the rest of the domain. This process is governed by a time-to-live setting similar to that used for DNS.

The main tables used by an NIS+ system are described in the following paragraphs.

**Hosts**   The Hosts table lists all of the hosts in a particular domain, matching their IP address with a hostname and an optional nickname. For example, if the host maria had an alias called bruny, and the IP address 192.34.54.3, then the entry in the Hosts table would look like the following:

```
192.34.54.3     maria      bruny
```

**Bootparams**   The Bootparams tables contains the necessary information to boot and configure any diskless clients in the domain. It contains entries for server-based dump and swap, as well as a root directory, for each client. For example, if there is a diskless client called pembroke, and it is configured by the server downing, then the Bootparams table would contain the entry:

```
pembroke            root=downing:/export/root/pembroke \
                    SWAP=downing:/export/SWAP/pembroke \
                    dump=downing:/export/dump/pembroke
```

Thus, each diskless client will have its own Bootparams entry and resources available on the server.

**Passwd**   The Passwd table stores all the standard user information expected on Solaris hosts, including username, encrypted password, user ID, group ID, user's real name, user's home directory, and user's login shell. A typical entry may look like the following:

```
pwatters: *LK*:101:10:Paul A. Watters:/home/pwatters:/bin/tcsh:10905:-1:-1:-1:-1::0
```

In addition to the standard details, this table contains extra information that specifies how often a password must be changed, or how many days until it must next be changed. This significantly increases the functionality of NIS+ over standard Solaris password authorization.

**Group**   The Group table consists of a group name, group password, group ID number, and member list, and stores information about the three kinds of groups accessible by NIS+ clients: Solaris groups (such as "staff"), NIS+ groups, and netgroups.

**Netgroups**   The Netgroup table defines a group of hosts and users that are authorized to perform specific operations on one or more other hosts within a group. The table format contains entries that identify the name of the group as well as its members. For small organizations, everyone belongs to a single group, perhaps called everyone, as shown here:

```
everyone    paulwatters.com
```

**Mail Aliases**    The Mail Aliases table replicates the functionality of the old /etc/aliases file for the local mail transport agent (MTA), which is typically **sendmail**. An aliases table can store an alias for a specific user, or it can be used to construct a mailing list. For example, if the user bounty wanted to receive mail as endeavour, then the Mail Aliases entry would look like:

```
endeavour:bounty
```

However, if an advertising company had a local mailing list for new clients, these messages could be distributed nationally to local offices by using an alias like:

```
newclients:layton,miami,oakton,sanfran
```

**Timezone**    The Timezone table defines the local timezone that will affect all system settings and applications, such as **sendmail**. For example, the entry:

```
hartog Australia/NSW
```

allows the host hartog to be identified as belonging the New South Wales timezone in Australia. In addition, timezones can be specified on a subnet basis. This allows systems that exist in different timezones to belong to the same domain. For example, a SPARCstation in Sydney can belong to the same domain as an Ultra in San Francisco.

**Networks**    The Networks table contains details of the local networks and their IP addresses. For example, if a Class B network 192.12.0.0 was known on the Internet as brunswick, but had an alias essendon, then it would be entered into the Networks table as:

```
brunswick    192.12.0.0    essendon
```

**Netmasks**    The Netmasks table specifies the netmasks for all local Class A, Class B, and Class C networks. For example, if the network 192.12.34.0 has a netmask of 255.255.255.0, then the entry would look like this:

```
192.12.34.0    255.255.255.0
```

**Ethers**    The Ethers table contains entries that associate a hostname with a specific hardware address. For example, if the host freycinet has an Ethernet address of 00:ff:a1:b3:c4:6c, then the Ethers table entry would look like the following:

```
00:ff:a1:b3:c4:6c     freycinet
```

**Services**    The Services table contains a list of the IP services that are available through both TCP and UDP. For example, the HTTP service provided by many web servers, such as Apache, is usually available through TCP port 80. This would be defined in the Services table as:

```
http     80/tcp
```

**Protocols**    The Protocols table defines the protocols available to the network. A necessary entry for Internet use would be the Internet protocol (IP):

```
ip     0     IP
```

which identifies ip as protocol number zero, which also has the alias IP.

**RPC**    The RTP table defines the RPC programs available to the network. An entry consists of a name, a program number, and one or more aliases. In the following example, rpcbind is also known as portmap, sunrpc, and portmapper. The entry for rpcbind looks like:

```
rpcbind     100000     portmap     sunrpc     portmapper
```

**Auto_Home**    The Auto_Home table is an automounter map that facilitates the mounting of a home directory for any user in the local domain. It is commonly used to share a common home directory for a user who has accounts on multiple machines. (It is also the cause of some consternation among administrators who attempt to create their users' home directories under /home, but who don't use the automounter to do it!) The Auto_Home table has two columns: a common username that is consistent across all machines in a domain, and a physical location for the user's shared home directory. For example, the home directory of user pwatters might be located physically on the server winston, in the directory /u1/export/pwatters. In this case, the entry in Auto_Home would be the following:

```
pwatters     winston:/u1/export/pwatters
```

**Auto_Master**    The Auto_Master table maps the physical mount points of all of the NFS automounter maps in a particular domain to a name. For example, it can be used to map user home directories to /home or /staff using Auto_Home, with either of the following mount points respectively:

```
/home      auto_home
/staff     auto_home
```

For more information regarding the automounter, see Chapter 17.

# Name Service Switch

Given a mixed network information service environment, comprising NIS maps, NIS+ tables, and DNS servers, you might be wondering how name services are selected to resolve particular requests. The answer provided in Solaris 8 is the name service switch, whose configuration is specified in the file /etc/nsswitch.conf. Non-NIS+ users who performed Solaris 1.x to Solaris 2.x upgrades will recognize this as the pesky file that appeared to prevent DNS from working; however, the name service switch is very useful.

For instance, it is possible to specify more than one kind of service for every kind of request; thus, if a request fails on the default service, it can be applied to a different service. For example, to resolve hostnames, many sites have at least some local hostnames statically hardwired into the /etc/hosts database; in addition, many sites connected to the Internet resolve hostnames using DNS, not NIS or NIS+. For such common possibilities, /etc/nsswitch.conf provides for the order in which files, DNS, NIS, and NIS+ can be selected as the default name service for resolving hosts. For example, the following line:

```
hosts: files dns nisplus nis
```

indicates that the /etc/hosts file should be consulted first, and if a match cannot be found for a hostname, then DNS should be tried next. If DNS fails to resolve, then NIS+ should be tried. As a last resort, NIS map resolution can be attempted. This is a useful setup for a network that makes great use of the Internet and consequently less use of NIS+ and NIS. Of course, many NIS+ advocates would suggest using the following line instead:

```
hosts: nisplus nis files dns
```

because this ensures that NIS+ is always selected over the /etc/hosts database or DNS.

In addition to host resolution, nsswitch.conf also allows the configuration of several other options, which roughly correspond to the contents of the NIS+ tables and/or the NIS maps. An NIS+ oriented nsswitch.conf file would look like the following:

```
passwd:       files nisplus
group:        files nisplus
hosts:        nisplus dns [NOTFOUND=return] files
services:     nisplus [NOTFOUND=return] files
networks:     nisplus [NOTFOUND=return] files
protocols:    nisplus [NOTFOUND=return] files
rpc:          nisplus [NOTFOUND=return] files
ethers:       nisplus [NOTFOUND=return] files
netmasks:     nisplus [NOTFOUND=return] files
bootparams:   nisplus [NOTFOUND=return] files
publickey:    nisplus
netgroup:     nisplus
automount:  nisplus files
aliases: nisplus files
sendmailvars: nisplus files
```

In most of these situations, NIS+ is consulted before the files. The exceptions are the password and group information. In addition, DNS is listed as a host resolution method after NIS+. However, it would also be possible to implement a bare-bones system, which relies on files for most resource information, and DNS for name resolution:

```
passwd:       files
group:        files
hosts:        dns [NOTFOUND=return] files
networks:     files
protocols:    files
rpc:          files
ethers:       files
netmasks:     files
bootparams:   files
publickey:    files
netgroup:     files
automount:    files
aliases:      files
services:     files
sendmailvars:   files
```

In the case illustrated by the above listing, the reliance on files and DNS means that NIS+ is effectively disabled.

# Configuring NIS

In this section, we will walk through a configuration session with NIS+, focusing on using a script-based installation, which makes using NIS+ much easier. The main tasks involved in setting up NIS+ involve configuring domain, master server, slave server, and user. These tasks can only be performed once a network has been designed along the lines discussed in previous sections.

Whether or not you are setting up a root or a non-root domain, the basic process is the same: After initializing a master server and creating the appropriate administrative groups, the NIS+ tables are populated, and clients and servers can then be installed. In the case of a root domain, these servers can then act as master servers for lower-level domains. In this section, we review the process of setting up a master server, populating the NIS+ tables, configuring clients and servers, and setting up other domains.

## Setting Up a Root Domain

The first step in creating an NIS+ namespace is to create the root master server for the new domain. Continuing with the example for the Panther.Edu. domain from earlier in the chapter, we create the root master server for Panther.Edu. by using the **nisserver** command. This command is used for most server configuration operations. The server will be known in DNS as ns.panther.edu. In this case, we use the following command:

```
ns.panther.edu# nisserver -r -d Panther.Edu.
```

where -r stands for "root master server," and -d stands for "domain." This creates a root domain master server without backward compatibility with NIS. In order to enable NIS support, you need to use the command:

```
ns.panther.edu# nisserver -Y -r -d Panther.Edu.
```

where -Y stands for "NIS compatible."

## Populating Tables

After creating the master root server for the Panther.Edu. domain on ns.panther.edu, the next step is to populate the NIS+ tables. To achieve this, we need to use the **nispopulate** command:

```
ns.panther.edu# nispopulate -F -p /nis+files -d Panther.Edu.
```

where -p stands for "populate." This populates all the tables for the Panther.Edu. domain, and stores the information on the master server. Again, if you need to support NIS, you need to include the -Y option:

```
ns.panther.edu# nispopulate -Y -F -p /nis+files -d Panther.Edu.
```

In order to administer the NIS+ namespace, we need to add administrators to the admin group. We can achieve this by using the **nisgrpadmin** command. In the Panther.Edu. example, imagine we have two administrators, michael and adonis. In order to add these administrators, use the command:

```
ns.panther.edu# nisgrpadm -a admin.Panther.Edu. michael.Panther.Edu. adonis.Panther.Edu.
```

where -a stands for "administrators." If you are satisfied with the configuration, then it is best to "checkpoint" or "commit" the configuration and transfer the domain configuration information to disk copies of the tables. This can be achieved by using the **nisping** command:

```
ns.panther.edu# nisping -C Panther.Edu.
```

where -C stands for "checkpoint." Now that we have successfully created the root domain, we can create clients that will act as master and slave servers for the two subdomains in the Panther.Edu. root domain: Graduate.Panther.Edu. and Undergrad.Panther.Edu.

## Setting Up Clients

To create master servers for the non-root domain Undergrad.Panther.Edu., we first need to set up the client within a domain by using the **nisclient** command. For the host client1.panther.edu, which will become the master server for the non-root domain, the command is as follows:

```
client1.panther.edu# nisclient -i -d Panther.Edu. -h Ns.Panther.Edu
```

where -h identifies the root master server. In order to actually set up client1's users within the domain, we can use use the following command, which must be executed from a nonprivileged user's shell:

```
client1.panther.edu% nisclient -u
```

where -u stands for "user." If this was for the user maya, then maya would now be able to access the namespace. Next, we need to turn the client host we have initialized into a non-root domain master server.

# Setting Up Servers

After the root server is created, most organizations will want to create new master servers for each of the subdomains that constitute the domain. For example, in the Panther.Edu. domain there are two subdomains: Undergrad.Panther.Edu. and Graduate.Panther.Edu. In this case, two clients must be created from the root master server, and then converted to be servers. Initially, these are root server replicas, but their designation then changes to a non-root master server for each of the subdomains. Replica servers for the subdomain master servers can also be enabled.

In the following example, we designate two client machines, whose DNS names are client1.panther.edu and client2.panther.edu (recall that the master server for the root domain is ns.panther.edu). These two clients will actually become the master and slave servers for the subdomain Undergrad.Panther.Edu. To begin the server creation process, a similar approach is followed as for the creation of the master server for the root domain. First, we need to start the **rpc** daemon on the client machine that will become the master server for the non-root domain:

```
client1.panther.edu# /usr/sbin/rpc.nisd
```

Next, we need to convert the client1 server to a root replica server in the first instance. This ensures that the subdomain inherits the appropriate settings from the top-level domain:

```
ns.panther.edu# nisserver -R -d Panther.Edu. -h client1.panther.edu
```

where -h indicates the server to be replicated. After replicating the settings from the root master server, the new non-root master server is ready to begin serving the new subdomain. In this case, the root master server (ns.panther.edu) must delegate this authority explicitly to the master of Undergrad.Panther.Edu., which is client1.panther.edu:

```
ns.panther.edu# nisserver -M -d Undergrad.Panther.Edu. -h client1.panther.edu
```

Following the same routine we outlined for the root master server, we must now populate the tables of the new subdomain server client1.panther.edu:

```
client1.panther.edu# nispopulate -F -p /nis+files -d Undergrad.Panther.Edu.
```

Finally, having created a new master server for the new subdomain, we have to create a replica server to ensure service reliability in the event of failure:

```
client1.panther.edu# nisclient -R -d Undergrad.Panther.Edu. -h client2.panther.edu
```

The process of installing a server for the Undergrad.Panther.Edu. subdomain would need to be adapted from the preceding examples in order to create the other subdomain (Graduate.Panther.Edu.), but the general process of setting up a client, converting it to a replicated server, and populating the tables would be very similar to the steps we followed for the domain above. Now that we have investigated how to create subdomains, the next section covers the day-to-day use of NIS+, and the most commonly used commands for accessing tables, groups, and objects in the namespace.

# NIS+ Tools

Now that we have examined the basic naming and configuration issues involved in NIS+, we investigate how NIS+ is actually used on a day-to-day basis to manage namespace objects, groups, and directories. The most commonly used commands are **nisdefault**, which displays the current settings for the local client; **nisls**, which lists the contents of an NIS+ directory; and **niscat**, which lists the contents of tables and other NIS+ objects.

## nisdefaults

The **nisdefaults** command displays the current settings for the local client. This is very useful when trying to troubleshoot why a particular client may have trouble accessing a particular resource, such as an automounted home directory. An example output from the **nisdefaults** command on the local client anglia for the user natashia would look like the following:

```
anglia% nisdefaults
Principal Name : natashia.graduate.panther.edu.
Domain Name    : graduate.panther.edu.
Host Name      : anglia.graduate.panther.edu.
Group Name     :
Access Rights  : ----rmcdr---r---
Time to live   : 12:00:00
Search Path    : graduate.panther.edu. undergraduate.panther.edu. panther.edu.
```

In this case, the *Principal Name* (client user) is natashia, while the client *Host Name* is anglia. The *Time to Live* is also stated, which is similar to that used for DNS, along with the *Search Path* for domain names. Thus, if natashia tried to connect to ns.panther.edu, she could do so by just using the name ns, as the panther.edu domain is automatically searched. Significantly, the client's *Access Rights* are also stated. In the next section, we examine what these access rights are, and how they are used to determine whether a client has the ability to read, write, or delete objects within the namespace.

## nischmod

In the previous section, access rights were listed for a particular principal (or client). These rights are stated in a way that is similar to the standard Solaris file and user access permissions, but with a few key differences. The permissions listed for the *Access Rights* entry may be interpreted in the following way:

- **r** Grants permission to read objects.
- **m** Grants permission to modify objects.
- **c** Grants permission to create objects.
- **d** Grants permission to delete objects.

These permissions can be set explicitly for each user and object by using the **nischmod** command and combining the above permissions with one or more of the following, which restrict the permission(s) to specific users or groups:

- **n** Grants the permission to clients who have not been authenticated.
- **o** Grants the permission to the object's owner.
- **g** Grants the permission to a specific group.
- **w** Grants the permission to the world (i.e., all authenticated clients).
- **a** Grants the permission to everyone.

Use the + key ("plus" key) on your keyboard to assign permissions and restrictions, and the hyphen or minus sign to remove them. (Either one of the + keys on your keyboard will do the job; that is, the + on the top row of the alphanumeric portion, or the + on the "10-key" numeric keypad. Similarly, both the hyphen on the alphanumeric section and the minus sign on the 10-key numeric keypad will work for removing permissions and restrictions.) Let's look at some examples to see how these permissions can be set on specific objects. This example removes (using –) any create (**c**) and modify (**m**) permissions for the group (**g**) and unauthenticated users (**n**), for the Passwd table (probably a wise idea!):

    **client1# nischmod gn-cm passwd.org_dir**

These permissions could be easily restored by using the following command:

    **client1# nischmod gn+cm passwd.org_dir**

As mentioned earlier, permissions can be set on a user-by-user and permission-by-permission basis. Although this may seem clunky compared to the compact numeric codes used to specify Solaris permissions (for example, **chmod 666**), it forces administrators to consider the implications of their actions explicitly on the command line. For example, to set a complex set of permissions for the Hosts table, we could use a command like:

> **client1# nischmod o=rmcd,g=rm,w=rc,n=r hosts.org_dir**

This command gives read, modify, create, and delete permissions to the owner; read and modify permissions to the group; read and create permissions to any authenticated users; but only read permissions to unauthenticated users.

## nisls

The **nisls** command lists the contents of any or all NIS+ directories, and is a very useful command for discovering which tables have been configured. To list all of the directories in the namespace, we use this command:

> **client1# nisls**

```
graduate.panther.edu.:
org_dir
groups_dir
```

We can see the two kinds of directory objects listed here that comprise an NIS+ domain or subdomain: the org_dir directory and groups_dir directory. Details of NIS+ groups are stored in the groups_dir directory, while org_dir contains the list of tables in the namespace. Thus, we can retrieve a list of all the tables by using the following command:

> **client1# nisls org_dir**

```
org_dir.undergrad.panther.edu.:
passwd
group
auto_master
auto_home
bootparams
cred
ethers
hosts
mail_aliases
```

```
sendmailvars
netmasks
netgroup
networks
protocols
rpc
services
timezone
client_info
```

In contrast, the groups directory is small, consisting only of an admin group:

**client1# nisls groups_dir**

```
groups_dir.undergrad.panther.edu.:
admin
```

The latter directory will change as the namespace is populated with users.

# niscat

**niscat** is the most commonly used NIS+ command, and is primarily used to display the contents of NIS+ tables and other NIS+ objects. In this section, we will investigate how **niscat** can be used to examine table data in the namespace. Every kind of table can be consulted in this way by using **niscat**. This is very useful for troubleshooting and generally obtaining information from the tables. For example, we can display the entries in the Hosts table by using this command:

**client1% niscat -h hosts.org_dir**

```
client.companyA.com client 192.168.205.46
server.companyA.com server 192.168.205.47
```

This shows two hosts within the domain of CompanyA.Com.: a server and a client. Similarly, we can view the contents of the Passwd table by typing:

**client1% niscat passwd.org_dir**

```
tosh:*LK*:4135:1:tosh:/staff/tosh:/bin/sh:10905:-1:-1:-1:-1::0
marley:*LK*:4048:1:marley:/staff.marley:/bin/csh:10930:-1:-1:-1:-1::0
```

If we wish to examine the list of groups to which these users can belong, we can use the following command:

**client1% niscat group.org_dir**

```
root::0:root
staff::1:tosh,marley
bin::2:root,bin,daemon
sys:*:3:root,bin,sys,adm,ingres
adm::4:root,adm,daemon
uucp::5:root,uucp
mail::6:root
```

In addition to normal user groups, we can also display the members of any netgroups that have been created. In many organizations, this will be a single group, unless there is a differentiation based on security rights. For example, everyone at Blueoyster.Com. belongs to the everyone netgroup:

**client1% niscat netgroup.org_dir**

```
everyone     blue-oyster.com
```

To list all of the registered hosts in the domain by Ethernet address, we can use the following command:

**client1% niscat ethers.org_dir**

```
8:8:19:4e:73:a3 strummer.music.org.
0:0:18:4d:84:4c headon.music.org.
08:17:6a:23:b3:8d jones.music.org.
```

To get an idea of the services that are offered to these hosts, we can examine the Services table:

**client1% niscat services.org_dir**

```
tcpmux tcpmux tcp 1
echo echo tcp 7
echo echo udp 7
discard discard tcp 9
discard sink tcp 9
discard null tcp 9
```

```
discard discard udp 9
discard sink udp 9
discard null udp 9
systat systat tcp 11
systat users tcp 11
daytime daytime tcp 13
daytime daytime udp 13
```

These are the first few of the many services available through Solaris. It is also possible to display the directory object for org_dir, which includes information such as the access rights and replica information:

**client1% niscat -o org_dir**

```
Object Name    : "org_dir"
Directory      : "kurosawa.co.jp."
Owner          : "rashomon.kurosawa.co.jp."
Group          : "admin.kurosawa.co.jp."
Access Rights : r---rmcdrmcdr---
Time to Live  : 12:0:0
Creation Time : Fri Jun  4 16:12:30 1999
Mod. Time     : Fri Jun  4 16:13:06 1999
Object Type    : DIRECTORY
Name : 'org_dir.kurosawa.co.jp.'
Type : NIS
Master Server :
        Name       : samurai.kurosawa.co.jp.
        Public Key : Diffie-Hellman (192 bits)
        Universal addresses (3)
        [1] - udp, inet, 192.128.64.127.0.111
        [2] - tcp, inet, 192.128.64.127.0.111
        [3] - -, inet, 192.128.64.127.0.111
Time to live : 12:0:0
Default Access rights :
```

This displays the directory details for kurosawa.co.jp, with an admin group, an owner, and details of the access rights (see the section on permissions earlier in this chapter). In addition, the master server is identified, along with the security mechanisms used to verify client credentials (the Diffie-Hellman algorithm). Details of the network addresses are also identified. All of the tables and objects in the namespace can be examined in this way by using **niscat**.

## Summary

In this chapter, we have examined the NIS+ network information service, and how it can be implemented to provide a more sophisticated service than standard DNS (or indeed, standard NIS). Although the idea of dealing with networked tables and objects is more complex than the standard configuration files in the /etc directory, administrators will find the extra features useful in improving security and authentication on a local or distributed network.

## How to Find Out More

There is an excellent book reviewing all NIS and NIS+ topics called *All About Administering NIS+*, written by Rick Ramsey, and published by Prentice Hall. There is also a very comprehensive FAQ available at

**http://www.eng.auburn.edu/users/rayh/solaris/NIS+_FAQ.html**

# The Complete Reference

Solaris 8

# Part IV

## Administering Services

# The Complete Reference

Solaris 8

# Chapter 16

## Managing Remote Access

emote access is the hallmark of modern multiuser operating systems such as Solaris and its antecedents like VAX/VMS. Solaris users can concurrently log in to and interactively execute commands on server systems from any client that supports TCP/IP (such as Solaris, NT, and Macintosh, as well as the thin Sun Ray client). Solaris can support hundreds and thousands of interactive user shells at any one time, constrained only by memory and CPU availability. This can be seen especially with high-end servers, like the E10000, which have almost linear scaling with up to 64 processors. Such a machine has the capacity to serve many concurrent users. However, while Solaris provides many of the traditional UNIX remote-access tools like **telnet**, **ftp**, and **rlogin**, it does not yet natively support recent secure replacements for these products (like **ssh** and **sftp**). However, these programs can be easily compiled and installed on any networked Solaris system, providing very safe network connectivity. Solaris 7 provides support for authentication services in the form of Kerberos Release 4, while Solaris 8 includes Kerberos Release 5. In this chapter, we will examine traditional UNIX remote-access tools, as well as the newer versions, and discuss the security implications for managing network services in geographically distributed organizations.

# Standard Remote-Access Tools

In this chapter, we will examine several popular methods of remote access, such as **telnet**, which have been popular for quite some time and have been supplied with most major UNIX releases. We will also outline the technical background to the much-publicized security holes and bugs that led to the innovation and development of secure remote-access systems, such as Secure Shell (SSH), which is available as both a freeware and a commercial product. These "safer" remote-access systems facilitate the encryption of the contents of user sessions or authentication sequences, and provide an important level of protection for sensitive corporate data. Although remote access is incredibly useful, the administrative overhead in securing a Solaris system can be significant, reflecting the increased functionality that remote-access services provide and the requirement of installing extra packages to support the secure services.

## Telnet

**telnet** is the standard remote-access tool for logging into a Solaris machine from a client using the original DARPA Telnet protocol. A compiled client can be executed on most operating systems that support TCP/IP. Alternatively, a Java Telnet client is available at the following URL:

http://srp.stanford.edu/~tjw/telnet.html

The Java Telnet client is supported on any operating system that has a browser that runs Java natively or as a plug-in. **telnet** is a terminal-like program that gives users interactive access to a login shell of their choice (e.g., the C Shell, or **csh**). Most Telnet clients support VT100 or VT220 terminal emulations, providing easy access to menu-based services and onscreen navigation using the arrow keys. The login shell can be used to execute scripts, develop applications, read email and news—in short, everything a Solaris environment should provide to its users, with the exception of X11 graphics and Open Windows, or more recently, the common desktop environment (CDE). A common arrangement in many organizations is for a Solaris server to be located in a secure area of a building, with Telnet-only access allowed; thus, many users will never see the actual console or use CDE. Such an arrangement is shown in Figure 16-1.

The sequence of events that occurs during a Telnet session begins with a request for a connection from the client to the server. The server either responds or times out, with a connection being explicitly accepted or rejected. If the connection is accepted, the client is asked to enter a username followed by a password. If the username and password combination is valid, then a shell is spawned, and the user is logged in. This sequence of events is shown in Figure 16-2.

The standard port for Telnet connections is 23. Thus, a command such as

**client% telnet server**

is expanded to give the effective command:

**client% telnet server 25**

Since a port number can be specified on the command line, Telnet clients can be used to connect to arbitrary ports on Solaris servers. This makes a Telnet client a very

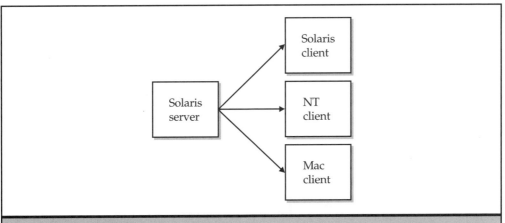

**Figure 16-1.** *Typical remote-access topology for client/server technology*

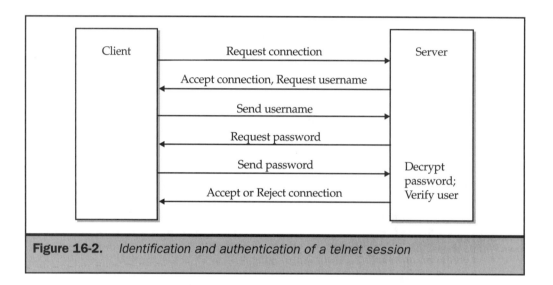

**Figure 16-2.** *Identification and authentication of a telnet session*

useful tool. For example, one can interactively issue commands to an FTP server on port 21:

**client% telnet server 21**

```
Trying 172.16.1.1...
Connected to server.
Escape character is '^]'.
220 server FTP server (UNIX(r) System V Release 4.0) ready.
and to a sendmail server on port 25:
```

**client% telnet server 25**

```
Trying 172.16.1.1...
Connected to server.
Escape character is '^]'.
220 server ESMTP Sendmail 8.9.1a/8.9.1; Mon, 22 Nov 1999 14:31:36
+1100 (EST)
```

Interactive testing of this kind has many uses. For example, if we **telnet** to port 80 on a server, we are usually connected to a web server where we can issue interactive commands using the HyperText Transfer Protocol (HTTP). For example, to **get** the default index page on a server, we could type the following:

**get index.html**

```
Trying 172.16.1.1...
Connected to server.
Escape character is '^]'.
GET index.html
<!DOCTYPE HTML PUBLIC "-//IETF//DTD HTML 2.0//EN">
<HTML><HEAD>
<TITLE>Server</TITLE></HEAD>
<h1>Welcome to server!</h1>
...
```

This technique is very useful when testing proxy server configurations for new kinds of HTTP clients (for example, a HotJava browser). You may also find it useful to use this technique during a script to check whether the web server is active and serving expected content.

**telnet** is controlled by the Internet super server (the daemon **inetd**), which invokes the **in.telnetd** server. An entry is made in /etc/services to define the port number for the Telnet service:

**telnet    23/tcp**

The configuration file /etc/inetd.conf also contains important details of the services provided by **inetd**. The Telnet daemon's location and properties are identified here:

```
telnet    stream    tcp       nowait    root      /pkgs/tcpwrapper/bin/tcpd    in.telnetd
```

In this case, we can see that **in.telnetd** is protected by the use of TCP "wrappers," which facilitate the logging of Telnet accesses through the Solaris **syslog** facility. TCP wrappers are discussed later in the chapter. **inetd** has historically had some significant security holes and performance issues that, although they have largely been fixed in recent years, have caused administrators to shy away from servers invoked by it. The Apache web server (**http://www.apache.org**), for example, runs as a standalone daemon process.

A rejection to a Telnet server may occur because the port that normally accepts Telnet client connections on the server has been blocked by a packet filter or firewall. Alternatively, the Telnet server could be disabled in the Internet daemon configuration file /etc/inetd.conf, or a physical disruption to the network service between the client and server could have occurred. If the latter occurs, check that **telnetd** is defined in /etc/inetd.conf and that **inetd** is running. If this fails to correct the problem, then check the rules for the packet filter to ensure that the Telnet port is not being blocked. If the Telnet server is still being rejected, then try using **ping** and **traceroute** to determine connectivity between client and host.

# R-Commands

**inetd** also controls many other standard remote-access clients, including the so-called "r-commands," which include the remote login (**rlogin**) and remote shell (**rsh**) applications. The **rlogin** application is similar to **telnet** in that it establishes a remote connection through TCP/IP to a server, spawning an interactive login shell. For example, the command:

**client% rlogin server**

by default produces the response:

```
password:
```

After the password is entered and authenticated by the server, then access is either denied or granted. If the target user account has a different name from your current user account, you can try:

**client% rlogin server -l user**

There are two main differences between **telnet** and **rlogin**. The first is that **rlogin** attempts to use the username on your current system as the account name to connect to on the remote service. (**telnet** always prompts for a separate username.) This makes remotely logging into machines on a single logical network much faster with **rlogin** than with **telnet**. Second, on a trusted, secure network, **rlogin** (but not **telnet**) makes it possible to set up a remote authentication mechanism by which the remote host allows a direct, no-username/no-password login from authorized clients. This automated authentication can be performed on a systemwide level by defining an "equivalent" host for authentication purposes on the server in /etc/hosts.equiv, or on a user-by-user basis with the file .rhosts. If the file /etc/hosts.equiv contains the client machine name and your user name, then you will be permitted to automatically execute a remote login. For example, if the /etc/hosts.equiv file on server contains the line:

```
client
```

then any user from client may log in to a corresponding account on server without entering a username and password. Similarly, if your username and client machine name appear in the .rhosts file in the home directory of the user with the same name on the server, then you will also be permitted to remotely log in without an identification/authentication challenge. The sequence of identification and authentication for **rlogin** is shown in Figure 16-3.

Remote-shell (**rsh**) connects to a specified hostname and executes a command. **rsh** is equivalent to **rlogin** when no command arguments are specified. **rsh** copies its

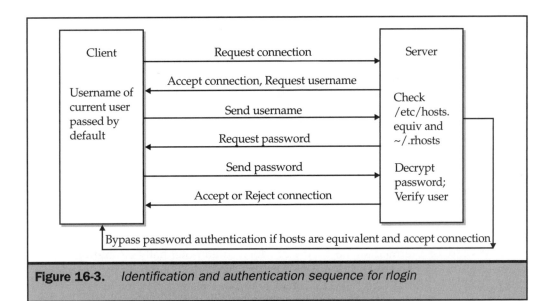

**Figure 16-3.** *Identification and authentication sequence for rlogin*

standard input to the remote command, the standard output of the remote command to its standard output, and the standard error of the remote command to its standard error. Interrupt, quit, and terminate signals are propagated to the remote command. In contrast to commands issued interactively through **rlogin**, **rsh** normally terminates when the remote command does.

As an example, the following command:

    client% rsh server df -k > server.df.txt

executes the command **df -k** on server, returning information about disk slices, and creates the local file server.df.txt, which contains the output of the command. Clearly, **rsh** has the potential to be very useful in scripts and automated command processing.

## Security Problems

One of the unfortunate drawbacks of the Telnet system is that usernames and even passwords are transmitted in clear-text around the network. If I were using a Telnet client to connect from a cyber-café in Paris to a server in New York, my traffic might pass through 20 or 30 routers and computers, all of which can be programmed to "sniff" the contents of network packets. A sample **traceroute** of the path taken by packets from AT&T to Sun's web page looks like:

    client% traceroute www.sun.com

```
Tracing route to wwwwseast.usec.sun.com [192.9.49.30]
over a maximum of 30 hops:
  1   184 ms    142 ms    138 ms   202.10.4.131
  2   147 ms    144 ms    138 ms   202.10.4.129
  3   150 ms    142 ms    144 ms   202.10.1.73
  4   150 ms    144 ms    141 ms   atm11-0-0-11.ia4.optus.net.au [202.139.32.17]
  5   148 ms    143 ms    139 ms   202.139.1.197
  6   490 ms    489 ms    474 ms   hssi9-0-0.sf1.optus.net.au [192.65.89.246]
  7   526 ms    480 ms    485 ms   g-sfd-br-02-f12-0.gn.cwix.net [207.124.109.57]
  8   494 ms    482 ms    485 ms   core7-hssi6-0-0.SanFrancisco.cw.net [204.70.10.9]
  9   483 ms    489 ms    484 ms   corerouter2.SanFrancisco.cw.net [204.70.9.132]
 10   557 ms    552 ms    561 ms   xcore3.Boston.cw.net [204.70.150.81]
 11   566 ms    572 ms    554 ms   sun-micro-system.Boston.cw.net [204.70.179.102]
 12   577 ms    574 ms    558 ms   wwwwseast.usec.sun.com [192.9.49.30]
Trace complete.
```

That's a lot of intermediate hosts, any of which could potentially be sniffing passwords and other sensitive data. If the network packet that contains the username and password is "sniffed" in this way, a rogue user can easily log in to the target account using a Telnet client. This risk has led to the development of Secure Shell clients and servers for Solaris, and similar products that encrypt the exchange of username and password information between client and server, making it very difficult for "sniffers" to extract useful information from network packets. Secure Shell (SSH) and similar tools are discussed further in the following section.

Although **rlogin** is the fastest kind of remote login possible, it can be easily exploited on systems that are not trusted and secure. Systems that are directly connected to the Internet, or which form part of a subnet that is not firewalled, should never be considered secure. Thus, **rlogin** can be dangerous in some circumstances, even if it is convenient for remotely administering many different machines. The most dangerous use involves /etc/hosts.equiv, when the file contains the single line:

```
+
```

This allows any users from any host that has equivalent usernames to remotely log in. The .rhosts file is also considered dangerous in some situations. For example, it is common practice in some organizations to allow the root and privileged users to permit automatic logins by root users from other machines by creating a /.rhosts file. This permits a remote user to gain root access to a remote machine—a danger in anyone's book. A more insidious problem can occur when users define their own .rhosts files in their own home directories: Such files are not directly controlled by the system administrator, and may therefore be exploited by malicious remote users. One way to remove these threats is to enforce a policy of disallowing user .rhosts files and activating a nightly **cron** job to search for and remove any files named .rhosts in the user directories.

A **cron** entry for root, like the following:

```
0 2 * * * find /staff -name .rhosts -print -exec rm{} \;
```

would execute this simple find-and-remove command every morning at 2 A.M., for all user accounts whose home directories lie underneath the /staff partition.

# Secure Tools

With the increased use of the Internet for business-to-business and consumer-to-business transactions, securing remote access has become a major issue in the provision of Solaris services. Solaris 8 comes with Kerberos 5, but not with any of the other security measures, unfortunately. Fortunately, solutions based around encryption of sessions and authentication of clients have improved the reliability of remote-access facilities in a security-conscious operating environment. The tools we'll look at here are Secure Shell (SSH), Kerberos, the Secure Remote Password protocol (SRP), and TCP wrappers.

## Secure Shell (SSH)

Secure Shell (SSH) is a secure client and server solution that facilitates the symmetric and asymmetric encryption of identification and authentication sequences for remote access. It is designed to replace the **telnet** and **rlogin** applications on the client side, with clients available for Solaris and Windows NT, and it improves upon the functionality provided by **inetd** on the server side. Figure 16-4 shows a typical SSH client session.

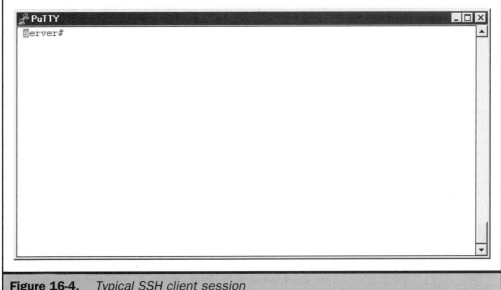

**Figure 16-4.**    *Typical SSH client session*

The secure shell makes use of a generic Transport layer encryption mechanism over TCP/IP, in many cases using the popular Blowfish or government-endorsed triple-DES algorithms. Other encryption algorithms are also supported. SSH transmits encrypted packets whose contents can still be "sniffed" like all traffic on the network—however, the contents of these packets appear to be random, without the appropriate "key" to decrypt them. The use of encryption technology makes it extremely unlikely that the contents of the interactive session will ever be known to anyone except the client and the server. In addition to the encryption of session data, identification and authentication sequences are also encrypted using RSA technology. This means that username and password combinations cannot be "sniffed" by a third party. SSH also provides automatic forwarding for graphics applications based around the X11 Windowing System, which is a substantial improvement over the text-only Telnet client.

The sequence of events for establishing an SSH client connection to a server is demonstrated in Figure 16-5, and proceeds as follows:

1. The client connects to a server port requesting a connection (usually port 22, but this can be adapted to suit local conditions).

2. The server replies with its standard public RSA host key (1024 bits), as well as another RSA "server key" (768 bits) that changes hourly. Since the server key changes hourly, then even if the key for the traffic of one session is "cracked," historic data would still remain encrypted, limiting the utility of any such attack.

3. The server can be configured to reject connections from hosts that it doesn't know about, but by default it will accept connections from any client.

4. If the connection is accepted, the client generates a session key composed of a 256-bit random number, and chooses an encryption algorithm that the server supports (3DES or Blowfish).

5. The client then encrypts the session key using RSA, using both the host key and server key, and returns the encrypted key to the server.

6. The server decrypts the session key, and encryption is enabled between the client and server.

7. If the default authentication mechanism is selected, the client then passes the username and password for the server across the secure channel.

It is possible to disable the username/password authentication sequence by permitting logins to clients that have an appropriate, private RSA key, as long as the server has a list of accepted public keys. However, if a client computer is stolen and the private key is retrieved by a rogue user, then access to the server might be obtained without a valid username and password combination, but only if the .shosts or .shosts.equiv files are used.

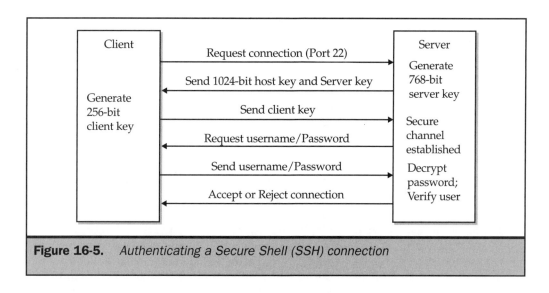

**Figure 16-5.**   *Authenticating a Secure Shell (SSH) connection*

On the client side, a knwnhsts.txt file is created, and server keys are recorded there. Entries look like:

```
server 1024 35 07448318855220650928863459182148090008748760313126632026365
56140699569229172676719815525201670198606754982042373639373659399872935084
73066069722639711474295242507691974151195842956063176626459842269220618785
53598043326806246000016982513757262927556592987704211810142126175715452796
748871506131894685401576418
```

In addition, a private key for the client is stored in Identity, and a public key for the client is stored in Identity.pub. Entries in this file are similar to the server key file:

```
1024 37 25909842022319975817366569029015041390873694788964256567214642296667226227437398365816534529060328087939018802894227642524259614636549518998450524923811481002360439473852363542223359868114619253961948185309446681933562979774158070860950587770774247373117735318506922304377996946111769127284747352249217710411151 Paul Watters
```

One of the advantages of using the commercial F-Secure version of SSH for international users is that the product was developed in Europe and does not fall under U.S. ITAR export restrictions, which limit the export of U.S.-developed encryption technology to most other countries. Both U.S. and non-U.S. users can download and install the commercial version of SSH from **http://www.datafellows.com/**, or the freeware version from **http://www.ssh.fi**.

It is sensible in a commercial context to enforce a policy of SSH-only remote access for interactive logins. This can easily be enforced by enabling the SSH daemon on the server side, and removing entries for the **telnet** and **rlogin** services in /etc/services and /etc/inetd.conf.

# Kerberos

While SSH is an excellent tool for remote access between a single client and multiple servers, maintaining local databases of keys on every client machine is costly in terms of disk space and network traffic. There is an argument that such information should always be distributed across the network, but the level of redundancy that SSH requires for installations of 1,000+ clients is inefficient. One alternative to using SSH servers as the primary means of authentication across a network is to use a centralized authentication system such as Kerberos, which grew out of the Athena Project at the Massachusetts Institute of Technology (MIT). Kerberos is a network authentication protocol that was designed to provide strong authentication for client/server applications by using secret-key cryptography.

In purpose and design Kerberos is similar to F-Secure SSH. The main difference between the two systems is that while authentication is performed by the target server when using SSH, a Kerberos authentication server can provide authorization for many services, provided by many different servers, for a large number of clients. The many-to-many relationships realized in the Kerberos authentication database makes the network authentication process more streamlined and efficient. Kerberos is also designed to provide authentication to hosts both inside and outside a firewall, since many attacks originate in internal networks that are normally considered trusted. In addition, Release 5 introduced the notion of *realms*, which are external but trusted networks, with authentication being extended beyond the firewall.

Another advantage of the Kerberos system is that the protocol has been published and widely publicized, and a free implementation (including source code) is available from MIT:

**http://web.mit.edu/network/kerberos-form.html**

The current version of Kerberos is Release 5 v1.1. Solaris 7 currently ships with authentication procedures built around Kerberos Release 4, while Solaris 8 ships with Kerberos Release 5.

Kerberos is based around a certificate-granting and validation system; the certificates are called "tickets." If a client machine wants to make a connection to a target server, it requests a ticket from a centralized authentication server, which can be physically the same machine as the target server but is logically quite separate. The encrypted ticket produced by the authentication server authorizes the client to request a specific service from a specific host, generally for a specific time period. It's similar to using a parking ticket machine that grants permission to park in a specific street for one or two hours only. Release 5 of Kerberos even supports ticket renewal.

When authentication is requested from the authentication server, that server creates a session key, which is based on your password, which it retrieves from your username, a random value that represents the requested service. The session key is like a voucher that the client then sends to a ticket-granting server, which then returns a ticket that can be used to access the target server. Clearly, there is some overhead in making a request to an authentication server, a ticket-granting server, and a target server. However, the overhead is well worth the effort if important data is at risk of interception. The sequence of events leading to authentication is shown in Figure 16-6.

Kerberos configuration is reasonably straightforward, given appropriate network resources. An /etc/krb5.conf configuration file contains entries like the following:

```
[libdefaults]
        default_realm = SITE.COM
[realms]
        SITE.COM = {
                kdc = kerberos1.site.com
                kdc = kerberos2.site.com
                admin_server = kerberos1.site.com
        }
```

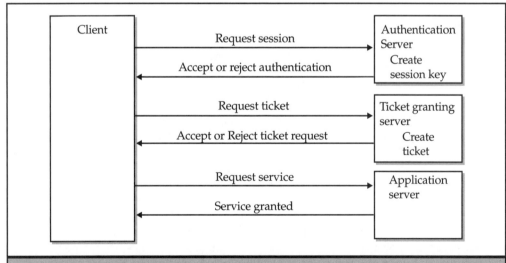

**Figure 16-6.** *Distributed mechanisms for Kerberos 5 authentication*

The preceding configuration is for a domain called site.com that has a logical admin server called kerberos1.site.com, and a backup server called kerberos2.site.com.

One disadvantage of the Kerberos system is that its legal status, with respect to the export of encryption technology, is unclear. One vendor has received permission to export a binary version of the product internationally; however, the Commerce Department considers each implementation on a case-by-case basis. For more information, see:

**ftp://ftp.cygnus.com/pub/export/export.html**

As with any security service, there are risks that should be noted before implementation. In particular, there is a known bug in **syslog**-based authentication that can lead to a possible denial-of-service attack. This has been fixed in an upcoming release; however, the potential for attacks against a centralized service remains a weak point of the Kerberos system. Even if the authentication server and target server were operational, for example, a sustained flood of requests to a ticket-granting server can halt any network-based service that requires authentication.

# SRP

The Secure Remote Password protocol (SRP) is the core technology behind the Stanford SRP Authentication Project. The Project is an Open Source initiative that integrates secure password authentication into existing networked applications. The Project's primary purpose is to improve network security from the ground up, by integrating secure password authentication into widely used protocols instead of adding security as an afterthought. SRP makes these objectives possible because it offers a unique combination of password security and user convenience, and because it is free of intellectual property encumbrances.

First and foremost, SRP is a strong password authentication protocol. It was designed as a solution to the age-old problem of deploying logins and passwords in a distributed system across networks that might be monitored or compromised by adversaries. While the strongest version of SRP, known as SRP-3, performs very well in such a role, it is also versatile enough to serve in other capacities, perhaps most notably as a zero-knowledge identification protocol. This latter type of protocol is highly desirable, as it does not leak information about the password even to a legitimate host, and thus provides protection against both passive snooping and active host impersonation. SRP also provides an asymmetric key-exchange protocol (i.e., secure key exchange is provided, but does not require both parties to share secrets before the exchange takes place).

SRP is the newest addition to a new class of strong authentication protocols that resist all the well-known passive and active attacks over the network. It generates keys that are cryptographically strong. It is also safe against snooping, since the password is never passed over the network, either in the clear or encrypted. This is in contrast to SSH, which enables an encrypted exchange of passwords across the network. By use of a session key, similar to the approach taken by Kerberos, intruders using a compromised password will not be allowed to decrypt past sessions because it is time locked. Technically, SRP is quite simple since it is based on exponentiation, addition, multiplication, and hashing, all of which are easily understood and implemented. SRP is also fast; typical unoptimized implementations have been shown to take under a second to complete authentication.

SRP addresses a fairly specific class of hard password authentication problems, namely that of authenticating a network user to a server host, both of which reside on a network susceptible to both passive and active attacks and are subject to several constraints. Unlike Kerberos, no third party is involved in the authentication process. Also, the system only supports password authentication, unlike F-Secure SSH, which supports either passwords or certificate-based authentication.

Like many of the products we've looked at in this chapter, Solaris does not include SRP in the standard distribution, but the current SRP distribution can be downloaded from **http://srp.stanford.edu/** and compiled.

## TCP Wrappers

While the security measures we have examined so far have been concerned with directly modifying the identification and authentication sequences used by clients to access server resources, there is an important aspect of evaluating security that we have neglected: access logging. As the first step in developing a secure access policy, logging access information can reveal whether an organization's networks have an authentication problem. In addition, specific instances of unauthorized access to various resources can be collated, and using statistical methods, can be assessed for regular patterns of abuse. Monitoring of log files can also be used by applications to accept or reject connections, based on historical data contained in centralized logging mechanisms provided under Solaris, such as the **syslogd** system logging daemon.

One reason why access monitoring is not often discussed is that implementations of the standard UNIX network daemons that are spawned by the Internet super server **inetd** (discussed earlier) do not have a provision to write directly to a syslog file. Later Internet service daemons, such as the Apache web server, run as standalone services not requiring **inetd**, but have enhanced logging facilities that are used to track web-site usage.

Wietse Venema's TCP wrappers is a popular method of enabling daemons launched from **inetd** to log their accepted and rejected connections, since the wrapper programs that are installed for each service do not require alteration to existing binary software distributions or to existing configuration files. TCP wrappers can be downloaded in source form from the following:

**ftp://ftp.porcupine.org/pub/security/index.html**

In their simplest form, TCP wrappers are used for monitoring only, but they could be used to build better applications that can reject connections on the basis of failed connections. For example, a flood of requests to log in using **rsh** from an untrusted host could be terminated after three failed attempts from a single host. TCP wrappers work by compiling a replacement daemon that points to the "real" daemon file, often located in a subdirectory below the daemon wrappers. The wrappers log the date and time of a service request, with a client hostname and an indication of whether the request was rejected or accepted. The current version of TCP wrappers as of this writing (Release 7.6) supports the SVR4 (System V Release 4) TLI network programming interface under Solaris, which has equivalent functionality to the Berkeley socket programming interface. In addition, the latest release supports access control and detection of host address or hostname spoofing. The latter is particularly important in the context of authentication services that provide access to services based on IP subnet ranges or specific hostnames in a local area network: If these are spoofed and access is granted to a rogue client, then the entire security infrastructure has failed. It is critical to detect and reject any unauthorized connections at any early stage, and TCP wrappers are an integral part of this mechanism. The sequence of events involved in logging TCP connections is shown in Figure 16-7.

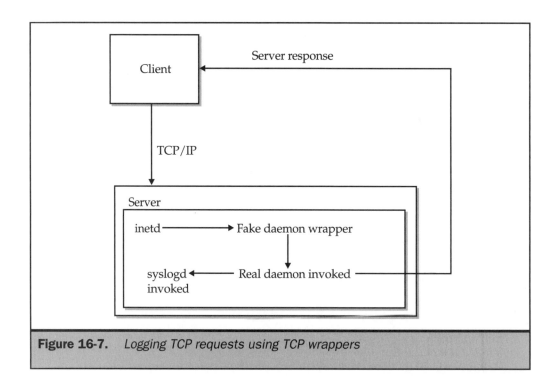

**Figure 16-7.** *Logging TCP requests using TCP wrappers*

When writing access information to syslog, the output looks like the following:

```
Nov 18 11:00:52 server in.telnetd[1493]: connect from client.site.com
Nov 18 11:25:03 server in.telnetd[1510]: connect from workstation.site.com
Nov 18 11:25:22 server in.telnetd[1511]: connect from client.site.com
Nov 18 12:16:30 server in.ftpd[1556]: connect from workstation.site.com
```

These entries indicate that between 11:00 A.M. and 12:16 P.M. on November 18, clients connected using **telnet** from client.site.com and workstation.site.com. In addition, there was an FTP connection from workstation.site.com. Although we've only examined wrappers for **in.ftpd** and **in.telnetd**, wrappers can be compiled for most services launched from **inetd**, including **finger**, **talk**, **tftp** (trivial ftp), and **rsh** (remote shell).

# Syslog

As we've seen in the previous section, centralized authentication usually requires some form of centralized logging of rejected and accepted service requests. The Solaris system log daemon (**syslogd**) is optimized to provide this logging on a per-machine or per-site basis, the latter requiring a dedicated loghost declared in /etc/hosts. In this section, we'll examine the role of **syslogd** in recording remote-access requests.

## What Is Syslog?

Syslog is a centralized logging facility that provides different classes of events that are logged to a logfile, as well as providing an alerting service for certain events. Since **syslogd** is configurable by root, it is very flexible in its operations. Multiple log files can exist for each daemon whose activity is being logged, or a single logfile can be created. The Syslog service is controlled by the configuration file /etc/syslog.conf, which is read at boot time, or whenever the Syslog daemon receives a HUP signal. This file defines the facility levels or system source of logged messages and conditions. Priority levels are also assigned to system events recorded in the system log, while an action field defines what action is taken when a particular class of events is encountered. These events can range from normal system usage, such as FTP connections and remote shells, to system crashes.

   The source facilities defined by Solaris are for the kernel (kern), authentication (auth), daemons (daemon), mail system (mail), print spooling (lp), and user processes (user). Priority levels are classified as system emergencies (emerg), errors requiring immediate attention (attn), critical errors (crit), messages (info), debugging output (debug), and other errors (err). These priority levels are defined for individual systems and architectures in /usr/include/sys/syslog.h. It is easy to see how logging applications, such as TCP wrappers, can take advantage of the different error levels and source facilities provided by **syslogd**.

On the Solaris platform, the Syslog daemon depends on the m4 macro processor being present. m4 is typically installed with the software developer packages, and is usually located in /usr/ccs/bin/m4. This version has been installed by default since Solaris 2.4. Users should note that the **syslogd** supplied by Sun has been error prone in previous releases: With early Solaris 2.x versions, the Syslog daemon left behind zombie processes when alerting logged-in users (for example, when notifying root of an emerg). In addition, the **syslogd** supplied in Solaris 2.6 is reportedly unstable, and patch 106439 should be installed. If **syslogd** does not work, check that m4 exists and is in the path for root, and/or run the **syslogd** program interactively by invoking it with a **-d** parameter.

# Examining Log Files

Log files are fairly straightforward in their contents, and what events are recorded can be stipulated by instructions in the syslog.conf file (reviewed in the following section). Records of mail messages can be useful for billing purposes and for detecting the bulk sending of unsolicited commercial email (SPAM). The system log will record the details supplied by **sendmail**: a message ID, the time when the message is sent or received, the destination, and the delivery result, which is typically either "delivered" or "deferred." This entry would appear in the log of the sending host (not the receiving host). Connections are usually deferred when a connection to a site is down. **sendmail** will usually try to redeliver failed deliveries in four-hour intervals.

When using TCP wrappers, connections to supported Internet daemons are also logged. For example, an FTP connection to a server will result in the connection time and date being recorded, along with the hostname of the client. A similar result is achieved for Telnet connections.

A delivered mail message is recorded as follows:

```
Feb 20 14:07:05 server sendmail[238]: AA00238:
message-id=<bulk.11403.19990219175554@sun.com>
Feb 20 14:07:05 server sendmail[238]: AA00238: from=<sun-developers-l@sun.com>,
size=1551, class=0, received from gateway.site.com (172.16.1.1)
Feb 20 14:07:06 server sendmail[243]: AA00238: to=<pwatters@mail.site.com>,
delay=00:00:01, stat=Sent, mailer=local
```

while a deferred mail message is recorded differently:

```
Feb 21 07:11:10 server sendmail[855]: AA00855:
message-id=<Pine.SOL.3.96.990220200723.5291A-100000@oracle.com>
Feb 21 07:11:10 server sendmail[855]: AA00855: from=<support@oracle.com>,
size=1290, class=0, received from gateway.site.com (172.16.1.1)
Feb 21 07:12:25 server sendmail[857]: AA00855: to=pwatters@mail.site.com,
delay=00:01:16, stat=Deferred: Connection timed out during user open with
mail.site.com, mailer=TCP
```

An FTP connection is recorded in a single line:

```
Feb 20 14:35:00 server in.ftpd[277]: connect from workstation.site.com
```

in the same way that a Telnet connection is recorded:

```
Feb 20 14:35:31 server in.telnetd[279]: connect from workstation.site.com
```

# The syslog.conf File

The file /etc/syslog.conf contains information used by the system log daemon, **syslogd**, to forward a system message to appropriate log files and/or users. **syslogd** preprocesses this file through m4 to obtain the correct information for certain log files, defining LOGHOST if the address of loghost is the same as one of the addresses of the host that is running **syslogd**.

The default **syslogd** configuration is not optimal for all installations. Many configuration decisions depend on when the system administrator wishes to be alerted should an alert or emergency occur, or whether it is sufficient for all **auth** notices to be logged, and a **cron** job run every night to filter the results for a review in the morning. For noncommercial installations, the latter is probably a reasonable approach. A **crontab** entry like the following:

```
0 1 * * * cat /var/adm/messages | grep auth | mail root
```

will send the root user a mail message at 1 A.M. every morning with all authentication messages.

A basic syslog.conf should contain provisions for sending emergency notices to all users, as well as alerts to the root user, and other nonprivileged administrator accounts. Errors, kernel notices, and authentication notices probably need to be displayed on the system console (in OpenWindows, a console can be created with **cmdtool -C**). It is generally sufficient to log daemon notices, alerts, and all other authentication information to the system log file, unless the administrator is directly and actively watching for cracking attempts.

```
*.alert                                      root,pwatters
*.emerg                                      *
*.err;kern.notice;auth.notice                /dev/console
daemon.notice                                /var/adm/messages
auth.none;kern.err;daemon.err;mail.crit;*.alert   /var/adm/messages
auth.info                                    /var/adm/authlog
```

## Monitoring System Access

System access can be monitored interactively using a number of measures. For example, syslog entries can be automatically viewed in real time by using the command:

**client% tail -f /var/adm/messages**

However, most administrators want to be able to occasionally interactively view what their remote users are doing on a system at any one time. Process-viewing commands are covered in Chapter 5, but here we will examine two methods for viewing remote user activity. The command **who** displays who is currently logged in to the system. The output of **who** displays the username, connecting line, date of login, idle time, process ID, and a comment. Here's an example:

**client% who | more**

```
root        console      Nov 22 12:39
pwatters     pts/0        Nov 19 21:05      (client.site.com)
```

This command can be automated to update the list of active users. An alternative to **who** is the **w** command, which displays a more detailed summary of the current activity on the system, including the current process name for each user. The header output from **w** shows the current time, the uptime of the current system, and the number of users actively logged in to the system. The average system load is also displayed as a series of three numbers at the end of the **w** header, indicating the average number of jobs in the run queue for the previous 1, 5, and 15 minutes. In addition to the output generated by **who**, the **w** command displays the current foreground process for each user, which is usually a shell. For example, the following output:

```
root    console    Thu12pm 3days     6     6 /usr/openwin/bin/shelltool
pwatters   pts/12    Thu11am  8:45     9       /usr/local/bin/tcsh
```

shows that the root user has an active **shelltool** running under OpenWindows, while the user pwatters is running the Cornell shell, **tcsh**. The **w** and **who** commands are very useful tools for getting an overview of current and historical usage patterns on any Solaris system.

## Summary

In this chapter, we have examined the traditional UNIX tools for remote access, and also the installation and configuration of more secure replacements for these tools. As the Internet is used more and more for e-commerce and distributed development of commercially sensitive applications, it is critical that a proper security infrastructure is in place to reduce attacks by rogue users and competitors on networked servers. While Solaris does not by default always provide the tools required, its design allows for improved configuration and installation versions of TCP daemons. In addition, Solaris provides sophisticated logging facilities for all network-related activities. These are important for auditing purposes, and can be combined with third-party logging software like the TCP wrapper package to provide total coverage.

## How to Find Out More

The best location on the Internet for learning about network and host security is the CERT web site at **http://www.cert.org/**. Here you will find information on the latest security holes that have been discovered in popular applications and commonly used system services, as well as links to vendor-provided patches. The Usenet forum comp.unix.security also contains a valuable discussion of security issues as they relate to Solaris and other UNIX systems.

ADMINISTERING
SERVICES

# The Complete Reference

Solaris 8

# Chapter 17

## Sharing Files with UNIX Systems Using NFS

The Network File System (NFS) is a distributed file system that provides transparent access to remote disks, allowing you to centralize the administration of disks. Instead of depending on the administrator to duplicate common directories or install software on every system, NFS allows the administrator to use a single copy of a directory that can be shared by all systems on the network. To a host that accesses an NFS directory, the remote file systems are indistinguishable from local file systems—that's what the "transparent" means in transparent access. There is no need to copy or **ftp** files from one system to another, as remote files appear automatically as part of the local directory structure.

NFS is built on the Remote Procedure Call (RPC) protocol, which uses a client/server model—where the server owns a resource and the client uses or requests access to that resource. In the case of NFS, the resource is a *file system*. An NFS server is a host that makes one or more of its file systems available on the network. An NFS client is a host that accesses a file system of an NFS server. In this chapter we will look at setting up both an NFS server and an NFS client. We will also look at a program called the automounter that allows machines to automatically mount and access NFS server file systems on demand. Finally, since many print spool systems are shared using NFS, we review the installation and configuration of local and remote printing systems.

## What Is NFS?

NFS, the Network File System, is a distributed file system designed by Sun Microsystems in the mid-1980s that enables machines from different UNIX vendors to share information. A distributed file system is one in which files are stored on one or more computers called servers and are accessed by other computers called clients. To the clients, the files located on the servers appear to be local files. The main advantages of a distributed file system are as follows:

- Files are more widely available, because many computers can access the servers, and sharing the files from a single location is easier than distributing copies of files to individual clients. This allows large number of users to easily share documents and applications.

- Backups and the safety of the information are easier to arrange, because only the servers need to be backed up.

- The servers can provide large storage space, which might be costly or impractical on every client.

Although those are strong advantages, distributed file systems introduce a few problems:

- Transporting many files over the network can easily create sluggish performance: latency, network bottlenecks, and server overload can result. The performance of NFS depends on the network type and topology as well.

- The security of data becomes an important issue, because it is essential to ensure that a client is really authorized to have access to information that it requests from the server.

- The reliability of the network and the servers is also very important, because although client computers may be more reliable than the network connecting them, network failures can render a client useless.

Sun designed NFS to deal with each of these problems, and also designed it to provide an easy-to-use and administer system. Originally NFS was available only on systems that used SunOS, but in the late 1980s Sun made the specifications freely available, and this motivated all major UNIX vendors to provide NFS with their systems. There are also many free implementations available, most notably the FreeBSD and Linux versions. NFS is now the standard for sharing files in UNIX environments, and there has been a considerable amount of work put into making it compatible with other systems like Windows NT, NetWare, and the Mac OS. The main reasons for the popularity of NFS over other distributed file systems are its wide availability and its ease of setup and administration.

Another aspect of NFS that has its advantages is its *stateless design*: The server does not need to know how one sequence of NFS operations relates to another; instead, it is up to the client to keep track of all of that information. Since the server does not have to worry about tracking transactions, if it needs to reboot it can do so with little effect on a client. The client just waits for the server to come back up. When it does, it issues all of the NFS requests that it had waiting.

The first version of the NFS in wide use was version 2, which continues to be available on a large variety of platforms. Solaris used version 2 of the NFS protocol until Solaris 2.5. NFS version 2 used the UDP transport protocol, which, due to the low overhead associated with UDP, made it efficient in a local area networking environment. However, because of the connectionless nature of UDP, NFS did not perform well over wide area networking links. Further, NFS versions lacked several security features (also due to the UDP protocol). The NFS version 3 provided with Solaris 8 supports both the TCP and the UDP transport protocols, and, by default, Solaris 8 NFS servers and client are configured to use both. However, NFS can be specified as necessary to run only on TCP and UDP.

## Why Use NFS?

Any Solaris system can share any of its file systems with other systems, making them available for remote mounting. NFS considers the system that shares the file system to be a server, and the system that remotely mounts the file system as a client. When a NFS client mounts a remote file system, it is connected to a mount point on the local file system, which means it appears to local users as just another file system. For example, a system called parkville may make its mail directory /var/mail available for remote mounting by NFS clients. This would allow users on machines like essendon, brunswick and upfield to read their mail stored actually on parkville to be read locally from their own machines, without their having to explicitly log in to parkville. This means that a single mail server that acts as a NFS server can serve all NFS clients on a local area network with mail. Figure 17-1 shows this configuration.

However, one important aspect of NFS is the ability to export file systems and mount them on a remote mount point that is different to the original shared directory. For example, the NFS server parkville may also export its Sun Answerbook files (from the directory /opt/answerbook) to the clients brunswick, essendon, and upfield. However, brunswick mounts these files in the /usr/local/www/htdocs directory, as it publishes them via the world wide web, whilst essendon mounts them in /opt/doc/answerbook. The client upfield mounts them in /opt/answerbook, just like they are exported from parkville. The point is that the remote mount point can be completely different to the actual directory exported by an NFS server. This configuration is shown in Figure 17-2.

## The NFS Daemons

For NFS to work properly, several processes must be running on the servers and the client. On the server side, three daemons are run: **nfsd**, **mountd**, and **statd**. On the client side, two daemons are run: **statd** and **lockd**. On Solaris 8 you will find the daemons to be located in the /usr/lib/nfs folder by default. Table 17-1 provides the purpose of each daemon.

## The Remote Procedure Call Protocol

NFS uses a special feature of UNIX known as Remote Procedure Calls (RPC). Although Sun designed RPC specifically for NFS, RPC is widely deployed and used

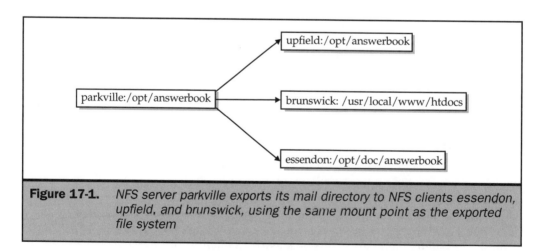

**Figure 17-1.**   *NFS server parkville exports its mail directory to NFS clients essendon, upfield, and brunswick, using the same mount point as the exported file system*

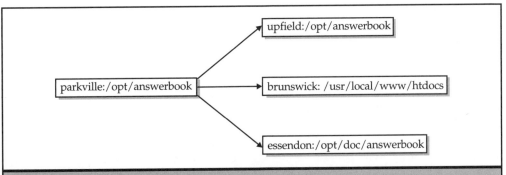

**Figure 17-2.** *NFS server parkville exports its mail directory to NFS clients essendon, upfield, and brunswick, using their own mount points*

| Daemon | Purpose |
|---|---|
| **Daemons started by /etc/init.d/nfs.server** | |
| nfsd | Processes requests from NFS clients. |
| mountd | Answers requests for NFS access information and file system mount requests. |
| **Daemons started by /etc/init.d/nfs.client** | |
| lockd | Controls network file-locking operations. It sends locking requests from the client to the NFS server. |
| statd | Interacts with lockd to provide the crash and recovery functions for the locking services. lockd tracks the clients that have locks on an NFS server. In the event of a server crash, after rebooting the statd on the server contacts statd on the client. The client statd can attempt to reclaim locks on the server. |

**Table 17-1.** *NFS Daemons*

by many other programs across a wide variety of operating systems, including Windows NT. By using RPC, NFS allows you to read and write files that reside on NFS servers transparently.

RPC is a protocol that one program can use to request a service from a program located on another computer on the network without having to understand network details. A procedure call is similar to a function call or a subroutine call. RPC provides a mechanism whereby the kernel picks a port when the service starts up, which is then registered with the RPC port mapper daemon. The daemon responsible for RPC, **rpcbind**, runs on both the server and the client. The RPC port mapper daemon uses port 111 (TCP or UDP). All clients requesting access to the service will request the port information from the port mapper. The port mapper replies with the number of the ephemeral port registered by the service. The client then proceeds by establishing connection with the service.

# Setting Up an NFS Server

If you would like to share file systems on your machine with other computers, you can set up your machine as an NFS server. In NFS terminology, when you allow other computers to share a file system it is called *exporting the file system*. An NFS server does not advertise the file systems that it has exported; rather, it keeps a list of currently exported file systems and checks this list each time it receives a request for a file system. This allows you to change the list of exported file systems in real time.

The list of currently exported file systems can also contain information about access restrictions. For example, this information can be used to protect certain file systems from being accessed by particular hosts, such as when a file system contains software that only licensed users are permitted to use.

 *Unless otherwise specified, the NFS-specific commands covered in this section assume that you have the directory /usr/sbin in your path.*

## Starting and Stopping the NFS Server

In the standard Solaris installation, the NFS server is started as part of the boot processes. When your system reaches runlevel 3, the NFS server is started by the script /etc/rc3.d/ S15nfs.server. Normally you will not have to start and stop the NFS server directly, but in a small number of instances you may have to start a crashed NFS server or stop a nonresponding one. You can do this via the NFS init script located at /etc/init.d/nfs.server.

The nfs server daemon is usually located in /etc/init.d/nfs.server. A typical initialization Bourne shell script looks like:

```
#!/bin/sh
killproc() {                 # kill the named process(es)
     pid=`/usr/bin/ps -e |
         /usr/bin/grep -w $1 |
         /usr/bin/sed -e 's/^  *//' -e 's/ .*//'`
     [ "$pid" != "" ] && kill $pid
}
# Start/stop processes required for server NFS
case "$1" in
'start')
     # Clean up /etc/dfs/sharetab - remove all nfs entries
     if [ -f /etc/dfs/sharetab ] ; then
         /usr/bin/awk '$3 != "nfs"' /etc/dfs/sharetab |
         /usr/bin/sed -e 's/ / /' > /tmp/sharetab
         mv /tmp/sharetab /etc/dfs/sharetab
         chmod 644 /etc/dfs/sharetab
     fi
     [ -f /etc/dfs/dfstab ] && /usr/sbin/shareall -F nfs
     if grep -s nfs /etc/dfs/sharetab >/dev/null ; then
         /usr/lib/nfs/nfsd -a 16
         /usr/lib/nfs/mountd
     fi

'stop')
     killproc nfsd
     killproc mountd
     killproc rpc.boot
     killproc in.rarpd
     if grep -s nfs /etc/dfs/sharetab >/dev/null ; then
         /usr/sbin/unshareall -F nfs
     fi
     ;;
*)
     echo "Usage: /etc/init.d/nfs.server { start | stop }"
     ;;
esac
```

When the NFS server starts up, any existing entries in /etc/dfs/sharetab are deleted—this is probably not a good idea, unless any existing NFS server daemons have already been killed. Next, nfsd and mountd are started: If nfsd is running, mountd must also be running to ensure that the NFS server can respond to requests,

**ADMINISTERING SERVICES**

otherwise the server will hang. Booting by trivial ftp is started if enabled, using in.rarpd, the Reverse Address Resolution Protocol daemon, which finds IP addresses, and rpc.bootparamd, the boot parameter server. If using bootparamd, the kernel is retrieved across the network by a diskless client using NFS, and is executed during booting. The Network Booting RPL (Remote Program Load) Server, which supports network booted x86 clients, is also loaded if configured.

When the "stop" parameter is passed to the script, the NFS server is shut down. This terminates whichever of the nfsd, mountd, rpc.boot, in.rarpd, and rpld processes are active, and unshares any NFS volumes that are currently shared to remote clients.

## Starting the NFS Server Directly

To start the server manually, enter the following command as root:

> **# /etc/init.d/nfs.server start**

Once the script returns you can check to see if the NFS server is running by using the following command:

> **$ /bin/ps -ef | grep "nfsd | mountd"**

The output should look like the following:

```
root 19956      1  0 11:13:18 ?        0:00 /usr/lib/nfs/nfsd -a 16
root 19958      1  0 11:13:22 ?        0:00 /usr/lib/nfs/mountd
```

If you receive no output or if your output contains a line for only **mountd** or **nfsd**, then your NFS server has not started correctly. You can start these processes manually by issuing the following command:

> **# /usr/lib/nfs/nfsd -a 16 -p tcp && /usr/lib/nfs/mountd**

In the above command, the **-a** option limits the number of consecutive connections to 16, and the **-p** option specifies that the TCP transport protocol be used. You very rarely need to start the NFS server in this manner (by starting mountd separately from nfsd). In older versions of Solaris (before 2.5.1) it was more common, but in current versions it is almost never required.

## Stopping the NFS Server Directly

Stopping the NFS server is similar to starting it:

> **# /etc/init.d/nfs.server stop**

The stop script usually stops the server, but you can confirm this using the command:

> **$ /bin/ps -ef | grep "nfsd | mountd"**

This is the same command that is used to check if the server is running; if the server is in fact stopped this command should not produce any output. If there is output, and a line for **nfsd** or **mountd** appears in the output, then the NFS server has not stopped correctly, and you should execute the NFS server stop command again.

# Exporting File Systems

To export a file system so that NFS clients can access it, you will need to use the **share** command. The basic syntax of this command is as follows:

```
share -F nfs [-o options] [-d "description"] [pathname]
```

The **-o** flag is used to indicate to **share** that one or more export options will be specified. The export options are discussed in the next section. If you do not want to specify any export options, you can omit the **-o** flag.

The **-d** flag is used to indicate you are including a human readable *description* of the file system you are exporting. Normally the *description* is a short string that describes the contents of the file system that you are exporting. In general it is a good idea to include a description for every exported file system, in order to gives users and other administrators a good idea about the contents. If you really don't want to describe a particular file system, you can omit the **-d** flag. Some of the examples in this section omit this flag for the sake of brevity.

The *pathname* is the name of the directory you want to export. The pathname must be specified, or **share** will generate an error message.

As an example, the following **share** command:

**# share -F nfs -d "GNU Tools" /export/FSF**

exports the file system /export/FSF, which, according to its description, contains GNU tools. As indicated by the prompt (#), **share** commands must be executed as root, because root is the only user that has the required permissions for exporting file systems.

## Export Options
The **share** command supports several options that can be used to control access to an exported file system:

- ■ **rw**   Allows read and write access to an exported file system.
- ■ **ro**   Allows read-only access to an exported file system.
- ■ **anon**   Allows you to map requests by unknown user IDs to a known user ID.
- ■ **root**   Treats requests by root on NFS client as requests by root on the server.
- ■ **nosuid**   Disables the set-uid bit for executables.

ADMINISTERING
SERVICES

**Read and Write Access**   Normally when a directory is exported as an NFS file system, it is accessible to every host on your network. Also, any hosts that request access to the file system will be able to read and write files on it. In most cases, however, this level of access to an NFS file system is undesired. For example, if you are exporting directories containing only executable programs and man pages, there is no need for users that access this file system via NFS to be able to write files on this file system.

In order to restrict the hosts that can read and write files on a file system, you need to specify the **rw** option for those machines specifically. The syntax is as follows:

```
-o rw=hostname1:hostname2:…
```

Here *hostname1* and *hostname2* are the names of machines that can mount the file system with read and write permissions. For example the following **share** command exports the /export/home/jdoe directory with read and write permissions for the hosts red.paulwatters.com and srv-ppc:

> # share -F nfs -o rw=red.paulwatters.com:srv-ppc /export/home/jdoe

You can specify as many hosts as you want by separating each hostname with a colon (:). The hostnames can be fully qualified hostnames or relative hostnames, as the previous example demonstrates: The hostname red.paulwatters.com is fully qualified, whereas the hostname srv-ppc is relative to the current domain. In addition to hostnames, you can also specify domain names. By specifying a domain name, every machine in that domain can access your exported file system. The **share** command assumes that you are specifying a domain name if the first character of the name is the dot character ( . ). For example, the following **share** command:

> # share -F nfs -o rw=.paulwatters.com /export/home/jdoe

exports the file system /export/home/jdoe with read and write permissions to all machines in the .paulwatters.com domain.

**Read-Only Access**   In most cases you do not want NFS clients that are accessing your exported file systems to modify the contents of those file systems. Normally, clients will only need to read the files located on the file system. A common example of this would be exported file systems that contain precompiled binaries, man pages, or other files that should not be altered by anyone. In these cases you can make all access to that file system read-only using the **ro** option. In its simplest form, it limits all accesses to the exported file system as read-only:

```
-o ro
```

Similar to the **rw** option, if you want to limit read-only access to a limited set of machines, you can specify the list of hostnames that should have that access as follows:

> `-o ro=hostname1:hostname2:…`

Here *hostname1* and *hostname2* are the names of machines that will have read-only access to the file system. Only those machines whose hostnames appear in this list will be allowed to access the exported file system. All other machines will be denied access. One of the common uses of this form of the command is to allow access to licensed software. If a particular piece of software is licensed for use on only certain machines, you can use this option to prevent other machines from accessing that software.

As an example of using the **ro** option, the following **share** command exports the directory /export/FSF with read-only permissions for the hosts vnatu-ultra and lgroth-ultra:

**# share -F nfs -o ro=vnatu-ultra:lgroth-ultra /export/FSF**

In addition to hostnames, you can also restrict access to particular domains as follows:

**# share -F nfs ro=.eng.paulwatters.com -d "GNU Tools" /export/FSF**

Here the file system /export/FSF can be accessed, with read-only permissions, only by hosts whose fully qualified hostname ends in .eng.paulwatters.com.

**Combining Options**    Most of the time, the **ro** and **rw** options by themselves will not be enough to satisfy your needs. Often a file system will need to be exported with read and write permissions for a small number of hosts, and read-only permission to a large number of hosts. You can accomplish this by combining the **rw** and **ro** options. You can combine any of the export options, using the following syntax:

> `-o option1=arguments1,option2=arguments2,…`

Here *option1* is the first export option, and *arguments1* are the arguments to that option. Similarly *option2* is the second NFS export option and *arguments2* are its arguments. A comma is used to separate the options. You can specify as many options as you want. The following example demonstrates combining options:

**# share -F nfs rw=srv-ultra:srv-ss10,ro=.eng.paulwatters.com /export/FSF**

This command exports the file system /usr/FSF with read and write permissions to the hosts srv-ultra and srv-ss10. It also allows any machine in the .eng.paulwatters.com domain to access the file system with read-only permissions.

Usually, a **share** command like this indicates that the administrator who is responsible for the contents of the exported file system normally performs updates from a different machine. In this case, the administrator might be using the machines srv-ultra and srv-ss10 to compile and test software before updating the contents in the directory /export/FSF. In order to update the contents, these machines need read and write permissions. Other machines on the .eng.paulwatters.comnetwork that access this file system only need to use the files it contains, so we allow these hosts to access the volume with read-only permission. All other hosts are denied access.

**The anon Option**    The **anon** export option allows you to specify the user ID that the NFS server should use when a user whose user ID is unknown to the server attempts an operation. Its syntax is as follows:

```
-o anon=uid
```

Here *uid* is the user ID that the server should use when the NFS server receives a request from a user with an unknown user ID. Normally, the user ID for the user nobody is used, because nobody has the lowest permissions on a system. You can specify any user ID here. Normally you should not specify a privileged user ID (any user ID less than 100). If you specify the user ID of –1, requests from unknown user IDs will be rejected by NFS server. Because 0 is the user ID of the root user, the export option should not be set with *anon=0*. Doing so will result in providing the unknown user ID with root-level access to the NFS file system.

**The root Option**    By default, any requests made by root on a remote machine are mapped to the user nobody by the NFS server. This prevents the system administrator of one machine from accidentally or intentionally modifying files and directories that are exported with read and write permission. In some special cases, requests made by root should be treated the same as operations done as root on the local machine. Usually this is the case when an NFS server is used as a repository for software, but the software is compiled and maintained by an administrator on a different machine. When the administrator goes to update the software, any modifications made as root should be treated as if they were made by root on the NFS server. You can allow this by using the **root** export option. Its syntax is as follows:

```
-o root=hostname1:hostname2:…
```

Here *hostname1* and *hostname2* are the names of machines. For example, the following **share** command exports the directory /export/FSF with read and write permission and root access enabled for the host srv-ultra:

# **share -F nfs -o rw=srv-ultra,root=srv-ultra /export/FSF**

Similar to the **rw** and **ro** options, a network name can be specified instead of a hostname.
You can also combine the **root** option with other options. For example, the following command:

# **share -F nfs -o rw=srv-ultra,root=srv-ultra,ro=.eng.paulwatters.com /export/FSF**

exports the file system /export/FSF with read and write permission and root access for the machine srv-ultra, while allowing hosts in the .eng.paulwatters.com network to access the file system with read-only permission.

If you specify a host in the list of hosts with the **root** option enabled, it does not automatically enable any of the other options. A host has the same access permissions regardless of whether or not the **root** option is specified. The next two examples should help to clarify this. The following **share** command:

> **# share -F nfs -o ro=vnatu-ultra,root=srv-ss10 /export/FSF**

prevents the host srv-ss10 from accessing the directory /export/FSF, even though it has root permission. The following **share** command gives read-only permissions to srv-ss10:

> **# share -F nfs -o ro=srv-ss10,root=srv-ss10 -d "GNU Tools" /usr/FSF**

**Disabling SetUID**    The last export option we will look at is the **nosuid** option. This option allows you to turn off the set-uid bit for files, which allows applications to be executed as a privileged user. It is specified as follows:

```
-o nosuid
```

If this option is enabled, then the set uid bit is ignored on files. It also prevents clients of the NFS server from enabling the set-uid bit on files. Unless you have extremely special programs that require the set uid bit enabled, most NFS export file systems should have this option enabled. Remember, the setuid bit in the file permissions specifies that the *program* will be run as the owner of the program file, and not the *user* running the program. If you are a security-conscious individual, then this option will prevent the running and/or creation of set-uid program files.

## Checking Exported File Systems

Once you export a file system using the **share** command, you should verify that it has been exported correctly. The simplest way to do this is with the command:

> **$ showmount -e**

The output will be similar to the following:

```
export list for brunswick:
/export/FSF .paulwatters.com
```

The first line gives the hostname of the NFS server; in this case it is a machine named brunswick. All of the other lines list the pathname of the exported file system in the first column, and the list of hosts that have access to it in the second column. In this case there is only one exported file system, /export/FSF, and it is available to hosts in the paulwatters.com domain. As the $ prompt indicates, the **showmount** command can be executed by ordinary users.

If you have a file system exported for access to all hosts, the output for that file system will look like the following:

```
/store/pub                  (everyone)
```

If you don't have any file systems exported, the output looks like the following:

```
no exported file systems for brunswick
```

You can also use the **showmount** command to check the list of exported file systems on any NFS server by specifying its *hostname* as follows:

```
$ showmount -e hostname
```

For example, the following command:

**$ showmount -e parkville**

lists the exported file systems on the NFS server parkville:

```
/store/pub                  (everyone)
/store/home                 brunswick,red,melkote
```

The initial list of exported file systems is created when the NFS daemons are started at boot time. It is based on the entries stored in the file /etc/dfs/dfstab. This file contains a list of **share** commands to execute. Sometimes the **showmount** command may display an error message as follows:

**$ showmount -e brunswick**

```
showmount: brunswick: RPC: Program not registered
```

This error message indicates that the NFS daemons on the server brunswick are not running. To fix the problem, confirm that the **nfsd** and the **mountd** daemons are running on the server brunswick.

The **dfshares** command provides similar functionality to **showmount**. It lists available resources from remote or local systems. By itself, **dfshares** displays all resources that are currently shared on the local system.

**$ dfshares**

```
RESOURCE                                   SERVER ACCESS    TRANSPORT
brunswick:/opt2                              brunswick   -        -
```

If hostnames are provided, then **dfshares** shows the file systems shared by the hosts:

**# dfshares parkville green**

```
RESOURCE                             SERVER ACCESS    TRANSPORT
parkville:/home                       parkville   rw=brunswick,green    -
green:/cdrom                        parkville   ro=brunswick,parkville    -
```

You can also list the clients that are mounting the shared resources by running the **dfmounts** command:

**# dfmounts**

```
RESOURCE      SERVER PATHNAME              CLIENTS
   -            brunswick /opt2             green,parkville
```

## "Unexporting" File Systems

If you need to unexport (undo the export of) a file system that you have exported using the **share** command, you will need to use the **unshare** command. Its syntax is:

```
# unshare pathname
```

Here *pathname* is the pathname of an exported file system. As the # prompt indicates, only root has permission to unexport file systems. As an example, the following command unexports the previously exported file system /export/FSF:

**# unshare /export/FSF**

You can check to see if the operation succeeded by using **showmount**. In this case there was only one exported file system, so the message is as follows:

**# showmount -e**

```
no exported file systems for brunswick
```

If you specify a file system that is not exported, **unshare** will report an error similar to the following:

**# unshare /export/games**

```
nfs unshare: /export/games: not shared
```

## Initialing the List of NFS Exports

If you are responsible for an NFS server, entering the **share** commands to export file systems every time your machine reboots would be extremely time consuming. Fortunately, when NFS starts up it executes a set of **share** commands stored in the file /etc/dfs/dfstab. It can contain as many **share** commands as you need. Unless you need to export a file system temporarily, you should place all your **share** commands into this file rather than issuing them on the command line. Here is a short example of this file:

```
# /etc/dfs/dfstab - file systems to export when NFS starts.
share -F nfs -o ro=.paulwatters.com -d "GNU Tools" /export/FSF
```

In this example there is a single **share** command that tells the NFS server that the file system /export/FSF should be exported. As the first line of the file demonstrates, you can add comments in the file by starting a line with the pound character (#).

Because the **share** commands stored in this file are executed only when NFS starts up, any changes that you make to it will not be reflected immediately. In order to have your changes take effect, you need to execute the following command:

**# shareall**

This command causes the NFS server to reread the /etc/dfs/dfstab and update the list of exported file systems.

## Rules for Exporting File Systems

There are three main rules to keep in mind when exporting NFS file systems:

1. You can export only local file systems or subsets of a local file system.

2. You cannot export any subdirectory of an exported file system unless the subdirectory is located on a different physical device. Likewise, you cannot export the parent of an exported directory unless the parent is located on a different physical device.

3. If you specify a symbolic link as the pathname of an exported NFS file system, the directory the symbolic link points to will be exported.

The main thing to keep in mind when exporting file systems is that you should try and let users see only those things that are relevant to them. You should try to hide directories that are extraneous to most users, or directories that contain sensitive information that only a few users need to access. If you have a large and complex directory structure, make sure to export those parts that users will need. Don't export too much, however, because directories with similar names and contents will confuse users.

## Rule 1: Export Only Local File Systems

The first rule allows you to export all or part of a large local file system. If you have a file system where all the files should be accessible to clients, this rule allows you to export the entire file system and all of its subdirectories. This is frequently the case with home directories, but it is not the case for programs. For example, say that the /net file system contains the following subdirectories that identify files by different operating system version and hardware type:

**$ /bin/ls -F /net**

```
sol-2.5.1-SPARC/   sol-2.6-SPARC/    sol-2.7-SPARC/
sol-2.5.1-x86/     sol-2.6-x86/      sol-2.7-x86/
```

Because a particular NFS client only cares about the files for its operating system and hardware type, there is no reason for clients to have access to the entire /net file system. It is much more useful for clients if you export each directory individually, rather than the whole file system. In some cases you may not even want some clients to know that all of these directories exist.

The first rule also prevents you from exporting file systems that you are accessing using NFS. If a machine needs to access an NFS file system, then it must access it from the machine that has exported the file system. In most instances, the only reason that you would need to export an NFS file system is to get around access restrictions. NFS does not allow you to circumvent access restrictions put in place by administrators.

## Rule 2: Restrictions on Exporting Parent and Subdirectories

The second rule is designed to avoid conflicts on an NFS client. Once you export a subdirectory of a local file system, you cannot go and export the whole thing. If one administrator exports a subset of directories on a file system, there is always a good reason for that choice. By disallowing the parent directory to be exported once its subdirectories have been exported, NFS prevents entire file systems from being exported on the fly, for the expectation is that the administrator has carefully chosen the directories to export. Also, once you make the whole file system accessible, there is no point in exporting one or two subdirectories. The only time this would be required is if the parent directory and the child directory are on different physical devices. For example, consider directory /usr/FSF:

```
include/  info/      lib/      libexec/  man/      pgms/      share/
```

and the contents of its subdirectory pgms:

```
sol-2.5.1-sparc/  sol-2.5.1-x86/    sol-2.6-sparc/    sol-2.6-x86/
```

In this case the common files located in /usr/FSF can be exported to all NFS clients because these are independent of the operating system version and hardware architecture. But the files in the pgms directory *are* dependent on the operating system version and hardware architecture. For example, an x86-based Solaris 2.5.1 machine would not care about files meant for a SPARC-based Solaris 2.6 system. In order to minimize the number of redundant copies of platform-independent files you keep around, it makes sense to export the directory /usr/FSF *and* the individual directories in pgms. In order to do this without causing confusion for the client, the pgms directory would need to be located on a different physical device than /usr/FSF.

## Rule 3: Exporting Symbolic Links

Exporting symbolic links as NFS file systems can have unexpected results. In general, just keep in mind that operations on a symbolic link are applied to the target of the link and not to the link itself. This will minimize the potential problems you will encounter. For example, if the link /www points to the directory /export/www:

**$ ls -l /www**

```
lrwxrwxrwx   1 root      other     12 Apr 24 21:43 /www ->
./export/www
```

then exporting the link /www:

**# share -F nfs -o ro -d "Web Pages" /www**

actually causes the file system /export/www to be exported, as shown here:

**# showmount -e**

```
export list for brunswick:
/export/www (everyone)
```

Clients that access this NFS file system can use either the pathname of the symbolic link or the pathname of the actual directory.

# Setting Up the NFS Client

In order to access a file system exported by an NFS server, an NFS client needs to mount the file system by using the **mount** command. You can also add entries for NFS file system into the file /etc/vfstab so that those filsesystems are automatically mounted when your system boots. In this section we will first look at using the **mount** command, and then we will show you how to add entries into vfstab for NFS file systems.

The nfs client daemon is located in /etc/init.d/nfs.client. A typical initialization Bourne shell script looks like:

```
#!/bin/sh
killproc() {              # kill the named process(es)
      pid=`/usr/bin/ps -e |
          /usr/bin/grep $1 |
          /usr/bin/sed -e 's/^  *//' -e 's/ .*//'`
      [ "$pid" != "" ] && kill $pid
}
#
# Start/stop processes required for client NFS
#
case "$1" in
'start')
      if [ -x /usr/lib/nfs/statd -a -x /usr/lib/nfs/lockd ]
      then
            /usr/lib/nfs/statd > /dev/console 2>&1
            /usr/lib/nfs/lockd > /dev/console 2>&1
      fi
      /sbin/mountall -F nfs
      /sbin/mountall -F cachefs
      /sbin/SWAPadd
      ;;
'stop')
      killproc lockd
      killproc statd
      /sbin/umountall -F cachefs
      /sbin/umountall -F nfs
      ;;
*)
      echo "Usage: /etc/init.d/nfs.client { start | stop }"
      ;;
esac
```

**ADMINISTERING SERVICES**

When the NFS client starts, when the "start" parameter is passed to the script, the statd and lockd daemons are initialized, and ksrvtgt is used to obtain any Kerberos tickets that are required for authentication. Next, all volumes that are listed in /etc/vfstab as NFS volumes are automatically mounted. When the NFS client processes, such as lockd and cachefs, are terminated when the "stop" parameter is passed to the script, all NFS mounted volumes are unmounted from the client.

# Using mount

Mounting NFS file systems using the **mount** command is similar to mounting regular file systems. The basic command is:

```
# mount -F nfs [-o options] host:file system destination
```

Here *host* is the name of the NFS server, *file system* is the pathname of an exported file system on the NFS server, and *destination* is the pathname of a local directory where you want the NFS file system mounted. The **-o** flag can be used to specify NFS mount *options*, which will be discussed shortly. It is not required.

You may also see the command issued as follows:

```
# mount host:file system destination
```

If the **mount** command sees that the file system that you want to mount is in the form *host:file system*, it assumes that you are mounting an NFS file system. The examples in this section use the first form, but you can choose to use either form.

As a simple example of using the **mount** command, consider the following:

**# mount -F nfs parkville:/store/home /users**

This command mounts the file system /store/home exported by the NFS server parkville on the directory /users. Once the command is issued, the contents of /users looks like the following:

**$ ls /users**

```
./        ../        adoe/    jdoe/    sdoe/
```

On the NFS client it looks like the files are part of the local directory tree; you can work with the files without ever knowing that the files were not stored locally.

You can also check if the mount operation succeeded by using the **df** command as follows:

**$ df -k /users**

```
File system            kbytes    used   avail capacity Mounted on
parkville:/store/home  1521567 1140883  302062    80%     /users
```

In this case it indicates that the NFS file system /store/home located on the host parkville is mounted on the directory /users. If the output shows a local device rather than an NFS file system, similar to the following:

```
File system            kbytes    used   avail capacity Mounted on
/dev/dsk/c0t3d0s0      739262   412549  267573    61%      /
```

it indicates that the mount operation failed. You will need to determine why it failed before trying again. Different strategies for recovering from mount failures are discussed later in the chapter.

## NFS mount Options

The main options available when mounting NFS file systems are:

- **ro**   This option mounts a file system read-only.
- **rw**   This option mounts a file system with read and write permissions.
- **hard**   With this option, the NFS client will keep trying to perform the requested file operation until it succeeds.
- **soft**   If this option is specified, the NFS client will try to perform requested file operations until they time out. Once the timeout occurs, an error is reported.
- **bg**   This option comes into play only if the first attempt to mount a file system fails. This option allows the NFS client to retry the mount in the background.

The default for NFS mounts is equivalent to specifying the options **rw** and **hard**. In the following sections we will look at each of these options in turn.

**Read/Write and Read-Only Permissions**   To mount an NFS file system with read and write permissions, you can specify the **rw** option as follows:

   -o rw

For example, the following command mounts the NFS file system /store/pub on the host parkville with read and write access:

**# mount -F nfs -o rw parkville:/store/home /users**

One thing to keep in mind is that, even if you specify the **rw** option, should the NFS file system you are attempting to mount be exported with the **ro** option, you will only be able to read files on it. Also, you cannot use the **mount** command to override the server's export permissions. If the NFS file system that you are trying to mount does not include your host in the list of hosts that are allowed either read and write or read-only access, you will get an error message similar to the following:

```
nfs mount: parkville:/store/home: access denied
```

If you want to mount an NFS file system with read-only access, you can use the **ro** option to mount, as shown here:

**-o ro**

For example, the following command mounts the NFS file system /export/FSF on the host brunswick with read-only permissions:

**# mount -F nfs -o ro brunswick:/export/FSF /usr/FSF**

The primary purpose for the **ro** option is to reduce the access privileges of an NFS file system. This option is mainly used when mounting as read-only an NFS file system that has been exported with read and write permission. Normally this is used for file systems that need to be accessed temporarily.

**Hard and Soft mounts**    The **hard** and **soft** mount options determine how the NFS client behaves when the server is heavily loaded, crashed, or becomes unavailable for some other reason. You can specify the **hard** option as follows:

**-o hard**

By default all NFS file systems are mounted with the **hard** option, which means that when a request to the server times out, the client will retry until it receives a response. This is intended to make NFS file systems behave like local disks. All requests will eventually be written to the remote disk. When the NFS server crashes or becomes unavailable, the behavior is like that of a very slow cache. This behavior ensures that the state of the NFS exported file system is consistent even after a crash. NFS servers can only guarantee the consistency of NFS file systems that are hard mounted by clients.

The other type of NFS mounts is the soft mount. You can soft mount an NFS file system with the **soft** option, specified in a similar manner:

**-o soft**

When an NFS file system is mounted with the **soft** option, the client will eventually report an error if it does not receive a response from the NFS server after several retries. This option is used mainly for NFS file systems that contain static information like man pages or web pages. You should not soft mount any NFS file system that you intend to run programs for or that you intend to access with read and write permissions. The **soft** option should be used only with read-only NFS file systems.

**Background mounts**    The **bg** option enables mounting an NFS file system in the background. You can specify it as follows:

**-o bg**

If this option is used, **mount** starts another process in the background to handle mounting the NFS file system and returns. If you are mounting from a slow NFS server, this option will allow you to issue many mount requests without having to wait for one request to finish before issuing another request. In addition to this, if you have two NFS servers that mount volumes from each other, you will need to specify the **bg** option for mounting volumes on at least one of the servers. Otherwise it is possible that the two servers can deadlock during reboots while they wait for each other to start the NFS server. Using the **bg** option allows the first **mount** option to fail, and then be completed later, when both systems start their NFS servers.

**Combining Options**    You can combine **mount** options using a syntax similar to that of the NFS server:

```
-o option1,option2,…
```

Here *option1* is the first NFS mount option and *option2* is the second NFS mount option. You can specify as many options as you require. The only restrictions are that you cannot specify both the **rw** and the **ro** options and you cannot specify both the **hard** and the **soft** options. As an example of using multiple NFS options, the following command:

> **# mount -F nfs -o ro,soft parkville:/store/docs /usr/doc**

mounts the NFS file system /store/docs located on the host parkville onto the directory /usr/doc. It specifies that this file system should be soft mounted with read-only permissions.

## Unmounting NFS File Systems

Unmounting (undoing a mount of) NFS file systems is similar to unmounting regular file systems. You can use the **umount** command with the syntax:

```
# umount pathname
```

Here *pathname* is the path to a mounted NFS file system. For example, if the directory /usr/doc was an NFS mounted file system, then the following command:

> **# umount /usr/doc**

would unmount that file system. You can check whether the NFS file system was correctly unmounted by using the **df** command as follows:

**$ df -k /usr/doc**

```
file system              kbytes    used   avail capacity  Mounted on
/dev/dsk/c0t3d0s0        739262  412550  267572    61%    /
```

If the output still lists an NFS file system, then the unmount operation did not complete successfully. This may happen if one or more files on the NFS file system are being used. If this is the case, you will usually see the following error message from **umount**:

```
nfs umount: /usr/doc: is busy
```

## Mounting NFS File Systems at Boot

If you mount an NFS file system using the **mount** command, it will stay mounted until you unmount it using the **umount** command or you reboot your system. After you reboot, you will have to manually mount these NFS file systems. In order to avoid doing this after every reboot, you can add NFS file systems to the file /etc/vfstab. NFS file systems specified in this file will be mounted automatically after your system reboots. The syntax for an NFS entry in this file is similar to entries for local devices. Here is a sample entry:

```
parkville:/store/doc     -        /usr/doc nfs    -          yes     bg,soft
```

The details of each column are as follows:

- The first column specifies the source of the file system to mount. In this case, it indicates that the file system /store/doc located on the host parkville should be mounted.

- The second column contains the pathname to the "raw" physical device for the file system. In the case of NFS file systems this should be a dash (–), because there is no physical device for an NFS file system on the local machine.

- The third column specifies the pathname of the directory where the NFS file system should be mounted. In this case it is the directory /usr/doc.

- The fourth column specifies the type of file system, in this case nfs.

- The fifth column is used by the **fsck** program to check local file systems. In the case of NFS there is no local file system, so this column should contain a dash (–), indicating to **fsck** that it should not check this file system.

■ The sixth column indicates whether or not the file system should be mounted at boot time. To have an NFS file system mounted automatically each time your system boots, this should be **yes**.

■ The seventh column contains the NFS mount options. In this case, the file system will be mounted using the options **bg** and **soft**.

## Starting and Stopping the NFS Client

Starting and stopping the NFS client is normally handled by your system at boot and shutdown time. In some instances you will have to start and stop the NFS client manually, especially if it stops responding correctly to operations on files in the NFS file system. To start the NFS client, issue the following command:

**# /etc/init.d/nfs.client start**

This should start the NFS client. You can confirm that the client has started correctly by using the command:

**$ /bin/ps -ef | grep "statd | lockd"**

The output should look like the following:

```
root 20674     1  0 13:06:43 ?        0:00 /usr/lib/nfs/statd
root 20676     1  0 13:06:44 ?        0:00 /usr/lib/nfs/lockd
```

If you receive no output, or if your output contains a line for only **statd** or **lockd**, then your NFS client has not started correctly. You can start these processes manually by issuing the following command:

```
# /usr/lib/nfs/statd ; /usr/lib/nfs/lockd ;
```

(Note that you should almost never need to start the NFS client in this manner.)
Stopping the NFS client is similar to starting it:

**# /etc/init.d/nfs.client stop**

The stop script usually stops the client, but you can confirm this using the command:

**$ /bin/ps -ef | grep "statd | lockd"**

This is the same command that is used to check to see if the client is running, except that once you stop the client this command should not produce any output. If there is output, and a line for **statd** or **lockd** appears in the output, the NFS client has not stopped correctly. In this case you should execute the NFS client stop command again.

# Troubleshooting NFS File Systems

There are many things that can go wrong when you try to mount an NFS file system. Some of the common problems are:

- NFS server cannot be located
- Inadequate access permissions or file system not exported
- Mount point does not exist
- NFS mount fails
- The server is not responsive or is performing poorly
- Stale file handles

## NFS Server Cannot Be Located

If the NFS server cannot be located, you will usually receive an error message similar to the following:

> # mount -F nfs banana.paulwatters.com:/export/FSF /usr/FSF

```
nfs mount: banana.paulwatters.com: : RPC: Unknown host
```

In the case of this example, the IP address for the host banana.paulwatters.com could not be determined, so the mount command returned an error message.

## Inadequate Access Permissions File System Not Exported

If the problem was with the NFS file system rather than the host, the error message will look similar to the following:

> # mount -F nfs parkville:/export/FSF /usr/FSF

```
nfs mount: parkville:/export/FSF: access denied
```

The error message in this case indicates that you do not have sufficient permissions to access the NFS file system. This could mean two things:

- Your machine is not on the read-and-write or read-only access lists.
- The NFS file system you requested is not exported by the NFS server.

As explained earlier in this chapter, the **showmount** command will help you determine which of these problems you are encountering.

## Mount Point Does Not Exist

If the local directory or the mount point you specified does not exist, the error message will be similar to the following:

**# mount -F nfs parkville:/export/FSF /usr/fsf**

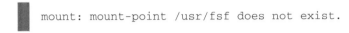

```
mount: mount-point /usr/fsf does not exist.
```

To fix this problem you will need to make the local directory using the **mkdir** command, or specify a different local directory. In this case we can use the following command:

**# mkdir -p /usr/fsf**

to create the directory /usr/fsf (or we could have picked another directory that already existed, like /usr/FSF).

Another potential error message from **mount** is:

```
mount: RPC: Program not registered
```

This error message is generated when you try to mount an NFS file system from a server where the NFS server daemons have been shut down or have crashed. You will need to contact the administrator of the NFS server to make sure the NFS server programs are running correctly. The procedure for checking if an NFS server is running correctly was given earlier in this chapter, in the section "Starting and Stopping the NFS Server."

## NFS mount Fails

Sometimes a legitimate request for an NFS mount from one NFS client to an NFS server fails. This often happens due to a failed reverse name lookup. For example, on server brunswick, running the **share** command may show the following:

**$ share**

- /opt2 rw ""
- /opt ro=red ""

Now when red tries to mount the /opt file system, the mount fails. Investigation reveals that the brunswick NFS server resolves an incorrect IP address for the red NFS client. To fix the problem, review and correct the name resolution process on the brunswick NFS server.

## The Server Is Not Responsive or Is Performing Poorly

Once you mount an NFS file system, it is possible for the NFS server that contains that file system to crash or become unresponsive. In this case, the NFS client programs will produce an error message similar to the following:

```
NFS server parkville not responding, still trying
```

An NFS client produces the "not responding" error message if it fails to contact the NFS server after more than 10,000 attempts. Once the NFS server recovers, the client will produce a message similar to the following:

```
NFS server parkville OK
```

A "not responding" error message could mean that the NFS server you are trying to contact is heavily loaded and is not able to respond to NFS requests. It could also mean that the NFS server has crashed. The NFS client has no way of determining if the server is overloaded or if it has crashed. In both cases, its requests are not handled by the server. If you see this error message occurring frequently, you should contact the administrator of the NFS server to isolate the problem. Solaris 8 supplies the **nfsstat** command, which displays statistical information about the NFS server and the client.

nfsstat generates basic NFS statistics concerning rpc connections. It can be used in several different modes. For example, to examine the statistics for each mounted file system, we can use the -m option:

```
brunswick# nfsstat -m
/var/mail from parkville:/var/mail
 Flags:
vers=3,proto=tcp,sec=sys,hard,intr,link,symlink,acl,rsize=32768,wsize=32768,retrans=5
/cdrom from parkville:/cdrom
 Flags:
vers=3,proto=tcp,sec=sys,hard,intr,link,symlink,acl,rsize=32768,wsize=32768,retrans=5
```

For the two remotely mounted NFS volumes /var/mail and /cdrom, we can see that the read and write sizes are identical (32K each), and that the retransmission count is five. For a more complete picture, you can use the -s option to display NFS server information:

```
server# nfsstat -s
Server rpc:
Connection oriented:
calls       badcalls    nullrecv    badlen      xdrcall     dupchecks
```

```
9126046      0             0             0             0             51316
dupreqs
0
```

Starting with the connection-oriented statistics, there have been 9,126,046 calls since the NFS server started, but no bad calls, which indicates that no calls were rejected by the server. In addition, there were no RPC calls whose length was less than the minimum size (badlen), and there were no RPC calls that could not be decoded (xdrcall). If any of these errors appeared, they may indicate that a network is overloaded, and that more bandwidth or a change in configuration is required. Although there were 51,316 dupchecks, which is the number of caching RPC checks that were duplicated, there were no actual duplicated requests (dupreqs).

```
Connectionless:
calls        badcalls      nullrecv      badlen        xdrcall       dupchecks
387871       0             0             0             0             0
dupreqs
0
```

Continuing with the connectionless statistics, there have been 387,871 calls since the NFS server started, but again no bad calls, indicating that no calls were rejected by the server. In addition, there were no RPC calls whose length was less than the minimum size (badlen), as above, and there were again no RPC calls that could not be decoded (xdrcall). This indicates that the network is not overloaded, and that more bandwidth or a change in configuration is not required.

```
Server nfs:
calls        badcalls
9513553      0
Version 2: (374112 calls)
null         getattr       setattr       root          lookup        readlink
8 0%         14006 3%      0 0%          0 0%          83943 22%     68 0%
read         wrcache       write         create        remove        rename
266686 71%   0 0%          0 0%          0 0%          0 0%          0 0%
link         symlink       mkdir         rmdir         readdir       statfs
0 0%         0 0%          0 0%          0 0%          9394 2%       7 0%
Version 3: (9137216 calls)
null         getattr       setattr       lookup        access        readlink
13759 0%     5428480 59%   1214 0%       1570122 17%   1825697 19%   20112 0%
read         write         create        mkdir         symlink       mknod
192425 2%    18188 0%      2949 0%       17 0%         5 0%          0 0%
```

```
remove       rmdir        rename       link         readdir      readdirplus
716 0%       13 0%        44 0%        5 0%         31964 0%     28165 0%
fsstat       fsinfo       pathconf     commit
151 0%       1087 0%      2065 0%      38 0%
```

In this case, writes occupy only a small percentage of both NFS 2 and NFS 3 requests, so no change in configuration is required on this point (0 writes for the former, and 18,188 writes for the latter). However, one point of concern is that the client attribute cache (getattr) is running at 59 percent for NFS 3, although it is only 3 percent for NFS 2. This suggests that virtual memory may need to be examined, and possibly the size of the Directory Name Lookup Cache (NDLC) increased to cope with high demand.

## vmstat

vmstat reports virtual memory statistics regarding process, virtual memory, disk, trap, and CPU activity. The "s" option reports on SWAPping rather than paging activity. This option will change two fields in vmstat's "paging" display: Rather than the "re" and "mf" fields, vmstat will report "si" (SWAP-ins) and "so" (SWAP-outs). In this case, we are interested in the DNLC hit rate, which might be low for parkville, given the poor getattr results shown above. However, there were 282,748,053 total name lookups, with a cache hit rate of 95 percent. This is perfectly acceptable, and so no further action is required. vmstat also provides more general information about server performance, including the number of processes in running or blocked states, the availability of real and virtual RAM, the size of the SWAP file currently unused, an account of paging activity, the load generated by disk operations, and a description of CPU usage. Let's review the virtual memory statistics for the NFS server parkville:

```
parkville# vmstat -s
        0 SWAP ins
        0 SWAP outs
        0 pages SWAPped in
        0 pages SWAPped out
 93374958 total address trans. faults taken
  2174582 page ins
  1324184 page outs
  6622497 pages paged in
  5319858 pages paged out
  1538949 total reclaims
  1525732 reclaims from free list
        0 micro (hat) faults
```

```
 93374958 minor (as) faults
  1529035 major faults
 23990812 copy-on-write faults
 18285368 zero fill page faults
  3662642 pages examined by the clock daemon
       28 revolutions of the clock hand
  6948532 pages freed by the clock daemon
   977717 forks
    49056 vforks
  2327053 execs
540848048 cpu context switches
546495420 device interrupts
257585396 traps
2139172397 system calls
282748053 total name lookups (cache hits 95%)
  1243876 toolong
 82084424 user   cpu
 22523996 system cpu
 35413407 idle   cpu
  7469599 wait   cpu
```

## mpstat

mpstat also reports statistics for CPU activity, and can be a useful indicator of a NFS server experiencing load handling difficulties, especially those related to "sys" activities. Since Parkville has two CPUs, two rows of data are produced, which describe the following charactersitics: minor and major faults, cross-calls between CPUs, interrupts, context switches, thread migrations, user percentage of CPU time, idle percentage of CPU time, and sys percentage of CPU time. In this example, sys time for both processors is well below the 50 percent benchmark, and so the system is adequately coping with its load. Let's review the complete output:

```
parkville# mpstat 10
CPU minf mjf xcal  intr ithr  csw icsw migr smtx  srw syscl  usr sys  wt idl
  0   63   1  438   350  261  378  114   23   13    0   913   55  16   5  24
  1   62   1  315   390  132  355  104   23   13    0  1996   57  15   5  24
<<State change>>
CPU minf mjf xcal  intr ithr  csw icsw migr smtx  srw syscl  usr sys  wt idl
  0   63   1  438   350  261  378  114   23   13    0   913   55  16   5  24
  1   62   1  315   390  132  355  104   23   13    0  1996   57  15   5  24
```

### Stale File Handles

Another error message that is sometimes encountered with NFS file systems is the following:

```
ls: .: Stale NFS file handle
```

This type of error messages is seen when a file or directory that was opened by an NFS client is removed, renamed, or replaced. Such error messages are common in an enterprise-wide NFS deployment. To fix this problem, the NFS file handles must be renegotiated. The client machines can try one of the following:

- Unmount and remount the file system.
- Create another mount point and access the files from the new mount point.
- Kill/restart the process that has open file handles.
- Restart the **statd** and the **lockd** daemons.

## Using the Automounter

The automounter is a program that automatically mounts NFS file systems when they are accessed and then unmounts them when they are no longer needed. It allows you to use special files called automounter maps, which contain information about the servers, the pathname to the NFS file system on the server, the local pathname, and the mount options. By using the automounter, you don't have to update the entries in /etc/vfstab on every client by hand each time you make a change to the NFS servers.

Normally, only root can mount file systems, so when users need to mount an NFS file system they need to find the system administrator. The main problem is that once users are finished with a file system, they rarely tell the system administrator. If the NFS server containing that file system ever crashed, you would be left with one or more hanging processes. This can easily increase your workload if you are responsible for maintaining an NFS server. The automounter can solve both of these problems, because it automatically mounts an NFS file system when a user references a file in that file system, and it will automatically unmount the NFS file system if it is not referenced for more than five minutes.

### Automounter Maps

The behavior of the automounter is determined by a set of files called automounter *maps*. There are two main types of maps: indirect and direct. An indirect map is useful when you are mounting several file systems that will share a common pathname prefix.

As we will see shortly, an indirect map can be used to manage the directory tree in /home. A direct map is used to mount file systems where each mount point does not share a common prefix with other mount points in the map. In this section we will look at examples of each of these types of maps. (An additional map, called the master map, is used by the automounter to determine the names of the files corresponding to the direct and indirect maps.)

## Indirect Maps

The most common type of automounter maps are indirect maps, which correspond to "regularly" named file systems like /home or /usr/sw directory trees. Regularly named file systems share the same directory prefix. For example, the directories /home/jdoe and /home/sdoe are regularly named directories in the /home directory tree.

Normally, indirect maps are stored in the /etc directory, and are named with the convention auto_*directory*, where directory is the name of the directory prefix (without slashes), which the indirect map is responsible for. As an example, the indirect map responsible for the /home directory is usually named auto_home. An indirect map is made up of a series of entries in the following format:

```
directory      options      host:file system
```

Here *directory* is the relative pathname of a directory that will be appended to the name of the directory that is corresponding to this indirect map as specified in the master map file. (The master map is covered later in this section.) For *options*, you can use any of the **mount** options covered earlier in this chapter. To specify options, you will need to prefix the first option with a dash (–). If you do not need any extra options, you can omit the options entirely. The final entry in the map contains the location of the NFS file system.

Here is an example of the indirect map that is responsible for the directories in /home:

```
# /etc/auto_home - home directory map for automounter
jdoe          parkville:/store/home/jdoe
sdoe          parkville:/store/home/sdoe
kdoe -bg srv-ss10:/home/kdoe
```

Here the entries for jdoe, sdoe, and kdoe correspond to the directories /home/jdoe, /home/sdoe, and /home/kdoe respectively. The first two entries indicate that the automounter should mount the directories /home/jdoe and /home/sdoe from the NFS server parkville, while the last one specifies that the directory /home/kdoe should be mounted from the NFS server srv-ss10. The last entry also demonstrates the use of options.

ADMINISTERING SERVICES

Now that we have taken a look at an indirect map, let's walk through what happens when you access a file on an NFS file system that is handled by the automounter. For example, consider the following command that accesses the file /home/jdoe/docs/book/ch17.doc:

**$ more /home/jdoe/docs/book/ch17.doc**

Because the directory /home/jdoe is automounted, the following steps are used by the automounter to allow you to access the file:

1. The automounter looks at the pathname and determines that the directory /home is controlled by the indirect map auto_home.

2. The automounter looks at the rest of the pathname for a corresponding entry in the auto_home map. In this case it finds the matching entry, jdoe.

3. Once a matching entry has been found, the automounter checks to see if the directory /home/jdoe is already mounted. If the directory is already mounted, you can directly access the file; otherwise the automounter mounts this directory and then allows you to access the file.

## Direct Maps

When you use an indirect map, the automounter takes complete control of the directory corresponding to the indirect map. This means that no user, not even root, can create entries in a directory corresponding to an indirect map. For this reason, directories specified in an indirect map cannot be automounted on top of an existing directory. In this case you need a special type of map known as a direct map. A direct map allows you to mix automounter mount points and normal directories in the same directory tree. The directories specified in a direct map have "nonregular" mount points, which simply mean that they do not share a common prefix. A common use for direct maps is to allow for directories in the /usr directory tree to be automounted.

The direct map is normally stored in the file /etc/auto_direct. The format of this file is similar to the format of the indirect maps:

```
directory     options     host:file system
```

Here *directory* is the absolute pathname of a directory. For *options*, you can use any of the mount options covered earlier in this chapter. To specify options, you will need to prefix the first option with a dash (–). If you do not need any extra options, you can omit the options entirely. The final entry in the map contains the location of the NFS file system. Here is an example of the direct map that is responsible for some of the directories in /usr:

```
# /etc/auto_direct - Direct Automount map
/usr/pubsw/man  parkville:/internal/opt/man
/usr/doc        parkville:/internal/httpd/htdocs
```

When any files in the directories /usr/pubsw/man or /usr/doc are accessed, the automounter will automatically handle the mounting of these directories.

## Master Map

When the automounter first starts, it reads the file /etc/auto_master to determine where to find the direct and indirect map files. The auto_master file is known as the master map. Its consists of lines whose format is as follows:

```
directory    map
```

Here *directory* is the name of the directory that corresponds to the indirect map. For a direct map, this entry is /–. The *map* is the name of the map file in the /etc directory corresponding to the *directory* given in the first column. The following example shows a master map file for the direct and indirect maps given earlier in this section:

```
# Master map for automounter
/home         auto_home
/-            auto_direct
```

# Starting and Stopping the Automounter

Starting and stopping the automounter is normally handled by your system at boot and shutdown time, but you will have to start and stop the automounter manually if you make changes to any of its map files.

The automount daemon is typically started from /etc/init.d/autofs during the multiuser startup, with a command like:

```
#!/bin/sh
killproc() {              # kill the named process(es)
     pid=`/usr/bin/ps -e |
         /usr/bin/grep $1 |
         /usr/bin/sed -e 's/^  *//' -e 's/ .*//'`
     [ "$pid" != "" ] && kill $pid
}
#
# Start/stop automounter
#
case "$1" in
```

ADMINISTERING
SERVICES

```
'start')
      /usr/lib/autofs/automountd > /dev/console 2>&1 # start daemon
      /usr/sbin/automount &                    # do mounts
      ;;
'stop')
      /sbin/umountall -F autofs                # undo mounts
      killproc automoun                  # kill daemon
      ;;
*)
      echo "Usage: /etc/init.d/autofs { start | stop }"
      ;;
esac
```

To start automounter, issue the command:

**# /etc/init.d/autofs start**

This should start the automounter. You can confirm that it started correctly by using the following command:

**$ /bin/ps -ef | grep automountd**

The output should look like the following:

```
root 21642    1  0 11:27:29 ?        0:00
/usr/lib/autofs/automountd
```

If you receive no output, then the automounter has not started correctly. In that case you should run the startup script again.

Stopping the NFS client is similar to starting it:

**# /etc/init.d/autofs stop**

The stop script usually stops the automounter, but you can confirm this using the command:

**$ /bin/ps -ef | grep automountd**

This is the same command that is used to check to see if the automounter is running, except that once you stop it this command should not produce any output. If you do see some output and it contains a **grep** command, you can ignore those lines. Any other output indicates that the automounter has not stopped, in which case you should execute the NFS client stop command again.

If you receive a message similar to the following:

```
/home: busy
```

then you will need to determine if anyone is logged on to the system and is using files from /home. If you cannot determine this, you can use the following command to get a list of all of the mounted directories in the directory that caused the error message (in this case /home):

```
$ df -k -F nfs
/home/jdoe
```

Just replace /home with the name of the directory that produced the error message. In this case only one directory, /home/jdoe, was automounted. Once you have a list of these directories, try unmounting each one with the **umount** command. When you receive an error message, you will know which directory contains the files that are in use. You can ask the user to finish with those files, and then proceed to stop the automounter.

# Printing

In large networks, it is possible to share file systems between hosts by using NFS, as we have demonstrated above. However, many organizations also choose to share other resources, such as printers. It is much cheaper to share printers between hosts than it is to purchase a printer for each system. Fortunately, it is possible to add printers to a Solaris system easily by using the admintool, which has a GUI interface. It is also possible to share a local printer with other hosts, and to configure a remote printer for use on a local system. Solaris also provides the printtool, which allows OpenWindows applications to "drag and drop" files onto a special pad on the printtool, automatically printing the files "dropped." Since the move to System V, the command-line printing tools have also become easier, with the lpr client being replaced by lp, lpstat replacing lpq, and cancel replacing lprm. This makes it easier for users of other System V UNIX systems to adapt to Solaris without having to learn the old BSD-style commands.

In order to use admintool for printer configuration and installation, simply start it from the command line:

**server# admintool&**

When admintool starts, its default screen is displayed, as shown in Figure 17-3. To install, configure, and manage printers, simply select the "Printers" option from the Browse menu.

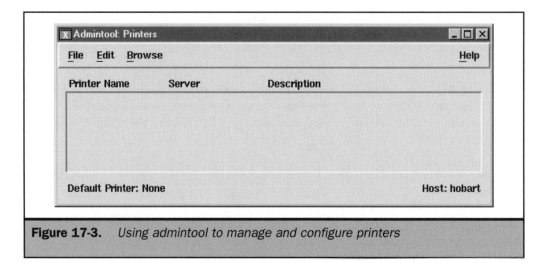

**Figure 17-3.**   *Using admintool to manage and configure printers*

## Configuring a Local Printer

In order to add a local printer, select the "Add" option from the "Edit" menu. Next, select the "Local Printer" option. You will then be presented with the screen displayed in Figure 17-4. It is then necessary to set a number of options:

- A printer name that must be unique for a particular server (but different machines can have different printers with the same name). The rules for naming printers can either follow schemes developed for hostnames (e.g., planets, stars, or names of famous people), or can reflect some aspect of the printer's functions (e.g., "bubblejet"), or geographic location (e.g., "level1-laser"). Here, our printer is called "henry" after "Henry Miller."

- If you use an entry from a standard naming scheme for the printer, you can also enter a more descriptive entry in the "Description" field.

- The printer port must also be set, in this case, /dev/term/a.

- The Printer Type must identify whether or not the printer accepts Adobe PostScript, or plain ASCII input.

- It is possible to customize the fault notification process—in this case, we simply chose to contact the system administrator if a problem arises.

- Many sites print a banner to identify unique print jobs for different users. However, many environmentally aware organizations choose not to print a banner page by default.

- Finally, you can set up an access control list for access to the printer, which is granted on a user-by-user basis. The default is "all" users.

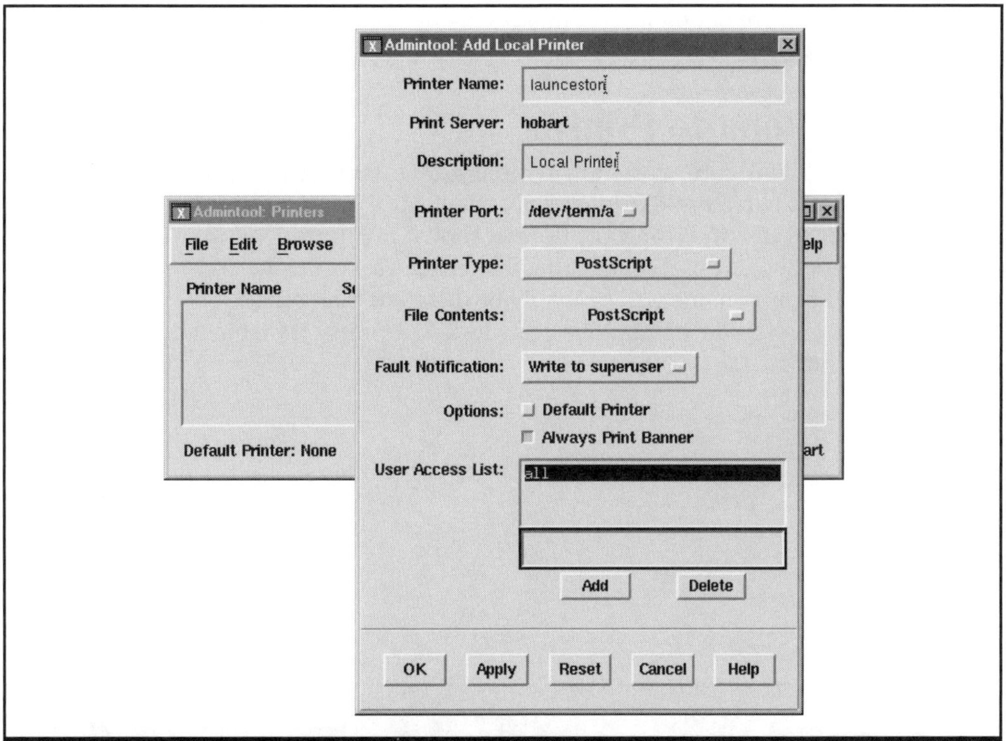

**Figure 17-4.** *Using admintool to add a local printer*

Once you have entered these settings, you can print from the command line by using the command:

**client% lp file.txt**

Alternatively, if you want to print all files in a directory, you can use the command:

**client% lp \***

If you have multiple printers defined on the local system it is possible to specify the printer directly by using the -d option:

**client% lp -d henry some_file.txt**

Alternatively, it is possible to set the LPDEST environment variable to a default and export this variable from your ".profile" (for Bourne shell) or ".cshrc" (for C shell):

LPDEST=henry; export LPDEST

You can check the print queue for a printer by using the lpstat command, and cancel specific jobs by using the cancel command.

## Configuring a Remote Printer

It is even easier to configure access to a remote printer than installing a local printer. In order to add access to a remote printer, select the "Add" option from the "Edit" menu. Then, select the "Access to Printer" option, as shown in Figure 17-5. In this case, we want to configure access to a printer called henry on a server called henry (of course, your server and printer name will probably be different than ours).

Once access to a remote printer has been added, its entry is displayed in the file /etc/printers.conf:

```
henry:\
        :bsdaddr=henry,henry:\
        :description=henry:
_default:\
        :use=henry:
```

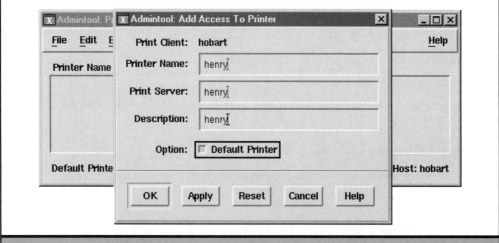

**Figure 17-5.**   *Using admintool to provide access to a remote printer*

This specifies that henry is the default printer, above and beyond any local printers that might also be configured.

# Printing in OpenWindows

It is easy to exchange documents in OpenWindows between applications and the printtool, as shown in Figure 17-6. In the example shown, we simply select the file we wish to print in the file manager, and drag its icon onto the pad located on the printtool. The file's details are then displayed in the "Filename" field, and several options can also be set at this time (e.g., printer name, header status). Clicking the "Print" button will then submit the job to the queue, and the file will be printed. You can observe the status of your print job on the printtool, and easily tell when it has been completed.

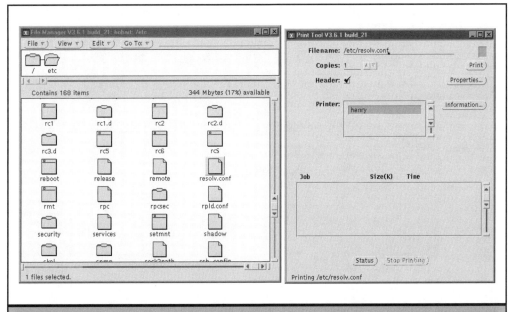

**Figure 17-6.**    *Using printtool to drag and drop files to print*

ADMINISTERING
SERVICES

# Summary

In this chapter we covered the topic of NFS administration. We first described NFS and what a distributed file system was. Then we looked at configuring an NFS server, starting with the NFS server processes. We also covered exporting file systems with the **share** command, and we showed you how to export file systems at boot time with the file /etc/dfs/dfstab. In the second section, we looked at mounting volumes from an NFS server using the **mount** command. The configuration of the automounter, which automatically mounts and unmounts NFS file systems as needed, was also discussed. We also briefly looked at sharing printers between Solaris systems, and gaining access to local and remote printers by using the printtool.

# How to Find Out More

If you are going to be administering a large installation of NFS, there are several excellent references that you should consult:

Santifaller, Michael. *TCP/IP and ONC/NFS: Internetworking in a UNIX Environment.* (Addison-Wesley, 1994.)

Stern, Hal. *Managing NFS and NIS.* (O'Reilly & Associates, 1991.)

Cockcroft, Adrian, et al. *Sun Performance and Tuning: Java and the Internet.* (Prentice Hall, 1998.)

An excellent background on the history and development of NFS is available at the following web site:

**http://www.netapp.com/technology/level3/nfsbook.html**

# The Complete Reference

Solaris 8

# Chapter 18

## Sharing Files with PCs and Macs Using SAMBA and Netatalk

D ue to their exceptional performance and stability, Solaris systems are often called upon to provide file and print services for Macintosh and Windows machines. In this chapter, we will discuss the protocols and packages that allow Solaris machines to do this; specifically, we'll cover the SMB/CIFS and AppleTalk protocols and the freely available SAMBA and netatalk packages. We will also briefly cover several commercial alternatives to these packages.

The SAMBA software suite (**http://www.samba.org/**) is a collection of programs that implement the Server Message Block (SMB) protocol. SAMBA was created by Andrew Tridgell and has since been developed by the SAMBA Team as an Open Source project. SAMBA allows you to use your Solaris system as a file and print server for DOS and Windows machines. Since its beginnings in 1991, SAMBA has proved to be a stable and reliable product and has made its way into many large companies and universities where it serves as a supplement to or even a replacement for NetWare and Windows NT servers.

Netatalk is a kernel-level implementation of the AppleTalk protocol suite by the Research Systems UNIX Group (RSUG) at the University of Michigan. The current release supports EtherTalk Phases I and II along with all of the major AppleTalk protocols, including DDP, NBP, and ZIP. Netatalk has been adopted by many companies and universities to provide MacOS-to-UNIX connectivity for their user base.

After a general overview of both Windows and Mac networking protocols vis-à-vis Solaris, the second section of this chapter provides instruction on installing and configuring SAMBA on Solaris. The third section of the chapter covers the installation and configuration of netatalk.

# Windows and MacOS File Sharing

The concepts of MS-DOS/Windows, MacOS, and UNIX networking differ remarkably. In this section we will provide an overview of networking from the perspective of NetBIOS (used by MS-DOS/Windows) and AppleTalk (used by MacOS systems).

## NetBIOS and Server Message Block (SMB)

The Network Basic Input Ouput System (NetBIOS) is a software interface that was designed for allowing communication between PCs. The original version of NetBIOS was part of a networking system developed by IBM and Sytec in the early 1980s. In the beginning NetBIOS only included a naming system that allowed PCs and network-enabled applications to be identified on a network. The first major use of NetBIOS came when Microsoft enhanced DOS so that disk requests could be redirected to NetBIOS, allowing for disks to be shared over a network. From this development came the Server Message Block (SMB) protocol.

> **Note**   *In recent versions of Windows, Microsoft sometimes refers to the features of the SMB protocol as the Windows LAN Manager.*

The current version of NetBIOS provides both a name service and a communication service. The name service enables machines connected to the network to reserve names for their use. After a name has been reserved, a machine can be addressed by that name. Any machine on the network can reserve as many names as it wants, provided the name is not already in use. The NetBIOS names have nothing in common with the names used in /etc/hosts or DNS. NetBIOS is a name space of its own. When configuring the NetBIOS name for a system it is recommended that you use names that correspond to DNS hostnames, as it makes administration much simpler.

Besides the name service, there are services for communication itself. There are secure and insecure data streams. The higher protocols, such as SMB, are in the layer on top of these secure and insecure data streams.

When NetBIOS was first developed it contained both the network access protocols and the NetBIOS API. Since this restricted NetBIOS to a few types of network architectures, it was divided into two separate parts, NetBIOS and NetBIOS Extended User Interface (NetBEUI). With the development of NetBEUI the network access protocols were moved from NetBIOS into NetBEUI, and NetBEUI became a protocol for data transport under NetBIOS. Abstracting the interface to the network into a separate module allowed the NetBIOS to be ported to many different types of networks, including networks running IPX from Novell or TCP/IP. The implementation of NetBIOS onto TCP/IP is described in RFC 1001 and 1002. RFC 1001 also contains an excellent introduction to all of the NetBIOS concepts. Figure 18-1 illustrates the relationship of SMB, NetBIOS, and the network access protocols like NetBEUI and TCP/IP in a layered format.

> **Note**   *For addressing single packets, NetBEUI works with the hardware address of your NIC. In contrast to IPX or IP addresses, you cannot get routing information from it, thus it is not possible to transfer NetBEUI packets via routers. A network running NetBEUI is reduced to the range that can be reached by repeaters and bridges.*

The Server Message Block (SMB) protocol is based on NetBIOS services and provides the ability to share file and print services in Windows LAN Manager. SMB has a client/server architecture whereby SMB clients are granted access to server-based resources, such as file systems or printers. The SMB protocol is based on the exchange of messages, called SMBs. Clients send SMB requests to servers, and the servers respond to the clients with SMB responses. Both requests and responses have a similar format, consisting of a fixed-size header followed by a variable-sized parameter and data portion. Some of the common SMB requests include open, close, read, and write. These SMBs allow for a client to open, close, read, and write files on

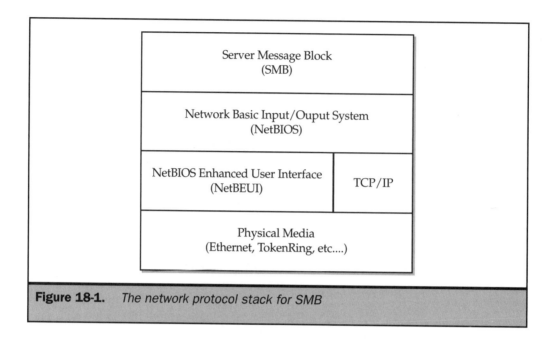

**Figure 18-1.**   *The network protocol stack for SMB*

the server. The SMB responses to these requests indicate whether or not the client's request was successful.

## The SMB Protocol

Before a client can access files on the server, it needs to establish a connection with a shared tree on the server by using the following process:

1. Establish a NetBIOS connection with the server.
2. Negotiate with the server over the version of the SMB protocol to use.
3. Log in to the server.
4. Request access to a shared tree on the server.

The process of establishing a connection to an SMB server by an SMB client is illustrated in Figure 18-2. This figure assumes that the NetBIOS connection has been created before the first SMB is sent from the SMB client to the SMB server.

When a client wants to access a server using SMB it first connects to the server at the NetBIOS level. Once this connection is in place the client and the server negotiate the version (also called the *dialect*) of the SMB protocol to use. We cover the different dialects for the SMB protocol below. The negotiation process begins with the client sending an SMB called a *negprot* (short for negotiate protocol) request to the server.

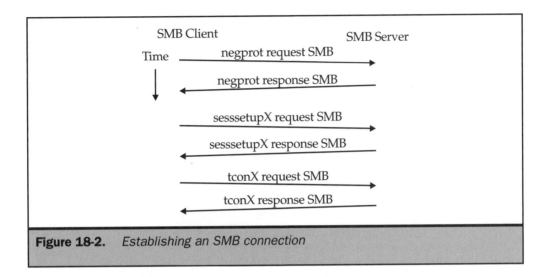

**Figure 18-2.** *Establishing an SMB connection*

This SMB lists all of the dialects that the client understands. The server responds with a negprot response that contains the dialect that it wants to use. If none of the dialects understood by the client are supported by the server, the server responds with an error message in its negprot response. Depending on the version of the SMB protocol selected by the server, the negprot response it sends can include additional information indicating its capabilities, such as the maximum buffer size it supports.

Once the protocol has been established, the client usually needs to log on to the server using an SMB called the sesssetupX (short for session setup) request. The sesssetupX response from the server indicates whether or not a valid username and password were supplied. If the login was successful, then the sesssetupX response contains the user ID (UID) of the logged-on user. The client uses this UID for all other requests it makes to the server.

After a valid username and password are supplied, the client can connect to any shared resource on the server. Every shared resource (or *share*) on a server is exported with a name and is accessed using that name. The name with which a resource, such as a directory, is shared does not have to match the name of that resource on the server.

To connect to a shared directory tree, the client sends an SMB called a tcon or tconX (short for tree connect) request to the server. This request specifies the network name of the shared tree that the client wants to use. The server responds with a tcon or tconX response that contains a tree ID (TID) for the requested shared tree. The client uses this TID in all of its requests for files in that shared tree. The process of accessing a printer is similar.

Once a client has accessed a shared resource such as a directory tree, it can send, open, read, write, and close SMBs for files in that resource.

**SMB Dialects**    There are several versions or dialects of the SMB protocol. The first version, usually called Core Protocol, was released by IBM as PC Network Program 1.0 or PCLAN 1.0. It handled a fairly basic set of operations, including:

- Connecting and disconnecting from file and print shares
- Opening, reading, writing, and closing files
- Getting and setting file attributes
- Opening and closing print files
- Creating and deleting files and directories

As additional features were required, newer versions of the SMB protocol were developed. The first revision was Microsoft's Networks 1.03, which implemented a version of the SMB protocol called Core Protocol Plus. It added new SMBs that allowed for locking and unlocking files. Following Core Protocol Plus, several versions of the SMB protocol were released under the name LAN Manager (often referred to as LANMAN). Version 1.0 of LAN Manager added OS/2-specific SMBs, and versions 2.0 and 2.1 added support for Windows for Workgroups. With the release of Windows NT 4.0, Microsoft introduced the NT LAN Manager 1.0 product, which contained special SMBs for NT. This product was based on the NT LM 0.12 protocol that SAMBA provides an implementation of.

The most recent version of the SMB protocol is called the Common Internet File System (CIFS). It is based on NT LAN Manager 1.0, and includes some extensions and refinements for use over the Internet. One of the major changes in this version is that CIFS has been designed to use DNS rather than NetBIOS as its main naming service. Microsoft has submitted the CIFS 1.0 protocol specification to the Internet Engineering Task Force (IETF) as an Internet-draft document and it is currently working towards developing RFCs that describe the protocol in detail. For more information on CIFS, you can consult Microsoft's CIFS home page at:

**http://msdn.microsoft.com/workshop/networking/cifs/default.asp**

## SMB Server Security

The SMB protocol addresses issues of access control and security by allowing any shared resource on a server to be protected by a password. In addition, it offers two standard levels of security: Share Level security and User Level security. The security level for an SMB server is the same for all shared resources; it is not possible to share some resources at Share Level security and others at User Level security.

**Share Level Security**    Share Level security is the "low" security setting in the SMB protocol. Clients connecting to a server with Share Level security are not required to log in with a valid username and password before attempting to connect to a shared resource. Most modern clients such as Windows 95/98 and Windows NT send a logon request with a username but no password when connecting to a server with Share

Level security. Clients are only required to send a username and password when connecting to a shared resource on the server that is password protected.

**User Level Security**    User Level security is the "high" security setting in the SMB protocol; it is also the default security setting for most UNIX-based SMB servers, including SAMBA. When a client connects to a server with User Level security it needs to log in with a valid username and password before it can attempt to connect to a shared resource. This security level also supports the use of encrypted passwords.

**Domains Versus Workgroups**    The security information (usernames and passwords) used to implement either security level for a particular SMB server can be stored on the server or on a separate system, depending on whether the server is part of a *workgroup* or a *domain*, respectively. A workgroup is a collection of computers that maintain their own security information. In a workgroup, security is distributed, not centralized, and any one of a group of servers could potentially take care of authentication. A domain, on the other hand, is a collection of computers where security is handled centrally. Each domain has a collection of one or more domain controllers. There is usually a primary domain controller and several backup domain controllers. The domain controllers maintain account information related to clients, such as account names, encrypted passwords, and group information.

# AppleTalk

AppleTalk is the networking system developed by Apple Computer and available as the standard file and printer sharing system under the Mac OS. It is also supported on many UNIX systems by various freeware and commercial packages. The AppleTalk protocol suite includes file sharing via AppleShare, support for printing and print spooler services, and facilities for low data streams and datagram delivery. Currently, the file sharing facility of AppleTalk, called AppleShare, is available on top of TCP/IP, in addition to the file sharing provided by the AppleTalk protocol suite.

## AppleTalk Protocols

The term AppleTalk was originally used for both the protocol and connecting cables. When Apple introduced support for several different types of physical media, the name of the "Link Layer" protocol was changed to reflect the media on which AppleTalk was running. The term LocalTalk is used to describe networks based on simple shielded twisted pair cable (such as phone cable). The terms EtherTalk and TokenTalk correspond to AppleTalk over Ethernet and TokenRing networks respectively.

At the equivalent of the Network Layer, AppleTalk has two separate protocols that serve the same function as ARP and UDP. The AppleTalk equivalent of ARP is the AppleTalk Address Resolution Protocol (AARP), which resolves the MAC address of a system into its AppleTalk address. AppleTalk addresses are discussed shortly. The equivalent of UDP is the Datagram Deliver Protocol (DDP).

It provides the same type of connectionless datagram service. In all major UNIX versions of AppleTalk, DDP is usually implemented within the kernel or as a kernel module. On Solaris 8 it is available implemented as an additional kernel module.

At the Transport Layer, AppleTalk has two separate protocols that are used to provide name services. The Name Binding Protocol (NBP) is similar to DNS and provides a mapping between AppleTalk addresses and hostnames. In general, the AppleTalk hostname for a system does not have to be the same as its DNS hostname, but for ease of administration most systems have the same DNS and AppleTalk name. The Zone Information Protocol (ZIP) handles name resolution between AppleTalk hosts in different zones. AppleTalk zones are discussed shortly.

At the Application Layer, AppleTalk has several protocols for sharing file and printing resources. The file sharing protocol is called the Apple Filing Protocol (AFP), while the printer sharing protocol is called the Printer Access Protocol (PAP). AppleShare is implemented using AFP.

The AppleTalk protocol stack is illustrated in Figure 18-3.

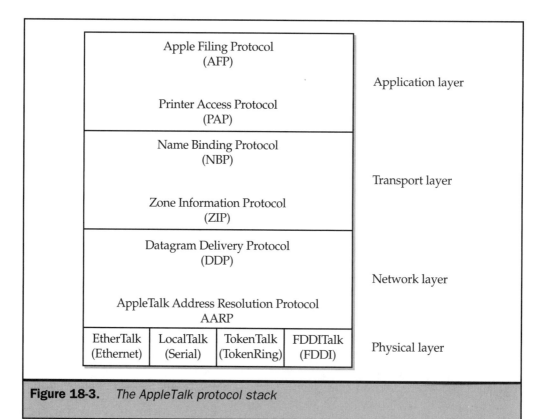

**Figure 18-3.**   *The AppleTalk protocol stack*

## AppleTalk Addresses

Each system in an AppleTalk network has an AppleTalk 24-bit address consisting of the system's node number and network number. Node numbers are 8 bits long and can be between 1 and 253. Network numbers are 16 bits long and can be between 1 and 65535. Normally the AppleTalk address of a system is written in a dotted decimal notation in this format:

*network.node*

Here, *network* is the AppleTalk network number the system is a part of and node is the AppleTalk *node* number for the system. For example, a system on AppleTalk network 100 with the node address of 2 has an AppleTalk address of 100.2. The dotted decimal format is similar to notation used for IP addresses.

Theoretically the maximum number of AppleTalk nodes that can be present in a single network is about 16 million, which makes the AppleTalk address space roughly equivalent to a Class B IP Address.

**Phase I Versus Phase II**    There are two different types of AppleTalk addresses, Phase I and Phase II. Phase I addressing was the original form of AppleTalk addressing and has been obsolete since 1988. In Phase I addressing, a single Ethernet or TokenRing network (called a *cable*) could have only one network address, limiting the number of hosts on the network to 253. In order to have a second network, you needed an AppleTalk router to connect the two networks. In this respect, Phase I addressing is roughly equivalent to a Class C address.

Phase II addressing (also referred to as Extended addressing) replaced Phase I addressing in 1988 and is the current standard. It allows for a range of network numbers to be used on a single cable. By using Phase II addressing you can designate a set of network addresses, for example 100 to 105, to be used on a single Ethernet or TokenRing network, thereby increasing the number of hosts you can have connected to an AppleTalk network.

**Zones**    For network load sharing or administrative purposes or simply convenience, network numbers can be grouped together into a *zone*. A zone is basically a named AppleTalk entity that encapsulates all of the network numbers within it. A Phase II AppleTalk network may have up to 255 zones assigned to a single cable, with one of these being denoted as the default zone. A Macintosh on a multiple-zone extended network can choose any of the available zones as its default zone.

## AppleTalk Named Objects

To facilitate the process of finding and remembering the locations of different AppleTalk services, an AppleTalk address can be associated with a name using the Name Binding Protocol (NBP). Each AppleTalk service, such as file sharing, can

register an NBP name and an object type within a zone. The registered names have the
following format:

*host:service@zone*

Here, *host* is the AppleTalk hostname of the system, *service* is the name of the
AppleTalk service, and *zone* is the name of the AppleTalk zone. Some of the common
service names are listed here:

| Service Name | Purpose |
|---|---|
| Workstation | Indicates that the system is a workstation |
| LaserWriter | Indicates that the system is a printer, specifically a laser printer |
| AFPServer | Indicates that the system is an AppleTalk File Server |

As an example, a file server named rishi within the bosland AppleTalk zone may
have the AppleTalk name rishi: AFPServer@bosland.

# SAMBA

The SAMBA project grew out of the needs of Andrew Tridgell in the early 1990s.
He had a DOS PC and wanted to mount the disks from his UNIX server on his PC.
Although it was possible to do this with NFS clients for DOS, these clients did not
work well with applications that required the NetBIOS interface. In order to solve this
problem Andrew used a packet sniffer to reverse engineer the SMB protocol. Once he
knew how the protocol worked, he implemented an SMB server daemon for his UNIX
system. From the perspective of the DOS PC, the UNIX server looked like an ordinary
PC file server. This allowed him to access shared file systems from the UNIX server
without affecting applications that required NetBIOS. Andrew made the code for his
SMB server daemon available in 1992. Although there was some interest from various
users on the Internet, Andrew mostly ignored his creation until 1994, when he needed
to link his wife's Windows PC to his Linux system. He took the server code that he had
written in 1992 and modified it to support the SMB changes introduced by Windows.
As he developed this new version, several of his Internet contacts pointed Andrew
to some documentation covering NetBIOS and SMB. This allowed him to update his
server code so that it was no longer based on information that he gained from his
reverse engineering. Since 1995, the popularity of SAMBA has grown steadily.
Currently Andrew is assisted in his efforts by a core team of developers worldwide.
As of this writing the most recent version of SAMBA includes several types
of security above and beyond the standard Windows security, along with several
improvements for interoperability with Windows NT. Version 2.0 is especially
significant in that it is the first non-Microsoft implementation that handles NT Domain

authentication. Some of the ongoing work includes support for Windows NT's Access Control Lists (ACLs), support for the Lightweight Directory Access Protocol (LDAP), and support for Microsoft's Distributed File System (DFS). Currently SAMBA does not offer all of the features of a full NT server. The main feature that is missing is the ability for SAMBA to act as a primary domain controller for Windows NT domains. This functionality is currently slated for version 2.1. Other functionality of NT currently absent from SAMBA are trust relationships, primary domain controller–to–backup domain controller integration, and Windows NT Access Control Lists on SAMBA shares.

SAMBA consists of two main programs, **smbd** and **nmbd**, that implement the major SMB/CIFS services for authentication, announcement, name resolution, and sharing. Sharing covers file and printer sharing. Authentication and sharing are handled by **smbd**, the SMB Daemon, while **nmbd** handles announcement (browsing shares) and name resolution.

# Installing SAMBA

SAMBA is freely available on the Internet in both binary and source form. The main FTP site for samba is **ftp://ftp.samba.org**. Due to the high demand on this server, you may find it inaccessible from time to time. If you encounter problems connecting to the server, you can use one of the alternative download sites listed on the main SAMBA web page at **http://www.samba.org**.

As of this writing the most recent version of the SAMBA source code is 2.05a. Usually the binary distribution on the SAMBA FTP sites is one or two revisions behind the source version. The binary distribution is usually in the form of a Solaris package. The standard binary distribution is divided into four separate packages. Alternatively you can obtain a single Solaris package from **http://www.sunfreeware.com/**.

## Installing the Package Distributions

The standard package distribution for SAMBA contains four Solaris packages: SAMBAroot, SAMBAusr, SAMBAman, and SAMBAdoc. The SAMBAroot package contains the system configuration file changes required to integrate SAMBA into the system startup process. The SAMBAusr package contains the binaries for SAMBA and for the graphical administration tool, SWAT. The SAMBAman package contains the man pages for SAMBA, while the SAMBAdoc package contains additional documentation. These four packages are distributed together in a single tar-compressed file. As an example, the Solaris 2.6 tar-compressed file for SAMBA version 2.0.5 is named samba-2.0.5-sparc-sun-solaris2.6.tar.Z. Depending on your version of Solaris the filename will be slightly different.

To uncompress and untar the contents, you should first create a temporary directory and extract the packages into that directory:

```
# mkdir /tmp/samba && cd /tmp/samba
# zcat dir/samba-2.0.5-sparc-sun-solaris2.6.tar.Z | tar –xvf -
```

Here, *dir* is the absolute or relative path to the directory where you placed the downloaded file. Based on this format, you can use the following command to install the packages:

```
# pkgadd -d /tmp/samba SAMBAroot SAMBAusr SAMBAman SAMBAdoc
```

Once the first package, SAMBAroot, is installed, /etc/services will be updated for **SWAT**, netbios-ssn, and netbios-ns. In addition, this package also configures /etc/inetd.conf to allow **inetd** to invoke SAMBA. Finally, it places startup scripts in /etc/init.d/samba and links to /etc/rc2.d/S99samba. If you install SAMBA using these four packages, you should not have to follow the instructions given later in this chapter for integrating SAMBA with system startup and shutdown. Once all these package binaries are added, the binaries and man pages for SAMBA will be located in the directories /opt/samba/bin and /opt/samba/man respectively.

The binary distribution available from *http://www.sunfreeware.com/* contains a single package. Depending on the version of Solaris your system is running, the name of the package will differ slightly. For Solaris 2.6 the package is named BSsamba and is distributed in package stream format. The file you download will be in GNU Zip format and will have a name similar to samba-2.0.0-sol26-sparc-local.gz. You can add the package using commands similar to the following:

```
# gunzip samba-2.0.0-sol26-sparc-local.gz
# pkgadd -d samba-2.0.0-sol26-sparc-local
```

Just replace samba-2.0.0-sol26-sparc-local.gz and samba-2.0.0-sol26-sparc-local with the correct name for the file you've downloaded.

Once the package is added, the binaries and man pages for SAMBA will be located in the directories /usr/local/samba/bin and /usr/local/samba/man respectively. The additional documentation will be located in the directory /usr/local/doc/samba. This package version of Solaris does not automatically integrate with the system startup procedure, so you will have to follow the instructions given later in this chapter for integrating SAMBA with system startup and shutdown.

## Compiling SAMBA

The source distribution for SAMBA is available from any of the SAMBA download sites located on the main SAMBA web page *http://www.samba.org*. Usually the latest source is located in a GNU zipped tar file named samba-latest.tar.gz. To extract this file you can use the following command:

```
$ gzip -cd samba-latest.tar.gz | tar -xvf -
```

This will create a directory that contains the source files for SAMBA. For SAMBA version 2.05a this directory is called samba-2.0.5a. To start building SAMBA you need to change into the directory samba-2.0.5a/source.

The process of compiling and installing SAMBA is quite simple. You need to have the compiler tools directory, /usr/ccs/bin, in your path, along with a C compiler such as the GNU C compiler (available in package format from **http://www.sunfreeware.com**) or the SunPRO C compiler. Once you have made certain that you have a C compiler and the compiler tools in your path, you can run the **configure** script to configure the SAMBA source code for your system:

```
$ ./configure
```

When **configure** is executed without any options it configures SAMBA to use default settings. It also configures the installation directory as /usr/local/samba. If you want to use a different directory, you can specify the **--prefix** option as follows:

$ ./configure —prefix=*dir*

Here, *dir* is the absolute path to the directory where you want SAMBA to be installed. For example, the following command configures the installation directory to be /opt/samba:

```
$ ./configure --prefix=/opt/samba
```

In addition to this option, the **configure** script also accepts several options that allow you to enable and disable several experimental features in SAMBA. Some of these options are listed here:

| Option | Purpose |
| --- | --- |
| --with-smbwrapper | Creates a shared library (smbwrapper.so) and shell (**smbshell**) that allow you to access shared resources on other SMB servers using a special directory, /smb/*server*, where *server* is the name of an SMB server. |
| --with-automount | Includes support for the automounter. |
| --with-pam | Includes support for Pluggable Authentication Modules (PAM). |
| --with-ldap | Includes support for the Lightweight Directory Access Protocol (LDAP). |
| --with-nisplus | Includes support for NIS+. |
| --with-syslog | Includes support for logging to **syslogd**. |

For a full list of the options accepted by **configure** you can execute the script with the —**help** option:

ADMINISTERING
SERVICES

```
$ ./configure --help
```

This option only prints out a list of the other supported options, it does not configure SAMBA in any way.

Once you have selected the options for **configure**, you need to execute the script so that it can configure the SAMBA source code for your system. While the command is running you will see messages similar to the following on your screen:

```
creating cache ./config.cache
checking for gcc... gc
checking whether the C compiler (gcc -O ) works... yes
...
```

Depending on the type of system you have, this script can take between three minutes (for an Ultra) to seven minutes (for a SPARCstation 10) to complete. When it completes, you will see messages similar to the following before your prompt is returned:

```
checking configure summary
configure OK
updating cache ./config.cache
creating ./config.status
creating include/stamp-h
creating Makefile
creating include/config.h
```

Once **configure** completes you can build SAMBA as follows:

```
$ make
```

As this command executes you will see the command being used to compile the source files into executables. It can take up to 15 minutes to compile SAMBA on older hardware such as a SPARCstation 10. Once the compilation completes you can install SAMBA using the command:

```
# make install
```

This will install all of the SAMBA programs and documentation.

## Integrating SAMBA into System Startup/Shutdown

To start SAMBA at system boot time you need to create a script that starts and stops SAMBA. Usually this script is placed in the directory /etc/init.d. The following is a simple example of such a startup script:

```
#!/sbin/sh
# Start Samba SMB services

# Set environment
PATH=/usr/bin:/sbin:/usr/sbin; export PATH
SAMBA_DIR=/opt/samba
SAMBA_SMBD_DEBUG_LEVEL=0
SAMBA_NMBD_DEBUG_LEVEL=0
SAMBA_SMBD_LOG=/var/opt/samba/log.smb
SAMBA_NMBD_LOG=/var/opt/samba/log.nmb
# function for kill all processes matching a certain name
kill_proc () {
    ps -ef | grep "$1" | grep -v grep |
    while read PROC; do
        PID=`echo ${PROC} | awk '{ print $2 }'`
        [ ${PID} -gt 0 ] && kill ${PID}
    done
}

case "$1" in
    start)
        ${SAMBA_DIR}/bin/smbd -D -d ${SAMBA_SMBD_DEBUG_LEVEL:=0} \
            -l ${SAMBA_SMBD_LOG:=/var/opt/samba/log.smb}
        ${SAMBA_DIR}/bin/nmbd -D -d ${SAMBA_NMBD_DEBUG_LEVEL:=0} \
            -l ${SAMBA_NMBD_LOG:=/var/opt/samba/log.nmb}
        echo "Samba services started."
        ;;
    stop)
        kill_proc "${SAMBA_DIR}/bin/nmbd"
        kill_proc "${SAMBA_DIR}/bin/smbd"
        echo "Samba services stopped."
        ;;
    *) echo "Usage: $0 { start | stop }" ; exit 1 ;;
esac
```

**ADMINISTERING SERVICES**

If this script were called **samba** and were located in /etc/init.d, you could start SAMBA using the command:

```
# /etc/init.d/samba start
```

Similarly, to stop SAMBA you could use the command:

```
# /etc/init.d/samba stop
```

To integrate this script into system startup, you need to create a link in /etc/rc3.d as follows:

```
# cd /etc/rc3.d
# ln -s ../init.d/samba S25samba
```

When the system reaches runlevel 3, SAMBA will be started. It is possible to start SAMBA at runlevel 2, but runlevel 3 is preferred since the NFS server is also started at runlevel 3. To stop SAMBA during system shutdown, you need to create a link in /etc/rc2.d as follows:

```
# cd /etc/rc2.d
# ln -s ../init.d/samba K75samba
```

**Note** *Some versions of the prepackaged SAMBA distribution from **ftp://ftp.samba.org** create links for the SAMBA startup in /etc/rc2.d rather than /etc/rc3.d. There is no functional difference, but most administrators prefer /etc/rc3.d.*

# Configuring SAMBA

In this section we will look at the process of configuring the SAMBA server using the web-based configuration tool **SWAT**. The first step in configuring SAMBA is to understand and choose a security level for your SAMBA server. Once you have selected a security level, you can use **SWAT** to configure your server and the shared volumes.

## Choosing a Security Level

In addition to the standard Share Level security and User Level security, SAMBA provides two additional levels of security, Server Level security and Domain Level security. These security levels are server-side only, and do not require any changes on the client side. From the client's point of view Server Level security and Domain Level security appear to be the same as User Level security.

If your server is located in a corporate intranet, then the default User Level security should be sufficiently secure. For servers located in university intranets or on the Internet, a higher level of security is preferred.

**Server Level Security**    The Server Level security is an "extra-high" security mode available only in SAMBA. In this mode SAMBA tries to validate the username and encrypted password provided by the client by passing it to another SMB server, such as an NT system. If this fails, the server reverts to the User Level security.

**Domain Level Security**    SAMBA's Domain Level security is a further extension of the Server Level security mode. When SAMBA is configured to use Domain Level security it tries to validate the username and password supplied by the client by passing it to a Windows NT primary or backup domain controller in exactly the same manner as Windows NT Server. Currently Domain Level security doesn't free you from having to create local UNIX user accounts for NT users that access your server. This means that if domain user fred in the domain DOM attaches to your domain-security SAMBA server, there needs to be a local user account fred on your system.

| Note | *Domain Level security works correctly only if the **smbpasswd** command has been used to add the SAMBA server system to a Windows NT domain. The process of adding a SAMBA server to an NT domain is covered later in this section.* |
| --- | --- |

**Windows NT Security Issues**    There are two main security issues that you need to be aware of when selecting Server Level or Domain Level security for your SMB server. The first security issue stems from the guest account on Windows NT. The second security issue stems from an unknown issue in Windows NT.

When guest access is enabled on certain versions of Windows NT, it will honor any logon attempt, even if the username and password supplied by the user are incorrect. Windows NT sends a positive response to the client and logs the client in as the guest user. If SAMBA uses such an NT system to validate passwords, the security of your SAMBA server can be compromised. For example, any access using the username root will always be validated even if the password was incorrect. There is no way that SAMBA can tell from the reply packet from NT whether the password was correct and normal user privilege has been granted, or whether the password was incorrect and the user has been given only "guest" privileges. Microsoft has issued several security fixes to fix this weakness in Windows NT. You should install these security patches on any NT server that will be used to validate passwords for your SAMBA server. Also, if possible you should disable guest access on all Windows NT systems used to validate passwords.

In some cases Windows NT servers accept and validate any username and password pair for session setup requests. SAMBA checks for this by deliberately sending an incorrect password when calling the password server in Server Level security. If the incorrect password succeeds, then SAMBA logs an error and refuses to use that password server. It is possible to remove this check from the code, however, if you remove this check, it is possible that your NT server will start behaving incorrectly, and may make your SAMBA server less secure.

## SWAT

The SAMBA Web Administration Tool, **SWAT**, is part of the SAMBA suite and allows a SAMBA administrator to configure the complex smb.conf file via a web browser. In addition, the main **SWAT** configuration page has help links to all the configurable options in the smb.conf file, allowing an administrator to easily look up the effects of any change.

Depending on how you installed SAMBA the location of **SWAT** will vary. The default location for the compiled or binary distribution from **ftp://ftp.samba.org** is /opt/samba/bin/SWAT, with the help and image files located in /opt/samba/ SWAT/help and /opt/samba/SWAT/images, respectively. The binary distribution from **http://www.sunfreeware.com** installs SWAT in /usr/local/samba/bin/SWAT, with the help and image files located in /usr/local/samba/SWAT/help and /usr/local/samba/SWAT/images, respectively.

**Enabling SWAT**   Normally SWAT is invoked via **inetd**. The default installation will configure **inetd** to enable **SWAT**, but you should check over these files to make sure that **SWAT** is configured to run correctly. The first step is to make sure that a line similar to the following was added to /etc/services:

```
SWAT    901/tcp
```

The default port number for **SWAT** is 901, but the choice of port number isn't really important except that it should be less than 1024 and not currently used. Using a port number above 1024 can expose a security hole in **inetd** on systems that are not running Solaris 2.6 or later. If an entry for **SWAT** does not exist in /etc/services, you should go ahead and add it.

The second step is to confirm that a line similar to the following exists in your /etc/inetd.conf:

```
SWAT   stream  tcp   nowait.400   root   /opt/samba/bin/SWAT SWAT
```

Depending on the location where you installed SWAT, the path to the SWAT binary may vary. If you do not find this line in your /etc/inetd.conf, be sure to add it.

If you edited either /etc/services or /etc/inetd.conf, you need to restart the inetd daemon by sending it a HUP signal. You can use the following command to obtain the process ID for inetd:

```
$ /bin/ps -ef | grep inetd | grep -v grep
root    144    1  0   Aug 27 ?         0:00 /usr/sbin/inetd -s
```

The second column contains the process ID. To restart the daemon just issue the following command:

```
# kill -HUP pid
```

In the case of the previous example we would use the command:

```
# kill -HUP 144
```

**Launching SWAT**   To launch SWAT just run your favorite web browser and point it at the URL **http://localhost:901/**. You can attach to SWAT from any machine, but connecting from a remote machine leaves your connection open to password sniffing, as passwords will be sent in the clear over the wire. Figure 18-4 shows a snapshot of the SWAT screen.

The resulting simple (and potentially nonsecure) configuration stored in smb.conf is as follows:

```
# Samba config file created using SWAT
# from samba.mydomain.org (192.168.0.10)
# Date: 1999/06/29 22:21:31

# Global parameters
[global]
workgroup = MYGROUP
netbios name = MYSERVER
server string = Samba Server V2.0.5a
interfaces = 192.168.0.10
security = SHARE
log file = /var/log/samba/log.%m
max log size = 50
socket options = TCP_NODELAY SO_RCVBUF=8192 SO_SNDBUF=8192
os level = 65
dns proxy = No
guest account = guest
hosts allow = localhost, 192.168.0.0/255.255.255.0

[homes]
comment = Home Directories
read only = No
browseable = No

[printers]
comment = All Printers
path = /var/spool/samba
print ok = Yes
browseable = No

[public]
comment = Public documents
path = /home/public/documents
guest ok = Yes
```

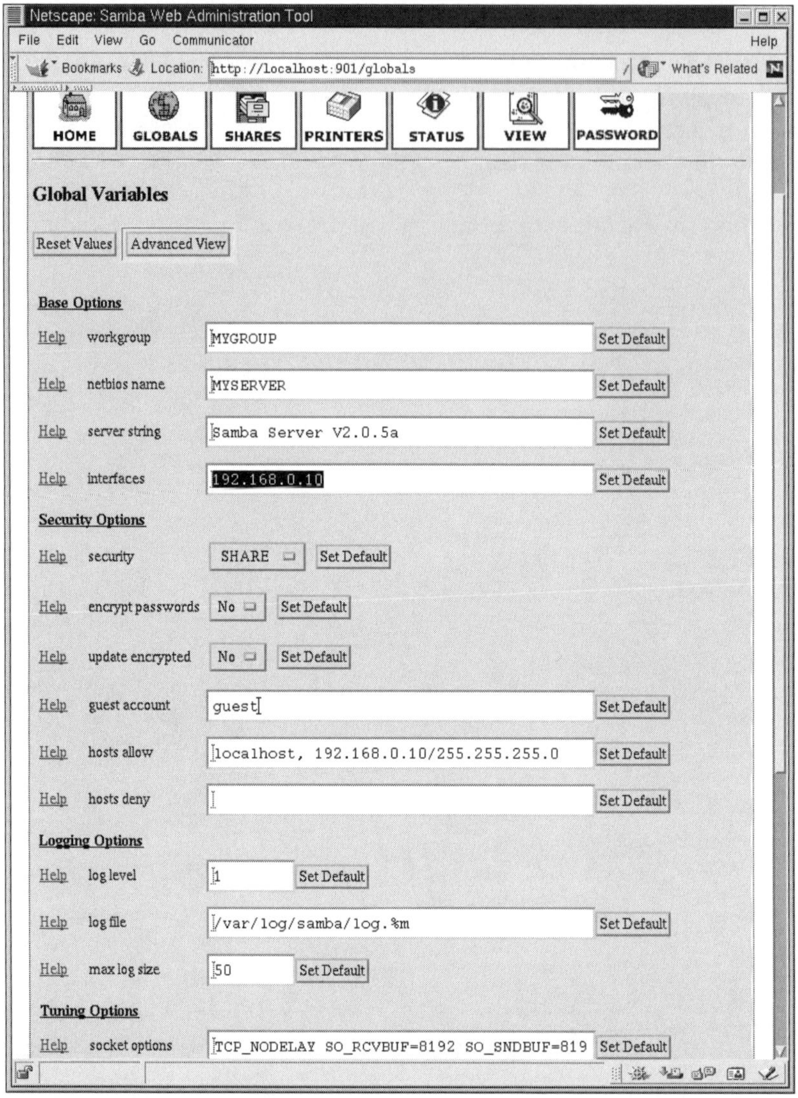

**Figure 18-4.** *A screen shot of SWAT*

The default configuration allows for printers to be exported from Solaris systems to be accessible from Microsoft Windows systems. This is a great improvement over the access to remote print services described in Chapter 17, which only allowed UNIX systems to share printers with each other. Thus, SAMBA supports a wide variety of hosts and operating systems for printing.

# Configuring Advanced Server Access

The **SWAT** utility allows you to configure most of the basic access information for shared resources on your SAMBA server. In most cases, **SWAT** is quite sufficient; if you need more advanced access controls you will need to configure them using the **smbpasswd** command. The main situation where you need more access control than can be provided by **SWAT** is when you need to allow connections from clients that are using encrypted passwords. The majority of clients that use encrypted passwords are Windows NT systems that have Service Pack 3 or later installed. These service packs change the behavior of NT so that it refuses to connect to servers that do not support SMB password encryption. A secondary use of the **smbpasswd** command is in adding your system to a Windows NT domain.

## Using the smbpasswd Command

The **smbpasswd** command, which is part of the SAMBA suite, is used to change or add encrypted passwords for SMB users.

When the **smbpasswd** command is executed by a normal user it allows the user to change the password used for their SMB sessions on machines that store SMB passwords. The encrypted SMB passwords are usually stored in a file named smbpasswd. This is similar to the way UNIX's **passwd** program works. The main difference between these two commands is that **smbpasswd** is not setuid root like the **passwd** command; rather, it acts as a client to the locally running smbd server. For this reason the smbd daemon must be running on the local machine.

When run with no options by ordinary users, **smbpasswd** prompts the user for their old SMB password and then asks them for their new password twice, to ensure that the new password was typed correctly. No characters are echoed on the screen while the password is being entered. If you have a blank SMB password (specified by the string "NO PASSWORD" in the smbpasswd file) then just press the ENTER key when asked for your old password.

When run by root, **smbpasswd** allows new users to be added and deleted in the smbpasswd file, and also allows changes to be made (within the file) to the attributes of those users. When run by root, it accesses the local smbpasswd file directly, thus enabling changes to be made even if **smbd** is not running.

Users can also use the **smbpasswd** command to change their SMB password on remote machines, such as Windows NT primary domain controllers. See the command's -r and -U options for more information on this topic, or look up the associated manual pages.

**Securing the smbpasswd File**    Due to the challenge/response nature of the SMB/CIFS authentication protocol, it is extremely important that you keep the passwords in the smbpasswd file secure. If a malicious user is able to access this file they will be able to impersonate that user (and possibly others) on the network. Also, the passwords used by the SMB/CIFS protocol are not as secure as standard UNIX passwords, as they are hashes or plain-text equivalents of a user's password rather than an encrypted version of the password. To protect these passwords, the **smbpasswd** file should be placed in a directory with read and traverse access only to the root user, and the **smbpasswd** file itself must be set to be read/write only by root, with no other access.

The two main types of password hashes used by SMB/CIFS are the LAN Manager and the Windows NT hashes. The LAN Manager hash of the user's password is encoded as 32 hex digits. The hash created by DES encrypting is a well-known string with the user's password as the DES key. This method is used by Windows 95/98 machines. This password hash is regarded as weak for various reasons:

- It is vulnerable to dictionary attacks.

- If two users choose the same password the entry will be identical, since the password is not *salted*, as a UNIX password is.

- If the user has a null password this field will contain the characters "NO PASSWORD" as the start of the hex string.

- If the hex string contains only the character "X" 32 times, then the user's account is marked as disabled and the user will not be able to log on to the SAMBA server.

The Windows NT hash of the user's password is also encoded as 32 hex digits. The Windows NT hash is created by taking the user's password as represented in 16-bit, little-endian UNICODE and then applying the MD4 (RFC1321) hashing algorithm to it. This password hash is considered more secure than the LAN Manager password hash because it preserves the case of the password and uses a much higher quality hashing algorithm. However, it is still the case that if two users choose the same password this entry will be identical, since the password is not salted, as UNIX passwords are.

## Joining an NT Domain

To include a SAMBA server in an NT domain, you must first add the NetBIOS name of the SAMBA server to the NT domain on the primary domain controller (PDC), using Server Manager for Domains, which is part of the NT operating system. This creates the machine account in the domain (PDC) SAM. Once the SAMBA server has an account on the PDC, you can join that domain using the following command:

    # smbpasswd -j *domain* -r *pdc*

Here, *domain* is the name of the NT domain you want to join and *pdc* is the name of the PDC for that domain. As an example, assume that you have a SAMBA server with a NetBIOS name of SERV1 and are joining an NT domain called DOM, where the PDC for this domain has the NetBIOS name of DOMPDC. (Assume also that there are two backup domain controllers, with the NetBIOS names DOMBDC1 and DOMBDC2. These will come up later in the example.) In order to join this domain, you need to first shut down SAMBA using the script in /etc/init.d. Then you can run the command as follows:

```
# smbpasswd -j DOM -r DOMPDC
```

If the SAMBA server successfully joined the domain you will see the following message:

```
smbpasswd: Joined domain DOM.
```

This command goes through the machine account password change protocol, then writes the new (random) machine account password for this SAMBA server into a file in the same directory where the smbpasswd file is stored (usually /usr/local/samba or /opt/samba/private). The filename has the following format:

*domain.server.mac*

Here, *domain* is the name of the NT domain and *server* is the name of the SAMBA server. The *.mac* suffix stands for machine account password file. In the sample setup, the resulting file would be called DOM.SERV1.mac. This file is created and owned by root and is not readable by any other user. It is the key to the domain-level security for your system, and should be treated as carefully as a shadow password file.

Before restarting the SAMBA daemons you must edit your smb.conf file to tell SAMBA it should now use Domain Level security. You will need to change or add lines similar to the following:

```
security=domain
workgroup=DOM
encrypt passwords=yes
password server=DOMPDC DOMBDC1 DOMBDC2
```

The first line indicates that you want to use Domain Level security. The second line indicates the name of the NT domain that you are part of, in this case the domain DOM. The third line indicates that all your passwords are encrypted. This is required in order for your users to authenticate with the NT PDC. The final line lists the systems to use for authenticating passwords. In this case the primary and both backup domain controllers are listed, and SAMBA will attempt to contact all three of them in order to authenticate users. Since SAMBA tries to contact each of these servers in order, you may want to rearrange this list in order to spread out the authentication load among domain controllers.

ADMINISTERING SERVICES

Once the SAMBA server has joined the NT domain, the SAMBA box can validate users against the NT PDC. However, SAMBA will need some way of mapping the determined user's NT RID (relative ID) to a valid UNIX UID. There are two ways to do this. One is to use the "username map =" parameter. The other is to create accounts for all your NT users in /etc/passwd on the UNIX box. There are some Perl scripts available to help in the migration. They are available for download from the /pub/samba/contributed directory in one of the SAMBA mirrors. The tarball is usually named *domain_member_scripts.tar.gz*.

Accounts created on the UNIX box are only used to get a valid UID. They are not used for validation. You can therefore set the password field to any lock string for your system. Under most (if not all) versions of UNIX this is the "*" character. Here is an example /etc/passwd entry:

```
jdoe:*:1124:100:NT dummy account:/dev/null:/bin/False
```

Once you have gotten this far, you should now be able to mount shares from the SAMBA server using valid domain accounts. More information on how to join an NT domain can be obtained at

**http://samba.org/samba/docs/ntdom_faq/samba_ntdom_faq.html**

## Alternatives to SAMBA

Although SAMBA is the most popular SMB server on Solaris systems, it is not the only option. There are two other SMB servers available for Solaris:

- VisionFS from Santa Cruz Operations
- TotalNET Advanced Server from Syntax

VisionFS from Santa Cruz Operation (SCO) provides an SMB server that allows PC clients to access both shared directories and printers. It is available for all major versions of UNIX including Solaris 2.3 and later for SPARC-based systems. For more information about VisionFS, you can consult its home page at

**http://www.sco.com/vision/products/visionfs/**

A 30-day evaluation copy of VisionFS is also available from this home page.

The TotalNET Advanced Server (TAS) from Syntax provides a single server that implements both SMB and AppleTalk. It is available for all major versions of UNIX, including Solaris version 2.5.1 and later on both SPARC- and x86-based systems. For more information about TAS, visit its home page at **http://www.syntax.com**.

A 100-user evaluation copy of TAS is available from this site. The most recent version of TAS as of this writing is version 5.4.1.

TAS is also available directly from Sun under the product name Solaris Easy Access Server. In addition to the standard functionality of TAS, Sun's version includes an easy-to-use administration interface geared for Windows administrators. For more information about Solaris Easy Access Server, go to its home page at

> **http://www.sun.com/solaris/easyaccess/**

# Netatalk

Netatalk is a kernel-level implementation of the AppleTalk Protocol Suite by the Research System UNIX Group (RSUG) at the University of Michigan. It was originally developed for BSD-derived systems such as SunOS. Since then it has been extended to include support for Linux- and System VNN–based systems such as Solaris. The last release version of netatalk by the RSUG was 1.4b2 in October of 1997. Since then Adrian Sun (asun) of the University of Washington has taken over development and has issued number fixes and patches, including AFP 2.2 (Appleshare TCP/IP) support.

Netatalk consists of three separate daemons that work with the DDP kernel module on Solaris. The three daemons are **atalkd**, **afpd**, and **papd**. The **atalkd** daemon is responsible for handling incoming AppleTalk requests. The **afpd** daemon is responsible for handling requests for file sharing, and the **papd** is responsible for handling printer requests. Since **papd** is designed for systems based on the BSD printing system, it does not work correctly on Solaris systems. My discussion of netatalk will focus on the file sharing daemon, **afpd**.

## Installing Netatalk

The current version of netatalk, 1.4b2, and Adrian Sun's patches are available from his FTP site

> **ftp://ftp.uwashington.edu/public/asun/**

As of this writing the most recent patch level is asun2.1.3. This version is available as netatalk-1.4b2+asun2.1.3.tar.gz. Currently, binary distributions of this version are not widely available, so it is recommended that you compile your own version.

### Checking for Required Patches

Before you begin to compile and install netatalk, you may need to install some Solaris patches to prevent kernel panics associated with the network drivers on some

Ultra-based systems. On Solaris 2.5.1 you will need to install patch 104212-13. On Solaris 2.6, you will need to install patch 105795-05 instead. You can check to see if a required patch is already installed on your system using the following command:

> $ showrev -p | awk '$2 ~ /^*major*/ { print; }'

Here, *major* is the patch major number you are checking for. For example, to check for patch 105795-05 you can use the following command:

```
$ showrev -p | awk '$2 ~ /^105795/ { print; }'
```

If this command produces one or more lines of output, then you probably have the appropriate patches installed. If this command does not produce any output, you will need to obtain the appropriate patch from SunSolve, as covered in Chapter 6.

## Unpacking and Customizing Netatalk

The first step in compiling netatalk is to unpack your distribution. You can do this as follows:

```
$ gzip -cd netatalk-1.4b2+asun2.1.3.tar.gz | tar -xvf -
```

This will create the directory netatalk-1.4b2+asun2.1.3. This is the main directory with the netatalk sources. It also contains several important text files that you should read before you start configuring and building netatalk. The three files you should read are README, README.ASUN, and INSTALL/README.SOLARIS. These files have additional details, beyond the scope of this chapter, about compiling and installing netatalk on Solaris.

**Customizing Netatalk**   The second step in compiling netatalk is to make sure that you have a C compiler (either the GNU C compiler or the SunPRO C compiler) and the compiler tools located in /usr/ccs/bin in your path. Once you are certain these are in your path, you can begin to customize netatalk for your site by editing portions of its Makefile. The three main customizations you can make are:

- Changing the installation or destination directory
- Enabling or Disabling DES-based passwords
- Enabling or Disabling TCP wrappers support

To change the installation directory, you will need to modify the following line in the Makefile:

```
DESTDIR=/usr/local/atalk
```

As you can see, the default installation directory is /usr/local/atalk. If you want to install netatalk in, for example, /opt/atalk, you can change this as follows:

```
DESTDIR=/opt/atalk
```

By default, netatalk supports two-way encrypted passwords with MacOS clients by using the libdes Data Encryption Standard (DES) library available from either **ftp://ftp.funet.fi/** or **ftp://ftp.psy.uq.oz.au/pub/Crypto/DES**.

If you have this library installed you may need to change the following line to point to the root of its directory:

```
DESDIR=/usr/local
```

The default location for the library is in /usr/local; you will need to change it if you have it installed in an alternate location. If you do not have this library installed, you can download and install it from one of the previously mentioned URLs. If you don't want two-way encrypted passwords, just comment out this line in the Makefile.

Netatalk also supports TCP wrappers by default and expects the files for this software package to be located in the /usr directory tree. If you choose to install TCP wrappers as described in Chapter 16, you will need to change the following line in the Makefile to point to the directory where TCP wrappers is installed on your system:

```
TCPWRAPDIR=/usr
```

If you don't want netatalk to support TCP wrappers, just comment out that line.

## Building and Installing Netatalk

Once you have customized the Makefile for netatalk, you can build it using the **make** command:

```
$ make
```

It can take up to 15 minutes to compile netatalk on older hardware such as a SPARCstation 10. On more modern hardware, the compilation should be much quicker. Once the compilation completes you can install most of netatalk using the command:

```
# make install
```

ADMINISTERING
SERVICES

When this command completes you will see the following message:

```
Install is done.  Don't forget to add lines from
services.atalk to /etc/services and to call rc.atalk
in /etc/rc.  See README and README.SOLARIS for more
information.
```

At this point you still need to modify several system files before starting netatalk. The first system file you need to modify is /etc/netconfig. You will need to add the following line to the file:

```
ddp tpi_clts - appletalk ddp /dev/ddp -
```

This makes the socket library aware of the AppleTalk protocol family. If you want to cut and paste this entry into /etc/netconfig, it is contained in the file INSTALL/README.SOLARIS. The second system file you need to modify is /etc/services. You need to add the following lines to this file:

```
rtmp           1/ddp           # Routing Table Maintenance Protocol
nbp            2/ddp           # Name Binding Protocol
echo           4/ddp           # AppleTalk Echo Protocol
zip            6/ddp           # Zone Information Protocol

afpovertcp     548/tcp         # AFP over TCP
afpovertcp     548/udp
```

You can use the **cat** command to add the entries from the file services.atalk to the file /etc/services:

```
# cat services.atalk >> /etc/services
```

**Note** *The file services.atalk is located in the root level of the netatalk source distribution.*

Once these system files have been updated correctly, you can install the kernel module as follows:

```
# make kinstall
```

A side effect of this command is that a startup and shutdown script for netatalk gets installed in /etc/init.d along with the appropriate links in rc2.d and rc0.d. The startup script for netatalk is called /etc/init.d/atalk. To start netatalk you can issue the following command:

```
# /etc/init.d/atalk start
```

Similarly, to stop netatalk you can issue the following command:

```
# /etc/init.d/atalk stop
```

# Configuring Netatalk

There are three main configuration files for netatalk: atalkd.conf, afpd.conf, and
AppleVolumes.default. The file atalkd.conf is the configuration file for the AppleTalk
daemon; the files aftpd.conf and AppleVolumes.default contain information related to
the AppleShare daemon **afpd**. In order to be accessed correctly, each of these files need
to be located in the etc directory under the root directory where you installed netatalk.
For example, the default location for these files is /usr/local/atalk/etc. Once these
files have been created and configured, you can start netatalk as shown in the previous
section. At that point all the MacOS clients on your networks will be able to access your
shared volumes.

A sample set of configuration files is provided as part of the netatalk distribution in
the config directory. You should copy these files for the netatalk distribution directory
into the etc directory as follows:

```
# cp config/* /usr/local/atalk/etc
```

If you choose a different location than the default, you will need to specify the
directory where you installed netatalk. The sample files will make the process of
configuring netatalk much simpler.

## atalkd.conf

The atalkd.conf is the simplest file to configure. It contains a single line that lists the
interface on which you want AppleTalk to run. On systems with a single interface,
you just need to add the name of that interface to the file. On systems with multiple
interfaces you will need to decide which interface you want to use.

You can get a list of the currently configured interfaces using the **ifconfig**
command as follows:

```
$ ifconfig -a
lo0: flags=849<UP,LOOPBACK,RUNNING,MULTICAST> mtu 8232
        inet 127.0.0.1 netmask ff000000
be0: flags=863<UP,BROADCAST,NOTRAILERS,RUNNING,MULTICAST> mtu 1500
        inet 10.8.11.14 netmask ff000000 broadcast 10.255.255.255
        ether 8:0:20:7b:3d:99
```

ADMINISTERING
SERVICES

Recall that the lo0 interface is the loopback interface; thus the only available interface in this case is be0. Depending on your system, the interface names may be different.

Once you have chosen an interface, you can use the following command to populate the atalkd.conf file:

# echo *int* >> atalkd.conf

Here, *int* is the name of the interface you want to use for AppleTalk. This command assumes that you are in the same directory as atalkd.conf. For example, to enable AppleTalk on the be0 interface you can use the command as follows:

```
# echo be0 >> atalkd.conf
```

If your AppleTalk network uses multiple zones or cable ranges, you may need a more complex configuration command similar to the following:

# ccho *int* -phase 2 -net *start-end* -addr *address* -zone "*name*" >> atalkd.conf

Here, *int* is the interface you want to use for AppleTalk, *start* is the starting AppleTalk network number for your AppleTalk network, *end* is the ending AppleTalk network number for your AppleTalk network, *address* is the AppleTalk address of your system, and *name* is the name of your zone. For most networks you will need to obtain this information from your AppleTalk network administrator. As an example of a complex setup, the following command specifies that AppleTalk be enabled on the interface be0 for the AppleTalk networks 1-4:

```
echo be0 -phase 2 -net 1-4 -addr 4.14 -zone "Bosland" >>
atalkd.conf
```

It also specifies that the AppleTalk address of the server is 4.14 and that the zone is Bosland.

## afpd.conf

The afpd.conf is the main configuration file for the AppleShare daemon aftpd. It consists of single-line entries that specify the different shared volumes on your server. Each line has the following form:

"*name*" *options*

In Table 18-1, *name* is the name you want the shared volume to have, and *options* arc any of the following:

As you can probably guess from Table 18-1, there are two clear categories of options: those related to transport and those related to authentication. At least one of the transport options, **-tcp**, **-ddp**, or **-transall**, should be specified. Normally the **-transall** option is used, since it provides the most flexibility in supporting MacOS

| Option | Purpose |
|--------|---------|
| -tcp | Enables TCP as the default transport mechanism for AppleShare. This option should be specified if either the -ddp or -transall options are specified. |
| -ddp | Enables DDP as the default transport mechanism for AppleShare. This option should be specified if either the -tcp or -transall options are specified. |
| -transall | Enables both TCP and DDP as transport mechanisms for AppleShare. This option should be specified if either the -ddp or -tcp options are specified. |
| -port *num* | Specifies the TCP port *num* that should be used by afpd for TCP clients. This option is not applicable if the -ddp option was specified. |
| -cleartext | Enables the use of clear-text passwords for accessing a shared volume. |
| -nocleartext | Disables the use of clear-text passwords for accessing user accounts. This option should not be specified if the -cleartext option is specified. Additionally, this option prevents password-based authentication for MacOS clients, unless one of the options -randnum or -rand2num is also specified. |
| -guest | Allows guest access to the shared volume. Guest users are not prompted for passwords. |
| -noguest | Prevents guest access to the shared volume. Clients must authenticate themselves using a username and password to gain access to the volume. |
| -randnum | Enables the use of two-way encrypted passwords for authentication. This option is available only if you compiled netatalk with libdes support. |
| -rand2num | Same as randnum. |
| -defaultvol | Allows you to specify an alternate AppleVolumes.default for this shared volume. |
| -systemvol | Allows you to specify an alternate AppleVolumes.system for this shared volume. |

**Table 18-1.**    *AppleShare Daemon Options*

ADMINISTERING
SERVICES

clients. If you specified either the -tcp or -transall option you will need to also specify the -port option. The standard ports to use start at 12000.

The authentication options are optional, but for volumes that contain user data, you should include at least the **-noguest** option. If you compiled netatalk with libdes support, you should always specify the **-nocleartext** option in favor of the **-randnum** and **-rand2num** options.

As an example, here is an afpd.conf file that contains two shared volumes, one with guest access and one without:

```
"Guest" -transall -guest -port 12001
"Users" -transall -cleartext -noguest -port 12002 -defaultvol
/usr/local/atalk/etc/AppleVolumes_Users.default -systemvol
/usr/local/atalk/etc/AppleVolumes_Users.system
```

The alternative AppleVolumes_Users.default for the "Users" shared volume is discussed in the next section.

## AppleVolumes.default and AppleVolumes.system

The primary function of AppleVolumes.default is to list the shared volumes that it controls. These shared volumes are listed one per line at the start of the file, in the following format:

path *shared_name*

Here, *path* is the absolute path to the shared directory and *shared-name* is the name that is presented to MacOS clients for that shared volume. As an example, the following entry will share the directory /home/ftp/pub/mac as ftp-mac:

```
/home/ftp/pub/mac ftp-mac
```

For user home directories you can simply use the "~" (tilde) character without specifying a share name. Normally, for user directories you want to create a copy of AppleVolumes.default (for example AppleVolumes_Users.default) with a single shared volume, "~", listed. This will avoid problems with some older MacOS clients.

The primary function of the AppleVolumes.system is to provide a mapping of file extensions to MacOS Creator and FileType information. The basic format of these mappings is:

.ext *type creator*

Here, *ext* is the file extension, *type* is the MacOS FileType, and *creator* is the MacOS Creator. For example the following entry maps the .doc extension to a Microsoft Word document:

```
.doc WDBN MSWD
```

The AppleVolumes.system that is shipped as a part of netatalk contains mappings for several common file types. You can add your own mappings when you encounter some that are missing.

# Alternatives to Netatalk

In addition to netatalk there are two other implementations of AppleTalk for Solaris:

- Columbia AppleTalk Package (CAP)
- TotalNET Advanced Server (TAS) from Syntax
- uShare from IPTech
- K-AShare from XiNet

The Columbia AppleTalk Package (CAP) is a user-level implementation of the AppleTalk protocol suite. Its main focus is to provide an AppleShare 2.1 compatible file server. It is available from the CAP home page, located at

**http://www.cs.mu.OZ.AU/appletalk/cap.html**

The most recent version, as of this writing, is a heavily patched version 6.0.

The TotalNET Advanced Server (TAS) from Syntax provides a single server that implements both SMB and AppleTalk. It is available for all major versions of UNIX, including Solaris version 2.5.1 and later on both SPARC- and x86-based systems. For more information about TAS, visit its home page at **http://www.syntax.com**. A 100-user evaluation copy of TAS is available from this site. The most recent version of TAS as of this writing is version 5.4.1. TAS is also available directly from Sun under the product name Solaris Easy Access Server. For more information about the Solaris Easy Access Server, you can consult its home page at

**http://www.sun.com/solaris/easyaccess/**

IPTech's uShare is a complete implementation of AppleTalk for most versions of UNIX, and it is supported on most versions of UNIX including Solaris 2.5 and later for SPARC-based systems. uShare features an administration GUI geared for administrators who are familiar with Mac OS and is used by many prepress and publishing companies. For more information about uShare, consult its home page, located at

**http://www.iptech.com/products/ushare/index.html**

(As of this writing the latest version of uShare is 5.0.1.)

XiNet's K-AShare is a popular AppleShare server used in a wide range of industries including biotech, multimedia, and prepress. It is available on most versions of UNIX, including Solaris 2.5 and later for both SPARC- and x86-based systems. It features a Java-based configuration GUI and also has extended security, including

**ADMINISTERING SERVICES**

Access Control Lists (ACLs). For more information or to download a free demo of K-AShare, see its home page at

**http://www.xinet.com/npg/index.html**

XiNet also has a unique product called K-FS that allows UNIX systems to access AppleTalk servers.

# Summary

Solaris systems are often the best choice for providing file sharing and printing services to Windows and MacOS clients. In this chapter, we discussed the NetBIOS/SMB protocols used for file sharing in Windows environments and we also discussed the AppleTalk protocols used for file sharing in MacOS environments. Then we covered the installation and configuration of SAMBA, which provides an SMB file server on Solaris. In the third section, we looked at the AppleTalk equivalent of SAMBA, netatalk, which provides AppleTalk and AppleShare services. We first covered installing netatalk and then its configuration.

# How to Find Out More

The main source of information about configuring SAMBA is the documentation available on the SAMBA home page, located at **http://www.samba.org**.

In addition to this documentation, members of the SAMBA team have written two excellent references:

Blair, John D. *SAMBA: Integrating UNIX and Windows.* (Specialized Systems Consultants Inc., 1998.)

Carter, Gerald; Sharpe, Richard; and Carter, Jerry. *Teach Yourself SAMBA in 24 Hours.* (Sams, 1999.)

The main sources of information for netatalk are its home page, the *Getting Started* guide, and the "netatalk Faq-o-matic." The netatalk homepage is located at the University of Michigan:

**http://www.umich.edu/~rsug/netatalk/**

The *Getting Started* guide for netatalk is located at

**http://thehamptons.com/anders/netatalk/**

The netatalk Faq-o-matic is located at

**http://www.umich.edu/~rsug/netatalk/faq.html**

It contains many helpful hints and debugging tips for netatalk.

The
# Complete
# Reference

Solaris 8

# Chapter 19

## Administering Mail

Electronic mail was one of the first applications to be widely adopted across the Internet, and despite changes in technology and a shift toward information delivery via the World Wide Web, "email" has managed to hold its ground. Email has undergone many changes in recent years: Users are no longer limited to plain-text messages being sent from command-line clients or "mail user agents"; many different mail protocols now govern how remote clients retrieve their mail from a centralized server (for example, POP, IMAP); and multimedia content is now supported through MIME extensions.

Although desktop clients are technically capable of running mail servers, most organizations still prefer to run a single main mail server, running a mail transport agent such as the traditional **sendmail** daemon or a newer replacement (for example, **qmail**). They prefer server systems because they have high uptime and better security features than the average desktop client, and because the security of mail services can be managed centrally. For example, if you're using a Solaris server system and a security problem is revealed in **sendmail**, a patch can be downloaded for free from SunSolve and applied to the server with minimal disruption to users. If everyone were running his or her own mail server instead, security problems could take weeks per incident to rectify (if not months, in a large organization).

*At the time of this writing, the most current version of **sendmail** was sendmail-8.9.3.1, which fixes a headers' denial-of-service attack vulnerability by limiting the headers of each mail message to a maximum of 32 kilobytes.*

In this chapter, we will discuss how email is addressed and delivered and examine the configuration of the popular **sendmail** mail transport agent. We will end by shifting the focus to the client side, exploring local and remote mail user agents that make use of the POP and IMAP protocols to retrieve their mail from a dedicated mail server.

## Understanding the Email Protocols

Transferring electronic mail between servers on the Internet is largely conducted using the Simple Mail Transfer Protocol, or SMTP. The advantage of using SMTP is that mail transfer can be initiated by a local third-party MUA (mail user agent), such as **elm** or **pine**, or it can be performed manually by a user using **telnet**. This makes installing **sendmail** somewhat easier because all mail commands can be tested interactively by a human operator, and the response to each command can be evaluated appropriately.

If your users are not logged in through a shell on the local mail server, it will be necessary for you to provide a means by which they can send and retrieve mail through the server by using a remote mail client. There are two protocols that support this: the Post Office Protocol (POP), which is the oldest client/server mail transfer protocol and only supports offline mail reading, and the Internet Message Access

Protocol (IMAP), which supports both offline and online mail reading. Offline reading means that messages are transferred to a local disk in a single block, and a connection is only made back to the mail server when another message is sent or when new mail is checked for. Online reading involves maintaining a connection to the mail server. The choice between the two will often come down to which MUAs your users are comfortable with, and which protocol their favorite client supports. However, there can be other considerations, like authentication, authorization, and security, which could sway an administrator to stipulate that IMAP be used over POP, even for offline mail reading. It should be noted that POP is generally easier to install and configure than IMAP.

In this section, we review the SMTP, POP, and IMAP protocols and investigate the new multimedia (MIME) extensions to email that allow the transmission of multipart, multimedia, and multilingual messages with attachments between Internet hosts.

## What Is SMTP?

SMTP is the Simple Mail Transfer Protocol (SMTP). This is the protocol that allows servers to exchange mail with each other on a message-by-message basis. Standardized since the publication of RFC 821, SMTP has become the dominant Internet mail transfer protocol, at the expense of earlier transfer methods, such as the ancient UUCP (UNIX-to-UNIX copy program), and the X.400 protocol, which is still popular with intranet and LAN-based email. SMTP allows **sendmail** and other mail transport agents, such as **qmail**, to accept connections on port 25 and "speak" to each other in a language that is interpretable by humans. In fact, as we will see later, it is actually possible for an administrator to manually test **sendmail** by **telnet**ing to port 25 and issuing SMTP commands directly. This is very useful for troubleshooting and testing existing configurations. Unfortunately, SMTP is almost too simple because it can be used by malicious users to forge email headers, so as to make an email appear to come from another user. However, as mentioned earlier, the most current version of **sendmail** addresses this vulnerability by limiting the headers of each mail message to a maximum of 32 kilobytes.

SMTP supports a sender-receiver model of host-to-host email transactions. A host, for example mail.companyA.com, may wish to transfer a message to mail.companyB.com. This transaction is shown in Figure 19-1. The server mail.companyA.com first makes a connection to port 25, which mail.companyB.com acknowledges. Then, mail.companyA.com identifies the sender of the message, and, again, mail.companyB.com acknowledges. Next, mail.companyA.com states the recipient of the message, and, again, mail.companyB.com acknowledges. If the local user exists, or is listed in the /etc/aliases database, then the acknowledgment is in the affirmative. If no local user can be matched to the intended recipient, then the acknowledgment is in the negative. If a user is found, then the message is transmitted from mail.companyA.com to mail.companyB.com, and the latter acknowledges receipt (with a receipt number). Finally, mail.companyA.com then requests a disconnection, and mail.companyB.com complies.

This kind of transaction is conducted millions of times every day on mail servers around the world, and is very fast. In the example, each of the acknowledgments

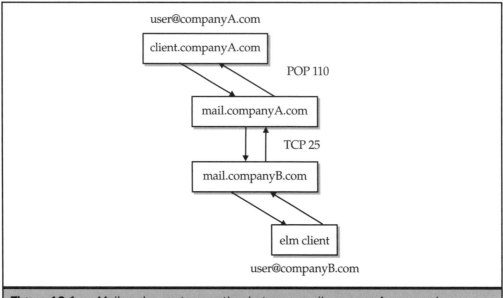

**Figure 19-1.**    *Mail exchange transaction between mail.companyA.com and mail.companyB.com*

from mail.companyB.com is associated with a three-digit numeric code. For example, a successful command from mail.companyA.com is always acknowledged with a code 250 from mail.companyB.com. Alternatively, if a user is not local, the code 551 is returned.

There are a number of standard SMTP commands; they are summarized below:

- **HELO**   Identifies the mail-sending host to the mail-receiving host.
- **MAIL**   Identifies the remote user who is sending the mail to the mail-receiving host.
- **RCPT**   Indicates the local user to whom the mail is to be delivered.
- **DATA**   Precedes the body of the mail message.
- **VRFY**   Checks that a particular local user is known to the mail system.
- **EXPN**   Expands local mailing lists.
- **QUIT**   Terminates a session.

In addition to the standard SMTP commands presented here, RFC 1869 proposed a set of extensions to SMTP, calling it ESMTP. Simply put, ESMTP allows developers to extend the services currently provided by SMTP. MTAs (mail transport agents) that support ESMTP commands will attempt to greet each other with the **EHLO** command.

If ESMTP is supported, a list of implemented commands on the remote server is returned. For example:

**server% telnet server.companyB.com 25**

```
Trying 192.68.232.45...
Connected to server.companyB.com.
Escape character is '^]'.
220 server.companyB.com ESMTP Sendmail 8.9.1a/8.9.1; Fri, 18 Feb 2000 13:05:14 +1100 (EST)
EHLO server.companyA.com
250-server.companyB.com Hello pwatters@server.companyA.com [192.68.231.64], pleased to meet you
250-EXPN
250-VERB
250-8BITMIME
250-SIZE
250-DSN
250-ONEX
250-ETRN
250-XUSR
250 HELP
```

One example of an ESMTP command is Delivery Status Notification (**DSN**), which was proposed in RFC 1891, and which reports on the status of remote mail deliveries to local users.

## An Example SMTP Transaction

In this section, we will walk through an actual SMTP session so that you can see how straightforward the procedure is. For example, it is possible to initiate message transfer from a client machine to a user on server.companyB.com by using the following command:

**client% telnet mail.serverB.com 25**

```
Trying 192.68.232.41...
Connected to mail.serverB.com.
Escape character is '^]'.
220 mail.serverB.com ESMTP Sendmail 8.9.1a/8.9.1; Fri, 18 Feb 2000 10:25:59 +1100 (EST)
```

If you now type:

**help**

you will receive a list of SMTP commands that can be used to transfer mail interactively:

```
214-This is Sendmail version 8.9.1a
214-Topics:
214-    HELO    EHLO    MAIL    RCPT    DATA
214-    RSET    NOOP    QUIT    HELP    VRFY
214-    EXPN    VERB    ETRN    DSN
214-For more info use "HELP <topic>".
214-To report bugs in the implementation send email to
214-    sendmail-bugs@sendmail.org.
214-For local information send email to Postmaster at your site.
214 End of HELP info
```

To actually send a message, you can use a combination of the **HELO, MAIL, RCPT,** and **QUIT** commands. **HELO** introduces the hostname that you are connecting from:

### HELO client.companyB.com

```
250 server.companyB.com Hello client.companyB.com [192.68.232.45], pleased to meet you
```

Next, you need to specify a sender using the **MAIL** command:

### MAIL FROM: <pwatters@companyB.com>

```
250 <pwatters@companyB.com>... Sender ok
```

A recipient for the mail should then be specified by the **RCPT** command:

### RCPT TO: <postmaster@server.companyB.com>

```
250 <postmaster@server.companyB.com>... Recipient ok
```

After transmitting the sender and recipient information, it's then time to actually send the body of the message by using the **DATA** command:

### DATA

```
354 Enter mail, end with "." on a line by itself
Hello,
My mail client is not working so I had to send this message manually -- can you help?
Thanks.
.
250 KAA11543 Message accepted for delivery
```

After the message has been accepted for delivery, you can then terminate the session by using the **QUIT** command:

**QUIT**

```
221 server.company.com closing connection
Connection closed by foreign host.
```

The message has now been successfully transmitted.

# Mail Headers (Mail Addressing and Routing)

When a mail message is delivered into a user's mailbox, it contains a history of its delivery process in the headers that precede the message body. The most common headers are described below:

- ■ **From**   Records the mail-sending user and the date and time at which the mail was received.
- ■ **Received**   Provides details of how the mail was received by the MTA on the mail server, including the remote computer's name, MTA name, and identification.
- ■ **Date**   Indicates the time and date on which the message was received.
- ■ **Message-Id**   A unique number generated by the sending host that identifies the message.
- ■ **To**   Indicates the user to whom the message was addressed, usually a user on the local machine.
- ■ **Content-Type**   Indicates the MIME type in which the message was encoded. This is usually text, but could contain multimedia types as well.
- ■ **Content-Length**   The number of lines making up the body of the message.
- ■ **Subject**   The subject of the mail message as entered by the sender.

These headers are useful in understanding how mail is transferred. For example, if a message is sent from a mail client on the local server to another user on the local server, then the headers are easy to interpret:

```
From pwatters@companyA.com Fri Feb 18 13:31 EST 2000
Received: (from pwatters@localhost)
        by mail.companyA.com (8.9.1a/8.9.1) id NAA17837
        for pwatters; Fri, 18 Feb 2000 13:31:34 +1100 (EST)
Date: Fri, 18 Feb 2000 13:31:34 +1100 (EST)
From: WATTERS Paul Andrew <pwatters@companyA.com>
Message-Id: <200002180231.NAA17837@mail.companyA.com>
To: pwatters@companyA.com
```

```
Subject: Testing Local Delivery
Content-Type: text
Content-Length: 5
This is a test of local delivery.
```

These headers can be interpreted thus: The local user pwatters@localhost sent the remote user pwatters@companyA.com a five-line message, encoded as text, on the subject of Testing Local Delivery. The message had an ID of 200002180231.NAA17837@mail.CompanyA.com, and was serviced by the sendmail MTA version 8.9.1a/8.9.1. If mail is forwarded from another host, then the headers become more complicated, but follow the same general principles.

## Multipurpose Internet Mail Extensions (MIME)

As we saw in the previous example concerning mail headers, there was a Content-Type that was text, but which could have conceivably been any kind of digital medium, thanks to MIME, the Multipurpose Internet Mail Extensions, as proposed in RFC 2045. MIME is very useful for sending multimedia files through email without having to worry about the specifics of encoding. Since many multimedia files are binary, and email message bodies are transmitted as text, MIME suggests that these files be encoded as text, and sent as a normal message. In addition, MIME supports the notion of multipart messages—that is, a single email message may contain more than one encoded file. This is very useful for sending a number of documents to another user: It is not necessary to overburden **sendmail** by sending a new message for each document (**sendmail** processes each email message individually). MIME also provides supports for languages that are encoded in ASCII but that need to be displayed in another script (for example, Japanese *kanji*).

MIME defines how a *Content-Type* header can be used to specify a particular character set or other nontextual data type for an email message. For example, the email header:

```
Content-Type: text/plain; charset=us-ascii
```

indicates that the message consists of plain text in the US-ASCII character set. MIME also specifies how to encode data when necessary. MIME stipulates that it is the responsibility of the receiving user to interpret the encoded information in order to correctly display an encoded message in a form that will be understood by the user. Here is an example of a MIME-encoded message:

```
This is a multipart message in MIME format.
-------=_NextPart_000_01A6_01BF7314.FF804600
Content-Type: text/plain;
```

```
          charset="iso-8859-1"
Content-Transfer-Encoding: 7bit
Joe,
Just confirmed the latest sales figures.
See the attached report.
Jane
------=_NextPart_000_01A6_01BF7314.FF804600
Content-Type: application/msword;
        name="report.doc"
Content-Disposition: attachment;
        filename="report.doc"
Content-Transfer-Encoding: base64
0M8R4KGxGuEAAAAAAAAAAAAAAAAAAAAAPgADAP7/CQAGAAAAAAAAAAAAACAAAmQAAAAAAAAAA
EAAAmwAAAAEAAAD+/////AAAAAJcAAACYAAAA////////////////////////////////////
////////////////////////////////////////////////////////////////////////
////////////////////////////////////////////////////////////////////////
////////////////////////////////////////////////////////////////////////
////////////////////////////////////////////////////////////////////////
////////////////////////////////////////////////////////////////////////
////////////////////////////////////////////////////////////////////////
```

After the headers are printed, indicating the number and type of attachments, the actual encoded data is printed (which is what all the forward slashes represent, in case you were wondering!). Since this file contains MIME-encoded data, then when you run **metamail** on it through a client, the user is prompted to save any detected attachments:

```
This message contains data in an unrecognized format, application/msword,
which can either be viewed as text or written to a file.
What do you want to do with the application/msword data?
1 -- See it as text
2 -- Write it to a file
3 -- Just skip it
```

Typically, at this point the user enters **2** and is then prompted to save the file:

```
Please enter the name of a file to which the data should be written
(Default: report.doc) >
```

The data is then saved to the file specified. MIME is thus very useful for encoding data from several binary files into a portable format that can be transmitted as an email message.

# What Is POP?

Many users today do not log in directly to an interactive shell on a mail server and run a local mail client like **mailx** or **elm**—instead, they are able to use a GUI-based mail reading client that runs locally on their PC, contacting the mail server directly to retrieve and send their mail. One of the most popular client/server protocols that facilitates this kind of mail delivery is the Post Office Protocol (POP), as proposed in RFC 1725. POP supports offline mail delivery to remote clients when mail addressed to a user account is delivered via a centralized mail server. POP supports many useful features, including the ability to retain copies of email on the server, as well as transmitting a copy to the client. This can be very useful for auditing and backup purposes, especially when you consider that when a client machine crashes or has to be reinstalled, all the user's mail (including unread mail) might be lost. Reliability of service is still one of the main arguments for using a centralized mail server.

To retrieve mail from a POP server, a client machine makes a TCP connection to port 110. The client then greets the server, receives an acknowledgment, and then the session continues until it is terminated. During this time, a user may be authenticated. If a user is successfully authenticated, that user may begin conducting transactions in the form of retrieving messages, until the **QUIT** command is received by the server, in which case the session is terminated. Errors are indicated by status codes like –ERR for negative responses and +OK for positive responses. POP is deliberately SMTP-like in its command set and operation, making it easy for administrators to apply their skills to configuring both kinds of systems.

One of the drawbacks to POP is its lack of security. Although users are authenticated using their username and password on the mail server, this exchange is not encrypted, and so anyone "snooping" the network might be able to retrieve this username and password. This would allow a rogue user to log in to the mail server as the mail user—perhaps without the legitimate mail user realizing this for a long time, because they themselves rarely log in directly to the mail server. Since **telnet** and **ftp** use exactly the same method of authentication, it's certainly no worse than the standard networking toolset—however, Chapter 16 describes some more secure alternatives to these tools using encrypted sessions, and something similar is clearly required for POP authentication.

To obtain a free POP server for Solaris, download the freeware Qpopper server from Qualcomm at **http://www.eudora.com/qpopper/index.html**. Qualcomm also has a free POP mail user agent called **Eudora** that is very popular in educational institutions, and is available for both Macintosh and Windows platforms. Figure 19-2 shows the main user screen from **Eudora**: Users can retrieve their mail from a remote server, and display it ordered by date, sender, and subject. In addition, files from the local Macintosh or Windows filesystem can be sent as attachments by using the MIME extensions. Software like **Eudora** makes it easy for Macintosh or Windows users to have the convenience of local file access and GUI-based interfaces, while retaining the security and reliability of the Solaris server platform.

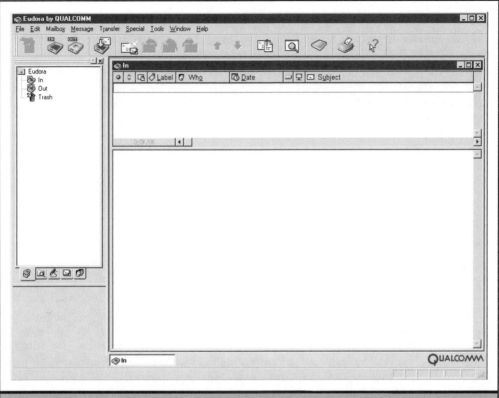

**Figure 19-2.**    *The POP-based Eudora client for Microsoft Windows, which receives mail from a centralized and secure Solaris mail server*

## What Is IMAP?

IMAP, the Internet Message Access Protocol, as proposed in RFC 2060, is intended to be a replacement for the POP protocol. While IMAP can perform offline processing, it is primarily intended for remote clients to retain some of the features of online processing enjoyed by mail user agents like **mailx** and **elm**. A remote MUA using IMAP has the ability to perform more sophisticated transactions than a POP-based client: While POP caters to requests like retrieving all new messages on the server and passing them to the client, IMAP supports requests of just header, just message bodies, or both. In addition, a search can be made for messages matching a particular criterion: For example, a request could be made to find all messages received by a particular user, or all messages received on a particular day. Although a POP-based MUA can perform these operations on its local copy of mail messages, IMAP can perform these operations remotely on the server. In addition, server-side messages can be marked with different flags—indicating, for example, whether or not they have been replied to. Again, although this reflects the kind of functionality also supplied by server-side MUAs like **mailx** or **elm**, IMAP additionally allows these operations to be performed by remote, easy-to-use GUI interfaces. Also, if IMAP users want to store their files locally, as they could with a POP-based service, this is also supported—but significantly, with IMAP there is a synchronization feature whereby the local mailbox contents can be regularly matched with the mailbox on the server. This feature ensures that no data corruption occurs due to errors on the client machine.

In summary, POP and IMAP offer significantly different functions, and the use of either protocol depends on which mail user agents are supported, and the needs of the users. Many mail clients only support POP, and it may be that your organization keeps the POP platform for this reason alone, even though IMAP offers many more features.

# Using sendmail

Now that we have reviewed how mail is transferred between the client and the server, we now turn our attention to server-to-server mail communications. Mail exchange between servers is performed by using mail transport agents such as **sendmail** that implement the SMTP protocol. **sendmail** is the most popular MTA for Solaris and many other UNIX systems, even though newer systems, such as **qmail**, make it easier to configure an MTA. In this section, we cannot cover all material relating to **sendmail**, as it is one of the most complex Solaris programs to master; however, we provide sufficient detail so that most administrators working in a standard environment will be able to configure and test their mail transfer environment.

## What Is sendmail?

**sendmail** is the standard and default mail transport agent supported under Solaris. (It is certainly possible, however, to install an alternative third-party MTA like **qmail**— see **http://www.qmail.org/** for details.) Solaris 2.5.x and later all support sendmail 8.

In most Solaris installations, the sendmail MTA relies on a single configuration file (sendmail.cf), which contains sets of rules to determine how email is to be sent from the local host to any arbitrary remote host and which mailer is to be used (for example, for local versus remote delivery). The rules are used to choose the mechanism by which each message is delivered and how mail addresses may be rewritten to ensure correct delivery. For example, a mail message sent from a server command line might not include the fully qualified domain name in the *Reply-to* field. This would mean that a remote user would not be able to reply to a message sent to them. Also, the sendmail MTA ensures that the virtual envelopes that contain email messages are addressed correctly by inserting headers where appropriate to identify senders and recipients.

Although **sendmail** is highly customizable, it is also difficult to configure and test because a single error in the rules can produce unexpected results. **sendmail** reads and processes every rule in sendmail.cf, so in order to speed up the process, the rules are written in a computer-friendly format. Unfortunately, like assembly language, computer-friendly rules are rarely human-friendly! In this section, we will review the configuration of **sendmail**, and highlight some of the security issues that continue to surround its deployment.

# Configuring sendmail (sendmail.cf)

The sendmail.cf file consists of single-line commands, which can range from rules and macros to options and headers. There can be many rules in a sendmail.cf file, but some of the commands must appear only once if they specify a directive that affects the interpretation of rules. **sendmail** configuration is very challenging and difficult to understand, but if you follow the basic outline given below, it should be more comprehensible. The main kinds of commands in a sendmail.cf file are described below:

- **C**   Specifies a macro, which can contain more than one item. For instance, **C{MAILCLIENTS} mars venus pluto** specifies an array that contains a list of mail clients (mars, venus, and pluto).

- **D**   Specifies a macro. For example, **D{Domain}mail.companyA.com** specifies a macro named "R" whose contents are "mail.companyA.com."

- **E**   Specifies an environment variable. As a security measure, **sendmail** does not use environment information passed to it, preferring to use values specified in the sendmail.cf file. To set the location of a Java Virtual Machine (VM), which may be used to support some mail-related applications, use the variable specification EJVM=/usr/local/java/bin/java.

- **H**   Specifies a header, such as the *Received* header. These definitions can be very complex due to the inclusion of multipart MIME messages.

- **M**   Specifies the mail delivery agent. For instance, **Mlocal, P=/bin/mail** specifies that /bin/mail is the mail delivery agent, which is usually the case under Solaris.

- **O**   Specifies an option. For example, setting **O SendMimeErrors=True** enables the sending of MIME-encapsulated error messages.

- **P**   Sets message precedence. For example, first-class mail is set with a precedence of zero (**Pfirst-class=0**), while junk mail is set with a precedence of -100 (**Pjunk=-100**).

- **R**   Specifies a rule. For example, the rule **R$-  $@ $1 @ ${Mydomain}  Rewrite address** appends the FQDN defined by the macro ${Mydomain} to a username.

- **S**   Indicates the start of a ruleset, which can either be specified as a number (for example, "S2" for ruleset two) or with a label (for example, "SDomainRules" for the DomainRules ruleset).

There are six kinds of system-defined rulesets that are contained in the sendmail.cf file:

- **S0**  Handles basic address parsing. For example, if a user address is not specified, an error message ("user address required") is returned.
- **S1**  Processes the email sender's address.
- **S2**  Processes the email recipient's address.
- **S3**  Performs name canonicalization, and initiates the rewriting rules. For example, invalid addresses are checked (for example, those with colons), and any angle brackets (the < and > symbols) are stripped from the address.
- **S4**  Performs the final-output post-rewriting, including conversion of expanded addresses like pwatters%mail @companyA.com to pwatters@mail.companyA.com.
- **S5**  The final rewriting ruleset that occurs after all aliases (defined in /etc/aliases) have been expanded.

User-defined rulesets can occupy **S6** and above. For example, Ruleset 33 is defined in Solaris to support Sun's RemoteMode. A typical **sendmail** rule takes the form:

```
Rlhs     rhs            description
```

In that example, R indicates that the line is a rule, lhs is the left-hand side of the rule, rhs is the right-hand side of the rule, and description would be a comment for humans who may need to interpret what action the rule performs.

Sendmail is a rule-based system, and therefore requires a system for extracting and interpreting the rules contained in the sendmail.cf file. Just as the utilities **lex** and **yacc** can be used for specifying actions based on matched tokens, so does the **sendmail** parser. When the sendmail.cf file is parsed by **sendmail**, it recognizes several specifiers: The left-hand side is a specification for matching a particular mail header, while the right-hand side specifies the action to be taken if a match is found for the rule. On the left side, it recognizes the following specifiers:

- **$-**  Matches a single token.
- **$***  Matches any number of tokens, including zero tokens.
- **$+**  Matches any number of tokens greater than zero.
- **$=**_character_  Matches any token equal to _character_.

If any rule stated using those specifiers finds a match, then one or more actions may be performed by one or more right-side specifiers:

- **$@**  Rewrite and return.

- **$>*integer***    Rewrite using the ruleset specified by integer.
- **$#**    Deliver through the specified mailer.
- **$*character***    Actions can be performed on variables defined on the left side.
- **$*integer***    Actions can be performed on variables defined on the left side.

As an example, let's examine a rule that adds a fully qualified domain name onto a mail server username, where a message is destined for external delivery. In this case, **$h** (host) is set to mail and **$d** (domain) is set to companyA.com. Thus, a rule to match a username with no FQDN specified would be as follows:

**R$+    $@$1<@$h.$d>    Add a FQDN to username**

Thus, any valid Solaris username, for example, pwatters, will have "mail", ".", and "companyA.com" appended to it for external delivery, as shown here:

```
paul<@mail.companyA.com>
```

A more complex rule, say for a more complex organization that has multiple internal networks, might have a second level in the FQDN above the company name (for example, the mail server for the sales department of companyA.com would have the FQDN mail.sales.companyA.com). In this case, we define **$o** (organization-level), set **$o** to sales, and change the rule to:

**R$+    $@$1<@$h.$o.$d>    Add a FQDN to username, including organization level**

Hence, any valid Solaris username, like neil, will have "mail", ".", "sales", "." and "companyA.com" appended to it for external delivery, giving us the following:

```
neil<@mail.sales.companyA.com>
```

Thus, the combination of rules, macros, and options can successfully create and resolve most email addresses. If all of the rule writing and option setting seems daunting to a first-time sendmail administrator, it is possible to use GUI-based configuration tools to ease the burden. One of the easiest ways to run and configure **sendmail** is to use Webmin, which is freely available at **http://www.webmin.com/webmin/**. This is a web-based interface for system administration for Solaris, including **sendmail**. Using any browser that supports tables and forms, you can make use of Webmin's sendmail configuration module, which allows administrators to manage **sendmail** aliases, masquerading, address rewriting, and other features. Webmin can also use SSL to secure connections between your web browser and the Webmin server, which is especially useful for remote administration. Figure 19-3 shows the Webmin interface, and the options it supports for configuring **sendmail**.

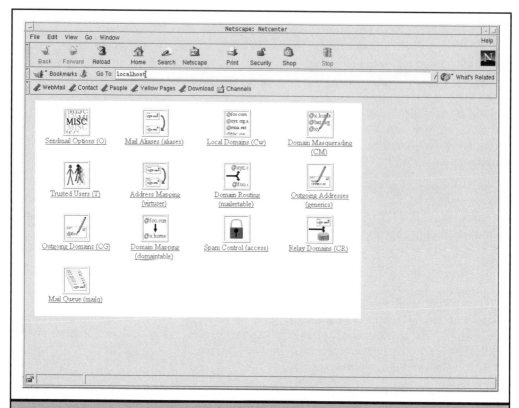

**Figure 19-3.**    *Webmin GUI interface for configuring sendmail.*

Since **sendmail** is particularly vulnerable to security problems, many sites choose to download and install the sendmail distribution from the sendmail web site (**http://www.sendmail.org/**). Although Sun's version of **sendmail** is usually up to date, the sendmail.org version is m4-based, and much safer than the standard method.

## Running sendmail

**sendmail** is started as a daemon process from scripts that are usually activated during multiuser startup (/etc/rc2). To stop **sendmail** manually, use the following command:

    **/etc/init.d/sendmail stop**

In order to start **sendmail**, use the command:

    **/etc/init.d/sendmail start**

# Installing Aliases

Email addresses typically correspond to a local Solaris user. For example, for the user account pwatters on host mail.companyA.com, the email address would naturally be pwatters@mail.companyA.com. However, there are many situations in which mail needs to be addressed to a user who may not have a user account as such. In addition, there are often aliases that require application programs and daemons as administrative contacts, and that should not go to a specific individual: They should be forwarded to the user account of an individual who has that responsibility at a particular point in time. To solve this problem, Solaris maintains an administrative database of email aliases, which for the purposes of **sendmail** allow a user to be logically different from actual Solaris users (as defined by the users listed in /etc/passwd). The /etc/aliases database contains rules of the form:

```
alias: user
```

where *alias* is the user alias, and *user* is the actual user account. For example, all mail for the logical user MAILER-DAEMON could be forwarded to the physical user root by using the alias:

```
MAILER-DAEMON: root
```

Aliases are also useful for creating mailing lists, and many mailing list packages like majordomo actually use the aliases database to record mailing list details. The only tip to remember with the aliases database is that you must run the **newaliases** command after making any changes to /etc/aliases if you want the new aliases to be available; otherwise the aliases database (/etc/aliases.dir and /etc/aliases/pag) won't be up to date. A sample /etc/aliases file is shown here:

```
# Following alias is required by the mail protocol, RFC 822
# Set it to the address of a HUMAN who deals with this system's mail problems.
Postmaster: root
# Alias for mailer daemon; returned messages from our MAILER-DAEMON
# should be routed to our local Postmaster.
MAILER-DAEMON: postmaster
# Aliases to handle mail to programs or files, eg news or vacation
nobody: /dev/null
# To be specified in as sender in USENET postings (anti-UCE trap)
spam: /dev/null
# Alias for staff distribution list, members specified here:
staff:          pwatters,neil@indiana,maya@sydney,cliff@adelaide,lori@adelaide
# Alias for a person, so they can receive mail by several names:
```

```
paul:              pwatters
root:              maya@sydney
help:              cliff@adelaide
helpdesk:          help
support:           neil@indiana
abuse:             spam
```

## Troubleshooting

Since **sendmail** can be a difficult program to configure, **sendmail** also includes some provisions for troubleshooting. For example, the following command:

>     server# sendmail –bt

causes **sendmail** to execute in address-testing mode, which is very useful for testing rule-sets interactively before including them in a production system. Keep in mind that ruleset 3 is no longer invoked automatically in address-testing mode. Thus, to test the following address:

```
Paul.Watters.1996@pem.cam.ac.uk
```

you should use the test string:

```
"0,3 Paul.Watters.1996@pem.cam.ac.uk"
```

instead of just using:

```
"0 Paul.Watters.1996@pem.cam.ac.uk"!
```

As a complete example, then, study the following:

```
ADDRESS TEST MODE (ruleset 3 NOT automatically invoked)
Enter <ruleset> <address>
> 0 Paul.Watters.1996@pem.cam.ac.uk
rewrite: ruleset   0   input: Paul . Watters . 1996 @ pem . cam . ac . uk
rewrite: ruleset 199   input: Paul . Watters . 1996 @ pem . cam . ac . uk
rewrite: ruleset 199 returns: Paul . Watters . 1996 @ pem . cam . ac . uk
rewrite: ruleset  98   input: Paul . Watters . 1996 @ pem . cam . ac . uk
rewrite: ruleset  98 returns: Paul . Watters . 1996 @ pem . cam . ac . uk
rewrite: ruleset 198   input: Paul . Watters . 1996 @ pem . cam . ac . uk
rewrite: ruleset 198 returns: $# local $: Paul . Watters . 1996 @ pem . cam . ac . uk
```

```
rewrite: ruleset    0 returns: $# local $: Paul . Watters . 1996 @ pem . cam . ac . uk
> 0,3 Paul.Watters.1996@pem.cam.ac.uk
rewrite: ruleset    0   input: Paul . Watters . 1996 @ pem . cam . ac . uk
rewrite: ruleset 199   input: Paul . Watters . 1996 @ pem . cam . ac . uk
rewrite: ruleset 199 returns: Paul . Watters . 1996 @ pem . cam . ac . uk
rewrite: ruleset  98   input: Paul . Watters . 1996 @ pem . cam . ac . uk
rewrite: ruleset  98 returns: Paul . Watters . 1996 @ pem . cam . ac . uk
rewrite: ruleset 198   input: Paul . Watters . 1996 @ pem . cam . ac . uk
rewrite: ruleset 198 returns: $# local $: Paul . Watters . 1996 @ pem . cam . ac . uk
rewrite: ruleset    0 returns: $# local $: Paul . Watters . 1996 @ pem . cam . ac . uk
rewrite: ruleset    3   input: $# local $: Paul . Watters . 1996 @ pem . cam . ac . uk
rewrite: ruleset    3 returns: $# local $: Paul . Watters . 1996 @ pem . cam . ac . uk
```

In addition to **sendmail**-based troubleshooting, the **mailx** MUA has a **-v** (verbose) switch, which tracks the process of mail delivery directly after mail has been sent. For example, if a message is sent from user@companyA.com to user@companyB.com, from the machine client.companyA.com, the process of delivery is displayed to the sender as follows:

**client% mailx -v user@companyB.com**

```
Subject: Hello
Hi user@companyB.com. This is a test.
^D
EOT
client% user@companyB.com... Connecting to mailhost (mail)...
220 mail.serverB.com ESMTP Sendmail 8.9.1a/8.9.1; Sat, 19 Feb 2000 12:13:22 +1100 (EST)
>>> HELO mail.companyA.com
250 mail.serverB.com Hello mail.companyA.com (moppet.companyA.com), pleased to meet you
>>> MAIL From:<user@companyA.com>
250 <user@companyA.com>... Sender ok
>>> RCPT To:<user@companyB.com>
250 <user@companyA.com>... Recipient ok
>>> DATA
354 Enter mail, end with "." on a line by itself
>>> Hi user@companyB.com. This is a test.
>>>.
250 Ok
>>> QUIT
221 mail.companyB.com closing connection
user@companyB.com... Sent (Ok)
```

In the above example, the local mail server (mail.companyA.com) contacts the remote mail server (mail.companyB.com) and delivers the mail correctly to the user. Used in this way, **mailx** can provide immediately useful hints for users and administrators to identify delivery problems with particular user addresses or remote network problems.

## Security

Since email is ubiquitous on the Internet, and since **sendmail** is the most widely deployed MTA, it is often associated with security warnings and issues. This has led some developers to develop alternative MTA systems like **qmail**, and many organizations worldwide to devote the appropriate resources to tracking down and solving bugs in **sendmail**. If you are a sendmail administrator, it pays to watch the headlines at sites like the Sendmail Consortium (**http://www.sendmail.org/**).

For example, **sendmail** was recently shown to suffer from the *buffer overflow* problem that allows remote users to execute arbitrary commands on a server running **sendmail**. This is a common problem for UNIX applications written in the C language, but only if proper bounds checking on array sizes is not correctly implemented. In the case of **sendmail**, very long MIME headers could be used to launch an attack. Fortunately, a patch is available that allows **sendmail** to detect and deny messages that might be associated with such an attack. If you need to apply the patch, it is available at:

> **ftp://ftp.sendmail.org/pub/sendmail/sendmail.8.9.1a.patch**

## Mail Clients

Mail clients can be local or remote. Local clients have online access to many Solaris commands, including **.forward** and **vacation**, while remote clients are GUI-based and are often easier to use. Remote clients can use either the IMAP or POP protocol to communicate with the server-based MTA, as reviewed earlier in the chapter. In this section, we will introduce a popular local client (**elm**) and an equally popular remote client (**Netscape mail**), and examine how each client is configured.

### Local Clients (elm)

Although Solaris is supplied with the **mailx** program, a local user agent developed by the University of California at Berkeley, many sites choose to install the **elm** MUA, which was originally developed by Hewlett-Packard. **elm** is now freeware, and supports many advanced features such as MIME and DSN. It is highly configurable, and can operate in beginner, intermediate, and advanced user mode. The following command can be used to start **elm**:

```
client% elm
```

The user interface for **elm** is shown in Figure 19-4. Using **elm**, users can issue most commands by typing a single letter from the main menu:

- | Pipe the displayed message through a user-defined command.
- ! Execute a shell process.
- ? Obtain help for elm commands.
- *<n>* Set current message number to *n*.
- */pattern* Search for *pattern* in message.
- a Create in the address book an alias for sender of the current message.
- b Bounce the current message to a user to make it appear as if it hasn't been delivered.
- c Change to a folder other than the inbox.
- d Delete the current message from the inbox.
- f Forward the current message to another user.
- m Create a new mail message.

Set options for skill level and general **elm** options (saved in elmrc).

- p Print current message.
- q Exit **elm** and save changes to inbox.
- s Save current message to a specific folder.
- u Undelete a message marked for deletion.
- x Exit without saving changes to inbox.

By default, **elm** uses the **vi** editor to edit messages, but if this is too daunting, it is possible to set the editor to **emacs** or **pico** by editing the defaults in the elmrc configuration file.

By convention, it is normal to include a signature at the bottom of every message, containing contact details. This is usually kept in ~/.signature. Here's an example of a typical signature file:

```
--
Paul A. Watters, M.Phil.(Cambridge)
Principal Consultant, Cassowary Computing
Sydney NSW Australia
Paul.Watters.1996@pem.cam.ac.uk
```

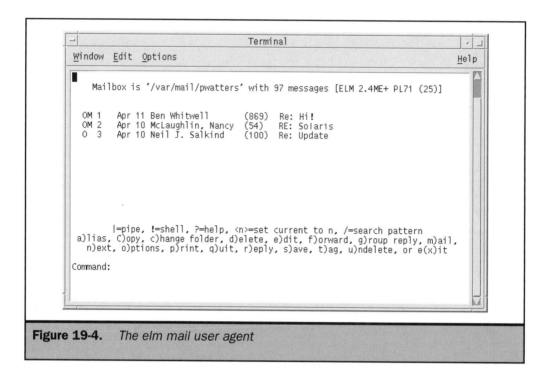

**Figure 19-4.** *The elm mail user agent*

This allows readers of your messages to quickly identify you and your role in the organization that you may represent. Since you may already be known to local users, **elm** actually has the ability to automatically attach a different signature to messages addressed to either local or remote users. This is but one of the many features that has ensured **elm**'s continued success in the age of GUI-based remote clients.

## Remote Clients (Netscape mail)

GUI-based mail clients operating on a remote PC have become commonplace in offices where mail is centralized on a Solaris server but a desktop system is used to read mail. Popular choices for reading email remotely include the **Netscape mail** client and the **Eudora** mail client, which are available for free from **http://www.netscape.com/** and **http://www.eudora.com/** respectively. Both clients use POP to retrieve their mail from a remote POP server, although **Netscape mail** can also use IMAP. In this section, we review the configuration of the POP-based Netscape mail client.

The first step after installing the **Netscape mail** software is to set the user preferences. In the Preferences popup, there is a section called Mail & Newsgroups, as shown in

Figure 19-5. Here the users need to set up basic information about their contact details: their full name, their email address, their Reply-to address (if it is different from their email address), their organization, and the location of their signature file on the local file system. This enables emails that are sent from the client to be identified easily.

The next step is to configure the POP settings. In Figure 19-6, we can see the General preferences tab. The POP server name is recorded here, along with the server type (in this case, POP-3). The remote username is also recorded, along with an instruction to remember the remote password, and to automatically check for and retrieve mail every 10 minutes. The POP tab contains an option to leave the mail on the server, as well as storing it on the local file system.

When the **Netscape mail** client is started, the user interface is shown in Figure 19-7. In the left pane, the different supported mailboxes are shown: inbox, unsent mail, draft emails, templates, sent mail, and a trash folder. In addition, messages can be ordered by subject, sender, date, or priority level.

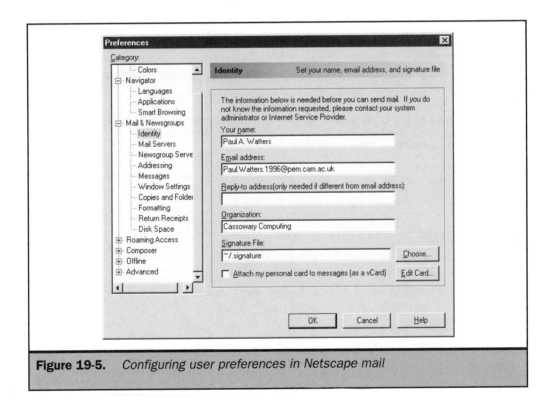

**Figure 19-5.**   *Configuring user preferences in Netscape mail*

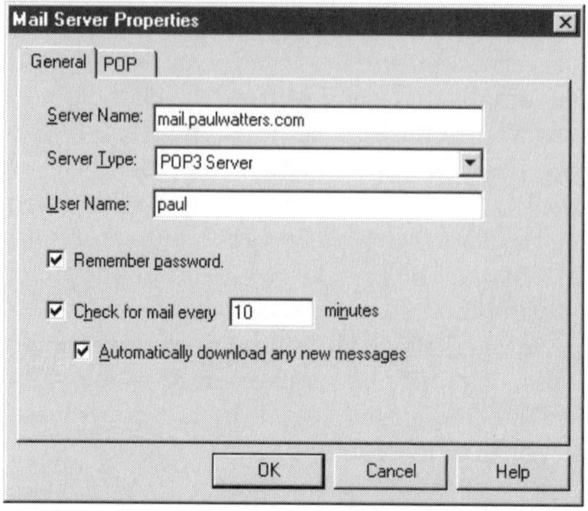

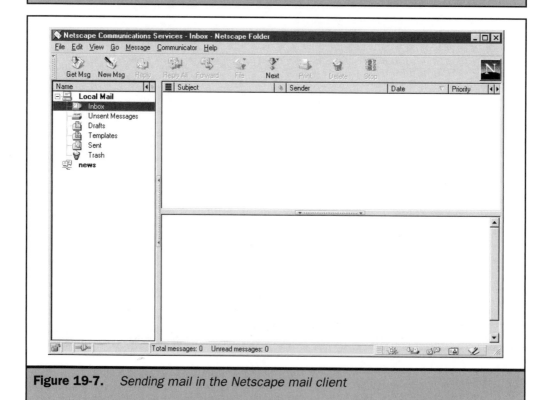

**Figure 19-6.** Configuring POP settings in the Netscape mail client

**Figure 19-7.** Sending mail in the Netscape mail client

## Summary

Sending electronic mail is a complicated but fascinating process, and it forms the basis of much of the Internet as we know it. Much of this functionality rests on mail transport agents such as **sendmail**.

## How to Find Out More

The best place to find out more about **sendmail** is the sendmail FAQ:

**http://www.sendmail.org/faq/**

There is also an excellent online tutorial at:

**http://www.networkcomputing.com/unixworld/tutorial/01/01.txt.html**

For an authoritative volume on **sendmail**, turn to the following book:

Costales, Bryan; and Allman, Eric. *sendmail*. (O'Reilly, 1997.)

Questions about **sendmail** can be posted to the **comp.mail.sendmail** USENET forum.

# The Complete Reference

Solaris 8

# Chapter 20

## FTP Administration

Fﬁle Transfer Protocol (FTP) is one of the oldest and most commonly used protocols for transferring files between hosts on the Internet. Although it has been avoided in recent years for security reasons, anonymous FTP is still the most popular method of organizing and serving publicly available data. In this chapter, we will examine FTP and demonstrate how to set up an FTP site with Solaris tools. We will also cover GUI FTP clients and explain some of the alternative FTP servers designed to handle large amounts of anonymous FTP traffic.

# Understanding FTP

After the UNIX-to-UNIX Copy Protocol (UUCP) was beginning to show its age in the era of Fast Ethernet and the globalization of the Internet, the File Transfer Protocol was destined to become the de facto standard for transferring files between computers connected to each other using a TCP/IP network. FTP is simple, transparent, and has a rich number of client commands and server features that are very powerful in the hands of an experienced user. In addition, there are a variety of clients available on all platforms with a TCP/IP stack, which assist with transferring entire directory trees, for example, rather than performing transfers file by file.

Although originally designed to provide remote file access for users with an account on the target system, the practice of providing anonymous FTP file areas has become common in recent years, allowing remote users without an account to download (and in some cases upload) data to and from their favorite servers. This allowed the easy dissemination of data and applications before the widespread adoption of more sophisticated systems for locating and identifying networked information sources such as gopher and the HyperText Transfer Protocol (HTTP). Anonymous FTP servers typically contain archives of application software, device drivers, and configuration files. In addition, many electronic mailing lists keep their archives on anonymous FTP sites so that an entire year's worth of discussion can be retrieved rapidly. However, relying on anonymous FTP can be precarious because sites are subject to change, and there is no guarantee that what is available today will still be there tomorrow.

In this section, we will examine how FTP transactions actually work behind the scenes, summarize the most common FTP commands, and examine some sample transactions of the most common variety.

## What Is FTP?

FTP is a TCP/IP protocol specified in RFC 959. On Solaris, it is invoked as a daemon through the Internet superdaemon (**inetd**). Thus, many of the options used to configure an FTP server can be entered directly into the configuration file for **inetd** (/etc/inetd.conf). For example, **in.ftpd** can be invoked with a debugging option (**-d**) or a logging option (**-l**), in which case all transactions will be logged to the /var/adm/messages file by default.

The objectives of providing an FTP server are to permit the reliable sharing of files between hosts across a TCP/IP network without concern for the underlying exchanges that must take place to facilitate the transfer of data. A user need only be concerned with identifying which files he/she wants to download or upload, and whether or not binary or ASCII transfer is required. The most common file types, and their recommended transfer modes, are shown in Table 20-1. A general rule of thumb is that text-only files should be transferred using ASCII, but applications and binary files should be transferred using binary mode. Many clients have a simple interface that makes it very easy for users to learn to send and retrieve data using FTP.

FTP has had a long evolution over the years, although many of its basic characteristics remain unchanged. The first RFC for FTP was published in 1971, with a targeted

| Extension | Transfer Type | Description |
|-----------|---------------|-------------|
| .arc | Binary | Archive compression |
| .arj | Binary | Arj compression |
| .gif | Binary | Image file |
| .gz | Binary | GNU Zip compression |
| .hqx | ASCII | HQX (MacOS version of **uuencode**) |
| .jpg | Binary | Image file |
| .lzh | Binary | LH compression |
| .shar | ASCII | Bourne shell archive |
| .sit | Binary | Stuff-It compression |
| .tar | Binary | Tape archive |
| .tgz | Binary | Gzip compressed tape archive |
| .txt | ASCII | Plain-text file |
| .uu | ASCII | Uuencoded file |
| .Z | Binary | Standard UNIX compression |
| .zip | Binary | Standard zip compression |
| .zoo | Binary | Zoo compression |

**Table 20-1.**   *Common File Types for Binary Versus ASCII Transfer Mode*

implementation on hosts at M.I.T. (RFC 114), by A.K. Bhushan. Since that time, enhancements to the original RFC have been suggested, including:

- **RFC 2640**   Internationalization of the File Transfer Protocol
- **RFC 2389**   Feature negotiation mechanism for the File Transfer Protocol
- **RFC 1986**   Experiments with a Simple File Transfer Protocol for Radio Links using Enhanced Trivial File Transfer Protocol (ETFTP)
- **RFC 1440**   SIFT/UFT: Sender-Initiated/Unsolicited File Transfer
- **RFC 1068**   Background File Transfer Program (BFTP)
- **RFC 2585**   Internet X.509 Public Key Infrastructure Operational Protocols: FTP and HTTP
- **RFC 2428**   FTP Extensions for IPv6 and NATs
- **RFC 2228**   FTP Security Extensions
- **RFC 1639**   FTP Operation Over Big Address Records (FOOBAR)
- **RFC 1068**   Background File Transfer Program (BFTP)
- **RFC 1440**   SIFT/UFT: Sender-Initiated/Unsolicited File Transfer
- **RFC 1639**   FTP Operation Over Big Address Records (FOOBAR)
- **RFC 1986**   Experiments with a Simple File Transfer Protocol for Radio Links using Enhanced Trivial File Transfer Protocol (ETFTP)
- **RFC 2228**   FTP Security Extensions
- **RFC 2389**   Feature negotiation mechanism for the File Transfer Protocol
- **RFC 2428**   FTP Extensions for IPv6 and NATs
- **RFC 2585**   Internet X.509 Public Key Infrastructure Operational Protocols: FTP and HTTP
- **RFC 2640**   Internationalization of the File Transfer Protocol

Some of these RFCs are informational only, although many suggest concrete improvements to FTP that have been implemented as standards. For example, many changes will be required to fully implement IPv6 at the network level, including support for IP addresses that are much longer than standard. Despite these changes and enhancements, however, the basic procedures for initiating, conducting, and terminating an FTP session have remained unchanged for many years. FTP is a client-server process: A client attempts to make a connection to a server by using a command like:

```
client% ftp server
```

If there is an FTP server active on the host server, the FTP process proper can begin. After a user initiates the FTP session through the user interface or client program, the client program requests a session through the client protocol interpreter (client PI), such as **DIR** for a directory listing. The client PI then issues the appropriate command to the server PI, which replies with the appropriate response number (for example, "200 Command OK," if the command is accepted by the server PI). FTP commands must reflect the desired nature of the transaction (such as port number and data transfer mode, whether binary or ASCII), and the type of operating to be performed (file retrieval with GET, file deletion with DELE, and so on). The actual data transfer process (DTP) is conducted by the server DTP agent, which connects to the client DTP agent, transferring the data packet by packet. After transmitting the data, both the client and server DTP agents then communicate the end of a transaction, successful or otherwise, to their respective PIs. A message is sent back to the user interface, and ultimately the user finds out whether or not his or her request has been processed. This process is shown in Figure 20-1.

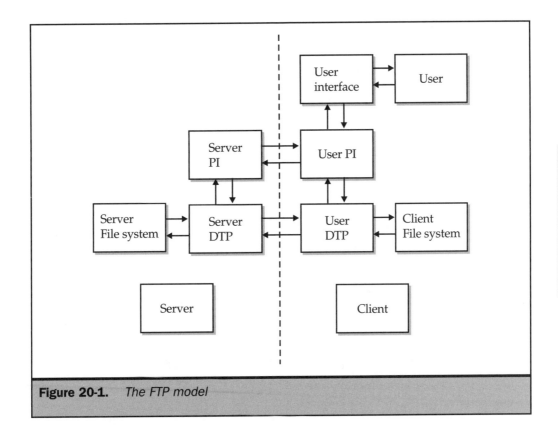

**Figure 20-1.**    *The FTP model*

# FTP Internal Commands/Responses

As we mentioned in the previous section, FTP commands are associated with specific operations to be performed on the server. Most FTP clients and the Solaris FTP server support the following case-insensitive commands:

- **!** Escape to the default shell.
- **$** Execute a predefined macro.
- **account** Send account information to the remote server.
- **append** Append server output to a file.
- **ascii** Set ASCII transfer type. ASCII mode is the default transfer mode and is used for transferring text files.
- **bell** Beep when the specified command is completed.
- **binary** Set binary transfer type. Typically used for transferring binary files such as .zip files, .gif files, and .Z files.
- **bye** Terminate the FTP session, and exit from the client.
- **case** Toggle **mget** upper-/lowercase mapping.
- **cd** Change remote working directory. Changes the directory to the one named. If the directory named is not a subdirectory of the current directory, the path must be specified (for example, **cd /pub/library**).
- **cdup** Change remote working directory to parent directory.
- **close** Terminate FTP session, but do not exit from the client.
- **delete** Delete the remote file specified.
- **debug** Toggle/set debugging mode on server.
- **dir** List the contents of a remote directory.
- **disconnect** Terminate the current FTP session.
- **form** Set file transfer format to be binary or ASCII.
- **get** Download file from the server to the local client.
- **glob** Toggle metacharacter expansion of local filenames.
- **hash** Toggle printing "#" for each buffer transferred. Prints a hash "#" on the screen for every 1,024 bytes transferred. This is useful for keeping track of an FTP transfer interactively.
- **help** Gives local help on the use of commands within the FTP client.
- **lcd** Change local working directory to that specified.
- **ls** List contents of current remote directory.

- **macdef**   Define a macro interactively.

- **mdelete**   Delete multiple files as determined by a file specification (for example, "mdelete *.txt").

- **mdir**   List contents of multiple remote directories in one request.

- **mget**   Download multiple files, as specified by using a wildcard character "*" in the file specification.

- **mkdir**   Create a directory on the remote machine as a subdirectory relative to the current directory.

- **mls**   List contents of multiple remote directories in a single request.

- **mode**   Set file transfer mode to be ASCII or binary.

- **mput**   Upload multiple files from your local file system to the remote server.

- **nmap**   Set templates for default filename mapping.

- **ntrans**   Set translation table for default filename mapping.

- **open**   Connect to remote server.

- **prompt**   Force interactive prompting on multiple commands.

- **proxy**   Issue command on alternate connection.

- **sendport**   Toggle use of port cmd for each data connection.

- **put**   Upload one file at a time.

- **pwd**   Print working directory on remote machine.

- **quit**   Terminate FTP session and exit.

- **quote**   Send arbitrary FTP command.

- **recv**   Receive file.

- **remotehelp**   Get help from remote server.

- **rename**   Rename file.

- **reset**   Clear queued command replies.

- **rmdir**   Remove directory on the remote machine.

- **runique**   Toggle the "store unique" flag for local files.

- **send**   Upload a single file.

- **status**   Show current status.

- **struct**   Set file transfer structure.

- **sunique**   Toggle the "store unique" flag on the remote machine.

- **tenex**   Set tenex file transfer type.

- **trace**   Toggle packet tracing.

ADMINISTERING
SERVICES

- **type**  Set file transfer type.
- **user**  Send new user information.
- **verbose**  Toggle verbose mode.
- **?**  Print local help information.

The following is a list of possible response codes, which the server generates in response to each command issued from the client:

- **110**  Restart marker reply.
- **120**  Service ready in *nnn* minutes.
- **125**  Data connection already open; transfer starting.
- **150**  File status okay; about to open data connection.
- **200**  Command okay.
- **202**  Command not implemented, superfluous at this site.
- **211**  System status, or system help reply.
- **212**  Directory status.
- **213**  File status.
- **214**  Help message.
- **215**  NAME system type.
- **220**  Service ready for new user.
- **221**  Service closing control connection.
- **225**  Data connection open; no transfer in progress.
- **226**  Closing data connection.
- **227**  Entering passive mode (h1,h2,h3,h4,p1,p2).
- **230**  User logged in, proceed.
- **250**  Requested file action okay, completed.
- **257**  "PATHNAME" repeated.
- **331**  Username okay, need password.
- **332**  Need account for login.
- **350**  Requested file action pending further information.
- **421**  Service not available, closing control connection.
- **425**  Can't open data connection.
- **426**  Connection closed; transfer aborted.
- **450**  Requested file action not taken.
- **451**  Requested action aborted: Local error in processing.

- **452** Requested action not taken.

- **500** Syntax error, command unrecognized.

- **501** Syntax error in parameters or arguments.

- **502** Command not implemented.

- **503** Bad sequence of commands.

- **504** Command not implemented for that parameter.

- **530** Not logged in.

- **532** Need account for storing files.

- **550** Requested action not taken.

- **551** Requested action aborted: Page type unknown.

- **552** Requested file action aborted.

- **553** Requested action not taken.

## An Example FTP Transaction

After examining the possible FTP client commands and server response codes, let's see how this transactional system actually works in practice on Solaris. The first step is to make a connection to a remote host from the local system by using the standard client:

```
client% ftp server
Connected to server.
220 server FTP server (SunOS 5.8) ready.
Name (server:pwatters): pwatters
331 Password required for pwatters.
Password:
230 User pwatters logged in.
ftp>
```

In this simple transaction, a user logs in, enters a password, and a session is established. This involves the client program sending a session request, receiving a 220 response, sending a user command ("user pwatters"), receiving back a 331 response requesting a password, and sending the password ("pass password"). If the username and password combination is correct, the session is established, and a 230 response is generated by the server. Let's look at what happens when an incorrect password is typed:

```
client% ftp server
Connected to server.
220 server FTP server (SunOS 5.8) ready.
Name (server:pwatters): pwatters
```

```
331 Password required for pwatters.
Password:
530 Login incorrect.
Login failed.
ftp>
```

In this transaction, the user logs in as before, entering a password and establishing a session. This client program then sends a session request, receiving a 220 response, then sends a user command ("user pwatters"), and receives back a 331 response requesting a password. The client then sends the password ("pass password"), which in this example is incorrect. A 530 response is sent back from the server to the client, and the user is left in his local client without establishing a session. However, the connect is still open, so mistyping a password can be remedied by using the following combination:

```
ftp> user pwatters
331 Password required for pwatters.
Password:
230 User pwatters logged in.
ftp>
```

Thus, the session is established, and the user can proceed with retrieving or uploading files. Let's look at an example:

```
ftp> dir
200 PORT command successful.
150 ASCII data connection for /bin/ls (192.58.64.22,34754) (0 bytes).
total 72573
drwxr-xr-x  13 pwatters staff 2048 Mar 27 08:43 .
dr-xr-xr-x   2 root     root     2 Mar 21 18:55 ..
-rw-r--r--   1 pwatters staff 0 Jan 27 15:42 .addressbook
-rw-r--r--   1 pwatters staff 2285 Jan 27 15:42 .addressbook.lu
-rw-r--r--   1 pwatters staff 5989 Mar 27 08:42 .bash_history
lrwxrwxrwx   1 pwatters staff 8 Mar 27 08:43 .bash_profile -> .profile
drwxr-xr-x  16 pwatters staff 512 Mar 21 10:10 .dt
-rwxr-xr-x   1 pwatters staff 5113 Jan 27 15:59 .dtprofile
-rw-------   1 pwatters staff 10 Feb 23 13:18 .hist10161
-rw-------   1 pwatters staff 28 Feb 23 16:17 .hist11931
-rw-------   1 pwatters staff 20 Mar  7 15:30 .hist12717
-rw-------   1 pwatters staff 30 Feb 21 08:11 .hist1298
-rw-------   1 pwatters staff 24 Mar  7 16:05 .hist13069
-rw-------   1 pwatters staff 18 Feb 21 15:16 .hist1370
-rw-------   1 pwatters staff 8 Feb 21 15:21 .hist1395
-rw-------   1 pwatters staff 8 Feb 22 08:43 .hist15962
-rw-------   1 pwatters staff 100 Feb 28 11:15 .hist17367
-rw-------   1 pwatters staff 24 Feb 28 11:16 .hist17371
-rw-------   1 pwatters staff 16 Feb 22 11:14 .hist19318
```

```
-rw-------   1 paul staff 68 Mar  7 14:38 .hist1954
226 ASCII Transfer complete.
6162 bytes received in 0.092 seconds (65.34 Kbytes/s)
ftp>
```

This is the contents of the current directory. Let's say you wanted to examine the contents of the subdirectory packages:

```
cd packages
250 CWD command successful.
ftp> dir
200 PORT command successful.
150 ASCII data connection for /bin/ls (192.58.64.22,34755) (0 bytes).
total 224056
drwxr-xr-x   3 pwatters staff 1024 Mar 27 08:37 .
drwxr-xr-x  13 pwatters staff 2048 Mar 27 08:43 ..
-rw-r--r--   1 pwatters staff 2457088 Mar 17 14:37
apache-1.3.6-sol7-intel-local
-rw-r--r--   1 pwatters staff 3912704 Mar 17 14:38
bash-2.03-sol7-intel-local
-rw-r--r--   1 pwatters staff 12154880 Mar 27 08:18
communicator-v472-export.SPARC-sun-solaris2.5.1.tar
drwxr-xr-x   2 pwatters staff 512 Feb  1 07:11
communicator-v472.SPARC-sun-solaris2.5.1
-rw-r--r--   1 pwatters staff 597504 Mar 17 16:18
flex-2.5.4a-sol7-intel-local
-rw-r--r--   1 pwatters staff 59280384 Mar 17 14:42
gcc-2.95.2-sol7-intel-local
226 ASCII Transfer complete.
1389 bytes received in 0.051 seconds (26.51 Kbytes/s)
ftp>
```

Now let's look at the situation where we want to retrieve a binary and an ASCII file. An example would be a Java source file (with a .java extension), which must be transferred in ASCII mode, and a Java class file (with a .class extension), which must be transferred in binary mode:

```
ftp> ascii
200 Type set to A.
ftp> get test.java
200 PORT command successful.
150 ASCII data connection for test.java (192.168.205.48,34759) (117 bytes).
226 ASCII Transfer complete.
local: test.java remote: test.java
127 bytes received in 0.02 seconds (6.25 Kbytes/s)
ftp> bin
```

ADMINISTERING SERVICES

```
200 Type set to I.
ftp> get test.class
200 PORT command successful.
150 Binary data connection for test.class (192.168.205.48,34760) (431 bytes).
226 Binary Transfer complete.
local: test.class remote: test.class
431 bytes received in 0.0031 seconds (137.10 Kbytes/s)
ftp>
```

Although there are many more commands available in FTP, as discussed above, these are the most commonly used commands and the responses associated with each kind of transfer.

# Using Anonymous FTP

Anonymous FTP allows an arbitrary remote user to make an FTP connection to a remote host. The permissible usernames for anonymous FTP are usually "anonymous" or "ftp." Not all servers offer FTP; often, it is only possible to determine if anonymous FTP is supported by trying to log in as "ftp" or "anonymous." Sites that support anonymous FTP usually allow the downloading of files from an archive of publicly available files. However, some servers also support an upload facility, where remote unauthenticated and unidentified users can upload files of arbitrary size. If this sounds dangerous, it is: If you don't apply quotas to the FTP users' directories on each file system the FTP user has write access to, it is possible for a malicious user to completely fill up the disk with large files. This is a kind of denial-of-service attack, since a completely filled file system cannot be written to by other users or system processes. If a remote user really does need to upload files, it is best to give that user a temporary account by which he or she can be authenticated and identified at login time.

Anonymous FTP uses the **chroot** facility to modify a user's root directory from the actual root to a virtual root. This means that when an anonymous FTP user logs in and types **cd /**, he or she will probably be **cd**ing to the physical path /home/ftp/. Anonymous users are prevented from accessing data in sensitive system areas, such as /etc/passwd. However, in order for chroot accounts like anonymous FTP to operate, they require local copies of files such as /etc/passwd (which would be physically located in /home/ftp/etc/passwd in this example). These entries are not required for actual password checking, and so the password field should always be deleted. They are only used by **ls** to show the correct user and group names rather than UIDs and GIDs, respectively.

When you connect to an anonymous FTP archive and you use the username "ftp" or "anonymous," it is traditional to enter your email address as the password. Although this won't be used for authentication, it may be stored on the remote server and could potentially make its way onto a list for unsolicited commercial email (UCE). If you have concerns about UCE (or you have as many unwanted UCE messages as many other Internet users do), you may wish to enter an email address like **dev@null.com**. As long as there is an @ symbol, most FTP servers will accept the address as valid, although some will do a reverse DNS lookup on the hostname to check its validity. In this case, use a domain that exists. Of course, you should never use a real password from your own local system, as this would also be logged by the remote server. If you're having problems logging in to an anonymous FTP server with a particular password, try using "-" as the first character in your password, as this will turn off the messages normally displayed when you first log on to the server.

Once you have logged in to an anonymous FTP server, the commands are exactly the same as for a normal FTP session. However, you will only be able to see and download the files contained underneath the chroot root directory (for example, all directories underneath /home/ftp). You can check the current remote directory by using the **pwd** command, and you can obtain a directory listing by using the **dir** command. By convention, the subdirectory where all publicly available files are stored is the /pub directory (which might physically correspond to /home/ftp/pub). Just like normal FTP, you will also need to determine whether you need to use binary or ASCII mode transmission. On some anonymous FTP sites, you can't obtain a directory listing from the /pub directory; this is to protect the file system by banning directory listings, as with some FTP servers. In this case, look out for a README or INDEX file that lists all of the publicly available FTP files.

Many FTP archives organize downloads around archive files of various kinds, as shown earlier in Table 20-1. Once you have downloaded the archive file, you can uncompress it and extract the contents to a temporary directory before installing it properly (for example, in the /tmp directory). You can change the directory to save files on your local client by using the **lcd** command.

## GUI FTP Clients

The standard Solaris FTP client is text-based and is limited in some of its commands. For example, defining a macro to retrieve all files contained in subdirectories of the current directory can be time consuming. This is one reason why graphical user interface (GUI) FTP clients are popular in desktop operating environments: They save time and make the file transfer process easy to initiate. Although there are not many GUI FTP clients available, one excellent client is the XFTP client created at the Lawrence Livermore National Laboratory (available for download from **http://www.llnl.gov/ia/ xftp.html**). The XFTP interface is shown in Figure 20-2. The left pane represents the local file system, displaying the current directory, and the right pane shows the remote file system. It is possible to select either a binary or ASCII transfer mode, and you can also select whether to connect anonymously or use an established account from the Connect menu. You can also select a remote or local text file for viewing, and change directories up the local or remote directory tree by selecting one of the hierarchical entries using the Dir menu.

XFTP is also useful as a file management tool in a network composed of hosts that support FTP clients and servers, but they have little else in common. For example, you may have several Solaris servers, a building full of PCs running Linux, BeOS, Microsoft Windows, and several off-site MacOS systems. Although SAMBA can be used to connect some of these hosts, FTP has a long history as a reliable file transfer method,

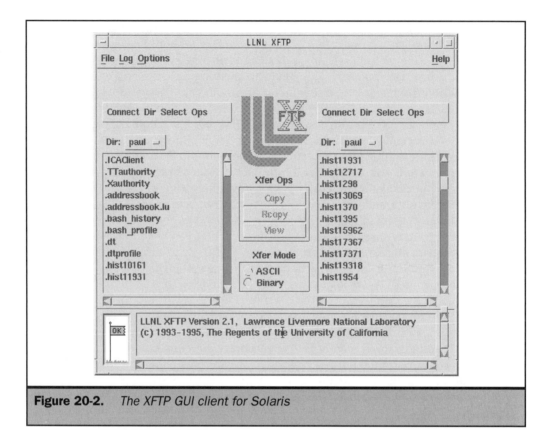

**Figure 20-2.** *The XFTP GUI client for Solaris*

even if it is not secure across the Internet. Nightly **cron** jobs may back up data from workstations to central servers in preparation for dumping to a DAT or DLT drive in the data center. Alternatively, XFTP can be used as a simple GUI-based client for downloading your favorite files from sites such as **http://www.sunfreeware.com/**.

XFTP can be easily compiled using GCC or the Sun Workshop compilers from its source form.

## Enabling FTP Access

Now that we have examined the most common uses for FTP, we will investigate how to configure the FTP daemon and how to set up anonymous FTP, which is one of the most common uses of FTP today.

## Setting Up ftpd

The FTP server in Solaris is installed by default during configuration and package copying during the initial installation or upgrade process. By default, the FTP server and protocol will also be active after installation. You can check the status of the FTP server on the local system by checking whether the FTP service is enabled in the services database and in the configuration file for the **inetd** superdaemon:

```
server# grep ftp /etc/services
ftp-data        20/tcp
ftp             21/tcp
tftp            69/udp

server# grep ftp /etc/inetd.conf
ftp     stream  tcp     nowait  root    /usr/sbin/in.ftpd       in.ftpd
# Tftp service is provided primarily for booting.  Most sites run this
#tftp   dgram   udp     wait    root    /usr/sbin/in.tftpd      in.tftpd -s
/tftpboot
```

We can see that FTP is both defined as a service (ftp 21/tcp) and as a daemon that runs from within the Internet superdaemon (/usr/sbin/in.ftpd). As long as the Internet superdaemon is started up during one of the single- or multiple-user init states, the FTP service will start. If you ever want to disable the FTP service, you need to comment out the appropriate line in both /etc/services and /etc/inetd.conf. You can do this by entering a hash character "#" in front of the appropriate line:

```
#ftp            21/tcp
#ftp    stream  tcp     nowait  root    /usr/sbin/in.ftpd       in.ftpd
```

You can also check the process list by using the command **ps -eaf | grep inetd** to verify that the Internet superdaemon is running at any time.

## Setting Up Anonymous FTP

Setting up normal FTP is easy, but setting up anonymous FTP can be difficult and time consuming. In the first instance, you need to evaluate from a security perspective whether anonymous FTP is worthwhile. Since many of the anonymous file archive functions can be provided through HTTP implemented by a web server, many organizations have switched off their anonymous FTP capability. In addition, there have been many loopholes and problems identified in FTP servers over the years that have made organizations reluctant to use FTP. However, by checking the appropriate CERT notices at **http://www.cert.org/**, you should be able to apply any security patches made available from vendors. Sun also releases Solaris-specific patches through Sunsolve. There is an anonymous FTP FAQ file available at

**ftp:// rtfm.mit.edu/pub/usenet/news.answers/computer-security/anonymous- ftp-faq**

First, use the admintool to create a user called ftp. It is also advisable to create a separate FTP users group called ftp, which has only the member ftp. The home directory should be specific as /home/ftp or reside on a completely separate file system from normal user accounts. This would physically isolate the anonymous FTP archive from the normal users on the system. The FTP account should be locked so that a normal user login cannot be initiated. In addition, the shell should be fake—for example, /bin/false. Admintool will create the appropriate home directory; however, you will need to manually set the permissions on the ftp home directory to 555. Note that the FTP user's directory should not be owned by the FTP user: This ensures that the FTP user has little control over any directories above the contents of the ftp home directory. Most sites would have all the files owned by root, as it is assumed that the root account is the most secure on the system. Make sure that only root has write permission on these files—in fact, removing write permissions as a matter of course will ensure the highest level of security.

Next, you need to recreate the layout of the normal system underneath the virtual root directory for the anonymous FTP user. This means creating the subdirectories /etc, /bin, and /pub as a minimum. The permissions for copies of files made here should be preserved from the normal system. So, for example, you need to change the ownership of the bin directory to root, and the group to wheel. Always turn off write permission to the directories (although this can be done as a last step, after all files have been copied). Next, copy the ls binary from /bin into /home/ftp/bin, and copy the password file (/etc/passwd) into the /home/ftp/etc directory. Remove all the encrypted password entries in /home/ftp/etc/passwd, and replace them with "*". This prevents external users from downloading an intact copy of your password file, giving them the ability to run programs like **crack** against all your (potentially weak) local passwords. Only the users who own files in the /home/ftp directory tree need to be included in this file (for example, ftp, root); all others should be removed for security purposes. An example password file would look like:

```
root:*:0:0:Super User::
ftp:*:500:500:FTP::
```

The /etc/group file should also be copied into /home/ftp/etc, and only the groups whose members own files in the /home/ftp directory tree should be included (GID 0 and GID 500 in this example). These are all the steps that are required. As files are copied into /home/ftp, they should be marked as read-only by all users so malicious external users cannot delete them from the archive. As always, the best way to determine the security of your FTP server is to try and break into it yourself. Here's an example of what /home/ftp should eventually look like:

```
dr-xr-xr-x  7   root    wheel  512 Mar 1      15:17 ./
        dr-xr-xr-x 25    root     wheel 512 Jan 4       11:30 ../
```

```
dr-xr-xr-x  2   root   wheel 512 Dec 20      15:43 bin/
dr-xr-xr-x  2   root   wheel 512 Mar 12      16:23 etc/
dr-xr-xr-x 10   root   wheel 512 Jun 5       10:54 pub/
```

The man page for FTP contains a script that will meet all these requirements.

## Improving FTP Security

FTP security can be increased to a certain extent by implementing the measures outlined above. However, there are some significant limitations. As we examined in Chapter 16, it is quite easy for an intermediate host between FTP client and FTP server to eavesdrop and detect system usernames and passwords transmitted using plain-text FTP username and password exchanges. It is recommended that **sftp** or **scp** be used in preference to FTP whenever transfers are conducted outside your local area network or through untrusted hosts (which usually means the Internet). However, your networking solution may already provide an encryption layer (for example, a virtual private network) over which normal FTP can be used without concern for packet sniffing. If you believe that your computer system has been broken into, and you are within the jurisdiction of the United States, you can contact the FBI National Computer Crimes Squad at (202) 324-9164. They deal specifically with computer crime.

Be sure to keep logs of all your FTP transactions. To obtain the detail necessary for a criminal investigation, it may be necessary to use the advanced logging features of the Washington University FTP daemon, described in the section "WU-FTPD," or switch on logging in the standard FTP daemon by supplying the **-l** flag to in.ftpd in the Internet superdaemon configuration file (/etc/inetd.conf).

## Troubleshooting

The most common mistake in configuring FTP is not to have a valid shells database (/etc/shells) on your system. Although you can insert any shell you like into the /etc/passwd file, if the shell is not registered in the database, users will not be able to log in. This is a security measure that prevents arbitrary shells with hidden features from being used on the system.

One of the nice features of FTP is that you can test it by telnetting to the FTP port, much like the way we tested **sendmail** in Chapter 19. This will allow you to issue FTP commands interactively and examine the results. Using this method, it is possible to determine if there is a problem with the remote server or a problem with your local client. For example, if you receive a "421" response, you know the remote FTP server is not running, in which case you can advise the administrator of the remote machine to check the status of **inetd**.

If your client attempts to connect to a host for a long time without receiving an acknowledgment, it's often worthwhile to check that the host is actually known through

DNS. You can use the **nslookup** command to achieve this: If a host is not registered using DNS, you won't be able to make a connection.

If the host has a resolvable hostname, you can use any one of the network troubleshooting tools—such as **ping** or **traceroute**—to determine whether a path exists between your local client and the remote server. If no valid path exists, you can contact the administrator of the intermediate site where the connection fails.

# Alternative FTP Servers

Although the standard Solaris FTP server is suitable for most purposes, there may be situations where you need some facility provided by one of the many alternative FTP servers available for download from the Internet. For example, you may want to use the advanced logging features of the Washington University FTP daemon (WU-FTPD), or you may be attracted to the virtual host support provided by BeroFTPD. Alternatively, Troll FTPD is an extremely thin server, providing only the most commonly used features of FTP and removing all code for deprecated features. This means it can serve more clients per CPU than most other FTP servers and is very useful in high transaction volume environments. In this section, we review the main features of each of these servers.

## WU-FTPD

The Washington University FTP server is a very popular alternative to the standard Solaris FTP server. This is as much a reflection of the extra features of the WU-FTPD server as it is of the fact that WU-FTPD comes with source. This allows local developers and administrators to make their own modifications to the public source code. Unfortunately, this also exposes any weaknesses or flaws in what is considered to be production software to potential crackers and rogue users. However, invisible bugs are often more dangerous than publicly visible bugs. You can download the current version of the server from

ftp://ftp.academ.com/pub/wu-ftpd/private

WU-FTPD allows administrators to manage file uploads in particular by applying quotas on a daemon basis rather than a file system basis. This is useful in situations where the FTP administrator is not the system administrator, and the FTP administrator does not have overall control of the file system. WU-FTPD can also limit the amount of data that can be uploaded or downloaded in any one session, reducing the likelihood of denial-of-service attacks and making sites available more equitably during periods of high request volume.

After configuring, compiling, and installing the WU-FTPD sources, it's easy to deploy the new server by defining its entry in the /etc/inetd.conf file:

```
ftp  stream  tcp  nowait  root  /usr/sbin/ftpd  ftpd -laio
```

You can alternatively run WU-FTPD on a separate port from standard FTP, but this defeats the whole purpose of installing a more secure server in the first place. Simply comment out the original FTP configuration lines as shown earlier when configuring WU-FTPD.

WU-FTPD also has some important configuration options, including the ability to disable potential security loopholes in the file system:

```
delete          no      guest,anonymous      # delete permission?
    overwrite       no      guest,anonymous        # overwrite permission?
    rename          no      guest,anonymous        # rename permission?
    chmod           no      anonymous              # chmod permission?
    umask           no      anonymous              # umask permission?
```

## BeroFTPD

BeroFTPD is developed from the WU-FTPD codebase and is available from

**ftp://rufus.w3.org/linux/1/RPM/yellowdog/1.0/updates/champion-1.1/extras/SRP MS/beroftpd-1.3.4-2a.src.html**

It has the main advantage of logging all transfers and commands, as well as virtual host support that is similar to that of Apache. Again, if the local server administrator does not have control over DNS for the local network, using BeroFTPD to control the allocation of resources to specific servers can be very useful. When you need to install more than one FTP server on a single server, you obviously need to have the hosts defined in DNS, but from that point on, you can easily manage the virtual hosts from within the server itself. Different settings can be applied on a per-host basis. For example, if a single host contains an FTP server for www.companyA.com, and an FTP server for www.companyB.com, they can each have their own unique login banners and user authentication procedures. You simply need to define a ftpaccess file for each domain in the BeroFTPD configuration file:

```
companyA.com      /etc/ftpd/config/companyA.com
companyB.com      /etc/ftpd/config/companyB.com
```

After creating the appropriate directories and files, both of these domains can be supported from a single physical server.

## Troll FTPD

The Troll FTP daemon is a true hackers' daemon, being small (45K for the C source), simple, and designed to use fewer resources than older servers. In addition, it supports only the most commonly used features and commands of FTP, omitting everything that has been deprecated over the years or is associated with security issues. The Troll

FTP daemon comes with complete source. This means it is very easy to understand the processes by which FTP operates. For example, a function is defined for each of the main FTP functions:

- **douser()** USER command (send username)
- **dopass()** PASS command (send password)
- **docwd()** CWD command (change working directory)
- **doretr()** RETR command (retrieve a file)
- **dodele()** DELE command (delete a remote file)
- **dostor()** STOR command (upload a file)
- **domkd()** MKDIR command (create a remote directory)
- **dormd()** RMDIR command (remove a remote directory)
- **dopasv()** Enter PASV mode (enter passive FTP mode)

Troll FTPD also has some internal checks and balances to prevent buffer overflows and other security problems. For example, it checks the size of each command issued to the server. If this command is larger than 1,024 characters, Troll FTPD rejects the command immediately.

## Summary

In this chapter, we examined the basic installation and configuration of the FTP server, and the use of client programs for user-authenticated and anonymous FTP. Although FTP is commonly used across the Internet, this is quite dangerous, except for anonymous FTP. However, even anonymous FTP is being supplanted by the HTTP protocol, and it may well be that FTP will be deprecated in future years. However, as it is still the standard file transfer protocol used over TCP/IP, it's important to understand the advantages and potential limitations of FTP in a production environment.

## How to Find Out More

Internet Product Watch often contains new releases of FTP client software for many different platforms, which can be used to access Solaris FTP servers and can be found at

**http://ipw.internet.com/site_management/telnet_ftp/**

If you would like to learn more about the RFC process, or submit an RFC for an improved FTP service, then read the RFC Frequently Asked Questions at

**http://www.rfc-editor.org/rfcfaq.html**

# The Complete Reference

Solaris 8

# Chapter 21

## Web Serving

A lthough the origins of the Internet lie in services such as Telnet and FTP, the development of distributed information systems has led to the massive growth in Internet use experienced worldwide. Although early Internet-based information systems such as Gopher and WAIS were popular for retrieving text-based data, the World Wide Web (WWW) has come to dominate the Internet as a way for users to make available multimedia data to the world being referenced by a single identifier (the Universal Resource Locator, or URL). The World Wide Web began in late 1989 when Tim Berners-Lee, a researcher at the Conseil Européen pour la Recherche Nucléaire (CERN), started to work out a system for sharing the results of experiments in high-energy particle physics with his colleagues. His system had two main advantages. First, documents located on one server could be easily linked to documents located on other servers. Second, documents stored on any server could be accessed from any machine. Since anyone with a "browser" program could access these documents, the popularity of Berners-Lee's "web" spread rapidly to other research centers and universities. The major explosion of the web came with the addition of graphics and the introduction of a web browser named Mosaic that gave users a point-and-click interface to the web.

The web is the hottest thing on the Internet, and Solaris provides the most stable platform for hosting web content and providing web services. Chapter 21 covers the HTTP protocol and the most popular and robust http server available, Apache. This chapter covers both basic installation and configuration, along with advanced topics like user access and virtual hosts.

# Introduction to HTTP

The web is based on the HyperText Transfer Protocol (HTTP), which allows for text files embedded with Uniform Resource Locators (URLs) to be transferred from the server where the file resides to a client machine that requests the file. These text files are commonly referred to as "web pages." Web pages are written in a special language called the HyperText Markup Language (HTML), which determines how different resources referred to in the page should be retrieved. HTML allows you to control certain characteristics about how documents are displayed, along with allowing you to create links to other pages by embedding URLs.

When you request a document located on the web, you use its web address or URL to locate it. The URL identifies the machine that contains the document you want and the pathname to the document on that machine. A URL can also contain a protocol that identifies the method you want to use to access the page on the remote machine. Here is a sample URL:

```
http://www.csua.berkeley.edu/~ranga/index.html
```

This URL identifies the page "index.html" located in the directory "/~ranga" on the machine "**www.csua.berkeley.edu**." It also specifies that the HTTP protocol should be used to access this file.

In the terminology of the web, machines where web pages reside are called *web servers*. A machine that requests pages from a web server is called a *web client*. The client communicates with the server through the use of HTTP. When the client wants a document, it takes a URL and issues an HTTP request to the machine specified by the URL. When the server receives the client's request it looks for the page requested by the client. If the server finds the appropriate page, it returns the contents of the page as its HTTP response. The client's request together with the server's response is called an HTTP transaction. Figure 21-1 illustrates such a transaction.

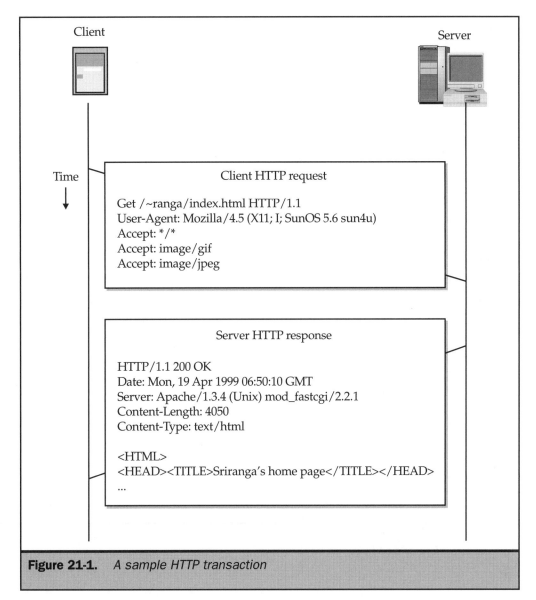

**Figure 21-1.** *A sample HTTP transaction*

In order for a machine to serve as a web client, it needs to have a web browser that understands how to make HTTP requests. Some of the common web browsers are Netscape's Navigator, Microsoft's Internet Explorer, and the text-only browser Lynx. Machines that receive HTTP requests need to have a web server program that understands how to respond to an HTTP request. Later in this chapter we will be looking at setting up and maintaining the web's most popular web server, Apache, which powers more than half of all the web sites in the world.

# HTTP Requests

One of the most important things to understand about HTTP is what a request looks like. HTTP requests are made up of single lines of text that provide information to the server about the client, its capabilities, and the page that is desired.

In general, an HTTP request is made up of five parts:

- The request type
- The general header
- The request header
- The entity header
- The entity body

The request type is the first line of an HTTP request. It tells the server how to retrieve the page the client wants. There are several different ways in which the server can retrieve pages, so the client has to specify which one the server should use. (The next section covers the request type in greater detail.) The request type is mandatory for all HTTP requests. All the other parts of the request are optional.

Usually the next few lines of the HTTP request are the general headers. These can be used by a client to send information to the server concerning the type of connection to use or the current time. The general headers are optional, and some clients omit them entirely. The general headers are followed by the request headers, which tell the server about the client and its capabilities. This can include information about the page the client is coming from, the name of the machine the client is running, the client's name, and the type of information the client understands.

The entity header and the entity body are used by the client to send a document to the server and are used by tools that allow you to create and publish web pages to a server. They are also used when you submit a form.

## HTTP Request Types

The HTTP request type indicates to the server the way your request is being made. HTTP specifies several different *methods* by which a client can request information from a server. Normally, the request type is specified by a line that has the following structure:

[*method*] pathname HTTP/[*version*]

Here, *method* is normally one of the following: GET, POST, or HEAD. The *pathname* is the part of the URL for the page that contains the path to the file on the server, and *version* is the version of HTTP that you are using. Usually this means that your client understands only that version of HTTP, so servers will take extra care to tailor their responses correctly.

Here is an example of an HTTP request type:

```
GET /~ranga/index.html HTTP/1.0
```

This request type indicates to the server that it should use the GET method to retrieve the file /~ranga/index.html. The "HTTP/1.0" portion of the request type indicates that the client understands HTTP version 1.0. Currently there are three different versions of HTTP: 0.9, 1.0, and 1.1. The major web browsers and web servers support all three versions of HTTP.

HTTP version 0.9 is the oldest and simplest version of HTTP. It defines only one method for requesting pages. If the requested page exists, the server returns it; otherwise the server returns nothing. Another limitation of version 0.9 is that it can only deal with text information. With this version there is no way for the server to send images, applets, compressed files, or any other file that contains binary data to the client. HTTP 0.9 is outdated, and is mostly supported for compatibility with older web browsers. Currently, most browsers use HTTP version 1.0 and 1.1.

HTTP version 1.0 was a major upgrade from version 0.9. Its biggest improvement was the addition of support for different media types, such as images, applets, and compressed files. By making web pages graphical, this improvement transformed the web. It also led to the creation of the first point-and-click web browser, Mosaic. Other improvements included additional methods like HEAD and POST, user authentication, and caching. The last major improvement that was introduced in version 1.0 was the ability for clients to communicate information about their capabilities to the server. This allowed for servers to tailor their responses to web browsers.

HTTP version 1.1, the latest version, is a performance upgrade to HTTP 1.0. Its main improvement is its support for "persistent connections." With HTTP 1.0, a client would open a connection to the server, send its request, read the server's response, and then close the connection. If the client wanted to get another document from the server, it had to create a new connection. The process of creating a connection to the server is slow, so by allowing the client to reuse its existing connection, HTTP 1.1 significantly improves the performance of both the web server and the web browser.

## HTTP Methods

Originally HTTP only supported the GET method. Using this method the client could ask a server to *get* it a particular document—that is, retrieve it and display it. Version 1.0 added several extra methods, the most significant of which are the HEAD and POST methods. Other methods include PUT, DELETE, and TRACE. In this section I'll describe each method.

Mostly, web browsers use the GET, HEAD, and POST methods; the other methods (PUT, DELETE, and TRACE) are not widely used. The GET method is the most common request method used by web browsers. In the current version of HTTP this method can be used to obtain HTML pages as well as other files, like pictures and applets. In the previous section we saw an example of a GET request.

The HEAD method is similar to the GET method, except that the server returns some information *about* the requested document, instead of the document itself. For example, consider the following HEAD request:

```
HEAD /~ranga/index.html HTTP/1.0
```

Usually the HEAD method is used by browsers to determine the size of a document, the type of data it contains, and the type of the server. With this information, the browser can then modify its GET request as needed.

The POST method allows the client to send data to special data processing programs that reside on the server. The data the client wants to send is included in the entity body part of the HTTP request. In the case of a POST request, the URL that is specified is usually the path to a special program on the server, a program that knows how to handle the data. Usually these programs are Common Gateway Interface (CGI) scripts or programs, but they can also be special Java programs called *servlets*. CGI scripts and servlets are discussed later in this section.

The most common use of a POST request is in the handling of a *form*. Forms are special HTML pages that allow users to input information into text fields or indicate their choices via check boxes. Each of the inputs in a form is associated with a name and a value. The value is normally the user's input. When users are finished with a form, they submit it. At this point the browser gathers all of the names and their corresponding values, places them into the entity body, and then sends the request to the server. For the form shown in Figure 21-2, the POST request will look something like the following:

```
POST /cgi-bin/login.pl HTTP/1.0
User-Agent: Mozilla/4.5 (X11; I; SunOS 5.6 sun4u)
Accept: */*
Accept: image/gif
Accept: image/jpeg
Content-type application/x-www-form-urlencoded
Content-length: 21

user=guest&pass=guest
```

The PUT method is used to transfer files from the client machine to the server. The DELETE method can be used by a client to delete files on the server. Finally, the TRACE method can be used to determine how the request traveled through the Internet. That is, it requests that the path the request takes to get from the client to the server be displayed.

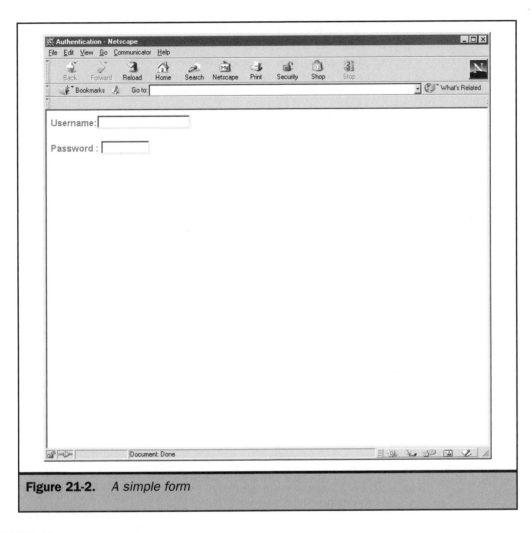

**Figure 21-2.** *A simple form*

# HTTP Responses

The main task of an HTTP server, or web server, is to respond to requests from clients. Just like an HTTP request, there are five main parts to an HTTP response:

- The response status
- The general headers
- The response headers
- The entity headers
- The entity body

The response status consists of a single line in the following format:

*HTTP/[version] [status_code] [reason_phrase]*

Here, *version* corresponds to the version of HTTP that the server is responding with. The version is usually 1.0 or 1.1. (A server never responds with the version number 0.9, because HTTP version 0.9 does not specify a way for the server to communicate the response status to the client.) *Status_code* is a number between 100 and 599 inclusive. The status code indicates whether the request was successful or not. *Reason_phrase* is a human-readable description of the status code, usually OK to indicate a successful request and ERR to indicate a failed request.

The general headers are similar to the general headers used in an HTTP request; they include information like the type of connection that is being used and the time at which the server started its request. The response header usually contains information about the server, such as its name and version. Some servers use the response headers to indicate to clients which HTTP methods they support.

The entity header and entity body are returned by the server only if the client's request was successful. The entity header contains information about the type of data that is being returned, including the size of the requested document (in bytes) and the time that the file was last modified. The entity body contains the contents of the document that was requested.

## Response Status Codes

The status codes returned by an HTTP server in response to a client request consist of numbers between 100 and 599. They are categorized as shown in the following table.

| Range | Explanation |
| --- | --- |
| 100–199 | Informational messages from the server |
| 200–299 | Successful requests |
| 300–399 | Redirected requests |
| 400–499 | Incomplete requests or failed requests |
| 500–599 | Server errors |

Basically, if a client receives any number between 100 and 299 for the status code, it means the request was successful. If a client receives a status code from 300 through 399, it means that the URL the client specified is outdated, and that another URL should be used instead. The two most common status codes in this range are 301, which corresponds to a URL that has been relocated permanently, and 302, which corresponds to a URL that has been moved temporarily. Normally, clients that receive a status code from 300 through 399 automatically make a new request to the new URL.

The numbers from 400 through 499 and from 500 through 599 correspond to client errors and server errors, respectively. Common status codes indicating client error include situations where the client has requested a page that:

- It does not have permission to access (401 and 403)
- Does not exist (404)
- Has been removed (410)

Server-error status codes (500 through 599) indicate that the server is not yet ready to handle the client's request or that the client is using a version of HTTP that the server does not understand.

# CGI and Servlets

The Common Gateway Interface (CGI) is a standard that defines an interface between the web server and an external program. It is a fairly old standard and is widely used in the World Wide Web. The servlet standard, designed by Sun Microsystems, is intended as a replacement for CGI. Servlets are special Java programs that are loaded and executed inside the web server. We will first look at CGI programs, and then examine servlets.

## CGI Programs

When the web server receives a request for a CGI program, it executes it and returns the output of that program as its response to the client. CGI programs are mostly used to present dynamic information to users of a web site. Some common uses for CGI programs include providing access to a search engine or a database. Since CGI programs are executed by the web server, it is easy to overload the server if many users access the same CGI program at the same time. In order to avoid this problem, CGI programs should be short and execute quickly. Most CGI programs are written in Perl, since it is quite powerful and can be executed efficiently. Other common languages for writing CGIs include C/C++ (for speed), TCL (for ease of use), and Bourne Shell (for compatibility across operating systems). The only requirement for a CGI program is that it should be executable by the user who executes the web server.

Normally, web servers will execute programs only if they're stored in a special directory, usually /cgi-bin. Some web servers, including Apache, are also capable of executing programs stored in other directories if they end with the .cgi suffix. The use of the .cgi suffix for executing CGI programs is discouraged because it can create security problems. If you manage a web site that allows users to create and maintain their own web sites, it is possible for malicious users to install programs into their web directories that will give them access as a privileged user. By installing the program with the .cgi suffix, it can be executed from the web—even if the user does not intend this to be the case. This can seriously compromise the security of your system. Even if you do a periodic check of all files that end with .cgi, a user can avoid detection by renaming the program. By using a server that limits itself to running programs from a single directory, such as /cgi-bin, you can easily control the programs that are placed in the directory, thus preventing a major security problem.

The HTTP request for a CGI program is the same as a request for any other page. For example, if I wanted to retrieve the page corresponding to the following URL,

**http://kanchi/cgi-bin/printenv**

then the GET request made by a web browser will look something like the following:

GET /cgi-bin/printenv HTTP/1.0

This request indicates that the client wants to retrieve the page /cgi-bin/printenv. From the client's perspective, there is no difference between this pathname and the pathname to any other page on the web server. When the web server receives this request, it sees that the request file resides in the /cgi-bin directory and proceeds to execute the program printenv stored in this directory. If the program produces any output, the web server places this output into the entity body of its response. The exact process used by the web server to execute a CGI script is as follows.

1. When a CGI request is received, the web server creates a new process for the CGI program.
2. The web server passes the request information (such as remote host, username, and HTTP headers) to the CGI program in environment variables.
3. The web server sends any client input (such as values from an HTML form) to the CGI program's standard input.
4. The CGI program writes any output to be returned to the client as standard output.
5. When the CGI process exits, the request is complete.

**Sending Information to CGI Programs**   Often it is necessary for the client to provide some information to a CGI program so that this information can be processed on the server. This is typical for CGI programs used for search engines and database access. In a GET request the information that needs to be processed by the CGI program is appended to the pathname of the URL. For example, a CGI GET request with client information might look like the following:

GET /cgi-bin/find.pl?dir=docs HTTP/1.0

Here the string "dir=docs" is being sent to the program /cgi-bin/find.pl by the client. The ? indicates to the server where the filename ends and the information provided by the client for the CGI program begins. Normally information from the client is sent to the server in this form:

*name=value*

In the preceding example, *name* was dir, and *value* was docs. Multiple name value pairs are separated using the & character. For example, the following URL sends two name value pairs, dir=docs and type=html, for processing by the CGI program find.pl.

http://kanchi/cgi-bin/find.pl?dir=docs&type=html

When the CGI program is invoked by the web server, the list of name value pairs sent by the client is provided to it in a single environment variable named QUERY_STRING. Normally, CGI programs will convert the name value pairs stored in this environment variable into separate variables. This extra processing adds some overhead to CGIs that respond to GET requests.

Another limitation of GET requests is that many clients limit the maximum length of the request to about 1 kilobyte. If you need to send a large amount of data to a CGI program, this is a serious limitation. To get around this problem many CGI programs use the POST method instead of GET. When the POST method is used the variable definitions are placed into the entity body instead of being appended to the pathname of the URL. The POST method is mainly used by CGI programs that need to process the information contained in complicated HTML forms.

The amount of information transmitted in a POST request is not subject to limitations like the GET method; thus client forms can transmit as much information as required to a CGI program. Most of the CGI programs for online shopping sites and e-commerce sites use the POST request for this reason.

## FastCGI and Servlets

One of the biggest complaints that administrators of large web sites have about CGI is that it puts a huge load on the web server. Each client that submits a form or requests a CGI-based page causes a process to be created on the machine where the web server is running. If you have hundreds of clients, this can translate to thousands of concurrent processes demanding resources from the web server system.

The biggest problems can come from CGI programs that need to create database or network connections. Each time such a CGI program is run it will need to create an expensive database of network connections. If these connections can take seconds to create on a lightly loaded system, then on a heavily loaded system that is processing hundreds of requests, creating these connections can take several minutes or even longer. For most users, several minutes is unbearably long, and thus unacceptable.

The ideal solution would be to allow CGI programs to create expensive network and database connections once—at startup time—and then to allow the CGI programs to reuse those connections. In fact, there *are* systems that allow CGIs to do this. The ones you are most likely to find are FastCGI and servlets.

**FastCGI**    FastCGI applications are similar to CGI programs in that they run in separate processes. The main difference is that FastCGI processes are persistent, and are reused to handle multiple requests. This solves the CGI performance problem caused by CGI's need to create new processes for each request.

FastCGI is implemented using the FastCGI application library, which was designed to allow for the migration of existing CGI applications. Applications built with the library can also run as CGI programs, for backward compatibility with old web servers. The

FastCGI library is available for all major web servers including Apache, from **www.fastcgi.com**. An extensive amount of documentation regarding its use is also available from this site.

**Servlets**    Servlets are Java programs that are executed on the web server using a mechanism similar to CGI: They are called from HTML pages, using GET or POST requests, and can interpret CGI parameters. They are able to generate HTML code, which is then piped back to the client application for display. Servlets can also connect to relational databases by using the Java Database Connectivity Classes (JDBC), which are currently supplied by many database vendors, or which can be purchased from third parties. Servlets are commonly used to develop three-tier information systems applications (HTML client, Java middleware, and database server), which form the basis for many e-commerce ventures.

Although servlets are often used in the same role as CGI scripts and programs, it is important to understand the differences. Servlets are executed on the server side by a "servlet runner," which is a single process, multithreaded Java server. Instances of each servlet, when invoked by a client, are lightweight processes that operate within the single Java server process. Thus, servlets are very fast, and easily support large numbers of concurrent users. They also benefit from the object-oriented characteristics of Java: Persistence of variables on the server side can be used to maintain session states without the need for cookies, and references to distributed objects can be created and maintained throughout the servlet lifecycle. This is a very useful feature when performing queries against legacy database systems, for example.

Servlets were conceived by Sun Microsystems as a replacement for CGI programs. In contrast to CGI and FastCGI programs, which are loaded and executed in a separate process outside the web server, servlets are loaded and executed as single threads inside a single servlet runner process. Servlets are similar to FastCGI in that each time a request for a servlet is received by the web server it reuses the copy that it has stored internally. Since servlets are only loaded once at invocation, they can minimize the effect of initializing resources, like network and database connections. Database and network connections can also be pooled, reducing overhead due to socket connections and name service lookups.

Many web servers provide support for servlets, by including a special module called a servlet runner. This provides the necessary interface between the web server and the Java Virtual Machine (JVM). There are several servlet engines available for Apache, including JRun from Allaire (**www.livesoftware.com**), which is a commercial product, and JServ from the Apache project itself, which is free.

In order to develop servlets, you will need to download and install a Java Development Kit (JDK) from Sun (**http://java.sun.com**), or use one of the vendor-supplied alternatives. For example, IBM has released the Jikes very fast Java compiler, available at **http://alphaworks.ibm.com/**. You will also need the Java Servlet Development Kit (JSDK) in order to compile servlets, which is available separately from the standard JDK. The JSDK is also required to use Jrun from Allaire.

Servlet runners are also distributed as a component of commercial application servers, such as WebLogic from BEA, and the Inprise Application Server (IAS) from Inprise. Although IAS is relatively expensive compared to JRun and other servlet runners, it is the most comprehensive offering available on the market, providing full support for Enterprise Java Beans (EJBs), CORBA distributed object management (through VisiBroker), and Java Server Pages (JSP). As a full implementation of Sun's Java 2 Enterprise Edition (J2EE) specification, IAS is intended for sites that use n-tier application architectures for web-based information systems, and/or for sites that have sufficient traffic to require more than one server. More information on IAS can be gathered from **http://www.inprise.com/appserver**.

To demonstrate just how easy it is to create a servlet, we present a simple example here that generates a HTML page that prints a greeting:

```
import java.io.*;
import javax.servlet.*;
import javax.servlet.http.*;


public class HelloReaders extends HttpServlet


{
public void doGet (HttpServletRequest request, HttpServletResponse
response) throws ServletException, IOException
{
                        PrintWriter page;
response.setContentType("text/html");
                        page = response.getWriter();
                        page.println("<HTML>");
                        page.println("<BODY>");
                        page.println("Hello Readers!");
                        page.println("</BODY>");
                        page.println("</HTML>");
                        page.close();
        }
public void doPost (HttpServletRequest request, HttpServletResponse
response) throws ServletException, IOException
{
                        doGet(request,response);
        }
}
```

Even if you are not a Java developer, it is easy to follow the logic of the application. Two methods are defined to handle GET (doGet) and POST (doPost) requests. After setting the MIME content type to HTML text, a page Writer is initialized, and the text of the HTML page is simply printed to the page. If this code was saved in a file called HelloReaders.java, it could be easily compiled with the command:

    client% javac HelloReaders.java

The class file HelloReaders.class would then need to be placed in the servlets directory defined within the servlet runner that you are using, and called with a URL like **http://localhost/servlet/HelloReaders**.

# Installing Apache

Anybody who wants to "serve" (make available) any large number of documents on the web needs a web server. In this section we will cover obtaining and installing the Internet's most popular and powerful web server: *Apache*. The Apache web server was originally based on version 1.3 of the NCSA httpd server. Due to widespread concern that this web server was not secure, many programmers around the world developed a set of security and performance patches, from which Apache gets its name (since the version of httpd that they ended up with was "a patchy server"). The most recent version of Apache, which by coincidence is also version 1.3, has been completely rewritten and no longer shares any code with the original NCSA version.

Before we start looking at the installation process for this latest version of Apache, there are several things you will need to do. The two most important steps are to obtain a valid IP address and a hostname for your web server. Without a valid hostname no one will be able to access your web site, so make sure that your web server is added to DNS (Domain Name Service) by the time you want to be able to deploy it. If you are responsible for DNS at your site, please consult Chapter 13, "The Domain Name Service," for more information. Otherwise contact your network administrator.

The next important consideration is the type of content you expect your web server will be serving:

- If you want your web server to support CGI programs or servlets, get a separate machine to use as a web server. These services can make heavy demands on your machine's resources, which could adversely affect the operation of other applications.

- The same goes for offering files for downloading: Downloads demand extra overhead.

- If your web server is primarily going to be serving static HTML pages (that is, no forms to be filled out by the users), then you don't have to worry too much that client web browsers will be making inordinate demands on your system.

Therefore, you can usually install the server on a system that is already used for some other purpose; in all likelihood the web server won't suffocate the other applications running on the system.

 **Note**  *A common option for serving mostly static content is to recommission older workstations and servers as dedicated web servers. This latter option is used for many intranet web servers.*

**Note**  *You may be wondering why we're about to show you how to install Apache web server instead of another web server that you may already have: Solaris Web Server, which comes on the Solaris Intranet Server Extension's CD. The simple answer is that Solaris Web Server is too simple: IT's a web server that was designed for lightweight use, mostly for non-networked desktop users who want to share just a few documents over the web. It is not designed for handling hundreds of simultaneous requests, which most intranet and Internet sites must occasionally expect. Note also that Solaris Web Server does not support many of the new technologies, including FastCGI and servlets.*

## Obtaining Apache

The Apache web server is available free of charge from the home page of The Apache Group, **www.apache.org**. As of this writing the most recent version of Apache is version 1.3.6. You can also obtain a copy of Apache using FTP from *ftp.apache.org*. The file to download is named Apache-1.3.6.tar.gz. If you prefer compressed files rather than a gzipped file, you can download the file Apache-1.3.6.tar.Z instead. Both of these files contain the sources to the Apache web server. In this section we will show you how to compile and install the web server.

The gzipped file is about 1.5 megabytes in size, while the compressed file is about 1.8 megabytes. When decompressed, each file creates a directory whose size is about 5 megabytes. Make sure that you decompress the distribution in a directory that has at least this much free space.

Here is the command for decompressing the Apache distribution once you've downloaded it:

```
$ gzip -cd Apache-1.3.6.tar.gz | tar -xvpf -
```

This will create a directory named Apache-1.3.6. This directory contains the source code, support utilities, and documentation for the web server.

## Considerations Before Compiling and Installing

Before proceeding further, you need to decide on the configuration of your Apache web server. Configuring involves checking your system to make sure that all the required components for compiling Apache are present on your system. That part of

ADMINISTERING SERVICES

the configuration process is handled automatically by the Apache configure command. Configuration also sets Apache up for running from the directory you want and enables the modules you want to use with Apache. Those parts of the process depend on choices you should make yourself:

- In what directory should Apache be installed after compilation?
- Which modules should be compiled into Apache?

## Deciding on the Installation Directory

The directory in which Apache should be installed is largely up to you. However, the choices made by other users may be illustrative here. Common locations that I've seen are /home/httpd, /home/www, /usr/httpd, /usr/local/httpd, and /www. On small Internet sites and most intranet sites it is common to find /home/httpd or /home/www used as the root directory for the web server. Large intranet sites seem to prefer /usr/httpd or /usr/local/httpd, and large Internet sites have a preference for /www. In reality, all of these directories are equally good. The only thing to keep in mind is that web sites require lots of disk space, so you should put the home directory of the web server on a dedicated partition, or at least a partition with lots of free space.

## Selecting Apache Modules

The standard Apache web server is basically a small engine that is designed to handle requests for static HTML pages quickly and efficiently. All other features of the Apache web server are provided by add-on components known as modules. Apache modules provide such features as access control, logging, CGI execution, and directory indexing. The standard Apache distribution comes with about 35 modules, and about half of these are enabled by default. In order to access the other modules, you will need to activate them manually when you configure Apache for compilation. Table 21-1 provides a description of each module that is included in the Apache distribution, and information about the default status of each module.

 *While you're reading Table 21-1, make a note of the names of any modules you are interested in enabling. You will need to know the module's name in order to compile Apache with that module enabled.*

# Configuring, Compiling, and Installing Apache

Configuring, compiling, and installing Apache is a simple three-step process, once you have determined where you want to install the server and which modules you want to include.

## Configuring Apache for Compilation

The first step is to configure the distribution for compilation using the configure command that comes with the Apache distribution. As mentioned earlier, the configure command checks your system to make sure that all the required components for compiling Apache are present on your system. It will also enable the modules you selected and configure Apache to run from the root directory you specified.

| Module Name | Description | Enabled by Default? |
|---|---|---|
| access | Access Control (user, host, network) | Yes |
| actions | Map CGI scripts to act as internal "handlers" | Yes |
| alias | Simple URL translation and redirection | Yes |
| asis | Raw HTTP responses | Yes |
| auth | HTTP Basic Authentication (user, passwd) | Yes |
| auth_anon | HTTP Basic Authentication for Anonymous-style users | No |
| auth_db | HTTP Basic Authentication via Berkeley-DB files | No |
| auth_dbm | HTTP Basic Authentication via Unix NDBM files | No |
| Autoindex | Automated directory index file generation | Yes |
| cern_meta | Arbitrary HTTP response headers (CERN-style files) | No |
| cgi | Common Gateway Interface (CGI) support | Yes |
| digest | HTTP Digest Authentication | No |
| dir | Directory and directory default file handling | Yes |
| env | Set environment variables for CGI/SSI scripts | Yes |
| expires | Expires HTTP responses | No |
| headers | Arbitrary HTTP response headers | No |
| imap | Server-side Image Map support | Yes |

**Table 21-1.**   *Apache Modules*

| Module Name | Description | Enabled by Default? |
|---|---|---|
| include | Server Side Includes (SSI) support | Yes |
| info | Content handler for server configuration summary | No |
| log_agent | Specialized HTTP User-Agent logging (deprecated) | No |
| log_config | Customizable logging of requests | Yes |
| log_refer | Specialized HTTP Referrer logging (deprecated) | No |
| mime | Content type/encoding determination | Yes |
| mime_magic | Content type/encoding determination | No |
| Negotiation | Content selection based on the HTTP Accept* headers | Yes |
| Proxy | Caching Proxy Module (HTTP, HTTPS, FTP) | No |
| rewrite | Advanced URL translation and redirection | No |
| setenvif | Set environment variables based on HTTP headers | Yes |
| so | Dynamic Shared Object (DSO) bootstrapping | No |
| spelling | Correction of misspelled URLs | No |
| status | Content handler for server run-time status | Yes |
| unique_id | Generate unique identifiers for request | No |

**Table 21-1.** *Apache Modules* (continued)

| Module Name | Description | Enabled by Default? |
|---|---|---|
| userdir | Selection of resource directories by username | Yes |
| usertrack | Logging of user click-trails via HTTP Cookies | No |

**Table 21-1.** *Apache Modules* (continued)

To configure Apache for compilation enter the following command in the directory where you decompressed the distribution:

```
$ ./configure -prefix=[install_dir] -enable_module=[module-name]
```

Here *install-dir* is the directory where you want Apache to be installed, and *module-name* is the name of a module you want enabled. The valid module names were given in Table 21-1.

If you want to enable more than one module, you can enter multiple–enable-module options. For example, the following command configures Apache to install in the directory /home/httpd and enables the modules expires and info:

```
$ ./configure -prefix=/home/httpd -enable-module=expires -enable-module=info
```

If you do not need any extra modules (that is, if the default modules are good enough for your site), then you can run the configure command with just the -prefix option.

## Compiling Apache

Once the configuration command completes its task, you can compile Apache by typing the following command:

```
$ make
```

(As with the configure command, you should type the make command in the directory where you decompressed the distribution.)

Depending on your shell, you may need to use the full path for make:

```
$ /usr/ccs/bin/make
```

The make command will compile Apache and all of its modules. When it completes, there will be a single executable named httpd in the src directory of the distribution.

## Finally—Installing Apache

You can install Apache at this point by issuing the following command:

```
$ make install
```

This will copy the executable, httpd, and all of the configuration files into the installation directory.

If you receive error messages indicating that you do not have sufficient permissions to install Apache, you may need to execute the command as root:

```
$ su root -c '/usr/ccs/bin/make install'
```

At this point you are finished with the Apache installation.

**Having Apache Start Up and Shut Down with Your System**   A very useful option for running Apache is to integrate it into the system startup and shutdown procedures. In the directory where you installed Apache, there will be a subdirectory named bin that contains a script named apachectl. This script can be used to start and stop Apache as easily as starting and stopping your computer.

To integrate Apache into your startup procedure, first place a copy of the apachectl script into the directory /etc/init.d. Again, if you followed the example in the previous section, you can use the following command as root:

```
# cp /home/httpd/bin/apachectl /etc/init.d
```

Of course, if you installed Apache in a directory other than /home/httpd, you should change this command to include the correct path to bin/apachectl.

Once you have made a copy of the apachectl script, change to the directory /etc/rc3.d and issue the following command as root:

```
# ln -s ../init.d/apachectl S85apachectl
```

This will create a link that will be used to automatically start Apache when your system reaches runlevel 3 (normally during system boot).

Next, change to the directory /etc/rc2.d and issue the following command as root:

```
# ln -s ../init.d/apachectl K15apachectl
```

This will create a link that will be used to automatically shut down Apache when your system reaches runlevel 2 (normally during reboots).

# Testing Apache

Once you have installed Apache, start it up to test if everything is working correctly. To start Apache, issue the following command as root:

```
# /etc/init.d/apachectl start
```

This assumes that you copied the apachectl script into the /etc/init.d directory as described in the previous section. If the command fails, then check that the executable bit has been set on the apachectl file. If you didn't copy the startup file to /etc/init.d, then change into the directory where Apache is installed and issue the following command as root:

```
# ./bin/apachectl start
```

This will start the web server. To test it out, you can use the telnet command as follows:

```
$ telnet localhost 80
```

This will produce the following output:

```
Trying 127.0.0.1...
Connected to localhost.
Escape character is '^]'.
```

You will not receive a prompt, but your terminal's cursor will be at the beginning of a blank line. This indicates that you are connected to the web server. If you receive a message saying "connection refused," then you need to check the process list to determine that Apache started correctly.

In order to test the web server, enter the following line :

```
GET / HTTP/1.0
```

and press ENTER twice (once at the end of the line and once again after that). After the second return you will see an HTML page scroll across your screen. The HTTP response headers and start of the page are reproduced here:

```
HTTP/1.1 200 OK
Date: Fri, 16 Apr 2000 06:45:52 GMT
Server: Apache/1.3.4 (Unix) mod_fastcgi/2.2.1
Last-Modified: Fri, 15 Mar 2000 06:30:39 GMT
ETag: "800f-327-369ee08f"
```

```
Accept-Ranges: bytes
Content-Length: 807
Connection: close
Content-Type: text/html

<HTML>
 <HEAD>
  <TITLE>Test Page for Apache Installation on Web Site</TITLE>
```

You are now ready to configure Apache to suit the needs of your web site. The next section discusses the configuration file for Apache, httpd.conf, to show you how to tune your Apache installation.

# Configuring Apache for Use

If your installation and test were successful, you can now configure Apache in order to start using it to serve web pages to a wide audience. For versions 1.3.4 and higher, all of the configuration information for Apache is stored in a single file named httpd.conf.

**Note** *If you look at the directory tree where you installed Apache you may notice two additional configuration files named access.conf and srm.conf. Previous versions of Apache used these files for configuring certain modules, but the complexity of maintaining three configuration files prompted the development team to move to a single configuration file.*

The httpd.conf file consists of sets of "directives" that tell the Apache web server how it should configure itself and its modules. Every line in the file, except blank lines and lines starting with the # character, are treated as part of a directive. This file is divided into three main sections:

- Global Configuration
- Server Configuration
- Virtual Hosts Configuration

We will look at each of these sections in turn. A complete httpd.conf file is reproduced at the end of this chapter.

## Global Configuration

The directives in the global configuration section affect the overall operation of Apache. Some of the key attributes that are defined in this section are:

- The location of files and directories that are used by Apache for finding configuration files, storing its process information, and its internal statistics

- The handling of network connection parameters such as timeouts and persistent connections
- The behavior of Apache when it needs to service many requests

## Directives for Essential Files and Directives

The location of files and directories are defined using the following directives:

```
ServerType standalone
ServerRoot "/home/httpd"
LockFile /var/log/httpd/httpd.lock
PidFile /var/log/httpd/httpd.pid
ScoreBoardFile /var/log/httpd/httpd.scoreboard
ExtendedStatus On
```

Here, the ServerType directive controls how Apache should be started. The two available modes are standalone and inetd. The default is to run Apache in standalone mode. Apache has a much faster response time and utilizes the resources of your machine more effectively in standalone mode. The inetd mode is provided for backward compatibility and should only be used on small sites that receive very few hits.

The ServerRoot directive defines the top directory under which all of Apache's configuration files, log files, and error files are stored. In this case the directory is /home/httpd, since this is where Apache is installed on my machine. If you chose a different directory when you built Apache, you will need to make sure that Server Root is set to that directory.

*Don't store the httpd executable and its configuration files in the ServerRoot directory or any of its subdirectories. Files in these directories are accessible by anyone using a web client; putting your web server's executable or its configuration files in ServerRoot or its subdirectories can be an open invitation to hackers.*

The LockFile and PidFile directives are used by Apache to define the location of files that it uses to prevent startup collisions. If you start Apache and then, later, while Apache is still running, try to start it again, the second instance of Apache will look at these files and detect the first instance. This prevents conflicts from occurring between the two instances of Apache. You should not have to change the default locations for these files.

The ScoreBoardFile directive defines the location of the file in which Apache should store its internal statistics. This file contains information like the number of requests that Apache handled, the origin of some of the recent requests, and the average time it took to handle a request. You can relocate this file to another location if you don't like the default location. The ExtendedStatus directive is related to the ScoreBoardFile directive. If this directive has the value On, it will be possible for you to browse the statistics of your web server by requesting the page /server-status from your web server. For example, on my web server, I can access this information using this URL:

```
http://kanchi/server-status
```

Your web server statistics can provide useful information to hackers, so if your web server will be on the Internet this directive should be set to Off. For web servers that are used in a secure intranet, this directive can set to On.

## Directives for Controlling Network Connections

Apache's handling of network connections is determined by the settings of the following directives:

```
Timeout 300
KeepAlive On
MaxKeepAliveRequests 100
KeepAliveTimeout 15
```

The Timeout directive controls the number of seconds that Apache should wait for a request before timing out a connection to the client. The default is 300 seconds, which is reasonable for installations. You may wish to increase the number if you find that your site receives requests from clients that are extremely slow. If you are working with a web-based application that requires user authentication, then after the timeout expires your users may have to re-authenticate themselves to the web servers. To decrease the frequency of re-authentication you may need to set the Timeout directive to a higher number, like 1200 seconds (20 minutes).

Apache implements HTTP version 1.1's persistent connections feature that allows clients to open a single connection to the web server and use this connection for more than one query. The next three directives in the preceding example control the behavior of persistent connections under Apache. The KeepAlive directive is used to activate persistent connections, and needs to be set to On (the default) in order for Apache to allow clients to use this feature. Since using persistent connections increases the efficiency of your web server and the performance of web browsers connecting to your site, there is no reason to turn this feature off.

The MaxKeepAliveRequests can be used to limit the number of requests a client can make using the same connection. The default is 100 requests, which covers most of the clients that will access your machine. If you find that clients accessing your web server are reconnecting multiple times, you should increase this number. It is possible to allow clients to reuse a single connection as many times as they want, by setting this directive to 0, but this is not recommended.

The KeepAliveTimeout is similar to the Timeout directive; its value determines how long Apache will wait before closing a connection to a client. The default value is 15 seconds, but you may need to increase this number to 20 or 30 seconds if your site is accessed by slow clients.

## Directives Controlling the Server Pool

As part of its startup phase Apache creates several copies of itself. These additional instances of Apache are used to handle incoming requests in a timely manner. When a request is received by Apache, the first idle instance of Apache will start to respond to this request. If another request is received right after that one, the next available instance of Apache will start to respond. This reduces the overall waiting time for clients. Depending on the frequency of requests received by your site, you will want to tailor the number of servers that are available at any given time. The following directives allow you to do just that.

```
StartServers 5
MinSpareServers 5
MaxSpareServers 10
MaxClients 150
MaxRequestsPerChild 30
```

The StartServers directive is used to tailor the number of initial copies of Apache that should be started. The default value is 5, and this is good for most small and medium sites. If you are going to be running your department's intranet web site or a web site on the Internet, you should increase this number. Most large sites work well with 10 or 20 initial servers. If you get a lot of complaints that your server is unreachable, try increasing the number. Make sure that this number isn't extremely high (greater than 50 or 60), since that may put an unnecessarily large burden on your system.

Determining the exact number of web servers you need to have running is not an easy task. In order to simplify this, Apache allows you to set the min and max number of idle servers that should be present at any time. By setting these parameters, you can make sure that during periods of high load, there are always enough servers to handle requests in a timely fashion. During a lull, you can terminate any extra servers to reduce the overall load on your machine.

The minimum number of idle servers is controlled by the MinSpareServers directive. The default value for this directive is 5. If the number of idle servers ever drops below 5, Apache will create extra ones to compensate. This allows you to maintain good response time to clients even when your site is receiving a large number of hits. For a small intranet web site the default is fine. For a large intranet web site or a Internet web site, you may need to set this directive to 10 or 15. Similarly the maximum number of idle servers is controlled by the MaxSpareServers directive. The default value for this directive is 10. If Apache detects that there are more than 10 idle servers, it will kill the extra ones off to reduce the load on the system.

The MaxClients directive is intended as a brake for a runaway server. It limits the number of simultaneous clients your web server can handle, since attempting to handle thousands of simultaneous requests can easily bring down your system. The default value is 150, which is reasonable for most machines. If your web server ever receives more than this number of simultaneous requests, the extra clients will be locked out until an instance of Apache becomes available. Since you probably don't want to lock out any more clients than you absolutely have to, you should not set this value to be too low (for example, under 50).

The final directive in this section, MaxRequestsPerChild, is designed to avoid problems with running Apache for extended periods of time. On some operating systems, the networking libraries have memory and resource leaks. This leads to problems for programs like Apache that make heavy use of the networking libraries. By limiting the number of requests any single instance of Apache handles, these problems can be minimized. The default value for this directive is 30. You should not have to change this number.

# Server-Specific Configuration

The second section of httpd.conf contains the server-specific configuration directives. These are directives that are used to control the various aspects of Apache's responses to requests. This section has five main parts:

- The first part contains directives for controlling general parameters of the web server. Examples: the port on which it listens for requests and the email address of the server's administrator.

- The second part contains directives for controlling access to certain directories and files. This part starts by defining the main directory where all the HTML pages are located for your site.

- The third part contains directives for controlling how directory listings and other automatically generated pages look.

- The fourth part contains directives for controlling Apache's logging feature. This feature allows you to have separate log files for information like accesses and errors.

- The fifth part contains directives for modifying the HTTP version with which Apache responds for certain clients. This section is designed to cope with clients that, although they issue HTTP version 1.1 requests, are not capable of handling an HTTP 1.1 response.

## General Server Directives

The general server directives control the port on which Apache listens for requests, the user and group at which it runs, the name of the server, and the contact e-mail for the server. The directives are:

```
Port 80
User nobody
Group nobody
ServerName www.bosland.us
UseCanonicalName On
ServerAdmin root@kanchi
```

The first directive, Port, defines the port on which Apache listens for requests. Here, the default HTTP port of 80 is being used.

If you use a port other than 80, clients accessing your server will have to modify their URLs to correctly access your web server. For example, if the port is set to 8080, a client would have to use the following URL to access the file docs.html stored on the server kanchi:

```
http://kanchi:8080/docs.html
```

The next two directives control the user and group that should be used to run each instance of Apache. The default is nobody, since this user has the lowest set of privileges on your machine. On some versions of UNIX, notably HP-UX, Apache cannot be run as nobody, since that user does not have enough permissions to create network connections. On these systems, Apache must be run as a different user, usually named www, web, or httpd. This problem does not exist on Solaris, but the option is available to you.

The ServerName directive allows you to set a hostname that is sent back to clients for your server if it's different than the one the program would normally get. As an example, I am using the name www.bosland.us, instead of the server's actual hostname. The hostname you define here must be a valid DNS name for your host. If your host is on multiple networks, you may have to define an IP address here in order for clients to access it correctly. The UseCanonicalName directive is related to the ServerName directive, and controls how Apache constructs the absolute URL for relative URLs on your server. If this directive is set to On, Apache will use the value provided by the ServerName directive to construct these URLs; otherwise it will rely on the information provided by the client. In order to ensure that all clients can properly access your web server, this option should be set to On.

The last directive, ServerAdmin, defines the email address of the server's administrator. This email address normally appears on pages generated by the server. You should set this to the email address of the person who will be maintaining the server on a daily basis. In this case the system administrator is also responsible for the web server, so root's email was used.

## Directory Directives

The directory directives are used to control access to the different directories where HTML files are stored. This part starts by defining the DocumentRoot directive, which determines the root directory for all HTML files on your web server. It also includes definitions for the cgi-bin directory and user directories.

**The Document Root**   The document root of your web server is the main directory where all your HTML documents are stored. When Apache receives a request for a document, it will start to search for the document relative to this directory. The document root is defined using the DocumentRoot directive:

```
DocumentRoot "/home/httpd/htdocs"
```

With this definition, the following URL:

```
http://kanchi/docs.html
```

really refers to the file /home/httpd/htdocs/docs.html. Since I installed Apache in the directory /home/httpd, I decided to put my HTML files in the directory htdocs, under this directory. You can choose any directory you want for your DocumentRoot. Other common values include /www and /web.

Once you have defined the root directory for your web server, you need to define the access "permissions" for that directory by using the Directory directive:

```
<Directory />
    Options Indexes FollowSymLinks
    AllowOverride None
    Order allow,deny
    allow from all
</Directory>
```

The Options directive controls what types of actions Apache is allowed to perform in this directory. The options that are available are Includes, Indexes, FollowSymLinks, and ExecCGI. The Includes option allows Apache to filter the contents of documents before it sends it to a client. The Indexes option allows Apache to generate a directory listing if a client requests a directory instead of a document.

The FollowSymLinks option allows Apache to translate symbolic links into files and directories. The ExecCGI option tells Apache that documents in a particular directory should be treated as programs and executed. Apache will return the output of the program instead of the contents of the file. If you don't want any options, you can specify None to deactivate all the options. Similarly, you can specify All to activate all the options. In this case, I have turned on only the Indexes and FollowSymLinks options for the root directory. You wouldn't want the ExecCGI and the Includes options activated for the main directory where your HTML files are located.

The AllowOverride directive controls whether or not special .htaccess files can override the Options settings for a directory. Since extra options can easily be enabled from this file, it is a good idea to prevent this in the root directory for your HTML documents. Apache also allows you to control access to your web server using the Order directive. This directive allows you to define the hosts you want to permit access for and those that you want to deny access to. In this case I have allowed everyone to access this directory.

Once you have defined the root directory for your web server, you can define the names for certain special files used by Apache. The three main files are the default directory index file, access control file, and the MIME types file. The directory index file is used by Apache to handle client requests for a directory. Normally, when a client requests a directory, Apache will simply list the contents of the directory. However, this is usually not what the client wanted, so the DirectoryIndex directive allows you to specify the name of an HTML file that should be used instead:

```
DirectoryIndex index.html
```

If this file exists, Apache will return its contents (instead of a mere directory listing) to the client. Here I've specified a file named index.html.

The access control files are used to selectively allow access to certain directories. The names of these files are defined using the AccessFileName directive. Since they can contain sensitive information, I also define a Files directive that prevents clients from accessing the files:

```
AccessFileName .htaccess
<Files .htaccess>
    Order allow,deny
    Deny from all
</Files>
```

The MIME types file is used by Apache to determine the correct MIME type for a particular file. The location of this file is controlled by the TypesConfig directive:

```
TypesConfig /home/httpd/conf/mime.types
```

You should not have to change the location of this file, since it is part of the standard configuration files and will be installed along with the httpd.conf file.

Related to the MIME types file is the DefaultType directive, which defines the default MIME type for documents on your web server:

```
DefaultType text/plain
```

If your server contains mostly text or HTML documents, "text/plain" is a good value. If most of your content is binary, such as applications or images, you may want to use "application/octet-stream" instead, to keep browsers from trying to display binary files as though they are text.

**User Directories**   In most companies and universities, a department web server allows individual users to place their own files, such as technical documents, pictures, and applications, on the web server so that other people can access them. For example, the following URL refers to the file index.html in my user directory on the host www.cusa.berkeley.edu:

```
http://www.cusa.berkeley.edu/~ranga/index.html
```

On this particular host there are hundreds of users. Since it is not practical to allow every user to access the document root, Apache provides the UserDir directive that allows you to define where user directories are located.

Once you define the UserDir, you also have to define its permissions. The complete set of directives for enabling user directories is as follows.

```
UserDir public_html
<Directory /*/public_html>
    Options Indexes
    AllowOverride None
    <Limit PUT DELETE>
        Order deny,allow
        deny from all
    </Limit>
</Directory>
```

Here I defined the UserDir to be public_html. If Apache receives a request for the document /~ranga/index.html, it will look for the file index.html in the directory public_html located in the home directory of the user ranga. This means that the maintenance of the public_html directory is up to the individual user. It also means that anyone with a valid login to your web server can create a web page easily, which can be a big advantage in a large organization, but also a security hazard.

The access permissions in this case are tighter than for the root directory since you can't be sure what users will put in their home directories. The only option that I allow is the automatic generation of indexes, and I prevent users from overriding this setting. I also use the Limit directive to prevent clients from using PUT and DELETE HTTP requests in the user directories.

**CGI Scripts**    CGI scripts provide the ability to execute commands on the server and return the output to clients. Since CGI scripts can reveal information about your server, you have to be careful in setting up access to them. In order to safely enable CGI scripts, you need to use the ScriptAlias directive in combination with a Directory directive. The ScriptAlias directive tells Apache that the files stored in a particular directory are scripts, and should be executed. This directive is an alternative to ExecCGI, which allows you to mark a directory and all its subdirectories as directories that contain only CGI programs. The full definition for enabling CGI programs is as follows.

```
ScriptAlias /cgi-bin/ "/home/httpd/cgi-bin/"
<Directory "/home/httpd/cgi-bin">
    AllowOverride None
    Options None
</Directory>
```

Here, I've defined the directory /home/httpd/cgi-bin as the main directory that contains CGI programs. When a client accesses a CGI script such as:

```
http://kanchi/cgi-bin/test.pl
```

the preceding definition will cause Apache to execute the file /home/httpd/cgi-bin/
test.pl and return the results to the client. After defining ScriptAlias, I define a Directory
directive for the CGI directory that disallows all options and prevents any overriding.
This is for security reasons since you don't want malicious visitors to your web server
to find out which CGI programs you have.

## Directory Listings

When Apache receives a request for a directory instead of a file, it will first try to find
the index file for that directory (usually index.html). If this file doesn't exist, then Apache
will return a listing of the contents of the directory. The style of the listing is controlled
by the IndexOptions directive.

In my httpd.conf file, I specified FancyIndexing, which allows for an icon and
a description to be returned for each file in a directory:

```
IndexOptions FancyIndexing
```

If you want a simple directory listing you can set this option to Standard instead. If
you use FancyIndexing, the icons are specified using the AddIcon directive. Here is the
syntax of this directive:

AddIcon *path-to-icon file-extensions*

Here *path-to-the icon* is relative to your document root, and *file-extensions* is a list of
extensions, like .exe and .gif. A standard set of icons is defined as follows.

```
AddIcon /icons/binary.gif .bin .exe
AddIcon /icons/binhex.gif .hqx
AddIcon /icons/tar.gif .tar
AddIcon /icons/compressed.gif .Z .z .tgz .gz .zip
AddIcon /icons/layout.gif .html .shtml .htm .pdf
AddIcon /icons/text.gif .txt
AddIcon /icons/uuencoded.gif .uu
AddIcon /icons/back.gif ..
AddIcon /icons/hand.right.gif README
AddIcon /icons/folder.gif ^^DIRECTORY^^
AddIcon /icons/blank.gif ^^BLANKICON^^
DefaultIcon /icons/unknown.gif
```

The last line defines the DefaultIcon directive, which will display a standard icon for
any file that does not explicitly have an icon defined for it.

To add descriptions for files while using FancyIndexing, you need to use the AddDescription directive. The syntax for this directive is:

AddDescription *"description"* *.file-extension*

Here, *description* is a string, like "tar archive," that describes the file. If your description has a space in it, you must enclose the description in double quotes. Otherwise the quotes are optional. *File-extension* is an extension, like .tar. A few standard descriptions follow.

```
AddDescription "GZIP compressed document" .gz
AddDescription "tar archive" .tar
AddDescription "GZIP compressed tar archive" .tgz
```

The last directive related to directory indexes is the IndexIgnore directive. It lets you list a set of filenames and file extensions that should be ignored when a directory listing is produced. Here's a standard value for this directive:

```
IndexIgnore .??* *~ *# HEADER* README* RCS CVS *,v *,t
```

## Logging Directives

The logging directives control how Apache logs information about requests. The directives in this part of the httpd.conf file are as follows:

```
HostnameLookups Off
ErrorLog /var/log/httpd/error_log
LogLevel warn
LogFormat "%h %l %u %t \"%r\" %>s %b \"%{Referer}i\" \"%{User-Agent}i\"" combine
LogFormat "%h %l %u %t \"%r\" %>s %b" common
LogFormat "%{Referer}i -> %U" referer
LogFormat "%{User-agent}i" agent
#CustomLog /var/log/httpd/access_log common
#CustomLog /var/log/httpd/referer_log referer
#CustomLog /var/log/httpd/agent_log agent
CustomLog /var/log/httpd/access_log combined
```

The HostnameLookups directive controls whether or not the hostname is logged instead of the IP address of the client. Since resolving the hostname of a client involves at least one DNS query, it is better to turn this option off to reduce the amount of network traffic that is generated for each request.

The ErrorLog directive defines the location where the error log should be stored. The error log stores information about request errors and response errors that occur. It is often useful when debugging CGI programs. You can store this anywhere you want, but the default should be good enough for most sites.

The next set of directives, LogLevel and LogFormat, defines the Syslog level and format that should be used for logging information. You can define your own formats if the defaults do not have enough information for you. The CustomLog directive uses the different LogFormats to provide the ability to have separate log files for logging requests (access), client's type (agent), the referring page (referer). The example above uses a single log file, but you can uncomment the appropriate lines in the previous example to get separate log files.

## BrowserMatch Directives

The BrowserMatch directives are used to modify the normal HTTP response behavior. The standard set of these directives is:

```
BrowserMatch "Mozilla/2" nokeepalive
BrowserMatch "MSIE 4\.0b2;" nokeepalive downgrade-1.0
force-response-1.0
BrowserMatch "RealPlayer 4\.0" force-response-1.0
BrowserMatch "Java/1\.0" force-response-1.0
BrowserMatch "JDK/1\.0" force-response-1.0
```

The first directive disables keepalive for Netscape 2.x, since this version has problems dealing with persistent connections. The second directive is for Microsoft Internet Explorer 4.0b2, which does not have a complete HTTP version 1.1 implementation and does not correctly support persistent connections in all cases. The last three directives are used to force RealPlayer and Java to use HTTP version 1.0 since they cannot handle HTTP version 1.1 at all.

# Virtual Host Configuration

In many cases you may need to host the web sites of several different organizations. This is often true for departmental web servers that have web sites for different groups. It is easiest for each group if people can access their web pages using a simple URL like www-eng or www-docs, instead of having to know the name of the server and the full path on that server. When the web first began, setting this up usually meant that you would have to get a separate machine for each group and set up a web server on each of these machines. If you had five or more groups to support, this could easily become a huge workload.

Fortunately, Apache provides a simple way of serving multiple web sites from the same web server by using an idea called *virtual hosts*. Basically, virtual hosts uses the DNS feature of creating aliases to simulate multiple web servers. The first step in enabling virtual hosts is to have the hostnames for the web sites you want to serve added to DNS as aliases for your web server. For example, if you wanted to host www-eng and www-docs on your web server, you would need to have www-eng and www-docs added to DNS as aliases for your web server. If you are managing DNS for your site, please see Chapter 13, "The Domain Name Service," for details on how to do this. Otherwise consult your network administrator.

The second step is to tell Apache about these different virtual hosts by using the VirtualHost directive. Here is an example for hosting the www-eng web site in addition to your normal web site.

```
<VirtualHost www-eng.bosland.us>
    ServerAdmin root@www-eng.bosland.us
    DocumentRoot /home/httpd/eng-docs
    ServerName www-eng.bosland.us
    ErrorLog /var/log/httpd/eng-error_log
    TransferLog /var/log/httpd/eng-access_log
</VirtualHost>
```

As you can see, the virtual host configuration is like a miniature version of the full web server configuration. Apache invokes this directive when it detects that an incoming request was made using the name www-eng rather than the regular server's name. The most important directives here are the DocumentRoot and the ServerName. In this case, the DocumentRoot was set to a directory that is not stored in the DocumentRoot of the normal web site. This allows different groups to maintain their web sites independently. If you need to make a change to one web site, you won't affect other sites if the document root settings for the two sites are completely different.

The other directives, like ServerAdmin, ErrorLog, and TransferLog, are useful for accounting purposes. If there is someone else who is in charge of the content for this web site, you can use the ServerAdmin directive to redirect support emails to them. The ErrorLog and TransferLog directives allow you to log the traffic received by this web site separately from your other web sites. This will allow you to monitor the traffic easily.

**Note** *Some older browsers, notably old versions of AOL's browser, are unable to handle virtual hosting. If you need to handle large numbers of users with such browsers, you many need to set up separate web servers for each virtual site. If your main traffic is from users with Netscape 3.0 or higher and Microsoft Internet Explorer 3.0 or higher, you can stick with virtual hosting.*

## The Complete httpd.conf

This section contains the listing for a complete httpd.conf file. It integrates all of the directives that were described in the previous sections.

```
# Apache 1.3.x Configuration File

# Section 1 - Global Configuration Directives
# The directives in this section control the overall behavior of Apache
ServerType standalone
```

```
ServerRoot "/home/httpd"
LockFile /var/log/httpd/httpd.lock
PidFile /var/log/httpd/httpd.pid
ScoreBoardFile /var/log/httpd/httpd.scoreboard
ExtendedStatus On
Timeout 300
KeepAlive On
MaxKeepAliveRequests 100
KeepAliveTimeout 15
StartServers 5
MinSpareServers 5
MaxSpareServers 10
MaxClients 150
MaxRequestsPerChild 30

# Section 2 - Server Specific Configuration
# This section contains directives related to server, including
# directory directives logging directives and indexing information
Port 80
User nobody
Group nobody
ServerName www.bosland.us
UseCanonicalName On
ServerAdmin root@kanchi
# Directives for the top-level directory of the web site
DocumentRoot "/home/httpd/htdocs"
<Directory />
    Options Indexes FollowSymLinks
    AllowOverride None
    Order allow,deny
    allow from all
</Directory>
# Define the name of the default index file and the access control file
DirectoryIndex index.html
AccessFileName .htaccess
<Files .htaccess>
    Order allow,deny
    Deny from all
</Files>
TypesConfig /home/httpd/conf/mime.types
DefaultType text/plain
# Directives for enabling user directories
```

```
UserDir public_html
<Directory /*/public_html>
    Options Indexes
    AllowOverride None
    <Limit PUT DELETE>
        Order deny,allow
        deny from all
    </Limit>
</Directory>
# Directives enabling cgi-bin programs
ScriptAlias /cgi-bin/ "/home/httpd/cgi-bin/"
<Directory "/home/httpd/cgi-bin">
    AllowOverride None
    Options None
</Directory>
# Automatic Index generation directives
IndexOptions FancyIndexing
AddIcon /icons/binary.gif .bin .exe
AddIcon /icons/binhex.gif .hqx
AddIcon /icons/tar.gif .tar
AddIcon /icons/compressed.gif .Z .z .tgz .gz .zip
AddIcon /icons/layout.gif .html .shtml .htm pdf
AddIcon /icons/text.gif .txt
AddIcon /icons/uuencoded.gif .uu
AddIcon /icons/back.gif ..
AddIcon /icons/hand.right.gif README
AddIcon /icons/folder.gif ^^DIRECTORY^^
AddIcon /icons/blank.gif ^^BLANKICON^^
DefaultIcon /icons/unknown.gif
AddDescription "GZIP compressed document" .gz
AddDescription "tar archive" .tar
AddDescription "GZIP compressed tar archive" .tgz
IndexIgnore .??* *~ *# HEADER* README* RCS CVS *,v *,t
# Directives for logging
HostnameLookups Off
ErrorLog /var/log/httpd/error_log
LogLevel warn
LogFormat "%h %l %u %t \"%r\" %>s %b \"%{Referer}i\" \"%{User-Agent}i\"" combine
LogFormat "%h %l %u %t \"%r\" %>s %b" common
LogFormat "%{Referer}i -> %U" referer
LogFormat "%{User-agent}i" agent
#CustomLog /var/log/httpd/access_log common
```

```
#CustomLog /var/log/httpd/referer_log referer
#CustomLog /var/log/httpd/agent_log agent
CustomLog /var/log/httpd/access_log combined
# Browser Match directives for handling bad requests
BrowserMatch "Mozilla/2" nokeepalive
BrowserMatch "MSIE 4\.0b2;" nokeepalive downgrade-1.0 force-response-1.0
BrowserMatch "RealPlayer 4\.0" force-response-1.0
BrowserMatch "Java/1\.0" force-response-1.0
BrowserMatch "JDK/1\.0" force-response-1.0

# Section 3 - Virtual Hosts
# This section demonstrates how to create a virutal host directive.
# The hostname for your virtual hosts will need to be in DNS for this
# directive to work correctly
<VirtualHost www-eng.bosland.us>
    ServerAdmin root@www-eng.bosland.us
    DocumentRoot /home/httpd/eng-docs
    ServerName www-eng.bosland.us
    ErrorLog /var/log/httpd/eng-error_log
    TransferLog /var/log/httpd/eng-access_log
</VirtualHost>
```

## Summary

In recent years, more and more information is being placed on the World Wide Web because of the power of the web as a medium for distribution and access. The number of web servers has drastically increased on both the Internet and on intranets. In many companies, every department, and sometimes smaller development groups as well, needs to have its own web servers to manage the demand for information. In this chapter we looked at the technology that powers the web, the HyperText Transfer Protocol (HTTP). We also detailed the steps for obtaining and installing the Apache web server, which allows you to serve web pages from your system. Finally we looked at configuring Apache. Using the material in this chapter, you will be able to start serving information efficiently on both intranets and the Internet.

## How to Find Out More

There are many excellent web sites and books that you can use to find out more about the web and web serving. Some books to consult are:

Hethmon, Paul S. *Illustrated Guide to HTTP.* (Manning Publications Company, 1997.)

Kabir, Mohammed J. *Apache Server Bible.* (IDG Books Worldwide, 1998.)

Wong, Clinton. *Web Client Programming with Perl.* (O'Reilly and Associates, 1997.)

ADMINISTERING
SERVICES

Three of the most important organizations related to the web are the World Wide Web Consortium, the Apache Group, and the National Center for Supercomputing Applications.

The World Wide Web Consortium (known as W3C) is headed by Tim Berners-Lee and is responsible for developing HTTP and other web-related technologies. Their home page is located at **www.w3c.org**.

The Apache Group is responsible for the development of the Apache web server. They have extensive documentation about Apache, HTTP, the web, and other web servers on their web site. The Apache Group has also been instrumental in implementing new web-based technologies. Their home page is located at **www.apache.org**.

The National Center for Supercomputing Applications (NCSA) developed the first widely used web server upon which Apache is based. NCSA has also led the field in the creation of other web-related technologies, like the Mosaic web browser. The home page of NCSA is located at **www.ncsa.uiuc.edu**.

If you are interested in the RFCs that are related to HTTP, please consult the following:

- RFC 1630 covers the original concept of the World Wide Web.
- RFC 1738 covers the concept of URLs.
- RFC 1866 covers HTML.
- RFC 1945 covers HTTP version 1.0.
- RFC 2068 covers HTTP version 1.1.

# Index

## A

## E

## F

## X

## Z